OECD Transfer Pricing Guidelines for Multinational Enterprises and Tax Administrations 2022

OECD
BETTER POLICIES FOR BETTER LIVES

This document, as well as any data and map included herein, are without prejudice to the status of or sovereignty over any territory, to the delimitation of international frontiers and boundaries and to the name of any territory, city or area.

Please cite this publication as:
OECD (2022), *OECD Transfer Pricing Guidelines for Multinational Enterprises and Tax Administrations 2022*, OECD Publishing, Paris, *https://doi.org/10.1787/0e655865-en*.

ISBN 978-92-64-52691-4 (print)
ISBN 978-92-64-92191-7 (pdf)

OECD Transfer Pricing Guidelines for Multinational Enterprises and Tax Administrations
ISSN 2076-9709 (print)
ISSN 2076-9717 (online)

Corrigenda to publications may be found on line at: *www.oecd.org/about/publishing/corrigenda.htm*.

Foreword

These Guidelines are a revision of the OECD Report *Transfer Pricing and Multinational Enterprises* (1979). They were approved in their original version by the Committee on Fiscal Affairs on 27 June 1995 and by the OECD Council for publication on 13 July 1995.

Since their original version, these Guidelines have been supplemented:

- By the report on intangible property and services, adopted by the Committee on Fiscal Affairs on 23 January 1996 [DAFFE/CFA(96)2] and noted by the Council on 11 April 1996 [C(96)46], incorporated in Chapters VI and VII;
- By the report on cost contribution arrangements, adopted by the Committee on Fiscal Affairs on 25 June 1997 [DAFFE/CFA(97)27] and noted by the Council on 24 July 1997 [C(97)144], incorporated in Chapter VIII;
- By the report on the guidelines for monitoring procedures on the OECD Transfer Pricing Guidelines and the involvement of the business community [DAFFE/CFA/WD(97)11/REV1], adopted by the Committee on Fiscal Affairs on 24 June 1997 and noted by the Council on 23 October 1997 [C(97)196], incorporated in the annexes;
- By the report on the guidelines for conducting advance pricing arrangements under the mutual agreement procedure, adopted by the Committee on Fiscal Affairs on 30 June 1999 [DAFFE/CFA(99)31] and noted by the Council on 28 October 1999 [C(99)138], incorporated in the annexes;
- By the report on the transfer pricing aspects of business restructurings, adopted by the Committee on Fiscal Affairs on 22 June 2010 [CTPA/CFA(2010)46] and approved by the Council on 22 July 2010 [Annex I to C(2010)99], incorporated in Chapter IX;
- By the report on the guidance for tax administrations on the application of the approach to hard-to-value intangibles, adopted by the Committee on Fiscal Affairs on 4 June 2018 [CTPA/CFA/NOE2(2018)25], incorporated in the annexes; and,

- By the report on the transfer pricing aspects of financial transactions, adopted by the Committee on Fiscal Affairs on 20 January 2020 [CTPA/CFA/NOE2(2019)75], incorporated in Section D.1.2.2 of Chapter I and in Chapter X.

In addition, these Guidelines have been modified:

- By an update of Chapter IV, adopted by the Committee on Fiscal Affairs on 6 June 2008 [CTPA/CFA(2008)30/REV1] and an update of the Foreword and of the Preface, adopted by the Committee on Fiscal Affairs on 22 June 2009 [CTPA/CFA(2009)51/REV1], approved by the Council on 16 July 2009 [C(2009)88];
- By a revision of Chapters I-III, adopted by the Committee on Fiscal Affairs on 22 June 2010 [CTPA/CFA(2010)55] and approved by the Council on 22 July 2010 [Annex I to C(2010)99]; and
- By an update of the Foreword, of the Preface, of the Glossary, of Chapters IV-VIII and of the annexes, adopted by the Committee on Fiscal Affairs on 22 June 2010 [CTPA/CFA(2010)47] and approved by the Council on 22 July 2010 [Annex I to C(2010)99].
- By a revision of Section E on safe harbours in Chapter IV, and the addition of another Annex to this Chapter including three sample Memoranda of Understanding to establish bilateral safe harbours, adopted by the Committee on Fiscal Affairs on 26 April 2013 [CTPA/CFA(2013)23] and approved by the Council on 16 May 2013 [C(2013)69].
- By a revision of Chapters I, II, V-VIII by the Report on BEPS Actions 8-10 *Aligning Transfer Pricing Outcomes with Value Creation* and the Report on BEPS Action 13, *Transfer Pricing Documentation and Country-by-Country Reporting*, endorsed by the Council on 1 October 2015 [C(2015)125/ADD8 and C(2015)125/ADD11].
- By a revision of Chapter IX adopted by the Committee on Fiscal Affairs on 31 December 2016 [CTPA/CFA/NOE2(2016)76] and approved by the Council on 3 April 2017 [C(2017)37].
- By an update of the Foreword, of the Preface, of the Glossary, of Chapters I-IV and of the annexes, adopted by the Committee on Fiscal Affairs on 19 May 2017 [CTPA/CFA/NOE2(2017)21];
- By a revision of Section C on the transactional profit split method in Part III of Chapter II and of the annexes, adopted by the Committee on Fiscal Affairs on 4 June 2018 [CTPA/CFA/NOE2(2018)24].

- By an update of the Foreword, of the Preface, of the Glossary, of Chapters I-IX and of the annexes, adopted by the Committee on Fiscal Affairs on 7 January 2022 [CTPA/CFA/NOE2(2021)52].

These Guidelines will continue to be supplemented with additional guidance addressing other aspects of transfer pricing and will be periodically reviewed and revised on an ongoing basis.

Table of contents

Preface

1. The role of multinational enterprises (MNEs) in world trade has continued to increase dramatically since the adoption of these Guidelines in 1995. This in part reflects the increased pace of integration of national economies and technological progress, particularly in the area of communications. The growth of MNEs presents increasingly complex taxation issues for both tax administrations and the MNEs themselves since separate country rules for the taxation of MNEs cannot be viewed in isolation but must be addressed in a broad international context.

2. These issues arise primarily from the practical difficulty, for both MNEs and tax administrations, of determining the income and expenses of a company or a permanent establishment that is part of an MNE group that should be taken into account within a jurisdiction, particularly where the MNE group's operations are highly integrated.

3. In the case of MNEs, the need to comply with laws and administrative requirements that may differ from jurisdiction to jurisdiction creates additional problems. The differing requirements may lead to a greater burden on an MNE, and result in higher costs of compliance, than for a similar enterprise operating solely within a single tax jurisdiction.

4. In the case of tax administrations, specific problems arise at both policy and practical levels. At the policy level, jurisdictions need to reconcile their legitimate right to tax the profits of a taxpayer based upon income and expenses that can reasonably be considered to arise within their territory with the need to avoid the taxation of the same item of income by more than one tax jurisdiction. Such double or multiple taxation can create an impediment to cross-border transactions in goods and services and the movement of capital. At a practical level, a jurisdiction's determination of such income and expense allocation may be impeded by difficulties in obtaining pertinent data located outside its own jurisdiction.

5. At a primary level, the taxing rights that each jurisdiction asserts depend on whether the jurisdiction uses a system of taxation that is residence-based, source-based, or both. In a residence-based tax system, a jurisdiction

will include in its tax base all or part of the income, including income from sources outside that jurisdiction, of any person (including juridical persons such as corporations) who is considered resident in that jurisdiction. In a source-based tax system, a jurisdiction will include in its tax base income arising within its tax jurisdiction, irrespective of the residence of the taxpayer. As applied to MNEs, these two bases, often used in conjunction, generally treat each enterprise within the MNE group as a separate entity. OECD member countries have chosen this separate entity approach as the most reasonable means for achieving equitable results and minimising the risk of unrelieved double taxation. Thus, each individual group member is subject to tax on the income arising to it (on a residence or source basis).

6. In order to apply the separate entity approach to intra-group transactions, individual group members must be taxed on the basis that they act at arm's length in their transactions with each other. However, the relationship among members of an MNE group may permit the group members to establish special conditions in their intra-group relations that differ from those that would have been established had the group members been acting as independent enterprises operating in open markets. To ensure the correct application of the separate entity approach, OECD member countries have adopted the arm's length principle, under which the effect of special conditions on the levels of profits should be eliminated.

7. These international taxation principles have been chosen by OECD member countries as serving the dual objectives of securing the appropriate tax base in each jurisdiction and avoiding double taxation, thereby minimising conflict between tax administrations and promoting international trade and investment. In a global economy, co-ordination among jurisdictions is better placed to achieve these goals than tax competition. The OECD, with its mission to contribute to the expansion of world trade on a multilateral, non-discriminatory basis and to achieve the highest sustainable economic growth in member countries, has continuously worked to build a consensus on international taxation principles, thereby avoiding unilateral responses to multilateral problems.

8. The foregoing principles concerning the taxation of MNEs are incorporated in the *OECD Model Tax Convention on Income and on Capital* (OECD Model Tax Convention), which forms the basis of the extensive network of bilateral income tax treaties between OECD member countries and between OECD member and non-member countries. These principles also are incorporated in the Model United Nations Double Taxation Convention between Developed and Developing Nations.

9. The main mechanisms for resolving issues that arise in the application of international tax principles to MNEs are contained in these bilateral treaties. The Articles that chiefly affect the taxation of MNEs are:

Article 4, which defines residence; Articles 5 and 7, which determine the taxation of permanent establishments; Article 9, which relates to the taxation of the profits of associated enterprises and applies the arm's length principle; Articles 10, 11, and 12, which determine the taxation of dividends, interest, and royalties, respectively; and Articles 24, 25, and 26, which contain special provisions relating to non-discrimination, the resolution of disputes, and exchange of information.

10. The Committee on Fiscal Affairs, which is the main tax policy body of the OECD, has issued a number of reports relating to the application of these Articles to MNEs and to others. The Committee has encouraged the acceptance of common interpretations of these Articles, thereby reducing the risk of inappropriate taxation and providing satisfactory means of resolving problems arising from the interaction of the laws and practices of different jurisdictions.

11. In applying the foregoing principles to the taxation of MNEs, one of the most difficult issues that has arisen is the establishment for tax purposes of appropriate transfer prices. Transfer prices are the prices at which an enterprise transfers physical goods and intangible property or provides services to associated enterprises. For purposes of these Guidelines, an "associated enterprise" is an enterprise that satisfies the conditions set forth in Article 9, sub-paragraphs 1a) and 1b) of the OECD Model Tax Convention. Under these conditions, two enterprises are associated if one of the enterprises participates directly or indirectly in the management, control, or capital of the other or if "the same persons participate directly or indirectly in the management, control, or capital" of both enterprises (i.e. if both enterprises are under common control). The issues discussed in these Guidelines also arise in the treatment of permanent establishments as discussed in the *Report on the Attribution of Profits to Permanent Establishments* that was adopted by the OECD Council in July 2010, which supersedes the OECD Report *Model Tax Convention: Attribution of Income to Permanent Establishments* (1994). Some relevant discussion may also be found in the OECD Report *International Tax Avoidance and Evasion* (1987).

12. Transfer prices are significant for both taxpayers and tax administrations because they determine in large part the income and expenses, and therefore taxable profits, of associated enterprises in different tax jurisdictions. Transfer pricing issues originally arose in transactions between associated enterprises operating within the same tax jurisdiction. The domestic issues are not considered in these Guidelines, which focus on the international aspects of transfer pricing. These international aspects are more difficult to deal with because they involve more than one tax jurisdiction and therefore any adjustment to the transfer price in one jurisdiction implies that a corresponding change in another jurisdiction is appropriate. However, if the other jurisdiction does not

agree to make a corresponding adjustment the MNE group will be taxed twice on this part of its profits. In order to minimise the risk of such double taxation, an international consensus is required on how to establish for tax purposes transfer prices on cross-border transactions.

13. These Guidelines are intended to be a revision and compilation of previous reports by the OECD Committee on Fiscal Affairs addressing transfer pricing and other related tax issues with respect to multinational enterprises. The principal report is *Transfer Pricing and Multinational Enterprises* (1979) (the "1979 Report") which was repealed by the OECD Council in 1995. Other reports address transfer pricing issues in the context of specific topics. These reports are *Transfer Pricing and Multinational Enterprises – Three Taxation Issues* (1984) (the "1984 Report"), and *Thin Capitalisation* (the "1987 Report"). A list of amendments made to these Guidelines is included in the Foreword.

14. These Guidelines also draw upon the discussion undertaken by the OECD on the proposed transfer pricing regulations in the United States [see the OECD Report *Tax Aspects of Transfer Pricing within Multinational Enterprises: The United States Proposed Regulations* (1993)]. However, the context in which that Report was written was very different from that in which these Guidelines have been undertaken, its scope was far more limited, and it specifically addressed the United States proposed regulations.

15. OECD member countries continue to endorse the arm's length principle as embodied in the OECD Model Tax Convention (and in the bilateral conventions that legally bind treaty partners in this respect) and in the 1979 Report. These Guidelines focus on the application of the arm's length principle to evaluate the transfer pricing of associated enterprises. The Guidelines are intended to help tax administrations (of both OECD member countries and non-member countries) and MNEs by indicating ways to find mutually satisfactory solutions to transfer pricing cases, thereby minimising conflict among tax administrations and between tax administrations and MNEs and avoiding costly litigation. The Guidelines analyse the methods for evaluating whether the conditions of commercial and financial relations within an MNE satisfy the arm's length principle and discuss the practical application of those methods. They also include a discussion of global formulary apportionment.

16. OECD member countries are encouraged to follow these Guidelines in their domestic transfer pricing practices, and taxpayers are encouraged to follow these Guidelines in evaluating for tax purposes whether their transfer pricing complies with the arm's length principle. Tax administrations are encouraged to take into account the taxpayer's commercial judgement about the application of the arm's length principle in their examination practices and to undertake their analyses of transfer pricing from that perspective.

17. These Guidelines are also intended primarily to govern the resolution of transfer pricing cases in mutual agreement proceedings between OECD member countries and, where appropriate, arbitration proceedings. They further provide guidance when a corresponding adjustment request has been made. The Commentary on paragraph 2 of Article 9 of the OECD Model Tax Convention makes clear that the State from which a corresponding adjustment is requested should comply with the request only if that State "considers that the figure of adjusted profits correctly reflects what the profits would have been if the transactions had been at arm's length". This means that in competent authority proceedings the State that has proposed the primary adjustment bears the burden of demonstrating to the other State that the adjustment "is justified both in principle and as regards the amount." Both competent authorities are expected to take a co-operative approach in resolving mutual agreement cases.

18. In seeking to achieve the balance between the interests of taxpayers and tax administrators in a way that is fair to all parties, it is necessary to consider all aspects of the system that are relevant in a transfer pricing case. One such aspect is the allocation of the burden of proof. In most jurisdictions, the tax administration bears the burden of proof, which may require the tax administration to make a *prima facie* showing that the taxpayer's pricing is inconsistent with the arm's length principle. It should be noted, however, that even in such a case a tax administration might still reasonably oblige the taxpayer to produce its records to enable the tax administration to undertake its examination of the controlled transactions. In other jurisdictions the taxpayer may bear the burden of proof in some respects. Some OECD member countries are of the view that Article 9 of the OECD Model Tax Convention establishes burden of proof rules in transfer pricing cases which override any contrary domestic provisions. Other countries, however, consider that Article 9 does not establish burden of proof rules (cf. paragraph 4 of the Commentary on Article 9 of the OECD Model Tax Convention). Regardless of which party bears the burden of proof, an assessment of the fairness of the allocation of the burden of proof would have to be made in view of the other features of the jurisdiction's tax system that have a bearing on the overall administration of transfer pricing rules, including the resolution of disputes. These features include penalties, examination practices, administrative appeals processes, rules regarding payment of interest with respect to tax assessments and refunds, whether proposed tax deficiencies must be paid before protesting an adjustment, the statute of limitations, and the extent to which rules are made known in advance. It would be inappropriate to rely on any of these features, including the burden of proof, to make unfounded assertions about transfer pricing. Some of these issues are discussed further in Chapter IV.

19. These Guidelines focus on the main issues of principle that arise in the transfer pricing area. The Committee on Fiscal Affairs intends to continue its work in this area. A revision of Chapters I-III and a new

Chapter IX were approved in 2010, reflecting work undertaken by the Committee on comparability, on transactional profit methods and on the transfer pricing aspects of business restructurings. In 2013, the guidance on safe harbours was also revised in order to recognise that properly designed safe harbours can help to relieve some compliance burdens and provide taxpayers with greater certainty. In 2016, these Guidelines were substantially revised in order to reflect the clarifications and revisions agreed in the 2015 BEPS Reports on Actions 8-10 *Aligning Transfer pricing Outcomes with Value Creation* and on Action 13 *Transfer Pricing Documentation and Country-by-Country Reporting.* In 2018, a revision of the guidance on the application of the profit split method in Chapter II was approved, as well as the addition of a new annex to Chapter VI which provides guidance for tax administrations on the application of the approach to hard-to-value intangibles. Finally, in 2020 a new Chapter X was added to these Guidelines to incorporate guidance on the transfer pricing aspects of financial transactions. The Committee intends to have regular reviews of the experiences of OECD member and selected non-member countries in applying the arm's length principle in order to identify areas on which further work could be necessary.

Abbreviations and acronyms

APA	Advance price arrangements
BEPS	Base erosion and profit shifting
CCA	Cost contribution arrangement
CbC	Country-by-Country
CFC	Controlled foreign company
CUP	Comparable uncontrolled price
DTC	Double taxation convention
G20	Group of twenty
HTVI	Hard-to-value intangibles
MAP	Mutual agreement procedure
MAP APA	Advance pricing arrangement under the mutual agreement procedure
MNE	Multinational enterprise
MOU	Memorandum of understanding
OECD	Organisation for Economic Co-operation and Development
Report on BEPS Action 14	2015 BEPS Report on Action 14 *Making Dispute Resolution Mechanisms More Effective*
R&D	Research and development
TIEA	Tax Information Exchange Agreement
TNMM	Transactional net margin method

Glossary

Advance pricing arrangement (APA)

An arrangement that determines, in advance of controlled transactions, an appropriate set of criteria (e.g. method, comparables and appropriate adjustments thereto, critical assumptions as to future events) for the determination of the transfer pricing for those transactions over a fixed period of time. An advance pricing arrangement may be unilateral involving one tax administration and a taxpayer or multilateral involving the agreement of two or more tax administrations.

Arm's length principle

The international standard that OECD member countries have agreed should be used for determining transfer prices for tax purposes. It is set forth in Article 9 of the OECD Model Tax Convention as follows: where "conditions are made or imposed between the two enterprises in their commercial or financial relations which differ from those which would be made between independent enterprises, then any profits which would, but for those conditions, have accrued to one of the enterprises, but, by reason of those conditions, have not so accrued, may be included in the profits of that enterprise and taxed accordingly".

Arm's length range

A range of figures that are acceptable for establishing whether the conditions of a controlled transaction are arm's length and that are derived either from applying the same transfer pricing method to multiple comparable data or from applying different transfer pricing methods.

Associated enterprises

Two enterprises are associated enterprises with respect to each other if one of the enterprises meets the conditions of Article 9, sub-paragraphs 1a) or 1b) of the OECD Model Tax Convention with respect to the other enterprise.

Balancing payment

A payment, normally from one or more participants to another, to adjust participants' proportionate shares of contributions, that increases the value of the contributions of the payer and decreases the value of the contributions of the payee by the amount of the payment.

Buy-in payment

A payment made by a new entrant to an already active CCA for obtaining an interest in any results of prior CCA activity.

Buy-out payment

Compensation that a participant who withdraws from an already active CCA may receive from the remaining participants for an effective transfer of its interests in the results of past CCA activities.

Comparability analysis

A comparison of a controlled transaction with an uncontrolled transaction or transactions. Controlled and uncontrolled transactions are comparable if none of the differences between the transactions could materially affect the factor being examined in the methodology (e.g. price or margin), or if reasonably accurate adjustments can be made to eliminate the material effects of any such differences.

Comparable uncontrolled transaction

A comparable uncontrolled transaction is a transaction between two independent parties that is comparable to the controlled transaction under examination. It can be either a comparable transaction between one party to the controlled transaction and an independent party ("internal comparable") or between two independent parties, neither of which is a party to the controlled transaction ("external comparable").

Comparable uncontrolled price (CUP) method

A transfer pricing method that compares the price for property or services transferred in a controlled transaction to the price charged for property or services transferred in a comparable uncontrolled transaction in comparable circumstances.

Compensating adjustment

An adjustment in which the taxpayer reports a transfer price for tax purposes that is, in the taxpayer's opinion, an arm's length price for a controlled transaction, even though this price differs from the amount actually charged between the associated enterprises. This adjustment would be made before the tax return is filed.

Contribution analysis

An analysis used in the profit split method under which the relevant profits from controlled transactions are divided between the associated enterprises based upon the relative value of the contributions made by each of the associated enterprises participating in those transactions, supplemented where possible by external market data that indicate how independent enterprises would have divided profits in similar circumstances.

Controlled transactions

Transactions between two enterprises that are associated enterprises with respect to each other.

Corresponding adjustment

An adjustment to the tax liability of the associated enterprise in a second tax jurisdiction made by the tax administration of that jurisdiction, corresponding to a primary adjustment made by the tax administration in a first tax jurisdiction, so that the allocation of profits by the two jurisdictions is consistent.

Cost contribution arrangement (CCA)

A CCA is a contractual arrangement among business enterprises to share the contributions and risks involved in the joint development, production or the obtaining of intangibles, tangible assets or services with the understanding that such intangibles, tangible assets or services are expected to create benefits for the individual businesses of each of the participants.

Cost plus mark-up

A mark-up that is measured by reference to margins computed after the direct and indirect costs incurred by a supplier of property or services in a transaction.

Cost plus method

A transfer pricing method using the costs incurred by the supplier of property (or services) in a controlled transaction. An appropriate cost plus mark-up is added to this cost, to make an appropriate profit in light of the functions performed (taking into account assets used and risks assumed) and the market conditions. What is arrived at after adding the cost plus mark up to the above costs may be regarded as an arm's length price of the original controlled transaction.

Direct-charge method

A method of charging directly for specific intra-group services on a clearly identified basis.

Direct costs

Costs that are incurred specifically for producing a product or rendering service, such as the cost of raw materials.

Functional analysis

The analysis aimed at identifying the economically significant activities and responsibilities undertaken, assets used or contributed, and risks assumed by the parties to the transactions.

Global formulary apportionment

An approach to allocate the global profits of an MNE group on a consolidated basis among the associated enterprises in different jurisdictions on the basis of a predetermined formula.

Gross profits

The gross profits from a business transaction are the amount computed by deducting from the gross receipts of the transaction the allocable purchases or production costs of sales, with due adjustment for increases or decreases in inventory or stock-in-trade, but without taking account of other expenses.

Independent enterprises

Two enterprises are independent enterprises with respect to each other if they are not associated enterprises with respect to each other.

Indirect-charge method

A method of charging for intra-group services based upon cost allocation and apportionment methods.

Indirect costs

Costs of producing a product or service which, although closely related to the production process, may be common to several products or services (for example, the costs of a repair department that services equipment used to produce different products).

Intra-group service

An activity (e.g. administrative, technical, financial, commercial, etc.) for which an independent enterprise would have been willing to pay or perform for itself.

Intentional set-off

A benefit provided by one associated enterprise to another associated enterprise within the group that is deliberately balanced to some degree by different benefits received from that enterprise in return.

Marketing intangible

An intangible (within the meaning of paragraph 6.6) that relates to marketing activities, aids in the commercial exploitation of a product or service and/or has an important promotional value for the product concerned. Depending on the context, marketing intangibles may include, for example, trademarks, trade names, customer lists, customer relationships, and proprietary market and customer data that is used or aids in marketing and selling goods or services to customers.

Multinational enterprise group (MNE group)

A group of associated companies with business establishments in two or more jurisdictions.

Multinational enterprise (MNE)

A company that is part of an MNE group.

Mutual agreement procedure

A means through which tax administrations consult to resolve disputes regarding the application of double tax conventions. This procedure, described and authorised by Article 25 of the OECD Model Tax Convention, can be used to eliminate double taxation that could arise from a transfer pricing adjustment.

Net profit indicator

The ratio of net profit to an appropriate base (e.g. costs, sales, assets). The transactional net margin method relies on a comparison of an appropriate net profit indicator for the controlled transaction with the same net profit indicator in comparable uncontrolled transactions.

"On call" services

Services provided by a parent company or a group service centre, which are available at any time for members of an MNE group.

Primary adjustment

An adjustment that a tax administration in a first jurisdiction makes to a company's taxable profits as a result of applying the arm's length principle to transactions involving an associated enterprise in a second tax jurisdiction.

Profit potential

The expected future profits. In some cases it may encompass losses. The notion of "profit potential" is often used for valuation purposes, in the determination of an arm's length compensation for a transfer of intangibles or of an ongoing concern, or in the determination of an arm's length indemnification for the termination or substantial renegotiation of existing arrangements, once it is found that such compensation or indemnification would have taken place between independent parties in comparable circumstances.

Profit split method

A transactional profit split method that identifies the relevant profits to be split for the associated enterprises from a controlled transaction (or controlled transactions that it is appropriate to aggregate under the principles of Chapter III) and then splits those profits between the associated enterprises on an economically valid basis that approximates the division of profits that would have been agreed at arm's length.

Resale price margin

A margin representing the amount out of which a reseller would seek to cover its selling and other operating expenses and, in the light of the functions performed (taking into account assets used and risks assumed), make an appropriate profit.

Resale price method

A transfer pricing method based on the price at which a product that has been purchased from an associated enterprise is resold to an independent enterprise. The resale price is reduced by the resale price margin. What is left after subtracting the resale price margin can be regarded, after adjustment for other costs associated with the purchase of the product (e.g. custom duties), as an arm's length price of the original transfer of property between the associated enterprises.

Residual analysis

An analysis used in the profit split method which divides the relevant profits from the controlled transactions under examination into two categories. In the first category are profits attributable to contributions which can be reliably benchmarked: typically less complex contributions for which reliable comparables can be found. Ordinarily this initial remuneration would be determined by applying one of the traditional transaction methods or a transactional net margin method to identify the remuneration of comparable transactions between independent enterprises. Thus, it would generally not account for the return that would be generated by a second category of contributions which may be unique and valuable, and/or are attributable to a high level of integration or the shared assumption of economically significant risks. Typically, the allocation of any residual profit (or loss) remaining after allowing for the profits attributable to the first category of contributions would be based on an analysis of the relative value of the second category of contributions by the parties, supplemented where possible by external market data that indicate how independent enterprises would have divided profits in similar circumstances.

Secondary adjustment

An adjustment that arises from imposing tax on a secondary transaction.

Secondary transaction

A constructive transaction that some jurisdictions will assert under their domestic legislation after having proposed a primary adjustment in order to make the actual allocation of profits consistent with the primary adjustment. Secondary transactions may take the form of constructive dividends, constructive equity contributions, or constructive loans.

Shareholder activity

An activity which is performed by a member of an MNE group (usually the parent company or a regional holding company) solely because of its ownership interest in one or more other group members, i.e. in its capacity as shareholder.

Simultaneous tax examinations

A simultaneous tax examination, as defined in Part A of the OECD Model Agreement for the Undertaking of Simultaneous Tax Examinations, means an "arrangement between two or more parties to examine simultaneously and independently, each on its own territory, the tax affairs of (a) taxpayer(s) in which they have a common or related interest with a view to exchanging any relevant information which they so obtain".

Trade intangible

An intangible other than a marketing intangible.

Traditional transaction methods

The comparable uncontrolled price method, the resale price method, and the cost plus method.

Transactional net margin method

A transactional profit method that examines the net profit margin relative to an appropriate base (e.g. costs, sales, assets) that a taxpayer realises from a controlled transaction (or transactions that it is appropriate to aggregate under the principles of Chapter III).

Transactional profit method

A transfer pricing method that examines the profits that arise from particular controlled transactions of one or more of the associated enterprises participating in those transactions.

Uncontrolled transactions

Transactions between enterprises that are independent enterprises with respect to each other.

Unique and valuable contributions

Contributions (for instance functions performed, or assets used or contributed) will be "unique and valuable" in cases where (i) they are not comparable to contributions made by uncontrolled parties in comparable circumstances, and (ii) they represent a key source of actual or potential economic benefits in the business operations.

Chapter I

The arm's length principle

A. Introduction

1.1. This Chapter provides a background discussion of the arm's length principle, which is the international transfer pricing standard that OECD member countries have agreed should be used for tax purposes by MNE groups and tax administrations. The Chapter discusses the arm's length principle, reaffirms its status as the international standard, and sets forth guidelines for its application.

1.2. When independent enterprises transact with each other, the conditions of their commercial and financial relations (e.g. the price of goods transferred or services provided and the conditions of the transfer or provision) ordinarily are determined by market forces. When associated enterprises transact with each other, their commercial and financial relations may not be directly affected by external market forces in the same way, although associated enterprises often seek to replicate the dynamics of market forces in their transactions with each other, as discussed in paragraph 1.5 below. Tax administrations should not automatically assume that associated enterprises have sought to manipulate their profits. There may be a genuine difficulty in accurately determining a market price in the absence of market forces or when adopting a particular commercial strategy. It is important to bear in mind that the need to make adjustments to approximate arm's length conditions arises irrespective of any contractual obligation undertaken by the parties to pay a particular price or of any intention of the parties to minimise tax. Thus, a tax adjustment under the arm's length principle would not affect the underlying contractual obligations for non-tax purposes between the associated enterprises, and may be appropriate even where there is no intent to minimise or avoid tax. The consideration of transfer pricing should not be confused with the consideration of problems of tax fraud or tax avoidance, even though transfer pricing policies may be used for such purposes.

1.3. When transfer pricing does not reflect market forces and the arm's length principle, the tax liabilities of the associated enterprises and the tax revenues of the host jurisdictions could be distorted. Therefore, OECD member countries have agreed that for tax purposes the profits of associated enterprises may be adjusted as necessary to correct any such distortions and thereby ensure that the arm's length principle is satisfied. OECD member countries consider that an appropriate adjustment is achieved by establishing the conditions of the commercial and financial relations that they would expect to find between independent enterprises in comparable transactions under comparable circumstances.

1.4. Factors other than tax considerations may distort the conditions of commercial and financial relations established between associated enterprises. For example, such enterprises may be subject to conflicting governmental pressures (in the domestic as well as foreign country) relating to customs valuations, anti-dumping duties, and exchange or price controls. In addition, transfer price distortions may be caused by the cash flow requirements of enterprises within an MNE group. An MNE group that is publicly held may feel pressure from shareholders to show high profitability at the parent company level, particularly if shareholder reporting is not undertaken on a consolidated basis. All of these factors may affect transfer prices and the amount of profits accruing to associated enterprises within an MNE group.

1.5. It should not be assumed that the conditions established in the commercial and financial relations between associated enterprises will invariably deviate from what the open market would demand. Associated enterprises in MNEs sometimes have a considerable amount of autonomy and can often bargain with each other as though they were independent enterprises. Enterprises respond to economic situations arising from market conditions, in their relations with both third parties and associated enterprises. For example, local managers may be interested in establishing good profit records and therefore would not want to establish prices that would reduce the profits of their own companies. Tax administrations should keep these considerations in mind to facilitate efficient allocation of their resources in selecting and conducting transfer pricing examinations. Sometimes, it may occur that the relationship between the associated enterprises may influence the outcome of the bargaining. Therefore, evidence of hard bargaining alone is not sufficient to establish that the transactions are at arm's length.

B. Statement of the arm's length principle

B.1. Article 9 of the OECD Model Tax Convention

1.6. The authoritative statement of the arm's length principle is found in paragraph 1 of Article 9 of the OECD Model Tax Convention, which forms the basis of bilateral tax treaties involving OECD member countries and an increasing number of non-member countries. Article 9 provides:

> [Where] conditions are made or imposed between the two [associated] enterprises in their commercial or financial relations which differ from those which would be made between independent enterprises, then any profits which would, but for those conditions, have accrued to one of the enterprises, but, by reason of those conditions, have not so accrued, may be included in the profits of that enterprise and taxed accordingly.

By seeking to adjust profits by reference to the conditions which would have obtained between independent enterprises in comparable transactions and comparable circumstances (i.e. in "comparable uncontrolled transactions"), the arm's length principle follows the approach of treating the members of an MNE group as operating as separate entities rather than as inseparable parts of a single unified business. Because the separate entity approach treats the members of an MNE group as if they were independent entities, attention is focused on the nature of the transactions between those members and on whether the conditions thereof differ from the conditions that would be obtained in comparable uncontrolled transactions. Such an analysis of the controlled and uncontrolled transactions, which is referred to as a "comparability analysis", is at the heart of the application of the arm's length principle. Guidance on the comparability analysis is found in Section D below and in Chapter III.

1.7. It is important to put the issue of comparability into perspective in order to emphasise the need for an approach that is balanced in terms of, on the one hand, its reliability and, on the other, the burden it creates for taxpayers and tax administrations. Paragraph 1 of Article 9 of the OECD Model Tax Convention is the foundation for comparability analyses because it introduces the need for:

- A comparison between conditions (including prices, but not only prices) made or imposed between associated enterprises and those which would be made between independent enterprises, in order to determine whether a re-writing of the accounts for the purposes of calculating tax liabilities of associated enterprises is authorised under Article 9 of the OECD Model Tax Convention (see paragraph 2 of the Commentary on Article 9); and

- A determination of the profits which would have accrued at arm's length, in order to determine the quantum of any re-writing of accounts.

1.8. There are several reasons why OECD member countries and other jurisdictions have adopted the arm's length principle. A major reason is that the arm's length principle provides broad parity of tax treatment for members of MNE groups and independent enterprises. Because the arm's length principle puts associated and independent enterprises on a more equal footing for tax purposes, it avoids the creation of tax advantages or disadvantages that would otherwise distort the relative competitive positions of either type of entity. In so removing these tax considerations from economic decisions, the arm's length principle promotes the growth of international trade and investment.

1.9. The arm's length principle has also been found to work effectively in the vast majority of cases. For example, there are many cases involving the purchase and sale of commodities and the lending of money where an arm's length price may readily be found in a comparable transaction undertaken by comparable independent enterprises under comparable circumstances. There are also many cases where a relevant comparison of transactions can be made at the level of financial indicators such as mark-up on costs, gross margin, or net profit indicators. Nevertheless, there are some significant cases in which the arm's length principle is difficult and complicated to apply, for example, in MNE groups dealing in the integrated production of highly specialised goods, in unique intangibles, and/or in the provision of specialised services. Solutions exist to deal with such difficult cases, including the use of the transactional profit split method described in Chapter II, Part III of these Guidelines in those situations where it is the most appropriate method in the circumstances of the case.

1.10. The arm's length principle is viewed by some as inherently flawed because the separate entity approach may not always account for the economies of scale and interrelation of diverse activities created by integrated businesses. There are, however, no widely accepted objective criteria for allocating between associated enterprises the economies of scale or benefits of integration resulting from group membership. The issue of possible alternatives to the arm's length principle is discussed in Section C below.

1.11. A practical difficulty in applying the arm's length principle is that associated enterprises may engage in transactions that independent enterprises would not undertake. Such transactions may not necessarily be motivated by tax avoidance but may occur because in transacting business with each other, members of an MNE group face different commercial circumstances than would independent enterprises. Where independent enterprises seldom undertake transactions of the type entered into by associated enterprises, the arm's length principle is difficult to apply because there is little or no direct evidence of what conditions would have been established by independent enterprises. The mere fact that a transaction may not be found between independent parties does not of itself mean that it is not arm's length.

1.12. In certain cases, the arm's length principle may result in an administrative burden for both the taxpayer and the tax administrations of evaluating significant numbers and types of cross-border transactions. Although associated enterprises normally establish the conditions for a transaction at the time it is undertaken, at some point the enterprises may be required to demonstrate that these are consistent with the arm's length principle. (See discussion of timing and compliance issues in Sections B and C of Chapter III and at Chapter V on Documentation). The tax administration may also have to engage in this verification process perhaps some years after the transactions have taken place. The tax administration would review any supporting documentation prepared by the taxpayer to show that its transactions are consistent with the arm's length principle, and may also need to gather information about comparable uncontrolled transactions, the market conditions at the time the transactions took place, etc., for numerous and varied transactions. Such an undertaking usually becomes more difficult with the passage of time.

1.13. Both tax administrations and taxpayers often have difficulty in obtaining adequate information to apply the arm's length principle. Because the arm's length principle usually requires taxpayers and tax administrations to evaluate uncontrolled transactions and the business activities of independent enterprises, and to compare these with the transactions and activities of associated enterprises, it can demand a substantial amount of data. The information that is accessible may be incomplete and difficult to interpret; other information, if it exists, may be difficult to obtain for reasons of its geographical location or that of the parties from whom it may have to be acquired. In addition, it may not be possible to obtain information from independent enterprises because of confidentiality concerns. In other cases information about an independent enterprise which could be relevant may simply not exist, or there may be no comparable independent enterprises, e.g. if that industry has reached a high level of vertical integration. It is important not to lose sight of the objective to find a reasonable estimate of an arm's length outcome based on reliable information. It should also be recalled at this point that transfer pricing is not an exact science but does require the exercise of judgment on the part of both the tax administration and taxpayer.

B.2. Maintaining the arm's length principle as the international consensus

1.14. While recognising the foregoing considerations, the view of OECD member countries continues to be that the arm's length principle should govern the evaluation of transfer prices among associated enterprises.

The arm's length principle is sound in theory since it provides the closest approximation of the workings of the open market in cases where property (such as goods, other types of tangible assets, or intangible assets) is transferred or services are rendered between associated enterprises. While it may not always be straightforward to apply in practice, it does generally produce appropriate levels of income between members of MNE groups, acceptable to tax administrations. This reflects the economic realities of the controlled taxpayer's particular facts and circumstances and adopts as a benchmark the normal operation of the market.

1.15. A move away from the arm's length principle would abandon the sound theoretical basis described above and threaten the international consensus, thereby substantially increasing the risk of double taxation. Experience under the arm's length principle has become sufficiently broad and sophisticated to establish a substantial body of common understanding among the business community and tax administrations. This shared understanding is of great practical value in achieving the objectives of securing the appropriate tax base in each jurisdiction and avoiding double taxation. This experience should be drawn on to elaborate the arm's length principle further, to refine its operation, and to improve its administration by providing clearer guidance to taxpayers and more timely examinations. In sum, OECD member countries continue to support strongly the arm's length principle. In fact, no legitimate or realistic alternative to the arm's length principle has emerged. Global formulary apportionment, sometimes mentioned as a possible alternative, would not be acceptable in theory, implementation, or practice. (See Section C, immediately below, for a discussion of global formulary apportionment.)

C. A non-arm's-length approach: global formulary apportionment

C.1. Background and description of approach

1.16. Global formulary apportionment has sometimes been suggested as an alternative to the arm's length principle as a means of determining the proper level of profits across national taxing jurisdictions. The approach has not been applied as between jurisdictions although it has been attempted by some local taxing jurisdictions.

1.17. Global formulary apportionment would allocate the global profits of an MNE group on a consolidated basis among the associated enterprises in different jurisdictions on the basis of a predetermined and mechanistic formula. There would be three essential components to applying global formulary apportionment: determining the unit to be taxed, i.e. which of the subsidiaries and branches of an MNE group should comprise the global taxable entity; accurately determining the global profits; and establishing the formula to be used to allocate the global profits of the unit. The formula would most likely be based on some combination of costs, assets, payroll, and sales.

1.18. Global formulary apportionment should not be confused with the transactional profit methods discussed in Part III of Chapter II. Global formulary apportionment would use a formula that is predetermined for all taxpayers to allocate profits whereas transactional profit methods compare, on a case-by-case basis, the profits of one or more associated enterprises with the profit experience that comparable independent enterprises would have sought to achieve in comparable circumstances. Global formulary apportionment also should not be confused with the selected application of a formula developed by both tax administrations in co-operation with a specific taxpayer or MNE group after careful analysis of the particular facts and circumstances, such as might be used in a mutual agreement procedure, advance pricing agreement, or other bilateral or multilateral determination. Such a formula is derived from the particular facts and circumstances of the taxpayer and thus avoids the globally pre-determined and mechanistic nature of global formulary apportionment.

C.2. Comparison with the arm's length principle

1.19. Global formulary apportionment has been promoted as an alternative to the arm's length principle by advocates who claim that it would provide greater administrative convenience and certainty for taxpayers. These advocates also take the position that global formulary apportionment is more in keeping with economic reality. They argue that an MNE group must be considered on a group-wide or consolidated basis to reflect the business realities of the relationships among the associated enterprises in the group. They assert that the separate accounting method is inappropriate for highly integrated groups because it is difficult to determine what contribution each associated enterprise makes to the overall profit of the MNE group.

1.20. Apart from these arguments, advocates contend that global formulary apportionment reduces compliance costs for taxpayers since in principle only one set of accounts would be prepared for the group for domestic tax purposes.

1.21. OECD member countries do not accept these propositions and do not consider global formulary apportionment a realistic alternative to the arm's length principle, for the reasons discussed below.

1.22. The most significant concern with global formulary apportionment is the difficulty of implementing the system in a manner that both protects against double taxation and ensures single taxation. To achieve this would require substantial international co-ordination and consensus on the predetermined formulae to be used and on the composition of the group in question. For example, to avoid double taxation there would have to be common agreement to adopt the approach in the first instance, followed by agreement on the measurement of the global tax base of an MNE group, on the use of a common accounting system, on the factors that should be used to apportion the tax base among different jurisdictions (including non-member countries), and on how to measure and weight those factors. Reaching such agreement would be time-consuming and extremely difficult. It is far from clear that jurisdictions would be willing to agree to a universal formula.

1.23. Even if some jurisdictions were willing to accept global formulary apportionment, there would be disagreements because each jurisdiction may want to emphasise or include different factors in the formula based on the activities or factors that predominate in its jurisdiction. Each jurisdiction would have a strong incentive to devise formulae or formula weights that would maximise that jurisdiction's own revenue. In addition, tax administrations would have to consider jointly how to address the potential for artificially shifting the production factors used in the formula (e.g. sales, capital) to low tax jurisdiction. There could be tax avoidance to the extent that the components of the relevant formula can be manipulated, e.g. by entering into unnecessary financial transactions, by the deliberate location of mobile assets, by requiring that particular companies within an MNE group maintain inventory levels in excess of what normally would be encountered in an uncontrolled company of that type, and so on.

1.24. The transition to a global formulary apportionment system therefore would present enormous political and administrative complexity and require a level of international co-operation that is unrealistic to expect in the field of international taxation. Such multilateral co-ordination would require the inclusion of all major jurisdictions where MNEs operate. If all the major jurisdictions failed to agree to move to global formulary apportionment, MNEs would be faced with the burden of complying with two totally different systems. In other words, for the same set of transactions they would be forced to calculate the profits accruing to their members under two completely different standards. Such a result would create the potential for double taxation (or under-taxation) in every case.

1.25. There are other significant concerns in addition to the double taxation issues discussed above. One such concern is that predetermined formulae are arbitrary and disregard market conditions, the particular circumstances of the individual enterprises, and management's own allocation of resources, thus producing an allocation of profits that may bear no sound relationship to the specific facts surrounding the transaction. More specifically, a formula based on a combination of cost, assets, payroll, and sales implicitly imputes a fixed rate of profit per currency unit (e.g. dollar, euro, yen) of each component to every member of the group and in every tax jurisdiction, regardless of differences in functions, assets, risks, and efficiencies and among members of the MNE group. Such an approach could potentially assign profits to an entity that would incur losses if it were an independent enterprise.

1.26. Another issue for global formulary apportionment is dealing with exchange rate movements. Although exchange rate movements can complicate application of the arm's length principle they do not have the same impact as for global formulary apportionment; the arm's length principle is better equipped to deal with the economic consequences of exchange rate movements because it requires the analysis of the specific facts and circumstances of the taxpayer. If the formula relies on costs, the result of applying a global formulary apportionment would be that as a particular currency strengthens in one jurisdiction consistently against another currency in which an associated enterprise keeps its accounts, a greater share of the profit would be attributed to the enterprise in the first jurisdiction to reflect the costs of its payroll nominally increased by the currency fluctuation. Thus, under a global formulary apportionment, the exchange rate movement in this example would lead to increasing the profits of the associated enterprise operating with the stronger currency whereas in the long run a strengthening currency makes exports less competitive and leads to a downward pressure on profits.

1.27. Contrary to the assertions of its advocates, global formulary apportionment may in fact present intolerable compliance costs and data requirements because information would have to be gathered about the entire MNE group and presented in each jurisdiction on the basis of the currency and the book and tax accounting rules of that particular jurisdiction. Thus, the documentation and compliance requirements for an application of global formulary apportionment would generally be more burdensome than under the separate entity approach of the arm's length principle. The costs of a global formulary apportionment would be further magnified if not all jurisdictions could agree on the components of the formula or on the way the components are measured.

1.28. Difficulties also would arise in determining the sales of each member and in the valuation of assets (e.g. historic cost versus market value), especially in the valuation of intangibles. These difficulties would be compounded by the existence across taxing jurisdictions of different accounting standards and of multiple currencies. Accounting standards among all jurisdictions would have to be conformed in order to arrive at a meaningful measure of profit for the entire MNE group. Of course, some of these difficulties, for example the valuation of assets and intangibles, also exist under the arm's length principle, although significant progress in respect of the latter has been made, whereas no credible solutions have been put forward under global formulary apportionment.

1.29. Global formulary apportionment would have the effect of taxing an MNE group on a consolidated basis and therefore abandons the separate entity approach. As a consequence, global formulary apportionment cannot, as a practical matter, recognise important geographical differences, separate company efficiencies, and other factors specific to one company or sub-grouping within the MNE group that may legitimately play a role in determining the division of profits between enterprises in different tax jurisdictions. The arm's length principle, in contrast, recognises that an associated enterprise may be a separate profit or loss centre with individual characteristics and economically may be earning a profit even when the rest of the MNE group is incurring a loss. Global formulary apportionment does not have the flexibility to account properly for this possibility.

1.30. By disregarding intra-group transactions for the purpose of computing consolidated profits, global formulary apportionment would raise questions about the relevance of imposing withholding taxes on cross-border payments between group members and would involve a rejection of a number of rules incorporated in bilateral tax treaties.

1.31. Unless global formulary apportionment includes every member of an MNE group, it must retain a separate entity rule for the interface between that part of the group subject to global formulary apportionment and the rest of the MNE group. Global formulary apportionment could not be used to value the transactions between the global formulary apportionment group and the rest of the MNE group. Thus, a clear disadvantage with global formulary apportionment is that it does not provide a complete solution to the allocation of profits of an MNE group unless global formulary apportionment is applied on the basis of the whole MNE group. This exercise would be a serious undertaking for a single tax administration given the size and scale of operations of major MNE groups and the information that would be required. The MNE group would also be required, in any event, to maintain separate accounting for corporations that are not members of the MNE group for global formulary apportionment tax purposes but that are still associated enterprises of one or more members of the MNE group. In fact, many domestic commercial and accountancy rules would still require the use of arm's length prices (e.g. customs rules), so that irrespective of the tax provisions a taxpayer would have to book properly every transaction at arm's length prices.

C.3. Rejection of non-arm's-length methods

1.32. For the foregoing reasons, OECD member countries reiterate their support for the consensus on the use of the arm's length principle that has emerged over the years among member and non-member countries and agree that the theoretical alternative to the arm's length principle represented by global formulary apportionment should be rejected.

D. Guidance for applying the arm's length principle

D.1. Identifying the commercial or financial relations

1.33. As stated in paragraph 1.6 a "comparability analysis" is at the heart of the application of the arm's length principle. Application of the arm's length principle is based on a comparison of the conditions in a controlled transaction with the conditions that would have been made had the parties been independent and undertaking a comparable transaction under comparable circumstances. There are two key aspects in such an analysis: the first aspect is to identify the commercial or financial relations between the associated enterprises and the conditions and economically relevant circumstances attaching to those relations in order that the controlled transaction is accurately delineated; the second aspect is to compare the conditions and the economically relevant circumstances of the controlled transaction as accurately delineated with the conditions and the economically relevant circumstances of comparable transactions between independent enterprises. This section of Chapter I provides guidance on identifying the commercial or financial relations between the associated enterprises and on accurately delineating the controlled transaction. This first aspect of the analysis is distinct from the second aspect of considering the pricing of that controlled transaction under the arm's length principle. Chapters II and III provide guidance on the second aspect of the analysis. The information about the controlled transaction determined under the guidance in this section is especially relevant for steps 2 and 3 of the typical process of a comparability analysis set out in paragraph 3.4.

1.34. The typical process of identifying the commercial or financial relations between the associated enterprises and the conditions and economically relevant circumstances attaching to those relations requires a broad-based understanding of the industry sector in which the MNE group operates (e.g. mining, pharmaceutical, luxury goods) and of the factors affecting the performance of any business operating in that sector. The understanding is derived from an overview of the particular MNE group which outlines how the MNE group responds to the factors affecting performance in the sector, including its business strategies, markets, products, its supply chain, and the key functions performed, material assets used, and important risks assumed. This information is likely to be included as part of the master file as described in Chapter V in support of a taxpayer's analysis of its transfer pricing, and provides useful context in which the commercial or financial relations between members of the MNE group can be considered.

1.35. The process then narrows to identify how each MNE within that MNE group operates, and provides an analysis of what each MNE does (e.g. a production company, a sales company) and identifies its commercial or financial relations with associated enterprises as expressed in transactions between them. The accurate delineation of the actual transaction or transactions between the associated enterprises requires analysis of the economically relevant characteristics of the transaction. These economically relevant characteristics consist of the conditions of the transaction and the economically relevant circumstances in which the transaction takes place. The application of the arm's length principle depends on determining the conditions that independent parties would have agreed in comparable transactions in comparable circumstances. Before making comparisons with uncontrolled transactions, it is therefore vital to identify the economically relevant characteristics of the commercial or financial relations as expressed in the controlled transaction.

1.36. The economically relevant characteristics or comparability factors that need to be identified in the commercial or financial relations between the associated enterprises in order to accurately delineate the actual transaction can be broadly categorised as follows:

- The contractual terms of the transaction (D.1.1).
- The functions performed by each of the parties to the transaction, taking into account assets used and risks assumed, including how those functions relate to the wider generation of value by the MNE group to which the parties belong, the circumstances surrounding the transaction, and industry practices (D.1.2).
- The characteristics of property transferred or services provided (D.1.3).
- The economic circumstances of the parties and of the market in which the parties operate (D.1.4).
- The business strategies pursued by the parties (D.1.5).

This information about the economically relevant characteristics of the actual transaction should be included as part of the local file as described in Chapter V in support of a taxpayer's analysis of its transfer pricing.

1.37. Economically relevant characteristics or comparability factors are used in two separate but related phases in a transfer pricing analysis. The first phase relates to the process of accurately delineating the controlled transaction for the purposes of this chapter, and involves establishing the characteristics of the transaction, including its terms, the functions performed, assets used, and risks assumed by the associated enterprises, the nature of the products transferred or services provided, and the circumstances of the associated enterprises, in accordance with the categories set out in the previous paragraph. The extent to which any one of the characteristics categorised above is economically relevant in a particular transaction depends on the extent to which it would be taken into account by independent enterprises when evaluating the terms of the same transaction were it to occur between them.

1.38. Independent enterprises, when evaluating the terms of a potential transaction, will compare the transaction to the other options realistically available to them, and they will only enter into the transaction if they see no alternative that offers a clearly more attractive opportunity to meet their commercial objectives. In other words, independent enterprises would only enter into a transaction if it is not expected to make them worse off than their next best option. For example, one enterprise is unlikely to accept a price offered for its product by an independent commercial enterprise if it knows that other potential customers are willing to pay more under similar conditions, or are willing to pay the same under more beneficial conditions. Independent enterprises will generally take into account any economically relevant differences between the options realistically available to them (such as differences in the level of risk) when valuing those options. Therefore, identifying the economically relevant characteristics of the transaction is essential in accurately delineating the controlled transaction and in revealing the range of characteristics taken into account by the parties to the transaction in reaching the conclusion that there is no clearly more attractive opportunity realistically available to meet their commercial objectives than the transaction adopted. In making such an assessment, it may be necessary or useful to assess the transaction in the context of a broader arrangement of transactions, since assessment of the options realistically available to third parties is not necessarily limited to the single transaction, but may take into account a broader arrangement of economically related transactions.

1.39. The second phase in which economically relevant characteristics or comparability factors are used in a transfer pricing analysis relates to the process set out in Chapter III of making comparisons between the controlled transactions and uncontrolled transactions in order to determine an arm's length price for the controlled transaction. To make such comparisons, taxpayers and tax administrations need first to have identified the economically relevant characteristics of the controlled transaction. As set out in Chapter III, differences in economically relevant characteristics between the controlled and uncontrolled arrangements need to be taken into account when establishing whether there is comparability between the situations being compared and what adjustments may be necessary to achieve comparability.

1.40. All methods that apply the arm's length principle can be tied to the concept that independent enterprises consider the options realistically available to them and in comparing one option to another they consider any differences between the options that would significantly affect their value. For instance, before purchasing a product at a given price, independent enterprises normally would be expected to consider whether they could buy an equivalent product on otherwise comparable terms and conditions but at a lower price from another party. Therefore, as discussed in Chapter II, Part II, the comparable uncontrolled price method compares a controlled transaction to similar uncontrolled transactions to provide a direct estimate of the price the parties would have agreed to had they resorted directly to a market alternative to the controlled transaction. However, the method becomes a less reliable substitute for arm's length transactions if not all the characteristics of these uncontrolled transactions that significantly affect the price charged between independent enterprises are comparable. Similarly, the resale price and cost plus methods compare the gross profit margin earned in the controlled transaction to gross profit margins earned in similar uncontrolled transactions. The comparison provides an estimate of the gross profit margin one of the parties could have earned had it performed the same functions for independent enterprises and therefore provides an estimate of the payment that party would have demanded, and the other party would have been willing to pay, at arm's length for performing those functions. Other methods, as discussed in Chapter II, Part III, are based on comparisons of net profit indicators (such as profit margins) between independent and associated enterprises as a means to estimate the profits that one or each of the associated enterprises could have earned had they dealt solely with independent enterprises, and therefore the payment those enterprises would have demanded at arm's length to compensate them for using their resources in the controlled transaction. Where there are differences between the situations being compared that could materially affect the comparison, comparability adjustments must be made, where possible, to improve the reliability of the comparison. Therefore, in no event can unadjusted industry average returns themselves establish arm's length prices.

1.41. For a discussion of the relevance of these factors for the application of particular pricing methods, see the consideration of those methods in Chapter II.

D.1.1. The contractual terms of the transaction

1.42. A transaction is the consequence or expression of the commercial or financial relations between the parties. The controlled transactions may have been formalised in written contracts which may reflect the intention of the parties at the time the contract was concluded in relation to aspects of the transaction covered by the contract, including in typical cases the division of responsibilities, obligations and rights, assumption of identified risks, and pricing arrangements. Where a transaction has been formalised by the associated enterprises through written contractual agreements, those agreements provide the starting point for delineating the transaction between them and how the responsibilities, risks, and anticipated outcomes arising from their interaction were intended to be divided at the time of entering into the contract. The terms of a transaction may also be found in communications between the parties other than a written contract.

1.43. However, the written contracts alone are unlikely to provide all the information necessary to perform a transfer pricing analysis, or to provide information regarding the relevant contractual terms in sufficient detail. Further information will be required by taking into consideration evidence of the commercial or financial relations provided by the economically relevant characteristics in the other four categories (see paragraph 1.36): the functions performed by each of the parties to the transaction, taking into account assets used and risks assumed, together with the characteristics of property transferred or services provided, the economic circumstances of the parties and of the market in which the parties operate, and the business strategies pursued by the parties. Taken together, the analysis of economically relevant characteristics in all five categories provides evidence of the actual conduct of the associated enterprises. The evidence may clarify aspects of the written contractual arrangements by providing useful and consistent information. If the contract neither explicitly nor implicitly (taking into account applicable principles of contract interpretation) addresses characteristics of the transaction that are economically relevant, then any information provided by the contract should be supplemented for purposes of the transfer pricing analysis by the evidence provided by identifying those characteristics.

1.44. The following example illustrates the concept of clarifying and supplementing the written contractual terms based on the identification of the actual commercial or financial relations. Company P is the parent company of an MNE group situated in Country P. Company S, situated in Country S, is a wholly-owned subsidiary of Company P and acts as an agent for Company P's branded products in the Country S market. The agency contract between Company P and Company S is silent about any marketing and advertising activities in Country S that the parties should perform. Analysis of other economically relevant characteristics and in particular the functions performed, determines that Company S launched an intensive media campaign in Country S in order to develop brand awareness. This campaign represents a significant investment for Company S. Based on evidence provided by the conduct of the parties, it could be concluded that the written contract may not reflect the full extent of the commercial or financial relations between the parties. Accordingly, the analysis should not be limited by the terms recorded in the written contract, but further evidence should be sought as to the conduct of the parties, including as to the basis upon which Company S undertook the media campaign.

1.45. If the characteristics of the transaction that are economically relevant are inconsistent with the written contract between the associated enterprises, the actual transaction should generally be delineated for purposes of the transfer pricing analysis in accordance with the characteristics of the transaction reflected in the conduct of the parties.

1.46. In transactions between independent enterprises, the divergence of interests between the parties ensures (i) that contractual terms are concluded that reflect the interests of both of the parties, (ii) that the parties will ordinarily seek to hold each other to the terms of the contract, and (iii) that contractual terms will be ignored or modified after the fact generally only if it is in the interests of both parties. The same divergence of interests may not exist in the case of associated enterprises or any such divergences may be managed in ways facilitated by the control relationship and not solely or mainly through contractual agreements. It is, therefore, particularly important in considering the commercial or financial relations between associated enterprises to examine whether the arrangements reflected in the actual conduct of the parties substantially conform to the terms of any written contract, or whether the associated enterprises' actual conduct indicates that the contractual terms have not been followed, do not reflect a complete picture of the transactions, have been incorrectly characterised or labelled by the enterprises, or are a sham. Where conduct is not fully consistent with economically significant contractual terms, further analysis is required to identify the actual transaction. Where there are material differences between contractual terms and the conduct of the associated enterprises in their relations with one another, the functions they actually perform, the assets they actually use, and the risks they actually assume, considered in the context of the contractual terms, should ultimately determine the factual substance and accurately delineate the actual transaction.

1.47. Where there is doubt as to what transaction was agreed between the associated enterprises, it is necessary to take into account all the relevant evidence from the economically relevant characteristics of the transaction. In doing so one must bear in mind that the terms of the transaction between the enterprises may change over time. Where there has been a change in the terms of a transaction, the circumstances surrounding the change should be examined to determine whether the change indicates that the original transaction has been replaced through a new transaction with effect from the date of the change, or whether the change reflects the intentions of the parties in the original transaction. Particular care should be exercised where it appears that any changes may have been triggered by knowledge of emerging outcomes from the transaction. Changes made in the purported assumption of a risk when risk outcomes are known do not involve an assumption of risk since there is no longer any risk, as discussed in paragraph 1.78.

1.48. The following example illustrates the concept of differences between written contractual terms and conduct of the parties, with the result that the actual conduct of the parties delineates the transaction. Company S is a wholly-owned subsidiary of Company P. The parties have entered into a written contract pursuant to which Company P licenses intellectual property to Company S for use in Company S's business; Company S agrees to compensate Company P for the licence with a royalty. Evidence provided by other economically relevant characteristics, and in particular the functions performed, establishes that Company P performs negotiations with third-party customers to achieve sales for Company S, provides regular technical services support to Company S so that Company S can deliver contracted sales to its customers, and regularly provides staff to enable Company S to fulfil customer contracts. A majority of customers insist on including Company P as joint contracting party along with Company S, although fee income under the contract is payable to Company S. The analysis of the commercial or financial relations indicates that Company S is not capable of providing the contracted services to customers without significant support from Company P, and is not developing its own capability. Under the contract, Company P has given a licence to Company S, but in fact controls the business risk and output of Company S such that it has not transferred risk and function consistent with a licensing arrangement, and acts not as the licensor but the principal. The identification of the actual transaction between Company P and Company S should not be defined solely by the terms of the written contract. Instead, the actual transaction should be determined from the conduct of the parties, leading to the conclusion that the actual functions performed, assets used, and risks assumed by the parties are not consistent with the written licence agreement.

1.49. Where no written terms exist, the actual transaction would need to be deduced from the evidence of actual conduct provided by identifying the economically relevant characteristics of the transaction. In some circumstances the actual outcome of commercial or financial relations may not have been identified as a transaction by the MNE, but nevertheless may result in a transfer of material value, the terms of which would need to be deduced from the conduct of the parties. For example, technical assistance may have been granted, synergies may have been created through deliberate concerted action (as discussed in Section D.8), or know-how may have been provided through seconded employees or otherwise. These relations may not have been recognised by the MNE, may not be reflected in the pricing of other connected transactions, may not have been formalised in written contracts, and may not appear as entries in the accounting systems. Where the transaction has not been formalised, all aspects would need to be deduced from available evidence of the conduct of the parties, including what functions are actually performed, what assets are actually used, and what risks are actually assumed by each of the parties.

1.50. The following example illustrates the concept of determining the actual transaction where a transaction has not been identified by the MNE. In reviewing the commercial or financial relations between Company P and its subsidiary companies, it is observed that those subsidiaries receive services from an independent party engaged by Company P. Company P pays for the services, the subsidiaries do not reimburse Company P directly or indirectly through the pricing of another transaction and there is no service agreement in place between Company P and the subsidiaries. The conclusion is that, in addition to a provision of services by the independent party to the subsidiaries, there are commercial or financial relations between Company P and the subsidiaries, which transfer potential value from Company P to the subsidiaries. The analysis would need to determine the nature of those commercial or financial relations from the economically relevant characteristics in order to determine the terms and conditions of the identified transaction.

D.1.2. Functional analysis

1.51. In transactions between two independent enterprises, compensation usually will reflect the functions that each enterprise performs (taking into account assets used and risks assumed). Therefore, in delineating the controlled transaction and determining comparability between controlled and uncontrolled transactions or entities, a functional analysis is necessary. This functional analysis seeks to identify the economically significant activities and responsibilities undertaken, assets used or contributed, and risks assumed by the parties to the transactions. The analysis focuses on what the parties actually do and the capabilities they provide. Such activities and capabilities will include decision-making, including decisions about business strategy and risks. For this purpose, it may be helpful to understand the structure and organisation of the MNE group and how they influence the context in which the MNE operates. In particular, it is important to understand how value is generated by the group as a whole, the interdependencies of the functions performed by the associated enterprises with the rest of the group, and the contribution that the associated enterprises make to that value creation. It will also be relevant to determine the legal rights and obligations of each of the parties in performing their functions. While one party may provide a large number of functions relative to that of the other party to the transaction, it is the economic significance of those functions in terms of their frequency, nature, and value to the respective parties to the transactions that is important.

1.52. The actual contributions, capabilities, and other features of the parties can influence the options realistically available to them. For example, an associated enterprise provides logistics services to the group. The logistics company is required to operate warehouses with spare capacity and in several locations in order to be able to cope in the event that supply is disrupted at any one location. The option of greater efficiency through consolidation of locations and reduction in excess capacity is not available. Its functions and assets may, therefore, be different to those of an independent logistics company if that independent service provider did not offer the same capabilities to reduce the risk of disruption to supply.

1.53. Therefore, the process of identifying the economically relevant characteristics of the commercial or financial relations should include consideration of the capabilities of the parties, how such capabilities affect options realistically available, and whether similar capabilities are reflected in potentially comparable arm's length arrangements.

1.54. The functional analysis should consider the type of assets used, such as plant and equipment, the use of valuable intangibles, financial assets, etc., and the nature of the assets used, such as the age, market value, location, property right protections available, etc.

1.55. The functional analysis may show that the MNE group has fragmented highly integrated functions across several group companies. There may be considerable interdependencies between the fragmented activities. For example, the separation into different legal entities of logistics, warehousing, marketing, and sales functions may require considerable co-ordination in order that the separate activities interact effectively. Sales activities are likely to be highly dependent on marketing, and fulfilment of sales, including the anticipated impact of marketing activities, would require alignment with stocking processes and logistics capability. That required co-ordination may be performed by some or all of the associated enterprises performing the fragmented activities, performed through a separate co-ordination function, or performed through a combination of both. Risk may be mitigated through contributions from all the parties, or risk mitigation activities may be undertaken mainly by the co-ordination function. Therefore, when conducting a functional analysis to identify the commercial or financial relations in fragmented activities, it will be important to determine whether those activities are highly interdependent, and, if so, the nature of the interdependencies and how the commercial activity to which the associated enterprises contribute is co-ordinated.

D.1.2.1. Analysis of risks in commercial or financial relations[1]

1.56. A functional analysis is incomplete unless the material risks assumed by each party have been identified and considered since the actual assumption of risks would influence the prices and other conditions of

1. The guidance in this chapter, and in this section on risk in particular, is not specific to any particular industry sector. While the basic concept that a party bearing risks must have the ability to effectively deal with those risks applies to insurance, banking, and other financial services businesses, these regulated sectors are required to follow rules prescribing arrangements for risks, and how risks are recognised, measured, and disclosed. The regulatory approach to risk allocation for regulated entities should be taken into account and reference made as appropriate to the transfer pricing guidance specific to financial services businesses in the *Report on the Attribution of Profits to Permanent Establishments* (OECD, 2010).

transactions between the associated enterprises. Usually, in the open market, the assumption of increased risk would also be compensated by an increase in the expected return, although the actual return may or may not increase depending on the degree to which the risks are actually realised. The level and assumption of risk, therefore, are economically relevant characteristics that can be significant in determining the outcome of a transfer pricing analysis.

1.57. Risk is inherent in business activities. Enterprises undertake commercial activities because they seek opportunities to make profits, but those opportunities carry uncertainty that the required resources to pursue the opportunities either will be greater than expected or will not generate the expected returns. Identifying risks goes hand in hand with identifying functions and assets and is integral to the process of identifying the commercial or financial relations between the associated enterprises and of accurately delineating the transaction or transactions.

1.58. The assumption of risks associated with a commercial opportunity affects the profit potential of that opportunity in the open market, and the allocation of risks assumed between the parties to the arrangement affects how profits or losses resulting from the transaction are allocated at arm's length through the pricing of the transaction. Therefore, in making comparisons between controlled and uncontrolled transactions and between controlled and uncontrolled parties it is necessary to analyse what risks have been assumed, what functions are performed that relate to or affect the assumption or impact of these risks and which party or parties to the transaction assume these risks.

1.59. This section provides guidance on the nature and sources of risk relevant to a transfer pricing analysis in order to help identify relevant risks with specificity. In addition, this section provides guidance on risk assumption under the arm's length principle. The detailed guidance provided in this section on the analysis of risks as part of a functional analysis covering functions, assets, and risks, should not be interpreted as indicating that risks are more important than functions or assets. The relevance of functions, assets and risks in a specific transaction will need to be determined through a detailed functional analysis. The expanded guidance on risks reflects the practical difficulties presented by risks: risks in a transaction can be harder to identify than functions or assets, and determining which associated enterprise assumes a particular risk in a transaction can require careful analysis.

1.60. The steps in the process set out in the rest of this section for analysing risk in a controlled transaction, in order to accurately delineate the actual transaction in respect to that risk, can be summarised as follows:

1. Identify economically significant risks with specificity (see Section D.1.2.1.1).

2. Determine how specific economically significant risks are contractually assumed by the associated enterprises under the terms of the transaction (see Section D.1.2.1.2).

3. Determine through a functional analysis how the associated enterprises that are parties to the transaction operate in relation to assumption and management of the specific, economically significant risks, and in particular which enterprise or enterprises perform control functions and risk mitigation functions, which enterprise or enterprises encounter upside or downside consequences of risk outcomes, and which enterprise or enterprises have the financial capacity to assume the risk (see Section D.1.2.1.3).

4. Steps 2-3 will have identified information relating to the assumption and management of risks in the controlled transaction. The next step is to interpret the information and determine whether the contractual assumption of risk is consistent with the conduct of the associated enterprises and other facts of the case by analysing (i) whether the associated enterprises follow the contractual terms under the principles of Section D.1.1; and (ii) whether the party assuming risk, as analysed under (i), exercises control over the risk and has the financial capacity to assume the risk (see Section D.1.2.1.4).

5. Where the party assuming risk under steps 1-4(i) does not control the risk or does not have the financial capacity to assume the risk, apply the guidance on allocating risk (see Section D.1.2.1.5).

6. The actual transaction as accurately delineated by considering the evidence of all the economically relevant characteristics of the transaction as set out in the guidance in Section D.1, should then be priced taking into account the financial and other consequences of risk assumption, as appropriately allocated, and appropriately compensating risk management functions (see Section D.1.2.1.6).

1.61. In this section references are made to terms that require initial explanation and definition. The term "risk management" is used to refer to the function of assessing and responding to risk associated with commercial activity. Risk management comprises three elements: (i) the capability to make decisions to take on, lay off, or decline a risk-bearing opportunity, together with the actual performance of that decision-making function, (ii) the capability to make decisions on whether and how to respond to the risks associated with the opportunity, together with the actual performance of that decision-making function, and (iii) the capability to mitigate risk, that is the capability to take measures that affect risk outcomes, together with the actual performance of such risk mitigation.

1.62. Some risk management functions can be undertaken only by the party performing functions and using assets in creating and pursuing commercial opportunities, while other risk management functions can be undertaken by a different party. Risk management should not be thought of as necessarily encompassing a separate function, requiring separate remuneration, distinct from the performance of the activities that optimise profits. For example, the development of intangibles through development activities may involve mitigating risks relating to performing the development according to specifications at the highest possible standards and on time; the particular risks might be mitigated through the performance of the development function itself. For example, if the contractual arrangement between the associated enterprises is a contract R&D arrangement that is respected under the requirements of this section, remuneration for risk mitigation functions performed through the development activity would be incorporated into the arm's length services payment. Neither the intangible risk itself, nor the residual income associated with such risk, would be allocated to the service provider. See also Example 1 in paragraph 1.83.

1.63. Risk management is not the same as assuming a risk. Risk assumption means taking on the upside and downside consequences of the risk with the result that the party assuming a risk will also bear the financial and other consequences if the risk materialises. A party performing part of the risk management functions may not assume the risk that is the subject of its management activity, but may be hired to perform risk mitigation functions under the direction of the risk-assuming party. For example, the day-to-day mitigation of product recall risk may be outsourced to a party performing monitoring of quality control over a specific manufacturing process according to the specifications of the party assuming the risk.

1.64. Financial capacity to assume risk can be defined as access to funding to take on the risk or to lay off the risk, to pay for the risk mitigation functions and to bear the consequences of the risk if the risk materialises. Access to funding by the party assuming the risk takes into account the available assets and the options realistically available to access additional liquidity, if needed, to cover the costs anticipated to arise should the risk materialise. This assessment should be made on the basis that the party assuming the risk is operating as an unrelated party in the same circumstances as the associated enterprise, as accurately delineated under the principles of this section. For example, exploitation of rights in an income-generating asset could open up funding possibilities for that party. Where a party assuming risk receives intra-group funding to meet the funding demands in relation to the risk, the party providing the funding may assume financial risk but does not, merely as a consequence of providing funding, assume the specific risk that gives rise to the need for additional funding. Where the financial capacity to assume a risk is lacking, then the allocation of risk requires further consideration under step 5.

1.65. Control over risk involves the first two elements of risk management defined in paragraph 1.61; that is (i) the capability to make decisions to take on, lay off, or decline a risk-bearing opportunity, together with the actual performance of that decision-making function and (ii) the capability to make decisions on whether and how to respond to the risks associated with the opportunity, together with the actual performance of that decision-making function. It is not necessary for a party to perform the day-to-day mitigation, as described in (iii) in order to have control of the risks. Such day-to-day mitigation may be outsourced, as the example in paragraph 1.63 illustrates. However, where these day-to-day mitigation activities are outsourced, control of the risk would require capability to determine the objectives of the outsourced activities, to decide to hire the provider of the risk mitigation functions, to assess whether the objectives are being adequately met, and, where necessary, to decide to adapt or terminate the contract with that provider, together with the performance of such assessment and decision-making. In accordance with this definition of control, a party requires both capability and functional performance as described above in order to exercise control over a risk.

1.66. The capability to perform decision-making functions and the actual performance of such decision-making functions relating to a specific risk involve an understanding of the risk based on a relevant analysis of the information required for assessing the foreseeable downside and upside risk outcomes of such a decision and the consequences for the business of the enterprise. Decision-makers should possess competence and experience in the area of the particular risk for which the decision is being made and possess an understanding of the impact of their decision on the business. They should also have access to the relevant information, either by gathering this information themselves or by exercising authority to specify and obtain the relevant information to support the decision-making process. In doing so, they require capability to determine the objectives of the gathering and analysis of the information, to hire the party gathering the information and making the analyses, to assess whether the right information is gathered and the analyses are adequately made, and, where necessary, to decide to adapt or terminate the contract with that provider, together with the performance of such assessment and decision-making. Neither a mere formalising of the outcome of decision-making in the form of, for example, meetings organised for formal approval of decisions that were made in other locations, minutes of a board meeting and signing of the documents relating to the decision, nor the setting of the policy environment relevant for the risk (see paragraph 1.76), qualifies as the exercise of a decision-making function sufficient to demonstrate control over a risk.

1.67. References to control over risk should not necessarily be taken to mean that the risk itself can be influenced or that the uncertainty can be nullified. Some risks cannot be influenced, and are a general condition of commercial activity affecting all businesses undertaking that activity. For example, risks associated with general economic conditions or commodity price cycles are typically beyond the scope of an MNE group to influence. Instead control over risk should be understood as the capability and authority to decide to take on the risk, and to decide whether and how to respond to the risk, for example through the timing of investments, the nature of development programmes, the design of marketing strategies, or the setting of production levels.

1.68. Risk mitigation refers to measures taken that are expected to affect risk outcomes. Such measures may include measures that reduce the uncertainty or measures that reduce the consequences in the event that the downside impact of risk occurs. Control should not be interpreted as requiring risk mitigation measures to be adopted, since in assessing risks businesses may decide that the uncertainty associated with some risks, including risks that may be fundamental to their core business operations, after being evaluated, should be taken on and faced in order to create and maximise opportunities.

1.69. The concept of control may be illustrated by the following examples. Company A appoints a specialist manufacturer, Company B to manufacture products on its behalf. The contractual arrangements indicate that Company B undertakes to perform manufacturing services, but that the product specifications and designs are provided by Company A, and that Company A determines production scheduling, including the volumes and timing of product delivery. The contractual relations imply that Company A bears the inventory risk and the product recall risk. Company A hires Company C to perform regular quality controls of the production process. Company A specifies the objectives of the quality control audits and the information that Company C should gather on its behalf. Company C reports directly to Company A. Analysis of the economically relevant characteristics shows that Company A controls its product recall and inventory risks by exercising its capability and authority to make a number of relevant decisions about whether and how to take on risk and how to respond to the risks. Besides that Company A has the capability to assess and take decisions relating to the risk mitigation functions and actually performs these functions. These include determining the objectives of the outsourced activities, the decision to hire the particular manufacturer and the party performing the quality checks, the assessment of whether the objectives are adequately met, and, where necessary, to decide to adapt or terminate the contracts.

1.70. Assume that an investor hires a fund manager to invest funds on its account. Depending on the agreement between the investor and the fund manager, the latter may be given the authority to make portfolio investments on behalf of the investor on a day-to-day basis in a way that reflects the risk preferences of the investor, although the risk of loss in value of the investment would be borne by the investor. In such an example, the investor is controlling its risks through four relevant decisions: the decision about its risk preference and therefore about the required diversification of the risks attached to the different investments that are part of the portfolio, the decision to hire (or terminate the contract with) that particular fund manager, the decision of the extent of the authority it gives to the fund manager and objectives it assigns to the latter, and the decision of the amount of the investment that it asks this fund manager to manage. Moreover, the fund manager would generally be required to report back to the investor on a regular basis as the investor would want to assess the outcome of the fund manager's activities. In such a case, the fund manager is providing a service and managing his business risk from his own perspective (e.g. to protect his credibility). The fund manager's operational risk, including the possibility of losing a client, is distinct from his client's investment risk. This illustrates the fact that an investor who gives to another person the authority to perform risk mitigation activities such as those performed by the fund manager does not necessarily transfer control of the investment risk to the person making these day-to-day decisions.

D.1.2.1.1. Step 1: Identify economically significant risks with specificity

1.71. There are many definitions of risk, but in a transfer pricing context it is appropriate to consider risk as the effect of uncertainty on the objectives of the business. In all of a company's operations, every step taken to exploit opportunities, every time a company spends money or generates income, uncertainty exists, and risk is assumed. A company is likely to direct much attention to identifying uncertainties it encounters, in evaluating whether and how business opportunities should be pursued in view of their inherent risks, and in developing appropriate risk mitigation strategies which are important to shareholders seeking their required rate of return. Risk is associated with opportunities, and does not have downside connotations alone; it is inherent in commercial activity, and companies choose which risks they wish to assume in order to have the opportunity to generate profits. No profit-seeking business takes on risk associated with commercial opportunities without expecting a positive return. Downside impact of risk occurs when the anticipated favourable outcomes fail to materialise. For example, a product may fail to attract as much consumer demand as projected. However, such an event is the downside manifestation of uncertainty associated with commercial opportunities. Companies are likely to devote considerable attention to identifying and managing economically significant risks in order to maximise the positive returns from having pursued the opportunity in the face of risk. Such attention may include activities around determining the product strategy, how the product is differentiated, how to identify changing market trends, how to anticipate political and social changes, and how to create demand. The significance of a risk depends on the likelihood and size of the potential profits or losses arising from the risk. For example, a different flavour of ice-cream may not be the company's sole product, the costs of developing, introducing, and marketing the product may have been marginal, the success or failure of the product may not create significant reputational risks so long as business management protocols are followed, and decision-making may have been effected by delegation to local or regional management who can provide knowledge of local tastes. However, ground-breaking technology or an innovative healthcare treatment may represent the sole or major product, involve significant strategic decisions at different stages, require substantial investment costs, create significant opportunities to make or break reputation, and require centralised management that would be of keen interest to shareholders and other stakeholders.

1.72. Risks can be categorised in various ways, but a relevant framework in a transfer pricing analysis is to consider the sources of uncertainty which give rise to risk. The following non-exclusive list of sources of risk is not intended to suggest a hierarchy of risk. Neither is it intended to provide rigid categories of risk, since there is overlap between the categories. Instead, it is intended to provide a framework that may assist in ensuring that a transfer pricing analysis considers the range of risks likely to arise from the commercial or financial relations of the associated enterprises, and from the context in which those relations take place. Reference is made to risks that are externally driven and those that are internally driven in order to help clarify sources of uncertainty. However, there should be no inference that externally driven risks are less relevant because they are not generated directly by activities. On the contrary, the ability of a company to face, respond to and mitigate externally driven risks is likely to be a necessary condition for a business to remain competitive. Importantly, guidance on the possible range of risk should assist in identifying material risks with specificity. Risks which are vaguely described or undifferentiated will not serve the purposes of a transfer pricing analysis seeking to delineate the actual transaction and the actual allocation of risk between the parties.

a) Strategic risks or marketplace risks. These are largely external risks caused by the economic environment, political and regulatory events, competition, technological advance, or social and environmental changes. The assessment of such uncertainties may define the products and markets the company decides to target, and the capabilities it requires, including investment in intangibles and tangible assets, as well as in the talent of its human capital. There is considerable potential downside, but the upside is also considerable if the company identifies correctly the impact of external risks, and differentiates its products and secures and continues to protect competitive advantage. Examples of such risks may include marketplace trends, new geographical markets, and concentration of development investment.

b) Infrastructure or operational risks. These are likely to include the uncertainties associated with the company's business execution and may include the effectiveness of processes and operations. The impact of such risks is highly dependent on the nature of the activities and the uncertainties the company chooses to assume. In some circumstances breakdowns can have a crippling effect on the company's operations or reputation and threaten its existence; whereas successful management of such risks can enhance reputation. In other circumstances, the failure to bring a product to market on time, to meet demand, to meet specifications, or to produce to high standards, can affect competitive and reputational position, and give advantage to companies which bring competing products to market more quickly, better exploit periods of market protection provided by, for example, patents, better manage supply chain risks and quality control. Some infrastructure risks are externally driven and may involve transport links, political and social situations, laws and regulations, whereas others are internally driven and may involve capability and availability of assets, employee capability, process design and execution, outsourcing arrangements, and IT systems.

c) Financial risks. All risks are likely to affect a company's financial performance, but there are specific financial risks related to the company's ability to manage liquidity and cash flow, financial capacity, and creditworthiness. The uncertainty can be externally driven, for example by economic shock or credit crisis, but can also be internally driven through controls, investment decisions, credit terms, and through outcomes of infrastructure or operational risks.

d) Transactional risks. These are likely to include pricing and payment terms in a commercial transaction for the supply of goods, property, or services.

e) Hazard risks. These are likely to include adverse external events that may cause damages or losses, including accidents and natural disasters. Such risks can often be mitigated through insurance, but insurance may not cover all the potential loss, particularly where there are significant impacts on operations or reputation.

1.73. Determining the economic significance of risk and how risk may affect the pricing of a transaction between associated enterprises is part of the broader functional analysis of how value is created by the MNE group, the activities that allow the MNE group to sustain profits, and the economically relevant characteristics of the transaction. The analysis of risk also helps to determine comparability under the guidance in Chapter III. Where potential comparables are identified, it is relevant to determine whether they include the same level of risks and management of risks. The economic significance of risk may be illustrated by the following two situations.

1.74. In the first situation the MNE group distributes heating oil to consumers. Analysis of the economically relevant characteristics establishes that the product is undifferentiated, the market is competitive, the market size is predictable, and players are price-takers. In such circumstances, the ability to influence margins may be limited. The credit terms achieved from managing the relationship with the oil suppliers fund working capital and are crucial to the distributor's margin. The impact of the risk on cost of capital is, therefore, significant in the context of how value is created for the distribution function.

1.75. In the second situation, a multinational toy retailer buys a wide range of products from a number of third-party manufacturers. Most of its sales are concentrated in the last two months of the calendar year, and a significant risk relates to the strategic direction of the buying function, and in making the right bets on trends and determining the products that will sell and in what volumes. Trends and the demand for products can vary across markets, and so expertise is needed to evaluate the right bets in the local market. The effect of the buying risk can be magnified if the retailer negotiates a period of exclusivity for a particular product with the third-party manufacturer.

1.76. Control over a specific risk in a transaction focusses on the decision-making of the parties to the transaction in relation to the specific risk arising from the transaction. This is not to say, however, that in an MNE group other parties may not be involved in setting general policies that are relevant for the assumption and control of the specific risks identified in a transaction, without such policy-setting itself representing decision making. The board and executive committees of the group, for example, may set the level of risk the group as a whole is prepared to accept in order to achieve commercial objectives, and to establish the control framework for managing and reporting risk in its operations. Line management in business segments, operational entities, and functional departments may identify and assess risk against the commercial opportunities, and put in place appropriate controls and processes to address risk and influence the risk outcomes arising from day-to-day operations. The opportunities pursued by operational entities require the ongoing management of the risk that the resources allocated to the opportunity will deliver the anticipated return. For example, finished product inventory risk in a supply transaction between two associated enterprises may be controlled by the party with the capability to determine the production volumes together with the performance of that decision-making. The way that inventory risk in the transaction between two associated enterprises is addressed may be subject to policy-setting elsewhere in the MNE group about overall levels of working capital tied up in inventory, or co-ordination of appropriate minimum stocking levels across markets to meet strategic objectives. This wider policy-setting however cannot be regarded as decisions to take on, lay off, decline, or mitigate the specific inventory risk in the example of the product supply transaction in this paragraph.

D.1.2.1.2. Step 2: Contractual assumption of risk

1.77. The identity of the party or parties assuming risks may be set out in written contracts between the parties to a transaction involving these risks. A written contract typically sets out an intended assumption of risk by the parties. Some risks may be explicitly assumed in the contractual arrangements. For example, a distributor might contractually assume accounts receivable risk, inventory risk, and credit risks associated with the distributor's sales to unrelated customers. Other risks might be implicitly assumed. For example, contractual arrangements that provide non-contingent remuneration for one of the parties implicitly allocate the outcome of some risks, including unanticipated profits or losses, to the other party.

1.78. A contractual assumption of risk constitutes an *ex ante* agreement to bear some or all of the potential costs associated with the *ex post* materialisation of downside outcomes of risk in return for some or all of the potential benefit associated with the *ex post* materialisation of positive outcomes. Importantly, *ex ante* contractual assumption of risk should provide clear evidence of a commitment to assume risk prior to the materialisation of risk outcomes. Such evidence is a very important part of the tax administration's transfer pricing analysis of risks in commercial or financial relations, since, in practice, an audit performed by the tax administration may occur years after the making of such up-front decisions by the associated enterprises and when outcomes are known. The purported assumption of risk by associated enterprises when risk outcomes are certain is by definition not an assumption of risk, since there is no longer any risk. Similarly, *ex post* reallocations of risk by a tax administration when risk outcomes are certain may, unless based on the guidance elsewhere in these Guidelines and in particular Section D.1.2.1, be inappropriate.

1.79. It is economically neutral to take on (or lay off) risk in return for higher (or lower) anticipated nominal income as long as the net present value of both options are equal. Between unrelated parties, for example, the sale of a risky income-producing asset may reflect in part a preference of the seller to accept a lower but more certain amount of nominal income and to forego the possibility of higher anticipated nominal income it might earn if it instead retained and exploited the asset. In a without-recourse debt factoring arrangement between independent enterprises, for example, the seller discounts the face value of its receivables in return for a fixed payment, and so accepts a lower return but has reduced its volatility and laid off risk. The factor will often be a specialised organisation which has the capability to decide to take on risk and to decide on how to respond to the risk, including by diversifying the risk and having the functional capabilities to mitigate the risk and generate a return from the opportunity. Neither party will expect to be worse off as a result of entering into the arrangement, essentially because they have different risk preferences resulting from their capabilities in relation to the specific risk. The factor is more capable of managing the risk than the seller and terms acceptable to both parties can be agreed.

1.80. However, it does not follow that every contractual exchange of potentially higher but riskier income for lower but less risky income between associated enterprises is automatically arm's length. The rest of the steps set out in this section describe the information required to determine how the associated enterprises operate in relation to the assumption and management of risk leading to the accurate delineation of the actual transaction in relation to risk.

1.81. The assumption of risk has a significant effect on determining arm's length pricing between associated enterprises, and it should not be concluded that the pricing arrangements adopted in the contractual arrangements alone determine which party assumes risk. Therefore, one may not infer from the fact that the price paid between associated enterprises for goods or services is set at a particular level, or by reference to a particular margin, that risks are borne by those associated enterprises in a particular manner. For example, a manufacturer may claim to be protected from the risk of price fluctuation of raw material as a consequence of its being remunerated by another group company on a basis that takes account of its actual costs. The implication of the claim is that the other group company bears the risk. The form of remuneration cannot dictate inappropriate risk allocations. It is the determination of how the parties actually manage and control risks, as set out in the remaining steps of the process of analysing risk, which will determine the assumption of risks by the parties, and consequently dictate the selection of the most appropriate transfer pricing method.

D.1.2.1.3. Step 3: Functional analysis in relation to risk

1.82. In this step the functions in relation to risk of the associated enterprises that are parties to the transaction are analysed. The analysis provides information about how the associated enterprises operate in relation to the assumption and management of the specific, economically significant risks, and in particular about which enterprise or enterprises perform control functions and risk mitigation functions, which enterprise or enterprises encounter upside or downside consequences of risk outcomes, and which enterprise or enterprises have the financial capacity to assume the risk. This step is illustrated by the following examples and conclusions are drawn from these examples in subsequent paragraphs of Section D.1.2.

Example 1

1.83. Company A seeks to pursue a development opportunity and hires a specialist company, Company B, to perform part of the research on its behalf. Under step 1 development risk has been identified as economically significant in this transaction, and under step 2 it has been established that under the contract Company A assumes development risk. The functional analysis under step 3 shows that Company A controls its development risk through exercising its capability and authority in making a number of relevant decisions about whether and how to take on the development risk. These include the decision to perform part of the development work itself, the decision to seek specialist input, the decision to hire the particular researcher, the decision of the type of research that should be carried out and objectives assigned to it, and the decision of the budget allocated to Company B. Company A has mitigated its risk by taking measures to outsource development activities to Company B which assumes the day-to-day responsibility for carrying out the research under the control of Company A. Company B reports back to Company A at predetermined milestones, and Company A assesses the progress of the development and whether its ongoing objectives are being met, and decides whether continuing investments in the project are warranted in the light of that assessment. Company A has the financial capacity to assume the risk. Company B has no capability to evaluate the development risk and does not make decisions about Company A's activities. Company B's risk is mainly to ensure it performs the research activities competently and it exercises its capability and authority to control that risk through making decisions about the processes, expertise, and assets it needs. The risk Company B assumes is distinct from the development risk assumed by Company A under the contract, and which is controlled by Company A based on the evidence of the functional analysis.

Example 2

1.84. Company B manufactures products for Company A. Under step 1 capacity utilisation risk and supply chain risk have been identified as economically significant in this transaction, and under step 2 it has been established that under the contract Company A assumes these risks. The functional analysis under step 3 provides evidence that Company B built and equipped its plant to Company A's specifications, that products are manufactured to technical requirements and designs provided by Company A, that volume levels are determined by Company A, and that Company A runs the supply chain, including the procurement of components and raw materials. Company A also performs regular quality checks of the manufacturing process. Company B builds the plant, employs and trains competent manufacturing personnel, and determines production scheduling based on volume levels determined by Company A. Although Company B has incurred fixed costs, it has no ability to manage the risk associated with the recovery of those costs through determining the production units over which the fixed costs are spread, since Company A determines volumes. Company A also determines significant costs relating to components and raw materials and the security of supply. The evaluation of the evidence concludes that Company B performs manufacturing services. Significant risks associated with generating a return from the manufacturing activities are controlled by Company A. Company B controls the risk that it fails to competently deliver services. Each company has the financial capacity to assume its respective risks.

Example 3

1.85. Company A has acquired ownership of a tangible asset and enters into contracts for the use of the asset with unrelated customers. Under step 1 utilisation of the tangible asset, that is the risk that there will be insufficient demand for the asset to cover the costs Company A has incurred, has been identified as an economically significant risk. Under step 2 it is established that Company A has a contract for the provision of services with another group company, Company C; the contract does not address the assumption of utilisation risk by the owner of the tangible asset, Company A. The functional analysis under step 3 provides evidence that another group company, Company B, decides that investment in the asset is appropriate in light of anticipated commercial opportunities identified and evaluated by Company B and its assessment of the asset's anticipated useful life; Company B provides specifications for the asset and the unique features required to respond to the commercial opportunities, and arranges for the asset to be constructed in accordance with its specifications, and for Company A to acquire the asset. Company C decides how to utilise the asset, markets the asset's capabilities to third-party customers, negotiates the contracts with these third party customers, assures that the asset is delivered to the third parties and installed appropriately. Although it is the legal owner of the asset, Company A does not exercise control over the investment risk in the tangible asset, since it lacks any capability to decide on whether to invest in the particular asset, and whether and how to protect its investment including whether to dispose of the asset. Although it is the owner of the asset, Company A does not exercise control over the utilisation risk, since it lacks any capability to decide whether and how to exploit the asset. It does not have the capability to assess and make decisions relating to the risk mitigation activities performed by other group companies. Instead, risks associated with investing in and exploiting the asset, enhancing upside risk and mitigating downside risk, are controlled by the other group companies. Company A does not have control over the economically significant risks associated with the investment in and exploitation of the asset. The functional contribution of the legal owner of the asset is limited to providing financing for an amount equating to the cost of the asset. However, the functional analysis also provides evidence that Company A has no capability and authority to control the risk of investing in a financial asset. Company A does not have the capability to make decisions to take on or decline the financing opportunity, or the capability to make decisions on whether and how to respond to the risks associated with the financing opportunity. Company A does not perform functions to evaluate the financing opportunity, does not consider the appropriate risk premium and other issues to determine the appropriate pricing of the financing opportunity, and does not evaluate the appropriate protection of its financial investment. Companies A, B and C all have financial capacity to assume their respective risks.

D.1.2.1.4. Step 4: Interpreting steps 1-3

1.86. Carrying out steps 1-3 involves the gathering of information relating to the assumption and management of risks in the controlled transaction. The next step is to interpret the information resulting from steps 1-3 and to determine whether the contractual assumption of risk is consistent with the conduct of the parties and the other facts of the case by analysing (i) whether the associated enterprises follow the contractual terms under the principles of Section D.1.1; and (ii) whether the party assuming risk, as analysed under (i), exercises control over the risk and has the financial capacity to assume risk.

1.87. The significance of step 4 will depend on the findings. In the circumstances of Examples 1 and 2 above, the step may be straightforward. Where a party contractually assuming a risk applies that contractual assumption of risk in its conduct, and also both exercises control over the risk and has the financial capacity to assume the risk, then there is no further analysis required beyond step 4(i) and (ii) to determine risk assumption. Companies A and B in both examples fulfil the obligations reflected in the contracts and exercise control over the risks that they assume in the transaction, supported by financial capacity. As a result step 4(ii) is satisfied, there is no need to consider step 5, and the next step to consider is step 6.

1.88. In line with the discussion in relation to contractual terms (see Section D.1.1), it should be considered under step 4(i) whether the parties' conduct conforms to the assumption of risk contained in written contracts, or whether the contractual terms have not been followed or are incomplete.

Where differences exist between contractual terms related to risk and the conduct of the parties which are economically significant and would be taken into account by third parties in pricing the transaction between them, the parties' conduct in the context of the consistent contractual terms should generally be taken as the best evidence concerning the intention of the parties in relation to the assumption of risk.

1.89. Consider for example, a manufacturer, whose functional currency is US dollars, that sells goods to an associated distributor in another jurisdiction, whose functional currency is euros, and the written contract states that the distributor assumes all exchange rate risks in relation to this controlled transaction. If, however, the price for the goods is charged by the manufacturer to the distributor over an extended period of time in euros, the currency of the distributor, then aspects of the written contractual terms do not reflect the actual commercial or financial relations between the parties. The assumption of risk in the transaction should be determined by the actual conduct of the parties in the context of the contractual terms, rather than by aspects of written contractual terms which are not in practice applied. The principle can be further illustrated by Example 7 in the Annex to Chapter VI, where there is an inconsistency between the contractual assumption of risk and the conduct of the parties as evidenced by the bearing of costs relating to the downside outcome of that risk.

1.90. Under step 4(ii) it should be determined whether the party assuming the risk under the contract, taking into account whether the contractual terms have been applied in the conduct of the parties under step 4(i), controls the risk and has the financial capacity to assume the risk. If all the circumstances set out in Example 1 remain the same except for the fact that the contract between Company A and Company B allocates development risk to Company B, and if there is no evidence from the conduct of the parties under step 4(i) to suggest that the contractual allocation of risk is not being followed, then Company B contractually assumes development risk but the facts remain that Company B has no capability to evaluate the development risk and does not make decisions about Company A's activities. Company B has no decision-making function which allows it to control the development risk by taking decisions that affect the outcomes of that risk. Based on the information provided in Example 1, the development risk is controlled by Company A. The determination that the party assuming a risk is not the party controlling that risk means that further consideration is required under step 5.

1.91. If the circumstances of Example 2 remain the same except for the fact that, while the contract specifies that Company A assumes supply chain risks, Company B is not reimbursed by Company A when there was a failure to secure key components on time, the analysis under step 4(i) would show that contractual assumption of risk has not been followed in practice in regard to that supply chain risk, such that Company B in fact assumes the downside consequences of that risk. Based on the information provided in Example 2, Company B does not have any control over the supply chain risk, whereas Company A does exercise control. Therefore, the party assuming risk as analysed under step 4(i), does not under step 4(ii) exercise control over that risk, and further consideration is required under step 5.

1.92. In the circumstances of Example 3, analysis under step 4(i) shows that the assumption of utilisation risk by Company A is consistent with its contractual arrangements with Company C, but under step 4(ii) it is determined that Company A does not control risks that it assumes associated with the investment in and exploitation of the asset. Company A has no decision-making function which allows it to control its risks by taking decisions that affect the outcomes of the risks. Under step 4(ii) the party assuming risk does not control that risk, and further consideration is required under step 5.

1.93. In some cases, the analysis under step 3 may indicate that there is more than one MNE that is capable of exercising control over a risk. However, control requires both capability and functional performance in order to exercise control over a risk. Therefore, if more than one party is capable of exercising control, but the entity contractually assuming risk (as analysed under step 4(i)) is the only party that actually exercises control through capability and functional performance, then the party contractually assuming the risk also controls the risk.

1.94. Furthermore, in some cases, there may be more than one party to the transaction exercising control over a specific risk. Where the associated enterprise assuming risk (as analysed under step 4(i)) controls that risk in accordance with the requirements set out in paragraphs 1.65-1.66, all that remains under step 4(ii) is to consider whether the enterprise has the financial capacity to assume the risk. If so, the fact that other associated enterprises also exercise control over the same risk does not affect the assumption of that risk by the first-mentioned enterprise, and step 5 need not be considered.

1.95. Where two or more parties to the transaction assume a specific risk (as analysed under step 4(i)), and in addition they together control the specific risk and each has the financial capacity to assume their share of the risk, then that assumption of risk should be respected. Examples may include the contractual assumption of development risk under a transaction in which the enterprises agree jointly to bear the costs of creating a new product.

1.96. If it is established that the associated enterprise assuming the risk as analysed under step 4(i) either does not control the risk or does not have the financial capacity to assume the risk, then the analysis described under step 5 needs to be performed.

1.97. In light of the potential complexity that may arise in some circumstances when determining whether an associated enterprise assuming a risk controls that risk, the test of control should be regarded as being met where comparable risk assumptions can be identified in a comparable uncontrolled transaction. To be comparable those risk assumptions require that the economically relevant characteristics of the transactions are comparable. If such a comparison is made, it is particularly relevant to establish that the enterprise assuming comparable risk in the uncontrolled transaction performs comparable risk management functions relating to control of that risk to those performed by the associated enterprise assuming risk in the controlled transaction. The purpose of the comparison is to establish that an independent party assuming a comparable risk to that assumed by the associated enterprise also performs comparable risk management functions to those performed by the associated enterprise.

D.1.2.1.5. Step 5: Allocation of risk

1.98. If it is established in step 4(ii) that the associated enterprise assuming the risk based on steps 1-4(i) does not exercise control over the risk or does not have the financial capacity to assume the risk, then the risk should be allocated to the enterprise exercising control and having the financial capacity to assume the risk. If multiple associated enterprises are identified that both exercise control and have the financial capacity to assume the risk, then the risk should be allocated to the associated enterprise or group of associated enterprises exercising the most control. The other parties performing control activities should be remunerated appropriately, taking into account the importance of the control activities performed.

1.99. In exceptional circumstances, it may be the case that no associated enterprise can be identified that both exercises control over the risk and has the financial capacity to assume the risk. As such a situation is not likely to occur in transactions between third parties, a rigorous analysis of the facts and circumstances of the case will need to be performed, in order to identify the underlying reasons and actions that led to this situation. Based on that assessment, the tax administrations will determine what adjustments to the transaction are needed for the transaction to result in an arm's length outcome. An assessment of the commercial rationality of the transaction based on Section D.2 may be necessary.

D.1.2.1.6. Step 6: Pricing of the transaction, taking account of the consequences of risk allocation

1.100. Following the guidance in this section, the accurately delineated transaction should then be priced in accordance with the tools and methods available to taxpayers and tax administrations set out in the following chapters of these Guidelines and taking into account the financial and other consequences of risk-assumption, and the remuneration for risk management. The assumption of a risk should be compensated with an appropriate anticipated return, and risk mitigation should be appropriately remunerated. Thus, a taxpayer that both assumes and mitigates a risk will be entitled to greater anticipated remuneration than a taxpayer that only assumes a risk, or only mitigates, but does not do both.

1.101. In the circumstances of Example 1 in paragraph 1.83, Company A assumes and controls the development risk and should bear the financial consequences of failure and enjoy the financial consequences of success. Company B should be appropriately rewarded for the carrying out of its development services, incorporating the risk that it fails to do so competently.

1.102. In the circumstances of Example 2 in paragraph 1.84, the significant risks associated with generating a return from the manufacturing activities are controlled by Company A, and the upside and downside consequences of those risks should therefore be allocated to Company A. Company B controls the risk that it fails to competently deliver services, and its remuneration should take into account that risk, as well as its funding costs for the acquisition of the manufacturing plant. Since the risks in relation to the capacity utilisation of the asset are controlled by Company A, Company A should be allocated the risk of under-utilisation. This means that the financial consequences related to the materialisation of that risk including failure to cover fixed costs, write-downs, or closure costs should be allocated to Company A.

1.103. The consequences of risk allocation in Example 3 in paragraph 1.85 depend on analysis of functions under step 3. Company A does not have control over the economically significant risks associated with the investment in and exploitation of the asset, and those risks should be aligned with control of those risks by Companies B and C. The functional contribution of Company A is limited to providing financing for an amount equating to the cost of the asset that enables the asset to be created and exploited by Companies B and C. However, the functional analysis also provides evidence that Company A has no capability and authority to control the risk of investing in a financial asset. Company A does not have the capability to make decisions to take on or decline the financing opportunity, or the capability to make decisions on whether and how to respond to the risks associated with the financing opportunity. Company A does not perform functions to evaluate the financing opportunity, does not consider the appropriate risk premium and other issues to determine the appropriate pricing of the financing opportunity, and does not evaluate the appropriate protection of its financial investment. In the circumstances of Example 3,

Company A would not be entitled to any more than a risk-free return[2] as an appropriate measure of the profits it is entitled to retain, since it lacks the capability to control the risk associated with investing in a riskier financial asset. The risk will be allocated to the enterprise which has control and the financial capacity to assume the risk associated with the financial asset. In the circumstances of example, this would be Company B. Company A does not control the investment risk that carries a potential risk premium. An assessment may be necessary of the commercial rationality of the transaction based on the guidance in Section D.2 taking into account the full facts and circumstances of the transaction.

1.104. Guidance on the relationship between risk assumption in relation to the provision of funding and the operational activities for which the funds are used is given in paragraphs 6.60-6.64. The concepts reflected in these paragraphs are equally applicable to investments in assets other than intangibles.

1.105. A party should always be appropriately compensated for its control functions in relation to risk. Usually, the compensation will derive from the consequences of being allocated risk, and therefore that party will be entitled to receive the upside benefits and to incur the downside costs. In circumstances where a party contributes to the control of risk, but does not assume the risk, compensation which takes the form of a sharing in the potential upside and downside, commensurate with that contribution to control, may be appropriate.

1.106. The difference between *ex ante* and *ex post* returns discussed in particular in Section D of Chapter VI arises in large part from risks associated with the uncertainty of future business outcomes. As discussed in paragraph 1.78 the *ex ante* contractual assumption of risk should provide clear evidence of a commitment to assume risk prior to the materialisation of risk outcomes. Following the steps in this section, the transfer pricing analysis will determine the accurate delineation of the transaction with respect to risk, including the risk associated with unanticipated returns. A party which, under these steps, does not assume the risk, nor contributes to the control of that risk, will not be entitled to unanticipated profits (or required to bear unanticipated losses) arising from that risk. In the circumstances of Example 3 (see paragraph 1.85), this would mean that neither unanticipated profits nor unanticipated losses will be allocated to Company A. Accordingly, if the asset in Example 3 were unexpectedly destroyed, resulting in an unanticipated loss, that loss would be allocated for transfer pricing purposes to the company or companies that control the investment risk, contribute to the control of that risk and have the financial capacity to assume that risk, and that would

2. Company A could potentially be entitled to less than a risk-free return if, for example, the transaction is disregarded under Section D.2.

be entitled to unanticipated profits or losses with respect to the asset. That company or companies would be required to compensate Company A for the return to which it is entitled as described in paragraph 1.103.

D.1.2.2. Risk-free and risk-adjusted rates of return

1.107. This section of Chapter I provides guidance on how to determine a risk-free rate of return and a risk-adjusted rate of return in those situations where an associated enterprise is entitled to any of those returns under the guidance in this chapter and Chapter VI of these Guidelines.

D.1.2.2.1. Determining a risk-free rate of return

1.108. Where, in accordance with the guidance in this chapter, the accurate delineation of the actual transaction shows that a funder lacks the capability, or does not perform the decision-making functions, to control the risk associated with investing in a financial asset, it will be entitled to no more than a risk-free return as an appropriate measure of the profits it is entitled to retain (see paragraph 1.103 and its footnote). In this context, the funder's costs related to the borrowing associated to the funding should be taken into account in determining the risk-free rate of return, and subject to other constraints, the funded party would still be entitled to a deduction up to an arm's length amount in respect of the funding. The difference between those amounts would be allocable to the party exercising control over the investment risk in accordance with the guidance in this chapter.

1.109. A risk-free rate of return is the hypothetical return which would be expected on an investment with no risk of loss. Ultimately, there is no investment with zero risk, and the reliability of available proxies for approximating a risk-free rate of return will depend on prevailing facts and circumstances.

1.110. An approach which is widely used in practice is to treat the interest rate on certain government issued securities as a reference rate for a risk-free return, as these securities are generally considered by market practitioners not to carry significant default risk. The intention of the guidance in this section is to outline an approach for reference purposes without suggesting that a particular government security should always be used to determine a risk-free rate.

1.111. To eliminate currency risk, the reference security for determining the risk-free rate would need to be a security issued in the same currency as the investor's cash flows, i.e. the functional currency of the investor rather than its jurisdiction of domicile. When there are multiple jurisdictions issuing bonds in the same currency, the reference point for the risk-free rate of return should be the government security with the lowest rate of return as any difference in rate must be due to differences in risk between the issuers (see paragraph 10.33).

1.112. Another relevant aspect in determining the risk-free rate of return will be the temporal proximity of the reference security to the tested transaction. The security should ideally be issued at the time, or have a similar remaining maturity, as the controlled transaction was entered into to eliminate the effect of differences which may be present between securities issued at different times (see paragraph 10.32).

1.113. Another key consideration would be the maturity of the financial instrument. The duration of the reference security should match the duration of the investment since the duration of an investment will usually affect its price. The duration of the controlled investment should be determined as part of the process of accurate delineation of the actual transaction. For example, a financial instrument which is short-term under the written contractual terms between the parties but which is consistently replaced with a new instrument may, depending upon the exact facts and circumstances, be accurately delineated as a long-term investment.

1.114. Due to difficulties in practice, practical solutions might be considered for estimating the risk-free rate of return. For instance, assume a situation where Company A, a member of an MNE group, is not entitled to any more than a risk-free return under the guidance in this chapter in relation to an advance of funds with a term of one year to an associated enterprise, Company B. In approximating that return, the starting point would be to identify a security issued at the time of the provision of the funding in the same currency as Company A's functional currency. Assume that the tax administration of Country X, where Company A is resident, identifies three securities issued in Company A's functional currency by the governments of Country X, Country Y and Country Z with a term of one year. The credit ratings of the issuing governments are A for Country X, B for Country Y and AA for Country Z. In specifying a minimum credit rating for the issuing government to consider the issued security as a risk-free investment comparable to the controlled financial transaction, the tax administration of Country X may select the security issued by Country Z as a reference for the risk-free rate of return since it represents the lowest rate of return available at the time of the provision of the funding on all outstanding government bonds in the relevant currency with a term of one year.

1.115. To approximate risk-free rate of returns, highly rated government issued securities are not the only reference, and other alternatives may be considered on prevailing facts and circumstances of each case, for instance interbank rates, interest rate swap rates or repurchase agreements of highly rated government issued securities.

1.116. The risk-free rate of return may be relevant, for example, as a component in calculating a risk-adjusted rate of return on an investment or as the return allocable to an investor who has provided funding but has not assumed any of the risks related to the funding.

D.1.2.2.2. Determining a risk-adjusted rate of return

1.117. As stated in paragraph 6.61, "where a party providing funding exercises control over the financial risk associated with the provision of funding, without the assumption of, including the control over, any other specific risk, it could generally only expect a risk-adjusted rate of return on its funding." (See paragraphs 1.85 and 1.103).

1.118. Therefore, in determining the risk-adjusted rate, it is important to identify and differentiate the financial risk which is assumed by the funder in carrying on its financing activity, and the operational risk that is assumed by the funded party and is connected to the use of the funds, e.g. for developing an intangible asset. Guidance on the relationship between risk assumption in relation to the provision of funding and the operational activities for which the funds are used is given in paragraphs 6.60-6.64.

1.119. For instance, consider a situation where Company F advances a loan to an associated enterprise, Company D, which undertakes the development of an intangible. Consider further that, under the guidance in this chapter, it is determined that Company F controls and consequently is allocated the financial risk associated with funding the development of the intangible, including the potential risk of Company D failing to develop the intangible and therefore being unable to repay the loan. However, Company F does not assume the risk of developing the intangible, which is entirely assumed by Company D under the accurate delineation of the actual transaction. Accordingly, in the event that the *ex post* results derived from the exploitation of the developed intangible were higher (or lower) than the results calculated on an *ex ante* basis, Company F would not be entitled to that difference but to a risk-adjusted rate of return as described in this section.

1.120. In general, the expected risk-adjusted rate of return on a funding transaction can be considered to have two components, i.e. the risk-free rate and a premium reflecting the risks assumed by the funder.

1.121. When the funder is assuming the financial risk under the guidance in this chapter and is therefore exposed to the potential playing out of that risk, it will encounter the upside and downside consequences of that risk outcome. Therefore, the assumption of that risk will warrant an expected remuneration higher than a risk-free rate of return.

1.122. A risk-adjusted rate of return can be determined under different approaches, for example, based on the return of a realistic alternative investment with comparable economic characteristics or the cost of funds (see Section C.1.2 in Chapter X).

1.123. It may be possible to find a reasonable indicator of a risk-adjusted rate of return from comparable uncontrolled transactions or by considering realistically available alternative investments reflecting the same risk profile. Depending on the facts and circumstances, realistic alternatives to an intra-group loan could be bond issuances or loans which are uncontrolled transactions (see paragraph 10.93).

1.124. Another approach to determining the risk-adjusted rate of return would be to add a risk premium to the risk-free return, based on the information available in the market on financial instruments issued under similar conditions and circumstances.

1.125. For instance, consider the same fact pattern as described in paragraph 1.114 but, in this particular scenario, assume that Company A is found to be entitled to a risk-adjusted rate of return under this chapter. To determine that return, the tax administration of Country X considers adding a risk premium to the risk-free rate of return, i.e. the security issued by the government in Country Z with a term of one year. To estimate the risk-adjusted return, Country X's tax administration considers that corporate bonds issued by independent parties resident in Country X operating in the same industry as Company B yield a return comparable to the one that an independent party would have expected had it invested its funds in Company B under comparable circumstances.

1.126. Under an approach based on the cost of funds, the controlled transaction would be priced by adding a profit margin to the costs incurred by the lender to raise the funds advanced to the borrower. That mark-up should be proportionate to the risk assumed by the lender and calculated according to the guidance provided in paragraphs 10.97-10.100.

D.1.3. Characteristics of property or services

1.127. Differences in the specific characteristics of property or services often account, at least in part, for differences in their value in the open market. Therefore, comparisons of these features may be useful in delineating the transaction and in determining the comparability of controlled and uncontrolled transactions. Characteristics that may be important to consider include the following: in the case of transfers of tangible property, the physical features of the property, its quality and reliability, and the availability and volume of supply; in the case of the provision of services, the nature and extent of the services; and in the case of intangible property, the form of transaction (e.g. licensing or sale), the type of property (e.g. patent, trademark, or know-how), the duration and degree of protection, and the anticipated benefits from the use of the property. For further discussion of some of the specific features of intangibles that may prove important in a comparability analysis involving transfers of intangibles or rights in intangibles, see Section D.2.1 of Chapter VI.

1.128. Depending on the transfer pricing method, this factor must be given more or less weight. Among the methods described at Chapter II of these Guidelines, the requirement for comparability of property or services is the strictest for the comparable uncontrolled price method. Under the comparable uncontrolled price method, any material difference in the characteristics of property or services can have an effect on the price and would require an appropriate adjustment to be considered (see in particular paragraph 2.16). Under the resale price method and cost plus method, some differences in the characteristics of property or services are less likely to have a material effect on the gross profit margin or mark-up on costs (see in particular paragraphs 2.29 and 2.47). Differences in the characteristics of property or services are also less sensitive in the case of the transactional profit methods than in the case of traditional transaction methods (see in particular paragraph 2.75). This however does not mean that the question of comparability in characteristics of property or services can be ignored when applying transactional profit methods, because it may be that product differences entail or reflect different functions performed, assets used and/or risks assumed by the tested party. See paragraphs 3.18-3.19 for a discussion of the notion of tested party.

1.129. In practice, it has been observed that comparability analyses for methods based on gross or net profit indicators often put more emphasis on functional similarities than on product similarities. Depending on the facts and circumstances of the case, it may be acceptable to broaden the scope of the comparability analysis to include uncontrolled transactions involving products that are different, but where similar functions are undertaken. However, the acceptance of such an approach depends on the effects that the product differences have on the reliability of the comparison and on whether or not more reliable data are available. Before broadening the search to include a larger number of potentially comparable uncontrolled transactions based on similar functions being undertaken, thought should be given to whether such transactions are likely to offer reliable comparables for the controlled transaction.

D.1.4. Economic circumstances

1.130. Arm's length prices may vary across different markets even for transactions involving the same property or services; therefore, to achieve comparability requires that the markets in which the independent and associated enterprises operate do not have differences that have a material effect on price or that appropriate adjustments can be made. As a first step, it is essential to identify the relevant market or markets taking account of available substitute goods or services. Economic circumstances that may be relevant to determining market comparability include the geographic location;

the size of the markets; the extent of competition in the markets and the relative competitive positions of the buyers and sellers; the availability (risk thereof) of substitute goods and services; the levels of supply and demand in the market as a whole and in particular regions, if relevant; consumer purchasing power; the nature and extent of government regulation of the market; costs of production, including the costs of land, labour, and capital; transport costs; the level of the market (e.g. retail or wholesale); the date and time of transactions; and so forth. The facts and circumstances of the particular case will determine whether differences in economic circumstances have a material effect on price and whether reasonably accurate adjustments can be made to eliminate the effects of such differences. More detailed guidance on the importance in a comparability analysis of the features of local markets, especially local market features that give rise to location savings, is provided in Section D.6 of this chapter.

1.131. The existence of a cycle (e.g. economic, business, or product cycle) is one of the economic circumstances that should be identified. See paragraph 3.77 in relation to the use of multiple year data where there are cycles.

1.132. The geographic market is another economic circumstance that should be identified. The identification of the relevant market is a factual question. For a number of industries, large regional markets encompassing more than one jurisdiction may prove to be reasonably homogeneous, while for others, differences among domestic markets (or even within domestic markets) are very significant.

1.133. In cases where similar controlled transactions are carried out by an MNE group in several jurisdictions and where the economic circumstances in these jurisdictions are in effect reasonably homogeneous, it may be appropriate for this MNE group to rely on a comparability analysis that covers multiple jurisdictions to support its transfer pricing policy towards this group of jurisdictions. But there are also numerous situations where an MNE group offers significantly different ranges of products or services in each jurisdiction, and/or performs significantly different functions in each of these jurisdictions (using significantly different assets and assuming significantly different risks), and/or where its business strategies and/or economic circumstances are found to be significantly different. In these latter situations, the recourse to a multiple-jurisdictional approach may reduce reliability.

D.1.5. Business strategies

1.134. Business strategies must also be examined in delineating the transaction and in determining comparability for transfer pricing purposes. Business strategies would take into account many aspects of an enterprise, such as innovation and new product development, degree of diversification, risk aversion, assessment of political changes, input of existing and planned labour laws, duration of arrangements, and other factors bearing upon the daily conduct of business. Such business strategies may need to be taken into account when determining the comparability of controlled and uncontrolled transactions and enterprises.

1.135. Business strategies also could include market penetration schemes. A taxpayer seeking to penetrate a market or to increase its market share might temporarily charge a price for its product that is lower than the price charged for otherwise comparable products in the same market. Furthermore, a taxpayer seeking to enter a new market or expand (or defend) its market share might temporarily incur higher costs (e.g. due to start-up costs or increased marketing efforts) and hence achieve lower profit levels than other taxpayers operating in the same market.

1.136. Timing issues can pose particular problems for tax administrations when evaluating whether a taxpayer is following a business strategy that distinguishes it from potential comparables. Some business strategies, such as those involving market penetration or expansion of market share, involve reductions in the taxpayer's current profits in anticipation of increased future profits. If in the future those increased profits fail to materialise because the purported business strategy was not actually followed by the taxpayer, the appropriate transfer pricing outcome would likely require a transfer pricing adjustment. However legal constraints may prevent re-examination of earlier tax years by the tax administrations. At least in part for this reason, tax administrations may wish to subject the issue of business strategies to particular scrutiny.

1.137. When evaluating whether a taxpayer was following a business strategy that temporarily decreased profits in return for higher long-run profits, several factors should be considered. Tax administrations should examine the conduct of the parties to determine if it is consistent with the purported business strategy. For example, if a manufacturer charges its associated distributor a below-market price as part of a market penetration strategy, the cost savings to the distributor may be reflected in the price charged to the distributor's customers or in greater market penetration expenses incurred by the distributor. A market penetration strategy of an MNE group could be put in place either by the manufacturer or by the distributor acting separately from the manufacturer (and the resulting cost borne by either of them), or by both of them acting in a co-ordinated manner. Furthermore, unusually intensive marketing and advertising efforts would often accompany a market penetration or market share expansion strategy. Another factor to consider is whether the nature of the relationship between the parties to the controlled transaction would be consistent with the taxpayer bearing the costs of the business strategy. For example, in arm's length transactions a company acting solely as a sales agent with little or no responsibility for long-term market development would generally not bear the costs of a market penetration strategy. Where a company has undertaken market development activities at its own risk and enhances the value of a product through a trademark or trade name or increases goodwill associated with the product, this situation should be reflected in the analysis of functions for the purposes of establishing comparability.

1.138. An additional consideration is whether there is a plausible expectation that following the business strategy will produce a return sufficient to justify its costs within a period of time that would be acceptable in an arm's length arrangement. It is recognised that a business strategy such as market penetration may fail, and the failure does not of itself allow the strategy to be ignored for transfer pricing purposes. However, if such an expected outcome was implausible at the time of the transaction, or if the business strategy is unsuccessful but nonetheless is continued beyond what an independent enterprise would accept, the arm's length nature of the business strategy may be doubtful and may warrant a transfer pricing adjustment. In determining what period of time an independent enterprise would accept, tax administrations may wish to consider evidence of the commercial strategies evident in the jurisdiction in which the business strategy is being pursued. In the end, however, the most important consideration is whether the strategy in question could plausibly be expected to prove profitable within the foreseeable future (while recognising that the strategy might fail), and that a party operating at arm's length would have been prepared to sacrifice profitability for a similar period under such economic circumstances and competitive conditions.

D.2. Recognition of the accurately delineated transaction

1.139. Following the guidance in the previous section, the transfer pricing analysis will have identified the substance of the commercial or financial relations between the parties, and will have accurately delineated the actual transaction by analysing the economically relevant characteristics.

1.140. In performing the analysis, the actual transaction between the parties will have been deduced from written contracts and the conduct of the parties. Formal conditions recognised in contracts will have been clarified and supplemented by analysis of the conduct of the parties and the other economically relevant characteristics of the transaction (see Section D.1.1). Where the characteristics of the transaction that are economically significant are inconsistent with the written contract, then the actual transaction will have been delineated in accordance with the characteristics of the transaction reflected in the conduct of the parties. Contractual risk assumption and actual conduct with respect to risk assumption will have been examined taking into account control over the risk (as defined in paragraphs 1.65-1.68) and the financial capacity to assume risk (as defined in paragraph 1.64), and consequently, risks assumed under the contract may have been allocated in accordance with the conduct of the parties and the other facts on the basis of steps 4 and 5 of the process for analysing risk in a controlled transaction as reflected in Sections D.1.2.1.4 and D.1.2.1.5. Therefore, the analysis will have set out the factual substance of the commercial or financial relations between the parties and accurately delineated the actual transaction.

1.141. Every effort should be made to determine pricing for the actual transaction as accurately delineated under the arm's length principle. The various tools and methods available to tax administrations and taxpayers to do so are set out in the following chapters of these Guidelines. A tax administration should not disregard the actual transaction or substitute other transactions for it unless the exceptional circumstances described in the following paragraphs 1.142-1.145 apply.

1.142. This section sets out circumstances in which the transaction between the parties as accurately delineated can be disregarded for transfer pricing purposes. Because non-recognition can be contentious and a source of double taxation, every effort should be made to determine the actual nature of the transaction and apply arm's length pricing to the accurately delineated transaction, and to ensure that non-recognition is not used simply because determining an arm's length price is difficult. Where the same transaction can be seen between independent parties in comparable circumstances (i.e. where all economically relevant characteristics are the same as those under which the tested transaction occurs other than that the parties are associated enterprises) non-recognition would not apply. Importantly, the mere fact that the transaction may not be seen between independent parties does not mean that it should not be recognised. Associated enterprises may have the ability to enter into a much greater variety of arrangements than can independent enterprises, and may conclude transactions of a specific nature that are not encountered, or are only very rarely encountered, between independent parties, and may do so for sound business reasons. The transaction as accurately delineated may be disregarded, and if appropriate, replaced by an alternative transaction, where the arrangements made in relation to the transaction, viewed in their totality, differ from those which would have been adopted by independent enterprises behaving in a commercially rational manner in comparable circumstances, thereby preventing determination of a price that would be acceptable to both of the parties taking into account their respective perspectives and the options realistically available to each of them at the time of entering into the transaction. It is also a relevant pointer to consider whether the MNE group as a whole is left worse off on a pre-tax basis since this may be an indicator that the transaction viewed in its entirety lacks the commercial rationality of arrangements between unrelated parties.

1.143. The key question in the analysis is whether the actual transaction possesses the commercial rationality of arrangements that would be agreed between unrelated parties under comparable economic circumstances, not whether the same transaction can be observed between independent parties. The non-recognition of a transaction that possesses the commercial rationality of an arm's length arrangement is not an appropriate application of the arm's length principle. Restructuring of legitimate business transactions would be a wholly arbitrary exercise the inequity of which could be compounded by double taxation created where the other tax administration does not share the same views as to how the transaction should be structured. It should again be noted that the mere fact that the transaction may not be seen between independent parties does not mean that it does not have characteristics of an arm's length arrangement.

1.144. The structure that for transfer pricing purposes, replaces that actually adopted by the taxpayers should comport as closely as possible with the facts of the actual transaction undertaken whilst achieving a commercially rational expected result that would have enabled the parties to come to a price acceptable to both of them at the time the arrangement was entered into.

1.145. The criterion for non-recognition may be illustrated by the following examples.

Example 1

1.146. Company S1 carries on a manufacturing business that involves holding substantial inventory and a significant investment in plant and machinery. It owns commercial property situated in an area prone to increasingly frequent flooding in recent years. Third-party insurers experience significant uncertainty over the exposure to large claims, with the result that there is no active market for the insurance of properties in the area. Company S2, an associated enterprise, provides insurance to Company S1, and an annual premium representing 80% of the value of the inventory, property and contents is paid by Company S1. In this example S1 has entered into a commercially irrational transaction since there is no market for insurance given the likelihood of significant claims, and either relocation or not insuring may be more attractive realistic alternatives. Since the transaction is commercially irrational, there is not a price that is acceptable to both S1 and S2 from their individual perspectives.

1.147. Under the guidance in this section, the transaction should not be recognised. S1 is treated as not purchasing insurance and its profits are not reduced by the payment to S2; S2 is treated as not issuing insurance and therefore not being liable for any claim.

Example 2

1.148. Company S1 conducts research activities to develop intangibles that it uses to create new products that it can produce and sell. It agrees to transfer to an associated company, Company S2, unlimited rights to all future intangibles which may arise from its future work over a period of twenty years for a lump sum payment. The arrangement is commercially irrational for both parties since neither Company S1 nor Company S2 has any reliable means to determine whether the payment reflects an appropriate valuation, both because it is uncertain what range of development activities Company S1 might conduct over the period and also because valuing the potential outcomes would be entirely speculative. Under the guidance in this section, the structure of the arrangement adopted by the taxpayer, including the form of payment, should be modified for the purposes of the transfer pricing analysis. The replacement structure should be guided by the economically relevant characteristics, including the functions performed, assets used, and risks assumed, of the commercial or financial relations of the associated enterprises. Those facts would narrow the range of potential replacement structures to the structure most consistent with the facts of the case (for example, depending on those facts the arrangement could be recast as the provision of financing by Company S2, or as the provision of research services by Company S1, or, if specific intangibles can be identified, as a licence with contingent payments terms for the development of those specific intangibles, taking into account the guidance on hard-to-value intangibles as appropriate).

D.3. Losses

1.149. When an associated enterprise consistently realises losses while the MNE group as a whole is profitable, the facts could trigger some special scrutiny of transfer pricing issues. Of course, associated enterprises, like independent enterprises, can sustain genuine losses, whether due to heavy start-up costs, unfavourable economic conditions, inefficiencies, or other legitimate business reasons. However, an independent enterprise would not be prepared to tolerate losses that continue indefinitely. An independent enterprise that experiences recurring losses will eventually cease to undertake business on such terms. In contrast, an associated enterprise that realises losses may remain in business if the business is beneficial to the MNE group as a whole.

1.150. The fact that there is an enterprise making losses that is doing business with profitable members of its MNE group may suggest to the taxpayers or tax administrations that the transfer pricing should be examined. The loss enterprise may not be receiving adequate compensation from the MNE group of which it is a part in relation to the benefits derived from its activities. For example, an MNE group may need to produce a full range of products and/or services in order to remain competitive and realise an overall profit, but some of the individual product lines may regularly lose revenue. One member of the MNE group might realise consistent losses because it produces all the loss-making products while other members produce the profit-making products. An independent enterprise would perform such a service only if it were compensated by an adequate service charge. Therefore, one way to approach this type of transfer pricing problem would be to deem the loss enterprise to receive the same type of service charge that an independent enterprise would receive under the arm's length principle.

1.151. A factor to consider in analysing losses is that business strategies may differ from MNE group to MNE group due to a variety of historic, economic, and cultural reasons. Recurring losses for a reasonable period may be justified in some cases by a business strategy to set especially low prices to achieve market penetration. For example, a producer may lower the prices of its goods, even to the extent of temporarily incurring losses, in order to enter new markets, to increase its share of an existing market, to introduce new products or services, or to discourage potential competitors. However, especially low prices should be expected for a limited period only, with the specific object of improving profits in the longer term. If the pricing strategy continues beyond a reasonable period, a transfer pricing adjustment may be appropriate, particularly where comparable data over several years show that the losses have been incurred for a period longer than that affecting comparable independent enterprises. Further, tax administrations should not accept especially low prices (e.g. pricing at marginal cost in a situation of underemployed production capacities) as arm's length prices unless independent enterprises could be expected to have determined prices in a comparable manner.

D.4. The effect of government policies

1.152. There are some circumstances in which a taxpayer will consider that an arm's length price must be adjusted to account for government interventions such as price controls (even price cuts), interest rate controls, controls over payments for services or management fees, controls over the payment of royalties, subsidies to particular sectors, exchange control, anti-dumping duties, or exchange rate policy. As a general rule, these government interventions should be treated as conditions of the market in the particular jurisdiction, and in the ordinary course they should be taken into account in evaluating the taxpayer's transfer price in that market. The question then presented is whether in light of these conditions the transactions undertaken by the controlled parties are consistent with transactions between independent enterprises.

1.153. One issue that arises is determining the stage at which a price control affects the price of a product or service. Often the direct impact will be on the final price to the consumer, but there may nonetheless be an impact on prices paid at prior stages in the supply of goods to the market. MNEs in practice may make no adjustment in their transfer prices to take account of such controls, leaving the final seller to suffer any limitation on profit that may occur, or they may charge prices that share the burden in some way between the final seller and the intermediate supplier. It should be considered whether or not an independent supplier would share in the costs of the price controls and whether an independent enterprise would seek alternative product lines and business opportunities. In this regard, it is unlikely that an independent enterprise would be prepared to produce, distribute, or otherwise provide products or services on terms that allowed it no profit. Nevertheless, it is quite obvious that a jurisdiction with price controls must take into account that those price controls will affect the profits that can be realised by enterprises selling goods subject to those controls.

1.154. A special problem arises when a jurisdiction prevents or "blocks" the payment of an amount which is owed by one associated enterprise to another or which in an arm's length arrangement would be charged by one associated enterprise to another. For example, exchange controls may effectively prevent an associated enterprise from transferring interest payments abroad on a loan made by another associated enterprise located in a different jurisdiction. This circumstance may be treated differently by the two jurisdictions involved: the jurisdiction of the borrower may or may not regard the untransferred interest as having been paid, and the jurisdiction of the lender may or may not treat the lender as having received the interest. As a general rule, where the government intervention applies equally to transactions between associated enterprises and transactions between independent enterprises (both in law and in fact), the approach to this problem where it occurs between associated enterprises should be the same for tax purposes as that adopted for transactions between independent enterprises. Where the government intervention applies only to transactions between associated enterprises, there is no simple solution to the problem. Perhaps one way to deal with the issue is to apply the arm's length principle viewing the intervention as a condition affecting the terms of the transaction. Treaties may specifically address the approaches available to the treaty partners where such circumstances exist.

1.155. A difficulty with this analysis is that often independent enterprises simply would not enter into a transaction in which payments were blocked. An independent enterprise might find itself in such an arrangement from time to time, most likely because the government interventions were imposed subsequent to the time that the arrangement began. But it seems unlikely that an independent enterprise would willingly subject itself to a substantial risk of non-payment for products or services rendered by entering into an arrangement when severe government interventions already existed unless the profit projections or anticipated return from the independent enterprise's proposed business strategy are sufficient to yield it an acceptable rate of return notwithstanding the existence of the government intervention that may affect payment.

1.156. Because independent enterprises might not engage in a transaction subject to government interventions, it is unclear how the arm's length principle should apply. One possibility is to treat the payment as having been made between the associated enterprises, on the assumption that an independent enterprise in a similar circumstance would have insisted on payment by some other means. This approach would treat the party to whom the blocked payment is owed as performing a service for the MNE group. An alternative approach that may be available in some jurisdictions would be to defer both the income and the relevant expenses of the taxpayer. In other words, the party to whom this blocked payment was due would not be allowed to deduct expenses, such as additional financing costs, until the blocked payment was made. The concern of tax administrations in these situations is mainly their respective tax bases. If an associated enterprise claims a deduction in its tax computations for a blocked payment, then there should be corresponding income to the other party. In any case, a taxpayer should not be permitted to treat blocked payments due from an associated enterprise differently from blocked payments due from an independent enterprise.

D.5. Use of customs valuations

1.157. The arm's length principle is applied, broadly speaking, by many customs administrations as a principle of comparison between the value attributable to goods imported by associated enterprises, which may be affected by the special relationship between them, and the value for similar goods imported by independent enterprises. Valuation methods for customs purposes however may not be aligned with the OECD's recognised transfer pricing methods. That being said, customs valuations may be useful to tax administrations in evaluating the arm's length character of a controlled transaction transfer price and vice versa. In particular, customs officials may have contemporaneous information regarding the transaction that could be relevant for transfer pricing purposes, especially if prepared by the taxpayer, while tax authorities may have transfer pricing documentation which provides detailed information on the circumstances of the transaction.

1.158. Taxpayers may have competing incentives in setting values for customs and tax purposes. In general, a taxpayer importing goods may be interested in setting a low price for the transaction for customs purposes so that the customs duty imposed will be low. (There could be similar considerations arising with respect to value added taxes, sales taxes, and excise taxes.) For tax purposes, however, a higher price paid for those same goods would increase the deductible costs in the importing jurisdiction (although this would also increase the sales revenue of the seller in the jurisdiction of export). Co-operation between income tax and customs administrations within a jurisdiction in evaluating transfer prices is becoming more common and this should help to reduce the number of cases where customs valuations are found unacceptable for tax purposes or vice versa. Greater co-operation in the area of exchange of information would be particularly useful, and should not be difficult to achieve in jurisdictions that already have integrated administrations for income taxes and customs duties. Jurisdictions that have separate administrations may wish to consider modifying the exchange of information rules so that the information can flow more easily between the different administrations.

D.6. Location savings and other local market features

1.159. Paragraphs 1.130, 1.132 and 6.120 indicate that features of the geographic market in which business operations occur can affect comparability and arm's length prices. Difficult issues can arise in evaluating differences between geographic markets and in determining appropriate comparability adjustments. Such issues may arise in connection with the consideration of cost savings attributable to operating in a particular market. Such savings are sometimes referred to as location savings. In other situations comparability issues can arise in connection with the consideration of local market advantages or disadvantages that may not be directly related to location savings.

D.6.1. Location savings

1.160. Paragraphs 9.126-9.131 discuss the treatment of location savings in the context of a business restructuring. The principles described in those paragraphs apply generally to all situations where location savings are present, not just in the case of a business restructuring.

1.161. Pursuant to the guidance in paragraphs 9.126 – 9.131, in determining how location savings are to be shared between two or more associated enterprises, it is necessary to consider (i) whether location savings exist; (ii) the amount of any location savings; (iii) the extent to which location savings are either retained by a member or members of the MNE group or are passed on to independent customers or suppliers; and (iv) where location savings are not fully passed on to independent customers or suppliers, the manner in which independent enterprises operating under similar circumstances would allocate any retained net location savings.

1.162. Where the functional analysis shows that location savings exist that are not passed on to customers or suppliers, and where comparable entities and transactions in the local market can be identified, those local market comparables will provide the most reliable indication regarding how the net location savings should be allocated amongst two or more associated enterprises. Thus, where reliable local market comparables are available and can be used to identify arm's length prices, specific comparability adjustments for location savings should not be required.

1.163. When reliable local market comparables are not present, determinations regarding the existence and allocation of location savings among members of an MNE group, and any comparability adjustments required to take into account location savings, should be based on an analysis of all of the relevant facts and circumstances, including the functions performed, risks assumed, and assets used of the relevant associated enterprises, in the manner described in paragraphs 9.126-9.131.

D.6.2. Other local market features

1.164. Features of the local market in which business operations occur may affect the arm's length price with respect to transactions between associated enterprises. While some such features may give rise to location savings, others may give rise to comparability concerns not directly related to such savings. For example, the comparability and functional analysis conducted in connection with a particular matter may suggest that the relevant characteristics of the geographic market in which products are manufactured or sold, the purchasing power and product preferences of households in that market, whether the market is expanding or contracting, the degree of competition in the market and other similar factors affect prices and margins that can be realised in the market. Similarly, the comparability and functional analysis conducted in connection with a particular matter may suggest that the relative availability of local country infrastructure, the relative availability of a pool of trained or educated workers, proximity to profitable markets, and similar features in a geographic market where business operations occur create market advantages or disadvantages that should be taken into account. Appropriate comparability adjustments should be made to account for such factors where reliable adjustments that will improve comparability can be identified.

1.165. In assessing whether comparability adjustments for such local market features are required, the most reliable approach will be to refer to data regarding comparable uncontrolled transactions in that geographic market between independent enterprises performing similar functions, assuming similar risks, and using similar assets. Such transactions are carried out under the same market conditions as the controlled transaction, and, accordingly, where comparable transactions in the local market can be identified, specific adjustments for features of the local market should not be required.

1.166. In situations where reasonably reliable local market comparables cannot be identified, the determination of appropriate comparability adjustments for features of the local market should consider all of the relevant facts and circumstances. As with location savings, in each case where reliable local market comparables cannot be identified, it is necessary to consider (i) whether a market advantage or disadvantage exists, (ii) the amount of any increase or decrease in revenues, costs or profits, *vis-à-vis* those of identified comparables from other markets, that are attributable to the local market advantage or disadvantage, (iii) the degree to which benefits or burdens of local market features are passed on to independent customers or suppliers, and (iv) where benefits or burdens attributable to local market features exist and are not fully passed on to independent customers or suppliers, the manner in which independent enterprises operating under similar circumstances would allocate such net benefits or burdens between them.

1.167. The need for comparability adjustments related to features of the local market in cases where reasonably reliable local market comparables cannot be identified may arise in several different contexts. In some circumstances, market advantages or disadvantages may affect arm's length prices of goods transferred or services provided between associated enterprises.

1.168. In other circumstances, a business restructuring or the transfer of intangibles between associated enterprises may make it possible for one party to the transaction to gain the benefit of local market advantages or require that party to assume the burden of local market disadvantages in a manner that would not have been possible in the absence of the business restructuring or transfer of the intangibles. In such circumstances, the anticipated existence of local market advantages and disadvantages may affect the arm's length price paid in connection with the business restructuring or intangible transfer.

1.169. In conducting a transfer pricing analysis it is important to distinguish between features of the local market, which are not intangibles, and any contractual rights, government licences, or know-how necessary to exploit that market, which may be intangibles. Depending on the circumstances, these types of intangibles may have substantial value that should be taken into account in a transfer pricing analysis in the manner described in Chapter VI, including the guidance on rewarding entities for functions, assets and risks associated with the development of intangibles contained in Section B of Chapter VI. In some circumstances, contractual rights and government licences may limit access of competitors to a particular market and may therefore affect the manner in which the economic consequences of local market features are shared between parties to a particular transaction. In other circumstances, contractual rights or government licences to access a market may be available to many or all potential market entrants with little restriction.

1.170. For example, a country may require a regulatory licence to be issued as a pre-condition for conducting an investment management business in the country and may restrict the number of foreign-owned firms to which such licences are granted. The comparability and functional analysis may indicate that qualifying for such a licence requires demonstrating to appropriate government authorities that the service provider has appropriate levels of experience and capital to conduct such a business in a reputable fashion. The market to which such a licence relates may also be one with unique features. It may, for example be a market where the structure of pension and insurance arrangements gives rise to large cash pools, a need to diversify investments internationally, and a resulting high demand for quality investment management services and knowledge of foreign financial markets that can make the provision of such services highly lucrative. The comparability analysis may further suggest that those features of the local market may affect the price that can be charged for certain types of investment management services and the profit margins that may be earned from providing such services. Under these circumstances, the intangible in question (i.e. the regulatory licence to provide investment management services) may allow the party or parties holding the licence to extract a greater share of the benefits of operating in the local market, including the benefits provided by unique features of that market, than would be the case in the absence of the licensing requirement. However, in assessing the impact of the regulatory licence, it may be important in a particular case to consider the contributions of both the local group member in the local market and other group members outside the local market in supplying the capabilities necessary to obtain the licence, as described in Section B of Chapter VI.

1.171. In a different circumstance, the comparability and functional analysis may suggest that a government issued business licence is necessary as a pre-condition for providing a particular service in a geographic market. However, it may be the case that such licences are readily available to any qualified applicant and do not have the effect of restricting the number of competitors in the market. Under such circumstances, the licence requirement may not present a material barrier to entry, and possession of such a licence may not have any discernible impact on the manner in which the benefits of operating in the local market are shared between independent enterprises.

D.7. Assembled workforce

1.172. Some businesses are successful in assembling a uniquely qualified or experienced cadre of employees. The existence of such an employee group may affect the arm's length price for services provided by the employee group or the efficiency with which services are provided or goods produced by the enterprise. Such factors should ordinarily be taken into account in a transfer pricing comparability analysis. Where it is possible to determine the benefits or detriments of a unique assembled workforce *vis-à-vis* the workforce of enterprises engaging in potentially comparable transactions, comparability adjustments may be made to reflect the impact of the assembled workforce on arm's length prices for goods or services.

1.173. In some business restructuring and similar transactions, it may be the case that an assembled workforce is transferred from one associated enterprise to another as part of the transaction. In such circumstances, it may well be that the transfer of the assembled workforce along with other transferred assets of the business will save the transferee the time and expense of hiring and training a new workforce. Depending on the transfer pricing methods used to evaluate the overall transaction, it may be appropriate in such cases to reflect such time and expense savings in the form of comparability adjustments to the arm's length price otherwise charged with respect to the transferred assets. In other situations, the transfer of the assembled workforce may result in limitations on the transferee's flexibility in structuring business operations and create potential liabilities if workers are terminated. In such cases it may be appropriate for the compensation paid in connection with the restructuring to reflect the potential future liabilities and limitations.

1.174. The foregoing paragraph is not intended to suggest that transfers or secondments of individual employees between members of an MNE group should be separately compensated as a general matter. In many instances the transfer of individual employees between associated enterprises will not give rise to a need for compensation. Where employees are seconded (i.e. they remain on the transferor's payroll but work for the transferee), in many cases the appropriate arm's length compensation for the services of the seconded employees in question will be the only payment required.

1.175. It should be noted, however, that in some situations, the transfer or secondment of one or more employees may, depending on the facts and circumstances, result in the transfer of valuable know-how or other intangibles from one associated enterprise to another. For example, an employee of Company A seconded to Company B may have knowledge of a secret formula owned by Company A and may make that secret formula available to Company B for use in its commercial operations. Similarly, employees of Company A seconded to Company B to assist with a factory start-up may make Company A manufacturing know-how available to Company B for use in its commercial operations. Where such a provision of know-how or other intangibles results from the transfer or secondment of employees, it should be separately analysed under the provisions of Chapter VI and an appropriate price should be paid for the right to use the intangibles.

1.176. Moreover, it should also be noted that access to an assembled workforce with particular skills and experience may, in some circumstances, enhance the value of transferred intangibles or other assets, even where the employees making up the workforce are not transferred. Example 23 in Annex I to Chapter VI illustrates one fact pattern where the interaction between intangibles and access to an assembled workforce may be important in a transfer pricing analysis.

D.8. MNE group synergies

1.177. Comparability issues, and the need for comparability adjustments, can also arise because of the existence of MNE group synergies. In some circumstances, MNE groups and the associated enterprises that comprise such groups may benefit from interactions or synergies amongst group members that would not generally be available to similarly situated independent enterprises. Such group synergies can arise, for example, as a result of combined purchasing power or economies of scale, combined and integrated computer and communication systems, integrated management, elimination of duplication, increased borrowing capacity, and numerous similar factors. Such group synergies are often favourable to the group as a whole and therefore may heighten the aggregate profits earned by group members, depending on whether expected cost savings are, in fact, realised, and on competitive conditions. In other circumstances such synergies may be negative, as when the size and scope of corporate operations create bureaucratic barriers not faced by smaller and more nimble enterprises, or when one portion of the business is forced to work with computer or communication systems that are not the most efficient for its business because of group wide standards established by the MNE group.

1.178. Paragraph 7.13 of these Guidelines suggests that an associated enterprise should not be considered to receive an intra-group service or be required to make any payment when it obtains incidental benefits attributable solely to its being part of a larger MNE group. In this context, the term incidental refers to benefits arising solely by virtue of group affiliation and in the absence of deliberate concerted actions or transactions leading to that benefit. The term incidental does not refer to the quantum of such benefits or suggest that such benefits must be small or relatively insignificant. Consistent with this general view of benefits incidental to group membership, when synergistic benefits or burdens of group membership arise purely as a result of membership in an MNE group and without the deliberate concerted action of group members or the performance of any service or other function by group members, such synergistic benefits of group membership need not be separately compensated or specifically allocated among members of the MNE group.

1.179. In some circumstances, however, synergistic benefits and burdens of group membership may arise because of deliberate concerted group actions and may give an MNE group a material, clearly identifiable structural advantage or disadvantage in the marketplace over market participants that are not part of an MNE group and that are involved in comparable transactions. Whether such a structural advantage or disadvantage exists, what the nature and source of the synergistic benefit or burden may be, and whether the synergistic benefit or burden arises through deliberate concerted group actions can only be determined through a thorough functional and comparability analysis.[3]

1.180. For example, if a group takes affirmative steps to centralise purchasing in a single group company to take advantage of volume discounts, and that group company resells the items it purchases to other group members, a deliberate concerted group action occurs to take advantage of group purchasing power. Similarly, if a central purchasing manager at the parent company or regional management centre performs a service by negotiating a group wide discount with a supplier on the condition of achieving minimum group wide purchasing levels, and group members then purchase from that supplier and obtain the discount, deliberate concerted group action has occurred notwithstanding the absence of specific purchase and sale transactions among group members. Where a supplier unilaterally offers one member of a group a favourable price in the hope of attracting business from other group members, however, no deliberate concerted group action would have occurred.

1.181. Where corporate synergies arising from deliberate concerted group actions do provide a member of an MNE group with material advantages or burdens not typical of comparable independent companies, it is necessary to determine (i) the nature of the advantage or disadvantage, (ii) the amount of the benefit or detriment provided, and (iii) how that benefit or detriment should be divided among members of the MNE group.

1.182. If important group synergies exist and can be attributed to deliberate concerted group actions, the benefits of such synergies should generally be shared by members of the group in proportion to their contribution to the creation of the synergy. For example, where members of the group take deliberate concerted actions to consolidate purchasing activities to take advantage of economies of scale resulting from high volume purchasing, the benefits of those large scale purchasing synergies, if any exist after an appropriate reward to the party co-ordinating the purchasing activities, should typically be shared by the members of the group in proportion to their purchase volumes.

1.183. Comparability adjustments may be warranted to account for group synergies.

3. In light of differences in local law, some jurisdictions consider a deliberate concerted action to always constitute a transaction, while others do not. However, the consensus view is that, in either scenario, a deliberate concerted action involves one associated enterprise performing functions, using assets, or assuming risks for the benefit of one or more other associated enterprises, such that arm's length compensation is required. See, e.g. Example 5 in paragraphs 1.190-1.193.

Example 1

1.184. P is the parent company of an MNE group engaging in a financial services business. The strength of the group's consolidated balance sheet makes it possible for P to maintain an AAA credit rating on a consistent basis. S is a member of the MNE group engaged in providing the same type of financial services as other group members and does so on a large scale in an important market. On a stand-alone basis, however, the strength of S's balance sheet would support a credit rating of only Baa. Nevertheless, because of S's membership in the P group, large independent lenders are willing to lend to it at interest rates that would be charged to independent borrowers with an A rating, i.e. a lower interest rate than would be charged if S were an independent entity with its same balance sheet, but a higher interest rate than would be available to the parent company of the MNE group.

1.185. Assume that S borrows EUR 50 million from an independent lender at the market rate of interest for borrowers with an A credit rating. Assume further that S simultaneously borrows EUR 50 million from T, another subsidiary of P, with similar characteristics as the independent lender, on the same terms and conditions and at the same interest rate charged by the independent lender (i.e. an interest rate premised on the existence of an A credit rating). Assume further that the independent lender, in setting its terms and conditions, was aware of S's other borrowings including the simultaneous loan to S from T.

1.186. Under these circumstances the interest rate charged on the loan by T to S is an arm's length interest rate because (i) it is the same rate charged to S by an independent lender in a comparable transaction; and (ii) no payment or comparability adjustment is required for the group synergy benefit that gives rise to the ability of S to borrow from independent enterprises at an interest rate lower than it could were it not a member of the group because the synergistic benefit of being able to borrow arises from S's group membership alone and not from any deliberate concerted action of members of the MNE group.

Example 2[4]

1.187. The facts relating to S's credit standing and borrowing power are identical to those in the preceding example. S borrows EUR 50 million from Bank A. The functional analysis suggests that Bank A would lend to S at an interest rate applicable to A rated borrowers without any formal guarantee.

4. Example 2 should not be viewed as providing comprehensive transfer pricing guidance on guarantee fees in respect of financial transactions. For further guidance on the transfer pricing aspects of financial transactions, see Chapter X of these Guidelines.

However, P agrees to guarantee the loan from Bank A in order to induce Bank A to lend at the interest rate that would be available to AAA rated borrowers. Under these circumstances, S should be required to pay a guarantee fee to P for providing the express guarantee. In calculating an arm's length guarantee fee, the fee should reflect the benefit of raising S's credit standing from A to AAA, not the benefit of raising S's credit standing from Baa to AAA. The enhancement of S's credit standing from Baa to A is attributable to the group synergy derived purely from passive association in the group which need not be compensated under the provisions of this section. The enhancement of S's credit standing from A to AAA is attributable to a deliberate concerted action, namely the provision of the guarantee by P, and should therefore give rise to compensation.

Example 3

1.188. Assume that Company A is assigned the role of central purchasing manager on behalf of the entire group. It purchases from independent suppliers and resells to associated enterprises. Company A, based solely on the negotiating leverage provided by the purchasing power of the entire group is able to negotiate with a supplier to reduce the price of widgets from USD 200 to USD 110. Under these circumstances, the arm's length price for the resale of widgets by Company A to other members of the group would not be at or near USD 200. Instead, the arm's length price would remunerate Company A for its services of co-ordinating purchasing activity. If the comparability and functional analysis suggests in this case that in comparable uncontrolled transactions involving a comparable volume of purchases, comparable co-ordination services resulted in a service fee based on Company A's costs incurred plus a mark-up equating to a total service fee of USD 6 per widget, then the intercompany price for the resale of the widgets by Company A would be approximately USD 116. Under these circumstances, each member of the group would derive benefits attributable to the group purchasing power of approximately USD 84 per widget. In addition, Company A would earn USD 6 per widget purchased by members of the group for its service functions.

Example 4

1.189. Assume facts similar to those in Example 3, except that instead of actually purchasing and reselling the widgets, Company A negotiates the discount on behalf of the group and group members subsequently purchase the widgets directly from the independent supplier. Under these circumstances, assume that the comparability analysis suggests that Company A would be entitled to a service fee of USD 5 per widget for the co-ordinating services that it performed on behalf of other group members. (The lower assumed service fee in Example 4 as compared to Example 3 may reflect a lower level of risk in the service provider following from the fact that it does not take title to the widgets or hold any inventory.) Group members purchasing widgets would retain the benefit of the group purchasing discount attributable to their individual purchases after payment of the service fee.

Example 5

1.190. Assume a multinational group based in Country A, has manufacturing subsidiaries in Country B and Country C. Country B has a tax rate of 30% and Country C has a tax rate of 10%. The group also maintains a shared services centre in Country D. Assume that the manufacturing subsidiaries in Country B and Country C each have need of 5 000 widgets produced by an independent supplier as an input to their manufacturing processes. Assume further that the Country D shared services company is consistently compensated for its aggregate activities by other group members, including the Country B and Country C manufacturing affiliates, on a cost plus basis, which, for purposes of this example, is assumed to be arm's length compensation for the level and nature of services it provides.

1.191. The independent supplier sells widgets for USD 10 apiece and follows a policy of providing a 5% price discount for bulk purchases of widgets in excess of 7 500 units. A purchasing employee in the Country D shared services centre approaches the independent supplier and confirms that if the Country B and Country C manufacturing affiliates simultaneously purchase 5 000 widgets each, a total group purchase of 10 000 widgets, the purchase discount will be available with respect to all of the group purchases. The independent supplier confirms that it will sell an aggregate of 10 000 widgets to the MNE group at a total price of USD 95 000, a discount of 5% from the price at which either of the two manufacturing affiliates could purchase independently from the supplier.

1.192. The purchasing employee at the shared services centre then places orders for the required widgets and requests that the supplier invoice the Country B manufacturing affiliate for 5 000 widgets at a total price of USD 50 000 and invoice the Country C manufacturing affiliate for 5 000 widgets at a total price of USD 45 000. The supplier complies with this request as it will result in the supplier being paid the agreed price of USD 95 000 for the total of the 10 000 widgets supplied.

1.193. Under these circumstances, Country B would be entitled to make a transfer pricing adjustment reducing the expenses of the Country B manufacturing affiliate by USD 2 500. The transfer pricing adjustment is appropriate because the pricing arrangements misallocate the benefit of the group synergy associated with volume purchasing of the widgets. The adjustment is appropriate notwithstanding the fact that the Country B manufacturing affiliate acting alone could not purchase widgets for a price less than the USD 50 000 it paid. The deliberate concerted group action in arranging the purchase discount provides a basis for the allocation of part of the discount to the Country B manufacturing affiliate notwithstanding the fact that there is no explicit transaction between the Country B and Country C manufacturing affiliates.

Chapter II

Transfer pricing methods

Part I: Selection of the transfer pricing method

A. Selection of the most appropriate transfer pricing method to the circumstances of the case

2.1. Parts II and III of this chapter respectively describe "traditional transaction methods" and "transactional profit methods" that can be used to establish whether the conditions imposed in the commercial or financial relations between associated enterprises are consistent with the arm's length principle. Traditional transaction methods are the comparable uncontrolled price method or CUP method, the resale price method, and the cost plus method. Transactional profit methods are the transactional net margin method and the transactional profit split method.

2.2. The selection of a transfer pricing method always aims at finding the most appropriate method for a particular case. For this purpose, the selection process should take account of the respective strengths and weaknesses of the OECD recognised methods; the appropriateness of the method considered in view of the nature of the controlled transaction, determined in particular through a functional analysis; the availability of reliable information (in particular on uncontrolled comparables) needed to apply the selected method and/or other methods; and the degree of comparability between controlled and uncontrolled transactions, including the reliability of comparability adjustments that may be needed to eliminate material differences between them. No one method is suitable in every possible situation, nor is it necessary to prove that a particular method is not suitable under the circumstances.

2.3. Traditional transaction methods are regarded as the most direct means of establishing whether conditions in the commercial and financial relations between associated enterprises are arm's length. This is because any difference in the price of a controlled transaction from the price in a comparable uncontrolled transaction can normally be traced directly to the commercial and financial relations made or imposed between the enterprises, and the arm's length conditions can be established by directly substituting the price in the comparable uncontrolled transaction for the price of the controlled transaction. As a result, where, taking account of the criteria described in paragraph 2.2, a traditional transaction method and a transactional profit method can be applied in an equally reliable manner, the traditional transaction method is preferable to the transactional profit method. Moreover, where, taking account of the criteria described in paragraph 2.2, the comparable uncontrolled price method (CUP) and another transfer pricing method can be applied in an equally reliable manner, the CUP method is to be preferred. See paragraphs 2.14-2.26 for a discussion of the CUP method.

2.4. There are situations where transactional profit methods are found to be more appropriate than traditional transaction methods. For example, cases where each of the parties makes unique and valuable contributions in relation to the controlled transaction, or where the parties engage in highly integrated activities, may make a transactional profit split more appropriate than a one-sided method. As another example, where there is no or limited publicly available reliable gross margin information on third parties, traditional transaction methods might be difficult to apply in cases other than those where there are internal comparables, and a transactional profit method might be the most appropriate method in view of the availability of information.

2.5. However, it is not appropriate to apply a transactional profit method merely because data concerning uncontrolled transactions are difficult to obtain or incomplete in one or more respects. The same criteria listed in paragraph 2.2 that were used to reach the initial conclusion that none of the traditional transactional methods could be reliably applied under the circumstances must be considered again in evaluating the reliability of the transactional profit method.

2.6. Methods that are based on profits can be accepted only insofar as they are compatible with Article 9 of the OECD Model Tax Convention, especially with regard to comparability. This is achieved by applying the methods in a manner that approximates arm's length pricing. The application of the arm's length principle is generally based on a comparison of the price, margin or profits from particular controlled transactions with the price, margin or profits from comparable transactions between independent enterprises. In the case of a transactional profit split method, it is based on an approximation of the division of profits that independent enterprises would have expected to realise from engaging in the transaction(s) (see paragraph 2.114).

2.7. In no case should transactional profit methods be used so as to result in over-taxing enterprises mainly because they make profits lower than the average, or in under-taxing enterprises that make higher than average profits. There is no justification under the arm's length principle for imposing additional tax on enterprises that are less successful than average or, conversely, for under-taxing enterprises that are more successful than average, when the reason for their success or lack thereof is attributable to commercial factors.

2.8. The guidance in paragraph 2.2 that the selection of a transfer pricing method always aims at finding the most appropriate method for each particular case does not mean that all the transfer pricing methods should be analysed in depth or tested in each case in arriving at the selection of the most appropriate method. As a matter of good practice, the selection of the most appropriate method and comparables should be evidenced and can be part of a typical search process as proposed in paragraph 3.4.

2.9. Moreover, MNE groups retain the freedom to apply methods not described in these Guidelines (hereafter "other methods") to establish prices provided those prices satisfy the arm's length principle in accordance with these Guidelines. Such other methods should however not be used in substitution for OECD-recognised methods where the latter are more appropriate to the facts and circumstances of the case. In cases where other methods are used, their selection should be supported by an explanation of why OECD-recognised methods were regarded as less appropriate or non-workable in the circumstances of the case and of the reason why the selected other method was regarded as providing a better solution. A taxpayer should maintain and be prepared to provide documentation regarding how its transfer prices were established. For a discussion of documentation, see Chapter V.

2.10. The application of a general rule of thumb does not provide an adequate substitute for a complete functional and comparability analysis conducted under the principles of Chapters I-III. Accordingly, a rule of thumb cannot be used to evidence that a price or an apportionment of income is arm's length.

2.11. It is not possible to provide specific rules that will cover every case. Tax administrators should hesitate from making minor or marginal adjustments. In general, the parties should attempt to reach a reasonable accommodation keeping in mind the imprecision of the various methods and the preference for higher degrees of comparability and a more direct and closer relationship to the transaction. It should not be the case that useful information, such as might be drawn from uncontrolled transactions that are not identical to the controlled transactions, should be dismissed simply because some rigid standard of comparability is not fully met. Similarly, evidence from enterprises engaged in controlled transactions with associated enterprises may be useful in understanding the transaction under review or as a pointer to further investigation. Further, any method should be permitted where its application is agreeable to the members of the MNE group involved with the transaction or transactions to which the methodology applies and also to the tax administrations in the jurisdictions of all those members.

B. Use of more than one method

2.12. The arm's length principle does not require the application of more than one method for a given transaction (or set of transactions that are appropriately aggregated following the standard described in paragraph 3.9), and in fact undue reliance on such an approach could create a significant burden for taxpayers. Thus, these Guidelines do not require either the tax examiner or taxpayer to perform analyses under more than one method. While in some cases the selection of a method may not be straightforward and more than one method may be initially considered, generally it will be possible to select one method that is apt to provide the best estimation of an arm's length price. However, for difficult cases, where no one approach is conclusive, a flexible approach would allow the evidence of various methods to be used in conjunction. In such cases, an attempt should be made to reach a conclusion consistent with the arm's length principle that is satisfactory from a practical viewpoint to all the parties involved, taking into account the facts and circumstances of the case, the mix of evidence available, and the relative reliability of the various methods under consideration. See paragraphs 3.58-3.59 for a discussion of cases where a range of figures results from the use of more than one method.

Part II: Traditional transaction methods

A. Introduction

2.13. This part provides a detailed description of traditional transaction methods that are used to apply the arm's length principle. These methods are the comparable uncontrolled price method or CUP method, the resale price method, and the cost plus method.

B. Comparable uncontrolled price method

B.1. In general

2.14. The CUP method compares the price charged for property or services transferred in a controlled transaction to the price charged for property or services transferred in a comparable uncontrolled transaction in comparable circumstances. If there is any difference between the two prices, this may indicate that the conditions of the commercial and financial relations of the associated enterprises are not arm's length, and that the price in the uncontrolled transaction may need to be substituted for the price in the controlled transaction.

2.15. Following the principles in Chapter I, an uncontrolled transaction is comparable to a controlled transaction (i.e. it is a comparable uncontrolled transaction) for purposes of the CUP method if one of two conditions is met: a) none of the differences (if any) between the transactions being compared or between the enterprises undertaking those transactions could materially affect the price in the open market; or, b) reasonably accurate adjustments can be made to eliminate the material effects of such differences. Where it is possible to locate comparable uncontrolled transactions, the CUP method is the most direct and reliable way to apply the arm's length principle. Consequently, in such cases the CUP method is preferable over all other methods.

2.16. It may be difficult to find a transaction between independent enterprises that is similar enough to a controlled transaction such that no differences have a material effect on price. For example, a minor difference in the property transferred in the controlled and uncontrolled transactions could materially affect the price even though the nature of the business activities undertaken may be sufficiently similar to generate the same overall profit margin. When this is the case, some adjustments will be appropriate. As discussed below in paragraph 2.17, the extent and reliability of such adjustments will affect the relative reliability of the analysis under the CUP method.

2.17. In considering whether controlled and uncontrolled transactions are comparable, regard should be had to the effect on price of broader business functions other than just product comparability (i.e. factors relevant to determining comparability under Chapter I). Where differences exist between the controlled and uncontrolled transactions or between the enterprises undertaking those transactions, it may be difficult to determine reasonably accurate adjustments to eliminate the effect on price. The difficulties that arise in attempting to make reasonably accurate adjustments should not routinely preclude the possible application of the CUP method. Practical considerations dictate a more flexible approach to enable the CUP method to be used and to be supplemented as necessary by other appropriate methods, all of which should be evaluated according to their relative accuracy. Every effort should be made to adjust the data so that it may be used appropriately in a CUP method. As for any method, the relative reliability of the CUP method is affected by the degree of accuracy with which adjustments can be made to achieve comparability.

2.18. Subject to the guidance in paragraph 2.2 for selecting the most appropriate transfer pricing method in the circumstances of a particular case, the CUP method would generally be an appropriate transfer pricing method for establishing the arm's length price for the transfer of commodities between associated enterprises. The reference to "commodities" shall be understood to encompass physical products for which a quoted price is used as a reference by independent parties in the industry to set prices in uncontrolled transactions. The term "quoted price" refers to the price of the commodity in the relevant period obtained in an international or domestic commodity exchange market. In this context, a quoted price also includes prices obtained from recognised and transparent price reporting or statistical agencies, or from governmental price-setting agencies, where such indexes are used as a reference by unrelated parties to determine prices in transactions between them.

2.19. Under the CUP method, the arm's length price for commodity transactions may be determined by reference to comparable uncontrolled transactions and by reference to comparable uncontrolled arrangements represented by the quoted price. Quoted commodity prices generally reflect the agreement between independent buyers and sellers in the market on the price for a specific type and amount of commodity, traded under specific conditions at a certain point in time. A relevant factor in determining the appropriateness of using the quoted price for a specific commodity is the extent to which the quoted price is widely and routinely used in the ordinary course of business in the industry to negotiate prices for uncontrolled transactions comparable to the controlled transaction. Accordingly, depending on the facts and circumstances of each case, quoted prices can be considered as a reference for pricing commodity transactions between associated enterprises. Taxpayers and tax administrations should be consistent in their application of the appropriately selected quoted price.

2.20. For the CUP method to be reliably applied to commodity transactions, the economically relevant characteristics of the controlled transaction and the uncontrolled transactions or the uncontrolled arrangements represented by the quoted price need to be comparable. For commodities, the economically relevant characteristics include, among others, the physical features and quality of the commodity; the contractual terms of the controlled transaction, such as volumes traded, period of the arrangements, the timing and terms of delivery, transportation, insurance, and foreign currency terms. For some commodities, certain economically relevant characteristics (e.g. prompt delivery) may lead to a premium or a discount. If the quoted price is used as a reference for determining the arm's length price or price range, the standardised contracts which stipulate specifications on the basis of which commodities are traded on the exchange and which result in a quoted price for the commodity may be relevant. Where there are differences between the conditions of the controlled transaction and the conditions of the uncontrolled transactions or the conditions determining the quoted price for the commodity that materially affect the price of the commodity transactions being examined, reasonably accurate adjustments should be made to ensure that the economically relevant characteristics of the transactions are comparable. Contributions made in the form of functions performed, assets used and risks assumed by other entities in the supply chain should be compensated in accordance with the guidance provided in these Guidelines.

2.21. In order to assist tax administrations in conducting an informed examination of the taxpayer's transfer pricing practices, taxpayers should provide reliable evidence and document, as part of their transfer pricing documentation, the price-setting policy for commodity transactions, the information needed to justify price adjustments based on the comparable uncontrolled transactions or comparable uncontrolled arrangements represented by the quoted price and any other relevant information, such as pricing formulas used, third party end-customer agreements, premia or discounts applied, pricing date, supply chain information, and information prepared for non-tax purposes.

2.22. A particularly relevant factor for commodity transactions determined by reference to the quoted price is the pricing date, which refers to the specific time, date or time period (e.g. a specified range of dates over which an average price is determined) selected by the parties to determine the price for commodity transactions. Where the taxpayer can provide reliable evidence of the pricing date agreed by the associated enterprises in the controlled commodity transaction at the time the transaction was entered into (e.g. proposals and acceptances, contracts or registered contracts, or other documents setting out the terms of the arrangements may constitute reliable evidence) and this is consistent with the actual conduct of the parties or with other facts of the case, in accordance with the guidance in Section D of Chapter I on accurately delineating the actual transaction, tax administrations should determine the price for the commodity transaction by reference to the pricing date agreed by the associated enterprises. If the pricing date specified in any written agreement between the associated enterprises is inconsistent with the actual conduct of the parties or with other facts of the case, tax administrations may determine a different pricing date consistent with those other facts of the case and what independent enterprises would have agreed in comparable circumstances (taking into considerations industry practices). When the taxpayer does not provide reliable evidence of the pricing date agreed by the associated enterprises in the controlled transaction and the tax administration cannot otherwise determine a different pricing date under the guidance in Section D of Chapter I, tax administrations may deem the pricing date for the commodity transaction on the basis of the evidence available to the tax administration; this may be the date of shipment as evidenced by the bill of lading or equivalent document depending on the means of transport. This would mean that the price for the commodities being transacted would be determined by reference to the average quoted price on the shipment date, subject to any appropriate comparability adjustments based on the information available to the tax administration. It would be important to permit resolution of cases of double taxation arising from application of the deemed pricing date through access to the mutual agreement procedure under the applicable Treaty.

B.2. Examples of the application of the CUP method

2.23. The following examples illustrate the application of the CUP method, including situations where adjustments may need to be made to uncontrolled transactions to make them comparable uncontrolled transactions.

2.24. The CUP method is a particularly reliable method where an independent enterprise sells the same product as is sold between two associated enterprises. For example, an independent enterprise sells unbranded Colombian coffee beans of a similar type, quality, and quantity as those sold between two associated enterprises, assuming that the controlled and uncontrolled transactions occur at about the same time, at the same stage in the production/distribution chain, and under similar conditions. If the only available uncontrolled transaction involved unbranded Brazilian coffee beans, it would be appropriate to inquire whether the difference in the coffee beans has a material effect on the price.

For example, it could be asked whether the source of coffee beans commands a premium or requires a discount generally in the open market. Such information may be obtainable from commodity markets or may be deduced from dealer prices. If this difference does have a material effect on price, some adjustments would be appropriate. If a reasonably accurate adjustment cannot be made, the reliability of the CUP method would be reduced, and it might be necessary to select another less direct method instead.

2.25. One illustrative case where adjustments may be required is where the circumstances surrounding controlled and uncontrolled sales are identical, except for the fact that the controlled sales price is a delivered price and the uncontrolled sales are made f.o.b. factory. The differences in terms of transportation and insurance generally have a definite and reasonably ascertainable effect on price. Therefore, to determine the uncontrolled sales price, adjustment should be made to the price for the difference in delivery terms.

2.26. As another example, assume a taxpayer sells 1 000 tons of a product for USD 80 per ton to an associated enterprise in its MNE group, and at the same time sells 500 tons of the same product for USD 100 per ton to an independent enterprise. This case requires an evaluation of whether the different volumes should result in an adjustment of the transfer price. The relevant market should be researched by analysing transactions in similar products to determine typical volume discounts.

C. Resale price method

C.1. In general

2.27. The resale price method begins with the price at which a product that has been purchased from an associated enterprise is resold to an independent enterprise. This price (the resale price) is then reduced by an appropriate gross margin on this price (the "resale price margin") representing the amount out of which the reseller would seek to cover its selling and other operating expenses and, in the light of the functions performed (taking into account assets used and risks assumed), make an appropriate profit. What is left after subtracting the gross margin can be regarded, after adjustment for other costs associated with the purchase of the product (e.g. customs duties), as an arm's length price for the original transfer of property between the associated enterprises. This method is probably most useful where it is applied to marketing operations.

2.28. The resale price margin of the reseller in the controlled transaction may be determined by reference to the resale price margin that the same reseller earns on items purchased and sold in comparable uncontrolled transactions ("internal comparable"). Also, the resale price margin earned by an independent enterprise in comparable uncontrolled transactions may serve as a guide ("external comparable"). Where the reseller is carrying on a general brokerage business, the resale price margin may be related to a brokerage fee, which is usually calculated as a percentage of the sales price of the product sold. The determination of the resale price margin in such a case should take into account whether the broker is acting as an agent or a principal.

2.29. Following the principles in Chapter I, an uncontrolled transaction is comparable to a controlled transaction (i.e. it is a comparable uncontrolled transaction) for purposes of the resale price method if one of two conditions is met: a) none of the differences (if any) between the transactions being compared or between the enterprises undertaking those transactions could materially affect the resale price margin in the open market; or, b) reasonably accurate adjustments can be made to eliminate the material effects of such differences. In making comparisons for purposes of the resale price method, fewer adjustments are normally needed to account for product differences than under the CUP method, because minor product differences are less likely to have as material an effect on profit margins as they do on price.

2.30. In a market economy, the compensation for performing similar functions would tend to be equalised across different activities. In contrast, prices for different products would tend to equalise only to the extent that those products were substitutes for one another. Because gross profit margins represent gross compensation, after the cost of sales for specific functions performed (taking into account assets used and risks assumed), product differences are less significant. For example, the facts may indicate that a distribution company performs the same functions (taking into account assets used and risks assumed) selling toasters as it would selling blenders, and hence in a market economy there should be a similar level of compensation for the two activities. However, consumers would not consider toasters and blenders to be particularly close substitutes, and hence there would be no reason to expect their prices to be the same.

2.31. Although broader product differences can be allowed in the resale price method, the property transferred in the controlled transaction must still be compared to that being transferred in the uncontrolled transaction. Broader differences are more likely to be reflected in differences in functions performed between the parties to the controlled and uncontrolled transactions. While less product comparability may be required in using the resale price method, it remains the case that closer comparability of products will produce a better result. For example, where there is a valuable or unique intangible involved in the transaction, product similarity may assume greater importance and particular attention should be paid to it to ensure that the comparison is valid.

2.32. It may be appropriate to give more weight to other attributes of comparability discussed in Chapter I (i.e. functions performed, economic circumstances, etc.) when the profit margin relates primarily to those other attributes and only secondarily to the particular product being transferred. This circumstance will usually exist where the profit margin is determined for an associated enterprise that has not used unique assets (such as valuable, unique intangibles) to add significant value to the product being transferred. Thus, where uncontrolled and controlled transactions are comparable in all characteristics other than the product itself, the resale price method might produce a more reliable measure of arm's length conditions than the CUP method, unless reasonably accurate adjustments could be made to account for differences in the products transferred. The same point is true for the cost plus method, discussed below.

2.33. When the resale price margin used is that of an independent enterprise in a comparable transaction, the reliability of the resale price method may be affected if there are material differences in the ways the associated enterprises and independent enterprises carry out their businesses. Such differences could include those that affect the level of costs taken into account (e.g. the differences could include the effect of management efficiency on levels and ranges of inventory maintenance), which may well have an impact on the profitability of an enterprise but which may not necessarily affect the price at which it buys or sells its goods or services in the open market. These types of characteristics should be analysed in determining whether an uncontrolled transaction is comparable for purposes of applying the resale price method.

2.34. The resale price method also depends on comparability of functions performed (taking into account assets used and risks assumed). It may become less reliable when there are differences between the controlled and uncontrolled transactions and the parties to the transactions, and those differences have a material effect on the attribute being used to measure arm's length conditions, in this case the resale price margin realised. Where there are material differences that affect the gross margins earned in the controlled and uncontrolled transactions (e.g. in the nature of the functions performed by the parties to the transactions), adjustments should be made to account for such differences. The extent and reliability of those adjustments will affect the relative reliability of the analysis under the resale price method in any particular case.

2.35. An appropriate resale price margin is easiest to determine where the reseller does not add substantially to the value of the product. In contrast, it may be more difficult to use the resale price method to arrive at an arm's length price where, before resale, the goods are further processed or incorporated into a more complicated product so that their identity is lost or transformed (e.g. where components are joined together in finished or semi-finished goods). Another example where the resale price margin requires particular care is where the reseller contributes substantially to the creation or maintenance of intangible property associated with the product (e.g. trademarks or trade names) which are owned by an associated enterprise. In such cases, the contribution of the goods originally transferred to the value of the final product cannot be easily evaluated.

2.36. A resale price margin is more accurate where it is realised within a short time of the reseller's purchase of the goods. The more time that elapses between the original purchase and resale the more likely it is that other factors – changes in the market, in rates of exchange, in costs, etc. – will need to be taken into account in any comparison.

2.37. It should be expected that the amount of the resale price margin will be influenced by the level of activities performed by the reseller. This level of activities can range widely from the case where the reseller performs only minimal services as a forwarding agent to the case where the reseller takes on the full risk of ownership together with the full responsibility for and the risks involved in advertising, marketing, distributing and guaranteeing the goods, financing stocks, and other connected services. If the reseller in the controlled transaction does not carry on a substantial commercial activity but only transfers the goods to a third party, the resale price margin could, in light of the functions performed, be a small one. The resale price margin could be higher where it can be demonstrated that the reseller has some special expertise in the marketing of such goods, in effect bears special risks, or contributes substantially to the creation or maintenance of intangible property associated with the product. However, the level of activity performed by the reseller, whether minimal or substantial, would need to be well supported by relevant evidence. This would include justification for marketing expenditures that might be considered unreasonably high; for example, when part or most of the promotional expenditure was clearly incurred as a service performed in favour of the legal owner of the trademark. In such a case the cost plus method may well supplement the resale price method.

2.38. Where the reseller is clearly carrying on a substantial commercial activity in addition to the resale activity itself, then a reasonably substantial resale price margin might be expected. If the reseller in its activities employs certain assets (e.g. intangibles used by the reseller, such as its marketing organisation), it may be inappropriate to evaluate the arm's length conditions in the controlled transaction using an unadjusted resale price margin derived from uncontrolled transactions in which the uncontrolled reseller does not employ similar assets. If the reseller possesses valuable marketing intangibles, the resale price margin in the uncontrolled transaction may underestimate the profit to which the reseller in the controlled transaction is entitled, unless the comparable uncontrolled transaction involves the same reseller or a reseller with similarly valuable marketing intangibles.

2.39. In a case where there is a chain of distribution of goods through an intermediate company, it may be relevant for tax administrations to look not only at the resale price of goods that have been purchased from the intermediate company but also at the price that such company pays to its own supplier and the functions that the intermediate company undertakes. There could well be practical difficulties in obtaining this information and the true function of the intermediate company may be difficult to determine. If it cannot be demonstrated that the intermediate company either assumes an economically significant risk or performs an economic function in the chain that has increased the value of the goods, then any element in the price that is claimed to be attributable to the activities of the intermediate company would reasonably be attributed elsewhere in the MNE group, because independent enterprises would not normally have allowed such a company to share in the profits of the transaction.

2.40. The resale price margin should also be expected to vary according to whether the reseller has the exclusive right to resell the goods. Arrangements of this kind are found in transactions between independent enterprises and may influence the margin. Thus, this type of exclusive right should be taken into account in any comparison. The value to be attributed to such an exclusive right will depend to some extent upon its geographical scope and the existence and relative competitiveness of possible substitute goods. The arrangement may be valuable to both the supplier and the reseller in an arm's length transaction. For instance, it may stimulate the reseller to greater efforts to sell the supplier's particular line of goods. On the other hand, such an arrangement may provide the reseller with a kind of monopoly with the result that the reseller possibly can realise a substantial turn over without great effort. Accordingly, the effect of this factor upon the appropriate resale price margin must be examined with care in each case. See also paragraphs 6.118 and 6.120.

2.41. Where the accounting practices differ from the controlled transaction to the uncontrolled transaction, appropriate adjustments should be made to the data used in calculating the resale price margin in order to ensure that the same types of costs are used in each case to arrive at the gross margin. For example, costs of R&D may be reflected in operating expenses or in costs of sales. The respective gross margins would not be comparable without appropriate adjustments.

C.2. Examples of the application of the resale price method

2.42. Assume that there are two distributors selling the same product in the same market under the same brand name. Distributor A offers a warranty; Distributor B offers none. Distributor A is not including the warranty as part of a pricing strategy and so sells its product at a higher price resulting in a higher gross profit margin (if the costs of servicing the warranty are not taken into account) than that of Distributor B, which sells at a lower price. The two margins are not comparable until a reasonably accurate adjustment is made to account for that difference.

2.43. Assume that a warranty is offered with respect to all products so that the downstream price is uniform. Distributor C performs the warranty function but is, in fact, compensated by the supplier through a lower price. Distributor D does not perform the warranty function which is performed by the supplier (products are sent back to the factory). However, Distributor D's supplier charges D a higher price than is charged to Distributor C. If Distributor C accounts for the cost of performing the warranty function as a cost of goods sold, then the adjustment in the gross profit margins for the differences is automatic. However, if the warranty expenses are accounted for as operating expenses, there is a distortion in the margins which must be corrected. The reasoning in this case would be that, if D performed the warranty itself, its supplier would reduce the transfer price, and therefore, D's gross profit margin would be greater.

2.44. A company sells a product through independent distributors in five jurisdictions in which it has no subsidiaries. The distributors simply market the product and do not perform any additional work. In one country, the company has set up a subsidiary. Because this particular market is of strategic importance, the company requires its subsidiary to sell only its product and to perform technical applications for the customers. Even if all other facts and circumstances are similar, if the margins are derived from independent enterprises that do not have exclusive sales arrangements or perform technical applications like those undertaken by the subsidiary, it is necessary to consider whether any adjustments must be made to achieve comparability.

D. Cost plus method

D.1. In general

2.45. The cost plus method begins with the costs incurred by the supplier of property (or services) in a controlled transaction for property transferred or services provided to an associated purchaser. An appropriate cost plus mark-up is then added to this cost, to make an appropriate profit in light of the functions performed and the market conditions. What is arrived at after adding the cost plus mark up to the above costs may be regarded as an arm's length price of the original controlled transaction. This method probably is most useful where semi finished goods are sold between associated parties, where associated parties have concluded joint facility agreements or long-term buy-and-supply arrangements, or where the controlled transaction is the provision of services.

2.46. The cost plus mark-up of the supplier in the controlled transaction should ideally be established by reference to the cost plus mark-up that the same supplier earns in comparable uncontrolled transactions ("internal comparable"). In addition, the cost plus mark-up that would have been earned in comparable transactions by an independent enterprise may serve as a guide ("external comparable").

2.47. Following the principles in Chapter I, an uncontrolled transaction is comparable to a controlled transaction (i.e. it is a comparable uncontrolled transaction) for purposes of the cost plus method if one of two conditions is met: a) none of the differences (if any) between the transactions being compared or between the enterprises undertaking those transactions materially affect the cost plus mark up in the open market; or, b) reasonably accurate adjustments can be made to eliminate the material effects of such differences. In determining whether a transaction is a comparable uncontrolled transaction for the purposes of the cost plus method, the same principles apply as described in paragraphs 2.29-2.34 for the resale price method. Thus, fewer adjustments may be necessary to account for product differences under the cost plus method than the CUP method, and it may be appropriate to give more weight to other factors of comparability described in Chapter I, some of which may have a more significant effect on the cost plus mark-up than they do on price. As under the resale price method (see paragraph 2.34), where there are differences that materially affect the cost plus mark ups earned in the controlled and uncontrolled transactions (for example in the nature of the functions performed by the parties to the transactions), reasonably accurate adjustments should be made to account for such differences. The extent and reliability of those adjustments will affect the relative reliability of the analysis under the cost plus method in particular cases.

2.48. For example, assume that Company A manufactures and sells toasters to a distributor that is an associated enterprise, that Company B manufactures and sells irons to a distributor that is an independent enterprise, and that the profit margins on the manufacture of basic toasters and irons are generally the same in the small household appliance industry. (The use of the cost plus method here presumes that there are no highly similar independent toaster manufacturers). If the cost plus method were being applied, the mark ups being compared in the controlled and uncontrolled transactions would be the difference between the selling price by the manufacturer to the distributor and the costs of manufacturing the product, divided by the costs of manufacturing the product. However, Company A may be much more efficient in its manufacturing processes than Company B thereby enabling it to have lower costs. As a result, even if Company A were making irons instead of toasters and charging the same price as Company B is charging for irons (i.e. no special condition were to exist), it would be appropriate for Company A's profit level to be higher than that of Company B. Thus, unless it is possible to adjust for the effect of this difference on the profit, the application of the cost plus method would not be wholly reliable in this context.

2.49. The cost plus method presents some difficulties in proper application, particularly in the determination of costs. Although it is true that an enterprise must cover its costs over a period of time to remain in business, those costs may not be the determinant of the appropriate profit in a specific case for any one year. While in many cases companies are driven by competition to scale down prices by reference to the cost of creating the relevant goods or providing the relevant service, there are other circumstances where there is no discernible link between the level of costs incurred and a market price (e.g. where a valuable discovery has been made and the owner has incurred only small research costs in making it).

2.50. In addition, when applying the cost plus method one should pay attention to apply a comparable mark up to a comparable cost basis. For instance, if the supplier to which reference is made in applying the cost plus method in carrying out its activities employs leased business assets, the cost basis might not be comparable without adjustment if the supplier in the controlled transaction owns its business assets. The cost plus method relies upon a comparison of the mark up on costs achieved in a controlled transaction and the mark up on costs achieved in one or more comparable uncontrolled transactions. Therefore, differences between the controlled and uncontrolled transactions that have an effect on the size of the mark up must be analysed to determine what adjustments should be made to the uncontrolled transactions' respective mark up.

2.51. For this purpose, it is particularly important to consider differences in the level and types of expenses – operating expenses and non-operating expenses including financing expenditures – associated with functions performed and risks assumed by the parties or transactions being compared. Consideration of these differences may indicate the following:

a) If expenses reflect a functional difference (taking into account assets used and risks assumed) which has not been taken into account in applying the method, an adjustment to the cost plus mark up may be required.

b) If the expenses reflect additional functions that are distinct from the activities tested by the method, separate compensation for those functions may need to be determined. Such functions may for example amount to the provision of services for which an appropriate reward may be determined. Similarly, expenses that are the result of capital structures reflecting non-arm's length arrangements may require separate adjustment.

c) If differences in the expenses of the parties being compared merely reflect efficiencies or inefficiencies of the enterprises, as would normally be the case for supervisory, general, and administrative expenses, then no adjustment to the gross margin may be appropriate.

In any of the above circumstances it may be appropriate to supplement the cost plus and resale price methods by considering the results obtained from applying other methods (see paragraph 2.12).

2.52. Another important aspect of comparability is accounting consistency. Where the accounting practices differ in the controlled transaction and the uncontrolled transaction, appropriate adjustments should be made to the data used to ensure that the same type of costs are used in each case to ensure consistency. The gross profit mark ups must be measured consistently between the associated enterprise and the independent enterprise. In addition, there may be differences across enterprises in the treatment of costs that affect gross profit mark ups that would need to be accounted for in order to achieve reliable comparability. In some cases it may be necessary to take into account certain operating expenses in order to achieve consistency and comparability; in these circumstances the cost plus method starts to approach a net rather than gross profit analysis. To the extent that the analysis takes into account operating expenses, its reliability may be adversely affected for the reasons set forth in paragraphs 2.70-2.73. Thus, the safeguards described in paragraphs 2.74-2.81 may be relevant in assessing the reliability of such analyses.

2.53. While precise accounting standards and terms may vary, in general the costs and expenses of an enterprise are understood to be divisible into three broad categories. First, there are the direct costs of producing a product or service, such as the cost of raw materials. Second, there are indirect costs of production, which although closely related to the production process may be common to several products or services (e.g. the costs of a repair department that services equipment used to produce different products). Finally, there are the operating expenses of the enterprise as a whole, such as supervisory, general, and administrative expenses.

2.54. The distinction between gross and net profit analyses may be understood in the following terms. In general, the cost plus method will use mark ups computed after direct and indirect costs of production, while a net profit method will use profits computed after operating expenses of the enterprise as well. It must be recognised that because of the variations in practice among jurisdictions, it is difficult to draw any precise lines between the three categories described above. Thus, for example, an application of the cost plus method may in a particular case include the consideration of some expenses that might be considered operating expenses, as discussed in paragraph 2.52. Nevertheless, the problems in delineating with mathematical precision the boundaries of the three categories described above do not alter the basic practical distinction between the gross and net profit approaches.

2.55. In principle historical costs should be attributed to individual units of production, although admittedly the cost plus method may over-emphasise historical costs. Some costs, for example costs of materials, labour, and transport will vary over a period and in such a case it may be appropriate to average the costs over the period. Averaging also may be appropriate across product groups or over a particular line of production. Further, averaging may be appropriate with respect to the costs of fixed assets where the production or processing of different products is carried on simultaneously and the volume of activity fluctuates. Costs such as replacement costs and marginal costs also may need to be considered where these can be measured and they result in a more accurate estimate of the appropriate profit.

2.56. The costs that may be considered in applying the cost plus method are limited to those of the supplier of goods or services. This limitation may raise a problem of how to allocate some costs between suppliers and purchasers. There is a possibility that some costs will be borne by the purchaser in order to diminish the supplier's cost base on which the mark up will be calculated. In practice, this may be achieved by not allocating to the supplier an appropriate share of overheads and other costs borne by the purchaser (often the parent company) for the benefit of the supplier (often a subsidiary). The allocation should be undertaken based on an analysis of functions performed (taking into account assets used and risks assumed) by the respective parties as provided in Chapter I. A related problem is how overhead costs should be apportioned, whether by reference to turnover, number or cost of employees, or some other criterion. The issue of cost allocation is also discussed in Chapter VIII on cost contribution arrangements.

2.57. In some cases, there may be a basis for using only variable or incremental (e.g. marginal) costs, because the transactions represent a disposal of marginal production. Such a claim could be justified if the goods could not be sold at a higher price in the relevant foreign market (see also the discussion of market penetration in Chapter I). Factors that could be taken into account in evaluating such a claim include information on whether the taxpayer has any other sales of the same or similar products in that particular foreign market, the percentage of the taxpayers' production (in both volume and value terms) that the claimed "marginal production" represents, the term of the arrangement, and details of the marketing analysis that was undertaken by the taxpayer or MNE group which led to the conclusion that the goods could not be sold at a higher price in that foreign market.

2.58. No general rule can be set out that deals with all cases. The various methods for determining costs should be consistent as between the controlled and uncontrolled transactions and consistent over time in relation to particular enterprises. For example, in determining the appropriate cost plus mark up, it may be necessary to take into account whether products can be supplied by various sources at widely differing costs. Associated enterprises may choose to calculate their cost plus basis on a standardised basis. An independent party probably would not accept to pay a higher price resulting from the inefficiency of the other party. On the other hand, if the other party is more efficient than can be expected under normal circumstances, this other party should benefit from that advantage. The associated enterprise may agree in advance which costs would be acceptable as a basis for the cost plus method.

D.2. Examples of the application of the cost plus method

2.59. A is a domestic manufacturer of timing mechanisms for mass-market clocks. A sells this product to its foreign subsidiary B. A earns a 5% gross profit mark up with respect to its manufacturing operation. X, Y, and Z are independent domestic manufacturers of timing mechanisms for mass-market watches. X, Y, and Z sell to independent foreign purchasers. X, Y, and Z earn gross profit mark ups with respect to their manufacturing operations that range from 3% to 5%. A accounts for supervisory, general, and administrative costs as operating expenses, and thus these costs are not reflected in cost of goods sold. The gross profit mark ups of X, Y, and Z, however, reflect supervisory, general, and administrative costs as part of costs of goods sold. Therefore, the gross profit mark ups of X, Y, and Z must be adjusted to provide accounting consistency.

2.60. Company C in Country D is a 100% subsidiary of company E, located in Country F. In comparison with Country F, wages are very low in Country D. At the expense and risk of company E, television sets are assembled by company C. All the necessary components, know-how, etc. are provided by company E. The purchase of the assembled product is guaranteed by company E in case the television sets fail to meet a certain quality standard. After the quality check, the television sets are brought – at the expense and risk of company E – to distribution centres company E has in several countries. The function of company C can be described as a purely contract manufacturing function. The risks company C could bear are eventual differences in the agreed quality and quantity. The basis for applying the cost plus method will be formed by all the costs connected to the assembling activities.

2.61. Company A of an MNE group agrees with company B of the same MNE group to carry out contract research for company B. All risks related to the research are assumed by company B. This company also owns all the intangibles developed through the research and therefore has also the profit chances resulting from the research. This is a typical setup for applying a cost plus method. All costs for the research, which the associated parties have agreed upon, have to be compensated. The additional cost plus may reflect how innovative and complex the research carried out is.

Part III: Transactional profit methods

A. Introduction

2.62. This Part provides a discussion of transactional profit methods that may be used to approximate arm's length conditions where such methods are the most appropriate to the circumstances of the case, see paragraphs 2.1-2.12. Transactional profit methods examine the profits that arise from particular transactions among associated enterprises. The only profit methods that satisfy the arm's length principle are those that are consistent with Article 9 of the OECD Model Tax Convention and follow the requirement for a comparability analysis as described in these Guidelines. In particular, so-called "comparable profits methods" or "modified cost plus/resale price methods" are acceptable only to the extent that they are consistent with these Guidelines.

2.63. A transactional profit method examines the profits that arise from particular controlled transactions. The transactional profit methods for purposes of these Guidelines are the transactional profit split method and the transactional net margin method. Profit arising from a controlled transaction can be a relevant indicator of whether the transaction was affected by conditions that differ from those that would have been made by independent enterprises in otherwise comparable circumstances.

B. Transactional net margin method

B.1. In general

2.64. The transactional net margin method examines the net profit relative to an appropriate base (e.g. costs, sales, assets) that a taxpayer realises from a controlled transaction (or transactions that are appropriate to aggregate under the principles of paragraphs 3.9-3.12). Thus, a transactional net margin method operates in a manner similar to the cost plus and resale price methods. This similarity means that in order to be applied reliably, the transactional net margin method must be applied in a manner consistent with the manner in which the resale price or cost plus method is applied.

This means in particular that the net profit indicator of the taxpayer from the controlled transaction (or transactions that are appropriate to aggregate under the principles of paragraphs 3.9-3.12) should ideally be established by reference to the net profit indicator that the same taxpayer earns in comparable uncontrolled transactions, i.e. by reference to "internal comparables" (see paragraphs 3.27-3.28). Where this is not possible, the net margin that would have been earned in comparable transactions by an independent enterprise ("external comparables") may serve as a guide (see paragraphs 3.29-3.35). A functional analysis of the controlled and uncontrolled transactions is required to determine whether the transactions are comparable and what adjustments may be necessary to obtain reliable results. Further, the other requirements for comparability, and in particular those of paragraphs 2.74-2.81, must be applied.

2.65. A transactional net margin method is unlikely to be reliable if each party to a transaction makes unique and valuable contributions, see paragraph 2.4. In such a case, a transactional profit split method will generally be the most appropriate method, see paragraph 2.119. However, a one-sided method (traditional transaction method or transactional net margin method) may be applicable in cases where one of the parties makes all the unique and valuable contributions involved in the controlled transaction, while the other party does not make any unique and valuable contribution. In such a case, the tested party should be the less complex one. See paragraphs 3.18-3.19 for a discussion of the notion of tested party.

2.66. There are also many cases where a party to a transaction makes contributions that are not unique – e.g. uses non-unique intangibles such as non-unique business processes or non-unique market knowledge. In such cases, it may be possible to meet the comparability requirements to apply a traditional transaction method or a transactional net margin method because the comparables would also be expected to use a comparable mix of non-unique contributions.

2.67. Finally, the lack of unique and valuable contributions involved in a particular transaction does not automatically imply that the transactional net margin method is the most appropriate method.

B.2. Strengths and weaknesses[1]

2.68. One strength of the transactional net margin method is that net profit indicators (e.g. return on assets, operating income to sales, and possibly other measures of net profit) are less affected by transactional differences than is

1. An example illustrating the sensitivity of gross and net profit margin indicators is found in Annex I to Chapter II.

the case with price, as used in the CUP method. Net profit indicators also may be more tolerant to some functional differences between the controlled and uncontrolled transactions than gross profit margins. Differences in the functions performed between enterprises are often reflected in variations in operating expenses. Consequently, this may lead to a wide range of gross profit margins but still broadly similar levels of net operating profit indicators. In addition, in some jurisdictions the lack of clarity in the public data with respect to the classification of expenses in the gross or operating profits may make it difficult to evaluate the comparability of gross margins, while the use of net profit indicators may avoid the problem.

2.69. Another practical strength of the transactional net margin method is that, as with any one-sided method, it is necessary to examine a financial indicator for only one of the associated enterprises (the "tested" party). Similarly, it is often not necessary to state the books and records of all participants in the business activity on a common basis or to allocate costs for all participants as is the case with the transactional profit split method. This can be practically advantageous when one of the parties to the transaction is complex and has many interrelated activities or when it is difficult to obtain reliable information about one of the parties. However, a comparability (including functional) analysis must always be performed in order to appropriately characterise the transaction between the parties and choose the most appropriate transfer pricing method, and this analysis generally necessitates that some information on the five comparability factors in relation to the controlled transaction be collected on both the tested and the non-tested parties. See paragraphs 3.20-3.23.

2.70. There are also a number of weaknesses to the transactional net margin method. The net profit indicator of a taxpayer can be influenced by some factors that would either not have an effect, or have a less substantial or direct effect, on price or gross margins between independent parties. These aspects may make accurate and reliable determinations of arm's length net profit indicators difficult. Thus, it is important to provide some detailed guidance on establishing comparability for the transactional net margin method, as set forth in paragraphs 2.74-2.81 below.

2.71. Application of any arm's length method requires information on uncontrolled transactions that may not be available at the time of the controlled transactions. This may make it particularly difficult for taxpayers that attempt to apply the transactional net margin method at the time of the controlled transactions (although use of multiple year data as discussed in paragraphs 3.75-3.79 may mitigate this concern). In addition, taxpayers may not have access to enough specific information on the profits attributable to comparable uncontrolled transactions to make a valid application of the method. It also may be difficult to ascertain revenue and operating expenses related to the controlled transactions to establish the net profit indicator used as the profit measure for the transactions. Tax administrators may have more information available to them from examinations of other taxpayers. See paragraph 3.36 for a discussion of information available to tax administrators that may not be disclosed to the taxpayer, and paragraphs 3.67-3.79 for a discussion of timing issues.

2.72. Like the resale price and cost plus methods, the transactional net margin method is applied to only one of the associated enterprises. The fact that many factors unrelated to transfer prices may affect net profits, in conjunction with the one-sided nature of the analysis under this method, can affect the overall reliability of the transactional net margin method if an insufficient standard of comparability is applied. Detailed guidance on establishing comparability for the transactional net margin method is given in Section B.3.1 below.

2.73. There may also be difficulties in determining an appropriate corresponding adjustment when applying the transactional net margin method, particularly where it is not possible to work back to a transfer price. This could be the case, for example, where the taxpayer deals with associated enterprises on both the buying and the selling sides of the controlled transaction. In such a case, if the transactional net margin method indicates that the taxpayer's profit should be adjusted upwards, there may be some uncertainty about which of the associated enterprises' profits should be reduced.

B.3. Guidance for application

B.3.1. The comparability standard to be applied to the transactional net margin method

2.74. A comparability analysis must be performed in all cases in order to select and apply the most appropriate transfer pricing method, and the process for selecting and applying a transactional net margin method should not be less reliable than for other methods. As a matter of good practice, the typical process for identifying comparable transactions and using data so obtained which is described in paragraph 3.4 or any equivalent process designed to ensure robustness of the analysis should be followed when applying a transactional net margin method, just as with any other method. That being said, it is recognised that in practice the level of information available on the factors affecting external comparable transactions is often limited. Determining a reliable estimate of an arm's length outcome requires flexibility and the exercise of good judgment. See paragraph 1.13.

2.75. Prices are likely to be affected by differences in products, and gross margins are likely to be affected by differences in functions, but net profit indicators are less adversely affected by such differences. As with the resale price and cost plus methods that the transactional net margin method resembles, this does not mean that a mere similarity of functions between two enterprises will necessarily lead to reliable comparisons. Assuming similar functions can be isolated from among the wide range of functions that enterprises may exercise, in order to apply the method, the net profit indicators related to such functions may still not be automatically comparable where, for instance, the enterprises concerned carry on those functions in different economic sectors or markets with different levels of profitability. When the comparable uncontrolled transactions being used are those of an independent enterprise, a high degree of similarity is required in a number of aspects of the associated enterprise and the independent enterprise involved in the transactions in order for the controlled transactions to be comparable; there are various factors other than products and functions that can significantly influence net profit indicators.

2.76. The use of net profit indicators can potentially introduce a greater element of volatility into the determination of transfer prices for two reasons. First, net profit indicators can be influenced by some factors that do not have an effect (or have a less substantial or direct effect) on gross margins and prices, because of the potential for variation of operating expenses across enterprises. Second, net profit indicators can be influenced by some of the same factors, such as competitive position, that can influence price and gross margins, but the effect of these factors may not be as readily eliminated. In the traditional transaction methods, the effect of these factors may be eliminated as a natural consequence of insisting upon greater product and function similarity. Depending on the facts and circumstances of the case and in particular on the effect of the functional differences on the cost structure and on the revenue of the potential comparables, net profit indicators can be less sensitive than gross margins to differences in the extent and complexity of functions and to differences in the level of risks (assuming the contractual allocation of risks is arm's length in accordance with Section D.1.2.1 of Chapter I). On the other hand, depending on the facts and circumstances of the case and in particular on the proportion of fixed and variable costs, the transactional net margin method may be more sensitive than the cost plus or resale price methods to differences in capacity utilisation, because differences in the levels of absorption of indirect fixed costs (e.g. fixed manufacturing costs or fixed distribution costs) would affect the net profit indicator but may not affect the gross margin or gross mark-up on costs if not reflected in price differences. See Annex I to Chapter II "Sensitivity of gross and net profit indicators".

2.77. Net profit indicators may be directly affected by such forces operating in the industry as follows: threat of new entrants, competitive position, management efficiency and individual strategies, threat of substitute products, varying cost structures (as reflected, for example, in the age of plant and equipment), differences in the cost of capital (e.g. self-financing versus borrowing), and the degree of business experience (e.g. whether the business is in a start-up phase or is mature). Each of these factors in turn can be influenced by numerous other elements. For example, the level of the threat of new entrants will be determined by such elements as product differentiation, capital requirements, and government subsidies and regulations. Some of these elements also may impact the application of the traditional transaction methods.

2.78. Assume, for example, that a taxpayer sells top quality audio players to an associated enterprise, and the only profit information available on comparable business activities is on generic medium quality audio player sales. Assume that the top quality audio player market is growing in its sales, has a high entry barrier, has a small number of competitors, and is with wide possibilities for product differentiation. All of the differences are likely to have material effect on the profitability of the examined activities and compared activities, and in such a case would require adjustment. As with other methods, the reliability of the necessary adjustments will affect the reliability of the analysis. It should be noted that even if two enterprises are in exactly the same industry, the profitability may differ depending on their market shares, competitive positions, etc.

2.79. It might be argued that the potential inaccuracies resulting from the above types of factors can be reflected in the size of the arm's length range. The use of a range may to some extent mitigate the level of inaccuracy, but may not account for situations where a taxpayer's profits are increased or reduced by a factor unique to that taxpayer. In such a case, the range may not include points representing the profits of independent enterprises that are affected in a similar manner by a unique factor. The use of a range, therefore, may not always solve the difficulties discussed above. See discussion of arm's length ranges in paragraphs 3.55-3.66.

2.80. The transactional net margin method may afford a practical solution to otherwise insoluble transfer pricing problems if it is used sensibly and with appropriate adjustments to account for differences of the type referred to above. The transactional net margin method should not be used unless the net profit indicators are determined from uncontrolled transactions of the same taxpayer in comparable circumstances or, where the comparable uncontrolled transactions are those of an independent enterprise, the differences between the associated enterprises and the independent enterprises that have a material effect on the net profit indicator being used are adequately taken into account. Many jurisdictions are concerned that the safeguards established for the traditional transaction methods may be overlooked in applying the transactional net margin method. Thus where differences in the characteristics of the enterprises being compared have a material effect on the net profit indicators being used, it would not be appropriate to apply the transactional net margin method without making adjustments for such differences. The extent and reliability of those adjustments will affect the relative reliability of the analysis under the transactional net margin method. See discussion of comparability adjustments in paragraphs 3.47-3.54.

2.81. Another important aspect of comparability is measurement consistency. The net profit indicators must be measured consistently between the associated enterprise and the independent enterprise. In addition, there may be differences in the treatment across enterprises of operating expenses and non-operating expenses affecting the net profits such as depreciation and reserves or provisions that would need to be accounted for in order to achieve reliable comparability.

B.3.2. Selection of the net profit indicator

2.82. In applying the transactional net margin method, the selection of the most appropriate net profit indicator should follow the guidance in paragraphs 2.2 and 2.8 in relation to the selection of the most appropriate method to the circumstances of the case. It should take account of the respective strengths and weaknesses of the various possible indicators; the appropriateness of the indicator considered in view of the nature of the controlled transaction, determined in particular through a functional analysis; the availability of reliable information (in particular on uncontrolled comparables) needed to apply the transactional net margin method based on that indicator; and the degree of comparability between controlled and uncontrolled transactions, including the reliability of comparability adjustments that may be needed to eliminate differences between them, when applying the transactional net margin method based on that indicator. These factors are discussed below in relation to both the determination of the net profit and its weighting.

B.3.3. Determination of the net profit

2.83. As a matter of principle, only those items that (a) directly or indirectly relate to the controlled transaction at hand and (b) are of an operating nature should be taken into account in the determination of the net profit indicator for the application of the transactional net margin method.

2.84. Costs and revenues that are not related to the controlled transaction under review should be excluded where they materially affect comparability with uncontrolled transactions. An appropriate level of segmentation of the taxpayer's financial data is needed when determining or testing the net profit it earns from a controlled transaction (or from transactions that are appropriately aggregated according to the guidance in paragraphs 3.9-3.12). Therefore, it would be inappropriate to apply the transactional net margin method on a company-wide basis if the company engages in a variety of different controlled transactions that cannot be appropriately compared on an aggregate basis with those of an independent enterprise.

2.85. Similarly, when analysing the transactions between the independent enterprises to the extent they are needed, profits attributable to transactions that are not similar to the controlled transactions under examination should be excluded from the comparison. Finally, when net profit indicators of an independent enterprise are used, the profits attributable to the transactions of the independent enterprise must not be distorted by controlled transactions of that enterprise. See paragraphs 3.9-3.12 on the evaluation of a taxpayer's separate and combined transactions and paragraph 3.37 on the use of non-transactional third party data.

2.86. Non-operating items such as interest income and expenses and income taxes should be excluded from the determination of the net profit indicator. Exceptional and extraordinary items of a non-recurring nature should generally also be excluded. This however is not always the case as there may be situations where it would be appropriate to include them, depending on the circumstances of the case and on the functions being undertaken and risks assumed by the tested party. Even where exceptional and extraordinary items are not taken into account in the determination of the net profit indicator, it may be useful to review them because they can provide valuable information for the purpose of comparability analysis (for instance by reflecting that the tested party bears a given risk).

2.87. In those cases where there is a correlation between the credit terms and the sales prices, it could be appropriate to reflect interest income in respect of short-term working capital within the calculation of the net profit indicator and/or to proceed with a working capital adjustment, see paragraphs 3.47-3.54. An example would be where a large retail business benefits from long credit terms with its suppliers and from short credit terms with its customers, thus making it possible to derive excess cash that in turn may make it possible to have lower sales prices to customers than if such advantageous credit terms were not available.

2.88. Whether foreign exchange gains and losses should be included or excluded from the determination of the net profit indicator raises a number of difficult comparability issues. First, it needs to be considered whether the foreign exchange gains and losses are of a trading nature (e.g. exchange gain or loss on a trade receivable or payable) and whether or not the tested party is responsible for them. Second, any hedging of the foreign currency exposure on the underlying trade receivable or payable also needs to be considered and treated in the same way in determining the net profit. In effect, if a transactional net margin is applied to a transaction in which the foreign exchange risk is borne by the tested party, foreign exchange gains or losses should be consistently accounted for (either in the calculation of the net profit indicator or separately).

2.89. For financial activities where the making and receiving of advances constitutes the ordinary business of the taxpayer, it will generally be appropriate to consider the effect of interest and amounts in the nature of interest when determining the net profit indicator.

2.90. Difficult comparability issues can arise where the accounting treatment of some items by potential third party comparables is unclear or does not allow reliable measurement or adjustment (see paragraph 2.81). This can be the case in particular for depreciation, amortisation, stock option and pension costs. The decision whether or not to include such items in the determination of the net profit indicator for applying the transactional net margin method will depend on a weighing of their expected effects on the appropriateness of the net profit indicator to the circumstances of the transaction and on the reliability of the comparison (see paragraph 3.50).

2.91. Whether start-up costs and termination costs should be included in the determination of the net profit indicator depends on the facts and circumstances of the case and on whether in comparable circumstances, independent parties would have agreed either for the party performing the functions to bear the start-up costs and possible termination costs; or for part or all of these costs to be recharged with no mark-up, e.g. to the customer or a principal; or for part or all of these costs to be recharged with a mark-up, e.g. by including them in the calculation of the net profit indicator of the party performing the functions. See Chapter IX, Part I, Section F for a discussion of termination costs in the context of a business restructuring.

B.3.4. Weighting the net profit

2.92. The selection of the denominator should be consistent with the comparability (including functional) analysis of the controlled transaction, and in particular it should reflect the allocation of risks between the parties (provided said allocation of risks is arm's length, see Section D.1.2.1 in Chapter I). For instance, capital-intensive activities such as certain manufacturing activities may involve significant investment risk, even in those cases where the operational risks (such as market risks or inventory risks) might be limited. Where a transactional net margin method is applied to such cases, the investment-related risks are reflected in the net profit indicator if the latter is a return on investment (e.g. return on assets or return on capital employed). Such indicator might need to be adjusted (or a different net profit indicator selected) depending on what party to the controlled transaction bears that risk, as well as on the degree of differences in risk that may be found in the taxpayer's controlled transaction and in comparables. See paragraphs 3.47-3.54 for a discussion of comparability adjustments.

2.93. The denominator should be focussed on the relevant indicator(s) of the value of the functions performed by the tested party in the transaction under review, taking account of its assets used and risks assumed. Typically, and subject to a review of the facts and circumstances of the case, sales or distribution operating expenses may be an appropriate base for distribution activities, full costs or operating expenses may be an appropriate base for a service or manufacturing activity, and operating assets may be an appropriate base for capital-intensive activities such as certain manufacturing activities or utilities. Other bases can also be appropriate depending on the circumstances of the case.

2.94. The denominator should be reasonably independent from controlled transactions, otherwise there would be no objective starting point. For instance, when analysing a transaction consisting in the purchase of goods by a distributor from an associated enterprise for resale to independent customers, one could not weight the net profit indicator against the cost of goods sold because these costs are the controlled costs for which consistency with the arm's length principle is being tested. Similarly, for a controlled transaction consisting in the provision of services to an associated enterprise, one could not weight the net profit indicator against the revenue from the sale of services because these are the controlled sales for which consistency with the arm's length principle is being tested. Where the denominator is materially affected by controlled transaction costs that are not the object of the testing (such as head office charges, rental fees or royalties paid to an associated enterprise), caution should be exercised to ensure that said controlled transaction costs do not materially distort the analysis and in particular that they are in accordance with the arm's length principle.

2.95. The denominator should be one that is capable of being measured in a reliable and consistent manner at the level of the taxpayer's controlled transactions. In addition, the appropriate base should be one that is capable of being measured in a reliable and consistent manner at the level of the comparable uncontrolled transactions. This in practice limits the ability to use certain indicators, as discussed in paragraph 2.105 below. Further, the taxpayer's allocation of indirect expenses to the transaction under review should be appropriate and consistent over time.

B.3.4.1. Cases where the net profit is weighted to sales

2.96. A net profit indicator of net profit divided by sales, or net profit margin, is frequently used to determine the arm's length price of purchases from an associated enterprise for resale to independent customers. In such cases, the sales figure at the denominator should be the re-sales of items purchased in the controlled transaction under review. Sales revenue that is derived from uncontrolled activities (purchase from independent parties for re-sale to independent parties) should not be included in the determination or testing of the remuneration for controlled transactions, unless the uncontrolled transactions are such that they do not materially affect the comparison; and/or the controlled and uncontrolled transactions are so closely linked that they cannot be evaluated adequately on a separate basis. One example of the latter situation can sometimes occur in relation to uncontrolled after-sales services or sales of spare parts provided by a distributor to independent end-user customers where they are closely linked to controlled purchase transactions by the distributor for resale to the same independent end-user customers, for instance because the service activity is performed using rights or other assets that are granted under the distribution arrangement. See also discussion of portfolio approaches in paragraph 3.10.

2.97. One question that arises in cases where the net profit indicator is weighted against sales is how to account for rebates and discounts that may be granted to customers by the taxpayer or the comparables. Depending on the accounting standards, rebates and discounts may be treated as a reduction of sales revenue or as an expense. Similar difficulties can arise in relation to foreign exchange gains or losses. Where such items materially affect the comparison, the key is to compare like with like and follow the same accounting principles for the taxpayer and for the comparables.

B.3.4.2. Cases where the net profit is weighted to costs

2.98. Cost-based indicators should only be used in those cases where costs are a relevant indicator of the value of the functions performed, assets used and risks assumed by the tested party. In addition, the determination of what costs should be included in the cost base should derive from a careful review of the facts and circumstances of the case. Where the net profit indicator is weighted against costs, only those costs that directly or indirectly relate to the controlled transaction under review (or transactions aggregated in accordance to the principle in paragraphs 3.9-3.12) should be taken into account. Accordingly, an appropriate level of segmentation of a taxpayer's accounts is needed in order to exclude from the denominator costs that relate to other activities or transactions and materially affect comparability with uncontrolled transactions. Moreover, in most cases only those costs which are of an operating nature should be included in the denominator. The discussion in paragraphs 2.86-2.91 above also applies to costs as denominator.

2.99. In applying a cost-based transactional net margin method, fully loaded costs are often used, including all the direct and indirect costs attributable to the activity or transaction, together with an appropriate allocation in respect of the overheads of the business. The question can arise whether and to what extent it is acceptable at arm's length to treat a significant portion of the taxpayer's costs as pass-through costs to which no profit element is attributed (i.e. as costs which are potentially excludable from the denominator of the net profit indicator). This depends on the extent to which an independent party in comparable circumstances would agree not to earn a mark-up on part of the costs it incurs. The response should not be based on the classification of costs as "internal" or "external" costs, but rather on a comparability (including functional) analysis. See paragraph 7.34.

2.100. Where treating costs as pass-through costs is found to be arm's length, a second question arises as to the consequences on comparability and on the determination of the arm's length range. Because it is necessary to compare like with like, if pass-through costs are excluded from the denominator of the taxpayer's net profit indicator, comparable costs should also be excluded from the denominator of the comparable net profit indicator. Comparability issues may arise in practice where limited information is available on the breakdown of the costs of the comparables.

2.101. Depending on the facts and circumstances of the case, actual costs, as well as standard or budgeted costs, may be appropriate to use as the cost base. Using actual costs may raise an issue because the tested party may have no incentive to carefully monitor the costs. In arrangements between independent parties, it is not rare that a cost savings objective is factored into the remuneration method. It can also happen in manufacturing arrangements between independent parties that prices are set on the basis of standard costs, and that any decrease or increase in actual costs compared to standard costs is attributed to the manufacturer. Where they reflect the arrangements that would be taken between independent parties, similar mechanisms could be taken into account in the application of the cost-based transactional net margin method. See paragraph 2.58 for a discussion of the same issue in relation to the cost plus method.

2.102. The use of budgeted costs can also raise a number of concerns where large differences between actual costs and budgeted costs result. Independent parties are not likely to set prices on the basis of budgeted costs without agreeing on what factors are to be taken into account in setting the budget, without having regard to how budgeted costs have compared with actual costs in previous years and without addressing how unforeseen circumstances are to be treated.

B.3.4.3. Cases where the net profit is weighted to assets

2.103. Returns on assets (or on capital) can be an appropriate base in cases where assets (rather than costs or sales) are a better indicator of the value added by the tested party, e.g. in certain manufacturing or other asset-intensive activities and in capital-intensive financial activities. Where the indicator is a net profit weighted to assets, operating assets only should be used. Operating assets include tangible operating fixed assets, including land and buildings, plant and equipment, operating intangible assets used in the business, such as patents and know-how, and working capital assets such as inventory and trade receivables (less trade payables). Investments and cash balances are generally not operating assets outside the financial industry sector.

2.104. In cases where the net profit is weighted to assets, the question arises how to value the assets, e.g. at book value or market value. Using book value could possibly distort the comparison, e.g. between those enterprises that have depreciated their assets and those that have more recent assets with on-going depreciation, and between enterprises that use acquired intangibles and others that use self-developed intangibles. Using market value could possibly alleviate this concern, although it can raise other reliability issues where valuation of assets is uncertain and can also prove to be extremely costly and burdensome, especially for intangible assets. Depending on the facts and circumstances of the case, it may be possible to perform adjustments to improve the reliability of the comparison. The choice between book value, adjusted book value, market value and other possibly available options should be made with a view to finding the most reliable measure, taking account of the size and complexity of the transaction and of the costs and burden involved, see Chapter III, Section C.

B.3.4.4. Other possible net profit indicators

2.105. Other net profit indicators may be appropriate depending on the facts and circumstances of the transactions. For instance, depending on the industry and on the controlled transaction under review, it may be useful to look at other denominators where independent data may exist, such as: floor area of retail points, weight of products transported, number of employees, time, distance, etc. While there is no reason to rule out the use of such bases where they provide a reasonable indication of the value added by the tested party to the controlled transaction, they should only be used where it is possible to obtain reliable comparable information to support the application of the method with such a net profit indicator.

B.3.5. Berry ratios

2.106. "Berry ratios" are defined as ratios of gross profit to operating expenses. Interest and extraneous income are generally excluded from the gross profit determination; depreciation and amortisation may or may not be included in the operating expenses, depending in particular on the possible uncertainties they can create in relation to valuation and comparability.

2.107. The selection of the appropriate financial indicator depends on the facts and circumstances of the case, see paragraph 2.82. Concerns have been expressed that Berry ratios are sometimes used in cases where they are not appropriate without the caution that is necessary in the selection and determination of any transfer pricing method and financial indicator. See paragraph 2.98 in relation to the use of cost-based indicators in general. One common difficulty in the determination of Berry ratios is that they are very sensitive to classification of costs as operating expenses or not, and therefore can pose comparability issues. In addition, the issues raised in paragraphs 2.99-2.100 above in relation to pass-through costs equally arise in the application of Berry ratios. In order for a Berry ratio to be appropriate to test the remuneration of a controlled transaction (e.g. consisting in the distribution of products), it is necessary that:

- The value of the functions performed in the controlled transaction (taking account of assets used and risks assumed) is proportional to the operating expenses,
- The value of the functions performed in the controlled transaction (taking account of assets used and risks assumed) is not materially affected by the value of the products distributed, i.e. it is not proportional to sales, and
- The taxpayer does not perform, in the controlled transactions, any other significant function (e.g. manufacturing function) that should be remunerated using another method or financial indicator.

2.108. A situation where Berry ratios can prove useful is for intermediary activities where a taxpayer purchases goods from an associated enterprise and on-sells them to other associated enterprises. In such cases, the resale price method may not be applicable given the absence of uncontrolled sales, and a cost plus method that would provide for a mark-up on the cost of goods sold might not be applicable either where the cost of goods sold consists in controlled purchases. By contrast, operating expenses in the case of an intermediary may be reasonably independent from transfer pricing formulation, unless they are materially affected by controlled transaction costs such as head office charges, rental fees or royalties paid to an associated enterprise, so that, depending on the facts and circumstances of the case, a Berry ratio may be an appropriate indicator, subject to the comments above.

B.3.6. Other guidance

2.109. While it is not specific to the transactional net margin method, the issue of the use of non-transactional third party data is in practice more acute when applying this method due to the heavy reliance on external comparables. The problem arises because there are often insufficient public data to allow for third party net profit indicators to be determined at transactional level. This is why there needs to be sufficient comparability between the controlled transaction and the comparable uncontrolled transactions. Given that often the only data available for the third parties are company-wide data, the functions performed by the third party in its total operations must be closely aligned to those functions performed by the tested party with respect to its controlled transactions in order to allow the former to be used to determine an arm's length outcome for the latter. The overall objective is to determine a level of segmentation that provides reliable comparables for the controlled transaction, based on the facts and circumstances of the particular case. In case it is impossible in practice to achieve the transactional level set out as the ideal by these Guidelines, it is still important to try to find the most reliable comparables as discussed in paragraph 3.2, through making suitable adjustments based on the evidence that is available.

2.110. See in particular paragraphs 3.18-3.19 for guidance on the tested party, paragraphs 3.55-3.66 for guidance on the arm's length range, and paragraphs 3.75-3.79 for guidance on multiple year data.

B.4. Examples of the application of the transactional net margin method

2.111. By way of illustration, the example of cost plus in paragraph 2.59 demonstrates the need to adjust the gross mark-up arising from transactions in order to achieve consistent and reliable comparison. Such adjustments may be made without difficulty where the relevant costs can be readily analysed. Where, however, it is known that an adjustment is required, but it is not possible to identify the particular costs for which an adjustment is required, it may, nevertheless, be possible to identify the net profit arising on the transaction and thereby ensure that a consistent measure is used. For example, if the supervisory, general, and administrative costs that are treated as part of costs of goods sold for the independent enterprises X, Y and Z cannot be identified so as to adjust the mark up in a reliable application of cost plus, it may be necessary to examine net profit indicators in the absence of more reliable comparisons.

2.112. A similar approach may be required when there are differences in functions performed by the parties being compared. Assume that the facts are the same as in the example in paragraph 2.44 except that it is the comparable independent enterprises that perform the additional function of technical support and not the associated enterprise, and that these costs are reported in the cost of goods sold but cannot be separately identified. Because of product and market differences it may not be possible to find a CUP, and a resale price method would be unreliable since the gross margin of the independent enterprises would need to be higher than that of the associated enterprise in order to reflect the additional function and to cover the unknown additional costs. In this example, it may be more reliable to examine net margins in order to assess the difference in the transfer price that would reflect the difference in function. The use of net margins in such a case needs to take account of comparability and may not be reliable if there would be a material effect on net margin as a result of the additional function or as a result of market differences.

2.113. The facts are the same as in paragraph 2.42. However, the amount of the warranty expenses incurred by Distributor A proves impossible to ascertain so that it is not possible to reliably adjust the gross profit of A to make the gross profit margin properly comparable with that of B. However, if there are no other material functional differences between A and B and the net profit of A relative to its sales is known, it might be possible to apply the transactional net margin method to B by comparing the margin relative to A's sales to net profits with the margin calculated on the same basis for B.

C. Transactional profit split method

C.1. General

2.114. The transactional profit split method seeks to establish arm's length outcomes or test reported outcomes for controlled transactions in order to approximate the results that would have been achieved between independent enterprises engaging in a comparable transaction or transactions. The method first identifies the profits to be split from the controlled transactions – the relevant profits – and then splits them between the associated enterprises on an economically valid basis that approximates the division of profits that would have been agreed at arm's length. As is the case with all transfer pricing methods, the aim is to ensure that profits of the associated enterprises are aligned with the value of their contributions and the compensation which would have been agreed in comparable transactions between independent enterprises for those contributions. The transactional profit split method is particularly useful when the compensation to the associated enterprises can be more reliably valued by reference to the relative shares of their contributions to the profits arising in relation to the transaction(s) than by a more direct estimation of the value of those contributions.

2.115. References to "profits" in this section should generally be taken as applying equally to losses. That is, where a transactional profit split method is determined to be the most appropriate method, it should generally also apply, and apply in the same way, regardless of whether the transaction(s) result in a relevant profit or loss. Asymmetrical splits of profits and losses (i.e. where the parties apply different considerations depending on the results of the transaction) might be arm's length, but should be used with caution and appropriately documented.

C.2. When is a transactional profit split method likely to be the most appropriate method?

2.116. As is noted in paragraph 2.2, the selection of a transfer pricing method always aims at finding the most appropriate method for a particular case, taking into account the respective strengths and weaknesses of each method, its appropriateness in view of the nature of the accurately delineated controlled transaction, the availability of reliable information (in particular on uncontrolled comparables) needed for application, and the degree of comparability between the controlled and uncontrolled transactions. See also paragraphs 2.4 to 2.7.

2.117. Guidance on how to determine whether the transactional profit split method is likely to be the most appropriate method is set out below, including the identification of certain features of a transaction which may be relevant. However it is important to note that there is no prescriptive rule for establishing when a particular transfer pricing method is the most appropriate method.

2.118. While there is no requirement in these Guidelines to undertake exhaustive analysis or testing of every method in each case, the selection of the most appropriate method should take into account the *relative* appropriateness and reliability of the selected method as compared to other methods which could be used.

C.2.1. Strengths and weaknesses of the transactional profit split method

2.119. The main strength of the transactional profit split method is that it can offer a solution for cases where both parties to a transaction make unique and valuable contributions (e.g. contribute unique and valuable intangibles) to the transaction. In such a case independent parties might effectively price the transaction in proportion to their respective contributions, making a two-sided method more appropriate. Furthermore, since those contributions are unique and valuable there will be no reliable comparables information which could be used to price the entirety of the transaction in a more reliable way, through the application of another method. In such cases, the allocation of profits under the transactional profit split method may be based on the contributions made by the associated enterprises, by reference to the relative values of their respective functions, assets and risks. See Section C.2.2 below on the nature of the transaction.

2.120. The transactional profit split method can also provide a solution for highly integrated operations in cases for which a one-sided method would not be appropriate. See Section C.2.2.2, below.

2.121. Another strength of the transactional profit split method is that it can offer flexibility by taking into account specific, possibly unique, facts and circumstances of the associated enterprises that may not be present in independent enterprises. Moreover, where there is a high degree of uncertainty for each of the parties in relation to a transaction, for example in transactions involving the shared assumption of economically significant risks by all parties (or the separate assumption of closely related economically significant risks), the flexibility of the transactional profit split method can allow for the determination of arm's length profits for each party that vary with the actual outcomes of the risks associated with the transaction.

2.122. A further strength of the transactional profit split method is that all relevant parties to the transaction are directly evaluated as part of the pricing of the transaction, that is, the contributions of each party to the transaction are specifically identified and their relative values measured in order to determine an arm's length compensation for each party in relation to the transaction.

2.123. A weakness of the transactional profit split method relates to difficulties in its application. On first review, the transactional profit split method may appear readily accessible to both taxpayers and tax administrations because it tends to rely less on information about independent enterprises. However, associated enterprises and tax administrations alike may have difficulty accessing the detailed information required to apply a transactional profit split method reliably. It may be difficult to measure the relevant revenue and costs for all the associated enterprises participating in the controlled transactions, which could require stating books and records on a common basis and making adjustments in accounting practices and currencies. Further, when the transactional profit split method is applied to operating profit, it may be difficult to identify the appropriate operating expenses associated with the transactions and to allocate costs between the transactions and the associated enterprises' other activities. Identifying the appropriate profit splitting factors can also be challenging. Given the necessity of applying judgement in determining each of the parameters for the application of the transactional profit split method, it will be particularly important to document how the method has been applied, including the determination of the relevant profits to be split, and how the profit splitting factors were arrived at. See Sections C.4 and C.5.

2.124. It is sometimes argued that a transactional profit split method is rarely used among independent enterprises, and thus its application in controlled transactions should be similarly rare. Where such a method is determined to be the most appropriate, this should not be a factor since transfer pricing methods are not necessarily intended to replicate arm's length behaviour, but rather to serve as a means of establishing and/or verifying arm's length outcomes for controlled transactions. That said, where there is evidence that independent parties in comparable transactions apply a profit split method among themselves, such evidence should be considered in determining whether a transactional profit split method is the most appropriate method for the controlled transactions. See paragraph 2.129.

C.2.2. Nature of the accurately delineated transaction

2.125. The accurate delineation of the actual transaction will be important in determining whether a transactional profit split is potentially applicable. This process should have regard to the commercial and financial relations between the associated enterprises, including an analysis of what each party to the transaction does, and the context in which the controlled transactions take place. That is, the accurate delineation of a transaction requires a two-sided analysis (or a multi-sided analysis of the contributions of more than two associated enterprises, where necessary) irrespective of which transfer pricing method is ultimately found to be the most appropriate. (See Section D.1, and in particularly Section D.1.2 of Chapter I of these Guidelines.)

2.126. The existence of unique and valuable contributions by each party to the controlled transaction is perhaps the clearest indicator that a transactional profit split may be appropriate. The context of the transaction, including the industry in which it occurs and the factors affecting business performance in that sector can be particularly relevant to evaluating the contributions of the parties and whether such contributions are unique and valuable. Depending on the facts of the case, other indicators that the transactional profit split may be the most appropriate method could include a high level of integration in the business operations to which the transactions relate and /or the shared assumption of economically significant risks (or the separate assumption of closely related economically significant risks) by the parties to the transactions. It is important to note that the indicators are not mutually exclusive and on the contrary may often be found together in a single case.

2.127. At the other end of the spectrum, where the accurate delineation of the transaction determines that one party to the transaction performs only simple functions, does not assume economically significant risks in relation to the transaction and does not otherwise make any contribution which is unique and valuable, a transactional profit split method typically would not be appropriate since a share of profits (which may be impacted by the playing out of the economically significant risks) would be unlikely to represent an arm's length outcome for such contributions or risk assumption.

2.128. A lack of closely comparable, uncontrolled transactions which would otherwise be used to benchmark an arm's length return for the party performing the less complex functions should not *per se* lead to a conclusion that the transactional profit split is the most appropriate method. Depending on the facts of the case, an appropriate method using uncontrolled transactions that are sufficiently comparable, but not identical to the controlled transaction is likely to be more reliable than an inappropriate use of the transactional profit split method. See paragraphs 3.38-3.39 for a discussion of limitations in available comparables. See also Section C.2.3.

2.129. It may also be relevant to consider industry practices. For instance, if information is available that independent parties do commonly use profit splitting approaches in similar situations, careful consideration should be given to whether the transactional profit split method may be the most appropriate method for the controlled transactions. Such industry practices may be a pointer to the fact that each party makes unique and valuable contributions, and/or that the parties are highly inter-dependent upon each other. Conversely, if independent parties engaged in comparable transactions are found to make use of other pricing methods, this should also be taken into account in determining the most appropriate transfer pricing method.

C.2.2.1. Unique and valuable contributions by each of the parties to the transaction

2.130. Contributions (for instance functions performed, or assets used or contributed) will be "unique and valuable" in cases where (i) they are not comparable to contributions made by uncontrolled parties in comparable circumstances, and (ii) they represent a key source of actual or potential economic benefits in the business operations. The two factors are often linked: comparables for such contributions are seldom found because they are a key source of economic advantage. It may be the case that in these situations, the risks associated with the respective unique and valuable contributions cannot be controlled by the other party or parties. This may impact the assumption of risk under the accurate delineation of the actual transaction. For example, the developer and manufacturer of a key component of a product together with the developer and manufacturer of another key component that together with the first component, form the ready-to-sell product, may both make unique and valuable contributions in terms of functions and intangibles that represent a key source of economic benefits. (See also paragraphs 6.50 to 6.58 and 6.133.) In practice, neither of them may be able to control the development risk in relation to the product as a whole, but instead they together control the development risks and share in the relevant profits resulting from their contributions. The principles of this section are illustrated by Examples 1, 2, 3 and 4 in Annex II to Chapter II of these Guidelines.

Transactions involving unique and valuable intangibles

2.131. Where each party to the transaction legally owns unique and valuable intangibles that are relevant to the transaction, it will also be necessary to consider whether, under the accurate delineation of the transaction, they each assume the economically significant risks relating to those intangibles, e.g. risks related to development, obsolescence, infringement, product liability and exploitation (see paragraphs 6.65 to 6.68).

2.132. As set out in paragraphs 6.148 to 6.149 and 6.152, in some cases, the transactional profit split method may be the most appropriate method for a transfer of fully developed intangibles (including rights in intangibles) where it is not possible to identify reliable comparable uncontrolled transactions. The transactional profit split method may also be appropriate for transfers of partially developed intangibles. Example 5 in Annex II to Chapter II provides an illustration. See paragraphs 6.150 to 6.151. Where the intangibles transferred are hard-to-value intangibles, the provisions of Section D.4 of Chapter VI should be considered.

C.2.2.2. Highly integrated business operations

2.133. Although most MNE groups are integrated to some extent, a particularly high degree of integration in certain business operations is an indicator for the consideration of the transactional profit split method. A high degree of integration means that the way in which one party to the transaction performs functions, uses assets and assumes risks is interlinked with, and cannot reliably be evaluated in isolation from, the way in which another party to the transaction performs functions, uses assets and assumes risks. In contrast, many instances of integration within an MNE result in situations in which the contribution of at least one party to the transaction can in fact be reliably evaluated by reference to comparable uncontrolled transactions. For example, where complementary but discrete activities are undertaken by the entities, it may be the case that it is possible to find reliable comparables since the functions, assets and risks involved in each discrete stage may be comparable to those in uncontrolled arrangements. This needs to be borne in mind in considering which transfer pricing method is the most appropriate in a particular case. Examples 6, 7 and 8 in Annex II to Chapter II illustrate the principles of this section.

2.134. In some cases the parties may perform functions jointly, use assets jointly and/or share assumption of risks to such an extent that it is impossible to evaluate their respective contributions in isolation from those of others. As an example, the transactional profit split method can be applied to the global trading of financial instruments by associated enterprises. See in Part III, Section C of the Report on the Attribution of Profits to Permanent Establishments.[2]

2. See *Report on the Attribution of Profits to Permanent Establishments* (OECD, 2010).

2.135. Another example may be where the integration between the parties takes the form of a high degree of inter-dependency. For instance, profit split approaches may be used by independent enterprises engaged in long-term arrangements where each party has made a significant contribution (e.g. of an asset) whose value depends on the counterparty to the arrangement. In these kinds of cases, where each party makes such a contribution, and is dependent on the other party (or where the value of the contribution(s) of one party depends to a significant degree on the contribution(s) of the other party), some form of flexible pricing that takes into account, and varies with, the outcome of the risks assumed by each party arising from its dependence on the other party may be observed.

2.136. Where business operations are highly integrated, the extent to which the parties share the assumption of the same economically significant risks or separately assume closely related economically significant risks will be relevant to the determination of the most appropriate method and, if a transactional profit split is considered the most appropriate method, how it should be applied; in particular whether a split of actual profits or of anticipated profits should be used. See Section C.4.1.

2.137. Where a party contributes to the control of economically significant risk, but that risk is assumed by the other party to the transaction, this may, in some cases, demonstrate that it is appropriate for the first party to share in the potential upside and downside associated with that risk, commensurate with its contribution to control. See paragraph 1.105. However, the mere fact that an entity performs control functions in relation to a risk will not necessarily lead to the conclusion that the transactional profit split is the most appropriate method in the case.

2.138. Where the contributions are highly inter-related or inter-dependent upon each other, the evaluation of the respective contributions of the parties may need to be done holistically. That is, a high degree of integration may also affect whether contributions by the enterprises are considered to be unique and valuable. For instance, a unique contribution by one party may have a significantly greater value when considered in combination with the particular unique contribution of the other party. Paragraphs 6.93-6.94 discuss this issue in relation to the combination of intangibles. See also Example 9 in Annex II to Chapter II.

C.2.2.3. Shared assumption of economically significant risks, separate assumption of closely related risks

2.139. A transactional profit split may be found to be the most appropriate method where, according to the accurately delineated transaction, each party to the controlled transaction shares the assumption of one or more of the economically significant risks in relation to that transaction (see paragraph 1.95).

2.140. A transactional profit split may also be found to be the most appropriate method where, according to the accurately delineated transaction, the various economically significant risks in relation to the transaction are separately assumed by the parties, but those risks are so closely inter-related and/or correlated that the playing out of the risks of each party cannot reliably be isolated. See Example 10 in Annex II to Chapter II.

2.141. The relevance of this factor as an indicator for the transactional profit split method will depend in large measure on the extent to which the risks concerned are economically significant such that a share of relevant profits would be warranted for each party. The economic significance of the risks should be analysed in relation to their importance to the actual or anticipated relevant profits from the controlled transaction(s), rather than in respect of their importance to any one of the associated enterprises whose business operations may extend beyond those covered by the relevant profits.

2.142. If each party shares the assumption of economically significant risks or separately assumes inter-related, economically significant risks, and a transactional profit split is considered to be the most appropriate method, it is likely that a split of actual profits, rather than anticipated profits, will be warranted since those actual profits, i.e. the actual relevant profits to be split, will reflect the playing out of the risks of each party. Conversely, a profit split of anticipated profits will tend to concentrate the playing out of economically significant risks on one party. That is, the transfer pricing outcome – a sharing of actual or anticipated profits – should align with the accurate delineation of the transaction. See Section C.4.1 below on splits of actual and anticipated profits.

C.2.3. Availability of reliable information

2.143. In general, it will tend to be the case that the presence of factors indicating that a transactional profit split is the most appropriate method will correspond to an absence of factors indicating that an alternative transfer pricing method – one which relies entirely on comparables – is the most appropriate method, determined in accordance with paragraph 2.2 of these Guidelines. Put another way, if information on reliable comparable uncontrolled transactions is available to price the transaction in its entirety, it is less likely that the transactional profit split method will be the most appropriate method. However, a lack of comparables alone is insufficient to warrant the use of a transactional profit split. See paragraph 2.128.

2.144. While the transactional profit split method can be applied in cases where there are no uncontrolled comparables, information from transactions between independent parties may still be relevant to the application of the method, for example to guide the splitting of relevant profits (see Section C.3.1.1), or where a residual analysis approach is used (see Section C.3.1.2).

C.2.4. Conclusions

2.145. This section has described certain characteristics of the transactional profit split method and provided a number of potential indicators as to when it may be found to be the most appropriate method, as well as a number of factors which may point in the opposite direction. The guidance in this regard does not seek to be comprehensive, nor is it prescriptive. The presence or absence of one or more of the indicators described in this section will not necessarily lead to the conclusion that the transactional profit split will (or will not) be the most appropriate method in a particular case. Each case needs to be analysed on its own facts, and it will be important to consider the relative merits and shortcomings of available transfer pricing methods.

C.3. Guidance for application – in general

2.146. These Guidelines do not seek to provide an exhaustive catalogue of ways in which the transactional profit split method may be applied. Application of the method will depend on the facts and circumstances of the case and the information available, but the overriding objective should be to approximate as closely as possible the split of profits that would have been realised had the parties been independent enterprises.

2.147. Under the transactional profit split method, the relevant profits are to be split between the associated enterprises on an economically valid basis that approximates the division of profits that would have been anticipated and reflected in an agreement made at arm's length. In general, the determination of the relevant profits to be split and of the profit splitting factors should be:

- consistent with the functional analysis of the controlled transaction under review, and in particular reflect the assumption of the economically significant risks by the parties, and
- capable of being measured in a reliable manner.

2.148. In addition,

- If the transactional profit split method is used to set transfer pricing in controlled transactions at the outset, it would be reasonable to expect the life-time of the arrangement and the criteria or profit splitting factors to be agreed in advance of the transaction,
- The person using the transactional profit split method (taxpayer or tax administration) should be prepared to explain why it is regarded

as the most appropriate method in the circumstances of the case, as well as the way it is implemented, and in particular the criteria or profit splitting factors used to split the relevant profits, and

- The determination of the relevant profits to be split and of the profit splitting factors should generally be used consistently over the life-time of the arrangement, including during loss years, unless the rationale for using differing relevant profits or profit splitting factors over time is supported by the facts and circumstances and is documented.

C.3.1. Approaches to splitting profits

2.149. There are a number of approaches to the application of the transactional profit split method, depending on the characteristics of the controlled transactions, and the information available. As has been described above, the method seeks to split the relevant profits from controlled transactions on an economically valid basis, in order to approximate the results that would have been achieved between independent enterprises in comparable circumstances. This may be done by considering the relative contributions of each party (a "contribution analysis"). Where the transactional profit split method is the most appropriate method but at least one party also makes some less complex contributions which are capable of being benchmarked by reference to comparable, uncontrolled transactions, a two-stage "residual analysis" may be appropriate.

C.3.1.1. Contribution analysis

2.150. Under a contribution analysis, the relevant profits, which are the total profits from the controlled transactions under examination, are divided between the associated enterprises in order to arrive at a reasonable approximation of the division that independent enterprises would have achieved from engaging in comparable transactions. This division can be supported by comparables data where available. In the absence thereof, it should be based on the relative value of the contributions by each of the associated enterprises participating in the controlled transactions, determined using information internal to the MNE group, as a proxy for the division that independent enterprises would have achieved (see Section C.5.2). In cases where the relative value of the contributions can be measured, it may not be necessary to estimate the actual market value of each party's contributions.

2.151. It can be difficult to determine the relative value of the contribution that each of the associated enterprises makes to the relevant profits, and the approach will depend on the facts and circumstances of each case. The determination might be made by comparing the nature and degree of each party's contribution of differing types (for example, provision of services, development expenses incurred, assets used or contributed, capital invested) and assigning a percentage based upon the relative comparison and external market data. See Section C.5 for a discussion of how to split the relevant profits.

C.3.1.2. Residual analysis

2.152. Where the contributions of the parties are such that some can be reliably valued by reference to a one-sided method and benchmarked using comparables, while others cannot, the application of a residual analysis may be appropriate. A residual analysis divides the relevant profits from the controlled transactions under examination into two categories. In the first category are profits attributable to contributions which can be reliably benchmarked: typically less complex contributions for which reliable comparables can be found. Ordinarily this initial remuneration would be determined by applying one of the traditional transaction methods or a transactional net margin method to identify the remuneration of comparable transactions between independent enterprises. Thus, it would generally not account for the return that would be generated by a second category of contributions which may be unique and valuable, and/or are attributable to a high level of integration or the shared assumption of economically significant risks. Typically, the allocation of the residual profit among the parties will be based on the relative value of the second category of contributions of the parties in the same way as in the application of the contribution analysis outlined above and in accordance with the guidance as described in Section C.5.

2.153. Example 11 in Annex II to Chapter II illustrates the application of a residual analysis under a transactional profit split method.

C.4. Guidance for application – Determining the profits to be split

2.154. The relevant profits to be split under the transactional profit split method are those of the associated enterprises arising as a result of the controlled transactions under review. It is essential to identify the level of aggregation, see paragraphs 3.9-3.12. In determining the relevant profits, it is therefore essential to first identify and accurately delineate the transactions to be covered by the transactional profit split method, and from this identify the relevant income and expense amounts for each party in relation to those transactions. See Section C.4.2, below. Example 12 in Annex II to Chapter II of these Guidelines illustrates the principles of this section.

2.155. Where the relevant profits to be split are comprised of profits of two or more associated enterprises, the relevant financial data of the parties to the transaction to which a transactional profit split is applied need to be put on a common basis as to accounting practice and currency, and then combined. Because accounting standards can have significant effects on the determination of the profits to be split, accounting standards should, in cases where the taxpayer chooses to use the transactional profit split method, be selected in advance of applying the method and applied consistently over the lifetime of the arrangement. Differences in accounting standards may affect the timing of revenue recognition as well as the treatment of expenses in arriving at profits. Material differences between the accounting standards used by the parties should be identified and aligned.

2.156. Financial accounting may provide the starting point for determining the profit to be split in the absence of harmonised tax accounting standards. The use of other financial data (e.g. cost accounting) should be permitted where such accounts exist, are reliable, auditable and sufficiently transactional. In this context, product-line income statements or divisional accounts may prove to be the most useful accounting records.

2.157. However, except in circumstances where the total activities of each of the parties are the subject of the profit split, the financial data will need to be segregated and allocations made in accordance with the accurately delineated transaction(s) so that the profits relating to the combined contributions made by the parties are identified. For example, a product supplier in a profit split with an associated enterprise engaged in European marketing and distribution would need to identify the profits arising from its production of goods for the European market, and exclude the profits arising from the production of goods for other markets. The exercise may be relatively simple if the same goods are supplied to all markets, but will be more complex if different goods with different production costs or with different embedded technology, for example, are supplied to different markets. Similarly, if the associated enterprise engaged in European marketing and distribution buys products from other sources, it will need to segregate its financial data in a way that reflects the revenues, costs, and profits relating to the goods purchased from the associated product supplier in the profit split. Experience suggests that this initial stage in performing a profit split can in some circumstances be extremely complex, and the method of identifying the profits relevant to the transaction and any assumptions made in doing so need to be documented.

C.4.1. Transactional profit splits of actual or anticipated profits

2.158. The determination of the profits to be split, including whether those profits are actual profits or anticipated profits, or some combination thereof, should be aligned with the accurately delineated transaction. Example 13 in Annex II to Chapter II illustrates the principles of this section.

2.159. Where the transactional profit split method is found to be the most appropriate, the splitting of actual profits, i.e. profits which have been affected by the playing out of economically significant risks, would only be appropriate where the accurate delineation of the transaction shows that the parties either share the assumption of the same economically significant risks associated with the business opportunity or separately assume closely related, economically significant risks associated with the business opportunity and consequently should share in the resulting profits or losses. These kinds of risk assumption may occur in scenarios where the business operations are highly integrated and/or each party makes unique and valuable contributions.

2.160. Alternatively, if the transactional profit split is found to be the most appropriate method (e.g. because each party to the transaction makes unique and valuable contributions) but one of the parties does not share in the assumption of the economically significant risks which might play out after entering into the transaction, a split of anticipated profits would be more appropriate. See scenario 1 of Example 13 in Annex II to Chapter II of this guidance.

2.161. In any application of a transactional profit split, care should be exercised to ensure that the method is applied without hindsight. See paragraph 3.74. That is, irrespective of whether a transactional profit split of anticipated or actual profits is used, unless there are major unforeseen developments which would have resulted in a renegotiation of the agreement had it occurred between independent parties, the basis upon which those profits are to be split between the associated enterprises, including the profit splitting factors, the way in which relevant profits are calculated, and any adjustments or contingencies, must be determined on the basis of information known or reasonably foreseeable by the parties at the time the transactions were entered into. This is so notwithstanding the fact that in many cases, the actual calculations can necessarily only be performed some time afterwards, where, for example they apply profit splitting factors determined at the outset to the actual profits. Additionally, it should be remembered that the starting point in the accurate delineation of any transaction will generally be the written contracts which may reflect the intention of the parties at the time the contract was concluded. See paragraph 1.42.

C.4.2. Different measures of profits

2.162. Most commonly, the relevant profits to be split under the transactional profit split method are operating profits. Applying the transactional profit split method in this manner ensures that both income and expenses of the MNE are attributed to the relevant associated enterprise on a consistent basis. However, depending on the accurate delineation of the transaction, it may be appropriate to split a different measure of profits such as gross profits, and then deduct the expenses incurred by or attributable to each relevant enterprise (excluding expenses already taken into account). In such cases, care must be taken to ensure that the expenses incurred by or attributable to each enterprise are consistent with the accurate delineation of the transaction, particularly the activities and risks undertaken by each party, and that the allocation of profits is likewise consistent with the contributions of the parties.

2.163. That is, the measure of profits to be split will depend on the accurate delineation of the transaction. For instance, if the accurate delineation of the transaction determines that the parties share the assumption of not only market risk, which affects the volume of sales and prices charged, but also risks associated with producing or otherwise acquiring goods and services, which affect the level of gross profit, it would be most appropriate to use gross profits as the basis of the split. In such a scenario, the parties may have integrated or joint functions and assets relating to the production or acquisition of goods and services. If the accurate delineation of the transaction determines that the parties share the assumption of, in addition to market and production risks, a further range of risks that affect the level of operating expenses that may include investment in intangibles, it would be most appropriate to use operating profits as the basis of the split. In this scenario, the parties may have integrated or joint functions relating to the entire value chain.

2.164. For example, two associated enterprises, each with its own manufacturing specialisation and unique and valuable intangibles, agree to contribute the intangibles to produce innovative, complex products. The accurate delineation of the transaction determines that the enterprises in this example share the assumption of risks associated with the success or otherwise of the products in the marketplace. However, they do not share the assumption of risks associated with their selling and other expenses, which are largely unintegrated. Using a profit split based on combined operating profits after all expenses of both parties would have the potential result of sharing the consequences of risks that are assumed by only one of the parties. In such cases, a splitting of gross profits may be more appropriate and reliable since this level of profits captures the outcomes of market and production activities that the parties share together with the assumption of associated risks. Similarly, in the case of associated enterprises that engage in highly integrated worldwide trading operations, if the accurate delineation of the actual transaction determines that the shared assumption of risks and level of integration does not extend to operating costs, it may be appropriate to split the gross profits from each trading activity, and then deduct from the resulting share of the overall gross profits allocated to each enterprise its own operating expenses incurred.

2.165. Example 14 in Annex II to Chapter II illustrates the principles of this section.

C.5. Splitting the profits

2.166. Profits should be split on an economically valid basis that reflects the relative contributions of the parties to the transaction and thus approximates the division of profits that would have obtained at arm's length. The relevance of comparable uncontrolled transactions or internal data (see Section C.5.2) and the criteria used to achieve an arm's length division of the profits depend on the facts and circumstances of the case. It is therefore not desirable to establish a prescriptive list of criteria or profit splitting factors. See paragraphs 2.146-2.148 for general guidance on the consistency of the determination of the splitting factors. In addition, the criteria or splitting factors used to split the profit should be:

- independent of transfer pricing policy formulation, i.e. they should be based on objective data (e.g. sales to independent parties), not on data relating to the remuneration of controlled transactions (e.g. sales to associated enterprises),
- verifiable, and
- supported by comparables data, internal data, or both.

2.167. One possible approach is to split the relevant profits based on the division of profits that actually is observed in comparable uncontrolled transactions. Examples of possible sources of information on uncontrolled transactions that might usefully assist the determination of criteria to split the profits, depending on the facts and circumstances of the case, include joint-venture arrangements between independent parties under which profits are shared, such as development projects in the oil and gas industry; pharmaceutical collaborations, co-marketing or co-promotion agreements; arrangements between independent music record labels and music artists; uncontrolled arrangements in the financial services sector, etc.

2.168. However, it can be difficult to find reliable comparables data that can be used in this manner. Nevertheless, external market data can be relevant in the profit split analysis to assess the value of contributions that each associated enterprise makes to the transactions. In effect, the assumption is that independent parties would have split relevant profits in proportion to the value of their respective contributions to the generation of profit in the transaction. Thus, where there is no more direct evidence of how independent parties in comparable circumstances would have split the profit in comparable transactions, the allocation of profits may be based on the relative contributions of the parties, as measured by their functions, assets used and risks assumed.

C.5.1. Profit splitting factors

2.169. As noted above, arm's length parties can be assumed to split profits on the basis of their relative contributions to the creation of those profits. The division of the relevant profits under the transactional profit split method is generally achieved using one or more profit splitting factors. The functional analysis and an analysis of the context in which the transactions take place (e.g. the industry and environment) are essential to the process of determining the relevant factors to use in splitting profits, including determining the weighting of applicable profit splitting factors, in cases where more than one factor is used. The determination of appropriate profit splitting factor(s) should reflect the key contributions to value in relation to the transaction. Examples 15 and 16 in Annex II to Chapter II of these Guidelines illustrate the principles of this section.

2.170. Depending on the facts and circumstances of the case, the factor can be a figure (e.g. a 30%-70% split based on evidence of a similar split achieved between independent parties in comparable transactions), or a variable (e.g. relative value of participant's marketing contributions or other possible factors as discussed below) which could be calculated on the basis of a single profit splitting factor or a weighting of multiple factors.

2.171. Profit splitting factors based on assets or capital (e.g. operating assets, fixed assets (e.g. production assets, retail assets, IT assets), intangibles), or costs (e.g. relative spending and/or investment in key areas such as research and development, engineering, marketing) may be used where these capture the relative contributions of the parties to the profits being split and they can be measured reliably. Note that while costs may be a poor measure of the value of intangibles contributed (see paragraph 6.142), the relative costs incurred by parties may provide a reasonable proxy for the relative value of those contributions where such contributions are similar in nature (see paragraphs 8.27-8.28).

2.172. Other profit splitting factors that could be appropriate in the circumstances of a given case include incremental sales, or employee compensation (relating to the individuals involved in the key functions that generate value to the transaction, for example in relation to the global trading of financial instruments). In other situations it is possible that headcount or time spent by a certain group of similarly skilled employees with similar responsibilities could be used if there is a strong and relatively consistent correlation between this and the creation of value represented by the relevant profits. The guidance in this section should not be considered as an exhaustive list of potential profit splitting factors. Other profit splitting factors may be acceptable provided they result in arm's length outcomes for all relevant parties.

2.173. In addition to the Local File, which should contain a detailed functional analysis of the taxpayer and its relevant associated enterprises, the MNE group's Master File might be a useful source of information relevant to the determination of appropriate profit splitting factors. As is set out in Annex I to Chapter V, the Master File should include information on the important drivers of business profit, the principal contributions to value creation by entities within the group, and key group intangibles. However, it should be borne in mind that the Master File is intended only to provide a high-level overview of an MNE group, and not granular or detailed information as to all of the group's transactions.

C.5.2. Reliance on data from the taxpayer's own operations (internal data)

2.174. Where comparable uncontrolled transactions of sufficient reliability are lacking to support the division of the relevant profits, consideration should be given to internal data, which may provide a reliable means of establishing or testing the arm's length nature of the division of profits. The types of such internal data that are relevant will depend on the facts and circumstances of the case and should satisfy the conditions outlined in this section and in particular in paragraphs 2.147-2.148 and 2.166. They will frequently be extracted from the taxpayers' cost accounting or financial accounting.

2.175. For instance, where an asset-based profit splitting factor is used, it may be based on data extracted from the balance sheets of the parties to the transaction. It will often be the case that not all the assets of the taxpayers relate to the transaction at hand and that accordingly some analytical work is needed for the taxpayer to draw up a "transactional" balance sheet that will be used for the application of the transactional profit split method. In addition, certain assets, such as self-developed intangibles, may not be reflected on the balance sheet at all, and accordingly must be separately evaluated. In this regard, valuation techniques, such as those based on the discounted value of projected future income streams or cash flows derived from the exploitation of the intangible may be useful. See Section D.2.6.3 of Chapter VI of these guidelines. See also paragraph 2.104 for a discussion of valuation of assets in the context of the transactional net margin method where the net profit is weighted to assets, which is also relevant to the valuation of assets in the context of a transactional profit split where an asset-based profit splitting factor is used.

2.176. Similarly, where cost-based profit splitting factors are used that are based on data extracted from the taxpayers' profit and loss accounts, it may be necessary to draw up transactional accounts that identify those expenses that are related to the controlled transaction at hand and those that should be excluded from the determination of the profit splitting factor. The type of expenditure that is taken into account (e.g. salaries, depreciation, etc.) as well as the criteria used to determine whether a given expense is related to the transaction at hand or is rather related to other transactions of the taxpayer (e.g. to other lines of products not subject to this profit split determination) should be applied consistently to all the parties to the transaction.

2.177. Internal data may also be helpful where the profit splitting factor is based on a cost accounting system, e.g. employee costs related to some aspects of the transaction, or time spent by a certain group of employees on certain tasks, etc.

2.178. Internal data are essential to assess the values of the respective contributions of the parties to the controlled transaction. The determination of such values should rely on a functional analysis that takes into account all the economically significant functions, assets and risks contributed by the parties to the controlled transaction. In those cases where the profit is split on the basis of an evaluation of the relative importance of the functions, assets and risks to the value added to the controlled transaction, such evaluation should be supported by reliable objective data in order to limit arbitrariness. Particular attention should be given to the identification of the relevant contributions of unique and valuable intangibles and the assumption of economically significant risks and the importance, relevance and measurement of the factors which gave rise to these.

C.5.3. Examples of profit splitting factors

C.5.3.1. Asset-based profit splitting factors

2.179. Asset-based or capital-based profit splitting factors can be used where there is a strong correlation between tangible assets or intangibles, or capital employed and creation of value in the context of the controlled transaction. In order for a profit splitting factor to be meaningful, it should be applied consistently to all the parties to the transaction. See paragraph 2.104 for a discussion of comparability issues in relation to asset valuation in the context of the transactional net margin method, which is also valid in the context of the transactional profit split method. Example 15 in Annex II to this chapter illustrates the principles of this section.

2.180. Where one or more of the parties to a transaction for which the transactional profit split method is found to be the most appropriate makes a contribution in the form of intangibles, difficult issues can arise in relation both to their identification and to their valuation. Guidance on the identification and valuation of intangibles is found at Chapter VI of these Guidelines. See also the examples in Annex I to Chapter VI "Examples to illustrate the guidance on intangibles."

C.5.3.2. Cost-based profit splitting factors

2.181. A profit splitting factor based on expenses may be appropriate where it is possible to identify a strong correlation between relative expenses incurred and relative value contributed. For example, marketing expenses may be an appropriate factor for distributors-marketers if advertising generates unique and valuable marketing intangibles, e.g. in consumer goods where the value of marketing intangibles is affected by advertising. Research and development expenses may be suitable for manufacturers if they relate to the development of unique and valuable intangibles such as patents. However, if, for instance, each party contributes different valuable intangibles, then it is not appropriate to use a costbased factor unless cost is a reliable measure of the relative value of those intangibles or costs can be risk-weighted to achieve a reliable measure of relative value. Even where each party contributes the same kind of intangibles, risk-weighting will be an appropriate consideration. For example, where the risk of failure at an early stage of development is several times higher than the risk of failure at a later stage or in the development of incremental improvements to an already proven concept, then the costs incurred in that early stage will have a higher risk weighting than the costs incurred at a later stage or on incremental improvements. Employee remuneration may be relevant in situations where functions relating to the skills and experience of staff are the primary factor in generating the relevant profits.

2.182. In identifying and applying appropriate cost-based profit splitting factors a number of issues may need to be considered. One is that there may be differences between the parties in the timing of expenditure. For example, research and development costs that are relevant to the value of a party's contributions may have been incurred several years in the past, whereas the expenditure for another party may be current. As a result, it may be necessary to bring historic costs to current values (as discussed further below) in addition to the risk weighting described in paragraph 2.181. The relevant costs may be part of a larger cost pool that needs to be analysed and allocated to the contributions made to the profit split transaction. For example, marketing costs may be incurred and recorded across several product lines, whereas only one product line is the subject of the profit split transaction. Where location savings retained by member(s) of the MNE group are a significant contributor to profits, and such costs are included in the profits to be split, then the manner in which independent parties would allocate retained location savings would need to be reflected in the profit split, taking into account the guidance in Section D.6 of Chapter I. Cost-based profit splitting factors can be very sensitive to differences and changes in accounting classification of costs. It is therefore necessary to clearly identify in advance what costs will be taken into account in the determination of the profit splitting factor and to determine the factor consistently among the parties.

2.183. In some cases, a significant issue for the reliability of cost-based splitting factors is the determination of the relevant period of time from which the elements of determination of the profit splitting factor(s) (e.g. assets, costs, or others) should be taken into account. A difficulty arises because there can be a lag between the time when expenses are incurred and the time when value is created, and it is sometimes difficult to decide which period's expenses should be used. For example, in the case of a cost-based factor, using the expenditure on a single-year basis may be suitable for some cases, while in some other cases it may be more suitable to use accumulated expenditure (net of depreciation or amortisation, where appropriate in the circumstances) incurred in the previous as well as the current years. Depending on the facts and circumstances of the case, this determination may have a significant effect on the allocation of profits amongst the parties. As noted in Section C.5.1 above, the selection of the profit splitting factor should be appropriate to the particular circumstances of the case and provide a reliable approximation of the division of profits that would have been agreed between independent parties. The principles of this section are illustrated by Example 16 in Annex II to Chapter II of this guidance.

D. Conclusions on transactional profit methods

2.184. Paragraphs 2.1-2.12 provide guidance on the selection of the most appropriate transfer pricing method to the circumstances of the case.

2.185. As discussed in these Guidelines, there are concerns regarding the use of the transactional net margin method, in particular that it is sometimes applied without adequately taking into account the relevant differences between the controlled and uncontrolled transactions being compared. Many jurisdictions are concerned that the safeguards established for the traditional transaction methods may be overlooked in applying the transactional net margin method. Thus, where differences in the characteristics of the transactions being compared have a material effect on the net profit indicators being used, it would not be appropriate to apply the transactional net margin method without making adjustments for such differences. See paragraphs 2.74-2.81 (the comparability standard to be applied to the transactional net margin method).

2.186. The recognition that the use of transactional profit methods may be necessary is not intended to suggest that independent enterprises would use these methods to set prices. As with any method, it is important that it be possible to calculate appropriate corresponding adjustments when transactional profit methods are used, recognising that in certain cases corresponding adjustments may be determined on an aggregate basis consistent with the aggregation principles in paragraphs 3.9-3.12.

2.187. In all cases, caution must be used to determine whether a transactional profit method as applied to a particular aspect of a case can produce an arm's length answer, either in conjunction with a traditional transaction method or on its own. The question ultimately can be resolved only on a case-by-case basis taking into account the strengths and weaknesses set forth above for a particular transactional profit method to be applied, the comparability (including functional) analysis of the parties to the transaction, and the availability and reliability of comparable data. In addition, these conclusions assume that jurisdictions will have a certain degree of sophistication in their underlying tax systems before applying these methods.

Chapter III

Comparability analysis

A. Performing a comparability analysis

3.1. General guidance on comparability is found in Section D of Chapter I. By definition, a comparison implies examining two terms: the controlled transaction under review and the uncontrolled transactions that are regarded as potentially comparable. The search for comparables is only part of the comparability analysis. It should be neither confused with nor separated from the comparability analysis. The search for information on potentially comparable uncontrolled transactions and the process of identifying comparables is dependent upon prior analysis of the taxpayer's controlled transaction and of the economically relevant characteristics or comparability factors (see Section D.1 of Chapter I). A methodical, consistent approach should provide some continuity or linkage in the whole analytical process, thereby maintaining a constant relationship amongst the various steps: from the preliminary analysis of the conditions of the controlled transaction, to the selection of the transfer pricing method, through to the identification of potential comparables and ultimately a conclusion about whether the controlled transactions being examined are consistent with the arm's length principle as described in paragraph 1 of Article 9 of the OECD Model Tax Convention.

3.2. As part of the process of selecting the most appropriate transfer pricing method (see paragraph 2.2) and applying it, the comparability analysis always aims at finding the most reliable comparables. Thus, where it is possible to determine that some uncontrolled transactions have a lesser degree of comparability than others, they should be eliminated (see also paragraph 3.56). This does not mean that there is a requirement for an exhaustive search of all possible sources of comparables as it is acknowledged that there are limitations in availability of information and that searches for comparables data can be burdensome. See also discussion of compliance efforts in paragraphs 3.80-3.83.

3.3. In order for the process to be transparent, it is considered a good practice for a taxpayer that uses comparables to support its transfer pricing, or a tax administration that uses comparables to support a transfer pricing adjustment, to provide appropriate supporting information for the other interested party (i.e. tax auditor, taxpayer or foreign competent authorities) to be able to assess the reliability of the comparables used. See paragraph 3.36 for a discussion of information available to tax administrations that is not disclosed to taxpayers. General guidance on documentation requirements is found at Chapter V of these Guidelines. See also Annex II to Chapter IV "Guidelines for conducting Advance Pricing Arrangements under the Mutual Agreement Procedure (MAP APAs)".

A.1. Typical process

3.4. Below is a description of a typical process that can be followed when performing a comparability analysis. This process is considered an accepted good practice but it is not a compulsory one, and any other search process leading to the identification of reliable comparables may be acceptable as reliability of the outcome is more important than process (i.e. going through the process does not provide any guarantee that the outcome will be arm's length, and not going through the process does not imply that the outcome will not be arm's length).

Step 1: Determination of years to be covered.

Step 2: Broad-based analysis of the taxpayer's circumstances.

Step 3: Understanding the controlled transaction(s) under examination, based in particular on a functional analysis, in order to choose the tested party (where needed), the most appropriate transfer pricing method to the circumstances of the case, the financial indicator that will be tested (in the case of a transactional profit method), and to identify the significant comparability factors that should be taken into account.

Step 4: Review of existing internal comparables, if any.

Step 5: Determination of available sources of information on external comparables where such external comparables are needed taking into account their relative reliability.

Step 6: Selection of the most appropriate transfer pricing method and, depending on the method, determination of the relevant financial indicator (e.g. determination of the relevant net profit indicator in case of a transactional net margin method).

Step 7: Identification of potential comparables: determining the key characteristics to be met by any uncontrolled transaction in order to be regarded as potentially comparable, based on the relevant factors identified in Step 3 and in accordance with the comparability factors set out in Section D.1 of Chapter I.

Step 8: Determination of and making comparability adjustments where appropriate.

Step 9: Interpretation and use of data collected, determination of the arm's length remuneration.

3.5. In practice, this process is not a linear one. Steps 5 to 7 in particular might need to be carried out repeatedly until a satisfactory conclusion is reached, i.e. the most appropriate method is selected, especially because the examination of available sources of information may in some instances influence the selection of the transfer pricing method. For instance, in cases where it is not possible to find information on comparable transactions (step 7) and/or to make reasonably accurate adjustments (step 8), taxpayers might have to select another transfer pricing method and repeat the process starting from step 4.

3.6. See paragraph 3.82 for a discussion of a process to establish, monitor and review transfer prices.

A.2. Broad-based analysis of the taxpayer's circumstances

3.7. The "broad-based analysis" is an essential step in the comparability analysis. It can be defined as an analysis of the industry, competition, economic and regulatory factors and other elements that affect the taxpayer and its environment, but not yet within the context of looking at the specific transactions in question. This step helps understand the conditions in the taxpayer's controlled transaction as well as those in the uncontrolled transactions to be compared, in particular the economic circumstances of the transaction (see paragraphs 1.130-1.133).

A.3. Review of the controlled transaction and choice of the tested party

3.8. The review of the controlled transaction(s) under examination aims at identifying the relevant factors that will influence the selection of the tested party (where needed), the selection and application of the most appropriate transfer pricing method to the circumstances of the case, the financial indicator that will be tested (in the case of a transactional profit method), the selection of comparables and where relevant the determination of comparability adjustments.

A.3.1. Evaluation of a taxpayer's separate and combined transactions

3.9. Ideally, in order to arrive at the most precise approximation of arm's length conditions, the arm's length principle should be applied on a transaction-by-transaction basis. However, there are often situations where separate transactions are so closely linked or continuous that they cannot be evaluated adequately on a separate basis. Examples may include: a) some long-term contracts for the supply of commodities or services, b) rights to use intangible property, and c) pricing a range of closely-linked products (e.g. in a product line) when it is impractical to determine pricing for each individual product or transaction. Another example would be the licensing of manufacturing know-how and the supply of vital components to an associated manufacturer; it may be more reasonable to assess the arm's length terms for the two items together rather than individually. Such transactions should be evaluated together using the most appropriate arm's length method. A further example would be the routing of a transaction through another associated enterprise; it may be more appropriate to consider the transaction of which the routing is a part in its entirety, rather than consider the individual transactions on a separate basis. See example 26 of Annex I to Chapter VI.

3.10. Another example where a taxpayer's transactions may be combined is related to portfolio approaches. A portfolio approach is a business strategy consisting of a taxpayer bundling certain transactions for the purpose of earning an appropriate return across the portfolio rather than necessarily on any single product within the portfolio. For instance, some products may be marketed by a taxpayer with a low profit or even at a loss, because they create a demand for other products and/or related services of the same taxpayer that are then sold or provided with high profits (e.g. equipment and captive aftermarket consumables, such as vending coffee machines and coffee capsules, or printers and cartridges). Similar approaches can be observed in various industries. Portfolio approaches are an example of a business strategy that may need to be taken into account in the comparability analysis and when examining the reliability of comparables. See paragraphs 1.134-1.138 on business strategies. However, as discussed in paragraphs 1.149-1.151, these considerations will not explain continued overall losses or poor performance over time. Moreover, in order to be acceptable, portfolio approaches must be reasonably targeted as they should not be used to apply a transfer pricing method at the taxpayer's company-wide level in those cases where different transactions have different economic logic and should be segmented. See paragraphs 2.84-2.85. Finally, the above comments should not be misread as implying that it would be acceptable for one entity within an MNE group to have a below arm's length return in order to provide benefits to another entity of the MNE group, see in particular paragraph 1.150.

3.11. While some separately contracted transactions between associated enterprises may need to be evaluated together in order to determine whether the conditions are arm's length, other transactions contracted between such enterprises as a package may need to be evaluated separately. An MNE may package as a single transaction and establish a single price for a number of benefits such as licences for patents, know-how, and trademarks, the provision of technical and administrative services, and the lease of production facilities. This type of arrangement is often referred to as a package deal. Such comprehensive packages would be unlikely to include sales of goods, however, although the price charged for sales of goods may cover some accompanying services. In some cases, it may not be feasible to evaluate the package as a whole so that the elements of the package must be segregated. In such cases, after determining separate transfer pricing for the separate elements, the tax administration should nonetheless consider whether in total the transfer pricing for the entire package is arm's length.

3.12. Even in uncontrolled transactions, package deals may combine elements that are subject to different tax treatment under domestic law or an income tax convention. For example, royalty payments may be subject to withholding tax but lease payments may be subject to net taxation. In such circumstances, it may still be appropriate to determine the transfer pricing on a package basis, and the tax administration could then determine whether for other tax reasons it is necessary to allocate the price to the elements of the package. In making this determination, tax administrations should examine the package deal between associated enterprises in the same way that they would analyse similar deals between independent enterprises. Taxpayers should be prepared to show that the package deal reflects appropriate transfer pricing.

A.3.2. Intentional set-offs

3.13. An intentional set-off is one that associated enterprises incorporate knowingly into the terms of the controlled transactions. It occurs when one associated enterprise has provided a benefit to another associated enterprise within the group that is balanced to some degree by different benefits received from that enterprise in return. These enterprises may indicate that the benefit each has received should be set off against the benefit each has provided as full or part payment for those benefits so that only the net gain or loss (if any) on the transactions needs to be considered for purposes of assessing tax liabilities. For example, an enterprise may license another enterprise to use a patent in return for the provision of know-how in another connection and indicate that the transactions result in no profit or loss to either party. Such arrangements may sometimes be encountered between independent enterprises and should be assessed in accordance with the arm's length principle in order to quantify the value of the respective benefits presented as set-offs.

3.14. Intentional set-offs may vary in size and complexity. Such set-offs may range from a simple balance of two transactions (such as a favourable selling price for manufactured goods in return for a favourable purchase price for the raw material used in producing the goods) to an arrangement for a general settlement balancing all benefits accruing to both parties over a period. Independent enterprises would be very unlikely to consider the latter type of arrangement unless the benefits could be sufficiently accurately quantified and the contract is created in advance. Otherwise, independent enterprises normally would prefer to allow their receipts and disbursements to flow independently of each other, taking any profit or loss resulting from normal trading.

3.15. Recognition of intentional set-offs does not change the fundamental requirement that for tax purposes the transfer prices for controlled transactions must be consistent with the arm's length principle. It would be a good practice for taxpayers to disclose the existence of set-offs intentionally built into two or more transactions between associated enterprises and demonstrate (or acknowledge that they have relevant supporting information and have undertaken sufficient analysis to be able to show) that, after taking account of the set-offs, the conditions governing the transactions are consistent with the arm's length principle.

3.16. It may be necessary to evaluate the transactions separately to determine whether they each satisfy the arm's length principle. If the transactions are to be analysed together, care should be taken in selecting comparable transactions and regard had to the discussion in paragraphs 3.9-3.12. The terms of set-offs relating to international transactions between associated enterprises may not be fully consistent with those relating to purely domestic transactions between independent enterprises because of the differences in tax treatment of the set-off under different national tax systems or differences in the treatment of the payment under a bilateral tax treaty. For example, withholding tax would complicate a set-off of royalties against sales receipts.

3.17. A taxpayer may seek on examination a reduction in a transfer pricing adjustment based on an unintentional over-reporting of taxable income. Tax administrations in their discretion may or may not grant this request. Tax administrations may also consider such requests in the context of mutual agreement procedures and corresponding adjustments (see Chapter IV).

A.3.3. Choice of the tested party

3.18. When applying a cost plus, resale price or transactional net margin method as described in Chapter II, it is necessary to choose the party to the transaction for which a financial indicator (mark-up on costs, gross margin, or net profit indicator) is tested. The choice of the tested party should be consistent with the functional analysis of the transaction. As a general rule, the tested party is the one to which a transfer pricing method can be applied in the most reliable manner and for which the most reliable comparables can be found, i.e. it will most often be the one that has the less complex functional analysis.

3.19. This can be illustrated as follows. Assume that company A manufactures two types of products, P1 and P2, that it sells to company B, an associated enterprise in another country. Assume that A is found to manufacture P1 products using valuable, unique intangibles that belong to B and following technical specifications set by B. Assume that in this P1 transaction, A only performs simple functions and does not make any valuable, unique contribution in relation to the transaction. The tested party for this P1 transaction would most often be A. Assume now that A is also manufacturing P2 products for which it owns and uses valuable unique intangibles such as valuable patents and trademarks, and for which B acts as a distributor. Assume that in this P2 transaction, B only performs simple functions and does not make any valuable, unique contribution in relation to the transaction. The tested party for the P2 transaction would most often be B.

A.3.4. Information on the controlled transaction

3.20. In order to select and apply the most appropriate transfer pricing method to the circumstances of the case, information is needed on the comparability factors in relation to the controlled transaction under review and in particular on the functions, assets and risks of all the parties to the controlled transaction, including the foreign associated enterprise(s). Specifically, while one-sided methods (e.g. cost plus, resale price or transactional net margin method which are discussed in detail in Chapter II) only require examining a financial indicator or profit level indicator for one of the parties to the transaction (the "tested party" as discussed in paragraphs 3.18-3.19), some information on the comparability factors of the controlled transaction and in particular on the functional analysis of the non-tested party is also needed in order to appropriately characterise the controlled transaction and select the most appropriate transfer pricing method.

3.21. Where the most appropriate transfer pricing method in the circumstances of the case, determined following the guidance in paragraphs 2.1-2.12, is a transactional profit split, financial information on all the parties to the transaction, domestic and foreign, is needed. Given the two-sided nature of this method, the application of a transactional profit split necessitates particularly detailed information on the foreign associated enterprise party to the transaction. This includes information on the five comparability factors in order to appropriately characterise the relationship between the parties and demonstrate the appropriateness of the transactional profit split method, as well as financial information (the determination of the relevant profits to be split and the splitting of the profits both rely on financial information pertaining to all the parties to the transaction, including the foreign associated enterprise). Accordingly, where the most appropriate transfer pricing method in the circumstances of the case is a transactional profit split, it would be reasonable to expect that taxpayers be ready to provide tax administrations with the necessary information on the foreign associated enterprise party to the transaction, including the financial data necessary to calculate the profit split. See Chapter V.

3.22. Where the most appropriate transfer pricing method in the circumstances of the case, determined following the guidance in paragraphs 2.1-2.12, is a one-sided method, financial information on the tested party is needed in addition to the information referred to in paragraph 3.20 – irrespective of whether the tested party is a domestic or foreign entity. So if the most appropriate method is a cost plus, resale price or transactional net margin method and the tested party is the foreign entity, sufficient information is needed to be able to reliably apply the selected method to the foreign tested party and to enable a review by the tax administration of the jurisdiction of the non-tested party of the application of the method to the foreign tested party. On the other hand, once a particular one-sided method is chosen as the most appropriate method and the tested party is the domestic taxpayer, the tax administration generally has no reason to further ask for financial data of the foreign associated enterprise outside of that requested as part of the country-by-country or master file reporting requirements (see Chapter V).

3.23. As explained above, transfer pricing analysis necessitates some information to be available about foreign associated enterprises, the nature and extent of which depends especially on the transfer pricing method used. However gathering such information may present a taxpayer with difficulties that it does not encounter in producing its own information. These difficulties should be taken into account in developing rules and/or procedures on documentation.

A.4. Comparable uncontrolled transactions

A.4.1. In general

3.24. A comparable uncontrolled transaction is a transaction between two independent parties that is comparable to the controlled transaction under examination. It can be either a comparable transaction between one party to the controlled transaction and an independent party ("internal comparable") or between two independent enterprises, neither of which is a party to the controlled transaction ("external comparable").

3.25. Comparisons of a taxpayer's controlled transactions with other controlled transactions carried out by the same or another MNE group are irrelevant to the application of the arm's length principle and therefore should not be used by a tax administration as the basis for a transfer pricing adjustment or by a taxpayer to support its transfer pricing policy.

3.26. The presence of minority shareholders may be one factor leading to the outcomes of a taxpayer's controlled transactions being closer to arm's length, but it is not determinative in and of itself. The influence of minority shareholders depends on a number of factors, including whether the minority shareholder has a participation in the capital of the parent company or in the capital of a subsidiary, and whether it has and actually exercises some influence on the pricing of intra-group transactions.

A.4.2. Internal comparables

3.27. Step 4 of the typical process described in paragraph 3.4 is a review of existing internal comparables, if any. Internal comparables may have a more direct and closer relationship to the transaction under review than external comparables. The financial analysis may be easier and more reliable as it will presumably rely on identical accounting standards and practices for the internal comparable and for the controlled transaction. In addition, access to information on internal comparables may be both more complete and less costly.

3.28. On the other hand, internal comparables are not always more reliable and it is not the case that any transaction between a taxpayer and an independent party can be regarded as a reliable comparable for controlled transactions carried on by the same taxpayer. Internal comparables where they exist must satisfy the five comparability factors in the same way as external comparables, see paragraphs 1.33-1.138. Guidance on comparability adjustments also applies to internal comparables, see paragraphs 3.47-3.54. Assume for instance that a taxpayer manufactures a particular product, sells a significant volume thereof to its foreign associated retailer and a marginal volume of the same product to an independent party. In such a case, the difference in volumes is likely to materially affect the comparability of the two transactions. If it is not possible to make a reasonably accurate adjustment to eliminate the effects of such difference, the transaction between the taxpayer and its independent customer is unlikely to be a reliable comparable.

A.4.3. External comparables and sources of information

3.29. There are various sources of information that can be used to identify potential external comparables. This sub-section discusses particular issues that arise with respect to commercial databases, foreign comparables and information undisclosed to taxpayers. Additionally, whenever reliable internal comparables exist, it may be unnecessary to search for external ones, see paragraphs 3.27-3.28.

A.4.3.1. Databases

3.30. A common source of information is commercial databases, which have been developed by editors who compile accounts filed by companies with the relevant administrative bodies and present them in an electronic format suitable for searches and statistical analysis. They can be a practical and sometimes cost-effective way of identifying external comparables and may provide the most reliable source of information, depending on the facts and circumstances of the case.

3.31. A number of limitations to commercial databases are frequently identified. Because these commercial databases rely on publicly available information, they are not available in all jurisdictions, since not all jurisdictions have the same amount of publicly available information about their companies. Moreover, where they are available, they do not include the same type of information for all the companies operating in a given jurisdiction because disclosure and filing requirements may differ depending on the legal form of the company and on whether or not it is listed. Care must be exercised with respect to whether and how these databases are used, given that they are compiled and presented for non-transfer pricing purposes. It is not always the case that commercial databases provide information that is detailed enough to support the chosen transfer pricing method. Not all databases include the same level of detail and can be used with similar assurance. Importantly, it is the experience in many jurisdictions that commercial databases are used to compare the results of companies rather than of transactions because third party transactional information is rarely available. See paragraph 3.37 for a discussion of the use of non-transactional third party data.

3.32. It may be unnecessary to use a commercial database if reliable information is available from other sources, e.g. internal comparables. Where they are used, commercial databases should be used in an objective manner and genuine attempts should be made to use the databases to identify reliable comparable information.

3.33. Use of commercial databases should not encourage quantity over quality. In practice, performing a comparability analysis using a commercial database alone may give rise to concerns about the reliability of the analysis, given the quality of the information relevant to assessing comparability that is typically obtainable from a database. To address these concerns, database searches may need to be refined with other publicly available information, depending on the facts and circumstances. Such a refinement of the database search with other sources of information is meant to promote quality over standardised approaches and is valid both for database searches made by taxpayers/practitioners and for those made by tax administrations. It should be understood in light of the discussion of the costs and compliance burden created for the taxpayer in paragraphs 3.80-3.83.

3.34. There are also proprietary databases that are developed and maintained by some advisory firms. In addition to the issues raised above for commercial databases that are more broadly commercialised, proprietary databases also raise a further concern with respect to their coverage of data if they are based on a more limited portion of the market than commercial databases. When a taxpayer has used a proprietary database to support its transfer prices, the tax administration may request access to the database to review the taxpayer's results, for obvious transparency reasons.

A.4.3.2. Foreign source or non-domestic comparables

3.35. Taxpayers do not always perform searches for comparables on a jurisdiction-by-jurisdiction basis, e.g. in cases where there are insufficient data available at the domestic level and/or in order to reduce compliance costs where several entities of an MNE group have comparable functional analyses. Non-domestic comparables should not be automatically rejected just because they are not domestic. A determination of whether non-domestic comparables are reliable has to be made on a case-by-case basis and by reference to the extent to which they satisfy the five comparability factors. Whether or not one regional search for comparables can be reliably used for several subsidiaries of an MNE group operating in a given region of the world depends on the particular circumstances in which each of those subsidiaries operates. See paragraphs 1.132-1.133 on market differences and multi-jurisdictional analyses. Difficulties may also arise from differing accounting standards.

A.4.3.3. Information undisclosed to taxpayers

3.36. Tax administrators may have information available to them from examinations of other taxpayers or from other sources of information that may not be disclosed to the taxpayer. However, it would be unfair to apply a transfer pricing method on the basis of such data unless the tax administration was able, within the limits of its domestic confidentiality requirements, to disclose such data to the taxpayer so that there would be an adequate opportunity for the taxpayer to defend its own position and to safeguard effective judicial control by the courts.

A.4.4. Use of non-transactional third party data

3.37. The transactional focus of transfer pricing methods and the question of a possible aggregation of the taxpayer's controlled transactions are discussed in paragraphs 3.9-3.12. A different question is whether non-transactional third party data can provide reliable comparables for a taxpayer's controlled transactions (or set of transactions aggregated consistently with the guidance in paragraphs 3.9-3.12). In practice, available third party data are often aggregated data, at a company-wide or segment level, depending on the applicable accounting standards. Whether such non-transactional third party data can provide reliable comparables for the taxpayer's controlled transaction or set of transactions aggregated consistently with the guidance in paragraphs 3.9-3.12 depends in particular on whether the third party performs a range of materially different transactions. Where segmented data are available, they can provide better comparables than company-wide, non-segmented data, because of a more transactional focus, although it is recognised that segmented data can raise issues in relation to the allocation of expenses to various segments. Similarly, company-wide third party data may provide better comparables than third party segmented data in certain circumstances, such as where the activities reflected in the comparables correspond to the set of controlled transactions of the taxpayer.

A.4.5. Limitations in available comparables

3.38. The identification of potential comparables has to be made with the objective of finding the most reliable data, recognising that they will not always be perfect. For instance, independent transactions may be scarce in certain markets and industries. A pragmatic solution may need to be found, on a case-by-case basis, such as broadening the search and using information on uncontrolled transactions taking place in the same industry and a comparable geographical market, but performed by third parties that may have different business strategies, business models or other slightly different economic circumstances; information on uncontrolled transactions taking place in the same industry but in other geographical markets; or information on uncontrolled transactions taking place in the same geographical market but in other industries. The choice among these various options will depend on the facts and circumstances of the case, and in particular on the significance of the expected effects of comparability defects on the reliability of the analysis.

3.39. A transactional profit split method might in appropriate circumstances be considered without comparable data, e.g. where the absence of comparable data is due to the presence of unique and valuable intangibles contributed by each party to the transaction (see paragraph 2.119). However, even in cases where comparable data are scarce and imperfect, the selection of the most appropriate transfer pricing method should be consistent with the functional analysis of the parties, see paragraph 2.2.

A.5. Selecting or rejecting potential comparables

3.40. There are basically two ways in which the identification of potentially comparable third party transactions can be conducted.

3.41. The first one, which can be qualified as the "additive" approach, consists of the person making the search drawing up a list of third parties that are believed to carry out potentially comparable transactions. Information is then collected on transactions conducted by these third parties to confirm whether they are in effect acceptable comparables, based on the pre-determined comparability criteria. This approach arguably gives well-focused results – all the transactions retained in the analysis are carried out by well-known players in the taxpayer's market. As indicated above, in order to ensure a sufficient degree of objectivity it is important that the process followed be transparent, systematic and verifiable. The "additive" approach may be used as the sole approach where the person making the search has knowledge of a few third parties that are engaged in transactions that are comparable to the examined controlled transaction. It is worth noting that the "additive" approach presents similarities with the approach followed when identifying internal comparables. In practice, an "additive" approach may encompass both internal and external comparables.

3.42. The second possibility, the "deductive" approach, starts with a wide set of companies that operate in the same sector of activity, perform similar broad functions and do not present economic characteristics that are obviously different. The list is then refined using selection criteria and publicly available information (e.g. from databases, Internet sites, information on known competitors of the taxpayer). In practice, the "deductive" approach typically starts with a search on a database. It is therefore important to follow the guidance on internal comparables and on the sources of information on external comparables, see paragraphs 3.24-3.39. In addition, the "deductive" approach is not appropriate to all cases and all methods and the discussion in this section should not be interpreted as affecting the criteria for selecting a transfer pricing method set out in paragraphs 2.1-2.12.

3.43. In practice, both quantitative and qualitative criteria are used to include or reject potential comparables. Examples of qualitative criteria are found in product portfolios and business strategies. The most commonly observed quantitative criteria are:

- Size criteria in terms of Sales, Assets or Number of Employees. The size of the transaction in absolute value or in proportion to the activities of the parties might affect the relative competitive positions of the buyer and seller and therefore comparability.
- Intangible-related criteria such as ratio of Net Value of Intangibles/Total Net Assets Value, or ratio of Research and Development (R&D)/Sales

where available: they may be used for instance to exclude companies with valuable intangibles or significant R&D activities when the tested party does not use valuable intangible assets nor participate in significant R&D activities.

- Criteria related to the importance of export sales (Foreign Sales/Total Sales), where relevant.
- Criteria related to inventories in absolute or relative value, where relevant.
- Other criteria to exclude third parties that are in particular special situations such as start-up companies, bankrupted companies, etc. when such peculiar situations are obviously not appropriate comparisons.

The choice and application of selection criteria depends on the facts and circumstances of each particular case and the above list is neither limitative nor prescriptive.

3.44. One advantage of the "deductive" approach is that it is more reproducible and transparent than the "additive". It is also easier to verify because the review concentrates on the process and on the relevance of the selection criteria retained. On the other hand, it is acknowledged that the quality of the outcome of a "deductive" approach depends on the quality of the search tools on which it relies (e.g. quality of the database where a database is used and possibility to obtain detailed enough information). This can be a practical limitation in some jurisdictions where the reliability and usefulness of databases in comparability analyses are questionable.

3.45. It would not be appropriate to give systematic preference to one approach over the other because, depending on the circumstances of the case, there could be value in either the "additive" or the "deductive" approach, or in a combination of both. The "additive" and "deductive" approaches are often not used exclusively. In a typical "deductive" approach, in addition to searching public databases it is common to include third parties, for instance known competitors (or third parties that are known to carry out transactions potentially comparable to those of the taxpayer), which may otherwise not be found following a purely deductive approach, e.g. because they are classified under a different industry code. In such cases, the "additive" approach operates as a tool to refine a search that is based on a "deductive" approach.

3.46. The process followed to identify potential comparables is one of the most critical aspects of the comparability analysis and it should be transparent, systematic and verifiable. In particular, the choice of selection criteria has a significant influence on the outcome of the analysis and should reflect the most meaningful economic characteristics of the transactions compared. Complete elimination of subjective judgments from the selection of comparables would not be feasible, but much can be done to increase objectivity and ensure transparency in the application of subjective judgments. Ensuring transparency of the process may depend on the extent to which the criteria used to select potential comparables are able to be disclosed and the reasons for excluding some of the potential comparables are able to be explained. Increasing objectivity and ensuring transparency of the process may also depend on the extent to which the person reviewing the process (whether taxpayer or tax administration) has access to information regarding the process followed and to the same sources of data. Issues of documentation of the process of identifying comparables are discussed in Chapter V.

A.6. Comparability adjustments

3.47. The need to adjust comparables and the requirement for accuracy and reliability are pointed out in these Guidelines on several occasions, both for the general application of the arm's length principle and more specifically in the context of each method. To be comparable means that none of the differences (if any) between the situations being compared could materially affect the condition being examined in the methodology or that reasonably accurate adjustments can be made to eliminate the effect of any such differences. Whether comparability adjustments should be performed (and if so, what adjustments should be performed) in a particular case is a matter of judgment that should be evaluated in light of the discussion of costs and compliance burden in Section C.

A.6.1. Different types of comparability adjustments

3.48. Examples of comparability adjustments include adjustments for accounting consistency designed to eliminate differences that may arise from differing accounting practices between the controlled and uncontrolled transactions; segmentation of financial data to eliminate significant non-comparable transactions; adjustments for differences in capital, functions, assets, risks.

3.49. An example of a working capital adjustment designed to reflect differing levels of accounts receivable, accounts payable and inventory is provided in the Annex to Chapter III. The fact that such adjustments are found in practice does not mean that they should be performed on a routine or mandatory basis. Rather, the improvement to comparability should be shown when proposing these types of adjustments (as for any type of adjustment). Further, a significantly different level of relative working capital between the controlled and uncontrolled parties may result in further investigation of the comparability characteristics of the potential comparable.

A.6.2. Purpose of comparability adjustments

3.50. Comparability adjustments should be considered if (and only if) they are expected to increase the reliability of the results. Relevant considerations in this regard include the materiality of the difference for which an adjustment is being considered, the quality of the data subject to adjustment, the purpose of the adjustment and the reliability of the approach used to make the adjustment.

3.51. It bears emphasis that comparability adjustments are only appropriate for differences that will have a material effect on the comparison. Some differences will invariably exist between the taxpayer's controlled transactions and the third party comparables. A comparison may be appropriate despite an unadjusted difference, provided that the difference does not have a material effect on the reliability of the comparison. On the other hand, the need to perform numerous or substantial adjustments to key comparability factors may indicate that the third party transactions are in fact not sufficiently comparable.

3.52. It is not always the case that adjustments are warranted. For instance, an adjustment for differences in accounts receivable may not be particularly useful if major differences in accounting standards were also present that could not be resolved. Likewise, sophisticated adjustments are sometimes applied to create the false impression that the outcome of the comparables search is "scientific", reliable and accurate.

A.6.3. Reliability of the adjustment performed

3.53. It is not appropriate to view some comparability adjustments, such as for differences in levels of working capital, as "routine" and uncontroversial, and to view certain other adjustments, such as for country risk, as more subjective and therefore subject to additional requirements of proof and reliability. The only adjustments that should be made are those that are expected to improve comparability.

A.6.4. Documenting and testing comparability adjustments

3.54. Ensuring the needed level of transparency of comparability adjustments may depend upon the availability of an explanation of any adjustments performed, the reasons for the adjustments being considered appropriate, how they were calculated, how they changed the results for each comparable and how the adjustment improves comparability. Issues regarding documentation of comparability adjustments are discussed in Chapter V.

A.7. Arm's length range

A.7.1. In general

3.55. In some cases it will be possible to apply the arm's length principle to arrive at a single figure (e.g. price or margin) that is the most reliable to establish whether the conditions of a transaction are arm's length. However, because transfer pricing is not an exact science, there will also be many occasions when the application of the most appropriate method or methods produces a range of figures all of which are relatively equally reliable. In these cases, differences in the figures that comprise the range may be caused by the fact that in general the application of the arm's length principle only produces an approximation of conditions that would have been established between independent enterprises. It is also possible that the different points in a range represent the fact that independent enterprises engaged in comparable transactions under comparable circumstances may not establish exactly the same price for the transaction.

3.56. In some cases, not all comparable transactions examined will have a relatively equal degree of comparability. Where it is possible to determine that some uncontrolled transactions have a lesser degree of comparability than others, they should be eliminated.

3.57. It may also be the case that, while every effort has been made to exclude points that have a lesser degree of comparability, what is arrived at is a range of figures for which it is considered, given the process used for selecting comparables and limitations in information available on comparables, that some comparability defects remain that cannot be identified and/or quantified, and are therefore not adjusted. In such cases, if the range includes a sizeable number of observations, statistical tools that take account of central tendency to narrow the range (e.g. the interquartile range or other percentiles) might help to enhance the reliability of the analysis.

3.58. A range of figures may also result when more than one method is applied to evaluate a controlled transaction. For example, two methods that attain similar degrees of comparability may be used to evaluate the arm's length character of a controlled transaction. Each method may produce an outcome or a range of outcomes that differs from the other because of differences in the nature of the methods and the data, relevant to the application of a particular method, used. Nevertheless, each separate range potentially could be used to define an acceptable range of arm's length figures. Data from these ranges could be useful for purposes of more accurately defining the arm's length range, for example when the ranges overlap, or for reconsidering the accuracy of the methods used when the ranges do not overlap. No general rule may be stated with respect to the use of ranges derived from the application of multiple methods because the conclusions to be drawn from their use will depend on the relative reliability of the methods employed to determine the ranges and the quality of the information used in applying the different methods.

3.59. Where the application of the most appropriate method (or, in relevant circumstances, of more than one method, see paragraph 2.12), produces a range of figures, a substantial deviation among points in that range may indicate that the data used in establishing some of the points may not be as reliable as the data used to establish the other points in the range or that the deviation may result from features of the comparable data that require adjustments. In such cases, further analysis of those points may be necessary to evaluate their suitability for inclusion in any arm's length range.

A.7.2. Selecting the most appropriate point in the range

3.60. If the relevant condition of the controlled transaction (e.g. price or margin) is within the arm's length range, no adjustment should be made.

3.61. If the relevant condition of the controlled transaction (e.g. price or margin) falls outside the arm's length range asserted by the tax administration, the taxpayer should have the opportunity to present arguments that the conditions of the controlled transaction satisfy the arm's length principle, and that the result falls within the arm's length range (i.e. that the arm's length range is different from the one asserted by the tax administration). If the taxpayer is unable to establish this fact, the tax administration must determine the point within the arm's length range to which it will adjust the condition of the controlled transaction.

3.62. In determining this point, where the range comprises results of relatively equal and high reliability, it could be argued that any point in the range satisfies the arm's length principle. Where comparability defects remain as discussed in paragraph 3.57, it may be appropriate to use measures of central tendency to determine this point (for instance the median, the mean or weighted averages, etc., depending on the specific characteristics of the data set), in order to minimise the risk of error due to unknown or unquantifiable remaining comparability defects.

A.7.3. Extreme results: comparability considerations

3.63. Extreme results might consist of losses or unusually high profits. Extreme results can affect the financial indicators that are looked at in the chosen method (e.g. the gross margin when applying a resale price, or a net profit indicator when applying a transactional net margin method). They can also affect other items, e.g. exceptional items which are below the line but nonetheless may reflect exceptional circumstances. Where one or more of the potential comparables have extreme results, further examination would be needed to understand the reasons for such extreme results. The reason might be a defect in comparability, or exceptional conditions met by an otherwise comparable third party. An extreme result may be excluded on the basis that a previously overlooked significant comparability defect has been brought to light, not on the sole basis that the results arising from the proposed "comparable" merely appear to be very different from the results observed in other proposed "comparables".

3.64. An independent enterprise would not continue loss-generating activities unless it had reasonable expectations of future profits. See paragraphs 1.149-1.151. Simple or low risk functions in particular are not expected to generate losses for a long period of time. This does not mean however that loss-making transactions can never be comparable. In general, all relevant information should be used and there should not be any overriding rule on the inclusion or exclusion of loss-making comparables. Indeed, it is the facts and circumstances surrounding the company in question that should determine its status as a comparable, not its financial result.

3.65. Generally speaking, a loss-making uncontrolled transaction should trigger further investigation in order to establish whether or not it can be a comparable. Circumstances in which loss-making transactions/ enterprises should be excluded from the list of comparables include cases where losses do not reflect normal business conditions, and where the losses incurred by third parties reflect a level of risks that is not comparable to the one assumed by the taxpayer in its controlled transactions. Loss-making comparables that satisfy the comparability analysis should not however be rejected on the sole basis that they suffer losses.

3.66. A similar investigation should be undertaken for potential comparables returning abnormally large profits relative to other potential comparables.

B. Timing issues in comparability

3.67. There are timing issues in comparability with respect to the time of origin, collection and production of information on comparability factors and comparable uncontrolled transactions that are used in a comparability analysis. See paragraphs 5.27 and 5.36 of Chapter V for indications with respect to timing issues in the context of transfer pricing documentation requirements.

B.1. Timing of origin

3.68. In principle, information relating to the conditions of comparable uncontrolled transactions undertaken or carried out during the same period of time as the controlled transaction ("contemporaneous uncontrolled transactions") is expected to be the most reliable information to use in a comparability analysis, because it reflects how independent parties have behaved in an economic environment that is the same as the economic environment of the taxpayer's controlled transaction. Availability of information on contemporaneous uncontrolled transactions may however be limited in practice, depending on the timing of collection.

B.2. Timing of collection

3.69. In some cases, taxpayers establish transfer pricing documentation to demonstrate that they have made reasonable efforts to comply with the arm's length principle at the time their intra-group transactions were undertaken, i.e. on an *ex ante* basis (hereinafter "the arm's length price-setting" approach), based on information that was reasonably available to them at that point. Such information includes not only information on comparable transactions from previous years, but also information on economic and market changes that may have occurred between those previous years and the year of the controlled transaction. In effect, independent parties in comparable circumstances would not base their pricing decision on historical data alone.

3.70. In other instances, taxpayers might test the actual outcome of their controlled transactions to demonstrate that the conditions of these transactions were consistent with the arm's length principle, i.e. on an *ex post* basis (hereinafter "the arm's length outcome-testing" approach). Such test typically takes place as part of the process for establishing the tax return at year-end.

3.71. Both the arm's length price-setting and the arm's length outcome-testing approaches, as well as combinations of these two approaches, are found among OECD member countries. The issue of double taxation may arise where a controlled transaction takes place between two associated enterprises where different approaches have been applied and lead to different outcomes, for instance because of a discrepancy between market expectations taken into account in the arm's length price-setting approach and actual outcomes observed in the arm's length outcome-testing approach. See paragraphs 4.38 and 4.39. Competent authorities are encouraged to use their best efforts to resolve any double taxation issues that may arise from different approaches adopted by jurisdictions to year-end adjustments and that may be submitted to them under a mutual agreement procedure (Article 25 of the OECD Model Tax Convention).

B.3. Valuation highly uncertain at the outset and unpredictable events

3.72. The question arises whether and if so how to take account in the transfer pricing analysis of future events that were unpredictable at the time of the testing of a controlled transaction, in particular where valuation at that time was highly uncertain. The question should be resolved, both by taxpayers and tax administrations, by reference to what independent enterprises would have done in comparable circumstances to take account of the valuation uncertainty in the pricing of the transaction.

3.73. The reasoning that is found in paragraphs 6.181-6.185, which provide guidance on the arm's length pricing of transactions involving intangibles for which valuation is highly uncertain at the time of the transactions, applies by analogy to other types of transactions with valuation uncertainties. The main question is to determine whether the valuation was sufficiently uncertain at the outset that the parties at arm's length would have required a price adjustment mechanism, or whether the change in value was so fundamental a development that it would have led to a renegotiation of the transaction. Where this is the case, the tax administration would be justified in determining the arm's length price for the transaction on the basis of the adjustment clause or re-negotiation that would be provided at arm's length in a comparable uncontrolled transaction. In other circumstances, where there is no reason to consider that the valuation was sufficiently uncertain at the outset that the parties would have required a price adjustment clause or would have renegotiated the terms of the agreement, there is no reason for tax administrations to make such an adjustment as it would represent an inappropriate use of hindsight. The mere existence of uncertainty should not require an *ex post* adjustment without a consideration of what independent enterprises would have done or agreed between them.

B.4. Data from years following the year of the transaction

3.74. Data from years following the year of the transaction may also be relevant to the analysis of transfer prices, but care must be taken to avoid the use of hindsight. For example, data from later years may be useful in comparing product life cycles of controlled and uncontrolled transactions for the purpose of determining whether the uncontrolled transaction is an appropriate comparable to use in applying a particular method. The conduct of the parties in years following the transaction will also be relevant in accurately delineating the actual transaction.

B.5. Multiple year data

3.75. In practice, examining multiple year data is often useful in a comparability analysis, but it is not a systematic requirement. Multiple year data should be used where they add value to the transfer pricing analysis. It would not be appropriate to set prescriptive guidance as to the number of years to be covered by multiple year analyses.

3.76. In order to obtain a complete understanding of the facts and circumstances surrounding the controlled transaction, it generally might be useful to examine data from both the year under examination and prior years. The analysis of such information might disclose facts that may have influenced (or should have influenced) the determination of the transfer price. For example, the use of data from past years will show whether a taxpayer's reported loss on a transaction is part of a history of losses on similar transactions, the result of particular economic conditions in a prior year that increased costs in the subsequent year, or a reflection of the fact that a product is at the end of its life cycle. Such an analysis may be particularly useful where a transactional profit method is applied. See paragraph 1.151 on the usefulness of multiple year data in examining loss situations. Multiple year data can also improve the understanding of long term arrangements.

3.77. Multiple year data will also be useful in providing information about the relevant business and product life cycles of the comparables. Differences in business or product life cycles may have a material effect on transfer pricing conditions that needs to be assessed in determining comparability. The data from earlier years may show whether the independent enterprise engaged in a comparable transaction was affected by comparable economic conditions in a comparable manner, or whether different conditions in an earlier year materially affected its price or profit so that it should not be used as a comparable.

3.78. Multiple year data can also improve the process of selecting third party comparables e.g. by identifying results that may indicate a significant variance from the underlying comparability characteristics of the controlled transaction being reviewed, in some cases leading to the rejection of the comparable, or to detect anomalies in third party information.

3.79. The use of multiple year data does not necessarily imply the use of multiple year averages. Multiple year data and averages can however be used in some circumstances to improve reliability of the range. See paragraphs 3.57-3.62 for a discussion of statistical tools.

C. Compliance issues

3.80. One question that arises when putting the need for comparability analyses into perspective is the extent of the burden and costs that should be borne by a taxpayer to identify possible comparables and obtain detailed information thereon. It is recognised that the cost of information can be a real concern, especially for small to medium sized operations, but also for those MNEs that deal with a very large number of controlled transactions in many jurisdictions. Paragraph 4.28 and Chapter V contain explicit recognition of the need for a reasonable application of the requirement to document comparability.

3.81. When undertaking a comparability analysis, there is no requirement for an exhaustive search of all possible relevant sources of information. Taxpayers and tax administrations should exercise judgment to determine whether particular comparables are reliable.

3.82. It is a good practice for taxpayers to set up a process to establish, monitor and review their transfer prices, taking into account the size of the transactions, their complexity, level of risk involved, and whether they are performed in a stable or changing environment. Such a practical approach would conform to a pragmatic risk assessment strategy or prudent business management principle. In practice, this means that it may be reasonable for a taxpayer to devote relatively less effort to finding information on comparables supporting less significant or less material controlled transactions. For simple transactions that are carried out in a stable environment and the characteristics of which remain the same or similar, a detailed comparability (including functional) analysis may not be needed every year.

3.83. Small to medium sized enterprises are entering into the area of transfer pricing and the number of cross-border transactions is ever increasing. Although the arm's length principle applies equally to small and medium sized enterprises and transactions, pragmatic solutions may be appropriate in order to make it possible to find a reasonable response to each transfer pricing case.

Chapter IV

Administrative approaches to avoiding and resolving transfer pricing disputes

A. Introduction

4.1. This chapter examines various administrative procedures that could be applied to minimise transfer pricing disputes and to help resolve them when they do arise between taxpayers and their tax administrations, and between different tax administrations. Such disputes may arise even though the guidance in these Guidelines is followed in a conscientious effort to apply the arm's length principle. It is possible that taxpayers and tax administrations may reach differing determinations of the arm's length conditions for the controlled transactions under examination given the complexity of some transfer pricing issues and the difficulties in interpreting and evaluating the circumstances of individual cases.

4.2. Where two or more tax administrations take different positions in determining arm's length conditions, double taxation may occur. Double taxation means the inclusion of the same income in the tax base by more than one tax administration, when either the income is in the hands of different taxpayers (economic double taxation, for associated enterprises) or the income is in the hands of the same juridical entity (juridical double taxation, for permanent establishments). Double taxation is undesirable and should be eliminated whenever possible, because it constitutes a potential barrier to the development of international trade and investment flows. The double inclusion of income in the tax base of more than one jurisdiction does not always mean that the income will actually be taxed twice.

4.3. This chapter discusses several administrative approaches to resolving disputes caused by transfer pricing adjustments and for avoiding double taxation. Section B discusses transfer pricing compliance practices by tax administrations, in particular examination practices, the burden of proof, and penalties. Section C discusses corresponding adjustments (Paragraph 2 of Article 9 of the OECD Model Tax Convention) and the mutual agreement procedure (Article 25). Section D describes the use of simultaneous tax examinations by two (or more) tax administrations to expedite the identification, processing, and resolution of transfer pricing issues (and other international tax issues). Sections E and F describe some possibilities for minimising transfer pricing disputes between taxpayers and their tax administrations. Section E addresses the possibility of developing safe harbours for certain taxpayers, and Section F deals with advance pricing arrangements, which address the possibility of determining in advance a transfer pricing methodology or conditions for the taxpayer to apply to specified controlled transactions. Section G considers briefly the use of arbitration procedures to resolve transfer pricing disputes between jurisdictions.

B. Transfer pricing compliance practices

4.4. Tax compliance practices are developed and implemented in each jurisdiction according to its own domestic legislation and administrative procedures. Many domestic tax compliance practices have three main elements: a) to reduce opportunities for non-compliance (e.g. through withholding taxes and information reporting); b) to provide positive assistance for compliance (e.g. through education and published guidance); and, c) to provide disincentives for non-compliance. As a matter of domestic sovereignty and to accommodate the particularities of widely varying tax systems, tax compliance practices remain within the province of each jurisdiction. Nevertheless a fair application of the arm's length principle requires clear procedural rules to ensure adequate protection of the taxpayer and to make sure that tax revenue is not shifted to jurisdictions with overly harsh procedural rules. However, when a taxpayer under examination in one jurisdiction is a member of an MNE group, it is possible that the domestic tax compliance practices in a jurisdiction examining a taxpayer will have consequences in other tax jurisdictions. This may be particularly the case when cross-border transfer pricing issues are involved, because the transfer pricing has implications for the tax collected in the tax jurisdictions of the associated enterprises involved in the controlled transaction. If the same transfer pricing is not accepted in the other tax jurisdictions, the MNE group may be subject to double taxation as explained in paragraph 4.2. Thus, tax administrations should be conscious of the arm's length principle when applying their domestic compliance practices and the potential implications of their transfer pricing compliance rules for other tax jurisdictions, and seek to facilitate both the equitable allocation of taxes between jurisdictions and the prevention of double taxation for taxpayers.

4.5. This section describes three aspects of transfer pricing compliance that should receive special consideration to help tax jurisdictions administer their transfer pricing rules in a manner that is fair to taxpayers and other jurisdictions. While other tax law compliance practices are in common use in

OECD member countries – for example, the use of litigation and evidentiary sanctions where information may be sought by a tax administration but is not provided – these three aspects will often impact on how tax administrations in other jurisdictions approach the mutual agreement procedure process and determine their administrative response to ensuring compliance with their own transfer pricing rules. The three aspects are: examination practices, the burden of proof, and penalty systems. The evaluation of these three aspects will necessarily differ depending on the characteristics of the tax system involved, and so it is not possible to describe a uniform set of principles or issues that will be relevant in all cases. Instead, this section seeks to provide general guidance on the types of problems that may arise and reasonable approaches for achieving a balance of the interests of the taxpayers and tax administrations involved in a transfer pricing inquiry.

B.1. Examination practices

4.6. Examination practices vary widely among OECD member countries. Differences in procedures may be prompted by such factors as the system and the structure of the tax administration, the geographic size and population of the jurisdiction, the level of domestic and international trade, and cultural and historical influences.

4.7. Transfer pricing cases can present special challenges to the normal audit or examination practices, both for the tax administration and for the taxpayer. Transfer pricing cases are fact-intensive and may involve difficult evaluations of comparability, markets, and financial or other industry information. Consequently, a number of tax administrations have examiners who specialise in transfer pricing, and transfer pricing examinations themselves may take longer than other examinations and follow separate procedures.

4.8. Because transfer pricing is not an exact science, it will not always be possible to determine the single correct arm's length price; rather, as Chapter III recognises, the correct price may have to be estimated within a range of acceptable figures. Also, the choice of methodology for establishing arm's length transfer pricing will not often be unambiguously clear. Taxpayers may experience particular difficulties when the tax administration proposes to use a methodology, for example a transactional profit method, that is not the same as that used by the taxpayer.

4.9. In a difficult transfer pricing case, because of the complexity of the facts to be evaluated, even the best-intentioned taxpayer can make an honest mistake. Moreover, even the best-intentioned tax examiner may draw the wrong conclusion from the facts. Tax administrations are encouraged to take this observation into account in conducting their transfer pricing examinations. This involves two implications. First, tax examiners are encouraged to be flexible in their approach and not demand from taxpayers in their transfer pricing a precision that is unrealistic under all the facts and circumstances. Second, tax examiners are encouraged to take into account the taxpayer's commercial judgment about the application of the arm's length principle, so that the transfer pricing analysis is tied to business realities. Therefore, tax examiners should undertake to begin their analyses of transfer pricing from the perspective of the method that the taxpayer has chosen in setting its prices. The guidance provided in Chapter II, Part I dealing with the selection of the most appropriate transfer pricing method also may assist in this regard.

4.10. A tax administration should keep in mind in allocating its audit resources the taxpayer's process of setting prices, for example whether the MNE group operates on a profit centre basis. See paragraph 1.5.

B.2. Burden of proof

4.11. Like examination practices, the burden of proof rules for tax cases also differ among OECD member countries. In most jurisdictions, the tax administration bears the burden of proof both in its own internal dealings with the taxpayer (e.g. assessment and appeals) and in litigation. In some of these jurisdictions, the burden of proof can be reversed, allowing the tax administration to estimate taxable income, if the taxpayer is found not to have acted in good faith, for example, by not co-operating or complying with reasonable documentation requests or by filing false or misleading returns. In other jurisdictions, the burden of proof is on the taxpayer. In this respect, however, the conclusions of paragraphs 4.16 and 4.17 should be noted.

4.12. The implication for the behaviour of the tax administration and the taxpayer of the rules governing burden of proof should be taken into account. For example, where as a matter of domestic law the burden of proof is on the tax administration, the taxpayer may not have any legal obligation to prove the correctness of its transfer pricing unless the tax administration makes a *prima facie* showing that the pricing is inconsistent with the arm's length principle. Even in such a case, of course, the tax administration might still reasonably oblige the taxpayer to produce its records that would enable the tax administration to undertake its examination. In some jurisdictions, taxpayers have a duty to co-operate with the tax administration imposed on them by law. In the event that a taxpayer fails to co-operate, the tax administration may be given the authority to estimate the taxpayer's income and to assume relevant facts based on experience. In these cases, tax administrations should not seek to impose such a high level of co-operation that would make it too difficult for reasonable taxpayers to comply.

4.13. In jurisdictions where the burden of proof is on the taxpayer, tax administrations are generally not at liberty to raise assessments against taxpayers which are not soundly based in law. A tax administration in a jurisdiction that applies the arm's length principle, for example, could not raise an assessment based on a taxable income calculated as a fixed percentage of turnover and simply ignore the arm's length principle. In the context of litigation in jurisdictions where the burden of proof is on the taxpayer, the burden of proof is often seen as a shifting burden. Where the taxpayer presents to a court a reasonable argument and evidence to suggest that its transfer pricing was arm's length, the burden of proof may legally or *de facto* shift to the tax administration to counter the taxpayer's position and to present argument and evidence as to why the taxpayer's transfer pricing was not arm's length and why the assessment is correct. On the other hand, where a taxpayer makes little effort to show that its transfer pricing was arm's length, the burden imposed on the taxpayer would not be satisfied where a tax administration raised an assessment which was soundly based in law.

4.14. When transfer pricing issues are present, the divergent rules on burden of proof among OECD member countries will present serious problems if the strict legal rights implied by those rules are used as a guide for appropriate behaviour. For example, consider the case where the controlled transaction under examination involves one jurisdiction in which the burden of proof is on the taxpayer and a second jurisdiction in which the burden of proof is on the tax administration. If the burden of proof is guiding behaviour, the tax administration in the first jurisdiction might make an unsubstantiated assertion about the transfer pricing, which the taxpayer might accept, and the tax administration in the second jurisdiction would have the burden of disproving the pricing. It could be that neither the taxpayer in the second jurisdiction nor the tax administration in the first jurisdiction would be making efforts to establish an acceptable arm's length price. This type of behaviour would set the stage for significant conflict as well as double taxation.

4.15. Consider the same facts as in the example in the preceding paragraph. If the burden of proof is again guiding behaviour, a taxpayer in the first jurisdiction being a subsidiary of a taxpayer in the second jurisdiction (notwithstanding the burden of proof and these Guidelines), may be unable or unwilling to show that its transfer prices are arm's length. The tax administration in the first jurisdiction after examination makes an adjustment in good faith based on the information available to it. The parent company in the second jurisdiction is not obliged to provide to its tax administration any information to show that the transfer pricing was arm's length as the burden of proof rests with the tax administration. This will make it difficult for the two tax administrations to reach agreement in competent authority proceedings.

4.16. In practice, neither jurisdictions nor taxpayers should misuse the burden of proof in the manner described above. Because of the difficulties with transfer pricing analyses, it would be appropriate for both taxpayers and tax administrations to take special care and to use restraint in relying on the burden of proof in the course of the examination of a transfer pricing case. More particularly, as a matter of good practice, the burden of proof should not be misused by tax administrations or taxpayers as a justification for making groundless or unverifiable assertions about transfer pricing. A tax administration should be prepared to make a good faith showing that its determination of transfer pricing is consistent with the arm's length principle even where the burden of proof is on the taxpayer, and taxpayers similarly should be prepared to make a good faith showing that their transfer pricing is consistent with the arm's length principle regardless of where the burden of proof lies.

4.17. The Commentary on paragraph 2 of Article 9 of the OECD Model Tax Convention makes clear that the State from which a corresponding adjustment is requested should comply with the request only if that State "considers that the figure of adjusted profits correctly reflects what the profits would have been if the transactions had been at arm's length". This means that in competent authority proceedings the State that has proposed the primary adjustment bears the burden of demonstrating to the other State that the adjustment "is justified both in principle and as regards the amount." Both competent authorities are expected to take a cooperative approach in resolving mutual agreement cases.

B.3. Penalties

4.18. Penalties are most often directed toward providing disincentives for non-compliance, where the compliance at issue may relate to procedural requirements such as providing necessary information or filing returns, or to the substantive determination of tax liability. Penalties are generally designed to make tax underpayments and other types of non-compliance more costly than compliance. The Committee on Fiscal Affairs has recognised that promoting compliance should be the primary objective of civil tax penalties. OECD Report *Taxpayers' Rights and Obligations* (1990). If a mutual agreement results in a withdrawal or reduction of an adjustment, it is important that there exist possibilities to cancel or mitigate a penalty imposed by the tax administrations.

4.19. Care should be taken in comparing different national penalty practices and policies with one another. First, any comparison needs to take into account that there may be different names used in the various jurisdictions for penalties that accomplish the same purposes. Second, the overall compliance measures of a jurisdiction should be taken into account. National tax compliance practices depend, as indicated above, on the overall tax system in the jurisdiction, and they are designed on the basis of domestic need and balance, such as the choice between the use of taxation measures that remove or limit opportunities for noncompliance (e.g. imposing a duty on taxpayers to cooperate with the tax administration or reversing the burden of proof in situations where a taxpayer is found not to have acted in good faith) and the use of monetary deterrents (e.g. additional tax imposed as a consequence of underpayments of tax in addition to the amount of the underpayment). The nature of tax penalties may also be affected by the judicial system of a jurisdiction. Most jurisdictions do not apply no-fault penalties; in some jurisdictions, for example, the imposition of a no-fault penalty would be against the underlying principles of their legal system.

4.20. There are a number of different types of penalties that tax jurisdictions have adopted. Penalties can involve either civil or criminal sanctions – criminal penalties are virtually always reserved for cases of very significant fraud, and they usually carry a very high burden of proof for the party asserting the penalty (i.e. the tax administration). Criminal penalties are not the principal means to promote compliance in any of the OECD member countries. Civil (or administrative) penalties are more common, and they typically involve a monetary sanction (although as discussed above there may be a non-monetary sanction such as a shifting of the burden of proof when, e.g. procedural requirements are not met or the taxpayer is uncooperative and an effective penalty results from a discretionary adjustment).

4.21. Some civil penalties are directed towards procedural compliance, such as timely filing of returns and information reporting. The amount of such penalties is often small and based on a fixed amount that may be assessed for each day in which, e.g. the failure to file continues. The more significant civil penalties are those directed at the understatement of tax liability.

4.22. Although some jurisdictions may refer to a "penalty", the same or similar imposition by another jurisdiction may be classified as "interest". Penalty regimes in some jurisdictions may therefore include an "additional tax", or "interest", for understatements which result in late payments of tax beyond the due date. This is often designed to ensure the revenue recovers at least the real time value of money (taxes) lost.

4.23. Civil monetary penalties for tax understatement are frequently triggered by one or more of the following: an understatement of tax liability exceeding a threshold amount, negligence of the taxpayer, or wilful intent to evade tax (and also fraud, although fraud can trigger much more serious criminal penalties). Many OECD member countries impose civil monetary penalties for negligence or wilful intent, while only a few countries penalise "no-fault" understatements of tax liability.

4.24. It is difficult to evaluate in the abstract whether the amount of a civil monetary penalty is excessive. Among OECD member countries, civil monetary penalties for tax understatement are frequently calculated as a percentage of the tax understatement, where the percentage most often ranges from 10% to 200%. In most OECD member countries, the rate of the penalty increases as the conditions for imposing the penalty increase. For instance, the higher rate penalties often can be imposed only by showing a high degree of taxpayer culpability, such as a wilful intent to evade. "No-fault" penalties, where used, tend to be at lower rates than those triggered by taxpayer culpability (see paragraph 4.28).

4.25. Improved compliance in the transfer pricing area is of some concern to OECD member countries and the appropriate use of penalties may play a role in addressing this concern. However, owing to the nature of transfer pricing problems, care should be taken to ensure that the administration of a penalty system as applied in such cases is fair and not unduly onerous for taxpayers.

4.26. Because cross-border transfer pricing issues implicate the tax base of two jurisdictions, an overly harsh penalty system in one jurisdiction may give taxpayers an incentive to overstate taxable income in that jurisdiction contrary to Article 9. If this happens, the penalty system fails in its primary objective to promote compliance and instead leads to non-compliance of a different sort – non-compliance with the arm's length principle and under-reporting in the other jurisdiction. Each OECD member country should ensure that its transfer pricing compliance practices are not enforced in a manner inconsistent with the objectives of the OECD Model Tax Convention, avoiding the distortions noted above.

4.27. It is generally regarded by OECD member countries that the fairness of the penalty system should be considered by reference to whether the penalties are proportionate to the offence. This would mean, for example, that the severity of a penalty would be balanced against the conditions under which it would be imposed, and that the harsher the penalty the more limited the conditions in which it would apply.

4.28. Since penalties are only one of many administrative and procedural aspects of a tax system, it is difficult to conclude whether a particular penalty is fair or not without considering the other aspects of the tax system. Nonetheless, OECD member countries agree that the following conclusions can be drawn regardless of the other aspects of the tax system in place in a particular jurisdiction. First, imposition of a sizable "no-fault" penalty based on the mere existence of an understatement of a certain amount would be unduly harsh when it is attributable to good faith error rather than negligence or an actual intent to avoid tax. Second, it would be unfair to impose sizable penalties on taxpayers that made a reasonable effort in good faith to set the terms of their transactions with associated enterprises in a manner consistent with the arm's length principle. In particular, it would be inappropriate to impose a transfer pricing penalty on a taxpayer for failing to consider data to which it did not have access, or for failure to apply a transfer pricing method that would have required data that was not available to the taxpayer. Tax administrations are encouraged to take these observations into account in the implementation of their penalty provisions.

C. Corresponding adjustments and the mutual agreement procedure: Articles 9 and 25 of the OECD Model Tax Convention[1]

C.1. The mutual agreement procedure

4.29. The mutual agreement procedure is a well-established means through which tax administrations consult to resolve disputes regarding the application of double tax conventions. This procedure, described and authorised by Article 25 of the OECD Model Tax Convention, can be used to eliminate double taxation that could arise from a transfer pricing adjustment.

4.30. Article 25 sets out three different areas where mutual agreement procedures are generally used. The first area includes instances of "taxation not in accordance with the provisions of the Convention" and is covered in paragraphs 1 and 2 of the Article. Procedures in this area are typically initiated by the taxpayer. The other two areas, which do not necessarily involve the taxpayer, are dealt with in paragraph 3 and involve questions of "interpretation or application of the Convention" and the elimination of double taxation in cases not otherwise provided for in the Convention. Paragraph 10 of the Commentary on Article 25 makes clear that Article 25 is intended to be used by competent authorities in resolving not only problems

1. Members of the Inclusive Framework on Base Erosion and Profit Shifting (BEPS) have agreed to a minimum standard with respect to the resolution of treaty-related disputes. This Section C of Chapter IV is not intended to be an explanation of the minimum standard, and thus there is no implication that all members of the Inclusive Framework are in agreement with the guidance contained in this section, except where a particular statement is explicitly identified as an element of the minimum standard. The minimum standard has three general objectives: (1) jurisdictions should ensure that treaty obligations related to the mutual agreement procedure are fully implemented in good faith and that MAP cases are resolved in a timely manner; (2) jurisdictions should ensure that administrative processes promote the prevention and timely resolution of treaty-related disputes; and (3) jurisdictions should ensure that taxpayers that meet the requirements of paragraph 1 of Article 25 can access the mutual agreement procedure. The detailed elements of the minimum standard are set out in OECD (2015), *Making Dispute Resolution Mechanisms More Effective, Action 14 – 2015 Report,* OECD/G20 BEPS Project, OECD Publishing, Paris. The minimum standard is complemented by a set of best practices (to which not all members of the Inclusive Framework have committed) that respond to the obstacles that prevent the resolution of treaty-related disputes through the mutual agreement procedure. In addition, although there is currently no consensus among all members of the Inclusive Framework on the adoption of mandatory binding arbitration as a mechanism to ensure the timely resolution of MAP cases, a significant group of countries has committed to adopt and implement mandatory binding arbitration.

of juridical double taxation but also those of economic double taxation arising from transfer pricing adjustments made pursuant to paragraph 1 of Article 9.

4.31. Paragraph 5 of Article 25, which was incorporated in the OECD Model Tax Convention in 2008, provides that, in mutual agreement procedure cases in which the competent authorities are unable to reach an agreement within two years of the initiation of the case under paragraph 1 of Article 25, the unresolved issues will, at the request of the person who presented the case, be resolved through an arbitration process. This extension of the mutual agreement procedure ensures that where the competent authorities cannot reach an agreement on one or more issues that prevent the resolution of a case, a resolution of the case will still be possible by submitting those issues to arbitration. Where one or more issues have been submitted to arbitration in accordance with such a provision, and unless a person directly affected by the case does not accept the mutual agreement that implements the arbitration decision, that decision shall be binding on both States, the taxation of any person directly affected by the case will have to conform with the decision reached on the issues submitted to arbitration and the decisions reached in the arbitral process will be reflected in the mutual agreement that will be presented to these persons. Where a particular bilateral treaty does not contain an arbitration provision similar to paragraph 5 of Article 25, the competent authorities are not obliged to reach an agreement to resolve their dispute; paragraph 2 of Article 25 requires only that the competent authorities "endeavour … to resolve the case by mutual agreement". The competent authorities may be unable to come to an agreement because of conflicting domestic laws or restrictions imposed by domestic law on the tax administration's power of compromise. Even in the absence of a mandatory binding arbitration provision similar to paragraph 5 of Article 25 in a particular bilateral treaty, however, the competent authorities of the Contracting States may by mutual agreement establish a binding arbitration procedure for general application or to deal with a specific case (see paragraph 69 of the Commentary on Article 25 of the OECD Model Tax Convention). It should also be noted that a multilateral Convention on the elimination of double taxation in connection with the adjustment of profits of associated enterprises[2] (the Arbitration Convention) was signed by the Member States of the European Communities on 23 July 1990; the Arbitration Convention, which entered into force on 1 January 1995, provides for an arbitration mechanism to resolve transfer pricing disputes between European Union Member States.

C.2. Corresponding adjustments: Paragraph 2 of Article 9

4.32. To eliminate double taxation in transfer pricing cases, tax administrations may consider requests for corresponding adjustments as described in

2. Convention 90/436/EEC.

paragraph 2 of Article 9. A corresponding adjustment, which in practice may be undertaken as part of the mutual agreement procedure, can mitigate or eliminate double taxation in cases where one tax administration increases a company's taxable profits (i.e. makes a primary adjustment) as a result of applying the arm's length principle to transactions involving an associated enterprise in a second tax jurisdiction. The corresponding adjustment in such a case is a downward adjustment to the tax liability of that associated enterprise, made by the tax administration of the second jurisdiction, so that the allocation of profits between the two jurisdictions is consistent with the primary adjustment and no double taxation occurs. It is also possible that the first tax administration will agree to decrease (or eliminate) the primary adjustment as part of the consultative process with the second tax administration, in which case the corresponding adjustment would be smaller (or perhaps unnecessary). It should be noted that a corresponding adjustment is not intended to provide a benefit to the MNE group greater than would have been the case if the controlled transactions had been undertaken at arm's length conditions in the first instance.

4.33. Paragraph 2 of Article 9 specifically provides that the competent authorities shall consult each other if necessary to determine appropriate corresponding adjustments. This confirms that the mutual agreement procedure of Article 25 may be used to consider corresponding adjustment requests. See also paragraph 10 of the Commentary on Article 25 of the OECD Model Tax Convention ("… the corresponding adjustments to be made in pursuance of paragraph 2 of [Article 9] … fall within the scope of mutual agreement procedure, both as concerns assessing whether they are well-founded and for determining their amount." However, the overlap between the two Articles has caused OECD member countries to consider whether the mutual agreement procedure can be used to achieve corresponding adjustments where the bilateral income tax convention between two Contracting States does not include a provision comparable to paragraph 2 of Article 9. Paragraphs 11 and 12 of the Commentary on Article 25 of the OECD Model Tax Convention expressly state the view of most OECD member countries that the mutual agreement procedure is considered to apply to transfer pricing adjustment cases, including issues of whether a corresponding adjustment should be provided, even in the absence of a provision comparable to paragraph 2 of Article 9. Paragraph 12 notes that those States that do not agree with this view in practice find means of remedying economic double taxation in most cases involving *bona fide* companies by making use of provisions in their domestic laws.

4.34. Under paragraph 2 of Article 9, a corresponding adjustment may be made by a Contracting State either by recalculating the profits subject to tax for the associated enterprise in that jurisdiction using the relevant revised price or by letting the calculation stand and giving the associated enterprise relief against its own tax paid in that State for the additional tax charged to the associated enterprise by the adjusting State as a consequence of the revised transfer price. The former method is by far the more common among OECD member countries.

4.35. In the absence of an arbitration decision arrived at pursuant to an arbitration procedure comparable to that provided for under paragraph 5 of Article 25 which provides for a corresponding adjustment, corresponding adjustments are not mandatory, mirroring the rule that tax administrations are not obliged to reach agreement under the mutual agreement procedure. Under paragraph 2 of Article 9, a tax administration should make a corresponding adjustment only insofar as it considers the primary adjustment to be justified both in principle and in amount. The non-mandatory nature of corresponding adjustments is necessary so that one tax administration is not forced to accept the consequences of an arbitrary or capricious adjustment by another State. It also is important to maintaining the fiscal sovereignty of each OECD member country.

4.36. Once a tax administration has agreed to make a corresponding adjustment it is necessary to establish whether the adjustment is to be attributed to the year in which the controlled transactions giving rise to the adjustment took place or to an alternative year, such as the year in which the primary adjustment is determined. This issue also often raises the question of a taxpayer's entitlement to interest on the overpayment of tax in the jurisdiction which has agreed to make the corresponding adjustment (discussed in paragraphs 4.65-4.67). The first approach is more appropriate because it achieves a matching of income and expenses and better reflects the economic situation as it would have been if the controlled transactions had been at arm's length. However, in cases involving lengthy delays between the year covered by the adjustment and the year of its acceptance by the taxpayer or a final court decision, the tax administration should have the flexibility to agree to make corresponding adjustments for the year of acceptance of or decision on the primary adjustment. This approach would need to rely on domestic law for implementation. While not ordinarily preferred, it could be appropriate as an equitable measure in exceptional cases to facilitate implementation and to avoid time limit barriers.

4.37. Corresponding adjustments can be a very effective means of obtaining relief from double taxation resulting from transfer pricing adjustments. OECD member countries generally strive in good faith to reach agreement whenever the mutual agreement procedure is invoked. Through the mutual agreement procedure, tax administrations can address issues in a non-adversarial proceeding, often achieving a negotiated settlement in the interests of all parties. It also allows tax administrations to take into account other taxing rights issues, such as withholding taxes.

4.38. At least one OECD member country has a procedure that may reduce the need for primary adjustments by allowing the taxpayer to report a transfer price for tax purposes that is, in the taxpayer's opinion, an arm's length price for a controlled transaction, even though this price differs from the amount actually charged between the associated enterprises. This adjustment, sometimes known as a "compensating adjustment", would be made before the tax return is filed. Compensating adjustments may facilitate the reporting of taxable income by taxpayers in accordance with the arm's length principle, recognising that information about comparable uncontrolled transactions may not be available at the time associated enterprises establish the prices for their controlled transactions. Thus, for the purpose of lodging a correct tax return, a taxpayer would be permitted to make a compensating adjustment that would record the difference between the arm's length price and the actual price recorded in its books and records.

4.39. However, compensating adjustments are not recognised by most OECD member countries, on the grounds that the tax return should reflect the actual transactions. If compensating adjustments are permitted (or required) in the jurisdiction of one associated enterprise but not permitted in the jurisdiction of the other associated enterprise, double taxation may result because corresponding adjustment relief may not be available if no primary adjustment is made. The mutual agreement procedure is available to resolve difficulties presented by compensating adjustments, and competent authorities are encouraged to use their best efforts to resolve any double taxation which may arise from different jurisdictional approaches to such year-end adjustments.

C.3. Concerns with the procedures

4.40. While corresponding adjustment and mutual agreement procedures have proved to be able to resolve most transfer pricing conflicts, serious concerns have been expressed by taxpayers. For example, because transfer pricing issues are so complex, taxpayers have expressed concerns that there may not be sufficient safeguards in the procedures against double taxation. These concerns are mainly addressed with the introduction in the 2008 update of the OECD Model Tax Convention of a new paragraph 5 to Article 25 which introduces a mechanism that allows taxpayers to request arbitration of unresolved issues that have prevented competent authorities from reaching a mutual agreement within two years. There is also in the Commentary on Article 25 a favourable discussion of the use of supplementary dispute resolution mechanisms in addition to arbitration, including mediation and the referral of factual disputes to third party experts.

4.41. Taxpayers have also expressed fears that their cases may be settled not on their individual merits but by reference to a balance of the results in other cases. An established good practice is that, in the resolution of mutual agreement cases, a competent authority should engage in discussions with other competent authorities in a principled, fair, and objective manner, with each case being decided on its own merits and not by reference to any balance of results in other cases. To the extent applicable, these Guidelines and proposals detailed in the Report on BEPS Action 14 (bearing in mind the difference between the minimum standard and best practices) are an appropriate basis for the development of a principled approach. Similarly, there may be a fear of retaliation or offsetting adjustments by the jurisdiction from which the corresponding adjustment has been requested. It is not the intention of tax administrations to take retaliatory action; the fears of taxpayers may be a result of inadequate communication of this fact. Tax administrations should take steps to assure taxpayers that they need not fear retaliatory action and that, consistent with the arm's length principle, each case is resolved on its own merits. Taxpayers should not be deterred from initiating mutual agreement procedures where Article 25 is applicable.

4.42. Concerns that have been expressed regarding the mutual agreement procedure, as it affects corresponding adjustments, include the following, which are discussed separately in the sections below:

1. Taxpayers may be denied access to the mutual agreement procedure in transfer pricing cases;
2. Time limits under domestic law for the amendments of tax assessments may make corresponding adjustments unavailable if the relevant tax treaty does not override those limits;
3. Mutual agreement procedure cases may take a long time;
4. Taxpayer participation may be limited;
5. Published guidance may not be readily available to instruct taxpayers on how the mutual agreement procedure may be used; and
6. There may be no procedures to suspend the collection of tax deficiencies or the accrual of interest pending resolution of the mutual agreement procedure case.

C.4. Guidance, approaches and actions taken to address concerns with the mutual agreement procedure

C.4.1. Denial of access to the mutual agreement procedure in transfer pricing cases

4.43. A fundamental concern with respect to the mutual agreement procedure as it relates to corresponding adjustments is the failure to grant access to the mutual agreement procedure for transfer pricing cases. The undertaking to resolve by mutual agreement cases of taxation not in accordance with the

Convention is an integral part of the obligations assumed by a Contracting State in entering into a tax treaty and must be performed in good faith. The failure to grant mutual agreement procedure access with respect to a treaty partner's transfer pricing adjustments, may frustrate a primary objective of tax treaties. The work on Action 14 of the BEPS Action Plan directly addressed concerns related to the denial of access to the mutual agreement procedure with respect to a treaty partner's transfer pricing adjustments by including, as element 1.1 of the Action 14 minimum standard, a commitment to provide access to the mutual agreement procedure in transfer pricing cases.

4.44. The Action 14 minimum standard also comprises a number of other elements intended to address more generally concerns related to the denial of access to the mutual agreement procedure. These include: a commitment to provide access to the mutual agreement procedure in cases in which there is a disagreement between the taxpayer and the tax authorities making an adjustment as to whether the conditions for the application of a treaty anti-abuse provision have been met or as to whether the application of a domestic law anti-abuse provision is in conflict with the provisions of a treaty (element 1.2); a commitment to publish rules, guidelines and procedures regarding the mutual agreement procedure (element 2.1) and to identify in that guidance the specific information and documentation that a taxpayer is required to submit with a request for mutual agreement procedure assistance (element 3.2); a commitment to clarify that audit settlements between tax authorities and taxpayers do not preclude access to the mutual agreement procedure (element 2.6); and a commitment to ensure that both competent authorities are made aware of requests for mutual agreement procedure assistance by either (i) amending Article 25(1) to permit requests to be made to the competent authority of either Contracting State or (ii) implementing a bilateral notification or consultation process for cases in which the competent authority to whom the case is presented does not consider the taxpayer's objection to be justified (element 3.1).

C.4.2. Time limits

4.45. Relief under paragraph 2 of Article 9 may be unavailable if the time limit provided by treaty or domestic law for making corresponding adjustments has expired. Paragraph 2 of Article 9 does not specify whether there should be a time limit after which corresponding adjustments should not be made. Some jurisdictions prefer an open-ended approach so that double taxation may be mitigated. Other jurisdictions consider the open-ended approach to be unreasonable for administrative purposes. Thus, relief may depend on whether the applicable treaty overrides domestic time limitations, establishes other time limits, or links the implementation of relief to the time limits prescribed by domestic law.

4.46. Time limits for finalising a taxpayer's tax liability are necessary to provide certainty for taxpayers and tax administrations. In a transfer pricing case a jurisdiction may under its domestic law be legally unable to make a corresponding adjustment if the time has expired for finalising the tax liability of the relevant associated enterprise. Thus, the existence of such time limits and the fact that they vary from jurisdiction to jurisdiction should be considered in order to minimise double taxation.

4.47. Paragraph 2 of Article 25 of the OECD Model Tax Convention addresses the time limit issue by requiring that any agreement reached by the competent authorities pursuant to the mutual agreement procedure shall be implemented notwithstanding the time limits in the domestic law of the Contracting States. Paragraph 29 of the Commentary on Article 25 recognises that the last sentence of Article 25(2) unequivocally states the obligation to implement such agreements (and notes that impediments to implementation that exist at the time a tax treaty is entered into should generally be built into the terms of the agreement itself). Time limits therefore do not impede the making of corresponding adjustments where a bilateral treaty includes this provision. Some jurisdictions, however, may be unwilling or unable to override their domestic time limits in this way and have entered explicit reservations on this point. OECD member countries therefore are encouraged as far as possible to extend domestic time limits for purposes of making corresponding adjustments when mutual agreement procedures have been invoked.

4.48. Where a bilateral treaty does not override domestic time limits for the purposes of the mutual agreement procedure, tax administrations should be ready to initiate discussions quickly upon the taxpayer's request, well before the expiration of any time limits that would preclude the making of an adjustment. Furthermore, OECD member countries are encouraged to adopt domestic law that would allow the suspension of time limits on determining tax liability until the discussions have been concluded.

4.49. The work on Action 14 of the BEPS Action Plan directly addresses the obstacle that domestic law time limits may present to effective mutual agreement procedures. Element 3.3 of the Action 14 minimum standard includes a recommendation that jurisdictions should include the second sentence of paragraph 2 of Article 25 in their tax treaties to ensure that domestic law time limits (1) do not prevent the implementation of competent authority mutual agreements and (2) do not thereby frustrate the objective of resolving cases of taxation not in accordance with the Convention.

4.50. Where a jurisdiction cannot include the second sentence of paragraph 2 of Article 25 in its tax treaties, element 3.3 of the Action 14 minimum standard states that it should be willing to accept an alternative treaty provision that limits the time during which a Contracting State may make an adjustment pursuant to Article 9(1), in order to avoid late adjustments with respect to which mutual agreement procedure relief will not be available. Such a jurisdiction would satisfy this element of the minimum standard where the alternative treaty provision was drafted to reflect the time limits for adjustments provided for in that country's domestic law. That alternative provision, as presented in the Report on BEPS Action 14, reads as follows:

> [*In Article 9*]:
>
> 3. A Contracting State shall not include in the profits of an enterprise, and tax accordingly, profits that would have accrued to the enterprise but by reason of the conditions referred to in paragraph 1 have not so accrued, after [*bilaterally agreed period*] from the end of the taxable year in which the profits would have accrued to the enterprise. The provisions of this paragraph shall not apply in the case of fraud, gross negligence or wilful default.

Element 3.3 of the Action 14 minimum standard also states that such a jurisdiction accept a similar alternative provision in Article 7 with respect to adjustments to the profits that are attributable to a permanent establishment.

4.51. While it is not possible to recommend generally a time limit on initial assessments, tax administrations are encouraged to make these assessments within their own domestic time limits without extension. If the complexity of the case or lack of cooperation from the taxpayer necessitates an extension, the extension should be made for a minimum and specified time period. Further, where domestic time limits can be extended with the agreement of the taxpayer, such an extension should be made only when the taxpayer's consent is truly voluntary. Tax examiners are encouraged to indicate to taxpayers at an early stage their intent to make an assessment based on cross-border transfer pricing, so that the taxpayer can, if it so chooses, inform the tax administration in the other interested State, which could accordingly begin to consider the relevant issues with a view to a possible mutual agreement procedure.

4.52. Another time limit that must be considered is the three-year time limit within which a taxpayer must invoke the mutual agreement procedure under Article 25 of the OECD Model Tax Convention. The three-year period begins to run from the first notification of the action resulting in taxation not in accordance with the provisions of the Convention, which can be the time when the tax administration first notifies the taxpayer of the proposed adjustment, described as the "adjustment action" or "act of taxation", or an earlier date as discussed in paragraphs 21-24 of the Commentary on Article 25. Although some jurisdictions consider three years too short a period for invoking the procedure, other countries consider it too long and have entered reservations on this point. The Commentary on Article 25 indicates that the time limit "must be regarded as a minimum so that Contracting States are left free to agree in their bilateral conventions upon a longer period in the interests of taxpayers". In this regard, it should be noted that element 1.1 of the Action 14 minimum standard includes a recommendation that jurisdictions include in their tax treaties paragraphs 1 through 3 of Article 25, as interpreted in the Commentary.

4.53. The three-year time limit raises the issue of determining its starting date, which is addressed in paragraphs 21-24 of the Commentary on Article 25. In particular, paragraph 21 states that the three-year time period "should be interpreted in the way most favourable to the taxpayer". Paragraph 22 contains guidance on the determination of the date of the act of taxation. Paragraph 23 discusses self-assessment cases. Paragraph 24 clarifies that "where it is the combination of decisions or actions taken in both Contracting States resulting in taxation not in accordance with the Convention, the time limit begins to run only from the first notification of the most recent decision or action."

4.54. In order to minimise the possibility that time limits may prevent the mutual agreement procedure from effectively ensuring relief from or avoidance of double taxation, taxpayers should be permitted to avail themselves of the procedure at the earliest possible stage, which is as soon as an adjustment appears likely. Early competent authority consultation, before any irrevocable steps are taken by either tax administration, may ensure that there are as few procedural obstacles as possible in the way of achieving a mutually acceptable conclusion to the discussions. Some competent authorities, however, may not like to be involved at such an early stage because a proposed adjustment may not result in final action or may not trigger a claim for a corresponding adjustment. Consequently, too early an invocation of the mutual agreement process may create unnecessary work.

C.4.3. Duration of mutual agreement proceedings

4.55. Once discussions under the mutual agreement procedure have commenced, the proceedings may turn out to be lengthy. The complexity of transfer pricing cases may make it difficult for the competent authorities to reach a swift resolution. Distance may make it difficult for the competent authorities to meet frequently, and correspondence is often an unsatisfactory substitute for face-to-face discussions. Difficulties also arise from differences in language, procedures, and legal and accounting systems, and these may lengthen the duration of the process. The process also may be prolonged if the taxpayer delays providing all of the information the competent authorities require for a full understanding of the transfer pricing issue or issues.

4.56. Whilst the time taken to resolve a mutual agreement procedure case may vary according to its complexity, most competent authorities endeavour to reach bilateral agreement for the resolution of a mutual agreement procedure case within 24 months. Accordingly, in order to ensure the timely, effective and efficient resolution of treaty-related disputes, the minimum standard that was adopted in the context of the work on Action 14 of the BEPS Action Plan includes a commitment to seek to resolve mutual agreement procedure cases within an average timeframe of 24 months (element 1.3). Jurisdictions' progress toward meeting that target will be periodically reviewed on the basis of the agreed reporting framework for mutual agreement procedure statistics[3] that was developed to provide a tangible measure to evaluate the effects of the implementation of the Action 14 minimum standard (see elements 1.5 and 1.6). Moreover, other elements of the Action 14 minimum standard related to the authority of staff in charge of mutual agreement processes (element 2.3), performance indicators for competent authority functions (element 2.4) and adequate competent authority resources (element 2.5) are expected to contribute to the timely resolution of mutual agreement procedure cases.

4.57. More fundamentally, the adoption in tax treaties of a mandatory binding arbitration provision similar to paragraph 5 of Article 25 to resolve issues that the competent authorities have been unable to resolve within the two year period referred to in that provision should considerably reduce the risk of lengthy mutual agreement procedures. See paragraphs 4.177-4.179.

C.4.4. Taxpayer participation

4.58. Paragraph 1 of Article 25 of the OECD Model Tax Convention gives taxpayers the right to submit a request to initiate a mutual agreement procedure. Although the taxpayer has the right to initiate the procedure, the taxpayer has no specific right to participate in the process. It has been argued that the taxpayer also should have a right to take part in the mutual agreement procedure, including the right at least to present its case to both competent authorities, and to be informed of the progress of the discussions. It should be noted in this respect that implementation of a mutual agreement in practice is subject to the taxpayer's acceptance. Some taxpayer representatives have suggested that the taxpayer also should have a right to be present at face-to-face discussions between the competent authorities. The purpose would be to ensure that there is no misunderstanding by the competent authorities of the facts and arguments that are relevant to the taxpayer's case.

4.59. The mutual agreement procedure envisaged in Article 25 of the OECD Model Tax Convention and adopted in many bilateral agreements is not a process of litigation. While input from the taxpayer in some cases can be helpful to the procedure, it must be recalled that the mutual agreement

3. See OECD (2016), *BEPS Action 14 on More Effective Dispute Resolution Mechanisms – Peer Review Documents*, OECD/G20 Base Erosion and Profit Shifting Project, OECD, Paris.

procedure is a government-to-government process and that any taxpayer participation in that process should be subject to the discretion and mutual agreement of the competent authorities.

4.60. Outside the context of the actual discussions between the competent authorities, it is essential for the taxpayer to give the competent authorities all the information that is relevant to the issue in a timely manner. Competent authorities have limited resources and taxpayers should make every effort to facilitate the process, particularly in complex, fact-intensive transfer pricing cases in which it may be challenging for the competent authorities to develop a complete and accurate understanding of the associated enterprises' activities. Further, because the mutual agreement procedure is fundamentally designed as a means of providing assistance to a taxpayer, competent authorities should allow taxpayers every reasonable opportunity to present the relevant facts and arguments to them to ensure as far as possible that the matter is not subject to misunderstanding.

4.61. In practice, the competent authorities of many OECD member countries routinely give taxpayers such opportunities, keep them informed of the progress of the discussions, and often ask them during the course of the discussions whether they can accept the settlements contemplated by the competent authorities. These practices, already standard procedure in most jurisdictions, should be adopted as widely as possible. They are reflected in the OECD's Manual for Effective Mutual Agreement Procedures.

C.4.5. Publication of mutual agreement procedure programme guidance

4.62. Taxpayers' contributions to the mutual agreement procedure process are of course facilitated where public guidance on applicable procedures is readily accessible. The work on Action 14 of the BEPS Action Plan directly recognised the importance of providing such guidance. Element 2.1 of the Action 14 minimum standard states that jurisdictions should develop and publish rules, guidelines and procedures regarding the mutual agreement procedure and take appropriate measures to make such information available to taxpayers. Such guidance should include information on how taxpayers may make requests for competent authority assistance. It should be drafted in clear and plain language and should be readily available to the public. The Report on BEPS Action 14 also notes that such information may be of particular relevance where an adjustment may potentially involve issues within the scope of a tax treaty, such as where a transfer pricing adjustment is made with respect to a controlled transaction with an associated enterprise in a treaty partner jurisdiction, and that jurisdictions should appropriately seek to ensure that mutual agreement procedure programme guidance is available to taxpayers in such cases. To promote the transparency and dissemination of such published guidance, element 2.2 of the Action 14 minimum standard includes the publication of country mutual agreement procedure profiles on a shared public platform, in order to make broadly available competent authority contact details, links to relevant domestic guidance and other useful country-specific information. These country profiles, prepared by the members of the Inclusive Framework on BEPS[4] pursuant to an agreed reporting template developed for that purpose, are published on the OECD website.[5]

4.63. The work on Action 14 also addresses a number of other aspects related to the content of mutual agreement procedure programme guidance:

- Element 3.2 of the Action 14 minimum standard states that jurisdictions should identify in their mutual agreement procedure programme guidance the specific information and documentation that a taxpayer is required to submit with a request for competent authority assistance. Pursuant to element 3.2, jurisdictions should not deny access to the mutual agreement procedure based on the argument that a taxpayer has provided insufficient information where the taxpayer has provided the required information and documentation consistent with such guidance.
- Element 2.6 of the Action 14 minimum standard states that jurisdictions should clarify in their mutual agreement procedure programme guidance that audit settlements between tax authorities and taxpayers do not preclude access to the mutual agreement procedure.
- Certain of the non-binding Action 14 best practices additionally recommend that jurisdictions' mutual agreement procedure programme guidance should include: an explanation of the relationship between the mutual agreement procedure and domestic law administrative and judicial remedies (best practice 8); guidance on the consideration of interest and penalties in the mutual agreement procedure (best practice 10); and guidance on multilateral mutual agreement procedures and advance pricing arrangements (best practice 11). Best practice 9 recommends that this guidance provide that taxpayers will be allowed access to the mutual agreement procedure so that the competent authorities can resolve through consultation the double taxation that can arise in the case of *bona fide* taxpayer initiated foreign adjustments.

4.64. There is no need for the competent authorities to agree to rules or guidelines governing the procedure, since the rules or guidelines would be limited in effect to the competent authority's relationship with taxpayers seeking its assistance. However, competent authorities should routinely communicate such unilateral rules or guidelines to the competent authorities of their treaty partners and ensure that their country mutual agreement procedure profiles (see paragraph 4.62 above) are kept up-to-date.

4. See www.oecd.org/tax/beps/beps-about.htm#membership.
5. See www.oecd.org/tax/beps/country-map-profiles.htm.

C.4.6. Problems concerning collection of tax deficiencies and accrual of interest

4.65. The process of obtaining relief from double taxation through a corresponding adjustment can be complicated by issues relating to the collection of tax deficiencies and the assessment of interest on those deficiencies or overpayment. A first problem is that the assessed deficiency may be collected before the corresponding adjustment proceeding is completed, because of a lack of domestic procedures allowing the collection to be suspended. This may cause the MNE group to pay the same tax twice until the issues can be resolved. This problem arises not only in the context of the mutual agreement procedure but also for internal appeals. The work on Action 14 of the BEPS Action Plan recognised that the collection of tax by both Contracting States pending the resolution of a case through the mutual agreement procedure may have a significant impact on a taxpayer's business (for example, as a result of cash flow problems). Such collection of tax may also make it more difficult for a competent authority to engage in good faith mutual agreement procedure discussions when it considers that it may likely have to refund taxes already collected. The Report on BEPS Action 14 accordingly includes as best practice 6 a recommendation that jurisdictions should take appropriate measures to provide for a suspension of collection procedures during the period in which a mutual agreement procedure case is pending; such a suspension of collections should be available, at a minimum, under the same conditions as apply to a person pursuing a domestic administrative or judicial remedy. In this regard, it should be noted that the country mutual agreement procedure profiles prepared pursuant to element 2.2 of the Action 14 minimum standard (see paragraph 4.62) include information on the availability of procedures for the suspension of collections in specific jurisdictions.

4.66. Whether or not collection of the deficiency is suspended or partially suspended, other complications may arise. Because of the lengthy time period for processing many transfer pricing cases, the interest due on a deficiency or, if a corresponding adjustment is allowed, on the overpayment of tax in the other jurisdiction can equal or exceed the amount of the tax itself. Jurisdictions should take into account in their mutual agreement procedures that inconsistent interest rules across the two jurisdictions may result in additional cost for the MNE group, or in other cases provide a benefit to the MNE group (e.g. where the interest paid in the jurisdiction making the corresponding adjustment exceeds the interest imposed in the jurisdictions making the primary adjustment) that would not have been available if the controlled transactions had been undertaken on an arm's length basis originally. As noted above, the Report on BEPS Action 14 includes as best practice 10 a recommendation that jurisdictions' published mutual agreement procedure guidance should provide guidance on the consideration of interest in the mutual agreement procedure. In addition, the country mutual agreement procedure profiles prepared pursuant to element 2.2 of the Action 14 minimum standard include information on how interest and penalties are dealt with by specific jurisdictions in the context of the mutual agreement procedure.

4.67. The amount of interest (as distinct from the rate at which it is applied) may also have more to do with the year to which the jurisdiction making the corresponding adjustment attributes the corresponding adjustment. The jurisdiction making the corresponding adjustment may decide to make the adjustment for the year in which the primary adjustment is determined, in which case relatively little interest is likely to be payable (regardless of the rate of interest), whereas the jurisdiction making the primary adjustment may seek to impose interest on the understated and uncollected tax liability from the year in which the controlled transactions took place (notwithstanding that a relatively low rate of interest may be imposed). The issue of the year to which a corresponding adjustment is attributed is raised in paragraph 4.36. It may be appropriate in certain cases for both competent authorities to agree not to assess or pay interest in connection with the adjustment at issue, but this may not be possible in the absence of a specific provision addressing this issue in the relevant bilateral treaty. This approach would also reduce administrative complexities. However, as the interest on the deficiency and the interest on the overpayment are attributable to different taxpayers in different jurisdictions, there would be no assurance under such an approach that a proper economic result would be achieved.

C.5. Secondary adjustments

4.68. Corresponding adjustments are not the only adjustments that may be triggered by a primary transfer pricing adjustment. Primary transfer pricing adjustments and their corresponding adjustments change the allocation of taxable profits of an MNE group for tax purposes but they do not alter the fact that the excess profits represented by the adjustment are not consistent with the result that would have arisen if the controlled transactions had been undertaken on an arm's length basis. To make the actual allocation of profits consistent with the primary transfer pricing adjustment, some jurisdictions having proposed a transfer pricing adjustment will assert under their domestic legislation a constructive transaction (a secondary transaction), whereby the excess profits resulting from a primary adjustment are treated as having been transferred in some other form and taxed accordingly. Ordinarily, the secondary transactions will take the form of constructive dividends, constructive equity contributions, or constructive loans. For example, a jurisdiction making a primary adjustment to the income of a subsidiary of a foreign parent may treat the excess profits in the hands of the foreign parent as having been transferred as a dividend, in which case withholding tax may apply. It may be that the subsidiary paid an excessive transfer price to the foreign parent as a means of avoiding that withholding tax. Thus, secondary adjustments attempt to account for the difference between the re-determined taxable profits and the originally booked profits. The subjecting to tax of a secondary transaction gives rise to a secondary transfer pricing adjustment (a secondary adjustment). Thus, secondary adjustments may serve to prevent tax avoidance. The exact form that a secondary transaction takes and of the consequent secondary adjustment will depend on the facts of the case and on the tax laws of the jurisdiction that asserts the secondary adjustment.

4.69. Another example of a tax administration seeking to assert a secondary transaction may be where the tax administration making a primary adjustment treats the excess profits as being a constructive loan from one associated enterprise to the other associated enterprise. In this case, an obligation to repay the loan would be deemed to arise. The tax administration making the primary adjustment may then seek to apply the arm's length principle to this secondary transaction to impute an arm's length rate of interest. The interest rate to be applied, the timing to be attached to the making of interest payments, if any, and whether interest is to be capitalised would generally need to be addressed. The constructive loan approach may have an effect not only for the year to which a primary adjustment relates but to subsequent years until such time as the constructive loan is considered by the tax administration asserting the secondary adjustment to have been repaid.

4.70. A secondary adjustment may result in double taxation unless a corresponding credit or some other form of relief is provided by the other country for the additional tax liability that may result from a secondary adjustment. Where a secondary adjustment takes the form of a constructive dividend any withholding tax which is then imposed may not be relievable because there may not be a deemed receipt under the domestic legislation of the other jurisdiction.

4.71. The Commentary on paragraph 2 of Article 9 of the OECD Model Tax Convention notes that the Article does not deal with secondary adjustments, and thus it neither forbids nor requires tax administrations to make secondary adjustments. In a broad sense, the purpose of double tax agreements can be stated as being for the avoidance of double taxation and the prevention of fiscal evasion with respect to taxes on income and capital. Many jurisdictions do not make secondary adjustments either as a matter of practice or because their respective domestic provisions do not permit them to do so. Some jurisdictions might refuse to grant relief in respect of other jurisdictions' secondary adjustments and indeed they are not required to do so under Article 9.

4.72. Secondary adjustments are rejected by some jurisdictions because of the practical difficulties they present. For example, if a primary adjustment is made between brother-sister companies, the secondary adjustment may involve a hypothetical dividend from one of those companies up a chain to a common parent, followed by constructive equity contributions down another chain of ownership to reach the other company involved in the transaction. Many hypothetical transactions might be created, raising questions whether tax consequences should be triggered in other jurisdictions besides those involved in the transaction for which the primary adjustment was made. This might be avoided if the secondary transaction were a loan, but constructive loans are not used by most jurisdictions for this purpose and they carry their own complications because of issues relating to imputed interest. It would be inappropriate for minority shareholders that are not parties to the controlled transactions and that have accordingly not received excess cash to be considered recipients of a constructive dividend, even though a non-pro-rata dividend might be considered inconsistent with the requirements of applicable corporate law. In addition, as a result of the interaction with the foreign tax credit system, a secondary adjustment may excessively reduce the overall tax burden of the MNE group.

4.73. In light of the foregoing difficulties, tax administrations, when secondary adjustments are considered necessary, are encouraged to structure such adjustments in a way that the possibility of double taxation as a consequence thereof would be minimised, except where the taxpayer's behaviour suggests an intent to disguise a dividend for purposes of avoiding withholding tax. In addition, jurisdictions in the process of formulating or reviewing policy on this matter are recommended to take into consideration the above-mentioned difficulties.

4.74. Some jurisdictions that have adopted secondary adjustments also give the taxpayer receiving the primary adjustment another option that allows the taxpayer to avoid the secondary adjustment by having the taxpayer arrange for the MNE group of which it is a member to repatriate the excess profits to enable the taxpayer to conform its accounts to the primary adjustment. The repatriation could be effected either by setting up an account receivable or by reclassifying other transfers, such as dividend payments where the adjustment is between parent and subsidiary, as a payment of additional transfer price (where the original price was too low) or as a refund of transfer price (where the original price was too high).

4.75. Where a repatriation involves reclassifying a dividend payment, the amount of the dividend (up to the amount of the primary adjustment) would be excluded from the recipient's gross income (because it would already have been accounted for through the primary adjustment). The consequences would be that the recipient would lose any indirect tax credit (or benefit of a dividend exemption in an exemption system) and a credit for withholding tax that had been allowed on the dividend.

4.76. When the repatriation involves establishing an account receivable, the adjustments to actual cash flow will be made over time, although domestic law may limit the time within which the account can be satisfied. This approach is identical to using a constructive loan as a secondary transaction to account for excess profits in the hands of one of the parties to the controlled transaction. The accrual of interest on the account could have its own tax consequences, however, and this may complicate the process, depending upon when interest begins to accrue under domestic law (as discussed in paragraph 4.69). Some jurisdictions may be willing to waive the interest charge on these accounts as part of a competent authority agreement.

4.77. Where a repatriation is sought, a question arises about how such payments or arrangements should be recorded in the accounts of the taxpayer repatriating the payment to its associated enterprise so that both it and the tax administration of that jurisdiction are aware that a repatriation has occurred or has been set up. The actual recording of the repatriation in the accounts of the enterprise from whom the repatriation is sought will ultimately depend on the form the repatriation takes. For example, where a dividend receipt is to be regarded by the tax administration making the primary adjustment and the taxpayer receiving the dividend as the repatriation, then this type of arrangement may not need to be specially recorded in the accounts of the associated enterprise paying the dividend, as such an arrangement may not affect the amount or characterisation of the dividend in its hands. On the other hand, where an account payable is set up, both the taxpayer recording the account payable and the tax administration of that jurisdiction will need to be aware that the account payable relates to a repatriation so that any repayments from the account or of interest on the outstanding balance in the account are clearly able to be identified and treated according to the domestic laws of that jurisdiction. In addition, issues may be presented in relation to currency exchange gains and losses.

4.78. As most OECD member countries at this time have not had much experience with the use of repatriation, it is recommended that agreements between taxpayers and tax administrations for a repatriation to take place be discussed in the mutual agreement proceeding where it has been initiated for the related primary adjustment.

D. Simultaneous tax examinations

D.1. Definition and background

4.79. A simultaneous tax examination is a form of mutual assistance, used in a wide range of international issues, that allows two or more jurisdictions to co-operate in tax investigations. Simultaneous tax examinations can be particularly useful where information based in a third jurisdiction is a key to a tax investigation, since they generally lead to more timely and more effective exchanges of information. Historically, simultaneous tax examinations of transfer pricing issues have focused on cases where the true nature of transactions was obscured by the interposition of tax havens. However, in complex transfer pricing cases, it is suggested that simultaneous examinations could serve a broader role since they may improve the adequacy of data available to the participating tax administrations for transfer pricing analyses. It has also been suggested that simultaneous examinations could help reduce the possibilities for economic double taxation, reduce the compliance cost to taxpayers, and speed up the resolution of issues. In a simultaneous examination, if a reassessment is made, both jurisdictions involved should endeavour to reach a result that avoids double taxation for the MNE group.

4.80. Simultaneous tax examinations are defined in Part A of the *OECD Model Agreement for the Undertaking of Simultaneous Tax Examinations* (OECD Model Agreement). According to this agreement, a simultaneous tax examination means an "arrangement between two or more parties to examine simultaneously and independently, each on its own territory, the tax affairs of (a) taxpayer(s) in which they have a common or related interest with a view to exchanging any relevant information which they so obtain". This form of mutual assistance is not meant to be a substitute for the mutual agreement procedure. Any exchange of information as a result of the simultaneous tax examination continues to be exchanged via the competent authorities, with all the safeguards that are built into such exchanges. Practical information on simultaneous examinations can be found in the relevant module of the Manual on Information Exchange that was adopted by the Committee on Fiscal Affairs on 23 January 2006 (see www.oecd.org/ctp/eoi/manual).

4.81. While provisions that follow Article 26 of the OECD Model Tax Convention may provide the legal basis for conducting simultaneous examinations, competent authorities frequently conclude working arrangements that lay down the objectives of their simultaneous tax examination programmes and practical procedures connected with the simultaneous tax examination and exchange of information. Once such an agreement has been reached on the general lines to be followed and specific cases have been selected, tax examiners and inspectors of each state will separately carry out their examination within their own jurisdiction and pursuant to their domestic law and administrative practice.

D.2. Legal basis for simultaneous tax examinations

4.82. Simultaneous tax examinations are within the scope of the exchange of information provision based on Article 26 of the OECD Model Tax Convention. Article 26 provides for co-operation between the competent authorities of the Contracting States in the form of exchanges of information necessary for carrying out the provisions of the Convention or of their domestic laws concerning taxes covered by the Convention. Article 26 and the Commentary do not restrict the possibilities of assistance to the three methods of exchanging information mentioned in the Commentary (exchange on request, spontaneous exchanges, and automatic exchanges).

4.83. Simultaneous tax examinations may be authorised outside the context of double tax treaties. For example, Article 12 of the Nordic Convention on Mutual Assistance in Tax Matters governs exchange of information and assistance in tax collection between the Nordic countries and provides for the possibility of simultaneous tax examinations. This convention gives common guidelines for the selection of cases and for carrying out such examinations. Article 8 of the joint Council of Europe and OECD Convention on Mutual Administrative Assistance in Tax Matters also provides expressly for the possibility of simultaneous tax examinations.

4.84. In all cases the information obtained by the tax administration of a state has to be treated as confidential under its domestic legislation and may be used only for certain tax purposes and disclosed only to certain persons and authorities involved in specifically defined tax matters covered by the tax treaty or mutual assistance agreement. The taxpayers affected are normally notified of the fact that they have been selected for a simultaneous examination and in some jurisdictions they may have the right to be informed when the tax administrations are considering a simultaneous tax examination or when information will be transmitted in conformity with Article 26. In such cases, the competent authority should inform its counterpart in the foreign state that such disclosure will occur.

D.3. Simultaneous tax examinations and transfer pricing

4.85. In selecting transfer pricing cases for simultaneous examinations, there may be major obstacles caused by the differences in time limits for conducting examinations or making assessments in different jurisdictions and the different tax periods open for examination. However, these problems may be mitigated by an early exchange of examination schedules between the relevant competent authorities to find out in which cases the tax examination periods coincide and to synchronise future examination periods. While at first glance an early exchange of examination schedules would seem beneficial, some jurisdictions have found that the chances of a treaty partner accepting a proposal are considerably better when one is able to present issues more comprehensively to justify a simultaneous examination.

4.86. Once a case is selected for a simultaneous examination it is customary for tax inspectors or examiners to meet, to plan, to co-ordinate and to follow closely the progress of the simultaneous tax examination. Especially in complex cases, meetings of the tax inspectors or examiners concerned may also be held with taxpayer participation to clarify factual issues. In those jurisdictions where the taxpayer has the right to be consulted before information is transferred to another tax administration, this procedure should also be followed in the context of a simultaneous examination. In this situation, that tax administration should inform in advance its treaty partners that it is subject to this requirement before the simultaneous examination is begun.

4.87. Simultaneous tax examinations may be a useful instrument to determine the correct tax liability of associated enterprises in cases where, for example, costs are shared or charged and profits are allocated between taxpayers in different taxing jurisdictions or more generally where transfer pricing issues are involved. Simultaneous tax examinations may facilitate an exchange of information on multinational business practices, complex transactions, cost contribution arrangements, and profit allocation methods in special fields such as global trading and innovative financial transactions. As a result, tax administrations may acquire a better understanding of and insight into the overall activities of an MNE and obtain extended possibilities of comparison and checking international transactions. Simultaneous tax examinations may also support the industry-wide exchange of information, which is aimed at developing knowledge of taxpayer behaviour, practices and trends within an industry, and other information that might be suitable beyond the specific cases examined.

4.88. One objective of simultaneous tax examinations is to promote compliance with transfer pricing regulations. Obtaining the necessary information and determining the facts and circumstances about such matters as the transfer pricing conditions of controlled transactions between associated enterprises in two or more tax jurisdictions may be difficult for a tax administration, especially in cases where the taxpayer in its jurisdiction does not co-operate or fails to provide the necessary information in due time. The simultaneous tax examination process can help tax administrations to establish these facts faster and more effectively and economically.

4.89. The process also might allow for the identification of potential transfer pricing disputes at an early stage, thereby minimising litigation with taxpayers. This could happen when, based upon the information obtained in the course of a simultaneous tax examination, the participating tax examiners or inspectors have the opportunity to discuss any differences in opinion with regard to the transfer pricing conditions which exist between the associated enterprises and are able to reconcile these contentions. When such a process is undertaken, the tax examiners or inspectors concerned should, as far as possible, arrive at concurring statements as to the determination and evaluation of the facts and circumstances of the controlled transactions between the associated enterprises, stating any disagreements about the evaluation of facts, and any differences with respect to the legal treatment of the transfer pricing conditions which exist between the associated enterprises. Such statements could then serve as a basis for subsequent mutual agreement procedures and perhaps obviate the problems caused by one jurisdiction examining the affairs of a taxpayer long after the treaty partner country has finally settled the tax liability of the relevant associated enterprise. For example, such an approach could minimise mutual agreement procedure difficulties due to the lack of relevant information.

4.90. In some cases the simultaneous tax examination procedure may allow the participating tax administrations to reach an agreement on the transfer pricing conditions of a controlled transaction between the associated enterprises. Where an agreement is reached, corresponding adjustments may be made at an early stage, thus avoiding time-limit impediments and economic double taxation to the extent possible. In addition, if the agreement about the associated enterprises' transfer pricing is reached with the taxpayers' consent, time-consuming and expensive litigation may be avoided.

4.91. Even if no agreement between the tax administrations can be reached in the course of a simultaneous tax examination with respect to the associated enterprises' transfer pricing, the OECD Model Agreement envisions that either associated enterprise may be able to present a request for the opening of a mutual agreement procedure to avoid economic double taxation at an earlier stage than it would have if there were no simultaneous tax examination. If this is the case, then simultaneous tax examinations may significantly reduce the time span between a tax administration's adjustments made to a taxpayer's tax liability and the implementation of a mutual agreement procedure. Moreover, the OECD Model Agreement envisions that simultaneous tax examinations may facilitate mutual agreement procedures, because tax administrations will be able to build up more complete factual evidence for those tax adjustments for which a mutual agreement procedure may be requested by a taxpayer. Based upon the determination and evaluation of facts and the proposed tax treatment of the transfer pricing issues concerned as set forth in the tax administrations' statements described above, the practical operation of the mutual agreement procedure may be improved significantly, allowing the competent authorities to reach an agreement more easily.

4.92. The associated enterprises may also benefit from simultaneous tax examinations from the savings of time and resources due to the co-ordination of inquiries from the tax administrations involved and the avoidance of duplication. In addition, the simultaneous involvement of two or more tax administrations in the examination of transfer pricing between associated enterprises may provide the opportunity for an MNE to take a more active role in resolving its transfer pricing issues. By presenting the relevant facts and arguments to each of the participating tax administrations during the simultaneous tax examination the associated enterprises may help avoid misunderstandings and facilitate the tax administrations' concurring determination and evaluation of their transfer pricing conditions. Thus, the associated enterprises may obtain certainty with regard to their transfer pricing at an early stage. See paragraph 4.79.

D.4. Recommendation on the use of simultaneous tax examinations

4.93. As a result of the increased use of simultaneous tax examinations among OECD member countries, the Committee on Fiscal Affairs decided it would be useful to draft the OECD Model Agreement for those countries that are able and wish to engage in this type of co-operation. On 23 July 1992, the Council of the OECD made a recommendation to member countries to use this Model Agreement, which provides guidelines on the legal and practical aspects of this form of co-operation.

4.94. With the increasing internationalisation of trade and business and the complexity of transactions of MNEs, transfer pricing issues have become more and more important. Simultaneous tax examinations can alleviate the difficulties experienced by both taxpayers and tax administrations connected with the transfer pricing of MNEs. A greater use of simultaneous tax examinations is therefore recommended in the examination of transfer pricing cases and to facilitate exchange of information and the operation of mutual agreement procedures. In a simultaneous examination, if a reassessment is made, both jurisdictions involved should endeavour to reach a result that avoids double taxation for the MNE group.

E. Safe harbours

E.1. Introduction

4.95. Applying the arm's length principle can be a resource-intensive process. It may impose a heavy administrative burden on taxpayers and tax administrations that can be exacerbated by both complex rules and resulting compliance demands. These facts have led OECD member countries to consider whether and when safe harbour rules would be appropriate in the transfer pricing area.

4.96. When these Guidelines were adopted in 1995, the view expressed regarding safe harbour rules was generally negative. It was suggested that while safe harbours could simplify transfer pricing compliance and administration, safe harbour rules may raise fundamental problems that could potentially have perverse effects on the pricing decisions of enterprises engaged in controlled transactions. It was suggested that unilateral safe harbours may have a negative impact on the tax revenues of the jurisdiction implementing the safe harbour, as well as on the tax revenues of jurisdictions whose associated enterprises engage in controlled transactions with taxpayers electing a safe harbour. It was further suggested that safe harbours may not be compatible with the arm's length principle. Therefore, it was concluded that transfer pricing safe harbours are not generally advisable, and consequently the use of safe harbours was not recommended.

4.97. Despite these generally negative conclusions, a number of jurisdictions have adopted safe harbour rules. Those rules have generally been applied to smaller taxpayers and/or less complex transactions. They are generally evaluated favourably by both tax administrations and taxpayers, who indicate that the benefits of safe harbours outweigh the related concerns when such rules are carefully targeted and prescribed and when efforts are made to avoid the problems that could arise from poorly considered safe harbour regimes.

4.98. The appropriateness of safe harbours can be expected to be most apparent when they are directed at taxpayers and/or transactions which involve low transfer pricing risks and when they are adopted on a bilateral or multilateral basis. It should be recognised that a safe harbour provision does not bind or limit in any way any tax administration other than the tax administration that has expressly adopted the safe harbour.

4.99. Although safe harbours primarily benefit taxpayers, by providing for a more optimal use of resources, they can benefit tax administrations as well. Tax administrations can shift audit and examination resources from smaller taxpayers and less complex transactions (which may typically be resolved in practice on a consistent basis as to both transfer pricing methodology and actual results) to more complex, higher-risk cases. At the same time, taxpayers can price eligible transactions and file their tax returns with more certainty and with lower compliance burdens. However, the design of safe harbours requires careful attention to concerns about the degree of approximation to arm's length prices that would be permitted in determining transfer prices under safe harbour rules for eligible taxpayers, the potential for creating inappropriate tax planning opportunities including double non-taxation of income, equitable treatment of similarly situated taxpayers, and the potential for double taxation resulting from the possible incompatibility of the safe harbours with the arm's length principle or with the practices of other jurisdictions.

4.100. The following discussion considers the benefits of, and concerns regarding, safe harbour provisions and provides guidance regarding the circumstances in which safe harbours may be applied in a transfer pricing system based on the arm's length principle.

E.2. Definition and concept of safe harbours

4.101. Some of the difficulties that arise in applying the arm's length principle may be avoided by providing circumstances in which eligible taxpayers may elect to follow a simple set of prescribed transfer pricing rules in connection with clearly and carefully defined transactions, or may be exempted from the application of the general transfer pricing rules. In the former case, prices established under such rules would be automatically accepted by the tax administrations that have expressly adopted such rules. These elective provisions are often referred to as "safe harbours".

4.102. A safe harbour in a transfer pricing regime is a provision that applies to a defined category of taxpayers or transactions and that relieves eligible taxpayers from certain obligations otherwise imposed by a jurisdiction's general transfer pricing rules. A safe harbour substitutes simpler obligations for those under the general transfer pricing regime. Such a provision could, for example, allow taxpayers to establish transfer prices in a specific way, e.g. by applying a simplified transfer pricing approach provided by the tax administration. Alternatively, a safe harbour could exempt a defined category of taxpayers or transactions from the application of all or part of the general transfer pricing rules. Often, eligible taxpayers complying with the safe harbour provision will be relieved from burdensome compliance obligations, including some or all associated transfer pricing documentation requirements.

4.103. For purposes of the discussion in this Section, safe harbours do not include administrative simplification measures which do not directly involve determination of arm's length prices, e.g. simplified, or exemption from, documentation requirements (in the absence of a pricing determination), and procedures whereby a tax administration and a taxpayer agree on transfer pricing in advance of the controlled transactions (advance pricing arrangements), which are discussed in Section F of this chapter. The discussion in this section also does not extend to tax provisions designed to prevent "excessive" debt in a foreign subsidiary ("thin capitalisation" rules).

4.104. Although they would not fully meet the foregoing description of a safe harbour, it may be the case that some jurisdictions adopt other administrative simplification measures that use presumptions to realise some of the benefits discussed in this Section. For example, a rebuttable presumption might be established under which a mandatory pricing target would be established by a tax authority, subject to a taxpayer's right to demonstrate that its transfer price is consistent with the arm's length principle. Under such a system, it would be essential that the taxpayer does not bear a higher burden to demonstrate its price is consistent with the arm's length principle than it would if no such system were in place. In any such system, it would be essential to permit resolution of cases of double taxation arising from application of the mandatory presumption through the mutual agreement process.

E.3. Benefits of safe harbours

4.105. The basic benefits of safe harbours are as follows:

1. Simplifying compliance and reducing compliance costs for eligible taxpayers in determining and documenting appropriate conditions for qualifying controlled transactions;
2. Providing certainty to eligible taxpayers that the price charged or paid on qualifying controlled transactions will be accepted by the tax administrations that have adopted the safe harbour with a limited audit or without an audit beyond ensuring the taxpayer has met the eligibility conditions of, and complied with, the safe harbour provisions;

3. Permitting tax administrations to redirect their administrative resources from the examination of lower risk transactions to examinations of more complex or higher risk transactions and taxpayers.

E.3.1. Compliance relief

4.106. Application of the arm's length principle may require collection and analysis of data that may be difficult or costly to obtain and/or evaluate. In certain cases, such compliance burdens may be disproportionate to the size of the taxpayer, its functions performed, and the transfer pricing risks inherent in its controlled transactions.

4.107. Properly designed safe harbours may significantly ease compliance burdens by eliminating data collection and associated documentation requirements in exchange for the taxpayer pricing qualifying transactions within the parameters set by the safe harbour. Especially in areas where transfer pricing risks are small, and the burden of compliance and documentation is disproportionate to the transfer pricing exposure, such a trade-off may be mutually advantageous to taxpayers and tax administrations. Under a safe harbour, taxpayers would be able to establish transfer prices which will not be challenged by tax administrations providing the safe harbour without being obligated to search for comparable transactions or expend resources to demonstrate transfer pricing compliance to such tax administrations.

E.3.2. Certainty

4.108. Another advantage provided by a safe harbour is the certainty that the taxpayer's transfer prices will be accepted by the tax administration providing the safe harbour, provided they have met the eligibility conditions of, and complied with, the safe harbour provisions. The tax administration would accept, with limited or no scrutiny, transfer prices within the safe harbour parameters. Taxpayers could be provided with relevant parameters which would provide a transfer price deemed appropriate by the tax administration for the qualifying transaction.

E.3.3. Administrative simplicity

4.109. A safe harbour would result in a degree of administrative simplicity for the tax administration. Although the eligibility of particular taxpayers or transactions for the safe harbour would need to be carefully evaluated, depending on the specific safe harbour provision, such evaluations would not necessarily have to be performed by auditors with transfer pricing expertise. Once eligibility for the safe harbour has been established, qualifying taxpayers would require minimal examination with respect to the transfer prices of controlled transactions qualifying for the safe harbour. This would enable tax administrations to secure tax revenues in low risk situations with a limited commitment of administrative resources and to concentrate their efforts on the examination of more complex or higher risk transactions and taxpayers. A safe harbour may also increase the level of compliance among small taxpayers that may otherwise believe their transfer pricing practices will escape scrutiny.

E.4. Concerns over safe harbours

4.110. The availability of safe harbours for a given category of taxpayers or transactions may have adverse consequences. These concerns stem from the fact that:

1. The implementation of a safe harbour in a given jurisdiction may lead to taxable income being reported that is not in accordance with the arm's length principle;
2. Safe harbours may increase the risk of double taxation or double non-taxation when adopted unilaterally;
3. Safe harbours potentially open avenues for inappropriate tax planning, and
4. Safe harbours may raise issues of equity and uniformity.

E.4.1. Divergence from the arm's length principle

4.111. Where a safe harbour provides a simplified transfer pricing approach, it may not correspond in all cases to the most appropriate method applicable to the facts and circumstances of the taxpayer under the general transfer pricing provisions. For example, a safe harbour might require the use of a particular method when the taxpayer could otherwise have determined that another method was the most appropriate method under the facts and circumstances. Such an occurrence could be considered as inconsistent with the arm's length principle, which requires the use of the most appropriate method.

4.112. Safe harbours involve a trade off between strict compliance with the arm's length principle and administrability. They are not tailored to fit exactly the varying facts and circumstances of individual taxpayers and transactions. The degree of approximation of prices determined under the safe harbour with prices determined in accordance with the arm's length principle could be improved by collecting, collating, and frequently updating a pool of information regarding prices and pricing developments in respect of the relevant types of transactions between uncontrolled parties of the relevant nature. However, such efforts to set safe harbour parameters accurately enough to satisfy the arm's length principle could erode the administrative simplicity of the safe harbour.

4.113. Any potential disadvantages to taxpayers from safe harbours diverging from arm's length pricing are avoided when taxpayers have the option to either elect the safe harbour or price transactions in accordance with the arm's length principle. With such an approach, taxpayers that believe the safe harbour would require them to report an amount of income exceeding the arm's length amount could apply the general transfer pricing rules. While such an approach can limit the divergence from arm's length pricing under a safe harbour regime, it would also limit the administrative benefits of the safe harbour to the tax administration. Moreover, tax administrations would need to consider the potential loss of tax revenue from such an approach where taxpayers will pay tax only on the lesser of the safe harbour amount or the arm's length amount. Jurisdictions may also be concerned over the ability of taxpayers to opt in and out of a safe harbour, depending on whether the use of the safe harbour is favourable to the taxpayer in a particular year. Jurisdictions may be able to gain greater comfort regarding this risk by controlling the conditions under which a taxpayer can be eligible for the safe harbour, for example by requiring taxpayers to notify the tax authority in advance of using the safe harbour or to commit to its use for a certain number of years.

E.4.2. Risk of double taxation, double non-taxation, and mutual agreement concerns

4.114. One major concern raised by a safe harbour is that it may increase the risk of double taxation. If a tax administration sets safe harbour parameters at levels either above or below arm's length prices in order to increase reported profits in its jurisdiction, it may induce taxpayers to modify the prices that they would otherwise have charged or paid to controlled parties, in order to avoid transfer pricing scrutiny in the safe harbour jurisdiction. The concern of possible overstatement of taxable income in the jurisdiction providing the safe harbour is greater where that jurisdiction imposes significant penalties for understatement of tax or failure to meet documentation requirements, with the result that there may be added incentives to ensure that the transfer pricing is accepted in that jurisdiction without further review.

4.115. If the safe harbour causes taxpayers to report income above arm's length levels, it would work to the benefit of the tax administration providing the safe harbour, as more taxable income would be reported by such domestic taxpayers. On the other hand, the safe harbour may lead to less taxable income being reported in the tax jurisdiction of the foreign associated enterprise that is the other party to the transaction. The other tax administrations may then challenge prices derived from the application of a safe harbour, with the result that the taxpayer would face the prospect of double taxation. Accordingly, any administrative benefits gained by the tax administration of the safe harbour jurisdiction would potentially be obtained at the expense of other jurisdictions which, in order to protect their own tax base, would have to determine systematically whether the prices or results permitted under the safe harbour are consistent with what would be obtained by the application of their own transfer pricing rules. The administrative burden saved by the jurisdiction offering the safe harbour would therefore be shifted to the foreign jurisdictions.

4.116. In cases involving smaller taxpayers or less complex transactions, the benefits of safe harbours may outweigh the problems raised by such provisions. Provided the safe harbour is elective, taxpayers may consider that a moderate level of double taxation, if any arises because of the safe harbour, is an acceptable price to be paid in order to obtain relief from the necessity of complying with complex transfer pricing rules. One may argue that the taxpayer is capable of making its own decision in electing the safe harbour as to whether the possibility of double taxation is acceptable or not.

4.117. Where safe harbours are adopted unilaterally, care should be taken in setting safe harbour parameters to avoid double taxation, and the jurisdiction adopting the safe harbour should generally be prepared to consider modification of the safe-harbour outcome in individual cases under mutual agreement procedures to mitigate the risk of double taxation. At a minimum, in order to ensure that taxpayers make decisions on a fully informed basis, the jurisdiction offering the safe harbour would need to make it explicit in advance whether or not it would attempt to alleviate any eventual double taxation resulting from the use of the safe harbour. Obviously, if a safe harbour is not elective and if the jurisdiction in question refuses to consider double tax relief, the risk of double taxation arising from the safe harbour would be unacceptably high and inconsistent with double tax relief provisions of treaties.

4.118. On the other hand, if a unilateral safe harbour permits taxpayers to report income below arm's length levels in the jurisdiction providing the safe harbour, taxpayers would have an incentive to elect application of the safe harbour. In such a case, there would be no assurance that the taxpayer would report income in other jurisdictions on a consistent basis or at levels above arm's length levels based on the safe harbour. Moreover it is unlikely that other tax administrations would have the authority to require that income be reported above arm's length levels. While the burden of under taxation in such situations would fall exclusively upon the jurisdiction adopting the safe harbour provision, and should not adversely affect the ability of other jurisdictions to tax arm's length amounts of income, double non-taxation would be unavoidable and could result in distortions of investment and trade.

4.119. It is important to observe that the problems of non-arm's length results and potential double taxation and double non-taxation arising under safe harbours could be largely eliminated if safe harbours were adopted on a bilateral or multilateral basis by means of competent authority agreements between jurisdictions. Under such a procedure, two or more jurisdictions could, by agreement, define a category of taxpayers and/or transactions to which a safe harbour provision would apply and by agreement establish pricing parameters that would be accepted by each of the contracting jurisdictions if consistently applied in each of the jurisdictions. Such agreements could be published in advance and taxpayers could consistently report results in each of the affected jurisdictions in accordance with the agreement.

4.120. The rigor of having two or more jurisdictions with potentially divergent interests agree to such a safe harbour should serve to limit some of the arbitrariness that otherwise might characterise a unilateral safe harbour and would largely eliminate safe harbour-created double taxation and double non-taxation concerns. Particularly for some smaller taxpayers and/or less complex transactions, creation of bilateral or multilateral safe harbours by competent authority agreement may provide a worthwhile approach to transfer pricing simplification that would avoid some of the potential pitfalls of unilateral safe harbour regimes.

4.121. The Annex I to Chapter IV of these Guidelines contains sample memoranda of understanding that competent authorities might use to establish bilateral or multilateral safe harbours in appropriate situations for common classes of transfer pricing cases. The use of these sample memoranda of understanding should not be considered as either mandatory or prescriptive in establishing bilateral or multilateral safe harbours. Rather, they are intended to provide a possible framework for adaptation to the particular needs of the tax authorities of the jurisdictions concerned.

E.4.3. Possibility of opening avenues for tax planning

4.122. Safe harbours may also provide taxpayers with tax planning opportunities. Enterprises may have an incentive to modify their transfer prices in order to shift taxable income to other jurisdictions. This may also possibly induce tax avoidance, to the extent that artificial arrangements are entered into for the purpose of exploiting the safe harbour provisions. For instance, if safe harbours apply to "simple" or "small" transactions, taxpayers may be tempted to break transactions up into parts to make them seem simple or small.

4.123. If a safe harbour were based on an industry average, tax planning opportunities might exist for taxpayers with better than average profitability. For example, a cost-efficient company selling at the arm's length price may be earning a mark-up of 15% on controlled sales. If a jurisdiction adopts a safe harbour requiring a 10% mark-up, the company might have an incentive to comply with the safe harbour and shift the remaining 5% to a lower tax jurisdiction. Consequently, taxable income would be shifted out of the jurisdiction. When applied on a large scale, this could mean significant revenue loss for the jurisdiction offering the safe harbour.

4.124. This concern may largely be avoided by the solution noted in paragraph 4.119 of adopting safe harbours on a bilateral or multilateral basis, thus limiting application of safe harbours to transactions involving jurisdictions with similar transfer pricing concerns. In adopting bilateral and multilateral safe harbours, tax administrations would need to be aware that the establishment of an extensive network of such arrangements could potentially encourage "safe harbour shopping" via the routing of transactions through territories with more favourable safe harbours and take appropriate steps to avoid that possibility. Similarly, jurisdictions adopting bilateral safe harbours would be well advised to target fairly narrow ranges of acceptable results and to require consistent reporting of income in each jurisdiction that is a party to the safe harbour arrangement. Treaty exchange of information provisions could be used by jurisdictions where necessary to confirm the use of consistent reporting under such a bilateral safe harbour.

4.125. Whether a jurisdiction is prepared to possibly suffer some erosion of its own tax base in implementing a safe harbour is for that jurisdiction to decide. The basic trade-off in making such a policy decision is between the certainty and administrative simplicity of the safe harbour for taxpayers and tax administrations on the one hand, and the possibility of tax revenue erosion on the other.

E.4.4. Equity and uniformity issues

4.126. Safe harbours may raise equity and uniformity issues. By implementing a safe harbour, one would create two distinct sets of rules in the transfer pricing area. Clearly and carefully designed criteria are required to differentiate those taxpayers or transactions eligible for the safe harbour to minimise the possibility of similar and possibly competing taxpayers finding themselves on opposite sides of the safe harbour threshold or, conversely, of allowing application of the safe harbour to unintended taxpayers or transactions. Insufficiently precise criteria could result in similar taxpayers receiving different tax treatment: one being permitted to meet the safe harbour rules and thus to be relieved from general transfer pricing compliance provisions, and the other being obliged to price its transactions in conformity with the general transfer pricing compliance provisions. Preferential tax treatment under safe harbour regimes for a specific category of taxpayers could potentially entail discrimination and competitive distortions. The adoption of bilateral or multilateral safe harbours could, in some circumstances, increase the potential of a divergence in tax treatment, not merely between different but similar taxpayers but also between similar transactions carried out by the same taxpayer with associated enterprises in different jurisdictions.

E.5. Recommendations on use of safe harbours

4.127. Transfer pricing compliance and administration is often complex, time consuming and costly. Properly designed safe harbour provisions, applied in appropriate circumstances, can help to relieve some of these burdens and provide taxpayers with greater certainty.

4.128. Safe harbour provisions may raise issues such as potentially having perverse effects on the pricing decisions of enterprises engaged in controlled transactions and a negative impact on the tax revenues of the jurisdiction implementing the safe harbour as well as on the jurisdictions whose associated enterprises engage in controlled transactions with taxpayers electing a safe harbour. Further, unilateral safe harbours may lead to the potential for double taxation or double non-taxation.

4.129. However, in cases involving smaller taxpayers or less complex transactions, the benefits of safe harbours may outweigh the problems raised by such provisions. Making such safe harbours elective to taxpayers can further limit the divergence from arm's length pricing. Where jurisdictions adopt safe harbours, willingness to modify safe-harbour outcomes in mutual agreement proceedings to limit the potential risk of double taxation is advisable.

4.130. Where safe harbours can be negotiated on a bilateral or multilateral basis, they may provide significant relief from compliance burdens and administrative complexity without creating problems of double taxation or double non-taxation. Therefore, the use of bilateral or multilateral safe harbours under the right circumstances should be encouraged.

4.131. It should be clearly recognised that a safe harbour, whether adopted on a unilateral or bilateral basis, is in no way binding on or precedential for jurisdictions which have not themselves adopted the safe harbour.

4.132. For more complex and higher risk transfer pricing matters, it is unlikely that safe harbours will provide a workable alternative to a rigorous, case by case application of the arm's length principle under the provisions of these Guidelines.

4.133. Tax administrations in each jurisdiction should carefully weigh the benefits of and concerns regarding safe harbours, making use of such provisions where they deem it appropriate.

F. Advance pricing arrangements[6]

F.1. Definition and concept of advance pricing arrangements

4.134. An advance pricing arrangement (APA) is an arrangement that determines, in advance of controlled transactions, an appropriate set of criteria (e.g. method, comparables and appropriate adjustments thereto, critical assumptions as to future events) for the determination of the transfer pricing for those transactions over a fixed period of time. An APA is formally initiated by a taxpayer and requires negotiations between the taxpayer, one or more associated enterprises, and one or more tax administrations. APAs are intended to supplement the traditional administrative, judicial, and treaty mechanisms for resolving transfer pricing issues. They may be most useful when traditional mechanisms fail or are difficult to apply. Detailed guidelines for conducting advance pricing arrangements under the mutual agreement procedure (MAP APAs) were adopted in October 1999 and are found as an Annex to this chapter. The work pursuant to Action 14 of the BEPS Action Plan to ensure the timely, effective and efficient resolution of treaty-related disputes recommended, as non-binding best practice 4, that jurisdictions should implement bilateral APA programmes as soon as they have the capacity to do so, recognising that APAs provide a greater level of certainty in both treaty partner jurisdictions, lessen the likelihood of double taxation and may proactively prevent transfer pricing disputes. In this regard, it should be noted that the country mutual agreement procedure profiles prepared pursuant to element 2.2 of the Action 14 minimum standard include information on the bilateral APA programmes.

4.135. One key issue in the concept of APAs is how specific they can be in prescribing a taxpayer's transfer pricing over a period of years, for example whether only the transfer pricing methodology or more particular results can be fixed in a particular case. In general, great care must be taken if the APA goes beyond the methodology, the way it will be applied, and the critical assumptions, because more specific conclusions rely on predictions about future events.

4.136. The reliability of any prediction used in an APA depends both on the nature of the prediction and the critical assumptions on which the prediction is based. For example, it would not be reasonable to assert that the arm's length short-term borrowing rate for a certain corporation on intra-group borrowings will remain at 6% during the entire coming three years. It would be more plausible to predict that the rate will be LIBOR plus a fixed percentage. The prediction would become even more reliable if an

6. Additional guidance for conducting Advance Pricing Arrangements under the Mutual Agreement Procedure is found in Annex II to Chapter IV.

appropriate critical assumption were added regarding the company's credit rating (e.g. the addition to LIBOR will change if the credit rating changes).

4.137. As another example, it would not be appropriate to specify a profit split formula between associated enterprises if it is expected that the allocation of functions between the enterprises will be unstable. It would, however, be possible to prescribe a profit split formula if the role of each enterprise were articulated in critical assumptions. In certain cases, it might even be possible to make a reasonable prediction on the appropriateness of an actual profit split ratio if enough assumptions were provided.

4.138. In deciding how specific an APA can be in a particular case, tax administrations should recognise that predictions of absolute future profit experience seems least plausible. It may be possible to use profit ratios of independent enterprises as comparables, but these also are often volatile and hard to predict. Use of appropriate critical assumptions and use of ranges may enhance the reliability of predictions. Historical data in the industry in question can also be a guide.

4.139. In sum, the reliability of a prediction depends on the facts and circumstances of each actual case. Taxpayers and tax administrations need to pay close attention to the reliability of a prediction when considering the scope of an APA. Unreliable predictions should not be included in APAs. The appropriateness of a method and its application can usually be predicted, and the relevant critical assumptions made, with more reliability than future results (price or profit level).

4.140. Some jurisdictions allow for unilateral arrangements where the tax administration and the taxpayer in its jurisdiction establish an arrangement without the involvement of other interested tax administrations. However, a unilateral APA may affect the tax liability of associated enterprises in other tax jurisdictions. Where unilateral APAs are permitted, the competent authorities of other interested jurisdictions should be informed about the procedure as early as possible to determine whether they are willing and able to consider a bilateral arrangement under the mutual agreement procedure. In any event, jurisdictions should not include in any unilateral APA they may conclude with a taxpayer a requirement that the taxpayer waive access to the mutual agreement procedure if a transfer pricing dispute arises, and if another jurisdiction raises a transfer pricing adjustment with respect to a transaction or issue covered by the unilateral APA, the first jurisdiction is encouraged to consider the appropriateness of a corresponding adjustment and not to view the unilateral APA as an irreversible settlement.

4.141. Because of concerns over double taxation, most jurisdictions prefer bilateral or multilateral APAs (i.e. an arrangement in which two or more jurisdictions concur), and indeed some jurisdictions will not grant a unilateral

APA (i.e. an arrangement between the taxpayer and one tax administration) to taxpayers in their jurisdiction. The bilateral (or multilateral) approach is far more likely to ensure that the arrangements will reduce the risk of double taxation, will be equitable to all tax administrations and taxpayers involved, and will provide greater certainty to the taxpayers concerned. It is also the case in some jurisdictions that domestic provisions do not permit the tax administrations to enter into binding agreements directly with the taxpayers, so that APAs can be concluded with the competent authority of a treaty partner only under the mutual agreement procedure. For purposes of the discussion in this section, an APA is not intended to include a unilateral arrangement except where specific reference to a unilateral APA is made.

4.142. Tax administrations may find APAs particularly useful in profit allocation or income attribution issues arising in the context of global securities and commodity trading operations, and also in handling multilateral cost contribution arrangements. The concept of APAs also may be useful in resolving issues raised under Article 7 of the OECD Model Tax Convention relating to allocation problems, permanent establishments, and branch operations.

4.143. APAs, including unilateral ones, differ in some ways from more traditional private rulings that some tax administrations issue to taxpayers. An APA generally deals with factual issues, whereas more traditional private rulings tend to be limited to addressing questions of a legal nature based on facts presented by a taxpayer. The facts underlying a private ruling request may not be questioned by the tax administration, whereas in an APA the facts are likely to be thoroughly analysed and investigated. In addition, an APA usually covers several transactions, several types of transactions on a continuing basis, or all of a taxpayer's international transactions for a given period of time. In contrast, a private ruling request usually is binding only for a particular transaction.

4.144. The co-operation of the associated enterprises is vital to a successful APA negotiation. For example, the associated enterprises ordinarily would be expected to provide the tax administrations with the methodology that they consider most reasonable under the particular facts and circumstances. The associated enterprises also should submit documentation supporting the reasonableness of their proposal, which would include, for example, data relating to the industry, markets, and jurisdictions to be covered by the agreement. In addition, the associated enterprises may identify uncontrolled businesses that are comparable or similar to the associated enterprises' businesses in terms of the economic activities performed and the transfer pricing conditions, e.g. economic costs and risks incurred, and perform a functional analysis as described in Chapter I of these Guidelines.

4.145. Typically, associated enterprises are allowed to participate in the process of obtaining an APA, by presenting the case to and negotiating with the tax administrations concerned, providing necessary information, and reaching agreement on the transfer pricing issues. From the associated enterprises' perspective, this ability to participate may be seen as an advantage over the conventional mutual agreement procedure.

4.146. At the conclusion of an APA process, the tax administrations should provide confirmation to the associated enterprises in their jurisdiction that no transfer pricing adjustment will be made as long as the taxpayer follows the terms of the arrangements. There should also be a provision in an APA (perhaps by reference to a range) that provides for possible revision or cancellation of the arrangement for future years when business operations change significantly, or when uncontrolled economic circumstances (e.g. significant changes in currency exchange rates) critically affect the reliability of the methodology in a manner that independent enterprises would consider significant for purposes of their transfer pricing.

4.147. An APA may cover all of the transfer pricing issues of a taxpayer (as is preferred by some jurisdictions) or may provide a flexibility to the taxpayer to limit the APA request to specified affiliates and intercompany transactions. An APA would apply to prospective years and transactions and the actual term would depend on the industry, products or transactions involved. The associated enterprises may limit their request to specified prospective tax years. An APA can provide an opportunity to apply the agreed transfer pricing methodology to resolve similar transfer pricing issues in open prior years. However, this application would require the agreement of the tax administration, the taxpayer, and, where appropriate, the treaty partner. Element 2.7 of the Action 14 minimum standard states that jurisdictions with bilateral APA programmes should provide for the roll-back of APAs (to previous filed tax years not included within the original scope of the APA) in appropriate cases, subject to the applicable time limits (such as domestic law statutes of limitation for assessments) where the relevant facts and circumstances in the earlier tax years are the same and subject to the verification of these facts and circumstances on audit.

4.148. Each tax administration involved in the APA will naturally wish to monitor compliance with the APA by the taxpayers in its jurisdiction, and this is generally done in two ways. First, it may require a taxpayer that has entered into an APA to file annual reports demonstrating the extent of its compliance with the terms and conditions of the APA and that critical assumptions remain relevant. Second, the tax administration may continue to examine the taxpayer as part of the regular audit cycle but without re-evaluating the methodology. Instead, the tax administration may limit the examination of the transfer pricing to verifying the initial data relevant to the APA proposal and determining whether or not the taxpayer has complied with the terms and conditions of the APA. With regard to transfer pricing, a tax administration may also examine the reliability and accuracy of the representations in the APA and annual reports and the accuracy and consistency of how the particular methodology has been applied. All other issues not associated with the APA fall under regular audit jurisdiction.

4.149. An APA should be subject to cancellation, even retroactively, in the case of fraud or misrepresentation of information during an APA negotiation, or when a taxpayer fails to comply with the terms and conditions of an APA. Where an APA is proposed to be cancelled or revoked, the tax administration proposing the action should notify the other tax administrations of its intention and of the reasons for such action.

F.2. Possible approaches for legal and administrative rules governing advance pricing arrangements

4.150. APAs involving the competent authority of a treaty partner should be considered within the scope of the mutual agreement procedure under Article 25 of the OECD Model Tax Convention, even though such arrangements are not expressly mentioned there. Paragraph 3 of that Article provides that the competent authorities shall endeavour to resolve by mutual agreement any difficulties or doubts arising as to the interpretation or application of the Convention. Although paragraph 50 of the Commentary indicates that the matters covered by this paragraph are difficulties of a general nature concerning a category of taxpayers, it specifically acknowledges that the issues may arise in connection with an individual case. In a number of cases, APAs arise from cases where the application of transfer pricing to a particular category of taxpayer gives rise to doubts and difficulties. Paragraph 3 of Article 25 also indicates that the competent authorities may consult together for the elimination of double taxation in cases not provided for in the Convention. Bilateral APAs should fall within this provision because they have as one of their objectives the avoidance of double taxation. Even though the Convention provides for transfer pricing adjustments, it specifies no particular methodologies or procedures other than the arm's length principle as set out in Article 9. Thus, it could be considered that APAs are authorised by paragraph 3 of Article 25 because the specific transfer pricing cases subject to an APA are not otherwise provided for in the Convention. The exchange of information provision in Article 26 also could facilitate APAs, as it provides for co-operation between competent authorities in the form of exchanges of information.

4.151. Tax administrations might additionally rely on general domestic authority to administer taxes as the authority for entering into APAs. In some jurisdictions tax administrations may be able to issue specific administrative or procedural guidelines to taxpayers describing the appropriate tax treatment of transactions and the appropriate pricing methodology. As mentioned above, the tax codes of some OECD member countries include provisions that allow taxpayers to obtain specific rulings for different purposes. Even though these rulings were not designed specifically to cover APAs, they may be broad enough to be used to include APAs.

4.152. Some jurisdictions lack the basis in their domestic law to enter into APAs. However, when a tax convention contains a clause regarding the mutual agreement procedure similar to Article 25 of the OECD Model Tax Convention, the competent authorities generally should be allowed to conclude an APA, if transfer pricing issues were otherwise likely to result in double taxation, or would raise difficulties or doubts as to the interpretation or application of the Convention. Such an arrangement would be legally binding for both States and would create rights for the taxpayers involved. Inasmuch as double tax treaties take precedence over domestic law, the lack of a basis in domestic law to enter into APAs would not prevent application of APAs on the basis of a mutual agreement procedure.

F.3. Advantages of advance pricing arrangements

4.153. An APA programme can assist taxpayers by eliminating uncertainty through enhancing the predictability of tax treatment in international transactions. Provided the critical assumptions are met, an APA can provide the taxpayers involved with certainty in the tax treatment of the transfer pricing issues covered by the APA for a specified period of time. In some cases, an APA may also provide an option to extend the period of time to which it applies. When the term of an APA expires, the opportunity may also exist for the relevant tax administrations and taxpayers to renegotiate the APA. Because of the certainty provided by an APA, a taxpayer may be in a better position to predict its tax liabilities, thereby providing a tax environment that is favourable for investment.

4.154. APAs can provide an opportunity for both tax administrations and taxpayers to consult and co-operate in a non-adversarial spirit and environment. The opportunity to discuss complex tax issues in a less confrontational atmosphere than in a transfer pricing examination can stimulate a free flow of information among all parties involved for the purpose of coming to a legally correct and practicably workable result. The non-adversarial environment may also result in a more objective review of the submitted data and information than may occur in a more adversarial context (e.g. litigation). The close consultation and co-operation required between the tax administrations in an APA programme also leads to closer relations with treaty partners on transfer pricing issues.

4.155. An APA may prevent costly and time-consuming examinations and litigation of major transfer pricing issues for taxpayers and tax administrations. Once an APA has been agreed, less resources may be needed for subsequent examination of the taxpayer's return, because more information is known about the taxpayer. It may still be difficult, however, to monitor the application of the arrangement. The APA process itself may also present time savings for both taxpayers and tax administrations over the time that would be spent in a conventional examination, although in the aggregate there may be no net time savings, for example, in jurisdictions that do not have an audit procedure and where the existence of an APA may not directly affect the amount of resources devoted to compliance.

4.156. Bilateral and multilateral APAs substantially reduce or eliminate the possibility of juridical or economic double or non taxation since all the relevant jurisdictions participate. By contrast, unilateral APAs do not provide certainty in the reduction of double taxation because tax administrations affected by the transactions covered by the APA may consider that the methodology adopted does not give a result consistent with the arm's length principle. In addition, bilateral and multilateral APAs can enhance the mutual agreement procedure by significantly reducing the time needed to reach an agreement since competent authorities are dealing with current data as opposed to prior year data that may be difficult and time-consuming to produce.

4.157. The disclosure and information aspects of an APA programme as well as the co-operative attitude under which an APA can be negotiated may assist tax administrations in gaining insight into complex international transactions undertaken by MNEs. An APA programme can improve knowledge and understanding of highly technical and factual circumstances in areas such as global trading and the tax issues involved. The development of specialist skills that focus on particular industries or specific types of transactions will enable tax administrations to give better service to other taxpayers in similar circumstances. Through an APA programme tax administrations have access to useful industry data and analysis of pricing methodologies in a co-operative environment.

F.4. Disadvantages relating to advance pricing arrangements

4.158. Unilateral APAs may present significant problems for tax administrations and taxpayers alike. From the point of view of other tax administrations, problems arise because they may disagree with the APA's conclusions. From the point of view of the associated enterprises involved, one problem is the possible effect on the behaviour of the associated enterprises. Unlike bilateral or multilateral APAs, the use of unilateral APAs may not lead to an increased level of certainty for the taxpayer involved and a reduction in economic or juridical double taxation for the MNE group. If the taxpayer accepts an arrangement that over-allocates income to the jurisdiction making the APA in order to avoid lengthy and expensive transfer pricing enquiries or excessive penalties, the administrative burden shifts from the jurisdiction providing the

APA to other tax jurisdictions. Taxpayers should not feel compelled to enter into APAs for these reasons.

4.159. Another problem with a unilateral APA is the issue of corresponding adjustments. The flexibility of an APA may lead the taxpayer and the associated party to accommodate their pricing to the range of permissible pricing in the APA. In a unilateral APA, it is critical that this flexibility preserve the arm's length principle since a foreign competent authority is not likely to allow a corresponding adjustment arising out of an APA that is inconsistent, in its view, with the arm's length principle.

4.160. Another possible disadvantage would arise if an APA involved an unreliable prediction on changing market conditions without adequate critical assumptions, as discussed above. To avoid the risk of double taxation, it is necessary for an APA programme to remain flexible, because a static APA may not satisfactorily reflect arm's length conditions.

4.161. An APA programme may initially place a strain on transfer pricing audit resources, as tax administrations will generally have to divert resources earmarked for other purposes (e.g. examination, advising, litigation, etc.) to the APA programme. Demands may be made on the resources of a tax administration by taxpayers seeking the earliest possible conclusion to an APA request, keeping in mind their business objectives and time scales, and the APA programme as a whole will tend to be led by the demands of the business community. These demands may not coincide with the resource planning of the tax administrations, thereby making it difficult to process efficiently both the APAs and other equally important work. Renewing an APA, however, is likely to be less time-consuming than the process of initiating an APA. The renewal process may focus on updating and adjusting facts, business and economic criteria, and computations. In the case of bilateral arrangements, the agreement of the competent authorities of both Contracting States is to be obtained on the renewal of an APA to avoid double taxation (or non-taxation).

4.162. Another potential disadvantage could occur where one tax administration has undertaken a number of bilateral APAs which involve only certain of the associated enterprises within an MNE group. A tendency may exist to harmonise the basis for concluding later APAs in a way similar to those previously concluded without sufficient regard being had to the conditions operating in other markets. Care should therefore be taken with interpreting the results of previously concluded APAs as being representative across all markets.

4.163. Concerns have also been expressed that, because of the nature of the APA procedure, it will interest taxpayers with a good voluntary compliance history. Experience in some jurisdictions has shown that, most often, taxpayers which would be interested in APAs are very large corporations which would be audited on a regular basis, with their pricing methodology then being examined in any event. The difference in the examination conducted of their transfer pricing would be one of timing rather than extent. As well, it has not been demonstrated that APAs will be of interest solely or principally to such taxpayers. Indeed, there are some early indications that taxpayers, having experienced difficulty with tax administrations on transfer pricing issues and not wishing these difficulties to continue, are often interested in applying for an APA. There is then a serious danger of audit resources and expertise being diverted to these taxpayers and away from the investigation of less compliant taxpayers, where these resources could be better deployed in reducing the risk of losing tax revenue. The balance of compliance resources may be particularly difficult to achieve since an APA programme tends to require highly experienced and often specialised staff. Requests for APAs may be concentrated in particular areas or sectors, e.g. global trading, and this can overstretch the specialist resources already allocated to those areas by the authorities. Tax administrations require time to train experts in specialist fields in order to meet unforeseeable demands from taxpayers for APAs in those areas.

4.164. In addition to the foregoing concerns, there are a number of possible pitfalls as described below that could arise if an APA programme were improperly administered, and tax administrations who use APAs should make strong efforts to eliminate the occurrence of these problems as APA practice evolves.

4.165. For example, an APA might seek more detailed industry and taxpayer specific information than would be requested in a transfer pricing examination. In principle, this should not be the case and the documentation required for an APA should not be more onerous than for an examination, except for the fact that in an APA the tax administration will need to have details of predictions and the basis for those predictions, which may not be central issues in a transfer pricing examination that focuses on completed transactions. In fact, an APA should seek to limit the documentation, as discussed above, and focus the documentation more closely on the issues in light of the taxpayer's business practices. Tax administrations need to recognise that:

a) Publicly available information on competitors and comparables is limited;

b) Not all taxpayers have the capacity to undertake in-depth market analyses; and,

c) Only parent companies may be knowledgeable about group pricing policies.

4.166. Another possible concern is that an APA may allow the tax administration to make a closer study of the transactions at issue than would occur in the context of a transfer pricing examination, depending on the facts and circumstances. The taxpayer must provide detailed information relating to its transfer pricing and satisfy any other requirements imposed for the verification of compliance with the terms and conditions of the APA. At the same time, the taxpayer is not sheltered from normal and routine examinations by the tax administration on other issues. An APA also does not shelter a taxpayer from examination of its transfer pricing activities. The taxpayer may still have to establish that it has complied in good faith with the terms and conditions of the APA, that the material representations in the APA remain valid, that the supporting data used in applying the methodology were correct, that the critical assumptions underlying the APA are still valid and are applied consistently, and that the methodology is applied consistently. Tax administrations should, therefore, seek to ensure that APA procedures are not unnecessarily cumbersome and that they do not make more demand of taxpayers than are strictly required by the scope of the APA application.

4.167. Problems could also develop if tax administrations misuse information obtained in an APA in their examination practices. If the taxpayer withdraws from its APA request or if the taxpayer's application is rejected after consideration of all of the facts, any nonfactual information provided by the taxpayer in connection with the APA request, such as settlement offers, reasoning, opinions, and judgments, cannot be treated as relevant in any respect to the examination. In addition, the fact that a taxpayer has applied unsuccessfully for an APA should not be taken into account by the tax administration in determining whether to commence an examination of that taxpayer.

4.168. Tax administrations also should ensure the confidentiality of trade secrets and other sensitive information and documentation submitted to them in the course of an APA proceeding. Therefore, domestic rules against disclosure should be applied. In a bilateral APA the confidentiality requirements on treaty partners would apply, thereby preventing public disclosure of confidential data.

4.169. An APA programme cannot be used by all taxpayers because the procedure can be expensive and time-consuming and small taxpayers generally may not be able to afford it. This is especially true if independent experts are involved. APAs may therefore only assist in resolving mainly large transfer pricing cases. In addition, the resource implications of an APA programme may limit the number of requests a tax administration can entertain. In evaluating APAs, tax administrations can alleviate these potential problems by ensuring that the level of inquiry is adjusted to the size of the international transactions involved.

F.5. Recommendations

F.5.1. In general

4.170. Since the Guidelines were published in their original version in 1995, a significant number of OECD member countries have acquired experience with APAs. Those jurisdictions which do have some experience seem to be satisfied so far, so that it can be expected that under the appropriate circumstances the experience with APAs will continue to expand. The success of APA programmes will depend on the care taken in determining the proper degree of specificity for the arrangement based on critical assumptions, the proper administration of the programme, and the presence of adequate safeguards to avoid the pitfalls described above, in addition to the flexibility and openness with which all parties approach the process.

4.171. There are some continuing issues regarding the form and scope of APAs that require greater experience for full resolution and agreement among member countries, such as the question of unilateral APAs. The Committee on Fiscal Affairs intends to monitor carefully any expanded use of APAs and to promote greater consistency in practice among those countries that choose to use them.

F.5.2. Coverage of an arrangement

4.172. When considering the scope of an APA, taxpayers and tax administrations need to pay close attention to the reliability of any predictions so as to exclude unreliable predictions. In general, great care must be taken if the APA goes beyond the methodology, its application, and critical assumptions. See paragraphs 4.134-4.139.

F.5.3. Unilateral versus bilateral (multilateral) arrangements

4.173. Wherever possible, an APA should be concluded on a bilateral or multilateral basis between competent authorities through the mutual agreement procedure of the relevant treaty. A bilateral APA carries less risk of taxpayers feeling compelled to enter into an APA or to accept a non-arm's-length agreement in order to avoid expensive and prolonged enquiries and possible penalties. A bilateral APA also significantly reduces the chance of any profits either escaping tax altogether or being doubly taxed, Moreover, concluding an APA through the mutual agreement procedure may be the only form that can be adopted by a tax administration which lacks domestic legislation to conclude binding agreements directly with the taxpayer.

F.5.4. Equitable access to APAs for all taxpayers

4.174. As discussed above, the nature of APA proceedings may *de facto* limit their accessibility to large taxpayers. The restriction of APAs to large taxpayers may raise questions of equality and uniformity, since taxpayers in identical situations should not be treated differently. A flexible allocation of examination resources may alleviate these concerns. Tax administrations also may need to consider the possibility of adopting a streamlined access for small taxpayers. Tax administrations should take care to adapt their levels of inquiry, in evaluating APAs, to the size of the international transactions involved.

F.5.5. Developing working agreements between competent authorities and improved procedures

4.175. Between those jurisdictions that use APAs, greater uniformity in APA practices could be beneficial to both tax administrations and taxpayers. Accordingly, the tax administrations of such jurisdictions may wish to consider working agreements with the competent authorities for the undertaking of APAs. These agreements may set forth general guidelines and understandings for the reaching of mutual agreement in cases where a taxpayer has requested an APA involving transfer pricing issues.

4.176. In addition, bilateral APAs with treaty partners should conform to certain requirements. For example, the same necessary and pertinent information should be made available to each tax administration at the same time, and the agreed upon methodology should be in accordance with the arm's length principle.

G. Arbitration

4.177. As trade and investment have taken on an increasingly international character, the tax disputes that, on occasion, arise from such activities have likewise become increasingly international. And more particularly, the disputes no longer involve simply controversy between a taxpayer and its tax administration but also concern disagreements between tax administrations themselves. In many of these situations, the MNE group is primarily a stakeholder and the real parties in interest are the governments involved. Although traditionally problems of double taxation have been resolved through the mutual agreement procedure, relief is not guaranteed if the tax administrations, after consultation, cannot reach an agreement on their own and if there is no mechanism, such as an arbitration clause similar to the one of paragraph 5 of Article 25, to provide the possibility of a resolution. However, where a particular tax treaty contains an arbitration clause similar to the one of paragraph 5 of Article 25, this extension of the mutual agreement procedure makes a resolution of the case still possible by submitting one or more issues on which the competent authorities cannot reach an agreement to arbitration.

4.178. In the 2008 update to the OECD Model Tax Convention, Article 25 was supplemented with a new paragraph 5 which provides that, in the cases where the competent authorities are unable to reach an agreement within two years, the unresolved issues will, at the request of the person who presented the case, be solved through an arbitration process. This extension of the mutual agreement procedure ensures that where the competent authorities cannot reach an agreement on one or more issues that prevent the resolution of a case, a resolution of the case will still be possible by submitting those issues to arbitration. Arbitration under paragraph 5 of Article 25 is an integral part of the mutual agreement procedure and does not constitute an alternative route to solving tax treaty disputes between States. Paragraphs 63-85 of the Commentary on Article 25 provide guidance on the arbitration phase of the mutual agreement procedure.

4.179. The existence of an arbitration clause similar to paragraph 5 of Article 25 in a particular bilateral treaty should make the mutual agreement procedure itself more effective even in cases where resort to arbitration is not necessary. The very existence of this possibility should encourage greater use of the mutual agreement procedure since both governments and taxpayers will know at the outset that the time and effort put into the mutual agreement procedure will be likely to produce a satisfactory result. Further, governments will have an incentive to ensure that the mutual agreement procedure is conducted efficiently in order to avoid the necessity of subsequent supplemental procedures.

Chapter V

Documentation

A. Introduction

5.1. This chapter provides guidance for tax administrations to take into account in developing rules and/or procedures on documentation to be obtained from taxpayers in connection with a transfer pricing enquiry or risk assessment. It also provides guidance to assist taxpayers in identifying documentation that would be most helpful in showing that their transactions satisfy the arm's length principle and hence in resolving transfer pricing issues and facilitating tax examinations.

5.2. When Chapter V of these Guidelines was adopted in 1995, tax administrations and taxpayers had less experience in creating and using transfer pricing documentation. The previous language in Chapter V of the Guidelines put an emphasis on the need for reasonableness in the documentation process from the perspective of both taxpayers and tax administrations, as well as on the desire for a greater level of co-operation between tax administrations and taxpayers in addressing documentation issues in order to avoid excessive documentation compliance burdens while at the same time providing for adequate information to apply the arm's length principle reliably. The previous language of Chapter V did not provide for a list of documents to be included in a transfer pricing documentation package nor did it provide clear guidance with respect to the link between the process for documenting transfer pricing, the administration of penalties and the burden of proof.

5.3. Since then, many jurisdictions have adopted transfer pricing documentation rules and the proliferation of these requirements, combined with a sharp increase in the volume and complexity of international intra-group trade and the heightened scrutiny of transfer pricing issues by tax administrations, has resulted in a significant increase in compliance costs for taxpayers. Nevertheless tax administrations have often found transfer pricing documentation to be less than fully informative and not adequate for their tax enforcement and risk assessment needs.

5.4. The following discussion identifies three objectives of transfer pricing documentation rules. The discussion also provides guidance for the development of such rules so that transfer pricing compliance is more straightforward and more consistent among jurisdictions, while at the same time providing tax administrations with more focused and useful information for transfer pricing risk assessments and audits. An important overarching consideration in developing such rules is to balance the usefulness of the data to tax administrations for transfer pricing risk assessment and other purposes with any increased compliance burdens placed on taxpayers. In this respect it is noted that clear and widely adopted documentation rules can reduce compliance costs which could otherwise arise in a transfer pricing dispute.

B. Objectives of transfer pricing documentation requirements

5.5. Three objectives of transfer pricing documentation are:

1. to ensure that taxpayers give appropriate consideration to transfer pricing requirements in establishing prices and other conditions for transactions between associated enterprises and in reporting the income derived from such transactions in their tax returns;
2. to provide tax administrations with the information necessary to conduct an informed transfer pricing risk assessment; and
3. to provide tax administrations with useful information to employ in conducting an appropriately thorough audit of the transfer pricing practices of entities subject to tax in their jurisdiction, although it may be necessary to supplement the documentation with additional information as the audit progresses.

5.6. Each of these objectives should be considered in designing appropriate domestic transfer pricing documentation requirements. It is important that taxpayers be required to carefully evaluate, at or before the time of filing a tax return, their own compliance with the applicable transfer pricing rules. It is also important that tax administrations be able to access the information they need to conduct a transfer pricing risk assessment to make an informed decision about whether to perform an audit. In addition, it is important that tax administrations be able to access or demand, on a timely basis, all additional information necessary to conduct a comprehensive audit once the decision to conduct such an audit is made.

B.1. Taxpayer's assessment of its compliance with the arm's length principle

5.7. By requiring taxpayers to articulate convincing, consistent and cogent transfer pricing positions, transfer pricing documentation can help to ensure that a culture of compliance is created. Well-prepared documentation will give tax administrations some assurance that the taxpayer has analysed the positions it reports on tax returns, has considered the available comparable data, and has reached consistent transfer pricing positions. Moreover, contemporaneous documentation requirements will help to ensure the integrity of the taxpayers' positions and restrain taxpayers from developing justifications for their positions after the fact.

5.8. This compliance objective may be supported in two important ways. First, tax administrations can require that transfer pricing documentation requirements be satisfied on a contemporaneous basis. This would mean that the documentation would be prepared at the time of the transaction, or in any event, no later than the time of completing and filing the tax return for the fiscal year in which the transaction takes place. The second way to encourage compliance is to establish transfer pricing penalty regimes in a manner intended to reward timely and accurate preparation of transfer pricing documentation and to create incentives for timely, careful consideration of the taxpayer's transfer pricing positions. Filing requirements and penalty provisions related to documentation are discussed in greater detail in Section D below.

5.9. While ideally taxpayers will use transfer pricing documentation as an opportunity to articulate a well thought-out basis for their transfer pricing policies, thereby meeting an important objective of such requirements, issues such as costs, time constraints, and competing demands for the attention of relevant personnel can sometimes undermine these objectives. It is therefore important for jurisdictions to keep documentation requirements reasonable and focused on material transactions in order to ensure mindful attention to the most important matters.

B.2. Transfer pricing risk assessment

5.10. Effective risk identification and assessment constitute an essential early stage in the process of selecting appropriate cases for transfer pricing audits or enquiries and in focusing such audits on the most important issues. Because tax administrations operate with limited resources, it is important for them to accurately evaluate, at the very outset of a possible audit, whether a taxpayer's transfer pricing arrangements warrant in-depth review and a commitment of significant tax enforcement resources. Particularly with regard to transfer pricing issues (which generally are complex and fact-intensive), effective risk assessment becomes an essential prerequisite for a focused and resource-efficient audit. The OECD Forum on Tax Administration has developed a number of tools to assist tax administrations in conducting such risk assessments.

5.11. Proper assessment of transfer pricing risk by the tax administration requires access to sufficient, relevant and reliable information at an early stage. While there are many sources of relevant information, transfer pricing documentation is one critical source of such information.

5.12. There is a variety of tools and sources of information used for identifying and evaluating transfer pricing risks of taxpayers and transactions, including transfer pricing forms (to be filed with the annual tax return), transfer pricing mandatory questionnaires focusing on particular areas of risk, general transfer pricing documentation requirements identifying the supporting evidence necessary to demonstrate the taxpayer's compliance with the arm's length principle, and co-operative discussions between tax administrations and taxpayers. Each of the tools and sources of information appears to respond to the same fundamental observation: there is a need for the tax administration to have ready access to relevant information at an early stage to enable an accurate and informed transfer pricing risk assessment. Assuring that a high quality transfer pricing risk assessment can be carried out efficiently and with the right kinds of reliable information should be one important consideration in designing transfer pricing documentation rules.

B.3. Transfer pricing audit

5.13. A third objective for transfer pricing documentation is to provide tax administrations with useful information to employ in conducting a thorough transfer pricing audit. Transfer pricing audit cases tend to be fact-intensive. They often involve difficult evaluations of the comparability of several transactions and markets. They can require detailed consideration of financial, factual and other industry information. The availability of adequate information from a variety of sources during the audit is critical to facilitating a tax administration's orderly examination of the taxpayer's controlled transactions with associated enterprises and enforcement of the applicable transfer pricing rules.

5.14. In situations where a proper transfer pricing risk assessment suggests that a thorough transfer pricing audit is warranted with regard to one or more issues, it is clearly the case that the tax administration must have the ability to obtain, within a reasonable period, all of the relevant documents and information in the taxpayer's possession. This includes information regarding the taxpayer's operations and functions, relevant information on the operations, functions and financial results of associated enterprises with which the taxpayer has entered into controlled transactions, information regarding potential comparables, including internal comparables, and documents regarding the operations and financial results of potentially comparable uncontrolled transactions and unrelated parties. To the extent such information is included in the transfer pricing documentation, special information and document production procedures can potentially be avoided. It must be recognised, however, that it would be unduly burdensome and inefficient for transfer pricing documentation to attempt to anticipate all of the information that might possibly be required for a full audit. Accordingly, situations will inevitably arise when tax administrations wish to obtain information not included in the documentation package. Thus, a tax administration's access to information should not be limited to, or by, the documentation package relied on in a transfer pricing risk assessment. Where a jurisdiction requires particular information to be retained for transfer pricing audit purposes, such requirements should balance the tax administration's need for information and the compliance burdens on taxpayers.

5.15. It may often be the case that the documents and other information required for a transfer pricing audit will be in the possession of members of the MNE group other than the local affiliate under examination. Often the necessary documents will be located outside the jurisdiction whose tax administration is conducting the audit. It is therefore important that the tax administration is able to obtain directly or through information sharing, such as exchange of information mechanisms, information that extends beyond the jurisdiction's borders.

C. A three-tiered approach to transfer pricing documentation

5.16. In order to achieve the objectives described in Section B, jurisdictions should adopt a standardised approach to transfer pricing documentation. This section describes a three-tiered structure consisting of (i) a master file containing standardised information relevant for all MNE group members; (ii) a local file referring specifically to material transactions of the local taxpayer; and (iii) a Country-by-Country Report containing certain information relating to the global allocation of the MNE group's income and taxes paid together with certain indicators of the location of economic activity within the MNE group.

5.17. This approach to transfer pricing documentation will provide tax administrations with relevant and reliable information to perform an efficient and robust transfer pricing risk assessment analysis. It will also provide a platform on which the information necessary for an audit can be developed and provide taxpayers with a means and an incentive to meaningfully consider and describe their compliance with the arm's length principle in material transactions.

C.1. Master file

5.18. The master file should provide an overview of the MNE group business, including the nature of its global business operations, its overall transfer pricing policies, and its global allocation of income and economic activity in order to assist tax administrations in evaluating the presence of significant transfer pricing risk. In general, the master file is intended to provide a high-level overview in order to place the MNE group's transfer pricing practices in their global economic, legal, financial and tax context. It is not intended to require exhaustive listings of minutiae (e.g. a listing of every patent owned by members of the MNE group) as this would be both unnecessarily burdensome and inconsistent with the objectives of the master file. In producing the master file, including lists of important agreements, intangibles and transactions, taxpayers should use prudent business judgment in determining the appropriate level of detail for the information supplied, keeping in mind the objective of the master file to provide tax administrations a high-level overview of the MNE group's global operations and policies. When the requirements of the master file can be fully satisfied by specific cross-references to other existing documents, such cross-references, together with copies of the relevant documents, should be deemed to satisfy the relevant requirement. For purposes of producing the master file, information is considered important if its omission would affect the reliability of the transfer pricing outcomes.

5.19. The information required in the master file provides a "blueprint" of the MNE group and contains relevant information that can be broken down into five categories: a) the MNE group's organisational structure; b) a description of the MNE group's business or businesses; c) the MNE group's intangibles; d) the MNE group's intercompany financial activities; and e) the MNE group's financial and tax positions.

5.20. Taxpayers should present the information in the master file for the MNE group as a whole. However, organisation of the information presented by line of business is permitted where well justified by the facts, e.g. where the structure of the MNE group is such that some significant business lines operate largely independently or are recently acquired. Where line of business presentation is used, care should be taken to assure that centralised group functions and transactions between business lines are properly described in the master file. Even where line of business presentation is selected, the entire master file consisting of all business lines should be available to each jurisdiction in order to assure that an appropriate overview of the MNE group's global business is provided.

5.21. Annex I to Chapter V of these Guidelines sets out the information to be included in the master file.

C.2. Local file

5.22. In contrast to the master file, which provides a high-level overview as described in paragraph 5.18, the local file provides more detailed information relating to specific intercompany transactions. The information required in the local file supplements the master file and helps to meet the objective of assuring that the taxpayer has complied with the arm's length principle in its material transfer pricing positions affecting a specific jurisdiction. The local file focuses on information relevant to the transfer pricing analysis related to transactions taking place between a local affiliate and associated enterprises in different jurisdictions and which are material in the context of the jurisdiction's tax system. Such information would include relevant financial information regarding those specific transactions, a comparability analysis, and the selection and application of the most appropriate transfer pricing method. Where a requirement of the local file can be fully satisfied by a specific cross-reference to information contained in the master file, such a cross-reference should suffice.

5.23. Annex II to Chapter V of these Guidelines sets out the items of information to be included in the local file.

C.3. Country-by-Country Report

5.24. The Country-by-Country Report requires aggregate tax jurisdiction-wide information relating to the global allocation of the income, the taxes paid, and certain indicators of the location of economic activity among tax jurisdictions in which the MNE group operates. The report also requires a listing of all the Constituent Entities for which financial information is reported, including the tax jurisdiction of incorporation, where different from the tax jurisdiction of residence, as well as the nature of the main business activities carried out by that Constituent Entity.

5.25. The Country-by-Country Report will be helpful for high-level transfer pricing risk assessment purposes. It may also be used by tax administrations in evaluating other BEPS related risks and where appropriate for economic and statistical analysis. However, the information in the Country-by-Country Report should not be used as a substitute for a detailed transfer pricing analysis of individual transactions and prices based on a full functional analysis and a full comparability analysis. The information in the Country-by-Country Report on its own does not constitute conclusive evidence that transfer prices are or are not appropriate. It should not be used by tax administrations to propose transfer pricing adjustments based on a global formulary apportionment of income.

5.26. Annex III to Chapter V of these Guidelines contains a model template for the Country-by-Country Report together with its accompanying instructions.

D. Compliance issues

D.1. Contemporaneous documentation

5.27. Each taxpayer should endeavour to determine transfer prices for tax purposes in accordance with the arm's length principle, based upon information reasonably available at the time of the transaction. Thus, a taxpayer ordinarily should give consideration to whether its transfer pricing is appropriate for tax purposes before the pricing is established and should confirm the arm's length nature of its financial results at the time of filing its tax return.

5.28. Taxpayers should not be expected to incur disproportionately high costs and burdens in producing documentation. Therefore, tax administrations should balance requests for documentation against the expected cost and administrative burden to the taxpayer of creating it. Where a taxpayer reasonably demonstrates, having regard to the principles of these Guidelines, that either no comparable data exists or that the cost of locating the comparable data would be disproportionately high relative to the amounts at issue, the taxpayer should not be required to incur costs in searching for such data.

D.2. Time frame

5.29. Practices regarding the timing of the preparation of the documentation differ among jurisdictions. Some jurisdictions require information to be finalised by the time the tax return is filed. Others require documentation to be in place by the time the audit commences. There is also a variety in practice regarding the amount of time given to taxpayers to respond to specific tax administration requests for documentation and other audit related information requests. These differences in the time requirements for providing information can add to taxpayers' difficulties in setting priorities and in providing the right information to the tax administrations at the right time.

5.30. The best practice is to require that the local file be finalised no later than the due date for the filing of the tax return for the fiscal year in question. The master file should be reviewed and, if necessary, updated by the tax return due date for the ultimate parent of the MNE group. In jurisdictions pursuing policies of auditing transactions as they occur under co-operative compliance programmes, it may be necessary for certain information to be provided in advance of the filing of the tax return.

5.31. With regard to the Country-by-Country Report, it is recognised that in some instances final statutory financial statements and other financial information that may be relevant for the country-by-country data described in Annex III may not be finalised until after the due date for tax returns in some jurisdictions for a given fiscal year. Under the given circumstances, the date for completion of the Country-by-Country Report described in Annex III to Chapter V of these Guidelines may be extended to one year following the last day of the fiscal year of the ultimate parent of the MNE group.

D.3. Materiality

5.32. Not all transactions that occur between associated enterprises are sufficiently material to require full documentation in the local file. Tax administrations have an interest in seeing the most important information while at the same time they also have an interest in seeing that MNE groups are not so overwhelmed with compliance demands that they fail to consider and document the most important items. Thus, jurisdictional transfer pricing documentation requirements based on Annex II to Chapter V of these Guidelines should include specific materiality thresholds that take into account the size and the nature of the local economy, the importance of the MNE group in that economy, and the size and nature of local operating entities, in addition to the overall size and nature of the MNE group. Measures of materiality may be considered in relative terms (e.g. transactions not exceeding a percentage of revenue or a percentage of cost measure) or in absolute amount terms (e.g. transactions not exceeding a certain fixed amount). Individual jurisdictions should establish their own materiality standards for local file purposes, based on local conditions. The materiality standards should be objective standards that are commonly understood and accepted in commercial practice. See paragraph 5.18 for the materiality standards applicable in completing the master file.

5.33. A number of jurisdictions have introduced in their transfer pricing documentation rules simplification measures which exempt small and medium-sized enterprises (SMEs) from transfer pricing documentation requirements or limit the information required to be provided by such enterprises. In order not to impose on taxpayers costs and burdens disproportionate to the circumstances, it is recommended to not require SMEs to produce the amount of documentation that might be expected from larger enterprises. However, SMEs should be obliged to provide information and documents about their material cross-border transactions upon a specific request of the tax administration in the course of a tax examination or for transfer pricing risk assessment purposes.

5.34. For purposes of Annex III to Chapter V of these Guidelines, the Country-by-Country Report should include all tax jurisdictions in which the MNE group has an entity resident for tax purposes, regardless of the size of business operations in that tax jurisdiction.

D.4. Retention of documents

5.35. Taxpayers should not be obliged to retain documents beyond a reasonable period consistent with the requirements of domestic law at either the parent company or local entity level. However, at times materials and information required in the documentation package (master file, local file and Country-by-Country Report) may be relevant to a transfer pricing enquiry for a subsequent year that is not time barred, for example where taxpayers voluntarily keep such records in relation to long-term contracts, or to determine whether comparability standards relating to the application of a transfer pricing method in that subsequent year are satisfied. Tax administrations should bear in mind the difficulties in locating documents for prior years and should restrict such requests to instances where they have good reason in connection with the transaction under examination for reviewing the documents in question.

5.36. Because the tax administration's ultimate interest would be satisfied if the necessary documents were submitted in a timely manner when requested by the tax administration in the course of an examination, the way that documentation is stored – whether in paper, electronic form, or in any other system – should be at the discretion of the taxpayer provided that relevant information can promptly be made available to the tax administration in the form specified by the local rules and practices in each jurisdiction.

D.5. Frequency of documentation updates

5.37. It is recommended that transfer pricing documentation be periodically reviewed in order to determine whether functional and economic analyses are still accurate and relevant and to confirm the validity of the applied transfer pricing methodology. In general, the master file, the local file and the Country-by-Country Report should be reviewed and updated annually. It is recognised, however, that in many situations business descriptions, functional analyses, and descriptions of comparables may not change significantly from year to year.

5.38. In order to simplify compliance burdens on taxpayers, tax administrations may determine, as long as the operating conditions remain unchanged, that the searches in databases for comparables supporting part of the local file be updated every three years rather than annually. Financial data for the comparables should nonetheless be updated every year in order to apply the arm's length principle reliably.

D.6. Language

5.39. The necessity of providing documentation in local language may constitute a complicating factor with respect to transfer pricing compliance to the extent that substantial time and cost may be involved in translating documents. The language in which transfer pricing documentation should be submitted should be established under local laws. Jurisdictions are encouraged to permit filing of transfer pricing documentation in commonly used languages where it will not compromise the usefulness of the documents. Where tax administrations believe that translation of documents is necessary, they should make specific requests for translation and provide sufficient time to make such translation as comfortable a burden as possible.

D.7. Penalties

5.40. Many jurisdictions have adopted documentation-related penalties to ensure efficient operation of transfer pricing documentation requirements. They are designed to make non-compliance more costly than compliance. Penalty regimes are governed by the laws of each individual jurisdiction. Practices among jurisdictions with regard to transfer pricing documentation-related penalties vary widely. The existence of different local penalty regimes in different jurisdictions may influence the quality of taxpayers' compliance so that taxpayers could be driven to favour one jurisdiction over another in their compliance practices.

5.41. Documentation-related penalties imposed for failure to comply with transfer pricing documentation requirements or failure to timely submit required information are usually civil (or administrative) monetary penalties. These documentation-related penalties are based on a fixed amount that may be assessed for each document missing or for each fiscal year under review, or calculated as a percentage of the related tax understatement ultimately determined, a percentage of the related adjustment to the income, or as a percentage of the amount of the cross-border transactions not documented.

5.42. Care should be taken not to impose a documentation-related penalty on a taxpayer for failing to submit data to which the MNE group did not have access. However, a decision not to impose documentation-related penalties does not mean that adjustments cannot be made to income where prices are not consistent with the arm's length principle. The fact that positions are fully documented does not necessarily mean that the taxpayer's positions are correct. Moreover, an assertion by a local entity that other group members are responsible for transfer pricing compliance is not a sufficient reason for that entity to fail to provide required documentation, nor should such an assertion prevent the imposition of documentation-related penalties for failure to comply with documentation rules where the necessary information is not forthcoming.

5.43. Another way for jurisdictions to encourage taxpayers to fulfil transfer pricing documentation requirements is by designing compliance incentives such as penalty protection or a shift in the burden of proof. Where the documentation meets the requirements and is timely submitted, the taxpayer could be exempted from tax penalties or subject to a lower penalty rate if a transfer pricing adjustment is made and sustained, notwithstanding the provision of documentation. In some jurisdictions where the taxpayer bears the burden of proof regarding transfer pricing matters, a shift of the burden of proof to the tax administration's side where adequate documentation is provided on a timely basis offers another measure that could be used to create an incentive for transfer pricing documentation compliance.

D.8. Confidentiality

5.44. Tax administrations should take all reasonable steps to ensure that there is no public disclosure of confidential information (trade secrets, scientific secrets, etc.) and other commercially sensitive information contained in the documentation package (master file, local file and Country-by-Country Report). Tax administrations should also assure taxpayers that the information presented in transfer pricing documentation will remain confidential. In cases where disclosure is required in public court proceedings or judicial decisions, every effort should be made to ensure that confidentiality is maintained and that information is disclosed only to the extent needed.

5.45. The *Confidentiality and Information Security Management Toolkit* (2020) produced by the Global Forum on Transparency and Exchange of Information for Tax Purposes provides guidance to jurisdictions to ensure that their legal framework on the confidentiality of taxpayer information is adequate and protects the confidentiality and appropriate use of information exchanged under an international exchange agreement.

D.9. Other issues

5.46. The requirement to use the most reliable information will usually, but not always, require the use of local comparables over the use of regional comparables where such local comparables are reasonably available. The use of regional comparables in transfer pricing documentation prepared for jurisdictions in the same geographic region in situations where appropriate local comparables are available will not, in some cases, comport with the obligation to rely on the most reliable information. While the simplification benefits of limiting the number of comparable searches an entity is required to undertake are obvious, and materiality and compliance costs are relevant factors to consider, a desire for simplifying compliance processes should not go so far as to undermine compliance with the requirement to use the most reliable available information. See paragraphs 1.132-1.133 on market differences and multi-jurisdictional analyses for further details on when local comparables are to be preferred.

5.47. It is not recommended, particularly at the stage of transfer pricing risk assessment, to require that the transfer pricing documentation should be certified by an outside auditor or other third party. Similarly, mandatory use of consulting firms to prepare transfer pricing documentation is not recommended.

E. Implementation

5.48. This section contains guidance to ensure an effective and consistent implementation of transfer pricing documentation requirements, and in particular Country-by-Country Reporting.

E.1. Master file and local file

5.49. It is recommended that the master file and local file elements of the transfer pricing documentation standard be implemented in each jurisdiction through local legislation or administrative procedures and that the master file and local file be filed directly with the tax administrations in each relevant jurisdiction as required by those administrations. With regard to the local file and the master file, confidentiality and the consistent use of the standards contained in Annex I and Annex II to Chapter V of these Guidelines should be taken into account by jurisdictions when introducing these elements in local legislation or administrative procedures.

E.2. Country-by-Country Report

E.2.1. Timing: When should the Country-by-Country Reporting requirement start?

5.50. It is recommended that the first Country-by-Country Reports be required to be filed for MNE fiscal years beginning on or after 1 January 2016. However, it is acknowledged that some jurisdictions may need time to follow their particular domestic legislative process in order to make necessary adjustments to the law. In order to assist jurisdictions in preparing timely legislation, model legislation requiring ultimate parent entities of MNE groups to file the Country-by-Country Report in their jurisdiction of residence has been developed (see Annex IV to Chapter V of these Guidelines). Jurisdictions will be able to adapt this model legislation to their own legal systems. Given the recommendation in paragraph 5.31 that MNEs be allowed one year from the close of the fiscal year to which the Country-by-Country Report relates to prepare and file the Country-by-Country Report, this recommendation means that the first Country-by-Country Reports would be filed by 31 December 2017. For MNEs with a fiscal year ending on a date other than 31 December, the first Country-by-Country Reports would be required to be filed later in 2018, twelve months after the close of the relevant MNE fiscal year, and would report on the MNE group's first fiscal year beginning after 1 January 2016. It follows from this recommendation that the jurisdictions participating in the OECD/G20 BEPS Project agree that they will not require filing of a Country-by-Country Report based on the new template for MNE fiscal years beginning prior to 1 January 2016. The MNE fiscal year relates to the consolidated reporting period for financial statement purposes and not to taxable years or to the financial reporting periods of individual subsidiaries.

E.2.2. Which MNE groups should be required to file the Country-by-Country Report?

5.51. It is recommended that all MNE groups be required to file the Country-by-Country Report each year except as follows.

5.52. There would be an exemption from the general filing requirement for MNE groups with annual consolidated group revenue in the immediately preceding fiscal year of less than EUR 750 million or a near equivalent amount in domestic currency as of January 2015. Thus, for example, if an MNE that keeps its financial accounts on a calendar year basis has EUR 625 million in consolidated group revenue for its 2015 calendar year, it would not be required to file the Country-by-Country Report in any jurisdiction with respect to its fiscal year ending 31 December 2016.

5.53. It is believed that the exemption described in paragraph 52, which provides a threshold of EUR 750 million, will exclude approximately 85 to 90% of MNE groups from the requirement to file the Country-by-Country Report, but that the Country-by-Country Report will nevertheless be filed by MNE groups controlling approximately 90% of corporate revenues. The prescribed exemption threshold therefore represents an appropriate balancing of reporting burden and benefit to tax administrations.

5.54. It is the intention of the jurisdictions participating in the OECD/G20 BEPS Project to reconsider the appropriateness of the applicable revenue threshold described in the preceding paragraph in connection with their 2020 review of implementation of the new standard, including whether additional or different data should be reported.

5.55. It is considered that no exemptions from filing the Country-by-Country Report should be adopted apart from the exemptions outlined in this section. In particular, no special industry exemptions should be provided, no general exemption for investment funds should be provided, and no exemption for non-corporate entities or non-public corporate entities should be provided. Notwithstanding this conclusion, MNE groups with income derived from international transportation or transportation in inland waterways that is covered by treaty provisions that are specific to such income and under which the taxing rights on such income are allocated exclusively to one jurisdiction, should include the information required by the Country-by-Country Report template with respect to such income only against the name of the jurisdiction to which the relevant treaty provisions allocate these taxing rights.

E.2.3. Necessary conditions underpinning the obtaining and the use of the Country-by-Country Report

5.56. The following conditions underpin the obtaining and the use of the Country-by-Country Report.

Confidentiality

5.57. Jurisdictions should have in place and enforce legal protections of the confidentiality of the reported information. Such protections would preserve the confidentiality of the Country-by-Country Report to an extent at least equivalent to the protections that would apply if such information were delivered to the jurisdiction under the provisions of the Multilateral Convention on Mutual Administrative Assistance in Tax Matters, a Tax Information Exchange Agreement (TIEA) or a tax treaty that meets the internationally agreed standard of information upon request as reviewed by the Global Forum on Transparency and Exchange of Information for Tax Purposes. Such protections include limitation of the use of information, rules on the persons to whom the information may be disclosed, ordre public, etc.

Consistency

5.58. Jurisdictions should use their best efforts to adopt a legal requirement that MNE groups' ultimate parent entities resident in their jurisdiction prepare and file the Country-by-Country Report, unless exempted as set out in paragraph 5.52. Jurisdictions should utilise the standard template contained in Annex III of Chapter V of these Guidelines. Stated otherwise, under this condition no jurisdiction will require that the Country-by-Country Report contain either additional information not contained in Annex III, nor will it fail to require reporting of information included in Annex III.

Appropriate use

5.59. Jurisdictions should use appropriately the information in the Country-by-Country Report template in accordance with paragraph 5.25. In particular, jurisdictions will commit to use the Country-by-Country Report for assessing high-level transfer pricing risk. Jurisdictions may also use the Country-by-Country Report for assessing other BEPS-related risks. Jurisdictions should not propose adjustments to the income of any taxpayer on the basis of an income allocation formula based on the data from the Country-by-Country Report. They will further commit that if such adjustments based on Country-by-Country Report data are made by the local tax administration of the jurisdiction, the jurisdiction's competent authority will promptly concede the adjustment in any relevant competent authority proceeding. This does not imply, however, that jurisdictions would be prevented from using the

Country-by-Country Report data as a basis for making further enquiries into the MNE group's transfer pricing arrangements or into other tax matters in the course of a tax audit.[1]

E.2.4. The framework for government-to-government mechanisms to exchange Country-by-Country Reports and implementation package

E.2.4.1. Framework

5.60. Jurisdictions should require in a timely manner Country-by-Country Reporting from ultimate parent entities of MNE groups resident in their jurisdiction and referred to in Section E.2.2 and exchange this information on an automatic basis with the jurisdictions in which the MNE group operates and which fulfil the conditions listed in Section E.2.3. Only in cases where a jurisdiction fails to provide information to a jurisdiction fulfilling the conditions listed in Section E.2.3, because (a) it has not required Country-by-Country Reporting from the ultimate parent entity of such MNE groups, (b) no competent authority agreement has been agreed in a timely manner under the current international agreements of the jurisdiction for the exchange of the Country-by-Country Reports or (c) it has been established that there is a failure to exchange the information in practice with a jurisdiction after agreeing with that jurisdiction to do so, a secondary mechanism would be accepted as appropriate, through local filing or through filing of the Country-by-Country Reports by a designated member of the MNE group acting in place of the ultimate parent entity and automatic exchange of these reports by its jurisdiction of tax residence.

E.2.4.2. Implementation package

5.61. Annex IV to Chapter V of these Guidelines contains an implementation package for government-to-government exchange of Country-by-Country Reports, which includes:

1. Access to a mutual agreement procedure (MAP) will be available when the government-to-government exchange of the Country-by-Country Reports is based on bilateral treaties. In cases where the international agreements on which the government-to-government exchanges of the Country-by-Country Reports are based do not contain provisions providing access to MAP, jurisdictions commit to introducing in the competent authority agreement to be developed a mechanism for competent authority procedures to discuss with the aim of resolving cases of undesirable economic outcomes, including if such cases arise for individual businesses.

- Model legislation requiring the ultimate parent entity of an MNE group to file the Country-by-Country Report in its jurisdiction of residence. Jurisdictions will be able to adapt this model legislation to their own legal systems, where changes to current legislation are required. Key elements of secondary mechanisms have also been developed.
- Implementing arrangements for the automatic exchange of the Country-by-Country Reports under international agreements, incorporating the conditions set out in Section E.2.3. Such implementing arrangements include competent authority agreements (CAAs) based on existing international agreements (the Multilateral Convention on Mutual Administrative Assistance in Tax Matters, bilateral tax treaties and TIEAs) and inspired by the existing models developed by the OECD working with G20 countries for the automatic exchange of financial account information.

5.62. Jurisdictions endeavour to introduce as necessary domestic legislation in a timely manner. They are also encouraged to expand the coverage of their international agreements for exchange of information. The implementation of the package will be monitored on an ongoing basis. The outcomes of this monitoring will be taken into consideration in the 2020 review.

Chapter VI

Special considerations for intangibles

6.1. Under Article 9 of the OECD Model Tax Convention, where the conditions made or imposed in the use or transfer of intangibles between two associated enterprises differ from those that would be made between independent enterprises, then any profits that would, but for those conditions, have accrued to one of the enterprises, but, by reason of those conditions, have not so accrued, may be included in the profits of that enterprise and taxed accordingly.

6.2. The purpose of this Chapter VI is to provide guidance specially tailored to determining arm's length conditions for transactions that involve the use or transfer of intangibles. Article 9 of the OECD Model Tax Convention is concerned with the conditions of transactions between associated enterprises, not with assigning particular labels to such transactions. Consequently, the key consideration is whether a transaction conveys economic value from one associated enterprise to another, whether that benefit derives from tangible property, intangibles, services or other items or activities. An item or activity can convey economic value notwithstanding the fact that it may not be specifically addressed in Chapter VI. To the extent that an item or activity conveys economic value, it should be taken into account in the determination of arm's length prices whether or not it constitutes an intangible within the meaning of paragraph 6.6.

6.3. The principles of Chapters I-III of these Guidelines apply equally to transactions involving intangibles and those transactions which do not. Under those principles, as is the case with other transfer pricing matters, the analysis of cases involving the use or transfer of intangibles should begin with a thorough identification of the commercial or financial relations between the associated enterprises and the conditions and economically relevant circumstances attaching to those relations in order that the actual transaction involving the use or transfer of intangibles is accurately delineated. The functional analysis should identify the functions performed, assets used, and risks assumed[1] by each relevant member of the MNE group. In cases involving the use or transfer of intangibles, it is especially important to ground the functional analysis on an understanding of the MNE's global business and the manner in which intangibles are used by the MNE to add or create value across the entire supply chain. Where necessary, the analysis should consider, within the framework of Section D.2 of Chapter I, whether independent parties would have entered into the arrangement and if so, the conditions that would have been agreed.

6.4. In order to determine arm's length conditions for the use or transfer of intangibles it is important to perform a functional and comparability analysis in accordance with Section D.1 of Chapter I, based on identifying the intangibles and associated risks in contractual arrangements and then supplementing the analysis through examination of the actual conduct of the parties based on the functions performed, assets used, and risks assumed, including control of important functions and economically significant risks. Accordingly the next section, Section A, provides guidance on identifying intangibles. Section B examines legal ownership and other contractual terms, together with guidance on the evaluation of the conduct of the parties based on functions, assets and risks. Section C outlines some typical scenarios involving intangibles, and Section D provides guidance on determining arm's length conditions including the application of pricing methods and valuation techniques, and provides an approach to determining arm's length conditions for a specific category of hard-to-value intangibles. Examples illustrating the guidance are contained in the Annex to this chapter.

A. Identifying intangibles

A.1. In general

6.5. Difficulties can arise in a transfer pricing analysis as a result of definitions of the term intangible that are either too narrow or too broad. If an overly narrow definition of the term intangible is applied, either taxpayers or governments may argue that certain items fall outside the definition and may therefore be transferred or used without separate compensation, even though such use or transfer would give rise to compensation in transactions between independent enterprises. If too broad a definition is applied, either taxpayers or governments may argue that the use or transfer of an item in transactions

1. The assumption of risks refers to the outcome of the determination of which associated enterprise assumes a specific risk under the guidance provided in Section D.1.2.1 of Chapter I, taking into account control over risk and financial capacity to assume the risk. Contractual assumption of risk refers to the allocation of risk in contracts between the parties.

between associated enterprises should require compensation in circumstances where no such compensation would be provided in transactions between independent enterprises.

6.6. In these Guidelines, therefore, the word "intangible" is intended to address something which is not a physical asset or a financial asset,[2] which is capable of being owned or controlled for use in commercial activities, and whose use or transfer would be compensated had it occurred in a transaction between independent parties in comparable circumstances. Rather than focusing on accounting or legal definitions, the thrust of a transfer pricing analysis in a case involving intangibles should be the determination of the conditions that would be agreed upon between independent parties for a comparable transaction.

6.7. Intangibles that are important to consider for transfer pricing purposes are not always recognised as intangible assets for accounting purposes. For example, costs associated with developing intangibles internally through expenditures such as research and development and advertising are sometimes expensed rather than capitalised for accounting purposes and the intangibles resulting from such expenditures therefore are not always reflected on the balance sheet. Such intangibles may nevertheless be used to generate significant economic value and may need to be considered for transfer pricing purposes. Furthermore, the enhancement to value that may arise from the complementary nature of a collection of intangibles when exploited together is not always reflected on the balance sheet. Accordingly, whether an item should be considered to be an intangible for transfer pricing purposes under Article 9 of the OECD Model Tax Convention can be informed by its characterisation for accounting purposes, but will not be determined by such characterisation only. Furthermore, the determination that an item should be regarded as an intangible for transfer pricing purposes does not determine or follow from its characterisation for general tax purposes, as, for example, an expense or an amortisable asset.

6.8. The availability and extent of legal, contractual, or other forms of protection may affect the value of an item and the returns that should be attributed to it. The existence of such protection is not, however, a necessary condition for an item to be characterised as an intangible for transfer pricing purposes. Similarly, while some intangibles may be identified separately and transferred on a segregated basis, other intangibles may be transferred only

2. As used in this paragraph, a financial asset is any asset that is cash, an equity instrument, a contractual right or obligation to receive cash or another financial asset or to exchange financial assets or liabilities, or a derivative. Examples include bonds, bank deposits, stocks, shares, forward contracts, futures contracts and swaps.

in combination with other business assets. Therefore, separate transferability is not a necessary condition for an item to be characterised as an intangible for transfer pricing purposes.

6.9. It is important to distinguish intangibles from market conditions or local market circumstances. Features of a local market, such as the level of disposable income of households in that market or the size or relative competitiveness of the market are not capable of being owned or controlled. While in some circumstances they may affect the determination of an arm's length price for a particular transaction and should be taken into account in a comparability analysis, they are not intangibles for the purposes of Chapter VI. See Section D.6 of Chapter I.

6.10. The identification of an item as an intangible is separate and distinct from the process for determining the price for the use or transfer of the item under the facts and circumstances of a given case. Depending on the industry sector and other facts specific to a particular case, exploitation of intangibles can account for either a large or small part of the MNE's value creation. It should be emphasised that not all intangibles deserve compensation separate from the required payment for goods or services in all circumstances, and not all intangibles give rise to premium returns in all circumstances. For example, consider a situation in which an enterprise performs a service using non-unique know-how, where other comparable service providers have comparable know-how. In that case, even though know-how constitutes an intangible, it may be determined under the facts and circumstances that the know-how does not justify allocating a premium return to the enterprise, over and above normal returns earned by comparable independent providers of similar services that use comparable non-unique know-how. See Section D.1.3 of Chapter I. See also paragraph 6.17 for a definition of "unique" intangibles.

6.11. Care should be taken in determining whether or when an intangible exists and whether an intangible has been used or transferred. For example, not all research and development expenditures produce or enhance an intangible, and not all marketing activities result in the creation or enhancement of an intangible.

6.12. In a transfer pricing analysis of a matter involving intangibles, it is important to identify the relevant intangibles with specificity. The functional analysis should identify the relevant intangibles at issue, the manner in which they contribute to the creation of value in the transactions under review, the important functions performed and specific risks assumed in connection with the development, enhancement, maintenance, protection and exploitation of the intangibles and the manner in which they interact with other intangibles, with tangible assets and with business operations to create value. While it may be appropriate to aggregate intangibles for the purpose of determining arm's length conditions for the use or transfer of the intangibles in certain cases, it is not sufficient to suggest that vaguely specified or undifferentiated intangibles have an effect on arm's length prices or other conditions. A thorough functional analysis, including an analysis of the importance of identified relevant intangibles in the MNE's global business, should support the determination of arm's length conditions.

A.2. Relevance of this chapter for other tax purposes

6.13. The guidance contained in this chapter is intended to address transfer pricing matters exclusively. It is not intended to have relevance for other tax purposes. For example, the Commentary on Article 12 of the OECD Model Tax Convention contains a detailed discussion of the definition of royalties under that Article (paragraphs 8 to 19). The Article 12 definition of "royalties" is not intended to provide any guidance on whether, and if so at what price, the use or transfer of intangibles would be remunerated between independent parties. It is therefore not relevant for transfer pricing purposes. Moreover, the manner in which a transaction is characterised for transfer pricing purposes has no relevance to the question of whether a particular payment constitutes a royalty or may be subjected to withholding tax under Article 12. The concept of intangibles for transfer pricing purposes and the definition of royalties for purposes of Article 12 of the OECD Model Tax Convention are two different notions that do not need to be aligned. It may occur that a payment made between associated enterprises may be regarded as not constituting a royalty for purposes of Article 12, and nevertheless be treated for transfer pricing purposes as a payment to which the principles of this chapter may apply. Examples could include certain payments related to goodwill or ongoing concern value. It may also occur that a payment properly treated as a royalty under Article 12 of a relevant Treaty may not be made in remuneration for intangibles for purposes of this chapter. Examples could include certain payments for technical services. Similarly, the guidance in this chapter is not intended to have relevance for customs purposes.

6.14. The guidance in this chapter is also not relevant to recognition of income, capitalisation of intangible development costs, amortisation, or similar matters. Thus, for example, a jurisdiction may choose not to impose tax on the transfer of particular types of intangibles under specified circumstances. Similarly, a jurisdiction may not permit amortisation of the cost of certain acquired items that would be considered intangibles under the definitions in this chapter and whose transfer may be subjected to tax at the time of the transfer in the transferor's jurisdiction. It is recognised that inconsistencies between individual jurisdictional laws regarding such matters can sometimes give rise to either double taxation or double non-taxation.

A.3. Categories of intangibles

6.15. In discussions of transfer pricing issues related to intangibles, it is sometimes the case that various categories of intangibles are described and labels applied. Distinctions are sometimes made between trade intangibles and marketing intangibles, between "soft" intangibles and "hard" intangibles, between routine and non-routine intangibles, and between other classes and categories of intangibles. The approach contained in this chapter for determining arm's length prices in cases involving intangibles does not turn on these categorisations. Accordingly, no attempt is made in these Guidelines to delineate with precision various classes or categories of intangibles or to prescribe outcomes that turn on such categories.

6.16. Certain categories of intangibles are, however, commonly referred to in discussions of transfer pricing matters. To facilitate discussions, definitions of two such commonly used terms, "marketing intangibles" and "trade intangibles" are contained in the Glossary and referred to from time to time in the discussion in these Guidelines. It should be emphasised that generic references to marketing or trade intangibles do not relieve taxpayers or tax administrations from their obligation in a transfer pricing analysis to identify relevant intangibles with specificity, nor does the use of those terms suggest that a different approach should be applied in determining arm's length conditions for transactions that involve either marketing intangibles or trade intangibles.

6.17. In certain instances these Guidelines refer to "unique and valuable" intangibles. "Unique and valuable" intangibles are those intangibles (i) that are not comparable to intangibles used by or available to parties to potentially comparable transactions, and (ii) whose use in business operations (e.g. manufacturing, provision of services, marketing, sales or administration) is expected to yield greater future economic benefits than would be expected in the absence of the intangible.

A.4. Illustrations

6.18. This section provides illustrations of items often considered in transfer pricing analyses involving intangibles. The illustrations are intended to clarify the provisions of Section A.1, but this listing should not be used as a substitute for a detailed analysis. The illustrations are not intended to be comprehensive or to provide a complete listing of items that may or may not constitute intangibles. Numerous items not included in this listing of illustrations may be intangibles for transfer pricing purposes. The illustrations in this section should be adapted to the specific legal and regulatory environment that prevails in each jurisdiction. Furthermore, the illustrations in this section should be considered and evaluated in the context of the comparability analysis (including the functional analysis) of the controlled transaction with the objective of better understanding how specific intangibles and items not treated as intangibles contribute to the creation of value in the context of the MNE's global business. It should be emphasised that a generic reference to an item included in the list of illustrations does not relieve taxpayers or tax administrations from their obligation in a transfer pricing analysis to identify relevant intangibles with specificity based on the guidance of Section A.1.

A.4.1. Patents

6.19. A patent is a legal instrument that grants an exclusive right to its owner to use a given invention for a limited period of time within a specific geography. A patent may relate to a physical object or to a process. Patentable inventions are often developed through risky and costly research and development activities. In some circumstances, however, small research and development expenditures can lead to highly valuable patentable inventions. The developer of a patent may try to recover its development costs (and earn a return) through the sale of products covered by the patent, by licensing others to use the patented invention, or by an outright sale of the patent. The exclusivity granted by a patent may, under some circumstances, allow the patent owner to earn premium returns from the use of its invention. In other cases, a patented invention may provide cost advantages to the owner that are not available to competitors. In still other situations, patents may not provide a significant commercial advantage. Patents are intangibles within the meaning of Section A.1.

A.4.2. Know-how and trade secrets

6.20. Know-how and trade secrets are proprietary information or knowledge that assist or improve a commercial activity, but that are not registered for protection in the manner of a patent or trademark. Know-how and trade secrets generally consist of undisclosed information of an industrial, commercial or scientific nature arising from previous experience, which has practical application in the operation of an enterprise. Know-how and trade secrets may relate to manufacturing, marketing, research and development, or any other commercial activity. The value of know-how and trade secrets is often dependent on the ability of the enterprise to preserve the confidentiality of the know-how or trade secret. In certain industries the disclosure of information necessary to obtain patent protection could assist competitors in developing alternative solutions. Accordingly, an enterprise may, for sound business reasons, choose not to register patentable know-how, which may nonetheless contribute substantially to the success of the enterprise. The confidential nature of know-how and trade secrets may be protected to some degree by (i) unfair competition or similar laws, (ii) employment contracts, and (iii) economic and technological barriers to competition. Know-how and trade secrets are intangibles within the meaning of Section A.1.

A.4.3. Trademarks, trade names and brands

6.21. A trademark is a unique name, symbol, logo or picture that the owner may use to distinguish its products and services from those of other entities. Proprietary rights in trademarks are often confirmed through a registration system. The registered owner of a trademark may exclude others from using the trademark in a manner that would create confusion in the marketplace. A trademark registration may continue indefinitely if the trademark is continuously used and the registration appropriately renewed. Trademarks may be established for goods or services, and may apply to a single product or service, or to a line of products or services. Trademarks are perhaps most familiar at the consumer market level, but they are likely to be encountered at all market levels. Trademarks are intangibles within the meaning of Section A.1.

6.22. A trade name (often but not always the name of an enterprise) may have the same force of market penetration as a trademark and may indeed be registered in some specific form as a trademark. The trade names of certain MNEs may be readily recognised, and may be used in marketing a variety of goods and services. Trade names are intangibles within the meaning of Section A.1.

6.23. The term "brand" is sometimes used interchangeably with the terms "trademark" and "trade name." In other contexts a brand is thought of as a trademark or trade name imbued with social and commercial significance. A brand may, in fact, represent a combination of intangibles and/or other items, including among others, trademarks, trade names, customer relationships, reputational characteristics, and goodwill. It may sometimes be difficult or impossible to segregate or separately transfer the various items contributing to brand value. A brand may consist of a single intangible, or a collection of intangibles, within the meaning of Section A.1.

A.4.4. Rights under contracts and government licences

6.24. Government licences and concessions may be important to a particular business and can cover a wide range of business relationships. They may include, among others, a government grant of rights to exploit specific natural resources or public goods (e.g. a licence of bandwidth spectrum), or to carry on a specific business activity. Government licences and concessions are intangibles within the meaning of Section A.1. However, government licences and concessions should be distinguished from company registration obligations that are preconditions for doing business in a particular jurisdiction. Such obligations are not intangibles within the meaning of Section A.1.

6.25. Rights under contracts may also be important to a particular business and can cover a wide range of business relationships. They may include, among others, contracts with suppliers and key customers, and agreements to make available the services of one or more employees. Rights under contracts are intangibles within the meaning of Section A.1.

A.4.5. Licences and similar limited rights in intangibles

6.26. Limited rights in intangibles are commonly transferred by means of a licence or other similar contractual arrangement, whether written, oral or implied. Such licensed rights may be limited as to field of use, term of use, geography or in other ways. Such limited rights in intangibles are themselves intangibles within the meaning of Section A.1.

A.4.6. Goodwill and ongoing concern value

6.27. Depending on the context, the term goodwill can be used to refer to a number of different concepts. In some accounting and business valuation contexts, goodwill reflects the difference between the aggregate value of an operating business and the sum of the values of all separately identifiable tangible and intangible assets. Alternatively, goodwill is sometimes described as a representation of the future economic benefits associated with business assets that are not individually identified and separately recognised. In still other contexts goodwill is referred to as the expectation of future trade from existing customers. The term ongoing concern value is sometimes referred to as the value of the assembled assets of an operating business over and above the sum of the separate values of the individual assets. It is generally recognised that goodwill and ongoing concern value cannot be segregated or transferred separately from other business assets. See paragraphs 9.68-9.70 for a discussion of the related notion of a transfer of all of the elements of an ongoing concern in connection with a business restructuring.

6.28. It is not necessary for purposes of this chapter to establish a precise definition of goodwill or ongoing concern value for transfer pricing purposes or to define when goodwill or ongoing concern value may or may not constitute an intangible. It is important to recognise, however, that an important and monetarily significant part of the compensation paid between independent enterprises when some or all of the assets of an operating business are transferred may represent compensation for something referred to in one or another of the alternative descriptions of goodwill or ongoing concern value. When similar transactions occur between associated enterprises, such value should be taken into account in determining an arm's length price for the transaction. When the reputational value sometimes referred to by the term goodwill is transferred to or shared with an associated enterprise in connection with a transfer or licence of a trademark or other intangible that reputational value should be taken into account in determining appropriate compensation. If features of a business such as a reputation for producing high quality products or providing high quality service allow that business to charge higher prices for goods or services than an entity lacking such reputation, and such features might be characterised as goodwill or ongoing concern value under one or another definition of such terms, such features should be taken into account in establishing arm's length prices for sales of goods or the provision of services between associated enterprises whether or not they are characterised as goodwill. In other words, labelling a contribution of value from one party to another as goodwill or ongoing concern value does not render such contribution non-compensable. See paragraph 6.2.

6.29. The requirement that goodwill and ongoing concern value be taken into account in pricing transactions in no way implies that the residual measures of goodwill derived for some specific accounting or business valuation purposes are necessarily appropriate measures of the price that would be paid for the transferred business or licence rights, together with their associated goodwill and ongoing concern value, by independent parties. Accounting and business valuation measures of goodwill and ongoing concern value do not, as a general rule, correspond to the arm's length price of transferred goodwill or ongoing concern value in a transfer pricing analysis. Depending on the facts and circumstances, however, accounting valuations and the information supporting such valuations can provide a useful starting point in conducting a transfer pricing analysis. The absence of a single precise definition of goodwill makes it essential for taxpayers and tax administrations to describe specifically relevant intangibles in connection with a transfer pricing analysis, and to consider whether independent enterprises would provide compensation for such intangibles in comparable circumstances.

A.4.7. Group synergies

6.30. In some circumstances group synergies contribute to the level of income earned by an MNE group. Such group synergies can take many different forms including streamlined management, elimination of costly duplication of effort, integrated systems, purchasing or borrowing power, etc. Such features may have an effect on the determination of arm's length conditions for controlled transactions and should be addressed for transfer pricing purposes as comparability factors. As they are not owned or controlled by an enterprise, they are not intangibles within the meaning of Section A.1. See Section D.8 of Chapter I for a discussion of the transfer pricing treatment of group synergies.

A.4.8. Market specific characteristics

6.31. Specific characteristics of a given market may affect the arm's length conditions of transactions in that market. For example, the high purchasing power of households in a particular market may affect the prices paid for certain luxury consumer goods. Similarly, low prevailing labour costs, proximity to markets, favourable weather conditions and the like may affect the prices paid for specific goods and services in a particular market. Such market specific characteristics are not capable, however, of being owned or controlled, and are therefore not intangibles within the meaning of Section A.1, and should be taken into account in a transfer pricing analysis through the required comparability analysis. See Section D.6 of Chapter I for guidance regarding the transfer pricing treatment of market specific characteristics.

B. Ownership of intangibles and transactions involving the development, enhancement, maintenance, protection and exploitation of intangibles

6.32. In transfer pricing cases involving intangibles, the determination of the entity or entities within an MNE group which are ultimately entitled to share in the returns derived by the group from exploiting intangibles is crucial.[3] A related issue is which entity or entities within the group should ultimately bear the costs, investments and other burdens associated with the development, enhancement, maintenance, protection and exploitation of intangibles. Although the legal owner of an intangible may receive the proceeds from exploitation of the intangible, other members of the legal owner's MNE group may have performed functions, used assets,[4] or assumed risks that are expected to contribute to the value of the intangible. Members of the MNE group performing such functions, using such assets, and assuming such risks must be compensated for their contributions under the arm's length principle. This Section B confirms that the ultimate allocation of the returns derived by the MNE group from the exploitation of intangibles, and the ultimate allocation of costs and other burdens related to intangibles among members of the MNE group, is accomplished by compensating members of the MNE group for functions performed, assets used, and risks assumed in the development, enhancement, maintenance, protection and exploitation of intangibles according to the principles described in Chapters I-III.

6.33. Applying the provisions of Chapters I-III to address these questions can be highly challenging for a number of reasons. Depending on the facts of any given case involving intangibles the following factors, among others, can create challenges:

3. As used herein, exploitation of an intangible includes both the transfer of the intangible or rights in the intangible and the use of the intangible in commercial operations.
4. As used in this Section B, the use of assets includes the contribution of funding and/or capital to the development, enhancement, maintenance, protection or exploitation of intangibles. See paragraph 6.59.

i) A lack of comparability between the intangible related transactions undertaken between associated enterprises and those transactions that can be identified between independent enterprises;

ii) A lack of comparability between the intangibles in question;

iii) The ownership and/or use of different intangibles by different associated enterprises within the MNE group;

iv) The difficulty of isolating the impact of any particular intangible on the MNE group's income;

v) The fact that various members of an MNE group may perform activities relating to the development, enhancement, maintenance, protection and exploitation of an intangible, often in a way and with a level of integration that is not observed between independent enterprises;

vi) The fact that contributions of various members of the MNE group to intangible value may take place in years different than the years in which any associated returns are realised; and

vii) The fact that taxpayer structures may be based on contractual terms between associated enterprises that separate ownership, the assumption of risk, and/or funding of investments in intangibles from performance of important functions, control over risk, and decisions related to investment in ways that are not observed in transactions between independent enterprises and that may contribute to base erosion and profit shifting.

Notwithstanding these potential challenges, applying the arm's length principle and the provisions of Chapters I-III within an established framework can, in most cases, yield an appropriate allocation of the returns derived by the MNE group from the exploitation of intangibles.

6.34. The framework for analysing transactions involving intangibles between associated enterprises requires taking the following steps, consistent with the guidance for identifying the commercial or financial relations provided in Section D.1 of Chapter I:

i) Identify the intangibles used or transferred in the transaction with specificity and the specific, economically significant risks associated with the development, enhancement, maintenance, protection, and exploitation of the intangibles;

ii) Identify the full contractual arrangements, with special emphasis on determining legal ownership of intangibles based on the terms and conditions of legal arrangements, including relevant registrations, licence agreements, other relevant contracts, and other indicia of legal ownership, and the contractual rights and obligations, including contractual assumption of risks in the relations between the associated enterprises;

iii) Identify the parties performing functions (including specifically the important functions described in paragraph 6.56), using assets, and managing risks related to developing, enhancing, maintaining, protecting, and exploiting the intangibles by means of the functional analysis, and in particular which parties control any outsourced functions, and control specific, economically significant risks;

iv) Confirm the consistency between the terms of the relevant contractual arrangements and the conduct of the parties, and determine whether the party assuming economically significant risks under step 4 (i) of paragraph 1.60, controls the risks and has the financial capacity to assume the risks relating to the development, enhancement, maintenance, protection, and exploitation of the intangibles;

v) Delineate the actual controlled transactions related to the development, enhancement, maintenance, protection, and exploitation of intangibles in light of the legal ownership of the intangibles, the other relevant contractual relations under relevant registrations and contracts, and the conduct of the parties, including their relevant contributions of functions, assets and risks, taking into account the framework for analysing and allocating risk under Section D.1.2.1 of Chapter I;

vi) Where possible, determine arm's length prices for these transactions consistent with each party's contributions of functions performed, assets used, and risks assumed, unless the guidance in Section D.2 of Chapter I applies.

B.1. Intangible ownership and contractual terms relating to intangibles

6.35. Legal rights and contractual arrangements form the starting point for any transfer pricing analysis of transactions involving intangibles. The terms of a transaction may be found in written contracts, public records such as patent or trademark registrations, or in correspondence and/or other communications among the parties. Contracts may describe the roles, responsibilities and rights of associated enterprises with respect to intangibles. They may describe which entity or entities provide funding, undertake research and development, maintain and protect intangibles, and perform functions necessary to exploit the intangibles, such as manufacturing, marketing and distribution. They may describe how receipts and expenses of the MNE associated with intangibles are to be allocated and may specify the form and amount of payment to all members of the group for their contributions. The prices and other conditions contained in such contracts may or may not be consistent with the arm's length principle.

6.36. Where no written terms exist, or where the facts of the case, including the conduct of the parties, differ from the written terms of any agreement between them or supplement these written terms, the actual transaction must be deduced from the facts as established, including the conduct of the parties (see Section D.1.1 of Chapter I). It is, therefore, good practice for associated enterprises to document their decisions and intentions regarding the allocation of significant rights in intangibles. Documentation of such decisions and intentions, including written agreements, should generally be in place at or before the time that associated enterprises enter into transactions leading to the development, enhancement, maintenance, protection, or exploitation of intangibles.

6.37. The right to use some types of intangibles may be protected under specific intellectual property laws and registration systems. Patents, trademarks and copyrights are examples of such intangibles. Generally, the registered legal owner of such intangibles has the exclusive legal and commercial right to use the intangible, as well as the right to prevent others from using or otherwise infringing the intangible. These rights may be granted for a specific geographic area and/or for a specific period of time.

6.38. There are also intangibles that are not protectable under specific intellectual property registration systems, but that are protected against unauthorised appropriation or imitation under unfair competition legislation or other enforceable laws, or by contract. Trade dress, trade secrets, and know-how may fall under this category of intangibles.

6.39. The extent and nature of the available protection under applicable law may vary from jurisdiction to jurisdiction, as may the conditions on which such protection is provided. Such differences can arise either from differences in substantive intellectual property law between jurisdictions, or from practical differences in local enforcement of such laws. For example, the availability of legal protection for some intangibles may be subject to conditions such as continued commercial use of the intangible or timely renewal of registrations. This means that in some circumstances or jurisdictions, the degree of protection for an intangible may be extremely limited either legally or in practice.

6.40. The legal owner will be considered to be the owner of the intangible for transfer pricing purposes. If no legal owner of the intangible is identified under applicable law or governing contracts, then the member of the MNE group that, based on the facts and circumstances, controls decisions concerning the exploitation of the intangible and has the practical capacity to restrict others from using the intangible will be considered the legal owner of the intangible for transfer pricing purposes.

6.41. In identifying the legal owner of intangibles, an intangible and any licence relating to that intangible are considered to be different intangibles for transfer pricing purposes, each having a different owner. See paragraph 6.26.

For example, Company A, the legal owner of a trademark, may provide an exclusive licence to Company B to manufacture, market, and sell goods using the trademark. One intangible, the trademark, is legally owned by Company A. Another intangible, the licence to use the trademark in connection with manufacturing, marketing and distribution of trademarked products, is legally owned by Company B. Depending on the facts and circumstances, marketing activities undertaken by Company B pursuant to its licence may potentially affect the value of the underlying intangible legally owned by Company A, the value of Company B's licence, or both.

6.42. While determining legal ownership and contractual arrangements is an important first step in the analysis, these determinations are separate and distinct from the question of remuneration under the arm's length principle. For transfer pricing purposes, legal ownership of intangibles, by itself, does not confer any right ultimately to retain returns derived by the MNE group from exploiting the intangible, even though such returns may initially accrue to the legal owner as a result of its legal or contractual right to exploit the intangible. The return ultimately retained by or attributed to the legal owner depends upon the functions it performs, the assets it uses, and the risks it assumes, and upon the contributions made by other MNE group members through their functions performed, assets used, and risks assumed. For example, in the case of an internally developed intangible, if the legal owner performs no relevant functions, uses no relevant assets, and assumes no relevant risks, but acts solely as a title holding entity, the legal owner will not ultimately be entitled to any portion of the return derived by the MNE group from the exploitation of the intangible other than arm's length compensation, if any, for holding title.

6.43. Legal ownership and contractual relationships serve simply as reference points for identifying and analysing controlled transactions relating to the intangible and for determining the appropriate remuneration to members of a controlled group with respect to those transactions. Identification of legal ownership, combined with the identification and compensation of relevant functions performed, assets used, and risks assumed by all contributing members, provides the analytical framework for identifying arm's length prices and other conditions for transactions involving intangibles. As with any other type of transaction, the analysis must take into account all of the relevant facts and circumstances present in a particular case and price determinations must reflect the realistic alternatives of the relevant group members. The principles of this paragraph are illustrated by Examples 1 to 6 in Annex I to Chapter VI.

6.44. Because the actual outcomes and manner in which risks associated with the development or acquisition of an intangible will play out over time are not known with certainty at the time members of the MNE group make decisions regarding intangibles, it is important to distinguish between (a) anticipated (or *ex ante*) remuneration, which refers to the future income expected to be derived by a member of the MNE group at the time of a transaction; and (b) actual (or *ex post*) remuneration, which refers to the income actually earned by a member of the group through the exploitation of the intangible.

6.45. The terms of the compensation that must be paid to members of the MNE group that contribute to the development, enhancement, maintenance, protection and exploitation of intangibles is generally determined on an *ex ante* basis. That is, it is determined at the time transactions are entered into and before risks associated with the intangible play out. The form of such compensation may be fixed or contingent. The actual (*ex post*) profit or loss of the business after compensating other members of the MNE group may differ from these anticipated profits depending on how the risks associated with the intangible or the other relevant risks related to the transaction or arrangement actually play out. The accurately delineated transaction, as determined under Section D.1 of Chapter I, will determine which associated entity assumes such risks and accordingly will bear the consequences (costs or additional returns) when the risks materialise in a different manner to what was anticipated (see Section B.2.4).

6.46. An important question is how to determine the appropriate arm's length remuneration to members of a group for their functions, assets, and risks within the framework established by the taxpayer's contractual arrangements, the legal ownership of intangibles, and the conduct of the parties. Section B.2 discusses the application of the arm's length principle to situations involving intangibles. It focuses on the functions, assets and risks related to the intangibles. Unless stated otherwise, references to arm's length returns and arm's length remuneration in Section B.2 refer to anticipated (*ex ante*) returns and remuneration.

B.2. Functions, assets, and risks related to intangibles

6.47. As stated above, a determination that a particular group member is the legal owner of intangibles does not, in and of itself, necessarily imply that the legal owner is entitled to any income generated by the business after compensating other members of the MNE group for their contributions in the form of functions performed, assets used, and risks assumed.

6.48. In identifying arm's length prices for transactions among associated enterprises, the contributions of members of the group related to the creation of intangible value should be considered and appropriately rewarded. The arm's length principle and the principles of Chapters I-III require that all members of the group receive appropriate compensation for any functions they perform, assets they use, and risks they assume in connection with the development, enhancement, maintenance, protection, and exploitation of intangibles. It is therefore necessary to determine, by means of a functional analysis, which member(s) perform and exercise control over development, enhancement, maintenance, protection, and exploitation functions, which member(s) provide funding and other assets, and which member(s) assume the various risks associated with the intangible. Of course, in each of these areas, this may or may not be the legal owner of the intangible. As noted in paragraph 6.133, it is also important in determining arm's length compensation for functions performed, assets used, and risks assumed to consider comparability factors that may contribute to the creation of value or the generation of returns derived by the MNE group from the exploitation of intangibles in determining prices for relevant transactions.

6.49. The relative importance of contributions to the creation of intangible value by members of the group in the form of functions performed, assets used and risks assumed will vary depending on the circumstances. For example, assume that a fully developed and currently exploitable intangible is purchased from a third party by a member of a group and exploited through manufacturing and distribution functions performed by other group members while being actively managed and controlled by the entity purchasing the intangible. It is assumed that this intangible would require no development, may require little or no maintenance or protection, and may have limited usefulness outside the area of exploitation intended at the time of the acquisition. There would be no development risk associated with the intangible, although there are risks associated with acquiring and exploiting the intangible. The key functions performed by the purchaser are those necessary to select the most appropriate intangible on the market, to analyse its potential benefits if used by the MNE group, and the decision to take on the risk-bearing opportunity through purchasing the intangible. The key asset used is the funding required to purchase the intangible. If the purchaser has the capacity and actually performs all the key functions described, including control of the risks associated with acquiring and exploiting the intangible, it may be reasonable to conclude that, after making arm's length payment for the manufacturing and distribution functions of other associated enterprises, the owner would be entitled to retain or have attributed to it any income or loss derived from the post-acquisition exploitation of the intangible. While the application of Chapters I-III may be fairly straightforward in such a simple fact pattern, the analysis may be more difficult in situations in which:

i) Intangibles are self-developed by a multinational group, especially when such intangibles are transferred between associated enterprises while still under development;

ii) Acquired or self-developed intangibles serve as a platform for further development; or

iii) Other aspects, such as marketing or manufacturing are particularly important to value creation.

The generally applicable guidance below is particularly relevant for, and is primarily concerned with, these more difficult cases.

B.2.1. Performance and control of functions

6.50. Under the principles of Chapters I-III, each member of the MNE group should receive arm's length compensation for the functions it performs. In cases involving intangibles, this includes functions related to the development, enhancement, maintenance, protection, and exploitation of intangibles. The identity of the member or members of the group performing functions related to the development, enhancement, maintenance, protection, and exploitation of intangibles, therefore, is one of the key considerations in determining arm's length conditions for controlled transactions.

6.51. The need to ensure that all members of the MNE group are appropriately compensated for the functions they perform, the assets they contribute and the risks they assume implies that if the legal owner of intangibles is to be entitled ultimately to retain all of the returns derived from exploitation of the intangibles it must perform all of the functions, contribute all assets used and assume all risks related to the development, enhancement, maintenance, protection and exploitation of the intangible. This does not imply, however, that the associated enterprises constituting an MNE group must structure their operations regarding the development, enhancement, maintenance, protection or exploitation of intangibles in any particular way. It is not essential that the legal owner physically performs all of the functions related to the development, enhancement, maintenance, protection and exploitation of an intangible through its own personnel in order to be entitled ultimately to retain or be attributed a portion of the return derived by the MNE group from exploitation of the intangibles. In transactions between independent enterprises, certain functions are sometimes outsourced to other entities. A member of an MNE group that is the legal owner of intangibles could similarly outsource functions related to the development, enhancement, maintenance, protection or exploitation of intangibles to either independent enterprises or associated enterprises.

6.52. Where associated enterprises other than the legal owner perform relevant functions that are anticipated to contribute to the value of the intangibles, they should be compensated on an arm's length basis for the functions they perform under the principles set out in Chapters I-III. The determination of arm's length compensation for functional contributions should consider the availability of comparable uncontrolled transactions, the importance of the functions performed to the creation of intangible value, and the realistically available options of the parties. The specific considerations described in paragraphs 6.53 to 6.58 should also be taken into account.

6.53. In outsourcing transactions between independent enterprises, it is usually the case that an entity performing functions on behalf of the legal owner of the intangible that relate to the development, enhancement, maintenance, protection, and exploitation of the intangible will operate under the control of such legal owner (as discussed in paragraph 1.65). Because of the nature of the relationships between associated enterprises that are members of an MNE group, however, it may be the case that outsourced functions performed by associated enterprises will be controlled by an entity other than the legal owner of the intangibles. In such cases, the legal owner of the intangible should also compensate the entity performing control functions related to the development, enhancement, maintenance, protection, and exploitation of intangibles on an arm's length basis. In assessing what member of the MNE group in fact controls the performance of the relevant functions, principles apply analogous to those for determining control over risk in Section D.1.2.1 of Chapter I. Assessing the capacity of a particular entity to exert control and the actual performance of such control functions will be an important part of the analysis.

6.54. If the legal owner neither controls nor performs the functions related to the development, enhancement, maintenance, protection or exploitation of the intangible, the legal owner would not be entitled to any ongoing benefit attributable to the outsourced functions. Depending on the facts, the arm's length compensation required to be provided by the legal owner to other associated enterprises performing or controlling functions related to the development, enhancement, maintenance, protection, or exploitation of intangibles may comprise any share of the total return derived from exploitation of the intangibles. A legal owner not performing any relevant function relating to the development, enhancement, maintenance, protection or exploitation of the intangible will therefore not be entitled to any portion of such returns related to the performance or control of functions relating to the development, enhancement, maintenance, protection or exploitation of the intangible. It is entitled to an arm's length compensation for any functions it actually performs, any assets it actually uses and risks it actually assumes. See Sections B.2.2 to B.2.3. In determining the functions it actually performs, assets it actually uses and the risks it actually assumes the guidance in Section D.1.2 of Chapter I is especially relevant.

6.55. The relative value of contributions to development, enhancement, maintenance, protection, and exploitation of intangibles varies depending on the particular facts of the case. The MNE group member(s) making the more significant contributions in a particular case should receive relatively greater remuneration. For example, a company that merely funds research and development should have a lower anticipated return than if it both funds and controls research and development. Other things being equal, a still higher anticipated return should be provided if the entity funds, controls, and physically performs the research and development. See also the discussion of funding in Section B.2.2.

6.56. In considering the arm's length compensation for functional contributions of various members of the MNE group, certain important functions will have special significance. The nature of these important functions in any specific case will depend on the facts and circumstances. For self-developed intangibles, or for self-developed or acquired intangibles that serve as a platform for further development activities, these more important functions may include, among others, design and control of research and marketing programmes, direction of and establishing priorities for creative undertakings including determining the course of "blue-sky" research, control over strategic decisions regarding intangible development programmes, and management and control of budgets. For any intangible (i.e. for either self-developed or acquired intangibles) other important functions may also include important decisions regarding defence and protection of intangibles, and ongoing quality control over functions performed by independent or associated enterprises that may have a material effect on the value of the intangible. Those important functions usually make a significant contribution to intangible value and, if those important functions are outsourced by the legal owner in transactions between associated enterprises, the performance of those functions should be compensated with an appropriate share of the returns derived by the MNE group from the exploitation of intangibles.

6.57. Because it may be difficult to find comparable transactions involving the outsourcing of such important functions, it may be necessary to utilise transfer pricing methods not directly based on comparables, including transactional profit split methods and *ex ante* valuation techniques, to appropriately reward the performance of those important functions. Where the legal owner outsources most or all of such important functions to other group members, attribution to the legal owner of any material portion of the return derived from the exploitation of the intangibles after compensating other group members for their functions should be carefully considered taking into account the functions it actually performs, the assets it actually uses and the risks it actually assumes under the guidance in Section D.1.2 of Chapter I. Examples 16 and 17 in Annex I to Chapter VI illustrate the principles contained in this paragraph.

6.58. Because the important functions described in paragraph 6.56 are often instrumental in managing the different functions performed, assets used, and risks assumed that are key to the successful development, enhancement, maintenance, protection, or exploitation of intangibles, and are therefore essential to the creation of intangible value, it is necessary to carefully evaluate transactions between parties performing these important functions and other associated enterprises. In particular, the reliability of a one-sided transfer pricing method will be substantially reduced if the party or parties performing significant portions of the important functions are treated as the tested party or parties. See Example 6.

B.2.2. Use of assets

6.59. Group members that use assets in the development, enhancement, maintenance, protection, and exploitation of an intangible should receive appropriate compensation for doing so. Such assets may include, without limitation, intangibles used in research, development or marketing (e.g. know-how, customer relationships, etc.), physical assets, or funding. One member of an MNE group may fund some or all of the development, enhancement, maintenance, and protection of an intangible, while one or more other members perform all of the relevant functions. When assessing the appropriate anticipated return to funding in such circumstances, it should be recognised that in arm's length transactions, a party that provides funding, but does not control the risks or perform other functions associated with the funded activity or asset, generally does not receive anticipated returns equivalent to those received by an otherwise similarly-situated investor who also performs and controls important functions and controls important risks associated with the funded activity. The nature and amount of compensation attributable to an entity that bears intangible-related costs, without more, must be determined on the basis of all the relevant facts, and should be consistent with similar funding arrangements among independent entities where such arrangements can be identified. See the guidance in Section D.1.2.1.6 of Chapter I, and in particular Example 3 in paragraphs 1.85 and 1.103, which illustrate a situation where the party providing funding does not control the financial risk associated with the funding.

6.60. Funding and risk-taking are integrally related in the sense that funding often coincides with the taking of certain risks (e.g. the funding party contractually assuming the risk of loss of its funds). The nature and extent of the risk assumed, however, will vary depending on the economically relevant characteristics of the transaction. The risk will, for example, be lower when the party to which the funding is provided has a high creditworthiness, or when assets are pledged, or when the investment funded is low risk, compared with the risk where the creditworthiness is lower, or the funding is unsecured, or the investment being funded is high risk. Moreover, the larger the amount of the funds provided, the larger the potential impact of the risk on the provider of the funding.

6.61. Under the principles of Section D.1.2 of Chapter I, the first step in a transfer pricing analysis in relation to risks is to identify the economically significant risks with specificity. When identifying risks in relation to an investment with specificity, it is important to distinguish between the financial risks that are linked to the funding provided for the investments and the operational risks that are linked to the operational activities for which the funding is used, such as for example the development risk when the funding is used for developing a new intangible. Where a party providing funding exercises control over the financial risk associated with the provision of funding, without the assumption of, including the control over, any other specific risk, it could generally only expect a risk-adjusted return on its funding.

6.62. The contractual arrangements will generally determine the terms of the funding transaction, as clarified or supplemented by the economic characteristics of the transaction as reflected in the conduct of the parties.[5] The return that would generally be expected by the funder should equal an appropriate risk-adjusted return. Such return can be determined, for example, based on the cost of capital or the return of a realistic alternative investment with comparable economic characteristics. In determining an appropriate return for the funding activities, it is important to consider the financing options realistically available to the party receiving the funds. There may be a difference between the return expected by the funder on an *ex ante* basis and the actual return received on an *ex post* basis. For example, when the funder provides a loan for a fixed amount at a fixed interest rate, the difference between the actual and expected returns will reflect the risk playing out that the borrower cannot make some or all of the payments due.

6.63. The extent and form of the activities that will be necessary to exercise control over the financial risk attached to the provision of funding will depend on the riskiness of the investment for the funder, taking into account the amount of money at stake and the investment for which these funds are used. In accordance with the definition of control as reflected in paragraphs 1.65 and 1.66 of these Guidelines, exercising control over a specific financial risk requires the capability to make the relevant decisions related to the risk bearing opportunity, in this case the provision of the funding, together with the actual performance of these decision making functions. In addition, the party exercising control over the financial risk must perform the activities as indicated in paragraph 1.65 and 1.66 in relation to the day-to-day risk mitigation activities related to these risks when these are outsourced and related to any preparatory work necessary to facilitate its decision making, if it does not perform these activities itself.

6.64. When funding is provided to a party for the development of an intangible, the relevant decisions relating to taking on, laying off or declining a risk bearing opportunity and the decisions on whether and how to respond

5. Further guidance will be provided on the economically relevant characteristics for determining the arm's length conditions for financial transactions, including when the funding is used for project finance, in particular investments in the development of intangibles. This work will be undertaken in 2016 and 2017.

to the risks associated with the opportunity, are the decisions related to the provision of funding and the conditions of the transaction. Depending on the facts and circumstances, such decisions may depend on an assessment of the creditworthiness of the party receiving the funds and an assessment of how the risks related to the development project may impact the expectations in relation to the returns on funding provided or additional funding required. The conditions underlying the provision of the funding may include the possibility to link funding decisions to key development decisions which will impact the funding return. For example, decisions may have to be made on whether to take the project to the next stage or to allow the investments in costly assets. The higher the development risk and the closer the financial risk is related to the development risk, the more the funder will need to have the capability to assess the progress of the development of the intangible and the consequences of this progress for achieving its expected funding return, and the more closely the funder may link the continued provision of funding to key operational developments that may impact its financial risk. The funder will need to have the capability to make the assessments regarding the continued provision of funding, and will need to actually make such assessments, which will then need to be taken into account by the funder in actually making the relevant decisions on the provision of funding.

B.2.3. Assumption of risks

6.65. Particular types of risk that may have importance in a functional analysis relating to transactions involving intangibles include (i) risks related to development of intangibles, including the risk that costly research and development or marketing activities will prove to be unsuccessful, and taking into account the timing of the investment (for example, whether the investment is made at an early stage, mid-way through the development process, or at a late stage will impact the level of the underlying investment risk); (ii) the risk of product obsolescence, including the possibility that technological advances of competitors will adversely affect the value of the intangibles; (iii) infringement risk, including the risk that defence of intangible rights or defence against other persons' claims of infringement may prove to be time consuming, costly and/or unavailing; (iv) product liability and similar risks related to products and services based on the intangibles; and (v) exploitation risks, uncertainties in relation to the returns to be generated by the intangible. The existence and level of such risks will depend on the facts and circumstances of each individual case and the nature of the intangible in question.

6.66. The identity of the member or members of the group assuming risks related to the development, enhancement, maintenance, protection, and exploitation of intangibles is an important consideration in determining prices for controlled transactions. The assumption of risk will determine which entity or entities will be responsible for the consequences if the risk materialises. The accurate delineation of the controlled transaction, based on the guidance in Section D.1 of Chapter I, may determine that the legal owner assumes risks or that, instead, other members of the group are assuming risks, and such members must be compensated for their contributions in that regard.

6.67. In determining which member or members of the group assume risks related to intangibles, the principles of Section D.1.2 of Chapter I apply. In particular, steps 1 to 5 of the process to analyse risk in a controlled transaction as laid out in paragraph 1.60 should be followed in determining which party assumes risks related to the development, enhancement, maintenance, protection, and exploitation of intangibles.

6.68. It is especially important to ensure that the group member(s) asserting entitlement to returns from assuming risk actually bear responsibility for the actions that need to be taken and the costs that may be incurred if the relevant risk materialises. If costs are borne or actions are undertaken by an associated enterprise other than the associated enterprise assuming the risk as determined under the framework for analysing risk reflected in paragraph 1.60 of these guidelines, then a transfer pricing adjustment should be made so that the costs are allocated to the party assuming the risk and the other associated enterprise is appropriately remunerated for any activities undertaken in connection with the materialisation of the risk. Example 7 in Annex I to Chapter VI illustrates this principle.

B.2.4. Actual, ex post returns

6.69. It is quite common that actual (*ex post*) profitability is different than anticipated (*ex ante*) profitability. This may result from risks materialising in a different way to what was anticipated through the occurrence of unforeseeable developments. For example, it may happen that a competitive product is removed from the market, a natural disaster takes place in a key market, a key asset malfunctions for unforeseeable reasons, or that a breakthrough technological development by a competitor will have the effect of making products based on the intangible in question obsolete or less desirable. It may also happen that the financial projections, on which calculations of *ex ante* returns and compensation arrangements are based, properly took into account risks and the probability of reasonably foreseeable events occurring and that the differences between actual and anticipated profitability reflects the playing out of those risks. Finally, it may happen that financial projections, on which calculations of *ex ante* returns and compensation arrangements are based, did not adequately take into account the risks of different outcomes occurring and therefore led to an overestimation or an underestimation of the anticipated profits. The question arises in such circumstances whether, and if so, how the profits or losses should be shared among members of an MNE group that have contributed to the development, enhancement, maintenance, protection, and exploitation of the intangible in question.

6.70. Resolution of this question requires a careful analysis of which entity or entities in the MNE group in fact assume the economically significant risks as identified when delineating the actual transaction (see Section D.1 of Chapter I). As this analytical framework indicates, the party actually assuming the economically significant risks may or may not be the associated enterprise contractually assuming these risks, such as the legal owner of the intangible, or may or may not be the funder of the investment. A party which is not allocated the risks that give rise to the deviation between the anticipated and actual outcomes under the principles of Sections D.1.2.1.4 to D.1.2.1.6 of Chapter I will not be entitled to the differences between actual and anticipated profits or required to bear losses that are caused by these differences if such risk materialises, unless these parties are performing the important functions as reflected in paragraph 6.56 or contributing to the control over the economically significant risks as established in paragraph 1.105, and it is determined that arm's length remuneration of these functions would include a profit sharing element. In addition, consideration must be given to whether the *ex ante* remuneration paid to members of the MNE group for their functions performed, assets used, and risks assumed is, in fact, consistent with the arm's length principle. Care should be taken to ascertain, for example, whether the group in fact underestimated or overestimated anticipated profits, thereby giving rise to underpayments or overpayments (determined on an *ex ante* basis) to some group members for their contributions. Transactions for which valuation is highly uncertain at the time of the transaction are particularly susceptible to such under or overestimations of value. This is further discussed in Section D.4.

B.2.5. Some implications from applying Sections B.1 and B.2

6.71. If the legal owner of an intangible in substance:

- performs and controls all of the functions (including the important functions described in paragraph 6.56) related to the development, enhancement, maintenance, protection and exploitation of the intangible;
- provides all assets, including funding, necessary to the development, enhancement, maintenance, protection, and exploitation of the intangibles; and
- assumes all of the risks related to the development, enhancement, maintenance, protection, and exploitation of the intangible,

then it will be entitled to all of the anticipated, *ex ante,* returns derived from the MNE group's exploitation of the intangible. To the extent that one or more members of the MNE group other than the legal owner performs functions, uses assets, or assumes risks related to the development, enhancement, maintenance, protection and exploitation of the intangible, such associated enterprises must be compensated on an arm's length basis for their contributions. This compensation may, depending on the facts and circumstances, constitute all or a substantial part of the return anticipated to be derived from the exploitation of the intangible.

6.72. The entitlement of any member of the MNE group to profit or loss relating to differences between actual (*ex post*) and a proper estimation of anticipated (*ex ante*) profitability will depend on which entity or entities in the MNE group in fact assumes the risks as identified when delineating the actual transaction (see Section D.1 of Chapter I). It will also depend on the entity or entities which are performing the important functions as reflected in paragraph 6.56 or contributing to the control over the economically significant risks as established in paragraph 1.105, and for which it is determined that an arm's length remuneration of these functions would include a profit sharing element.

B.3. Identifying and determining the prices and other conditions for the controlled transactions

6.73. Undertaking the analysis described in Section D.1 of Chapter I, as supplemented by this Chapter, should facilitate a clear assessment of legal ownership, functions, assets and risks associated with intangibles, and an accurate identification of the transactions whose prices and other conditions require determination. In general, the transactions identified by the MNE group in the relevant registrations and contracts are those whose prices and other conditions are to be determined under the arm's length principle. However, the analysis may reveal that transactions in addition to, or different from, the transactions described in the registrations and contracts actually occurred. Consistent with Section D.1 of Chapter I, the transactions (and the true terms thereof) to be analysed are those determined to have occurred consistent with the actual conduct of the parties and other relevant facts.

6.74. Arm's length prices and other conditions for transactions should be determined according to the guidance in Chapters I-III, taking into account the contributions to anticipated intangible value of functions performed, assets used, and risks assumed at the time such functions are performed, assets are used, or risks are assumed as discussed in this Section B of this chapter. Section D of this chapter provides supplemental guidance on transfer pricing methods and other matters applicable in determining arm's length prices and other conditions for transactions involving intangibles.

B.4. Application of the foregoing principles in specific fact patterns

6.75. The principles set out in this Section B must be applied in a variety of situations involving the development, enhancement, maintenance, protection, and exploitation of intangibles. A key consideration in each case is that associated enterprises that contribute to the development, enhancement, maintenance, protection, or exploitation of intangibles legally owned by another member of the group must receive arm's length compensation for the functions they perform, the risks they assume, and the assets they use. In evaluating whether associated enterprises that perform functions or assume risks related to the development, enhancement, maintenance, protection, and exploitation of intangibles have been compensated on an arm's length basis, it is necessary to consider (i) the level and nature of the activity undertaken; and (ii) the amount and form of compensation paid. In assessing whether the compensation provided in the controlled transaction is consistent with the arm's length principle, reference should be made to the level and nature of activity of comparable uncontrolled entities performing similar functions, the compensation received by comparable uncontrolled entities performing similar functions, and the anticipated creation of intangible value by comparable uncontrolled entities performing similar functions. This section describes the application of these principles in commonly occurring fact patterns.

B.4.1. Development and enhancement of marketing intangibles

6.76. A common situation where these principles must be applied arises when an enterprise associated with the legal owner of trademarks performs marketing or sales functions that benefit the legal owner of the trademark, for example through a marketing arrangement or through a distribution/ marketing arrangement. In such cases, it is necessary to determine how the marketer or distributor should be compensated for its activities. One important issue is whether the marketer/distributor should be compensated only for providing promotion and distribution services, or whether the marketer/distributor should also be compensated for enhancing the value of the trademarks and other marketing intangibles by virtue of its functions performed, assets used, and risks assumed.

6.77. The analysis of this issue requires an assessment of (i) the obligations and rights implied by the legal registrations and agreements between the parties; (ii) the functions performed, the assets used, and the risks assumed by the parties; (iii) the intangible value anticipated to be created through the marketer/distributor's activities; and (iv) the compensation provided for the functions performed by the marketer/distributor (taking account of the assets used and risks assumed). One relatively clear case is where a distributor acts merely as an agent, being reimbursed for its promotional expenditures and being directed and controlled in its activities by the owner of the trademarks and other marketing intangibles. In that case, the distributor ordinarily would be entitled to compensation appropriate to its agency activities alone. It does not assume the risks associated with the further development of the trademark and other marketing intangibles, and would therefore not be entitled to additional remuneration in that regard.

6.78. When the distributor actually bears the cost of its marketing activities (for example, when there is no arrangement for the legal owner to reimburse the expenditures), the analysis should focus on the extent to which the distributor is able to share in the potential benefits deriving from its functions performed, assets used, and risks assumed currently or in the future. In general, in arm's length transactions the ability of a party that is not the legal owner of trademarks and other marketing intangibles to obtain the benefits of marketing activities that enhance the value of those intangibles will depend principally on the substance of the rights of that party. For example, a distributor may have the ability to obtain benefits from its functions performed, assets used, and risks assumed in developing the value of a trademark and other marketing intangibles from its turnover and market share when it has a long-term contract providing for sole distribution rights for the trademarked product. In such a situation the distributor's efforts may have enhanced the value of its own intangibles, namely its distribution rights. In such cases, the distributor's share of benefits should be determined based on what an independent distributor would receive in comparable circumstances. In some cases, a distributor may perform functions, use assets or assume risks that exceed those an independent distributor with similar rights might incur or perform for the benefit of its own distribution activities and that create value beyond that created by other similarly situated marketers/distributors. An independent distributor in such a case would typically require additional remuneration from the owner of the trademark or other intangibles. Such remuneration could take the form of higher distribution profits (resulting from a decrease in the purchase price of the product), a reduction in royalty rate, or a share of the profits associated with the enhanced value of the trademark or other marketing intangibles, in order to compensate the distributor for its functions, assets, risks, and anticipated value creation. Examples 8 to 13 in Annex I to Chapter VI illustrate in greater detail the application of this Section B in the context of marketing and distribution arrangements.

B.4.2. Research, development and process improvement arrangements

6.79. The principles set out in the foregoing paragraphs also apply in situations involving the performance of research and development functions by a member of an MNE group under a contractual arrangement with an associated enterprise that is the legal owner of any resulting intangibles.

Appropriate compensation for research services will depend on all the facts and circumstances, such as whether the research team possesses unique skills and experience relevant to the research, assumes risks (e.g. where "blue sky" research is undertaken), uses its own intangibles, or is controlled and managed by another party. Compensation based on a reimbursement of costs plus a modest mark-up will not reflect the anticipated value of, or the arm's length price for, the contributions of the research team in all cases.

6.80. The principles set out in this section similarly apply in situations where a member of an MNE group provides manufacturing services that may lead to process or product improvements on behalf of an associated enterprise that will assume legal ownership of such process or product improvements. Examples 14 to 17 in Annex I to Chapter VI illustrate in greater detail the application of this Section B in the context of research and development arrangements.

B.4.3. Payments for use of the company name

6.81. Questions often arise regarding the arm's length compensation for the use of group names, trade names and similar intangibles. Resolution of such questions should be based on the principles of this Section B and on the commercial and legal factors involved. As a general rule, no payment should be recognised for transfer pricing purposes for simple recognition of group membership or the use of the group name merely to reflect the fact of group membership. See paragraph 7.12

6.82. Where one member of the group is the owner of a trademark or other intangible for the group name, and where use of the name provides a financial benefit to members of the group other than the member legally owning such intangible, it is reasonable to conclude that a payment for use would have been made in arm's length transactions. Similarly, such payments may be appropriate where a group member owns goodwill in respect of the business represented by an unregistered trademark, use of that trademark by another party would constitute misrepresentation, and the use of the trademark provides a clear financial benefit to a group member other than that owning the goodwill and unregistered trademark.

6.83. In determining the amount of payment with respect to a group name, it is important to consider the amount of the financial benefit to the user of the name attributable to use of that name, the costs and benefits associated with other alternatives, and the relative contributions to the value of the name made by the legal owner, and the entity using the name in the form of functions performed, assets used and risks assumed. Careful consideration should be given to the functions performed, assets used, and risks assumed by the user of the name in creating or enhancing the value of the name in its jurisdiction. Factors that would be important in a licence of the name to an independent enterprise under comparable circumstances applying the principles of Chapters I-III should be taken into account.

6.84. Where an existing successful business is acquired by another successful business and the acquired business begins to use a name, trademark or other branding indicative of the acquiring business, there should be no automatic assumption that a payment should be made in respect of such use. If there is a reasonable expectation of financial benefit to the acquired company from using the acquiring company's branding, then the amount of any payment should be informed by the level of that anticipated benefit.

6.85. It may also be the case that the acquiring business will leverage the existing position of the acquired business to expand the business of the acquirer in the territory of operation of the acquired business by causing the acquired business to use the acquirer's branding. In that case, consideration should be given to whether the acquirer should make a payment to or otherwise compensate the acquired business for the functions performed, risks assumed, and assets used (including its market position) in connection with expanded use of the acquirer's name.

C. Transactions involving the use or transfer of intangibles

6.86. In addition to identifying with specificity the intangibles involved in a particular transfer pricing issue, and identifying the owner of such intangibles, it is necessary to identify and properly characterise, at the beginning of any transfer pricing analysis involving intangibles, the specific controlled transactions involving intangibles. The principles of Chapter I apply in identifying and accurately delineating transactions involving the use or transfer of intangibles. In addition to the guidance on identifying the actual transaction (Section D.1 of Chapter I) and on business restructurings (Chapter IX, especially Part I), Section C of this chapter outlines some typical scenarios that may be useful in ascertaining whether intangibles or rights in intangibles are involved in a transaction. See Example 19. The characterisation of a transaction for transfer pricing purposes has no relevance for determinations under Article 12 of the OECD Model Tax Convention. See, e.g. paragraphs 8 to 19 of the Commentary to Article 12 of the OECD Model Tax Convention.

6.87. There are two general types of transactions where the identification and examination of intangibles will be relevant for transfer pricing purposes. These are: (i) transactions involving transfers of intangibles or rights in intangibles; and (ii) transactions involving the use of intangibles in connection with the sale of goods or the provision of services.

C.1. Transactions involving transfers of intangibles or rights in intangibles

C.1.1. Transfers of intangibles or rights in intangibles

6.88. Rights in intangibles themselves may be transferred in controlled transactions. Such transactions may involve a transfer of all rights in the intangibles in question (e.g. a sale of the intangible or a perpetual, exclusive licence of the intangible) or only limited rights (e.g. a licence or similar transfer of limited rights to use an intangible which may be subject to geographical restrictions, limited duration, or restrictions with respect to the right to use, exploit, reproduce, further transfer or further develop). The principles of Chapters I-III apply to transactions involving the transfer of intangibles or rights in intangibles. Supplemental guidance regarding the determination of arm's length conditions for such transactions is also contained in Sections D.1, D.2 and D.3 of this chapter.

6.89. In transactions involving the transfer of intangibles or rights in intangibles, it is essential to identify with specificity the nature of the intangibles and rights in intangibles that are transferred between associated enterprises. Where limitations are imposed on the rights transferred, it is also essential to identify the nature of such limitations and the full extent of the rights transferred. It should be noted in this regard that the labels applied to transactions do not control the transfer pricing analysis. For example, in the case of a transfer of the exclusive right to exploit a patent in Country X, the taxpayer's decision to characterise the transaction either as a sale of all of the Country X patent rights, or as a perpetual exclusive licence of a portion of the worldwide patent rights, does not affect the determination of the arm's length price if, in either case, the transaction being priced is a transfer of exclusive rights to exploit the patent in Country X over its remaining useful life. Thus, the functional analysis should identify the nature of the transferred rights in intangibles with specificity.

6.90. Restrictions imposed in licence and similar agreements on the use of an intangible in the further development of new intangibles or new products using the intangibles are often of significant importance in a transfer pricing analysis. It is therefore important in identifying the nature of a transfer of rights in intangibles to consider whether the transferee receives the right to use the transferred intangible for the purpose of further research and development. In transactions between independent enterprises, arrangements are observed where the transferor/licensor retains the full right to any enhancements of the licensed intangible that may be developed during the term of the licence. Transactions between independent enterprises are also observed where the transferee/licensee retains the right to any enhancements it may develop, either for the term of its licence or in perpetuity. The nature of any limitations on further development of transferred intangibles, or on the ability of the transferee and the transferor to derive an economic benefit from such enhancements, can affect the value of the rights transferred and the comparability of two transactions involving otherwise identical or closely comparable intangibles. Such limitations must be evaluated in light of both the written terms of agreements and the actual conduct of the affected parties.

6.91. The provisions of Section D.1.1 of Chapter I apply in identifying the specific nature of a transaction involving a transfer of intangibles or rights in intangibles, in identifying the nature of any intangibles transferred, and in identifying any limitations imposed by the terms of the transfer on the use of those intangibles. For example, a written specification that a licence is non-exclusive or of limited duration need not be respected by the tax administration if such specification is not consistent with the conduct of the parties. Example 18 in Annex I to Chapter VI illustrates the provisions of this paragraph.

C.1.2. Transfers of combinations of intangibles

6.92. Intangibles (including limited rights in intangibles) may be transferred individually or in combination with other intangibles. In considering transactions involving transfers of combinations of intangibles, two related issues often arise.

6.93. The first of these involves the nature and economic consequences of interactions between different intangibles. It may be the case that some intangibles are more valuable in combination with other intangibles than would be the case if the intangibles were considered separately. It is therefore important to identify the nature of the legal and economic interactions between intangibles that are transferred in combination.

6.94. For example, a pharmaceutical product will often have associated with it three or more types of intangibles. The active pharmaceutical ingredient may be protected by one or more patents. The product will also have been through a testing process and a government regulatory authority may have issued an approval to market the product in a given geographic market and for specific approved indications based on that testing. The product may be marketed under a particular trademark. In combination these intangibles may be extremely valuable. In isolation, one or more of them may have much less value. For example, the trademark without the patent and regulatory marketing approval may have limited value since the product could not be sold without the marketing approval and generic competitors could not be excluded from the market without the patent. Similarly, the value of the patent may be much greater once regulatory marketing approval has been obtained than would be the case in the absence of the marketing approval. The interactions between each of these classes of intangibles, as well as which parties performed functions, bore the risks and incurred the costs associated with securing the intangibles, are therefore very important in performing a transfer pricing analysis with regard to a transfer of the intangibles. It is important to consider the relative contribution to value creation where different associated enterprises hold rights in the intangibles used.

6.95. A second and related issue involves the importance of ensuring that all intangibles transferred in a particular transaction have been identified. It may be the case, for example, that intangibles are so intertwined that it is not possible, as a substantive matter, to transfer one without transferring the other. Indeed, it will often be the case that a transfer of one intangible will necessarily imply the transfer of other intangibles. In such cases it is important to identify all of the intangibles made available to the transferee as a consequence of an intangibles transfer, applying the principles of Section D.1 of Chapter I. For example, the transfer of rights to use a trademark under a licence agreement will usually also imply the licensing of the reputational value, sometimes referred to as goodwill, associated with that trademark, where it is the licensor who has built up such goodwill. Any licence fee required should consider both the trademark and the associated reputational value. Example 20 in Annex I to Chapter VI illustrates the principles of this paragraph.

6.96. It is important to identify situations where taxpayers or tax administrations may seek to artificially separate intangibles that, as a matter of substance, independent parties would not separate in comparable circumstances. For example, attempts to artificially separate trademarks or trade names from the goodwill or reputational value that is factually associated with the trademark or trade name should be identified and critically analysed. Example 21 in Annex I to Chapter VI illustrates the principles of this paragraph.

6.97. It should be recognised that the process of identifying all of the intangibles transferred in a particular transaction is an exercise of identifying, by reference to written agreements and the actual conduct of the parties, the actual transactions that have been undertaken, applying the principles of Section D.1 of Chapter I.

C.1.3. Transfers of intangibles or rights in intangibles in combination with other business transactions

6.98. In some situations intangibles or rights in intangibles may be transferred in combination with tangible business assets, or in combination with services. It is important in such a situation to determine whether intangibles have in fact been transferred in connection with the transaction. It is also important that all of the intangibles transferred in connection with a particular transaction be identified and taken into account in the transfer pricing analysis. Examples 23 to 25 in Annex I to Chapter VI illustrate the principles of this paragraph.

6.99. In some situations it may be both possible and appropriate to separate transactions in tangible goods or services from transfers of intangibles or rights in intangibles for purposes of conducting a transfer pricing analysis. In these situations, the price of a package contract should be disaggregated in order to confirm that each element of the transaction is consistent with the arm's length principle. In other situations transactions may be so closely related that it will be difficult to segregate tangible goods or service transactions from transfers of intangibles or rights in intangibles. Reliability of available comparables will be an important factor in considering whether transactions should be combined or segregated. In particular, it is important to consider whether available comparables permit accurate evaluation of interactions between transactions.

6.100. One situation where transactions involving transfers of intangibles or rights in intangibles may be combined with other transactions involves a business franchise arrangement. Under such an arrangement, one member of an MNE group may agree to provide a combination of services and intangibles to an associated enterprise in exchange for a single fee. If the services and intangibles made available under such an arrangement are sufficiently unique that reliable comparables cannot be identified for the entire service/intangible package, it may be necessary to segregate the various parts of the package of services and intangibles for separate transfer pricing consideration. It should be kept in mind, however, that the interactions between various intangibles and services may enhance the value of both.

6.101. In other situations, the provision of a service and the transfer of one or more intangibles may be so closely intertwined that it is difficult to separate the transactions for purposes of a transfer pricing analysis. For example, some transfers of rights in software may be combined with an undertaking by the transferor to provide ongoing software maintenance services, which may include periodic updates to the software. In situations where services and transfers of intangibles are intertwined, determining arm's length prices on an aggregate basis may be necessary.

6.102. It should be emphasised that delineating the transaction as the provision of products or services or the transfer of intangibles or a combination of both does not necessarily dictate the use of a particular transfer pricing method. For example, a cost plus approach will not be appropriate for all service transactions, and not all intangibles transactions require complex valuations or the application of profit split methods. The facts of each specific situation, and the results of the required functional analysis, will guide the manner in which transactions are combined, delineated and analysed for transfer pricing purposes, as well as the selection of the most appropriate transfer pricing method in a particular case. The ultimate objective is to identify the prices and other relevant conditions that would be established between independent enterprises in comparable transactions.

6.103. Moreover, it should also be emphasised that determinations as to whether transactions should be aggregated or segregated for analysis usually involve the delineation of the actual transaction undertaken, by reference to written agreements and the actual conduct of the parties. Determinations regarding the actual transaction undertaken constitute one necessary element in determining the most appropriate transfer pricing method in the particular case.

C.2. Transactions involving the use of intangibles in connection with sales of goods or performance of services

6.104. Intangibles may be used in connection with controlled transactions in situations where there is no transfer of the intangible or of rights in the intangible. For example, intangibles may be used by one or both parties to a controlled transaction in connection with the manufacture of goods sold to an associated enterprise, in connection with the marketing of goods purchased from an associated enterprise, or in connection with the performance of services on behalf of an associated enterprise. The nature of such a transaction should be clearly specified, and any relevant intangibles used by either of the parties in connection with such a controlled transaction should be identified and taken into account in the comparability analysis, in the selection and application of the most appropriate transfer pricing method for that transaction, and in the choice of the tested party. Supplemental guidance regarding the determination of arm's length conditions for transactions involving the use of intangibles in connection with the sale of goods or the provision of services is contained in Sections D.1 and D.4 of this chapter.

6.105. The need to consider the use of intangibles by a party to a controlled transaction involving a sale of goods can be illustrated as follows. Assume that a car manufacturer uses valuable proprietary patents to manufacture the cars that it then sells to associated distributors. Assume that the patents significantly contribute to the value of the cars. The patents and the value they contribute should be identified and taken into account in the comparability analysis of the transaction consisting in the sales of cars by the car manufacturer to its associated distributors, in selecting the most appropriate transfer pricing method for the transactions, and in selecting the tested party. The associated distributors purchasing the cars do not, however, acquire any right in the manufacturer's patents. In such a case, the patents are used in the manufacturing and may affect the value of the cars, but the patents themselves are not transferred.

6.106. As another example of the use of intangibles in connection with a controlled transaction, assume that an exploration company has acquired or developed valuable geological data and analysis, and sophisticated exploratory software and know-how. Assume further that it uses those intangibles in providing exploration services to an associated enterprise. Those intangibles should be identified and taken into account in the comparability analysis of the service transactions between the exploration company and the associated enterprise, in selecting the most appropriate transfer pricing method for the transaction, and in selecting the tested party. Assuming that the associated enterprise of the exploration company does not acquire any rights in the exploration company's intangibles, the intangibles are used in the performance of the services and may affect the value of services, but are not transferred.

D. Supplemental guidance for determining arm's length conditions in cases involving intangibles

6.107. After identifying the relevant transactions involving intangibles, specifically identifying the intangibles involved in those transactions, identifying which entity or entities legally own the intangibles as well as those that contribute to the value of the intangibles, it should be possible to identify arm's length conditions for the relevant transactions. The principles set out in Chapters I-III of these Guidelines should be applied in determining arm's length conditions for transactions involving intangibles. In particular, the recommended nine-step process set out in paragraph 3.4 can be helpful in identifying arm's length conditions for transactions involving intangibles. As an essential part of applying the principles of Chapter III to conduct a comparability analysis under the process described in paragraph 3.4, the principles contained in Sections A, B, and C of this Chapter VI should be considered.

6.108. However, the principles of Chapters I-III can sometimes be difficult to apply to controlled transactions involving intangibles. Intangibles may have special characteristics that complicate the search for comparables, and in some cases make pricing difficult to determine at the time of the transaction. Further, for wholly legitimate business reasons, due to the relationship between them, associated enterprises might sometimes structure a transaction involving intangibles in a manner that independent enterprises would not contemplate. See paragraph 1.11. The use or transfer of intangibles may raise challenging issues regarding comparability, selection of transfer pricing methods, and determination of arm's length conditions for transactions. This Section D provides supplemental guidance for use in applying the principles of Chapters I-III to determine arm's length conditions for controlled transactions involving intangibles.

6.109. Section D.1 provides general supplemental guidance related to all transactions involving intangibles. Section D.2 provides supplemental guidance specifically related to transactions involving the transfer of intangibles or rights in intangibles. Section D.3 provides supplemental guidance regarding transfers of intangibles or rights in intangibles whose value is highly uncertain at the time of the transfer. Section D.4 provides an approach to pricing hard-to-value intangibles. Section D.5 provides supplemental guidance applicable to transactions involving the use of intangibles in connection with the sale of goods or the provision of services in situations where there is no transfer of rights in the intangibles.

D.1. General principles applicable in transactions involving intangibles

6.110. Section D of Chapter I and Chapter III contain principles to be considered and a recommended process to be followed in conducting a comparability analysis. The principles described in those sections of the Guidelines apply to all controlled transactions involving intangibles.

6.111. In applying the principles of the Guidelines related to the content and process of a comparability analysis to a transaction involving intangibles, a transfer pricing analysis must consider the options realistically available to each of the parties to the transaction.

6.112. In considering the options realistically available to the parties, the perspectives of each of the parties to the transaction must be considered. A comparability analysis focusing only on one side of a transaction generally does not provide a sufficient basis for evaluating a transaction involving intangibles (including in those situations for which a one-sided transfer pricing method is ultimately determined).

6.113. While it is important to consider the perspectives of both parties to the transaction in conducting a comparability analysis, the specific business circumstances of one of the parties should not be used to dictate an outcome contrary to the realistically available options of the other party. For example, a transferor would not be expected to accept a price for the transfer of either all or part of its rights in an intangible that is less advantageous to the transferor than its other realistically available options (including making no transfer at all), merely because a particular associated enterprise transferee lacks the resources to effectively exploit the transferred rights in the intangible. Similarly, a transferee should not be expected to accept a price for a transfer of rights in one or more intangibles that would make it impossible for the transferee to anticipate earning a profit using the acquired rights in the intangible in its business. Such an outcome would be less favourable to the transferee than its realistically available option of not engaging in the transfer at all.

6.114. It will often be the case that a price for a transaction involving intangibles can be identified that is consistent with the realistically available options of each of the parties. The existence of such prices is consistent with the assumption that MNE groups seek to optimise resource allocations. If situations arise in which the minimum price acceptable to the transferor, based on its realistically available options, exceeds the maximum price acceptable to the transferee, based on its realistically available options, it may be necessary to consider whether the actual transaction should be disregarded under the criterion for non-recognition set out in Section D.2 of Chapter I, or whether the conditions of the transaction should otherwise be adjusted. Similarly, if situations arise in which there are assertions that either the current use of an intangible, or a proposed realistically available option (i.e. an alternative use of the intangible), does not optimise resource allocations, it may be necessary to consider whether such assertions are consistent with the true facts and circumstances of the case. This discussion highlights the importance of taking all relevant facts and circumstances into account in accurately delineating the actual transaction involving intangibles.

D.2. Supplemental guidance regarding transfers of intangibles or rights in intangibles

6.115. This section provides supplemental guidance regarding specific issues arising in connection with the transfer between associated enterprises of intangibles or rights in intangibles. Such transactions may include sales of intangibles as well as transactions that are economically equivalent to sales. Such transactions could also include a licence of rights in one or more intangibles or a similar transaction. This section is not intended to provide comprehensive guidance with regard to the transfer pricing treatment of such intangibles transfers. Rather, it supplements the otherwise applicable provisions of Chapters I-III, and the guidance in Sections A, B, C, and D.1 of this chapter, in the context of transfers of intangibles or rights in intangibles, by providing guidance with regard to certain specific topics commonly arising in connection with such transfers.

D.2.1. Comparability of intangibles or rights in intangibles

6.116. In applying the provisions of Chapters I-III to transactions involving the transfer of intangibles or rights in intangibles, it should be borne in mind that intangibles often have unique characteristics, and as a result have the potential for generating returns and creating future benefits that could differ widely. In conducting a comparability analysis with regard to a transfer of intangibles, it is therefore essential to consider the unique features of the intangibles. This is particularly important where the CUP method is considered to be the most appropriate transfer pricing method, but also has importance in applying other methods that rely on comparables. In the case of a transfer of an intangible or rights in an intangible that provides the enterprise with a unique competitive advantage in the market, purportedly comparable intangibles or transactions should be carefully scrutinised. It is critical to assess whether potential comparables in fact exhibit similar profit potential.

6.117. Set out below is a description of some of the specific features of intangibles that may prove important in a comparability analysis involving transfers of intangibles or rights in intangibles. The following list is not exhaustive and in a specific case consideration of additional or different factors may be an essential part of a comparability analysis.

D.2.1.1. Exclusivity

6.118. Whether the rights in intangibles relevant to a particular transaction involving the transfer of intangibles or rights in intangibles are exclusive or non-exclusive can be an important comparability consideration. Some intangibles allow the legal owner of the intangible to exclude others from using the intangible. A patent, for example, grants an exclusive right to use the invention covered by the patent for a period of years. If the party controlling intangible rights can exclude other enterprises from the market, or exclude them from using intangibles that provide a market advantage, that party may enjoy a high degree of market power or market influence. A party with non-exclusive rights to intangibles will not be able to exclude all competitors and will generally not have the same degree of market power or influence. Accordingly, the exclusive or non-exclusive nature of intangibles or rights in intangibles should be considered in connection with the comparability analysis.

D.2.1.2. Extent and duration of legal protection

6.119. The extent and duration of legal protection of the intangibles relevant to a particular transfer can be an important comparability consideration. Legal protections associated with some intangibles can prevent competitors from entering a particular market. For other intangibles, such as know-how or trade secrets, available legal protections may have a different nature and not be as strong or last as long. For intangibles with limited useful lives, the duration of legal protections can be important since the duration of the intangible rights will affect the expectation of the parties to a transaction with regard to the future benefits from the exploitation of the intangible. For example, two otherwise comparable patents will not have equivalent value if one expires at the end of one year while the other expires only after ten years.

D.2.1.3. Geographic scope

6.120. The geographic scope of the intangibles or rights in intangibles will be an important comparability consideration. A global grant of rights to intangibles may be more valuable than a grant limited to one or a few jurisdictions, depending on the nature of the product, the nature of the intangible, and the nature of the markets in question.

D.2.1.4. Useful life

6.121. Many intangibles have a limited useful life. The useful life of a particular intangible can be affected by the nature and duration of the legal protections afforded to the intangible, as noted above. The useful life of some intangibles can also be affected by the rate of technological change in an industry and by the development of new and potentially improved products. It may also be the case that the useful life of particular intangibles can be extended.

6.122. In conducting a comparability analysis, it will therefore be important to consider the expected useful life of the intangibles in question. In general, intangibles expected to provide market advantages for a longer period of time will be more valuable than similar intangibles providing such advantages for a shorter period of time, other things being equal. In evaluating the useful life of intangibles it is also important to consider the use being made of the intangible. The useful life of an intangible that forms a base for ongoing research and development may extend beyond the commercial life of the current generation product line based on that intangible.

D.2.1.5. Stage of development

6.123. In conducting a comparability analysis, it may be important to consider the stage of development of particular intangibles. It is often the case that an intangible is transferred in a controlled transaction at a point in time before it has been fully demonstrated that the intangible will support commercially viable products. A common example arises in the pharmaceutical industry, where chemical compounds may be patented, and the patents (or rights to use the patents) transferred in controlled transactions, well in advance of the time when further research, development and testing demonstrates that the compound constitutes a safe and effective treatment for a particular medical condition.

6.124. As a general rule, intangibles relating to products with established commercial viability will be more valuable than otherwise comparable intangibles relating to products whose commercial viability is yet to be established. In conducting a comparability analysis involving partially developed intangibles, it is important to evaluate the likelihood that further development will lead to commercially significant future benefits. In certain circumstances, industry data regarding the risks associated with further development can be helpful to such evaluations. However, the specific circumstances of any individual situation should always be considered.

D.2.1.6. Rights to enhancements, revisions, and updates

6.125. Often, an important consideration in a comparability analysis involving intangibles relates to the rights of the parties with regard to future enhancements, revisions and updates of the intangibles. In some industries, products protected by intangibles can become obsolete or uncompetitive in a relatively short period of time in the absence of continuing development and enhancement of the intangibles. As a result, having access to updates and enhancements can be the difference between deriving a short term advantage from the intangibles and deriving a longer term advantage. It is therefore necessary to consider for comparability purposes whether or not a particular grant of rights in intangibles includes access to enhancements, revisions, and updates of the intangibles.

6.126. A very similar question, often important in a comparability analysis, involves whether the transferee of intangibles obtains the right to use the intangibles in connection with research directed to developing new and enhanced intangibles. For example, the right to use an existing software platform as a basis for developing new software products can shorten development times and can make the difference between being the first to market with a new product or application, or being forced to enter a market already occupied by established competitive products. A comparability analysis with regard to intangibles should, therefore, consider the rights of the parties regarding the use of the intangibles in developing new and enhanced versions of products.

D.2.1.7. Expectation of future benefit

6.127. Each of the foregoing comparability considerations has a consequence with regard to the expectation of the parties to a transaction regarding the future benefits to be derived from the use of the intangibles in question. If for any reason there is a significant discrepancy between the anticipated future benefit of using one intangible as opposed to another, it is difficult to consider the intangibles as being sufficiently comparable to support a comparables-based transfer pricing analysis in the absence of reliable comparability adjustments. Specifically, it is important to consider the actual and potential profitability of products or potential products that are based on the intangible. Intangibles that provide a basis for high profit products or services are not likely to be comparable to intangibles that support products or services with only industry average profits. Any factor materially affecting the expectation of the parties to a controlled transaction of obtaining future benefits from the intangible should be taken into account in conducting the comparability analysis.

D.2.2. Comparison of risk in cases involving transfers of intangibles or rights in intangibles

6.128. In conducting a comparability analysis involving the transfer of intangibles or rights in intangibles, the existence of risks related to the likelihood of obtaining future economic benefits from the transferred intangibles must be considered, including the allocation of risk between the parties which should be analysed within the framework set out in Section D.1.2 of Chapter I. The following types of risks, among others, should be considered in evaluating whether transfers of intangibles or combinations of intangibles are comparable, and in evaluating whether the intangibles themselves are comparable.

- Risks related to the future development of the intangibles. This includes an evaluation of whether the intangibles relate to commercially viable products, whether the intangibles may support commercially viable products in the future, the expected cost of required future development and testing, the likelihood that such development and testing will prove successful and similar considerations. The consideration of development risk is particularly important in situations involving transfers of partially developed intangibles.
- Risks related to product obsolescence and depreciation in the value of the intangibles. This includes an evaluation of the likelihood that competitors will introduce products or services in the future that would materially erode the market for products dependent on the intangibles being analysed.
- Risks related to infringement of the intangible rights. This includes an evaluation of the likelihood that others might successfully claim that products based on the intangibles infringe their own intangible rights and an evaluation of the likely costs of defending against such claims. It also includes an evaluation of the likelihood that the holder of intangible rights could successfully prevent others from infringing the intangibles, the risk that counterfeit products could erode the profitability of relevant markets, and the likelihood that substantial damages could be collected in the event of infringement.
- Product liability and similar risks related to the future use of the intangibles.

D.2.3. Comparability adjustments with regard to transfers of intangibles or rights in intangibles

6.129. The principles of paragraphs 3.47 to 3.54 relating to comparability adjustments apply with respect to transactions involving the transfer of intangibles or rights in intangibles. It is important to note that differences between intangibles can have significant economic consequences that may be difficult to adjust for in a reliable manner. Particularly in situations where amounts attributable to comparability adjustments represent a large percentage of the compensation for the intangible, there may be reason to believe, depending on the specific facts, that the computation of the adjustment is not reliable and that the intangibles being compared are in fact not sufficiently comparable to support a valid transfer pricing analysis. If reliable comparability adjustments are not possible, it may be necessary to select a transfer pricing method that is less dependent on the identification of comparable intangibles or comparable transactions.

D.2.4. Use of comparables drawn from databases

6.130. Comparability, and the possibility of making comparability adjustments, is especially important in considering potentially comparable intangibles and related royalty rates drawn from commercial databases or proprietary compilations of publicly available licence or similar agreements. The principles of Section A.4.3.1 of Chapter III apply fully in assessing the usefulness of transactions drawn from such sources. In particular, it is important to assess whether publicly available data drawn from commercial databases and proprietary compilations is sufficiently detailed to permit an evaluation of the specific features of intangibles that may be important in conducting a comparability analysis. In evaluating comparable licence arrangements identified from databases, the specific facts of the case, including the methodology being applied, should be considered in the context of the provisions of paragraph 3.38.

D.2.5. Selecting the most appropriate transfer pricing method in a matter involving the transfer of intangibles or rights in intangibles

6.131. The principles of these Guidelines related to the selection of the most appropriate transfer pricing method to the circumstances of the case are described in paragraphs 2.1 to 2.12. Those principles apply fully to cases involving the transfer of intangibles or rights in intangibles. In selecting the most appropriate transfer pricing method in a case involving a transfer of intangibles or rights in intangibles, attention should be given to (i) the nature of the relevant intangibles, (ii) the difficulty of identifying comparable uncontrolled transactions and intangibles in many, if not most, cases, and (iii) the difficulty of applying certain of the transfer pricing methods described in Chapter II in cases involving the transfer of intangibles. The issues discussed below are particularly important in the selection of transfer pricing methods under the Guidelines.

6.132. In applying the principles of paragraphs 2.1 to 2.12 to matters involving the transfer of intangibles or rights in intangibles, it is important to recognise that transactions structured in different ways may have similar economic consequences. For example, the performance of a service using intangibles may have very similar economic consequences to a transaction involving the transfer of an intangible (or the transfer of rights in the intangible), as either may convey the value of the intangible to the transferee. Accordingly, in selecting the most appropriate transfer pricing method in connection with a transaction involving the transfer of intangibles or rights in intangibles, it is important to consider the economic consequences of the transaction, rather than proceeding on the basis of an arbitrary label.

6.133. This chapter makes it clear that in matters involving the transfer of intangibles or rights in intangibles it is important not to simply assume that all residual profit, after a limited return to those providing functions, should necessarily be allocated to the owner of intangibles. The selection of the most appropriate transfer pricing method should be based on a functional analysis that provides a clear understanding of the MNE's global business processes and how the transferred intangibles interact with other functions, assets and risks that comprise the global business. The functional analysis should identify all factors that contribute to value creation, which may include risks borne, specific market characteristics, location, business strategies, and MNE group synergies among others. The transfer pricing method selected, and any adjustments incorporated in that method based on the comparability analysis, should take into account all of the relevant factors materially contributing to the creation of value, not only intangibles and routine functions.

6.134. The principles set out in paragraphs 2.12, 3.58 and 3.59 regarding the use of more than one transfer pricing method apply to matters involving the transfer of intangibles or rights in intangibles.

6.135. Paragraphs 3.9 to 3.12 and paragraph 3.37 provide guidance regarding the aggregation of separate transactions for purposes of transfer pricing analysis. Those principles apply fully to cases involving the transfer of intangibles or rights in intangibles and are supplemented by the guidance in Section C of this chapter. Indeed, it is often the case that intangibles may be transferred in combination with other intangibles, or in combination with transactions involving the sale of goods or the performance of services. In such situations it may well be that the most reliable transfer pricing analysis will consider the interrelated transactions in the aggregate as necessary to improve the reliability of the analysis.

D.2.6. Supplemental guidance on transfer pricing methods in matters involving the transfer of intangibles or rights in intangibles

6.136. Depending on the specific facts, any of the five OECD transfer pricing methods described in Chapter II might constitute the most appropriate transfer pricing method to the circumstances of the case where the transaction involves a controlled transfer of one or more intangibles. The use of other alternatives may also be appropriate.

6.137. Where the comparability analysis identifies reliable information related to comparable uncontrolled transactions, the determination of arm's length prices for a transfer of intangibles or rights in intangibles can be determined on the basis of such comparables after making any comparability adjustments that may be appropriate and reliable.

6.138. However, it will often be the case in matters involving transfers of intangibles or rights in intangibles that the comparability analysis (including the functional analysis) reveals that there are no reliable comparable uncontrolled transactions that can be used to determine the arm's length price and other conditions. This can occur if the intangibles in question have unique characteristics, or if they are of such critical importance that such intangibles are transferred only among associated enterprises. It may also result from a lack of available data regarding potentially comparable transactions or from other causes. Notwithstanding the lack of reliable comparables, it is usually possible to determine the arm's length price and other conditions for the controlled transaction.

6.139. Where information regarding reliable comparable uncontrolled transactions cannot be identified, the arm's length principle requires use of another method to determine the price that uncontrolled parties would have agreed under comparable circumstances. In making such determinations, it is important to consider:

- The functions, assets and risks of the respective parties to the transaction.
- The business reasons for engaging in the transaction.
- The perspectives of and options realistically available to each of the parties to the transaction.
- The competitive advantages conferred by the intangibles including especially the relative profitability of products and services or potential products and services related to the intangibles.
- The expected future economic benefits from the transaction.
- Other comparability factors such as features of local markets, location savings, assembled workforce, and MNE group synergies.

6.140. In identifying prices and other conditions that would have been agreed between independent enterprises under comparable circumstances, it is often essential to carefully identify idiosyncratic aspects of the controlled transaction that arise by virtue of the relationship between the parties. There is no requirement that associated enterprises structure their transactions in precisely the same manner as independent enterprises might have done. However, where transactional structures are utilised by associated enterprises that are not typical of transactions between independent parties, the effect of those structures on prices and other conditions that would have been agreed between uncontrolled parties under comparable circumstances should be taken into account in evaluating the profits that would have accrued to each of the parties at arm's length.

6.141. Care should be used, in applying certain of the OECD transfer pricing methods in a matter involving the transfer of intangibles or rights in intangibles. One sided methods, including the resale price method and the

TNMM, are generally not reliable methods for directly valuing intangibles. In some circumstances such mechanisms can be utilised to indirectly value intangibles by determining values for some functions using those methods and deriving a residual value for intangibles. However, the principles of paragraph 6.133 are important when following such approaches and care should be exercised to ensure that all functions, risks, assets and other factors contributing to the generation of income are properly identified and evaluated.

6.142. The use of transfer pricing methods that seek to estimate the value of intangibles based on the cost of intangible development is generally discouraged. There rarely is any correlation between the cost of developing intangibles and their value or transfer price once developed. Hence, transfer pricing methods based on the cost of intangible development should usually be avoided.

6.143. However, in some limited circumstances, transfer pricing methods based on the estimated cost of reproducing or replacing the intangible may be utilised. Such approaches may sometimes have valid application with regard to the development of intangibles used for internal business operations (e.g. internal software systems), particularly where the intangibles in question are not unique and valuable intangibles. Where intangibles relating to products sold in the marketplace are at issue, however, replacement cost valuation methods raise serious comparability issues. Among other concerns, it is necessary to evaluate the effect of time delays associated with deferred development on the value of the intangibles. Often, there may be a significant first mover advantage in having a product on the market at an early date. As a result, an identical product (and the supporting intangibles) developed in future periods will not be as valuable as the same product (and the supporting intangibles) available currently. In such a case, the estimated replacement cost will not be a valid proxy for the value of an intangible transferred currently. Similarly, where an intangible carries legal protections or exclusivity characteristics, the value of being able to exclude competitors from using the intangible will not be reflected in an analysis based on replacement cost. Cost based valuations generally are not reliable when applied to determine the arm's length price for partially developed intangibles.

6.144. The provisions of paragraph 2.10 related to the use of rules of thumb apply to determinations of a correct transfer price in any controlled transaction, including cases involving the use or transfer of intangibles. Accordingly, a rule of thumb cannot be used to evidence that a price or apportionment of income is arm's length, including in particular an apportionment of income between a licensor and a licensee of intangibles.

6.145. The transfer pricing methods most likely to prove useful in matters involving transfers of one or more intangibles are the CUP method and the transactional profit split method. Valuation techniques can be useful tools.

Supplemental guidance on the transfer pricing methods most likely to be useful in connection with transfers of intangibles is provided below.

D.2.6.1. Application of the CUP Method

6.146. Where reliable comparable uncontrolled transactions can be identified, the CUP method can be applied to determine the arm's length conditions for a transfer of intangibles or rights in intangibles. The general principles contained in paragraphs 2.14 to 2.26 apply when the CUP method is used in connection with transactions involving the transfer of intangibles. Where the CUP method is utilised in connection with the transfer of intangibles, particular consideration must be given to the comparability of the intangibles or rights in intangibles transferred in the controlled transaction and in the potential comparable uncontrolled transactions. The economically relevant characteristics or comparability factors described in Section D.1 of Chapter I should be considered. The matters described in Sections D.2.1 to D.2.4 of this chapter are of particular importance in evaluating the comparability of specific transferred intangibles and in making comparability adjustments, where possible. It should be recognised that the identification of reliable comparables in many cases involving intangibles may be difficult or impossible.

6.147. In some situations, intangibles acquired by an MNE group from independent enterprises are transferred to a member of the MNE group in a controlled transaction immediately following the acquisition. In such a case the price paid for the acquired intangibles will often (after any appropriate adjustments, including adjustments for acquired assets not re-transferred) represent a useful comparable for determining the arm's length price for the controlled transaction under a CUP method. Depending on the facts and circumstances, the third party acquisition price in such situations will have relevance in determining arm's length prices and other conditions for the controlled transaction, even where the intangibles are acquired indirectly through an acquisition of shares or where the price paid to the third party for shares or assets exceeds the book value of the acquired assets. Examples 23 and 26 in Annex I to Chapter VI illustrate the principles of this paragraph.

D.2.6.2. Application of transactional profit split method

6.148. In some circumstances, a transactional profit split method can be utilised to determine the arm's length conditions for a transfer of intangibles or rights in intangibles where it is not possible to identify reliable comparable uncontrolled transactions for such transfers. Section C of Chapter II contains guidance to be considered in applying transactional profit split methods. That guidance is fully applicable to matters involving the transfer of intangibles or rights in intangibles. In evaluating the reliability of transactional profit split methods, however, the availability of reliable and adequate data regarding the relevant profits to be split, appropriately allocable expenses, and the reliability of factors used to divide the relevant income should be fully considered.

6.149. Transactional profit split methods may have application in connection with the sale of full rights in intangibles. As with other applications of the transactional profit split method, a full functional analysis that considers the functions performed, risks assumed and assets used by each of the parties is an essential element of the analysis. Where a transactional profit split analysis is based on projected revenues and expenses, the concerns with the accuracy of such projections described in Section D.2.6.4.1 should be taken into account.

6.150. It is also sometimes suggested that a profit split analysis can be applied to transfers of partially developed intangibles. In such an analysis, the relative value of contributions to the development of intangibles before and after a transfer of the intangibles in question is sometimes examined. Such an approach may include an attempt to amortise the transferor's contribution to the partially developed intangible over the asserted useful life of that contribution, assuming no further development. Such approaches are generally based on projections of cash flows and benefits expected to arise at some future date following the transfer and the assumed successful completion of further development activities.

6.151. Caution should be exercised in applying profit split approaches to determine estimates of the contributions of the parties to the creation of income in years following the transfer, or an arm's length allocation of future income, with respect to partially developed intangibles. The contribution or value of work undertaken prior to the transfer may bear no relationship to the cost of that work. For example, a chemical compound with potentially blockbuster pharmaceutical indications might be developed in the laboratory at relatively little cost. In addition, a variety of difficult to evaluate factors would need to be taken into account in such a profit split analysis. These would include the relative riskiness and value of research contributions before and after the transfer, the relative risk and its effect on value, for other development activities carried out before and after the transfer, the appropriate amortisation rate for various contributions to the intangible value, assumptions regarding the time at which any potential new products might be introduced, and the value of contributions other than intangibles to the ultimate generation of profit. Income and cash flow projections in such situations can sometimes be especially speculative. These factors can combine to call the reliability of such an application of a profit split analysis into question. See Section D.4 on hard-to-value intangibles.

6.152. Where limited rights in fully developed intangibles are transferred in a licence or similar transaction, and reliable comparable uncontrolled transactions cannot be identified, a transactional profit split method can often be utilised to evaluate the respective contributions of the parties to earning the relevant income. The profit contribution of the rights in intangibles made available by the licensor or other transferor would, in such a circumstance, be one of the factors contributing to the earning of income following the transfer. However, other factors would also need to be considered. In particular, functions performed and risks assumed by the licensee/transferee should specifically be taken into account in such an analysis. Other intangibles used by the licensor/transferor and by the licensee/transferee in their respective businesses should similarly be considered, as well as other relevant factors. Careful attention should be given in such an analysis to the limitations imposed by the terms of the transfer on the use of the intangibles by the licensee/transferee and on the rights of the licensee/transferee to use the intangibles for purposes of ongoing research and development. Further, assessing contributions of the licensee to enhancements in the value of licensed intangibles may be important. The allocation of income in such an analysis would depend on the findings of the functional analysis, including an analysis of the relevant risks assumed. It should not be assumed that all of the residual profit after functional returns would necessarily be allocated to the licensor/transferor in a profit split analysis related to a licensing arrangement.

D.2.6.3. Use of valuation techniques

6.153. In situations where reliable comparable uncontrolled transactions for a transfer of one or more intangibles cannot be identified, it may also be possible to use valuation techniques to estimate the arm's length price for intangibles transferred between associated enterprises. In particular, the application of income based valuation techniques, especially valuation techniques premised on the calculation of the discounted value of projected future income streams or cash flows derived from the exploitation of the intangible being valued, may be particularly useful when properly applied. Depending on the facts and circumstances, valuation techniques may be used by taxpayers and tax administrations as a part of one of the five OECD transfer pricing methods described in Chapter II, or as a tool that can be usefully applied in identifying an arm's length price.

6.154. Where valuation techniques are utilised in a transfer pricing analysis involving the transfer of intangibles or rights in intangibles, it is necessary to apply such techniques in a manner that is consistent with the arm's length principle and the principles of these Guidelines. In particular, due regard should be given to the principles contained in Chapters I-III. Principles related to realistically available options, economically relevant characteristics including assumption of risk (see Section D.1 of Chapter I) and aggregation of transactions (see paragraphs 3.9 to 3.12) apply fully to situations where valuation techniques are utilised in a transfer pricing analysis. Furthermore, the rules of these Guidelines on selection of transfer pricing methods apply in determining when such techniques should be used (see paragraphs 2.1 to

2.12). The principles of Sections A, B, C, and D.1 of this chapter also apply where use of valuation techniques is considered.

6.155. It is essential to consider the assumptions and other motivations that underlie particular applications of valuation techniques. For sound accounting purposes, some valuation assumptions may sometimes reflect conservative assumptions and estimates of the value of assets reflected in a company's balance sheet. This inherent conservatism can lead to definitions that are too narrow for transfer pricing purposes and valuation approaches that are not necessarily consistent with the arm's length principle. Caution should therefore be exercised in accepting valuations performed for accounting purposes as necessarily reflecting arm's length prices or values for transfer pricing purposes without a thorough examination of the underlying assumptions. In particular, valuations of intangibles contained in purchase price allocations performed for accounting purposes are not determinative for transfer pricing purposes and should be utilised in a transfer pricing analysis with caution and careful consideration of the underlying assumptions.

6.156. It is not the intention of these Guidelines to set out a comprehensive summary of the valuation techniques utilised by valuation professionals. Similarly, it is not the intention of these Guidelines to endorse or reject one or more sets of valuation standards utilised by valuation or accounting professionals or to describe in detail or specifically endorse one or more specific valuation techniques or methods as being especially suitable for use in a transfer pricing analysis. However, where valuation techniques are applied in a manner that gives due regard to these Guidelines, to the specific facts of the case, to sound valuation principles and practices, and with appropriate consideration of the validity of the assumptions underlying the valuation and the consistency of those assumptions with the arm's length principle, such techniques can be useful tools in a transfer pricing analysis where reliable comparable uncontrolled transactions are not available. See, however, paragraphs 6.142 and 6.143 for a discussion of the reliability and application of valuation techniques based on intangible development costs.

6.157. Valuation techniques that estimate the discounted value of projected future cash flows derived from the exploitation of the transferred intangible or intangibles can be particularly useful when properly applied. There are many variations of these valuation techniques. In general terms, such techniques measure the value of an intangible by the estimated value of future cash flows it may generate over its expected remaining lifetime. The value can be calculated by discounting the expected future cash flows to present value.[6] Under this approach valuation requires, among other things,

6. In the case of a financial valuation based on projections, the analysis will often be based on projections of cash flows. Accrual based measures of income, such

defining realistic and reliable financial projections, growth rates, discount rates, the useful life of intangibles, and the tax effects of the transaction. Moreover it entails consideration of terminal values when appropriate. Depending on the facts and circumstances of the individual case, the calculation of the discounted value of projected cash flows derived from the exploitation of the intangible should be evaluated from the perspectives of both parties to the transaction in arriving at an arm's length price. The arm's length price will fall somewhere within the range of present values evaluated from the perspectives of the transferor and the transferee. Examples 27 to 29 in Annex I to Chapter VI illustrate the provisions of this section.

D.2.6.4. Specific areas of concern in applying methods based on the discounted value of projected cash flows

6.158. When applying valuation techniques, including valuation techniques based on projected cash flows, it is important to recognise that the estimates of value based on such techniques can be volatile. Small changes in one or another of the assumptions underlying the valuation model or in one or more of the valuation parameters can lead to large differences in the intangible value the model produces. A small percentage change in the discount rate, a small percentage change in the growth rates assumed in producing financial projections, or a small change in the assumptions regarding the useful life of the intangible can each have a profound effect on the ultimate valuation. Moreover, this volatility is often compounded when changes are made simultaneously to two or more valuation assumptions or parameters.

6.159. The reliability of the intangible value produced using a valuation model is particularly sensitive to the reliability of the underlying assumptions and estimates on which it is based and on the due diligence and judgment exercised in confirming assumptions and in estimating valuation parameters.

6.160. Because of the importance of the underlying assumptions and valuation parameters, taxpayers and tax administrations making use of valuation techniques in determining arm's length prices for transferred intangibles should explicitly set out each of the relevant assumptions made in

as those determined for accounting or tax purposes, may not properly reflect the timing of cash flows which can create a difference in outcome between an income and a cash flow based approach. However, in light of a number of considerations, the use of income projections rather than cash flow projections may, in some cases, yield a more reliable result in a transfer pricing context as a practical matter. Care must be taken, however, to assure that either income or cash flow measures are applied in a consistent manner and in appropriate circumstances. References to cash flow in this document should therefore be read broadly to include both cash flow and income measures, appropriately applied.

creating the valuation model, should describe the basis for selecting valuation parameters, and should be prepared to defend the reasonableness of such assumptions and valuation parameters. Moreover, it is a good practice for taxpayers relying on valuation techniques to present as part of their transfer pricing documentation some sensitivity analysis reflecting the consequential change in estimated intangible value produced by the model when alternative assumptions and parameters are adopted.

6.161. It may be relevant in assessing the reliability of a valuation model to consider the purposes for which the valuation was undertaken and to examine the assumptions and valuation parameters in different valuations undertaken by the taxpayer for non-tax purposes. It would be reasonable for a tax administration to request an explanation for any inconsistencies in the assumptions made in a valuation of an intangible undertaken for transfer pricing purposes and valuations undertaken for other purposes. For example, such requests would be appropriate if high discount rates are used in a transfer pricing analysis when the company routinely uses lower discount rates in evaluating possible mergers and acquisitions. Such requests would also be appropriate if it is asserted that particular intangibles have short useful lives but the projections used in other business planning contexts demonstrate that related intangibles produce cash flows in years beyond the "useful life" that has been claimed for transfer pricing purposes. Valuations used by an MNE group in making operational business decisions may be more reliable than those prepared exclusively for purposes of a transfer pricing analysis.

6.162. The following sections identify some of the specific concerns that should be taken into account in evaluating certain important assumptions underlying calculations in a valuation model based on discounted cash flows. These concerns are important in evaluating the reliability of the particular application of a valuation technique. Notwithstanding the various concerns expressed above and outlined in detail in the following paragraphs, depending on the circumstances, application of such a valuation technique, either as part of one of the five OECD transfer pricing methods or as a useful tool, may prove to be more reliable than application of any other transfer pricing method, particularly where reliable comparable uncontrolled transactions do not exist.

D.2.6.4.1. Accuracy of financial projections

6.163. The reliability of a valuation of a transferred intangible using discounted cash flow valuation techniques is dependent on the accuracy of the projections of future cash flows or income on which the valuation is based. However, because the accuracy of financial projections is contingent on developments in the marketplace that are both unknown and unknowable at the time the valuation is undertaken, and to this extent such projections are speculative, it is essential for taxpayers and tax administrations to examine carefully the assumptions underlying the projections of both future revenue and future expense.

6.164. In evaluating financial projections, the source and purpose of the projections can be particularly important. In some cases, taxpayers will regularly prepare financial projections for business planning purposes. It can be that such analyses are used by management of the business in making business and investment decisions. It is usually the case that projections prepared for non-tax business planning purposes are more reliable than projections prepared exclusively for tax purposes, or exclusively for purposes of a transfer pricing analysis.

6.165. The length of time covered by the projections should also be considered in evaluating the reliability of the projections. The further into the future the intangible in question can be expected to produce positive cash flows, the less reliable projections of income and expense are likely to be.

6.166. A further consideration in evaluating the reliability of projections involves whether the intangibles and the products or services to which they relate have an established track record of financial performance. Caution should always be used in assuming that past performance is a reliable guide to the future, as many factors are subject to change. However, past operating results can provide some useful guidance as to likely future performance of products or services that rely on intangibles. Projections with respect to products or services that have not been introduced to the market or that are still in development are inherently less reliable than those with some track record.

6.167. When deciding whether to include development costs in the cash flow projections it is important to consider the nature of the transferred intangible. Some intangibles may have indefinite useful lives and may be continually developed. In these situations it is appropriate to include future development costs in the cash flow forecasts. Others, for example a specific patent, may already be fully developed and, in addition not provide a platform for the development of other intangibles. In these situations no development costs should be included in the cash flow forecasts for the transferred intangible.

6.168. Where, for the foregoing reasons, or any other reason, there is a basis to believe that the projections behind the valuation are unreliable or speculative, attention should be given to the guidance in Section D.3 and D.4.

D.2.6.4.2. Assumptions regarding growth rates

6.169. A key element of some cash flow projections that should be carefully examined is the projected growth rate. Often projections of future cash flows are based on current cash flows (or assumed initial cash flows after product introduction in the case of partially developed intangibles) expanded by reference to a percentage growth rate. Where that is the case, the basis for the assumed growth rate should be considered. In particular, it is unusual for revenues derived from a particular product to grow at a steady rate over a long period of time. Caution should therefore be exercised in too readily accepting simple models containing linear growth rates not justified on the basis of either experience with similar products and markets or a reasonable evaluation of likely future market conditions. It would generally be expected that a reliable application of a valuation technique based on projected future cash flows would examine the likely pattern of revenue and expense growth based on industry and company experience with similar products.

D.2.6.4.3. Discount rates

6.170. The discount rate or rates used in converting a stream of projected cash flows into a present value is a critical element of a valuation model. The discount rate takes into account the time value of money and the risk or uncertainty of the anticipated cash flows. As small variations in selected discount rates can generate large variations in the calculated value of intangibles using these techniques, it is essential for taxpayers and tax administrations to give close attention to the analysis performed and the assumptions made in selecting the discount rate or rates utilised in the valuation model.

6.171. There is no single measure for a discount rate that is appropriate for transfer pricing purposes in all instances. Neither taxpayers nor tax administrations should assume that a discount rate that is based on a Weighted Average Cost of Capital (WACC) approach or any other measure should always be used in transfer pricing analyses where determination of appropriate discount rates is important. Instead the specific conditions and risks associated with the facts of a given case and the particular cash flows in question should be evaluated in determining the appropriate discount rate.

6.172. It should be recognised in determining and evaluating discount rates that in some instances, particularly those associated with the valuation of intangibles still in development, intangibles may be among the most risky components of a taxpayer's business. It should also be recognised that some businesses are inherently more risky than others and some cash flow streams are inherently more volatile than others. For example, the likelihood that a projected level of research and development expense will be incurred may be higher than the likelihood that a projected level of revenues will ultimately be generated. The discount rate or rates should reflect the level of risk in the overall business and the expected volatility of the various projected cash flows under the circumstances of each individual case.

6.173. Since certain risks can be taken into account either in arriving at financial projections or in calculating the discount rate, care should be taken to avoid double discounting for risk.

D.2.6.4.4. Useful life of intangibles and terminal values

6.174. Valuation techniques are often premised on the projection of cash flows derived from the exploitation of the intangible over the useful life of the intangible in question. In such circumstances, the determination of the actual useful life of the intangible will be one of the critical assumptions supporting the valuation model.

6.175. The projected useful life of particular intangibles is a question to be determined on the basis of all of the relevant facts and circumstances. The useful life of a particular intangible can be affected by the nature and duration of the legal protections afforded the intangible. The useful life of intangibles also may be affected by the rate of technological change in the industry, and by other factors affecting competition in the relevant economic environment. See paragraphs 6.121 and 6.122.

6.176. In some circumstances, particular intangibles may contribute to the generation of cash flow in years after the legal protections have expired or the products to which they specifically relate have ceased to be marketed. This can be the case in situations where one generation of intangibles forms the base for the development of future generations of intangibles and new products. It may well be that some portion of continuing cash flows from projected new products should properly be attributed to otherwise expired intangibles where such follow on effects exist. It should be recognised that, while some intangibles have an indeterminate useful life at the time of valuation, that fact does not imply that non-routine returns are attributable to such intangibles in perpetuity.

6.177. In this regard, where specific intangibles contribute to continuing cash flows beyond the period for which reasonable financial projections exist, it will sometimes be the case that a terminal value for the intangible related cash flows is calculated. Where terminal values are used in valuation calculations, the assumptions underlying their calculation should be clearly set out and the underlying assumptions thoroughly examined, particularly the assumed growth rates.

D.2.6.4.5. Assumptions regarding taxes

6.178. Where the purpose of the valuation technique is to isolate the projected cash flows associated with an intangible, it may be necessary to evaluate and quantify the effect of projected future income taxes on the projected cash flows. Tax effects to be considered include: (i) taxes projected to be imposed on future cash flows, (ii) tax amortisation benefits projected to be available to the transferee, if any, and (iii) taxes projected to be imposed on the transferor as a result of the transfer, if any.

D.2.7. Form of payment

6.179. Taxpayers have substantial discretion in defining the form of payment for transferred intangibles. In transactions between independent parties, it is common to observe payments for intangibles that take the form of a single lump sum. It is also common to observe payments for intangibles that take the form of periodic payments over time. Arrangements involving periodic payments can be structured either as a series of instalment payments fixed in amount, or may take the form of contingent payments where the amount of payments depends on the level of sales of products supported by the intangibles, on profitability, or on some other factor. The principles of Section D.1.1 of Chapter I should be followed in evaluating taxpayer agreements with regard to the form of payment.

6.180. In evaluating the provisions of taxpayer agreements related to the form of payment, it should be noted that some payment forms will entail greater or lesser levels of risk to one of the parties. For example, a payment form contingent on future sales or profit will normally involve greater risk to the transferor than a payment form calling for either a single lump-sum payment at the time of the transfer or a series of fixed instalment payments, because of the existence of the contingency. The chosen form of the payment must be consistent with the facts and circumstances of the case, including the written contracts, the actual conduct of the parties, and the ability of the parties to bear and manage the relevant payment risks. In particular, the amount of the specified payments should reflect the relevant time value of money and risk features of the chosen form of payment. For example, if a valuation technique is applied and results in the calculation of a lump-sum present value for the transferred intangible, and if a taxpayer applies a payment form contingent on future sales, the discount rate used in converting the lump-sum valuation to a stream of contingent payments over the useful life of the intangible should reflect the increased risk to the transferor that sales may not materialise and that payments would therefore not be forthcoming, as well as the time value of money consequences arising from the deferral of the payments to future years.

D.3. Arm's length pricing of transactions involving intangibles for which valuation is highly uncertain at the time of the transaction

6.181. Intangibles or rights in intangibles may have specific features complicating the search for comparables and in some cases making it difficult to determine the value of an intangible at the time of the transaction. When valuation of an intangible or rights in an intangible at the time of the transaction is highly uncertain, the question arises as to how arm's length pricing should be determined. The question should be resolved, both by taxpayers and tax administrations, by reference to what independent enterprises would have done in comparable circumstances to take account of the valuation uncertainty in the pricing of the transaction. To this aim, the guidance and recommended process in Section D of Chapter I and the principles in Chapter III as supplemented by the guidance in this chapter for conducting a comparability analysis are relevant.

6.182. Depending on the facts and circumstances, there is a variety of mechanisms that independent enterprises might adopt to address high uncertainty in the valuation of the intangible at the time of the transaction. For example, one possibility is to use anticipated benefits (taking into account all relevant economic factors) as a means for establishing the pricing at the outset of the transaction. In determining the anticipated benefits, independent enterprises would take into account the extent to which subsequent developments are foreseeable and predictable. In some cases, independent enterprises might find that subsequent developments are sufficiently predictable and therefore the projections of anticipated benefits are sufficiently reliable to fix the pricing for the transaction at the outset on the basis of those projections.

6.183. In other cases, independent enterprises might find that pricing based on anticipated benefits alone does not provide adequate protection against the risks posed by the high uncertainty in valuing the intangible. In such cases independent enterprises might, for instance, adopt shorter-term agreements, include price adjustment clauses in the terms of the agreement, or adopt a payment structure involving contingent payments to protect against subsequent developments that might not be sufficiently predictable. For these purposes, a contingent pricing arrangement is any pricing arrangement in which the quantum or timing of payments is dependent on contingent events, including the achievement of predetermined financial thresholds such as sales or profits, or of predetermined development stages (e.g. royalty or periodic milestone payments). For example, a royalty rate could be set to increase as the sales of the licensee increase, or additional payments could be required at such time as certain development targets are successfully achieved. For a transfer of intangibles or rights in intangibles at a stage when they are not ready to be commercialised but require further development, payment terms adopted by independent parties on initial transfer might include the determination of additional contingent amounts that would become payable only on the achievement of specified milestone stages in their further development.

6.184. Also, independent enterprises may determine to assume the risk of unpredictable subsequent developments. However, the occurrence of major events or developments unforeseen by the parties at the time of the transaction or the occurrence of foreseen events or developments considered to have a low probability of occurrence which change the fundamental assumptions upon which the pricing was determined may lead to renegotiation of the pricing arrangements by agreement of the parties where it is to their mutual benefit. For example, a renegotiation might occur at arm's length if a royalty rate based on sales for a patented drug turned out to be vastly excessive due to an unexpected development of an alternative low-cost treatment. The excessive royalty might remove the incentive of the licensee to manufacture or sell the drug at all, in which case the licensee will have an interest in renegotiating the agreement. It may be the case that the licensor has an interest in keeping the drug on the market and in retaining the same licensee to manufacture or sell the drug because of the skills and expertise of the licensee or the existence of a long-standing co-operative relationship between them. Under these circumstances, the parties might prospectively renegotiate to their mutual benefit all or part of the agreement and set a lower royalty rate. In any event, whether renegotiation would take place, would depend upon all the facts and circumstances of each case.

6.185. If independent enterprises in comparable circumstances would have agreed on the inclusion of a mechanism to address high uncertainty in valuing the intangible (e.g. a price adjustment clause), the tax administration should be permitted to determine the pricing of a transaction involving an intangible or rights in an intangible on the basis of such mechanism. Similarly, if independent enterprises in comparable circumstances would have considered subsequent events so fundamental that their occurrence would have led to a prospective renegotiation of the pricing of a transaction, such events should also lead to a modification of the pricing of the transaction between associated enterprises.

D.4. Hard-to-value intangibles (HTVI)

6.186. A tax administration may find it difficult to establish or verify what developments or events might be considered relevant for the pricing of a transaction involving the transfer of intangibles or rights in intangibles, and the extent to which the occurrence of such developments or events, or the direction they take, might have been foreseen or reasonably foreseeable at the time the transaction was entered into. The developments or events that might be of relevance for the valuation of an intangible are in most cases strongly connected to the business environment in which that intangible is developed or exploited. Therefore, the assessment of which developments or events are relevant and whether the occurrence and direction of such developments or events might have been foreseen or reasonably foreseeable requires specialised knowledge, expertise and insight into the business environment in which the intangible is developed or exploited. In addition, the assessments that are prudent to undertake when evaluating the transfer of intangibles or rights in intangibles in an uncontrolled transaction, may not be seen as necessary or useful for other than transfer pricing purposes by the MNE group when a transfer takes place within the group, with the result that those assessments may not be comprehensive. For example, an enterprise may transfer intangibles at an early stage of development to an associated enterprise, set a royalty rate that does not reflect the value of the intangible at the time of the transfer, and later take the position that it was not possible at the time of the transfer to predict the subsequent success of the product with full certainty. The difference between the *ex ante* and *ex post* value of the intangible would therefore be claimed by the taxpayer to be attributable to more favourable developments than anticipated. The general experience of tax administrations in these situations is that they may not have the specific business insights or access to the information to be able to examine the taxpayer's claim and to demonstrate that the difference between the *ex ante* and *ex post* value of the intangible is due to non-arm's length pricing assumptions made by the taxpayer. Instead, tax administrations seeking to examine the taxpayer's claim are largely dependent on the insights and information provided by that taxpayer. These situations associated with information asymmetry between taxpayers and tax administrations can give rise to transfer pricing risk. See paragraph 6.191.

6.187. In these situations involving the transfer of an intangible or rights in an intangible *ex post* outcomes can provide a pointer to tax administrations about the arm's length nature of the *ex ante* pricing arrangement agreed upon by the associated enterprises, and the existence of uncertainties at the time of the transaction. If there are differences between the *ex ante* projections and the *ex post* results which are not due to unforeseeable developments or events, the differences may give an indication that the pricing arrangement agreed upon by the associated enterprises at the time the transaction was entered into may not have adequately taken into account the relevant developments or events that might have been expected to affect the value of the intangible and the pricing arrangements adopted.

6.188. In response to the considerations discussed above, this section contains an approach consistent with the arm's length principle that tax administrations can adopt to ensure that tax administrations can determine in which situations the pricing arrangements as set by the taxpayers are at arm's length and are based on an appropriate weighting of the foreseeable developments or events that are relevant for the valuation of certain hard-to-value intangibles, and in which situations this is not the case. Under this approach, *ex post* evidence provides presumptive evidence as to the existence of uncertainties at the time of the transaction, whether the taxpayer appropriately took into account reasonably foreseeable developments or events at the time of the transaction, and the reliability of the information used *ex ante* in determining the transfer price for the transfer of such intangibles or rights in intangibles. Such presumptive evidence may be subject to rebuttal as stated in paragraphs 6.193 and 6.194, if it can be demonstrated that it does not affect the accurate determination of the arm's length price. This situation should be distinguished from the situation in which hindsight is used by taking *ex post* results for tax assessment purposes without considering whether the information on which the *ex post* results are based could or should reasonably have been known and considered by the associated enterprises at the time the transaction was entered into.

6.189. The term hard-to-value intangibles (HTVI) covers intangibles or rights in intangibles for which, at the time of their transfer between associated enterprises, (i) no reliable comparables exist, and (ii) at the time the transactions was entered into, the projections of future cash flows or income expected to be derived from the transferred intangible, or the assumptions used in valuing the intangible are highly uncertain, making it difficult to predict the level of ultimate success of the intangible at the time of the transfer.

6.190. Transactions involving the transfer or the use of HTVI in paragraph 6.189 may exhibit one or more of the following features:

- The intangible is only partially developed at the time of the transfer.
- The intangible is not expected to be exploited commercially until several years following the transaction.
- The intangible does not itself fall within the definition of HTVI in paragraph 6.189 but is integral to the development or enhancement of other intangibles which fall within that definition of HTVI.
- The intangible is expected to be exploited in a manner that is novel at the time of the transfer and the absence of a track record of development or exploitation of similar intangibles makes projections highly uncertain.
- The intangible, meeting the definition of HTVI under paragraph 6.189, has been transferred to an associated enterprise for a lump sum payment.
- The intangible is either used in connection with or developed under a CCA or similar arrangements.

6.191. For such intangibles, information asymmetry between taxpayer and tax administrations, including what information the taxpayer took into account in determining the pricing of the transaction, may be acute and may exacerbate the difficulty encountered by tax administrations in verifying the arm's length basis on which pricing was determined for the reasons discussed in paragraph 6.186. As a result, it will prove difficult for a tax administration to perform a risk assessment for transfer pricing purposes, to evaluate the reliability of the information on which pricing has been based by the taxpayer, or to consider whether the intangible or rights in intangibles have been transferred at undervalue or overvalue compared to the arm's length price, until *ex post* outcomes are known in years subsequent to the transfer.

6.192. In these circumstances, the tax administration can consider *ex post* outcomes as presumptive evidence about the appropriateness of the *ex ante* pricing arrangements. However, the consideration of *ex post* evidence should be based on a determination that such evidence is necessary to be taken into account to assess the reliability of the information on which *ex ante* pricing has been based. Where the tax administration is able to confirm the reliability of the information on which *ex ante* pricing has been based, notwithstanding the approach described in this section, then adjustments based on *ex post* profit levels should not be made. In evaluating the *ex ante* pricing arrangements, the tax administration is entitled to use the *ex post* evidence about financial outcomes to inform the determination of the arm's length pricing arrangements, including any contingent pricing arrangements, that would have been made between independent enterprises at the time of the transaction, considering the guidance in paragraph 6.185. Depending on the facts and circumstances of the case and considering the guidance in Section B.5 of Chapter III, a multi-year analysis of the information for the application of this approach may be appropriate.

6.193. This approach will not apply to transactions involving the transfer or use of HTVI falling within the scope of paragraph 6.189, when at least one of the following exemptions applies:

i) The taxpayer provides:

1. Details of the *ex ante* projections used at the time of the transfer to determine the pricing arrangements, including how risks were accounted for in calculations to determine the price (e.g. probability-weighted), and the appropriateness of its consideration of reasonably foreseeable events and other risks, and the probability of occurrence; and,

2. Reliable evidence that any significant difference between the financial projections and actual outcomes is due to: a) unforeseeable developments or events occurring after the determination of the price that could not have been anticipated by the associated

enterprises at the time of the transaction; or b) the playing out of probability of occurrence of foreseeable outcomes, and that these probabilities were not significantly overestimated or underestimated at the time of the transaction;

ii) The transfer of the HTVI is covered by a bilateral or multilateral advance pricing arrangement in effect for the period in question between the jurisdictions of the transferee and the transferor.

iii) Any significant difference between the financial projections and actual outcomes mentioned in i)2 above does not have the effect of reducing or increasing the compensation for the HTVI by more than 20% of the compensation determined at the time of the transaction.

iv) A commercialisation period of five years has passed following the year in which the HTVI first generated unrelated party revenues for the transferee and in which commercialisation period any significant difference between the financial projections and actual outcomes mentioned in i)2 above was not greater than 20% of the projections for that period.[7]

6.194. The first exemption means that, although the *ex post* evidence about financial outcomes provides relevant information for tax administrations to consider the appropriateness of the *ex ante* pricing arrangements, in circumstances where the taxpayer can satisfactorily demonstrate what was foreseeable at the time of the transaction and reflected in the pricing assumptions, and that the developments leading to the difference between projections and outcomes arose from unforeseeable events, tax administrations will not be entitled to make adjustments to the *ex ante* pricing arrangements based on *ex post* outcomes. For example, if the evidence of financial outcomes shows that sales of products exploiting the transferred intangible reached 1 000 a year, but the *ex ante* pricing arrangements were based on projections that considered sales reaching a maximum of only 100 a year, then the tax administration should consider the reasons for sales reaching such higher volumes. If the higher volumes were due to, for example, an exponentially higher demand for the products incorporating the intangible caused by a natural disaster or some other unexpected event that was clearly unforeseeable at the time of the transaction or appropriately given a very low probability of occurrence, then the *ex ante* pricing should be recognised as being at arm's length, unless there is evidence other than the *ex post* financial outcomes indicating that price setting did not take place on an arm's length basis.

7. In some business sectors it is not unusual for an intangible to be transferred with a contingent clause relating to a second, or further, use. In respect of the type of intangibles where this occurs, the time period begins again with the new commercialisation.

6.195. It would be important to permit resolution of cases of double taxation arising from application of the approach for HTVI through access to the mutual agreement procedure under the applicable Treaty.

D.5. Supplemental guidance for transactions involving the use of intangibles in connection with the sale of goods or the provision of services

6.196. This section provides supplemental guidance for applying the rules of Chapters I-III in situations where one or both parties to a controlled transaction uses intangibles in connection with the sale of goods or the provision of services, but where no transfer of intangibles or interests in intangibles occurs. Where intangibles are present, the transfer pricing analysis must carefully consider the effect of the intangibles involved on the prices and other conditions of controlled transactions.

D.5.1. Intangibles as a comparability factor in transactions involving the use of intangibles

6.197. The general rules of Section D.1 of Chapter I and Chapter III also apply to guide the comparability analysis of transactions involving the use of intangibles in connection with a controlled transaction involving the sale of goods or the provision of services. However, the presence of intangibles may sometimes raise challenging comparability issues.

6.198. In a transfer pricing analysis where the most appropriate transfer pricing method is the resale price method, the cost-plus method, or the transactional net margin method, the less complex of the parties to the controlled transaction is often selected as the tested party. In many cases, an arm's length price or level of profit for the tested party can be determined without the need to value the intangibles used in connection with the transaction. That would generally be the case where only the non-tested party uses intangibles. In some cases, however, the tested party may in fact use intangibles notwithstanding its relatively less complex operations. Similarly, parties to potentially comparable uncontrolled transactions may use intangibles. Where either of these is the case, it becomes necessary to consider the intangibles used by the tested party and by the parties to potentially comparable uncontrolled transactions as one comparability factor in the analysis.

6.199. For example, a tested party engaged in the marketing and distribution of goods purchased in controlled transactions may have developed marketing intangibles in its geographic area of operation, including customer lists, customer relationships, and customer data. It may also have developed advantageous logistical know-how or software and other tools that it uses in conducting its distribution business. The impact of such intangibles on the profitability of the tested party should be considered in conducting a comparability analysis.

6.200. It is important to note, however, that in many cases where the tested party uses such intangibles, parties to comparable uncontrolled transactions will also have the same types of intangibles at their disposal. Thus, in the distribution company case, an uncontrolled entity engaged in providing distribution services in the tested party's industry and market is also likely to have knowledge of and contacts with potential customers, collect customer data, have its own effective logistical systems, and in other respects have similar intangibles to the tested party. Where that is the case, the level of comparability may be sufficiently high that it is possible to rely on prices paid or margins earned by the potential comparables as an appropriate measure of arm's length compensation for both the functions performed and the intangibles owned by the tested party.

6.201. Where the tested party and the potential comparable have comparable intangibles, the intangibles will not constitute unique and valuable intangibles within the meaning of paragraph 6.17, and therefore no comparability adjustments will be required with regard to the intangibles. The potential comparable will, in these circumstances, provide the best evidence of the profit contribution of the tested party's intangibles. If, however, either the tested party or the potential comparable has and uses in its business unique and valuable intangibles, it may be necessary either to make appropriate comparability adjustments or to revert to a different transfer pricing method. The principles contained in Sections D.2.1 to D.2.4 apply in evaluating the comparability of intangibles in such situations.

6.202. It is appropriate for both taxpayers and tax administrations to exercise restraint in rejecting potential comparables based on the use of intangibles by either the parties to potentially comparable transactions or by the tested party. Potential comparables should generally not be rejected on the basis of the asserted existence of unspecified intangibles or on the basis of the asserted significance of goodwill. If identified transactions or companies are otherwise comparable, they may provide the best available indication of arm's length pricing notwithstanding the existence and use by either the tested party or the parties to the potentially comparable transactions of relatively insignificant intangibles. Potentially comparable transactions should be disregarded on the basis of the existence and use of non-comparable intangibles only where the intangibles in question can be clearly and distinctly identified and where the intangibles are manifestly unique and valuable intangibles.

D.5.2. Determining arm's length prices for transactions involving the use of intangibles in connection with the sale of goods or the performance of services

6.203. The principles of Chapters I-III apply in determining arm's length prices for transactions involving the use of intangibles in connection with sales of goods or the performance of services. Two general categories of cases can arise. In the first category of cases, the comparability analysis, including the functional analysis, will reveal the existence of sufficiently reliable comparables to permit the determination of arm's length conditions for the transaction using a transfer pricing method based on comparables. In the second category of cases, the comparability analysis, including the functional analysis, will fail to identify reliable comparable uncontrolled transactions, often as a direct result of the use by one or both parties to the transaction of unique and valuable intangibles. Transfer pricing approaches to these two categories of cases are described below.

D.5.2.1. Situations where reliable comparables exist

6.204. It will often be the case that, notwithstanding the use of intangibles by one or both parties to a controlled sale of goods or provision of services, reliable comparables can be identified. Depending on the specific facts, any of the five OECD transfer pricing methods described in Chapter II might constitute the most appropriate transfer pricing method where the transaction involves the use of intangibles in connection with a controlled sale of goods or provision of services and reliable comparables are present.

6.205. Where the tested party does not use unique and valuable intangibles, and where reliable comparables can be identified, it will often be possible to determine arm's length prices on the basis of one-sided methods including the CUP, resale price, cost plus and TNMM methods. The guidance in Chapters I-III will generally be sufficient to guide the determination of arm's length prices in such situations, without the need for a detailed analysis of the nature of the intangibles used by the other party to the transaction.

6.206. The principles described in Sections D.2.1 to D.2.4 of this chapter should be applied in determining whether the use of intangibles by the tested party will preclude reliance on identified comparable uncontrolled transactions or require comparability adjustments. Only when the intangibles used by the tested party are unique and valuable intangibles will the need arise to make comparability adjustments or to adopt a transfer pricing method less dependent on comparable uncontrolled transactions. Where intangibles used by the tested party are not unique and valuable intangibles, prices paid or received, or margins or returns earned by parties to comparable uncontrolled transactions may provide a reliable basis for determining arm's length conditions.

6.207. Where the need to make comparability adjustments arises because of differences in the intangibles used by the tested party in a controlled transaction and the intangibles used by a party to a potentially comparable uncontrolled transaction, difficult factual questions can arise in quantifying reliable comparability adjustments. These issues require thorough consideration of the relevant facts and circumstances and of the available data regarding the impact of the intangibles on prices and profits. Where the impact on price of a difference in the nature of the intangibles used is clearly material, but not subject to accurate estimation, it may be necessary to utilise a different transfer pricing method that is less dependent on identification of reliable comparables.

6.208. It should also be recognised that comparability adjustments for factors other than differences in the nature of the intangibles used may be required in matters involving the use of intangibles in connection with a controlled sale of goods or services. In particular, comparability adjustments may be required for matters such as differences in markets, locational advantages, business strategies, assembled workforce, corporate synergies and other similar factors. While such factors may not be intangibles as that term is described in Section A.1 of this chapter, they can nevertheless have important effects on arm's length prices in matters involving the use of intangibles.

D.5.2.2. Situations where reliable comparables do not exist

6.209. In some circumstances where reliable uncontrolled transactions cannot be identified, transactional profit split methods may be utilised to determine an arm's length allocation of profits for the sale of goods or the provision of services involving the use of intangibles. One circumstance in which the use of transactional profit split methods may be appropriate is where both parties to the transaction make unique and valuable contributions to the transaction.

6.210. Section C in Part III of Chapter II contains guidance to be considered in applying transactional profit split methods. That guidance is fully applicable to matters involving the use of intangibles in connection with the sale of goods or the provision of services in controlled transactions.

6.211. In applying a profit split method in a case involving the use of intangibles, care should be taken to identify the intangibles in question, to evaluate the manner in which those intangibles contribute to the creation of value, and to evaluate other income producing functions performed, risks assumed and assets used. Vague assertions of the existence and use of unspecified intangibles will not support a reliable application of a profit split method.

6.212. In appropriate circumstances, transfer pricing methods or valuation techniques not dependent on the identification of reliable comparable uncontrolled transactions may also be utilised to determine arm's length conditions for the sale of goods or the provision of services where intangibles are used in connection with the transaction. The alternative selected should reflect the nature of the goods or services provided and the contribution of intangibles and other relevant factors to the creation of value.

Chapter VII

Special considerations for intra-group services

A. Introduction

7.1. This chapter discusses issues that arise in determining for transfer pricing purposes whether services have been provided by one member of an MNE group to other members of that group and, if so, in establishing arm's length pricing for those intra-group services. The chapter does not address except incidentally whether services have been provided in a cost contribution arrangement, nor, in such a case, the appropriate arm's length pricing. Cost contribution arrangements are the subject of Chapter VIII.

7.2. Nearly every MNE group must arrange for a wide scope of services to be available to its members, in particular administrative, technical, financial and commercial services. Such services may include management, co-ordination and control functions for the whole group. The cost of providing such services may be borne initially by the parent, by one or more specially designated group members ("a group service centre"), or other group members. An independent enterprise in need of a service may acquire the services from a service provider who specialises in that type of service or may perform the service for itself (i.e. in-house). In a similar way, a member of an MNE group in need of a service may acquire it from independent enterprises, or from one or more associated enterprises in the same MNE group (i.e. intra-group), or may perform the service for itself. Intra-group services often include those that are typically available externally from independent enterprises (such as legal and accounting services), in addition to those that are ordinarily performed internally (e.g. by an enterprise for itself, such as central auditing, financing advice, or training of personnel). It is not in the interests of an MNE group to incur costs unnecessarily, and it is in the interest of an MNE group to provide intra-group services efficiently. Application of the guidance in this chapter should ensure that services are appropriately identified and associated costs appropriately allocated within the MNE group in accordance with the arm's length principle.

7.3. Intra-group arrangements for rendering services are sometimes linked to arrangements for transferring goods or intangibles (or the licensing thereof). In some cases, such as know-how contracts containing a service element, it may be very difficult to determine where the exact border lies between the transfer of intangibles or rights in intangibles and the provision of services. Ancillary services are frequently associated with the transfer of technology. It may therefore be necessary to consider the principles for aggregation and segregation of transactions in Chapter III where a mixed transfer of services and property is involved.

7.4. Intra-group services may vary considerably among MNE groups, as does the extent to which those services provide a benefit, or an expected benefit, to one or more group members. Each case is dependent upon its own facts and circumstances and the arrangements within the group. For example, in a decentralised group, the parent company may limit its intra-group activity to monitoring its investments in its subsidiaries in its capacity as a shareholder. In contrast, in a centralised or integrated group, the board of directors and senior management of the parent company may make important decisions concerning the affairs of its subsidiaries, and the parent company may support the implementation of these decisions by performing general and administrative activities for its subsidiaries as well as operational activities such as treasury management, marketing, and supply chain management.

B. Main issues

7.5. There are two issues in the analysis of transfer pricing for intra-group services. One issue is whether intra-group services have in fact been provided. The other issue is what the intra-group charge for such services for tax purposes should be in accordance with the arm's length principle. Each of these issues is discussed below.

B.1. Determining whether intra-group services have been rendered

B.1.1. Benefits test

7.6. Under the arm's length principle, the question whether an intra-group service has been rendered when an activity is performed for one or more group members by another group member should depend on whether the activity provides a respective group member with economic or commercial value to enhance or maintain its business position. This can be determined by considering whether an independent enterprise in comparable circumstances would have been willing to pay for the activity if performed for it by an independent enterprise or would have performed the activity in-house for itself. If the activity is not one for which the independent enterprise would have been willing to pay or perform for itself, the activity ordinarily should not be considered as an intra-group service under the arm's length principle.

7.7. The analysis described above quite clearly depends on the actual facts and circumstances, and it is not possible in the abstract to set forth categorically the activities that do or do not constitute the rendering of intra-group services. However, some guidance may be given to elucidate how the analysis would be applied for some common types of services undertaken in MNE groups.

7.8. Some intra-group services are performed by one member of an MNE group to meet an identified need of one or more specific members of the group. In such a case, it is relatively straightforward to determine whether a service has been provided. Ordinarily an independent enterprise in comparable circumstances would have satisfied the identified need either by performing the activity in-house or by having the activity performed by a third party. Thus, in such a case, an intra-group service ordinarily would be found to exist. For example, an intra-group service would normally be found where an associated enterprise repairs equipment used in manufacturing by another member of the MNE group. It is essential, however, that reliable documentation is provided to the tax administrations to verify that the costs have been incurred by the service provider.

B.1.2. Shareholder activities

7.9. A more complex analysis is necessary where an associated enterprise undertakes activities that relate to more than one member of the group or to the group as a whole. In a narrow range of such cases, an intra-group activity may be performed relating to group members even though those group members do not need the activity (and would not be willing to pay for it were they independent enterprises). Such an activity would be one that a group member (usually the parent company or a regional holding company) performs solely because of its ownership interest in one or more other group members, i.e. in its capacity as shareholder. This type of activity would not be considered to be an intra-group service, and thus would not justify a charge to other group members. Instead, the costs associated with this type of activity should be borne and allocated at the level of the shareholder. This type of activity may be referred to as a "shareholder activity", distinguishable from the broader term "stewardship activity" used in the 1979 Report. Stewardship activities covered a range of activities by a shareholder that may include the provision of services to other group members, for example services that would be provided by a co-ordinating centre. These latter types of non-shareholder activities could include detailed planning services for particular operations, emergency management or technical advice (trouble shooting), or in some cases assistance in day-to-day management.

7.10. The following are examples of costs associated with shareholder activities, under the standard set forth in paragraph 7.6:

a) Costs relating to the juridical structure of the parent company itself, such as meetings of shareholders of the parent, issuing of shares in the parent company, stock exchange listing of the parent company and costs of the supervisory board;

b) Costs relating to reporting requirements (including financial reporting and audit) of the parent company including the consolidation of reports, costs relating to the parent company's audit of the subsidiary's accounts carried out exclusively in the interest of the parent company, and costs relating to the preparation of consolidated financial statements of the MNE (however, in practice costs incurred locally by the subsidiaries may not need to be passed on to the parent or holding company where it is disproportionately onerous to identify and isolate those costs);

c) Costs of raising funds for the acquisition of its participations and costs relating to the parent company's investor relations such as communication strategy with shareholders of the parent company, financial analysts, funds and other stakeholders in the parent company;

d) Costs relating to compliance of the parent company with the relevant tax laws;

e) Costs which are ancillary to the corporate governance of the MNE as a whole.

In contrast, if for example a parent company raises funds on behalf of another group member which uses them to acquire a new company, the parent company would generally be regarded as providing a service to the group member. The 1984 Report also mentioned "costs of managerial and control (monitoring) activities related to the management and protection of the investment as such in participations". Whether these activities fall within the definition of shareholder activities as defined in these Guidelines would be determined according to whether under comparable facts and circumstances the activity is one that an independent enterprise would have been willing to pay for or to perform for itself. Where activities such as those described above are performed by a group company other than solely because of an ownership interest in other group members, then that group company is not performing shareholder activities but should be regarded as providing a service to the parent or holding company to which the guidance in this chapter applies.

B.1.3. Duplication

7.11. In general, no intra-group service should be found for activities undertaken by one group member that merely duplicate a service that another group member is performing for itself, or that is being performed for such other group member by a third party. An exception may be where the duplication of services is only temporary, for example, where an MNE group is reorganising to centralise its management functions. Another exception would be where the duplication is undertaken to reduce the risk of a wrong business decision (e.g. by getting a second legal opinion on a subject). Any consideration of possible duplication of services needs to identify the nature of the services in detail, and the reason why the company appears to be duplicating costs contrary to efficient practices. The fact that a company performs, for example, marketing services in-house and also is charged for marketing services from a group company does not of itself determine duplication, since marketing is a broad term covering many levels of activity. Examination of information provided by the taxpayer may determine that the intra-group services are different, additional, or complementary to the activities performed in-house. The benefits test would then apply to those non-duplicative elements of the intra-group services. Some regulated sectors require control functions to be performed locally as well as on a consolidated basis by the parent; such requirements should not lead to disallowance on grounds of duplication.

B.1.4. Incidental benefits

7.12. There are some cases where an intra-group service performed by a group member such as a shareholder or co-ordinating centre relates only to some group members but incidentally provides benefits to other group members. Examples could be analysing the question whether to reorganise the group, to acquire new members, or to terminate a division. These activities could constitute intra-group services to the particular group members involved, for example those members who may make the acquisition or terminate one of their divisions, but they may also produce economic benefits for other group members not directly involved in the potential decision since the analysis could provide useful information about their own business operations. The incidental benefits ordinarily would not cause these other group members to be treated as receiving an intra-group service because the activities producing the benefits would not be ones for which an independent enterprise ordinarily would be willing to pay.

7.13. Similarly, an associated enterprise should not be considered to receive an intra-group service when it obtains incidental benefits attributable solely to its being part of a larger concern, and not to any specific activity being performed. For example, no service would be received where an associated enterprise by reason of its affiliation alone has a credit-rating higher than it would if it were unaffiliated, but an intra-group service would usually exist where the higher credit rating were due to a guarantee by another group member, or where the enterprise benefitted from deliberate concerted action involving global marketing and public relations campaigns. In this respect, passive association should be distinguished from active promotion of the MNE group's attributes that positively enhances the profit-making potential of particular members of the group. Each case must be determined according to its own facts and circumstances. See Section D.8 of Chapter I on MNE group synergies.

B.1.5. Centralised services

7.14. Other activities that may relate to the group as a whole are those centralised in the parent company or one or more group service centres (such as a regional headquarters company) and made available to the group (or multiple members thereof). The activities that are centralised depend on the kind of business and on the organisational structure of the group, but in general they may include administrative services such as planning, co-ordination, budgetary control, financial advice, accounting, auditing, legal, factoring, computer services; financial services such as supervision of cash flows and solvency, capital increases, loan contracts, management of interest and exchange rate risks, and refinancing; assistance in the fields of production, buying, distribution and marketing; and services in staff matters such as recruitment and training. Group service centres also often carry out order management, customer service and call centres, research and development or administer and protect intangible property for all or part of the MNE group. These types of activities ordinarily will be considered intra-group services because they are the type of activities that independent enterprises would have been willing to pay for or to perform for themselves.

B.1.6. Form of the remuneration

7.15. In considering whether a charge for the provision of services would be made between independent enterprises, it would also be relevant to consider the form that an arm's length consideration would take had the transaction occurred between independent enterprises dealing at arm's length. For example, in respect of financial services such as loans, foreign exchange and hedging, all of the remuneration may be built into the spread and it would not be appropriate to expect a further service fee to be charged if such were the case. Similarly, in some buying or procurement services a commission element may be incorporated in the price of the product or services procured, and a separate service fee may not be appropriate.

7.16. Another issue arises with respect to services provided "on call". The question is whether the availability of such services is itself a separate service for which an arm's length charge (in addition to any charge for services actually rendered) should be determined. A parent company or one or more group service centres may be on hand to provide services such as financial, managerial, technical, legal or tax advice and assistance to members of the group at any time. In that case, a service may be rendered to associated enterprises by having staff, equipment, etc., available. An intra-group service would exist to the extent that it would be reasonable to expect an independent enterprise in comparable circumstances to incur "standby" charges to ensure the availability of the services when the need for them arises. It is not unknown, for example, for an independent enterprise to pay an annual "retainer" fee to a firm of lawyers to ensure entitlement to legal advice and representation if litigation is brought. Another example is a service contract for priority computer network repair in the event of a breakdown.

7.17. These services may be available on call and they may vary in amount and importance from year to year. It is unlikely that an independent enterprise would incur stand-by charges where the potential need for the service was remote, where the advantage of having services on-call was negligible, or where the on-call services could be obtained promptly and readily from other sources without the need for stand-by arrangements. Thus, the benefit conferred on a group company by the on-call arrangements should be considered, perhaps by looking at the extent to which the services have been used over a period of several years rather than solely for the year in which a charge is to be made, before determining that an intra-group service is being provided.

7.18. The fact that a payment was made to an associated enterprise for purported services can be useful in determining whether services were in fact provided, but the mere description of a payment as, for example, "management fees" should not be expected to be treated as *prima facie* evidence that such services have been rendered. At the same time, the absence of payments or contractual agreements does not automatically lead to the conclusion that no intra-group services have been rendered.

B.2. Determining an arm's length charge

B.2.1. In general

7.19. Once it is determined that an intra-group service has been rendered, it is necessary, as for other types of intra-group transfers, to determine whether the amount of the charge, if any, is in accordance with the arm's length principle. This means that the charge for intra-group services should be that which would have been made and accepted between independent enterprises in comparable circumstances. Consequently, such transactions should not be treated differently for tax purposes from comparable transactions between independent enterprises, simply because the transactions are between enterprises that happen to be associated.

B.2.2. Identifying actual arrangements for charging for intra-group services

7.20. To identify the amount, if any, that has actually been charged for services, a tax administration will need to identify what arrangements, if any, have actually been put in place between the associated enterprises to facilitate charges being made for the provision of services between them.

B.2.2.1. Direct-charge methods

7.21. In certain cases, the arrangements made for charging for intra-group services can be readily identified. These cases are where the MNE group uses a direct-charge method, i.e. where the associated enterprises are charged for specific services. In general, the direct-charge method is of great practical convenience to tax administrations because it allows the service performed and the basis for the payment to be clearly identified. Thus, the direct-charge method facilitates the determination of whether the charge is consistent with the arm's length principle.

7.22. An MNE group may be able to adopt direct charging arrangements, particularly where services similar to those rendered to associated enterprises are also rendered to independent parties. If specific services are provided not only to associated enterprises but also to independent enterprises in a comparable manner and as a significant part of its business, it could be presumed that the MNE has the ability to demonstrate a separate basis for the charge (e.g. by recording the work done, the fee basis, or costs expended in fulfilling its third party contracts). As a result, MNEs in such a case are encouraged to adopt the direct-charge method in relation to their transactions with associated enterprises. It is accepted, however, that this approach may not always be appropriate if, for example, the services to independent parties are merely occasional or marginal.

B.2.2.2. Indirect-charge methods

7.23. A direct-charge method for charging for intra-group services can be difficult to apply in practice. Consequently, some MNE groups have developed other methods for charging for services provided by parent companies or group service centres. In such cases, MNE groups may find they have few alternatives but to use cost allocation and apportionment methods which often necessitate some degree of estimation or approximation, as a basis for calculating an arm's length charge following the principles in Section B.2.3 below. Such methods are generally referred to as indirect-charge methods and should be allowable provided sufficient regard has been given to the value of the services to recipients and the extent to which comparable services are provided between independent enterprises. These methods of calculating charges would generally not be acceptable where specific services that form a main business activity of the enterprise are provided not only to associated enterprises but also to independent parties. While every attempt should be made to charge fairly for the service provided, any charging has to be supported by an identifiable and reasonably foreseeable benefit. Any indirect-charge method should be sensitive to the commercial features of the individual case (e.g. the allocation key makes sense under the circumstances), contain safeguards against manipulation and follow sound accounting principles, and be capable of producing charges or allocations of costs that are commensurate with the actual or reasonably expected benefits to the recipient of the service.

7.24. In some cases, an indirect-charge method may be necessary due to the nature of the service being provided. One example is where the proportion of the value of the services rendered to the various relevant entities cannot be quantified except on an approximate or estimated basis. This problem may occur, for example, where sales promotion activities carried on centrally (e.g. at international fairs, in the international press, or through other centralised advertising campaigns) may affect the quantity of goods manufactured or sold by a number of affiliates. Another case is where a separate recording and analysis of the relevant services for each beneficiary would involve a burden of administrative work that would be disproportionately heavy in relation to the activities themselves. In such cases, the charge could be determined by reference to an allocation among all potential beneficiaries of the costs that cannot be allocated directly, i.e. costs that cannot be specifically assigned to the actual beneficiaries of the various services. To satisfy the arm's length principle, the allocation method chosen must lead to a result that is consistent with what comparable independent enterprises would have been prepared to accept.

7.25. The allocation should be based on an appropriate measure of the usage of the service that is also easy to verify, for example turnover, staff employed, or an activity based key such as orders processed. Whether the allocation method is appropriate may depend on the nature and usage of the service. For example, the usage or provision of payroll services may be more related to the number of staff than to turnover, while the allocation of the stand-by costs of priority computer back-up could be allocated in proportion to relative expenditure on computer equipment by the group members.

7.26. When an indirect-charge method is used, the relationship between the charge and the services provided may be obscured and it may become difficult to evaluate the benefit provided. Indeed, it may mean that the enterprise being charged for a service itself has not related the charge to the service. Consequently, there is an increased risk of double taxation because it may be more difficult to determine a deduction for costs incurred on behalf of group members if compensation cannot be readily identified, or for the recipient of the service to establish a deduction for any amount paid if it is unable to demonstrate that services have been provided.

B.2.2.3. Form of the compensation

7.27. The compensation for services rendered to an associated enterprise may be included in the price for other transfers. For instance, the price for licensing a patent or know-how may include a payment for technical assistance services or centralised services performed for the licensee or for managerial advice on the marketing of the goods produced under the licence. In such cases, the tax administration and the taxpayers would have to check that there is no additional service fee charged and that there is no double deduction.

7.28. In identifying arrangements for charging any retainer for the provision of "on call" services (as discussed in paragraphs 7.16 and 7.17), it may be necessary to examine the terms for the actual use of the services since these may include provisions that no charge is made for actual use until the level of usage exceeds a predetermined level.

B.2.3. Calculating the arm's length compensation

7.29. In trying to determine the arm's length price in relation to intra-group services, the matter should be considered both from the perspective of the service provider and from the perspective of the recipient of the service. In this respect, relevant considerations include the value of the service to the recipient and how much a comparable independent enterprise would be prepared to pay for that service in comparable circumstances, as well as the costs to the service provider.

7.30. For example, from the perspective of an independent enterprise seeking a service, the service providers in that market may or may not be willing or able to supply the service at a price that the independent enterprise is prepared to pay. If the service providers can supply the wanted service within a range of prices that the independent enterprise would be prepared to pay, then a deal will be struck. From the point of view of the service provider, a price below which it would not supply the service and the cost to it are relevant considerations to address, but they are not necessarily determinative of the outcome in every case.

B.2.3.1. Methods

7.31. The method to be used to determine arm's length transfer pricing for intra-group services should be determined according to the guidelines in Chapters I, II, and III. Often, the application of these guidelines will lead to use of the CUP or a cost-based method (cost plus method or cost-based TNMM) for pricing intra-group services. A CUP method is likely to be the most appropriate method where there is a comparable service provided between independent enterprises in the recipient's market, or by the associated enterprise providing the services to an independent enterprise in comparable circumstances. For example, this might be the case where accounting, auditing, legal, or computer services are being provided subject to the controlled and uncontrolled transactions being comparable. A cost based method would likely be the most appropriate method in the absence of a CUP where the nature of the activities involved, assets used, and risks assumed are comparable to those undertaken by independent enterprises. As indicated in Chapter II, Part II, in applying the cost plus method, there should be a consistency between the controlled and uncontrolled transactions in the categories of cost that are included. In exceptional cases, for example where it may be difficult to apply the CUP method or the cost-based methods, it may be helpful to take account of more than one method (see paragraph 2.12) in reaching a satisfactory determination of arm's length pricing.

7.32. It may be necessary to perform a functional analysis of the various members of the group to establish the relationship between the relevant services and the members' activities and performance. In addition, it may be necessary to consider not only the immediate impact of a service, but also its long-term effect, bearing in mind that some costs will never actually produce the benefits that were reasonably expected when they were incurred. For example, expenditure on preparations for a marketing operation might *prima facie* be too heavy to be borne by a member in the light of its current resources; the determination whether the charge in such a case is arm's length should consider expected benefits from the operation and the possibility that the amount and timing of the charge in some arm's length arrangements might depend on the results of the operation. The taxpayer should be prepared to demonstrate the reasonableness of its charges to associated enterprises in such cases.

7.33. Where a cost based method is determined to be the most appropriate method to the circumstances of the case, the analysis would require examining whether the costs incurred by the group service provider need some adjustment to make the comparison of the controlled and uncontrolled transactions reliable.

7.34. When an associated enterprise is acting only as an agent or intermediary in the provision of services, it is important in applying a cost based method that the return or mark-up is appropriate for the performance of an agency function rather than for the performance of the services themselves. In such a case, it may not be appropriate to determine arm's length pricing as a mark-up on the cost of the services but rather on the costs of the agency function itself. For example, an associated enterprise may incur the costs of renting advertising space on behalf of group members, costs that the group members would have incurred directly had they been independent. In such a case, it may well be appropriate to pass on these costs to the group recipients without a mark-up, and to apply a mark-up only to the costs incurred by the intermediary in performing its agency function.

B.2.3.2. Considerations on including a profit element

7.35. Depending on the method being used to establish an arm's length charge for intra-group services, the issue may arise whether it is necessary that the charge be such that it results in a profit for the service provider. In an arm's length transaction, an independent enterprise normally would seek to charge for services in such a way as to generate profit, rather than providing the services merely at cost. The economic alternatives available to the recipient of the service also need to be taken into account in determining the arm's length charge. However, there are circumstances (e.g. as outlined in the discussion on business strategies in Chapter I) in which an independent enterprise may not realise a profit from the performance of services alone, for example where a supplier's costs (anticipated or actual) exceed market price but the supplier agrees to provide the service to increase its profitability, perhaps by complementing its range of activities. Therefore, it need not always be the case that an arm's length price will result in a profit for an associated enterprise that is performing an intra-group service.

7.36. For example, it may be the case that the market value of intra-group services is not greater than the costs incurred by the service provider. This could occur where, for example, the service is not an ordinary or recurrent activity of the service provider but is offered incidentally as a convenience to the MNE group. In determining whether the intra-group services represent the same value for money as could be obtained from an independent enterprise, a comparison of functions and expected benefits would be relevant to assessing comparability of the transactions. An MNE group may still determine to provide the service intra-group rather than using a third party for a variety of reasons, perhaps because of other intra-group benefits (for which arm's length compensation may be appropriate). It would not be appropriate in such a case to increase the price for the service above what would be established by the CUP method just to make sure the associated enterprise makes a profit. Such a result would be contrary to the arm's length principle. However, it is important to ensure that all benefits to the recipient are properly taken into account.

7.37. While as a matter of principle tax administrations and taxpayers should try to establish the proper arm's length pricing, it should not be overlooked that there may be practical reasons why a tax administration in its discretion exceptionally might be willing to forgo computing and taxing an arm's length price from the performance of services in some cases, as distinct from allowing a taxpayer in appropriate circumstances to merely allocate the costs of providing those services. For instance, a cost-benefit analysis might indicate the additional tax revenue that would be collected does not justify the costs and administrative burdens of determining what an appropriate arm's length price might be in some cases. In such cases, charging all relevant costs rather than an arm's length price may provide a satisfactory result for MNEs and tax administrations. This concession is unlikely to be made by tax administrations where the provision of a service is a principal activity of the associated enterprise, where the profit element is relatively significant, or where direct charging is possible as a basis from which to determine the arm's length price.

C. Some examples of intra-group services

7.38. This section sets forth several examples of transfer pricing issues in the provision of intra-group services. The examples are provided for illustrative purposes only. When dealing with individual cases, it is necessary to explore the actual facts and circumstances to judge the applicability of any transfer pricing method.

7.39. One example involves debt-factoring activities, where an MNE group decides to centralise the activities for economic reasons. For example, it may be prudent to centralise the debt-factoring activities to better manage liquidity, currency and debt risks and to provide administrative efficiencies. A debt-factoring centre that takes on this responsibility is performing intra-group services for which an arm's length charge should be made. A CUP method could be appropriate in such a case.

7.40. Another example of an activity that may involve intra-group services is manufacturing or assembly operations. The activities can take a variety of forms including what is commonly referred to as contract manufacturing. In some cases of contract manufacturing the producer may operate under extensive instruction from the counterparty about what to produce, in what quantity and of what quality. In some cases, raw materials or components may be made available to the producer by the counterparty. The production company may be assured that its entire output will be purchased, assuming quality requirements are met. In such a case the production company could be considered as performing a low-risk service to the counterparty, and the cost plus method could be the most appropriate transfer pricing method, subject to the principles in Chapter II.

7.41. Research is similarly an example of an activity that may involve intra-group services. The terms of the activity can be set out in a detailed contract with the party commissioning the service, commonly known as contract research. The activity can involve highly skilled personnel and vary considerably both in its nature and in its importance to the success of the group. The actual arrangements can take a variety of forms from the undertaking of detailed programmes laid down by the principal party, extending to agreements where the research company has discretion to work within broadly defined categories. In the latter instance, the additional functions of identifying commercially valuable areas and assessing the risk of unsuccessful research can be a critical factor in the performance of the group as a whole. It is therefore crucial to undertake a detailed functional analysis and to obtain a clear understanding of the precise nature of the research, and of how the activities are being carried out by the company, prior to consideration of the appropriate transfer pricing methodology. The consideration of options realistically available to the party commissioning the research may also prove useful in selecting the most appropriate transfer pricing method. See Section B.2 of Chapter VI.

7.42. Another example of intra-group services is the administration of licences. The administration and enforcement of intangible property rights should be distinguished from the exploitation of those rights for this purpose. The protection of a licence might be handled by a group service centre responsible for monitoring possible licence infringements and for enforcing licence rights.

D. Low value-adding intra-group services

7.43. This section provides specific guidance relating to a particular category of intra-group services referred to as low value-adding intra-group services. Section D.1 contains the definition of low value-adding intra-group services. Section D.2 sets out an elective, simplified approach for the determination of arm's length charges for low value-adding intra-group services, including a simplified benefits test. Section D.3 contains guidance on documentation and reporting requirements that should be met by an MNE group electing to apply this simplified approach. Finally, Section D.4 addresses some issues with regard to the levying of withholding taxes on charges for low value-adding intra-group services. In summary, the simplified approach recognises that the arm's length price for low value-adding intra-group services is closely related to costs, allocates the costs of providing each category of such services to those group companies which benefit from using those services, and then applies the same mark-up to all categories of services. MNE groups not electing to apply the simplified approach set out in this section should address transfer pricing issues related to low-value-adding services under the provisions of Sections A and B, above.

D.1. Definition of low value-adding intra-group services

7.44. This section discusses the definitional issues related to low value-adding intra-group services for applying the elective, simplified approach discussed under Section D.2. It starts by indicating the characteristics that services must have in order to qualify as low-value-adding intra-group services for applying the elective, simplified approach. It then identifies a series of activities that do not qualify as low value-adding intra-group services for the elective, simplified approach. Finally it contains a list of examples of services that likely would have the characteristics to qualify as low value-adding intra-groups services for the application of the simplified approach.

7.45. Low value-adding intra-group services for the purposes of the simplified approach are services performed by one member or more than one member of an MNE group on behalf of one or more other group members which

- are of a supportive nature,
- are not part of the core business of the MNE group (i.e. not creating the profit-earning activities or contributing to economically significant activities of the MNE group),
- do not require the use of unique and valuable intangibles and do not lead to the creation of unique and valuable intangibles, and
- do not involve the assumption or control of substantial or significant risk by the service provider and do not give rise to the creation of significant risk for the service provider.

7.46. The guidance in this section is not applicable to services that would ordinarily qualify as low value-adding intra-group services where such services are rendered to unrelated customers of the members of the MNE group. In such cases it can be expected that reliable internal comparables exist and can be used for determining the arm's length price for the intra-group services.

7.47. The following activities would not qualify for the simplified approach outlined in this section:

- services constituting the core business of the MNE group;
- research and development services (including software development unless falling within the scope of information technology services in 7.49);
- manufacturing and production services;
- purchasing activities relating to raw materials or other materials that are used in the manufacturing or production process;

- sales, marketing and distribution activities;
- financial transactions;
- extraction, exploration, or processing of natural resources;
- insurance and reinsurance;
- services of corporate senior management (other than management supervision of services that qualify as low value-adding intra-group services under the definition of paragraph 7.45).

7.48. The fact that an activity does not qualify for the simplified approach, as defined under paragraph 7.45, should not be interpreted to mean that that activity generates high returns. The activity could still add low value, and the determination of the arm's length charge for such activity, if any, should be determined according to the guidance set out in paragraphs 7.1 to 7.42.

7.49. The following bullet points provide examples of services that would likely meet the definition of low value-adding services provided in paragraph 7.45:

- accounting and auditing, for example gathering and reviewing information for use in financial statements, maintenance of accounting records, preparation of financial statements, preparation or assistance in operational and financial audits, verifying authenticity and reliability of accounting records, and assistance in the preparation of budgets through compilation of data and information gathering;
- processing and management of accounts receivable and accounts payable, for example compilation of customer or client billing information, and credit control checking and processing;
- human resources activities, such as:
    - staffing and recruitment, for example hiring procedures, assistance in evaluation of applicants and selection and appointment of personnel, on-boarding new employees, performance evaluation and assistance in defining careers, assistance in procedures to dismiss personnel, assistance in programmes for redundant personnel;
    - training and employee development, for example evaluation of training needs, creation of internal training and development programmes, creation of management skills and career development programmes;
    - remuneration services, for example, providing advice and determining policies for employee compensation and benefits such as healthcare and life insurance, stock option plans, and

pension schemes; verification of attendance and timekeeping, payroll services including processing and tax compliance;

- developing and monitoring of staff health procedures, safety and environmental standards relating to employment matters;

- monitoring and compilation of data relating to health, safety, environmental and other standards regulating the business;
- information technology services where they are not part of the principal activity of the group, for example installing, maintaining and updating IT systems used in the business; information system support (which may include the information system used in connection with accounting, production, client relations, human resources and payroll, and email systems); training on the use or application of information systems as well as on the associated equipment employed to collect, process and present information; developing IT guidelines, providing telecommunications services, organising an IT helpdesk, implementing and maintaining of IT security systems; supporting, maintaining and supervising of IT networks (local area network, wide area network, internet);
- internal and external communications and public relations support (but excluding specific advertising or marketing activities as well as development of underlying strategies);
- legal services, for example general legal services performed by in-house legal counsel such as drafting and reviewing contracts, agreements and other legal documents, legal consultation and opinions, representation of the company (judicial litigation, arbitration panels, administrative procedures), legal research and legal as well as administrative work for the registration and protection of intangible property;
- activities with regard to tax obligations, for example information gathering and preparation of tax returns (income tax, sales tax, VAT, property tax, customs and excise), making tax payments, responding to tax administrations' audits, and giving advice on tax matters;
- general services of an administrative or clerical nature.

7.50. The following examples illustrate an important element of the definition of low value-adding intra-group services, namely, that they should not include services which are part of the MNE's core business. Services that may seem superficially similar in nature (in the example, credit risk analysis) may or may not be low value-adding intra-group services depending on the specific context and circumstances. The examples also illustrate the point that services may not qualify as low value-adding intra-group services because in their specific context they create significant risk or unique and valuable intangibles.

a) Company A, situated in Country A, is a shoe manufacturer and wholesale distributor of shoes in the North-West region. Its wholly-owned subsidiary B, situated in Country B, is a wholesale distributor in the South-East region of the shoes manufactured by A. As part of its operations, A routinely performs a credit risk analysis on its customers on the basis of reports purchased from a credit reporting agency. A performs, on behalf of B, the same credit risk analysis with respect to B's customers, using the same methods and approaches. Under the facts and circumstances, it could be reasonably concluded that the service A performs for B is a low value-adding intra-group service.

b) Company X is a subsidiary of a worldwide investment banking group. Company X performs credit risk analysis with respect to potential counterparties for transactions involving financial derivatives contracts and prepares credit reports for the worldwide investment banking group. The credit analyses performed by Company X are utilised by the group in establishing the prices of financial derivatives for the group's clients. The personnel of Company X have developed special expertise and make use of internally developed, confidential credit risk analysis models, algorithms and software. Under the facts and circumstances of this case, it could not be concluded that the service Company X performs for the worldwide investment banking group is a low value-adding intra-group service.

7.51. The definition of low value-adding intra-group services refers to the supportive nature of such services, which are not part of the core business of the MNE group. The provision of low value-adding intra-group services may, in fact, be the principal business activity of the legal entity providing the service, e.g. a shared service centre, provided these services do not relate to the core business of the group. As an example, assume that an MNE is engaged in the development, production, sale and marketing of dairy products worldwide. The group established a shared services company, the only activity of which is to act as a global IT support service centre. From the perspective of the IT support service provider, the rendering of the IT services is the company's principal business activity. However, from the perspective of the service recipients, and from the perspective of the MNE group as a whole, the service is not a core business activity and may therefore qualify as a low value-adding intra-group service.

D.2. Simplified determination of arm's length charges for low value-adding intra-group services

7.52. This subsection sets out the elements of a simplified charge mechanism for low value-adding intra-group services. This simplified method is premised on the proposition that all low value-adding service costs incurred in supporting the business of MNE group members should be allocated to those members. The basic benefits of using the simplified approach include: (1) reducing the compliance effort of meeting the benefits test and in demonstrating arm's length charges; (2) providing greater certainty for MNE groups that the price charged for the qualifying activities will be accepted by the tax administrations that have adopted the simplified approach when the conditions of the simplified approach mentioned in paragraph 7.45 have been met; and (3) providing tax administrations with targeted documentation enabling efficient review of compliance risks. An MNE group electing to adopt this simplified method would as far as practicable apply it on a consistent, group wide basis in all jurisdictions in which it operates.

7.53. Where a tax administration has not adopted the simplified approach, and as a consequence the MNE group complies with the local requirements in that jurisdiction, such compliance would not disqualify the MNE group from the application of the simplified approach to other jurisdictions. In addition, not all MNE groups are vertically integrated and may instead have regional or divisional sub-groups with their own management and support structures. Therefore, MNE groups may elect to adopt the simplified method at the level of a sub-holding company and apply it on a consistent basis across all subsidiaries of that sub-holding company. When the MNE group elects for and applies the simplified approach, charges for low value-adding intra-group services that are or have been determined in conformity with the guidance in this subsection are determined to be in accordance with the arm's length principle. A possible alternative approach for dealing with the issues discussed in this subsection would be the use of cost contribution arrangements, covered in Chapter VIII.

D.2.1. Application of the benefits test to low value-adding intra-group services

7.54. As discussed in paragraph 7.6, under the arm's length principle an obligation to pay for an intra-group service arises only where the benefits test is satisfied, i.e. the activity must provide the group member expected to pay for the service with economic or commercial value to enhance or maintain its commercial position, which in turn is determined by evaluating whether an independent enterprise in comparable circumstances would have been willing to pay for the activity if performed for it by an independent enterprise or would have performed the activity in-house for itself. However, because of the nature of the low value-adding intra-group services discussed in this section, such determinations may be difficult or may require greater effort than the amount of the charge warrants. Tax administrations should therefore generally refrain from reviewing or challenging the benefits test when the simplified approach has been applied under the conditions and circumstances discussed in this section and in particular in conformity with the documentation and reporting discussed in Section D.3 below.

7.55. While low value-adding intra-group services may provide benefits to all recipients of those services, questions may arise about the extent of the benefits and whether independent parties would have been willing to pay for the service or perform it themselves. Where the MNE group has followed the guidance of the simplified approach the documentation and reporting discussed in Section D.3 below, it should provide sufficient evidence that the benefits test is met given the nature of low value-adding intra-group services. In evaluating the benefits test, tax administrations should consider benefits only by categories of services and not on a specific charge basis. Thus, the taxpayer need only demonstrate that assistance was provided with, for example, payroll processing, rather than being required to specify individual acts undertaken that give rise to the costs charged. Provided such information outlined in paragraph 7.64 is made available to the tax administration, a single annual invoice describing a category of services should suffice to support the charge, and correspondence or other evidence of individual acts should not be required. With regard to low value-adding intra-group services that benefit only one recipient entity in the MNE group, it is expected that the benefits to the service recipient will be capable of separate demonstration.

D.2.2. Determination of cost pools

7.56. The initial step in applying the simplified approach to low value-adding intra-group services is for the MNE group to calculate, on an annual basis, a pool of all costs incurred by all members of the group in performing each category of low value-adding intra-group services. The costs to be pooled are the direct and indirect costs of rendering the service as well as, where relevant, the appropriate part of operating expenses (e.g. supervisory, general and administrative). The costs should be pooled according to category of services, and should identify the accounting cost centres used in creating the pool. Pass-through costs in the cost pool should be identified for the purposes of applying paragraph 7.61. The cost pool should exclude costs that are attributable to an in-house activity that benefits solely the company performing the activity (including shareholder activities performed by the shareholding company).

7.57. As a second step, the MNE group should identify and remove from the pool those costs that are attributable to services performed by one group member solely on behalf of one other group member. In creating a pool of payroll costs, for example, if group company A provides payroll services solely to group company B the relevant costs should be separately identified and omitted from the pool. However, if group company A performs payroll services for itself as well as for company B, the relevant costs should remain within the pool.

7.58. At this stage in the calculation, the MNE group has identified a pool of costs associated with categories of low value-adding services which are provided to multiple members of the MNE group.

D.2.3. Allocation of low value-adding service costs

7.59. The third step in this simplified charge method for low value-adding intra-group service costs is to allocate among members of the group the costs in the cost pool that benefit multiple members of the group. The taxpayer will select one or more allocation keys to apply for this purpose based on the following principles. The appropriate allocation key or keys will depend on the nature of the services. The same allocation key or keys must be used on a consistent basis for all allocations of costs relating to the same category of services. In accordance with the guidance in paragraph 7.24, the allocation key or keys selected with respect to costs for each relevant category of services should reasonably reflect the level of benefit expected to be received by each recipient of the particular service. As a general rule, the allocation key or keys should reflect the underlying need for the particular services. By way of examples, the allocation key for services related to people might employ each company's share of total group headcount, IT services might employ the share of total users, fleet management services might employ the share of total vehicles, accounting support services might employ the share of total relevant transactions or the share of total assets. In many cases, the share of total turnover may be a relevant key.

7.60. The examples of allocation keys provided in the previous paragraph are not intended to be an exhaustive list. Depending on the facts and circumstances more sophisticated allocation keys might be used. However, a balance should be struck between theoretical sophistication and practical administration, bearing in mind that the costs involved are not generating high value for the group. In this context, there may be no need to use multiple allocation keys if the taxpayer can explain the reasons for concluding that a single key provides a reasonable reflection of the respective benefits. For reasons of consistency, the same allocation key or keys should be applied in determining the allocation to all recipients within the group of the same type of low value-adding intra-group services, and it is expected that the same reasonable key will be used from year to year unless there is a justified reason to change. Tax administrations and taxpayers should also bear in mind that changing the reasonable allocation key can give rise to considerable complexities. It is expected that the taxpayer will describe in its documentation (see paragraph 7.64 below) the reasons for concluding that the allocation key produces outcomes which reasonably reflects the benefits likely to be derived by each service recipient.

D.2.4. Profit mark-up

7.61. In determining the arm's length charge for low value-adding intra-group services, the MNE provider of services shall apply a profit mark-up to all costs in the pool with the exception of any pass-through costs as determined under paragraphs 2.99 and 7.34. The same mark-up shall be utilised for all low value-adding services irrespective of the categories of services. The mark-up shall be equal to 5% of the relevant cost as determined in Section D.2.2. The mark-up under the simplified approach does not need to be justified by a benchmarking study. The same mark-up may be applied to low value-adding intra-group services performed by one group member solely on behalf of one other group member, the costs of which are separately identified under the guidance in paragraph 7.57. It should be noted that the low value-adding intra-group services mark-up should not, without further justification and analysis, be used as benchmark for the determination of the arm's length price for services not within the definition of low value-adding intra-group services, nor for similar services not within the elective, simplified scheme.

D.2.5. Charge for low value-adding services

7.62. Subject to the provisions of paragraph 7.55, the charge for services to any member of the electing MNE group shall be the sum of (i) the costs incurred by another group member in providing services specifically to the member under the second step as detailed in paragraph 7.57, plus the selected profit mark-up, and (ii) the share of pooled costs allocated to the member under the third step as detailed in paragraph 7.59 using the selected allocation key, plus the selected profit mark-up. The charge is payable to the group member that incurred the costs in the pool, and where there is more than one group member incurring those costs, in proportion to each member's share of the pooled costs.

D.2.6. Threshold for the application of the simplified approach

7.63. Tax administrations adopting the simplified approach to low-value-adding intra-group services set out in this section may include an appropriate threshold to enable them to review the simplified approach in cases where the threshold is exceeded. Such a threshold might, for example, be based on fixed financial ratios of the recipient party (e.g. proportion of intra-group services costs to total costs or turnover or pre-intra-group service charge profit) or be determined by reference to a group-wide ratio of total service costs to turnover of the MNE group or some other appropriate measure. Where such a threshold is adopted, the tax administration would not be obliged to accept the simplified approach if the level of low-value-adding intra-group service fees exceeds the threshold and may require a full functional analysis and comparability analysis including the application of the benefits test to specific service charges.

D.3. Documentation and reporting

7.64. An MNE group electing for application of this simplified methodology shall prepare the following information and documentation and make it available upon request to the tax administration of any entity within the group either making or receiving a payment for low value-adding intra-group services.

- A description of the categories of low value-adding intra-group services provided; the identity of the beneficiaries; the reasons justifying that each category of services constitute low value-adding intra-group services within the definition set out in Section D.1; the rationale for the provision of services within the context of the business of the MNE; a description of the benefits or expected benefits of each category of services; a description of the selected allocation keys and the reasons justifying that such allocation keys produce outcomes that reasonably reflect the benefits received, and confirmation of the mark-up applied;
- Written contracts or agreements for the provision of services and any modifications to those contracts and agreements reflecting the agreement of the various members of the group to be bound by the allocation rules of this section. Such written contracts or agreements could take the form of a contemporaneous document identifying the entities involved, the nature of the services, and the terms and conditions under which the services are provided;
- Documentation and calculations showing the determination of the cost pool as described in Section D.2.2, and of the mark-up applied thereon, in particular a detailed listing of all categories and amounts of relevant costs, including costs of any services provided solely to one group member;
- Calculations showing the application of the specified allocation keys.

D.4. Levying of withholding tax on charges for low value-adding intra-group services

7.65. The levying of withholding taxes on the provision of low value-adding intra-group services can prevent the service provider recovering the totality of the costs incurred for rendering the services. When a profit element or mark-up is included in the charge of the services, tax administrations levying withholding tax are encouraged to apply it only to the amount of that profit element or mark-up.

Chapter VIII

Cost contribution arrangements

A. Introduction

8.1. This chapter discusses cost contribution arrangements (CCAs) between two or more associated enterprises. The purpose of the chapter is to provide some general guidance for determining whether the conditions established by associated enterprises for transactions covered by a CCA are consistent with the arm's length principle. The analysis of the structure of such arrangements should be informed by the provisions of this chapter and other provisions of these Guidelines and should be based on an adequate documentation of the arrangement.

8.2. Section B provides a general definition and overview of the concept of CCAs, and Section C gives guidance as to the application of the arm's length principle to CCAs. Section C includes guidance on how to measure contributions to a CCA, whether balancing payments are needed (i.e. payments between participants to adjust their proportionate shares of contributions), and guidance on how contributions and balancing payments should be treated for tax purposes. It also addresses the determination of participants in the CCA and issues related to the entry or withdrawal of participants, and the termination of CCAs. Finally, Section D discusses suggestions for structuring and documenting CCAs.

B. Concept of a CCA

B.1. In general

8.3. A CCA is a contractual arrangement among business enterprises to share the contributions and risks involved in the joint development, production or the obtaining of intangibles, tangible assets or services with the understanding that such intangibles, tangible assets or services are expected to create benefits for the individual businesses of each of the participants. A CCA is a contractual arrangement rather than necessarily a distinct juridical entity or fixed place of business of all the participants. A CCA does not require the participants to combine their operations in order, for example, to exploit any resulting intangibles jointly or to share the revenues or profits. Rather, CCA participants may exploit their interest in the outcomes of a CCA through their individual businesses. The transfer pricing issues focus on the commercial or financial relations between the participants and the contributions made by the participants that create the opportunities to achieve those outcomes.

8.4. As indicated in Section D.1 of Chapter I, the delineation of the actual transaction undertaken forms the first phase in any transfer pricing analysis. The contractual agreement provides the starting point for delineating the actual transaction. In this respect, no difference exists for a transfer pricing analysis between a CCA and any other kind of contractual arrangement where the division of responsibilities, risks, and anticipated outcomes as determined by the functional analysis of the transaction is the same. The guidance on identifying the other economically relevant characteristics is equally applicable to CCAs as to any other type of contractual arrangement, including an assessment as to whether the parties contractually assuming risks are actually assuming these risks based on the framework for analysing risk set out in paragraph 1.60 of these Guidelines. As a consequence, parties performing activities under arrangements with similar economic characteristics should receive similar expected returns, irrespective of whether the contractual arrangement in a particular case is termed a CCA. However, there are specific characteristics of CCAs that warrant special consideration.

8.5. A key feature of a CCA is the sharing of contributions. In accordance with the arm's length principle, at the time of entering into a CCA, each participant's proportionate share of the overall contributions to a CCA must be consistent with its proportionate share of the overall expected benefits to be received under the arrangement. Further, in the case of CCAs involving the development, production or obtaining of intangibles or tangible assets, an ownership interest in any intangibles or tangible assets resulting from the activity of the CCA, or rights to use or exploit those intangibles or tangible assets, is contractually provided for each participant. For CCAs for services, each participant is contractually entitled to receive services resulting from the activity of the CCA. In either case, participants may exploit the interest, rights or entitlement without paying additional consideration (other than the contributions and balancing payments described in Sections C.4 and C.5, respectively) to any party for such interest, rights or entitlement.

8.6. Some benefits of the CCA activity can be determined in advance, whereas others will be uncertain. Some types of CCA activities will produce current benefits, while others have a longer time frame or may not be successful. Nevertheless, in a CCA there is always an expected benefit that each participant seeks from its contribution, including the attendant rights to have the CCA properly administered. Each participant's interest in the results of the CCA activity should be established from the outset, even where the interest is inter-linked with that of other participants, e.g. because legal ownership of developed intangibles or tangible assets may be vested in only one of them but all of them have certain rights to use or exploit the intangibles or tangible assets as provided in the contractual arrangements (for example, perpetual, royalty-free licences for the territory in which the individual participant operates).

8.7. In some cases CCAs can provide helpful simplification of multiple transactions (bearing in mind that the tax consequences of transactions are determined in accordance with applicable local laws). In a situation where associated enterprises both perform activities for other group members and simultaneously benefit from activities performed by other group members, a CCA can provide a mechanism for replacing a web of separate intra-group arm's length payments with a more streamlined system of netted payments, based on aggregated benefits and aggregated contributions associated with all the covered activities (see also paragraphs 3.9 to 3.17 of these Guidelines). A CCA for the sharing in the development of intangibles can eliminate the need for complex cross-licensing arrangements and associated allocation of risk, and replace them with a more streamlined sharing of contributions and risks, with ownership interests of the resulting intangible(s) shared in accordance with the terms of the CCA. However, the streamlining of flows that may result from the adoption of a CCA does not affect the appropriate valuation of the separate contributions of the parties.

8.8. As an illustration of a CCA, take the example of an MNE group which manufactures products through three enterprises which each operate a production site and have their own R&D teams engaged in various projects to improve production processes. Those three enterprises enter into a CCA aimed at generating production process improvements, and as a result pool their expertise and share the risks. Since the CCA grants each participant rights to the outcomes of the projects, the CCA replaces the cross-licensing arrangements that may have resulted in the absence of a CCA and if the enterprises had individually developed certain intangibles and granted rights to one another.

B.2. Relationship to other chapters

8.9. As indicated in paragraph 8.4, there is no difference in the analytical framework for analysing transfer prices for CCAs compared to analysing other forms of contractual relations. The guidance in Section D of Chapter I is relevant to the analysis of all transactions between associated enterprises, and applies to identify the economically relevant characteristics of the commercial or financial relations between the parties as expressed in a

CCA. The contractual terms of the CCA provide the starting point for delineating the transaction between the parties and how the responsibilities, risks, and anticipated outcomes were intended to be allocated at the time of entering into the arrangements. However, as set out in that guidance, the evidence of the conduct of the parties may clarify or supplement aspects of the agreement. The framework for analysing risk in Section D.1.2.1 of Chapter I is relevant to determining whether parties assume risks under the CCA, as discussed in Section C.2 of this chapter, and the consequences for providing funding without assuming risk or performing other functions. Chapter VI provides guidance regarding the determination of arm's length conditions for transactions that involve the use or transfer of intangibles. Paragraphs 6.60 to 6.64 give relevant guidance on exercising control over the financial risk if the funding is used for investment in R&D projects. The guidance in Sections D.3 and D.4 of Chapter VI on hard-to-value intangibles is equally applicable to CCAs. Chapter VII provides guidance on issues that arise in determining for transfer pricing purposes whether services have been provided by a member of an MNE group to other members of that group and, if so, in establishing arm's length prices for those intra-group services. This chapter's objective is to provide supplementary guidance on situations where resources and skills are pooled and the consideration received is, in part or whole, the reasonable expectation of mutual benefits. Thus, the provisions of Chapters VI and VII, and indeed all the other chapters of these Guidelines, will continue to apply to the extent relevant, for instance in measuring the value of a contribution to a CCA as part of the process of determining the proportionate shares of contributions. MNEs are encouraged to observe the guidance of this chapter in order to ensure that their CCAs operate in accordance with the arm's length principle.

B.3. Types of CCAs

8.10. Two types of CCAs are commonly encountered: those established for the joint development, production or the obtaining of intangibles or tangible assets ("development CCAs"); and those for obtaining services ("services CCAs"). Although each particular CCA should be considered on its own facts and circumstances, key differences between these two types of CCAs will generally be that development CCAs are expected to create ongoing, future benefits for participants, while services CCAs will create current benefits only. Development CCAs, in particular with respect to intangibles, often involve significant risks associated with what may be uncertain and distant benefits, while services CCAs often offer more certain and less risky benefits. These distinctions are useful because the greater complexity of development CCAs may require more refined guidance, particularly on the valuation of contributions, than may be required for services CCAs, as discussed below. However, the analysis of a CCA should not be based on superficial distinctions: in some cases, a CCA for obtaining current services may also create or enhance an intangible which provides ongoing and uncertain benefits, and some intangibles developed under a CCA may provide short-term and relatively certain benefits.

8.11. Under a development CCA, each participant has an entitlement to rights in the developed intangible(s) or tangible asset(s). In relation to intangibles, such rights often take the form of separate rights to exploit the intangible in a specific geographic location or for a particular application. The separate rights obtained may constitute actual legal ownership; alternatively, it may be that only one of the participants is the legal owner of the property but the other participants have certain rights to use or exploit the property. In cases where a participant has such rights in any property developed by the CCA, there is no need for a royalty payment or other further consideration for the use of the developed property consistent with the interest to which the participant is entitled under the CCA (however, the contributions of a participant may need to be adjusted if they are not proportionate to their expected benefits; see Section C.5).

C. Applying the arm's length principle

C.1. In general

8.12. For the conditions of a CCA to satisfy the arm's length principle, the value of participants' contributions must be consistent with what independent enterprises would have agreed to contribute under comparable circumstances given their proportionate share of the total anticipated benefits they reasonably expect to derive from the arrangement. What distinguishes contributions to a CCA from any other intra-group transfer of property or services is that part or all of the compensation intended by the participants is the expected mutual and proportionate benefit from the pooling of resources and skills. In addition, particularly for development CCAs, the participants agree to share the upside and downside consequences of risks associated with achieving the anticipated CCA outcomes. As a result, there is a distinction between, say, the intra-group licensing of an intangible where the licensor has borne the development risk on its own and expects compensation through the licensing fees it will receive once the intangible has been fully developed, and a development CCA in which all parties make contributions and share in the consequences of risks materialising in relation to the development of the intangible and decide that each of them, through those contributions, acquires a right in the intangible.

8.13. The expectation of mutual and proportionate benefit is fundamental to the acceptance by independent enterprises of an arrangement for sharing the consequences of risks materialising and pooling resources and skills. Independent enterprises would require that the value of each participant's proportionate share of the actual overall contributions to the arrangement is consistent with the participant's proportionate share of the overall expected benefits to be received under the arrangement. To apply the arm's length principle to a CCA, it is therefore a necessary precondition that all the parties to the arrangement have a reasonable expectation of benefit. The next step is to calculate the value of each participant's contribution to the joint activity, and finally to determine whether the allocation of CCA contributions (as adjusted for any balancing payments made among participants) accords with their respective share of expected benefits. It should be recognised that these determinations are likely to bear a degree of uncertainty, particularly in relation to development CCAs. The potential exists for contributions to be allocated among CCA participants so as to result in an overstatement of taxable profits in some jurisdictions and the understatement of taxable profits in others, measured against the arm's length principle. For that reason, taxpayers should be prepared to substantiate the basis of their claim with respect to the CCA (see Section E).

C.2. Determining participants

8.14. Because the concept of mutual benefit is fundamental to a CCA, it follows that a party may not be considered a participant if the party does not have a reasonable expectation that it will benefit from the objectives of the CCA activity itself (and not just from performing part or all of the subject activity), for example, from exploiting its interest or rights in the intangibles or tangible assets, or from the use of the services produced through the CCA. A participant therefore must be assigned an interest or rights in the intangibles, tangible assets or services that are the subject of the CCA, and have a reasonable expectation of being able to benefit from that interest or those rights. An enterprise that solely performs the subject activity, for example performing research functions, but does not receive an interest in the output of the CCA, would not be considered a participant in the CCA but rather a service provider to the CCA. As such, it should be compensated for the services it provides on an arm's length basis external to the CCA. See paragraph 8.18. Similarly, a party would not be a participant in a CCA if it is not capable of exploiting the output of the CCA in its own business in any manner.

8.15. A party would also not be a participant in a CCA if it does not exercise control over the specific risks it assumes under the CCA and does not have the financial capacity to assume these risks, as this party would not be entitled to a share in the output that is the objective of the CCA based on the functions it actually performs. The general principles set out in Chapter I of these guidelines on the assumption of risks apply to situations involving CCAs. Each participant makes particular contributions to the

CCA objectives, and contractually assumes certain risks. Guidance under Section D.1 of Chapter I on delineating the actual transaction will apply to the transfer pricing analysis in relation to these risks. This also means that a party assuming risks under a CCA based on an analysis under step 4(i) of the framework for analysing risks in paragraph 1.60 ("assumes the risk under the CCA") must control the specific risks it assumes under the CCA and must have the financial capacity to assume these risks. In particular, this implies that a CCA participant must have (i) the capability to make decisions to take on, lay off, or decline the risk-bearing opportunity presented by participating in the CCA, and must actually perform that decision-making function and (ii) the capability to make decisions on whether and how to respond to the risks associated with the opportunity, and must actually perform that decision-making function. While it is not necessary for the party to perform day-to-day risk mitigation activities in relation to activities of the CCA, in such cases, it must have the capability to determine the objectives of those risk mitigation activities to be performed by another party, to decide to entrust that other party to provide the risk mitigation functions, to assess whether the objectives are being adequately met, and, where necessary, to decide to adapt or terminate the arrangement, and must actually perform such assessment and decision-making. In accordance with the principles of prudent business management, the extent of the risks involved in the arrangement will determine the extent of capability and control required. The guidance in paragraphs 6.60 to 6.64 is relevant for assessing whether a party providing funding has the functional capability to exercise control over the financial risk attached to its contributions to the CCA and whether it actually performs these functions. See Examples 4 and 5 in the Annex to this chapter for an illustration of this principle.

8.16. To the extent that specific contributions made by participants to a CCA are different in nature, e.g. the participants perform very different types of R&D activities or one of the parties contributes property and another contributes R&D activities, the guidance in paragraph 6.64 is equally applicable. This means that the higher the development risk attached to the development activities performed by the other party and the closer the risk assumed by the first party is related to this development risk, the more the first party will need to have the capability to assess the progress of the development of the intangible and the consequences of this progress for achieving its expected benefits, and the more closely this party may need to link its actual decision-making required in relation to its continued contributions to the CCA to key operational developments that may impact the specific risks it assumes under the CCA. A development CCA in which benefits are uncertain and distant is likely to give rise to greater risks than does a services CCA in which benefits are current.

8.17. As described in the previous paragraphs, it is not necessary for the CCA participants to perform all of the CCA activities through their own personnel. In some cases, the participants in a CCA may decide to outsource certain functions related to the subject activity to a separate entity that is not a participant under the standard of paragraph 8.14 above. In such situations, the participants to the CCA should individually meet the requirements on exercising control over the specific risks they assume under the CCA. Such requirements include exercising control over the outsourced functions by at least one of the participants to the CCA. In circumstances in which the objective of the CCA is to develop an intangible, at least one of the participants to the CCA should also exercise control over the important development, enhancement, maintenance, protection and exploitation functions that are outsourced. When the contribution of a participant to the CCA consists of activities other than controlling the outsourced functions, the guidance in paragraph 8.15 is relevant for assessing whether this party has the functional capability to exercise control over the specific risks it assumes under the CCA, in particular if these risks are closely linked to the outsourced functions.

8.18. In cases where CCA activities are outsourced, an arm's length charge would be appropriate to compensate the entity for services or other contributions being rendered to the CCA participants. Where the entity is an associated enterprise of one or more of the CCA participants, the arm's length charge would be determined under the general principles of Chapters I-III, including *inter alia* consideration of functions performed, assets used, and risks assumed, as well as the special considerations affecting an arm's length charge for services and/or in relation to any intangibles, as described in Chapter VII and Chapter VI (including the guidance on hard-to-value intangibles).

C.3. Expected benefits from the CCA

8.19. The relative shares of expected benefits might be estimated based on the anticipated additional income generated or costs saved or other benefits received by each participant as a result of the arrangement. An approach that is frequently used in practice, most typically for services CCAs, would be to reflect the participants' proportionate shares of expected benefits using a relevant allocation key. The possibilities for allocation keys include sales (turnover), profits, units used, produced, or sold; number of employees, and so forth.

8.20. To the extent that a material part or all of the benefits of a CCA activity are expected to be realised in the future and not solely in the year the costs are incurred, most typically for development CCAs, the allocation of contributions will take account of projections about the participants' shares of those benefits. The use of projections may raise problems for tax administrations in verifying the assumptions based on which projections have been made and in dealing with cases where the projections vary markedly from the actual results. These problems may be exacerbated where the CCA activity ends several years before the expected benefits actually materialise. It may be appropriate, particularly where benefits are expected to be realised in the future, for a CCA to provide for possible adjustments of proportionate shares of contributions over the term of the CCA on a prospective basis to reflect changes in relevant circumstances resulting in changes in relative shares of benefits. In situations where the actual shares of benefits differ markedly from projections, tax administrations might be prompted to enquire whether the projections made would have been considered acceptable by independent enterprises in comparable circumstances, taking into account all the developments that were reasonably foreseeable by the participants, without using hindsight. When the expected benefits of a CCA consist of a right in an intangible that is hard to value at the start of the development project or if pre-existing intangibles that are hard to value are part of the contributions to the CCA project, the guidance in Sections D.3 and D.4 of Chapter VI on hard-to-value intangibles is applicable to value the contributions of each of the participants to the CCA.

8.21. If an arrangement covers multiple activities, it will be important to take this into account in choosing an allocation method, so that the value of contributions made by each participant is properly related to the relative benefits expected by the participants. One approach (though not the only one) is to use more than one allocation key. For example, if there are five participants in a CCA, one of which cannot benefit from certain services activities undertaken within the CCA, then in the absence of some form of set-off or reduction in contribution, the contributions associated with those activities might be allocated only to the other four participants. In this case, two allocation keys might be used to allocate the contributions. Whether any particular allocation key or keys are appropriate depends on the exact nature of the CCA activity and the relationship between the allocation key(s) and the expected benefits. The guidance in Chapter VII on the use of indirect methods of determining an arm's length charge for services (paragraphs 7.23-7.26) may be helpful in this regard. In contrast, the three enterprises operating production sites in the illustration of a CCA in paragraph 8.8 are all anticipated to benefit from the multiple projects to improve production processes, and may adopt an allocation key based on, for example, relative size of production capacity. If one of the enterprises chooses not to implement the outcome of a particular project, this should not affect the relative share of benefits or the allocation key used. However, in such circumstances careful consideration should be given to the reason the enterprise chose not to implement the outcome, whether it ever had any reasonable intention of so doing, whether the expected benefits should have been adapted as the CCA arrangement developed and when its intention changed.

8.22. Whatever the method used to evaluate participants' relative shares of expected benefits, adjustments to the measure used may be necessary to account for differences between the respective shares of expected and actual benefits received by the participants. The CCA should require periodic reassessment of contributions *vis-à-vis* the revised share of benefits to determine whether the future contributions of participants should be adjusted accordingly. Thus, the allocation key(s) most relevant to any particular CCA may change over time leading to prospective adjustments. Such adjustments may reflect either the fact that the parties will have more reliable information about foreseeable (but uncertain) events as time passes, or the occurrence of unforeseeable events.

C.4. The value of each participant's contribution

8.23. For the purpose of determining whether a CCA satisfies the arm's length principle – i.e. whether each participant's proportionate share of the overall contributions to the CCA is consistent with the participant's proportionate share of the overall expected benefits – it is necessary to measure the value of each participant's contributions to the arrangement.

8.24. Contributions to a CCA may take many forms. For services CCAs, contributions primarily consist of the performance of the services. For development CCAs, contributions typically include the performance of development activities (e.g. R&D, marketing), and often include additional contributions relevant to the development CCA such as pre-existing tangible assets or intangibles. Irrespective of the type of CCA, all contributions of current or pre-existing value must be identified and accounted for appropriately in accordance with the arm's length principle. Since the value of each participant's relative share of contributions should accord with its share of expected benefits, balancing payments may be required to ensure this consistency. The term "contributions" as used in this Chapter includes contributions of both pre-existing and current value made by participants to a CCA.

8.25. Under the arm's length principle, the value of each participant's contribution should be consistent with the value that independent enterprises in comparable circumstances would have assigned to that contribution. That is, contributions must generally be assessed based on their value at the time they are contributed, bearing in mind the mutual sharing of risks, as well as the nature and extent of the associated expected benefits to participants in the CCA, in order to be consistent with the arm's length principle. In determining the value of contributions to a CCA the guidance elsewhere in these Guidelines should be followed.

8.26. In valuing contributions, distinctions should be drawn between contributions of pre-existing value and current contributions. For example, in a CCA for the development of an intangible, the contribution of patented technology by one of the participants reflects a contribution of pre-existing value which is useful towards the development of the intangible that is the objective of the CCA. The value of that technology should be determined under the arm's length principle using the guidance in Chapter I-III and Chapter VI, including, where appropriate, the use of valuation techniques as set out in that Chapter. The current R&D activity under the development CCA performed by one or more associated enterprises would constitute a current contribution. The value of current functional contributions is not based on the potential value of the resulting further application of the technology, but on the value of the functions performed. The potential value of the resulting further application of the technology is taken into account through the value of pre-existing contributions and through the sharing of the development risk in proportion to the expected share of benefits by the CCA participants. The value of the current contributions should be determined under the guidance in Chapters I-III, VI and VII. As noted in paragraph 6.79, compensation based on a reimbursement of cost plus a modest mark-up will not reflect that anticipated value of, or the arm's length price for, the contribution of the research team in all cases.

8.27. While all contributions should be measured at value (but see paragraph 8.28 below), it may be more administrable for taxpayers to pay current contributions at cost. This may be particularly relevant for development CCAs. If this approach is adopted, the pre-existing contributions should recover the opportunity cost of the *ex ante* commitment to contribute resources to the CCA. For example, a contractual arrangement (i.e. the CCA) that commits an existing R&D workforce to undertake work for the benefit of the CCA should reflect the opportunity cost of alternative R&D endeavours (e.g. the present value of the arm's length mark-up over R&D costs) in the pre-existing contributions, while contributing current activities at cost (see Example 1A in the Annex to this chapter).

8.28. Whereas it cannot be assumed that the value of pre-existing contributions corresponds to costs, it is sometimes the case that cost could be used as a practical means to measure relative value of current contributions. Where the difference between the value and costs is relatively insignificant, for practical reasons, current contributions of a similar nature may be measured at cost in such cases for services CCAs. However, in other circumstances (for example where contributions provided by the participants vary in nature and include a mixture of service types and/or intangibles or other assets) measuring current contributions at cost is unlikely to provide a reliable basis for determining the value of the relative contributions of participants, and may lead to non-arm's length results. For development CCAs, the measurement of current contributions at cost (apart from the administrative guidance in paragraph 8.27) will generally not provide a reliable basis for the application of the arm's length principle. See Examples 1-3 in the Annex to this chapter for illustration of this guidance. Where uncontrolled arrangements are claimed to be comparable to the arrangements between the associated enterprises in the CCA, and those uncontrolled arrangements provide for contributions to be made at cost, it is important to consider the comparability of all of the economically relevant characteristics of the transactions in the broader context of the arrangement, including the impact of any broader arrangement of economically related transactions which may exist between the parties to the uncontrolled transaction, and the sharing of risks. Particular attention should be paid to whether other payments are made in the uncontrolled arrangements; for example, stage payments or compensating contributions may be made in addition to the reimbursement of costs.

8.29. Since contributions are based on expected benefits, this generally implies that where a cost reimbursement basis for valuing current contributions is permitted, the analysis should initially be based on budgeted costs. This does not necessarily mean fixing the costs, since the budget framework may accommodate variability arising from factors such as varying demand levels (for instance budgeted costs may be expressed as a fixed percentage of actual sales). Additionally, there are likely to be differences between budgeted costs and actual costs during the term of the CCA. In an arm's length situation, the terms agreed between the parties are likely to set out how such differences should be treated since, as stated in paragraph 2.96, independent parties are not likely to use budgeted costs without agreeing what factors are taken into account in setting the budget and how unforeseen circumstances are to be treated. Attention should be paid to the reason for any significant differences between budgeted costs and actual costs, since the difference may point to changes in the scope of activities which may not benefit all the participants in the same way as the activities originally scoped. In general terms, however, where cost is found to be an appropriate basis for measuring current contributions, it is likely to be sufficient to use actual costs as the basis for so doing.

8.30. It is important that the evaluation process recognises all contributions made by participants to the arrangement. This includes contributions made by one or more parties at the inception of the CCA (such as contributions of pre-existing intangibles) as well as contributions made on an ongoing basis during the term of the CCA. Contributions to be considered include property or services that are used solely in the CCA activity, but also property or services (i.e. shared property or services) that are used partly in the CCA activity and also partly in the participant's separate business activities. It can be difficult to measure contributions that involve shared property or services, for example where a participant contributes the partial use of assets such as office buildings and IT systems or performs supervisory, clerical, and administrative functions for the CCA and for its own business. It will be necessary to determine the proportion of the assets used or services that relate to the CCA activity in a commercially justifiable way with regard to recognised accounting principles and the actual facts, and adjustments, if material, may be necessary to achieve consistency when different jurisdictions are involved. Once the proportion is determined, the contribution can be measured in accordance with the principles in the rest of this chapter.

8.31. For development CCAs, contributions in the form of controlling and managing the CCA, its activities and risks, are likely to be important functions, as described in paragraph 6.56, in relation to the development, production, or obtaining of the intangibles or tangible assets and should be valued in accordance with the principles set out in Chapter VI.

8.32. The following scenario illustrates the guidance on determining participants, the share of benefits, and the value of contributions.

8.33. Company A based in Country A and Company B based in Country B are members of an MNE group and have concluded a CCA to develop intangibles. Company B has entitlement under the CCA to exploit the intangibles in Country B, and Company A has entitlement under the CCA to exploit the intangibles in the rest of the world. The parties anticipate that Company A will have 75% of total sales and Company B 25% of total sales, and that their share of expected benefits from the CCA is 75:25. Both A and B have experience of developing intangibles and have their own research and development personnel. They each control their development risk under the CCA within the terms set out in paragraphs 8.14 to 8.16. Company A contributes pre-existing intangibles to the CCA that it has recently acquired from a third-party. Company B contributes proprietary analytical techniques that it has developed to improve efficiency and speed to market. Both of these pre-existing contributions should be valued under the guidance provided in Chapters I-III and VI. Current contributions in the form of day-to-day research will be performed 80% by Company B and 20% by Company A under the guidance of a leadership team made up of personnel from both companies in the ratio 90:10 in favour of Company A. These two kinds of current contributions should separately be analysed and valued under the guidance provided in Chapters I-III and VI. When the expected benefits of a CCA consist of a right in an intangible that is hard to value at the start of the development project or if pre-existing intangibles that are hard to value are part of the contributions to the CCA project, the guidance in Sections D.3 and D.4 of Chapter VI on hard-to-value intangibles is applicable to value the contributions of each of the participants to the CCA.

C.5. Balancing payments

8.34. A CCA will be considered consistent with the arm's length principle where the value of each participant's proportionate share of the overall contributions to the arrangement (taking into account any balancing payments already made) is consistent with the participant's share of the overall expected benefits to be received under the arrangement. Where the value of a participant's share of overall contributions under a CCA at the time the contributions are made is not consistent with that participant's share of expected benefits under the CCA, the contributions made by at least one of the participants will be inadequate, and the contributions made by at least one other participant will be excessive. In such a case, the arm's length principle would generally require that an adjustment be made. This will generally take the form of an adjustment to the contribution through making or imputing a (further) balancing payment. Such balancing payments increase the value of the contributions of the payor and decrease that of the payee.

8.35. Balancing payments may be made by participants to "top up" the value of the contributions when their proportionate contributions are lower than their proportionate expected benefits. Such adjustments may be anticipated by the participants upon entering into the CCA, or may be the result of periodic re-evaluation of their share of the expected benefits and/or the value of their contributions (see paragraph 8.22).

8.36. Balancing payments may also be required by tax administrations where the value of a participant's proportionate contributions of property or services at the time the contribution was made has been incorrectly determined, or where the participants' proportionate expected benefits have been incorrectly assessed, e.g. where the allocation key when fixed or adjusted for changed circumstances was not adequately reflective of proportionate expected benefits. Normally the adjustment would be made by a balancing payment from one or more participants to another being made or imputed for the period in question.

8.37. In the case of development CCAs, variations between a participant's proportionate share of the overall contributions and that participant's proportionate share of the overall expected benefits may occur in a particular year. If that CCA is otherwise acceptable and carried out faithfully, having regard to the recommendations of Section E, tax administrations should generally refrain from making an adjustment based on the results of a single fiscal year. Consideration should be given to whether each participant's proportionate share of the overall contributions is consistent with the participant's proportionate share of the overall expected benefits from the arrangement over a period of years (see paragraphs 3.75-3.79). Separate balancing payments might be made for pre-existing contributions and for current contributions, respectively. Alternatively, it might be more reliable or administrable to make an overall balancing payment relating to pre-existing contributions and current contributions collectively. See Example 4 in the Annex to this chapter.

8.38. In the example in paragraph 8.33, the participants, Companies A and B, expect to benefit from the CCA in the ratio 75:25. In the first year the value of their pre-existing contributions is 10 million for Company A and 6 million for Company B. As a result, a net balancing payment is required to be made to Company B by Company A of 2 million (i.e. 4.5 million from Company A to Company B less 2.5 million from Company B to Company A) in order to increase Company A's contribution to 12 million (75% of the total contributions) and reducing Company B's contribution to 4 million (25% of the total).

C.6. Accurately delineating the actual transaction

8.39. As indicated in paragraph 8.9, the economically relevant characteristics of the arrangement identified under the guidance in Section D of Chapter I may indicate that the actual transaction differs from the terms of the CCA purportedly agreed by the participants. For example, one or more of the claimed participants may not have any reasonable expectation of benefit from the CCA activity. Although in principle the smallness of a participant's share of expected benefits is no bar to eligibility, if a participant that is performing all of the subject activity is expected to have only a small fraction of the overall expected benefits, it may be questioned whether the reality of the arrangements for that party is to pool resources and share risks or whether the appearance of sharing in mutual benefits has been constructed to obtain more favourable tax results. The existence of significant balancing payments arising from a material difference between the parties' proportionate shares of contributions and benefits may also give rise to questions about whether mutual benefits exist or whether the arrangements should be accurately delineated, taking into account all the economically relevant characteristics, as a funding transaction.

8.40. As indicated in paragraph 8.33, the guidance in Chapter VI on hard-to-value intangibles may equally apply in situations involving CCAs. This will be the case if the objective of the CCA is to develop a new intangible that is hard to value at the start of the development project, but also in valuing contributions involving pre-existing intangibles. Where the arrangements viewed in their totality lack commercial rationality in accordance with the criteria in Section D.2 of Chapter I, the CCA may be disregarded.

C.7. The tax treatment of contributions and balancing payments

8.41. Contributions, including any balancing payments, by a participant to a CCA should be treated for tax purposes in the same manner as would apply under the general rules of the tax system(s) applicable to that participant if the contributions were made outside a CCA, to carry on the activity that is the subject of the CCA. The character of the contribution will depend on the nature of the activity being undertaken by the CCA, and will determine how it is recognised for tax purposes.

8.42. In services CCAs, a participant's contribution to the CCA will often give rise to benefits in the form of cost savings (in which case there may not be any income generated directly by the CCA activity). In development CCAs, the expected benefits to participants may not accrue until some time after contributions are made, and therefore there will be no immediate recognition of income to the participants on their contributions at the time they are made.

8.43. Any balancing payment should be treated as an addition to the contribution of the payor and as a reduction in the contribution of the recipient. As with contributions generally, the character and tax treatment of any balancing payments will be determined in accordance with domestic laws, including applicable tax treaties.

D. CCA entry, withdrawal or termination

8.44. Changes in the membership of a CCA will generally trigger a reassessment of the proportionate shares of participants' contributions and expected benefits. An entity that becomes a participant in an already active CCA might obtain an interest in any results of prior CCA activity, such as completed or work-in-progress intangibles or tangible assets. In such cases, the previous participants effectively transfer part of their respective interests in the results of the prior CCA activity to the new entrant. Under the arm's length principle, any such transfer of intangibles or tangible assets must be compensated based on an arm's length value for the transferred interest. Such compensation is referred to in this chapter as a "buy-in payment".

8.45. The amount of a buy-in payment should be determined based upon the value (i.e. the arm's length price) of the interest in the intangibles and/or tangible assets the new entrant obtains, taking into account the new entrant's proportionate share of the overall expected benefits to be received under the CCA. There may also be cases where a new participant brings existing intangibles or tangible assets to the CCA, and that balancing payments may be appropriate from the other participants in recognition of this contribution. Any balancing payments to the new entrant could be netted against any buy-in payments required, although appropriate records must be kept of the full amounts of the separate payments for tax administration purposes.

8.46. Similar issues could arise when a participant leaves a CCA. In particular, a participant that leaves a CCA may dispose of its interest in the results, if any, of past CCA activity (including work in progress) to the other participants. Any such transfer should be compensated according to the arm's length principle. Such compensation is referred to in this chapter as a "buy-out payment".

8.47. The guidance in Chapters I-III and Chapter VI is fully applicable to determining the arm's length amount of any buy-in, buy-out or balancing payments required. There may be instances where no such payments are required under the arm's length principle. For example, a CCA for the sharing of administrative services would generally only produce benefits to participants on a current basis, rather than any valuable on-going results.

8.48. Buy-in and buy-out payments should be treated for tax purposes in the same manner as would apply under the general rules of the tax system(s) (including conventions for the avoidance of double taxation) applicable to the respective participants as if the payment were made outside a CCA as consideration for the acquisition or disposal of the interest in the results of the prior CCA activity.

8.49. When a CCA terminates, the arm's length principle requires that each participant retains an interest in the results, if any, of the CCA activity consistent with their proportionate share of contributions to the CCA throughout its term (adjusted by any balancing payments actually made, including those made as a result of the termination), or is appropriately compensated for any transfer of that interest to other participants.

E. Recommendations for structuring and documenting CCAs

8.50. Generally, a CCA between controlled parties should meet the following conditions:

a) The participants would include only enterprises expected to derive mutual and proportionate benefits from the CCA activity itself (and not just from performing part or all of that activity). See paragraph 8.14.

b) The arrangement would specify the nature and extent of each participant's interest in the results of the CCA activity, as well its expected respective share of benefits.

c) No payment other than the CCA contributions, appropriate balancing payments and buy-in payments would be made for the particular interest or rights in intangibles, tangible assets or services obtained through the CCA.

d) The value of participants' contributions would be determined in accordance with these Guidelines and, where necessary, balancing payments should be made to ensure the proportionate shares of contributions align with the proportionate shares of expected benefits from the arrangement.

e) The arrangement may specify provision for balancing payments and/or changes in the allocation of contributions prospectively after a reasonable period of time to reflect material changes in proportionate shares of expected benefits among the participants.

f) Adjustments would be made as necessary (including the possibility of buy-in and buy-out payments) upon the entrance or withdrawal of a participant and upon termination of the CCA.

8.51. The transfer pricing documentation standard set out in Chapter V requires reporting under the master file of important service arrangements and important agreements related to intangibles, including CCAs. The local file requires transactional information including a description of the transactions, the amounts of payments and receipts, identification of the associated enterprises involved, copies of material intercompany agreements, and pricing information including a description of reasons for concluding that the transactions were priced on an arm's length basis. It would be expected that in order to comply with these documentation requirements, the participants in a CCA will prepare or obtain materials about the nature of the subject activity, the terms of the arrangement, and its consistency with the arm's length principle. Implicit in this is that each participant should have full access to the details of the activities to be conducted under the CCA, the identity and location of the other parties involved in the CCA, the projections on which the contributions are to be made and expected benefits determined, and budgeted and actual expenditures for the CCA activity, at a level of detail commensurate with the complexity and importance of the CCA to the taxpayer. All this information could be relevant and useful to tax administrations in the context of a CCA and, if not included in the master file or local file, taxpayers should be prepared to provide it upon request. The information relevant to any particular CCA will depend on the facts and circumstances. It should be emphasised that the information described in this list is neither a minimum compliance standard nor an exhaustive list of the information that a tax administration may be entitled to request.

8.52. The following information would be relevant and useful concerning the initial terms of the CCA:

a) a list of participants

b) a list of any other associated enterprises that will be involved with the CCA activity or that are expected to exploit or use the results of the subject activity

c) the scope of the activities and specific projects covered by the CCA, and how the CCA activities are managed and controlled

d) the duration of the arrangement

e) the manner in which participants' proportionate shares of expected benefits are measured, and any projections used in this determination

f) the manner in which any future benefits (such as intangibles) are expected to be exploited

g) the form and value of each participant's initial contributions, and a detailed description of how the value of initial and ongoing contributions is determined (including any budgeted *vs* actual adjustments) and how accounting principles are applied consistently to all participants in determining expenditures and the value of contributions

h) the anticipated allocation of responsibilities and tasks, and the mechanisms for managing and controlling those responsibilities and tasks, in particular, those relating to the development, enhancement, maintenance, protection or exploitation of intangibles or tangible assets used in the CCA activity

i) the procedures for and consequences of a participant entering or withdrawing from the CCA and the termination of the CCA

j) any provisions for balancing payments or for adjusting the terms of the arrangement to reflect changes in economic circumstances.

8.53. Over the duration of the CCA term, the following information could be useful:

a) any change to the arrangement (e.g. in terms, participants, subject activity), and the consequences of such change

b) a comparison between projections used to determine the share of expected benefits from the CCA activity with the actual share of benefits (however, regard should be had to paragraph 3.74)

c) the annual expenditure incurred in conducting the CCA activity, the form and value of each participant's contributions made during the CCA's term, and a detailed description of how the value of contributions is determined.

Chapter IX

Transfer pricing aspects of business restructurings

Introduction

A. Scope

A.1. Business restructurings that are within the scope of this chapter

9.1. There is no legal or universally accepted definition of business restructuring. In the context of this chapter, business restructuring refers to the cross-border reorganisation of the commercial or financial relations between associated enterprises, including the termination or substantial renegotiation of existing arrangements. Relationships with third parties (e.g. suppliers, sub-contractors, customers) may be a reason for the restructuring or be affected by it.

9.2. Business restructurings may often involve the centralisation of intangibles, risks, or functions with the profit potential attached to them. They may typically consist of:

- Conversion of full-fledged distributors (that is, enterprises with a relatively higher level of functions and risks) into limited-risk distributors, marketers, sales agents, or *commissionnaires* (that is, enterprises with a relatively lower level of functions and risks) for a foreign associated enterprise that may operate as a principal,
- Conversion of full-fledged manufacturers (that is, enterprises with a relatively higher level of functions and risks) into contract manufacturers or toll manufacturers (that is, enterprises with a relatively lower level of functions and risks) for a foreign associated enterprise that may operate as a principal,

- Transfers of intangibles or rights in intangibles to a central entity (e.g. a so-called "IP company") within the group,
- The concentration of functions in a regional or central entity, with a corresponding reduction in scope or scale of functions carried out locally; examples may include procurement, sales support, supply chain logistics.

9.3. There are also business restructurings whereby more intangibles or risks are allocated to operational entities (e.g. to manufacturers or distributors). Business restructurings can also consist of the rationalisation, specialisation or de-specialisation of operations (manufacturing sites and/or processes, research and development activities, sales, services), including the downsizing or closing of operations. The arm's length principle and guidance in this chapter apply in the same way to all types of transactions comprising a business restructuring, irrespective of whether they lead to a more centralised or less centralised business model.

9.4. Some of the reasons reported by business for restructuring include the wish to maximise synergies and economies of scale, to streamline the management of business lines and to improve the efficiency of the supply chain, taking advantage of the development of web-based technologies that has facilitated the emergence of global organisations. Furthermore, business restructurings may be needed to preserve profitability or limit losses, e.g. in the event of an over-capacity situation or in a downturn economy.

A.2. Issues that are within the scope of this chapter

9.5. This chapter contains a discussion of the transfer pricing aspects of business restructurings, i.e. of the application of Article 9 (Associated Enterprises) of the OECD Model Tax Convention and of these Guidelines to business restructurings.

9.6. Business restructurings are typically accompanied by a reallocation of profit potential among the members of the MNE group, either immediately after the restructuring or over a few years. One major objective of this chapter in relation to Article 9 is to discuss the extent to which such a reallocation of profit potential is consistent with the arm's length principle and more generally how the arm's length principle applies to business restructurings. The implementation of integrated business models and the development of global organisations may complicate the application of the arm's length principle, which determines the profit of members of an MNE group by reference to the conditions which would have been made between independent enterprises in comparable transactions and comparable circumstances. This complexity in applying the arm's length principle in practice is acknowledged in these Guidelines (see paragraphs 1.10-1.11). Notwithstanding this issue, these Guidelines reflect the OECD Member countries' strong support for the arm's length principle and for efforts to describe its application and refine its operation in practice (see paragraphs 1.14-1.15). When discussing the issues that arise in the context of business restructurings, the OECD has kept this complexity in mind in an attempt to develop approaches that are realistic and reasonably pragmatic.

9.7. This chapter only covers transactions between associated enterprises in the context of Article 9 of the OECD Model Tax Convention and does not address the attribution of profits within a single enterprise on the basis of Article 7 of the OECD Model Tax Convention, as this is the subject of the Report on the Attribution of Profits to Permanent Establishments.[1]

9.8. Domestic anti-abuse rules and CFC legislation are not within the scope of this chapter. The domestic tax treatment of an arm's length payment, including rules regarding the deductibility of such a payment and how domestic capital gains tax provisions may apply to an arm's length capital payment, are also not within the scope of this chapter. Moreover, while they raise important issues in the context of business restructurings, VAT and indirect taxes are not covered in this chapter.

B. Applying Article 9 of the OECD Model Tax Convention and these Guidelines to business restructurings: theoretical framework

9.9. This chapter starts from the premise that the arm's length principle and these Guidelines do not and should not apply differently to restructurings or post-restructuring transactions than to transactions that were structured as such from the beginning. The relevant question under Article 9 of the OECD Model Tax Convention and the arm's length principle is whether there are conditions made or imposed in a business restructuring that differ from the conditions that would be made between independent enterprises. This is the theoretical framework in which all the guidance in this chapter should be read. The guidance in this chapter is composed of two parts: the first part provides guidance on the determination of the arm's length compensation for the restructuring itself; the second part addresses the remuneration of post-restructuring controlled transactions. Both parts should be read together, and applied in accordance with the guidance provided in the rest of these Guidelines, and in particular in Chapter I.

1. See *Report on the Attribution of Profits to Permanent Establishments*, approved by the Committee on Fiscal Affairs on 22-23 June 2010 and by the Council for publication on 22 July 2010.

Part I: Arm's length compensation for the restructuring itself

A. Introduction

9.10. A business restructuring may involve cross-border transfers of something of value, e.g. of valuable intangibles, although this is not always the case. It may also or alternatively involve the termination or substantial renegotiation of existing arrangements, e.g. manufacturing arrangements, distribution arrangements, licences, service agreements, etc. The first step in analysing the transfer pricing aspects of a business restructuring is to accurately delineate the transactions that comprise the business restructuring by identifying the commercial or financial relations and the conditions attached to those relations that lead to a transfer of value among the members of the MNE group. This is discussed in Section B. Section C discusses the recognition of accurately delineated transactions that comprise the business restructuring. The relationship between a business restructuring and the reallocation of profit potential is addressed in Section D. The transfer pricing consequences of the transfer of something of value are discussed in Section E of this part and the transfer pricing consequences of the termination or substantial renegotiation of existing arrangements are discussed in Section F.

9.11. For transfer pricing purposes, the aim of the analysis is to determine whether, under Article 9 of the OECD Model Tax Convention, conditions have been made or imposed in transactions comprising a business restructuring that differ from those that would be made or imposed between independent enterprises; and, if so, to determine the profits which would, but for those conditions, have accrued to one of the enterprises, but, by reason of those conditions, have not so accrued, and include them in the profits of that enterprise and tax them accordingly.

9.12. The arm's length principle requires an evaluation of the conditions made or imposed between associated enterprises, at the level of each of them. The fact that a business restructuring may be motivated by sound commercial reasons at the level of the MNE group, e.g. in order to try to derive synergies at a group level, does not answer the question whether it is arm's length from the perspectives of each of the restructured entities.

B. Understanding the restructuring itself

9.13. The application of the arm's length principle to a business restructuring must start, as for any controlled transaction, with the identification of the commercial or financial relations between the associated enterprises involved in the business restructuring and the conditions and economically relevant circumstances attaching to those relations so that the controlled transactions comprising the business restructuring are accurately delineated. In this regard, the general guidance in Section D.1 of Chapter I is applicable. This guidance requires the examination of the economically relevant characteristics of the commercial or financial relations between the associated enterprises, and in particular the contractual terms of the business restructuring (Section D.1.1); the functions performed by each party to the restructuring, before and after the restructuring, taking into account assets used and risks assumed (Section D.1.2); the economic circumstances of the parties (Section D.1.4) and business strategies (Section D.1.5). In addition, the analysis should be informed by a review of the business reasons for and the expected benefits from the restructuring, including the role of synergies, and the options realistically available to the parties. As stated in paragraph 1.33, these conditions and economically relevant circumstances of the accurately delineated transactions that comprise the business restructuring will then be compared with the conditions and economically relevant circumstances of comparable transactions between independent enterprises.

9.14. Aspects of identifying the commercial or financial relations between the parties which are particularly relevant to determining the arm's length conditions of business restructurings, are analysed in the following sections:

- The accurate delineation of the transactions comprising the business restructuring and the functions, assets and risks before and after the restructuring (see Section B.1);
- The business reasons for and the expected benefits from the restructuring, including the role of synergies (see Section B.2);
- The other options realistically available to the parties (see Section B.3).

B.1. Accurate delineation of the transactions comprising the business restructuring: functions, assets and risks before and after the restructuring

9.15. Restructurings can take a variety of different forms and may involve two or more members of an MNE group. For example, a simple pre-restructuring arrangement could involve a full-fledged manufacturer producing goods and selling them to an associated full-fledged distributor for on-sale into the market. The restructuring could involve a modification to that two-party arrangement, whereby the distributor is converted to a limited risk distributor or *commissionnaire*, with risks previously assumed by the full-fledged distributor being assumed by the manufacturer (taking into account the guidance in Section D.1 of Chapter I. Frequently, the restructuring will be more complicated, with functions performed, assets used and risks assumed by either or both parties to a pre-restructuring arrangement shifting to one or more members of the group.

9.16. In order to determine whether, at arm's length, compensation would be payable upon a restructuring to any restructured entity within an MNE group, and if so the amount of such compensation as well as the member of the group that should bear such compensation, it is important to accurately delineate the transactions occurring between the restructured entity and one or more other members of the group. For these purposes, the detailed guidance in Section D of Chapter I of these Guidelines is applicable.

9.17. Where the conditions of a business restructuring have been formalised by the MNE group in writing (e.g. written contractual agreements, correspondence and/or other communications), those agreements provide the starting point for delineating the transactions comprising the business restructuring between the MNEs involved. The contractual terms may describe the roles, responsibilities and rights of the restructured entity under the pre-restructuring arrangement (including in relevant circumstances those existing under contract and commercial law) and of the manner and extent to which those rights and obligations change as a result of the restructuring. However, where no written terms exist, or where the facts of the case, including the conduct of the parties, differ materially from the written terms of any agreement between them or supplement these written terms, the actual transactions comprising the business restructuring must be deduced from the facts as established, including the conduct of the parties (see Section D.1.1 of Chapter I).

9.18. The accurate delineation of the transactions comprising the business restructuring requires performing a functional analysis that seeks to identify the economically significant activities and responsibilities undertaken, assets used or contributed, and risks assumed before and after the restructuring by the parties involved. Accordingly, the analysis focuses on what the parties actually do and the capabilities, as well as the type and nature of assets used or contributed by the parties in a pre-restructuring and post-restructuring scenarios. See Section D.1.2 of Chapter I. Given the importance of risk in the analysis of business restructurings, the following section provides specific guidance on the analysis of risk in transactions comprising the business restructuring.

B.1.1. The analysis of risk in the context of business restructurings

9.19. Risks are of critical importance in the context of business restructurings. Usually, in the open market, the assumption of risk associated with a commercial opportunity affects the profit potential of that opportunity, and the allocation of risk assumed between the parties to the arrangement affects how profits or losses resulting from the transaction are allocated through the arm's length pricing of the transaction. Business restructurings often result in local operations being converted into low risk operations (e.g. "low risk distributors", or "low risk contract manufacturers") and being remunerated with a relatively low (but generally stable) return on the grounds that the economically significant risks are assumed by another party to which the profits or losses associated with those risks are allocated. For this reason, an examination of the allocation of risks between associated enterprises before and after the restructuring is an essential part of the functional analysis. Such analysis should allow tax administrations to assess the transfer of the economically significant risks of the business that is restructured and the consequences of that transfer for the application of the arm's length principle to the restructuring itself and to the post-restructuring transactions.

9.20. The framework and detailed guidance for analysing risk laid out in Section D.1.2.1 of Chapter I is applicable for purposes of undertaking an analysis of risks in the context of business restructurings, and in particular for determining which party assumes a specific risk by reference to control and financial capacity. It is crucial to apply this framework to determine which party assumes specific risks before the restructuring and which party assumes specific risks following the restructuring. For example, where a restructuring purports to transfer inventory risk, it is relevant to examine not only the contractual terms, but also the conduct of the parties under Step 3 in the framework (e.g. where any inventory write-downs are taken before and after the restructuring, whether there is any indemnification for those inventory write-downs, which party or parties perform risk control functions and have the financial capacity to assume the risks). The results of this analysis may establish that before the restructuring one party assumed the inventory risk and that same party continues to do so after the restructuring notwithstanding a change in contractual terms. In that situation, the risk would continue to be allocated to that same party. References in this Chapter to "transfer of risk", "relocation of risk, "shifting of risk" or "laying off of risk" should be read in the context of the guidance in Section D.1 of Chapter I. In particular, the transferee of the risk is considered to assume the risk when the conditions set out in the framework for analysing risk in controlled transactions (Section D.1.2.1 of Chapter I) are met.

9.21. A second example relates to the purported transfer of credit risk as part of a business restructuring. The analysis under Section D.1.2.1 of

Chapter I would take into account the contractual terms before and after the restructuring, but would also examine how the parties operate in relation to the risk before and after the restructuring. The analysis would then examine whether the party that contractually assumes the risk controls the risk in practice through relevant capability and decision-making as defined in paragraph 1.65 and has the financial capacity to assume such risk as defined in paragraph 1.64. It is important to note that a party that before the restructuring did not assume a risk under the analysis of Section D.1.2.1 of Chapter I cannot transfer it to another party, and a party that after the restructuring does not assume a risk under the analysis of Section D.1.2.1 of Chapter I should not be allocated the profit potential associated with that risk.

- For example, suppose that before a business restructuring, a full-fledged distributor contractually assumes bad debt risks, which is reflected in the balance sheet at year end. However, the analysis described above establishes that before the business restructuring, decisions about the extension of credit terms to customers and debt recovery were taken by an associated enterprise and not by the distributor, and the associated enterprise reimbursed the costs of irrecoverable debts. It is also determined that the associated enterprise is the only entity that controlled the risk and had the financial capacity to assume the bad debt risk, leading to the conclusion that, before the business restructuring, the risk was not assumed by the distributor. In such a case there is no bad debt risk for the distributor to transfer as part of the business restructuring.
- In other circumstances it may be found that before the business restructuring the distributor controlled the bad debt risk and had the financial capacity to assume the risk it contractually assumed, but mitigated its risk through indemnification arrangements or debt factoring arrangements with an associated enterprise in exchange for appropriate compensation. Following the business restructuring, the bad debt risk is contractually assumed by that associated enterprise which, as determined under the analysis described above, now controls the risk and has the financial capacity to assume the risk. The risk has, therefore been transferred but the impact on the profits of the distributor going forward compared with the past resulting from the transfer of this risk alone may be limited, because before the restructuring steps had been taken and costs incurred to mitigate the risk outcomes of the distributor.

9.22. In any analysis of risks in controlled transactions, one important issue is to assess whether a risk is economically significant, i.e. it carries significant profit potential, and, as a consequence, whether that risk may explain a significant reallocation of profit potential. The significance of a risk will depend on the likelihood of the risk materialising and the size of the potential profits or losses arising from the risk. Accounting statements may provide useful information on the probability and quantum of certain risks (e.g. bad debt risks, inventory risks), if past performance is an indicator of current risks, but there are also economically significant risks that may not be separately recorded as such in the financial accounts (e.g. market risks). If a risk is assessed to be economically insignificant for the entity, then that risk would not explain a substantial amount of the entity's profit potential. At arm's length a party would not be expected to lay off a risk that is perceived as economically insignificant in exchange for a substantial decrease in its profit potential.

9.23. For instance, where a full-fledged distributor is converted into a limited-risk distributor or *commissionnaire* resulting in the reduction or elimination of risks relating to inventory in the restructured enterprise, in order to determine whether such risk is economically significant the tax administration may want to analyse:

- The role of inventory in the business model (for example, speed to market, comprehensive range),
- The nature of the inventory (for example, spare parts, fresh flowers),
- The level of investment in inventory,
- The factors giving rise to inventory write-downs or obsolescence (for example, perishability, pricing pressures, speed of technical improvements, market conditions),
- The history of write-down and stock obsolescence, and whether any commercial changes affect the reliability of historic performance as an indicator of current risk,
- The cost of insuring against damage or loss of inventory, and
- The history of damage or loss (if uninsured).

B.2. Understanding the business reasons for and the expected benefits from the restructuring, including the role of synergies

9.24. Some businesses have indicated that multinational businesses, regardless of their products or sectors, have reorganised their structures to provide more centralised control and management of manufacturing, research and distribution functions. The pressure of competition in a globalised economy, savings from economies of scale, the need for specialisation and the need to increase efficiency and lower costs have all been described as important in driving business restructurings. Where anticipated synergies are put forward by a taxpayer as an important business reason for the restructuring, it would be a good practice for the taxpayer to document, at the time the restructuring is decided upon or implemented, what these anticipated synergies are and on what assumptions they are anticipated. This is a type of documentation that is likely to be produced at the group level for non-tax purposes, to support the decision-making process of the restructuring. For Article 9 purposes, it would be a good practice for the taxpayer to document the source of these synergies and how these anticipated synergies impact at the entity level in applying the arm's length principle (see Section D.8 of Chapter I). Care should be taken to ensure that, where deliberate concerted group actions are taken through a business restructuring, the associated enterprises contributing to the synergistic benefit after the restructuring are appropriately remunerated (see the example in the following paragraph). Furthermore, while anticipated synergies may be relevant to the understanding of a business restructuring, care must be taken to avoid the use of hindsight in *ex post* analyses (see paragraph 3.74).

9.25. For example, a business restructuring may involve the setting up by an MNE group of a central procurement operation that replaces the procurement activities of several associated enterprises. Similar to the guidance in paragraph 1.180 the MNE group has taken affirmative steps to centralise purchasing in a single group company to take advantage of volume discounts and potential savings in administrative costs. In accordance with the guidance in Chapter I, the benefits due to deliberate concerted group action should be allocated to the associated enterprises whose contributions create the synergies. However, in a business restructuring, the central procurement company may also contractually assume risk associated with buying, holding, and on-selling goods. As stated in the previous section, an analysis of risk under the framework provided in Section D.1.2.1 of Chapter I will determine the economic significance of the risk and which party or parties assume that risk. Although the central procurement operation is entitled to profit potential arising from its assumption of the risk associated with buying, holding, and on-selling goods, it is not entitled to retain profits arising from the group purchasing power because it does not contribute to the creation of synergies (see paragraph 1.188).

9.26. The fact that a business restructuring may be motivated by anticipated synergies does not necessarily mean that the profits of the MNE group will effectively increase after the restructuring. It may be the case that enhanced synergies make it possible for the MNE group to derive additional profits compared to what the situation would have been in the future if the restructuring had not taken place, but there may not necessarily be additional profits compared to the pre-restructuring situation, for instance if the restructuring is needed to maintain competitiveness rather than to increase it. In addition, expected synergies do not always materialise – there can be cases where the implementation of a global business model designed to derive more group synergies in fact leads to additional costs and less efficiency.

B.3. Other options realistically available to the parties

9.27. The arm's length principle is based on the notion that independent enterprises, when evaluating the terms of a potential transaction, will compare the transaction to the other options realistically available to them, and they will only enter into the transaction if they see no alternative that offers a clearly more attractive opportunity to meet their commercial objective. In other words, independent enterprises would only enter into a transaction if it does not make them worse off than their next best option. Consideration of the other options realistically available may be relevant to comparability analysis, to understand the respective positions of the parties.

9.28. Thus, in applying the arm's length principle, the tax administration should evaluate each transaction as accurately delineated under the guidance in Section D of Chapter I and consider the economically relevant characteristics taken into account by the parties in reaching the conclusion that there is no option realistically available that offers a clearly more attractive opportunity to meet their commercial objectives than the restructuring adopted (see paragraph 1.38). In making such assessment, it may be necessary or useful to assess the transactions comprising the business restructuring in the context of a broader arrangement of economically related transactions.

9.29. At arm's length, there are situations where the restructured entity would have had no clearly more attractive option realistically available to it than to accept the conditions of the restructuring, e.g. a contract termination – with or without indemnification as discussed in Section F below. In longer-term contracts, this may occur by invoking an exit clause that allows for one party to prematurely exit the contract with just cause. In contracts that allow either party to opt out of the contract, the party terminating the arrangement may choose to do so because it has determined, subject to the terms of the termination clause, that it is more favourable to stop using the function, or to internalise it, or to engage a cheaper or more efficient provider or to seek more lucrative opportunities. If the restructured entity transfers rights or other assets or an ongoing concern to another party, it might however be compensated for such a transfer as discussed in Section E below.

9.30. At arm's length, there are also situations where an entity would have had one or more options realistically available to it that would clearly offer more attractive opportunities to meet their objectives than to accept the conditions of the restructuring (taking into account all the relevant conditions, including the commercial and market conditions going forward, the profit potential of the various options and any compensation or indemnification for the restructuring), including possibly the option not to enter into the restructuring transaction. In such cases, an independent party may not have agreed to the conditions of the restructuring and adjustments to the conditions made or imposed may be necessary.

9.31. The reference to the notion of options realistically available is not intended to create a requirement for taxpayers to document all possible hypothetical options realistically available. Rather, the intention is to provide an indication that, if there is a realistically available option that is clearly more attractive, it should be considered in the analysis of the conditions of the restructuring.

B.4. Transfer pricing documentation for business restructurings

9.32. In the master file (see Annex I to Chapter V), taxpayers are asked to describe any important business restructuring transactions occurring during the year. In addition, in the local file, taxpayers are asked to indicate whether the local entity has been involved in or affected by business restructurings occurring during the year or immediately past year and to explain the aspects of such transactions affecting the local entity (see Annex II to Chapter V).

9.33. As part of their transfer pricing documentation, MNE groups are recommended to document their decisions and intentions regarding business restructurings, especially as regards their decisions to assume or transfer significant risks, before the relevant transactions occur, and to document the evaluation of the consequences on profit potential of significant risk allocations resulting from the restructuring. In describing the assumption of risk as part of a business restructuring, it is recommended that taxpayers use the framework set out in Section D.1.2.1 of Chapter I.

C. Recognition of the accurately delineated transactions that comprise the business restructuring

9.34. MNEs are free to organise their business operations as they see fit. Tax administrations do not have the right to dictate to an MNE how to design its structure or where to locate its business operations. In making commercial decisions, tax considerations may be a factor. Tax administrations, however, have the right to determine the tax consequences of the structure put in place by an MNE, subject to the application of treaties and in particular of Article 9 of the OECD Model Tax Convention. This means that tax administrations may make, where appropriate, adjustments to profits in accordance with Article 9 of the OECD Model Tax Convention and other types of adjustments allowed by their domestic law (e.g. under general or specific anti-abuse rules), to the extent that such adjustments are compatible with their treaty obligations.

9.35. Business restructurings often lead MNE groups to implement global business models that are hardly if ever found between independent enterprises, taking advantage of the very fact that they are MNE groups and that they can work in an integrated fashion. For instance, MNE groups may implement global supply chains or centralised functions that may not be found between independent enterprises. This lack of comparables does not mean that the implementation of such global business models is not arm's length. Every effort should be made to determine the pricing for the restructured transactions as accurately delineated under the arm's length principle. A tax administration should not disregard part or all of the restructuring or substitute other transactions for it unless the exceptional circumstances described in paragraph 1.142 are met. In those cases, the guidance in Section D.2 of Chapter I may be applicable. The structure that for transfer pricing purposes, replaces that actually adopted by the taxpayers should comport as closely as possible with the facts of the actual transaction undertaken whilst achieving a commercially rational expected result that would have enabled the parties to come to a price acceptable to both of them at the time the arrangement was entered into. For example, where one element of a restructuring arrangement involves the closing down of a factory, the structure adopted for transfer pricing purposes cannot ignore the reality that the factory no longer operates. Similarly, where one element of a restructuring involves the actual relocation of substantive business functions, the structure adopted for transfer pricing purposes cannot ignore the fact that those functions were actually relocated.

9.36. In assessing the commercial rationality of a restructuring under the guidance for non-recognition under Section D.2 of Chapter I, the question may arise whether to look at one transaction in isolation or whether to examine it in a broader context, taking account of other transactions that are economically inter-related. It will generally be appropriate to look at the commercial rationality of a restructuring as a whole. For instance, where examining a sale of an intangible that is part of a broader restructuring involving changes to the arrangements relating to the development and use of the intangible, then the commercial rationality of the intangible sale should not be examined in isolation of these changes. On the other hand, where a restructuring involves changes to more than one element or aspect of a business that are not economically inter-related, the commercial rationality of particular changes may need to be separately considered. For example, a restructuring may involve centralising a group's purchasing function and centralising the ownership of valuable intangible property unrelated to the purchasing function. In such a case, the commercial rationality of centralising the purchasing function and of centralising the ownership of valuable intangible property may need to be evaluated separately from one another.

9.37. There can be group-level business reasons for an MNE group to restructure. However, it is worth re-emphasising that the arm's length principle treats the members of an MNE group as separate entities rather than as inseparable parts of a single unified business (see paragraph 1.6). As a consequence, it is not sufficient from a transfer pricing perspective that a restructuring arrangement makes commercial sense for the group as a whole: the arrangement must be arm's length at the level of each individual taxpayer, taking account of its rights and other assets, expected benefits from the arrangement (i.e. any consideration of the post-restructuring arrangement plus, if applicable, any compensation payments for the restructuring itself), and realistically available options. Where a restructuring makes commercial sense for the group as a whole on a pre-tax basis, it is expected that an appropriate transfer price (that is, any compensation for the post-restructuring arrangement plus, if applicable, any compensation payments for the restructuring itself) would generally be available to provide arm's length compensation for each accurately delineated transaction comprising the business restructuring for each individual group member participating in it.

9.38. Under Article 9 of the OECD Model Tax Convention, the fact that a business restructuring arrangement is motivated by a purpose of obtaining tax benefits does not of itself warrant a conclusion that it is a non-arm's length arrangement.[2] The presence of a tax motive or purpose does not of itself justify non-recognition of the parties' characterisation or structuring of the arrangement. However, tax benefits at a group level do not determine whether the arm's length principle is satisfied at the entity level for a taxpayer affected by the restructuring (see previous paragraph). Moreover, as indicated in paragraph 1.142, the fact that a MNE group as a whole is left worse off on a pre-tax basis may be a relevant pointer in determining the commercial rationality of the restructuring.

D. Reallocation of profit potential as a result of a business restructuring

D.1. Profit potential

9.39. An independent enterprise does not necessarily receive compensation when a change in its business arrangements results in a reduction in its profit potential or expected future profits. The arm's length principle does not require compensation for a mere decrease in the expectation of an entity's future profits. When applying the arm's length principle to business restructurings, the question is whether there is a transfer of something of value (an asset or an ongoing concern) or a termination or substantial renegotiation of existing arrangements and that transfer, termination or substantial renegotiation would be compensated between independent parties in comparable circumstances. These two situations are discussed in Sections E and F below.

9.40. In these Guidelines, "profit potential" means "expected future profits". In some cases it may encompass losses. The notion of "profit potential" is often used for valuation purposes, in the determination of an arm's length

2. As indicated in paragraph 9.8, domestic anti-abuse rules are not within the scope of this chapter.

compensation for a transfer of intangibles or of an ongoing concern, or in the determination of an arm's length indemnification for the termination or substantial renegotiation of existing arrangements, once it is found that such compensation or indemnification would have taken place between independent parties in comparable circumstances.

9.41. In the context of business restructurings, profit potential should not be interpreted as simply the profits/losses that would occur if the pre-restructuring arrangement were to continue indefinitely. On the one hand, if an entity has no discernible rights or other assets at the time of the restructuring, then it has no compensable profit potential. On the other hand, an entity with considerable rights or other assets at the time of the restructuring may have considerable profit potential, which must ultimately be appropriately remunerated in order to justify the sacrifice of such profit potential.

9.42. In order to determine whether at arm's length the restructuring itself would give rise to a form of compensation, it is essential to understand the restructuring, including the changes that have taken place, how they have affected the functional analysis of the parties, what the business reasons for and the anticipated benefits from the restructuring were, and what options would have been realistically available to the parties, as discussed in Section B.

D.2. Reallocation of risks and profit potential

9.43. General guidance on the transfer pricing aspects of risks is found in Section D.1.2.1 of Chapter I, and the reallocation of risk following a business restructuring should be analysed under the framework set out in that Section in order to determine whether the party allocated risk following the restructuring controls the risk and has the financial capacity to assume the risk.

9.44. Take the example of a conversion of a full-fledged manufacturer into a contract manufacturer. In such a case, while a cost plus reward might be an arm's length remuneration for undertaking the post-restructuring contract manufacturing operations, a different question is whether there should be indemnification at arm's length for the change in the existing arrangements which results in the surrender of the riskier profit potential by the manufacturer, taking into account its rights, other assets and economically relevant characteristics. Indemnification is discussed in Section F.

9.45. As another example, assume a full-fledged distributor is operating under a long term contractual arrangement for a given type of transaction. Assume that, based on its rights under the long term contract with respect to these transactions, it has the option realistically available to it to accept or refuse being converted into a limited risk distributor operating for a foreign associated enterprise, and that an arm's length remuneration for such a low risk distribution activity is estimated to be a stable profit of +2% per year while the excess profit potential associated with the risks would now be attributed to the foreign associated enterprise. Assume for the purpose of this example that the restructuring leads to the renegotiation of the existing contractual arrangements, but it does not entail the transfer of assets other than its rights under the long term contract. From the perspective of the distributor, the question arises as to whether the new arrangement (taking into account both the remuneration for the post-restructuring transactions and any compensation for the restructuring itself) is expected to make it as well off as its realistic – albeit riskier – alternatives. If not, this would imply that the post-restructuring arrangement is not priced at arm's length and that additional compensation would be needed to appropriately remunerate the distributor for the restructuring, or that an assessment of the commercial rationality of the transaction based on Section D.2 may be necessary. Furthermore, for transfer pricing purposes, it is important to determine whether risks contractually transferred as part of the business restructuring, are assumed by the foreign associated enterprise in accordance with the guidance in Section D.1 of Chapter I.

9.46. At arm's length, the response is likely to depend on the rights and other assets of the parties, on the profit potential of the distributor and of its associated enterprise in relation to both business models (full-fledged and low risk distributor) as well as the expected duration of the new arrangement. In particular, in evaluating profit potential, it is necessary to evaluate whether historic profits (determined in accordance with the arm's length principle) are an indicator of future profit potential, or whether there have been changes in the business environment around the time of the restructuring that mean that past performance is not an indicator of profit potential. For example, competing products could have the effect of eroding profitability, and new technology or consumer preferences could render the products less attractive. The consideration of these factors from perspective of the distributor can be illustrated with the following example.

Note: This example is for illustration only. It is not intended to say anything about the choice of the most appropriate transfer pricing method, about aggregation of transactions, or about arm's length remuneration rates for distribution activities. It is assumed in this example that the change in the allocation of risk to the distributor derives from the renegotiation of the existing distribution arrangement which reallocates risk between the parties. This example is intended to illustrate the perspective of the distributor. It does not take account of the perspective of the foreign associated enterprise (principal), although both perspectives should be taken into account in the transfer pricing analysis.

	Scenario 1	Scenario 2	Scenario 3
Full-fledged distributor Historical profitability data (last 5 years)	Year 1: - 2% Year 2: 4% Year 3: 2% Year 4: 0% Year 5: 6%	Year 1: 5% Year 2: 10% Year 3: 5% Year 4: 5% Year 5: 10%	Year 1: 5% Year 2: 7% Year 3: 10% Year 4: 8% Year 5: 6%
Full-fledged distributor Projected profitability (over remaining term of agreement)	(-2)% to 6% With significant uncertainties within this range	5% to 10% With significant uncertainties within that range	0% to 4% With significant uncertainties within that range (due to new competitive pressures)
Limited risk distributor Projected profitability (next three years)	2% per year	2% per year	2% per year

9.47. In scenario no. 1, the distributor is surrendering a profit potential with significant uncertainties for a relatively low but stable rate of profitability. Whether an independent party would be willing to do so would depend on its anticipated return under both scenarios, on its level of risk tolerance, on its options realistically available and on possible compensation for the restructuring itself. In case scenario no. 2, it is unlikely that independent parties in the distributor's situation would agree to relocate the risks and associated profit potential for no additional compensation if they had the option to do otherwise. Scenario no. 3 illustrates the fact that the analysis should take account of the profit potential going forward and that, where there is a significant change in the commercial or economic environment, relying on historical data alone will not be sufficient.

E. Transfer of something of value (e.g. an asset or an ongoing concern)

9.48. Sections E.1 to E.3 below contain a discussion of some typical transfers that can arise in business restructurings: transfers of tangible assets, of intangibles and rights in intangibles, and of activities (ongoing concern).

E.1. Tangible assets

9.49. Business restructurings can involve the transfer of tangible assets (e.g. equipment) by a restructured entity to a foreign associated enterprise. One common issue relates to the valuation of inventories that are transferred upon the conversion by a restructured manufacturer or distributor to a foreign associated enterprise (e.g. a principal), where the latter takes title to the inventories as from the implementation of the new business model and supply chain arrangements.

Illustration

Note: The following example is solely intended to illustrate the issue of valuation of inventory transfers. It is not intended to undertake an analysis of the transactions comprising the business restructuring as accurately delineated under Section D.1 of Chapter I, nor is it intended to suggest that a particular transfer pricing method is always acceptable for restructured operations.

9.50. Assume a taxpayer, which is a member of an MNE group, used to operate as a "full-fledged" manufacturer and distributor. According to the pre-restructuring business model, the taxpayer purchased raw materials, manufactured finished products using tangible property and intangibles that belonged to it or were rented/licensed to it, performed marketing and distribution functions and sold the finished products to third party customers. In doing so, the taxpayer assumed a series of risks such as inventory risks, bad debt risks and market risks.

9.51. Assume the arrangement is restructured and the taxpayer now operates as a so-called "toll-manufacturer" and "limited risk distributor". As part of the restructuring, a foreign associated enterprise is established that acquires various intangibles from various affiliates including the taxpayer. Further to the restructuring, raw materials are to be acquired by the foreign associated enterprise, put in consignment in the premises of the taxpayer for manufacturing in exchange for a manufacturing fee. The stock of finished products will belong to the foreign associated enterprise and be acquired by the taxpayer for immediate re-sale to third party customers (i.e. the taxpayer will only purchase the finished products once it has concluded a sale with a customer). Under this new business model, the foreign associated enterprise contractually assumes the inventory risks that were previously borne by the taxpayer, and meets the requirements of control over the risk and financial capacity to assume the risk.

9.52. Assume that in order to migrate from the pre-existing arrangement to the restructured one, the raw materials and finished products that are on the balance sheet of the taxpayer at the time the new arrangement is put in place are transferred to the foreign associated enterprise. The question arises how to determine the arm's length transfer price for the inventories upon the conversion. This is an issue that can typically be encountered where there is a transition from one business model to another. The arm's length principle applies to transfers of inventory among associated enterprises situated in different tax jurisdictions. The choice of the appropriate transfer pricing method depends upon the comparability (including functional) analysis of the parties. The functional analysis may have to cover a transition period over which the transfer is being implemented. For instance, in the above example:

- One possibility could be to determine the arm's length price for the raw material and finished products by reference to comparable uncontrolled prices, to the extent the comparability factors can be met by such comparable uncontrolled prices, i.e. that the conditions of the uncontrolled transaction are comparable to the conditions of the transfer that takes place in the context of the restructuring.
- Another possibility could be to determine the transfer price for the finished products as the resale price to customers minus an arm's length remuneration for the marketing and distribution functions that still remain to be performed.
- A further possibility would be to start from the manufacturing costs and add an arm's length mark-up to remunerate the manufacturer for the functions it performed, assets it used and risks it assumed with respect to these inventories. There are however cases where the market value of the inventories is too low for a profit element to be added on costs at arm's length.

9.53. The choice of the appropriate transfer pricing method depends in part on which part of the transaction is the less complex and can be evaluated with the greater certainty (the functions performed, assets used and risks assumed by the manufacturer, or the marketing and sales functions that remain to be performed taking account of the assets to be used and risks to be assumed to perform these functions). See paragraphs 3.18-3.19 on the choice of the tested party.

9.54. In practice, what to do about inventory at the time of the restructuring would likely be taken into account by unrelated parties in agreeing the terms of the total deal, and inventory should be analysed as part of delineating the actual transactions comprising the business restructuring. A key consideration is how to deal with the risks inherent in the inventory, and how to avoid double counting – i.e. the party reducing its risks should not receive a price that takes into account risks it has given up, and cannot exploit. If raw materials costing 100 now have a market price of 80 or 120, then a transfer would crystallise a loss or gain which could be a significant impediment to one of the parties to the restructuring. The matter is likely to be resolved as part of the overall terms of the restructuring and should be analysed accordingly. In practice there may be a transition period where inventory is run down before starting the new arrangements, and thus avoiding transfer of inventory, particularly when there may be several complications beyond transfer pricing involved in transferring legal ownership of inventory cross-border.

E.2. Intangibles

9.55. Transfers of intangibles or rights in intangibles raise difficult questions both as to the identification of the intangibles transferred and as to their valuation. Identification can be difficult because not all valuable intangibles are legally protected and registered and not all valuable intangibles are recognised or recorded for accounting purposes. Relevant intangibles might potentially include rights to use industrial assets such as patents, trademarks, trade names, designs or models, as well as copyrights of literary, artistic or scientific work (including software) and intellectual property such as know-how and trade secrets. They may also include customer lists, distribution channels, unique names, symbols or pictures. An essential part of the analysis of a business restructuring is to identify with specificity the relevant intangibles or rights in intangibles that were transferred (if any), whether independent parties would have remunerated their transfer, and what their arm's length value is.

9.56. The determination of the arm's length price for a transfer of intangibles or rights in intangibles should be conducted in accordance with the guidance in Section D.1 of Chapter VI. It will be affected by a number of factors among which are the amount, duration and riskiness of the expected benefits from the exploitation of the intangible, the nature of the intangible right and the restrictions that may be attached to it (restrictions in the way it can be used or exploited, geographical restrictions, time limitations), the extent and remaining duration of its legal protection (if any), and any exclusivity clause that might be attached to the right. See Section D.2.1 of Chapter VI. Valuation of intangibles can be complex and uncertain. The general guidance on intangibles and on cost contribution arrangements that is found in Chapters VI and VIII is applicable in the context of business restructurings.

E.2.1. Disposal of intangibles or rights in intangibles by a local operation to a central location (foreign associated enterprise)

9.57. Business restructurings sometimes involve the transfer of the legal ownership of intangibles or rights in intangibles that were previously owned by one or more local operation(s) to a central location situated in another tax jurisdiction (e.g. a foreign associated enterprise that operates as a principal or as a so-called "IP company"). In some cases the transferor continues to use the intangible transferred, but does so in another legal capacity (e.g. as a licensee of the transferee, or through a contract that includes limited rights to the intangible such as a contract manufacturing arrangement using patents that were transferred; or a limited risk distribution arrangement using a trademark that was transferred). In accordance with the guidance in Chapter VI, it is important to remember that the legal ownership of an intangible by itself does not confer any right ultimately to retain returns derived by the MNE group from exploiting that intangible (see 6.42). Instead, the compensation required to be paid to associated enterprises performing or controlling functions related to the development, enhancement, maintenance, protection, or exploitation of intangibles may comprise any share of the total return anticipated to be derived from the intangibles (see 6.54). Therefore, the change in legal ownership of an intangible in a business restructuring may not affect which party is entitled to returns from that intangible.

9.58. MNE groups may have sound business reasons to centralise ownership of intangibles or rights in intangibles. An example in the context of business restructuring is a transfer of legal ownership of intangibles that accompanies the specialisation of manufacturing sites within an MNE group. In a pre-restructuring environment, each manufacturing entity may be the owner and manager of a series of patents – for instance if the manufacturing sites were historically acquired from third parties with their intangibles. In a global business model, each manufacturing site can be specialised by type of manufacturing process or by geographical area rather than by patent. As a consequence of such a restructuring the MNE group might proceed with the transfer of all the locally owned patents to a central location which will in turn give contractual rights (through licences or manufacturing agreements) to all the group's manufacturing sites to manufacture the products falling in their new areas of competence, using patents that were initially owned either by the same or by another entity within the group. In such a scenario it will be important to delineate the actual transaction and to understand whether the transfer of legal ownership is for administrative simplicity (as in Example 1 in Annex I to Chapter VI), or whether the restructuring changes the identity of the parties performing or controlling functions related to the development, enhancement, maintenance, protection, and exploitation of intangibles.

9.59. The arm's length principle requires an evaluation of the conditions made or imposed between associated enterprises, at the level of each of them. The fact that centralisation of legal ownership of intangibles may be motivated by sound commercial reasons at the level of the MNE group does not answer the question whether the conditions of the transfer are arm's length from the perspectives of both the transferor and the transferee.

9.60. Also in the case where a local operation disposes of the legal ownership of its intangibles to a foreign associated enterprise and continues to use the intangibles further to the disposal, but does so in a different legal capacity (e.g. as a licensee), the conditions of the transfer should be assessed from both the transferor's and the transferee's perspectives. The determination of an arm's length remuneration for the subsequent ownership, control and exploitation of the transferred intangible should take account of the extent of the functions performed, assets used and risks assumed by the parties in relation to the intangible transferred, and in particular analysing control of risks and control of functions performed relating to the development, enhancement, maintenance, protection, or exploitation of the intangibles.

9.61. Where the business restructuring provides for a transfer of an intangible followed by a new arrangement whereby the transferor will continue to use the intangible transferred, the entirety of the commercial arrangement between the parties should be examined in order to accurately delineate the transaction. If an independent party were to transfer an asset that it intends to continue exploiting, it would be prudent for it to negotiate the conditions of such a future use (e.g. in a license agreement) concomitantly with the conditions of the transfer. In effect, there will generally be a relationship between the determination of an arm's length compensation for the transfer, the determination of an arm's length compensation for the post-restructuring transactions in relation to the transferred intangible, such as future licence fees that may be payable by the transferor to be able to continue using the asset, and the expected future profitability of the transferor from its future use of the asset. For instance, in an arrangement whereby a patent is transferred for a price of 100 in Year N and a licence agreement is concomitantly concluded according to which the transferor will continue to use the patent transferred in exchange for a royalty of 100 per year over a 10-year period, it is likely that at least one of the two prices is not arm's length or that the arrangement should be delineated as something other than a sale and concomitant license back. In some circumstances, the accurate delineation of the transaction might conclude that the arrangements reflect the provision of financing, as illustrated in Example 16 in Annex I to Chapter VI.

E.2.2. Intangible transferred at a point in time when its valuation is highly uncertain

9.62. Difficulties can arise in the context of business restructuring where the valuation of an intangible or rights in an intangible at the time of the transaction is highly uncertain. In these cases, the question arises as to how arm's length pricing should be determined. The question should be resolved, both by taxpayers and tax administrations, by reference to what independent enterprises would have done in comparable circumstances to take account of the valuation uncertainty in the pricing of the transaction. To this aim, the guidance in Section D.3 of Chapter VI is relevant.

9.63. In addition, where the intangible being transferred as a result of the restructuring meets the criteria for being considered a hard-to value-intangible in paragraph 6.189, then the guidance in Section D.4 of Chapter VI is applicable.

E.2.3. Local intangibles

9.64. Where a local full-fledged operation is converted into an operation assuming limited risk, using limited intangibles and receiving low remuneration, the questions arise of whether this conversion entails the transfer by the restructured local entity to a foreign associated enterprise of valuable intangibles or rights in intangibles and whether there are local intangibles that remain with the local operation.

9.65. In particular, in the case of the conversion of a full-fledged distributor into, for example, a limited risk distributor or commissionnaire, it may be important to examine whether the distributor has developed local marketing intangibles over the years prior to its being restructured and if so, what the nature and the value of these intangibles are, and whether they were transferred to an associated enterprise. Where such local intangibles are found to be in existence and to be transferred to a foreign associated enterprise, the arm's length principle should apply to determine whether and if so how to compensate such a transfer, based on what would be agreed between independent parties in comparable circumstances. In this regard it is relevant to note that the transferor should receive arm's length compensation (in addition to the arm's length compensation for the transferred intangibles) when after the restructuring it continues to perform functions related to the development, enhancement, maintenance, protection or exploitation of the local intangible transferred (see Section B.2.1 of Chapter VI). On the other hand, where such local intangibles are found to be in existence and to remain in the restructured entity, they should be taken into account in the functional analysis of the post-restructuring activities. They may accordingly influence the selection and application of the most appropriate transfer pricing method for the post-restructuring controlled transactions, in order that appropriate compensation can be determined.[3]

E.2.4. Contractual rights

9.66. Contractual rights can be valuable intangibles. Where valuable contractual rights are transferred (or surrendered) between associated enterprises, they should be remunerated at arm's length, taking account of the value of the rights transferred from the perspectives of both the transferor and the transferee.

9.67. Tax administrations have expressed concerns about cases they have observed in practice where an entity voluntarily terminates a contract that provided benefits to it, in order to allow a foreign associated enterprise to

3. See Part II of this chapter for a discussion of the remuneration of the post-restructuring arrangements.

enter into a similar contract and benefit from the profit potential attached to it. For instance, assume that company A has valuable long-term contracts with independent customers that carry significant profit potential for A. Assume that at a certain point in time, A voluntarily terminates its contracts with its customers under circumstances where the latter are legally or commercially obligated to enter into similar arrangements with company B, a foreign entity that belongs to the same MNE group as A. As a consequence, the contractual rights and attached profit potential that used to lie with A now lie with B. If the factual situation is that B could only enter into the contracts with the customers subject to A's surrendering its own contractual rights to its benefit, and that A only terminated its contracts with its customers knowing that the latter were legally or commercially obligated to conclude similar arrangements with B, this in substance would consist in a tri-partite transaction and it may amount to a transfer of valuable contractual rights from A to B that may have to be remunerated at arm's length, depending on the value of the rights surrendered by A from the perspectives of both A and B.

E.3. Transfer of activity (ongoing concern)

E.3.1. Valuing a transfer of activity

9.68. Business restructurings sometimes involve the transfer of an ongoing concern, i.e. a functioning, economically integrated business unit. The transfer of an ongoing concern in this context means the transfer of assets, bundled with the ability to perform certain functions and assume certain risks. Such functions, assets and risks may include, among other things: tangible property and intangibles; liabilities associated with holding certain assets and performing certain functions, such as R&D and manufacturing; the capacity to carry on the activities that the transferor carried on before the transfer; and any resource, capabilities, and rights. The valuation of a transfer of an ongoing concern should reflect all the valuable elements that would be remunerated between independent parties in comparable circumstances. See Section A.4.6 of Chapter VI. For example, in the case of a business restructuring that involves the transfer of a business unit that includes, among other things, research facilities staffed with an experienced research team, the valuation of such ongoing concern should reflect, among other things, the value of the facility and the impact (e.g. time and expense savings) of the assembled workforce on the arm's length price. For a discussion on the transfer pricing treatment of assembled workforce, see Section D.7 of Chapter I.

9.69. The determination of the arm's length compensation for a transfer of an ongoing concern does not necessarily amount to the sum of the separate valuations of each separate element that comprises the aggregate transfer. In particular, if the transfer of an ongoing concern comprises multiple contemporaneous transfers of interrelated assets, risks, or functions, valuation of those transfers on an aggregate basis may be necessary to achieve the most reliable measure of the arm's length price for the ongoing concern. Valuation techniques that are used, in acquisition deals, between independent parties may prove useful to valuing the transfer of an ongoing concern between associated enterprises. The guidance on the use of valuation techniques for transactions involving the transfer of intangibles or rights in intangibles contained in Section D.2.6.3 of Chapter VI should be considered.

9.70. An example is the case where a manufacturing activity that used to be performed by M1, one entity of the MNE group, is re-located to another entity, M2 (e.g. to benefit from location savings). Assume M1 transfers to M2 its machinery and equipment, inventories, patents, manufacturing processes and know-how, and key contracts with suppliers and clients. Assume that several employees of M1 are relocated to M2 in order to assist M2 in the start of the manufacturing activity so relocated. Assume such a transfer would be regarded as a transfer of an ongoing concern, should it take place between independent parties. In order to determine the arm's length remuneration, if any, of such a transfer between associated enterprises, it should be compared with a transfer of an ongoing concern between independent parties rather than with a transfer of isolated assets.

E.3.2. Loss-making activities

9.71. Not every case where a restructured entity experiences a reduction of its functions, assets and risks involves an actual loss of expected future profits. In some restructuring situations, the circumstances may be such that, rather than losing a "profit-making opportunity", the restructured entity is actually being saved from the likelihood of a "loss-making opportunity". An entity may agree to a restructuring as a better option than going out of business altogether. If the restructured entity is forecasting future losses absent the restructuring (e.g. it operates a manufacturing plant that is uneconomic due to increasing competition from low-cost imports), then there may be in fact no loss of any profit-making opportunity from restructuring rather than continuing to operate its existing business. In such circumstances, the restructuring might deliver a benefit to the restructured entity from reducing or eliminating future losses if such losses exceed the restructuring costs.

9.72. The question may arise of whether the transferee should in fact be compensated by the transferor for taking over a loss-making activity. The response depends on whether an independent party in comparable circumstances would have been willing to pay for getting rid of the loss-making activity, or whether it would have considered other options such as closing down the activity; and on whether a third party would have been willing to acquire the loss-making activity (e.g. because of possible synergies with its own activities) and if so under what conditions, e.g. subject to compensation. There can be circumstances where an independent party would be willing to pay, e.g. if the financial costs and social risks of closing down the activity would be such that the transferor finds it more advantageous to pay a transferee who will attempt to reconvert the activity and will be responsible for any redundancy plan that may be needed.

9.73. The situation might however be different where the loss-making activity provided other benefits such as synergies with other activities performed by the same taxpayer. There can also be circumstances where a loss-making activity is maintained because it produces some benefits to the group as a whole. In such a case, the question arises whether at arm's length the entity that maintains the loss-making activity should be compensated by those who benefit from it being maintained. See Section D.3 of Chapter I.

E.4. Outsourcing

9.74. In outsourcing cases, it may happen that a party voluntarily decides to undergo a restructuring and to bear the associated restructuring costs in exchange for anticipated savings. For instance, assume a taxpayer that is manufacturing and selling products in a high-cost jurisdiction decides to outsource the manufacturing activity to an associated enterprise situated in a low-cost jurisdiction. Further to the restructuring, the taxpayer will purchase from its associated enterprise the products manufactured and will continue to sell them to third party customers. The restructuring may entail restructuring costs for the taxpayer while at the same time making it possible for it to benefit from cost savings on future procurements compared to its own manufacturing costs. Independent parties implementing this type of outsourcing arrangement may not necessarily require explicit compensation from the transferee, for example, where the anticipated benefits for the transferor are greater than its restructuring costs.[4]

F. Indemnification of the restructured entity for the termination or substantial renegotiation of existing arrangements

9.75. Section F addresses the question of whether the restructured entity, at arm's length, should receive compensation, in the form of indemnification, upon the termination or substantial renegotiation of its existing arrangements, which may or may not involve a transfer of something of value (addressed in the previous section). For the purpose of this chapter, indemnification means any type of compensation that may be paid for detriments suffered by the

4. A further issue discussed in Section D.6 of Chapter I and Section E of Part II of this Chapter is whether and if so how location savings should be allocated between the parties at arm's length.

restructured entity, whether in the form of an up-front payment, of a sharing in restructuring costs, of lower (or higher) purchase (or sale) prices in the context of the post-restructuring operations, or of any other form.

9.76. Terminations or renegotiations of arrangements generally involve changes in the risk and functional profiles of the parties, with consequences for the allocation of profit potential between them. In addition, the termination or renegotiation of contractual relationships in the context of a business restructuring might cause the restructured entity to suffer detriments such as restructuring costs (e.g. write-off of assets, termination of employment contracts), re-conversion costs (e.g. in order to adapt its existing operation to other customer needs), and/or a loss of profit potential. In these situations, the question arises of whether, at arm's length, indemnification should be paid to the restructured entity, and if so how to determine such an indemnification.

9.77. When the termination or renegotiation of existing arrangements involves the transfer of something of value (e.g. the termination of a distribution contract is sometimes accompanied by a transfer of intangibles), the guidance in Section E applies to the transfer of something of value, and this section considers whether further compensation may be warranted for any detriments suffered.

9.78. There should be no presumption that all contract terminations or substantial renegotiations should give a right to indemnification at arm's length, as this will depend on the facts and circumstances of each case. The analysis of whether an indemnification would be warranted at arm's length should be made on the basis of the accurate delineation of the arrangements before and after the restructuring (based on the guidance in Section D.1 of Chapter I and Section B.1 of this Part) and the options realistically available to the parties.

9.79. Once the restructuring arrangements have been accurately delineated and the options realistically available to the parties have been assessed, the following aspects should be considered:

- Whether commercial law supports rights to indemnification for the restructured entity under the facts of the case as accurately delineated (see Section F.1 below);
- Whether the existence or absence of an indemnification clause or similar provisions (as well as the terms of such a clause where it exists) under the terms of the arrangement, as accurately delineated, is arm's length (see Section F.2 below).
- Which party should ultimately bear the costs related to the indemnification of the party that suffers from the termination or re-negotiation of the agreement (see Section F.3 below).

F.1. Whether commercial law supports rights to indemnification for the restructured entity under the facts of the case as accurately delineated

9.80. In the assessment of whether the conditions of the termination or non-renewal of an existing arrangement are arm's length, the possible recourse that may be offered by the applicable commercial law might provide some helpful insights. The applicable commercial legislation or case law may provide useful information on indemnification rights and terms and conditions that could be expected in case of termination of specific types of agreements, e.g. of a distributorship agreement. Under such rules, it may be that the terminated party has the right to claim before the courts an indemnification irrespective of whether or not it was provided for in the contract. Where the parties belong to the same MNE group, however, the terminated party is unlikely in practice to litigate against its associated enterprise in order to seek such an indemnification, and the conditions of the termination may therefore differ from the conditions that would be made between independent enterprises in similar circumstances.

F.2. Whether the existence or absence of an indemnification clause or similar provisions (as well as the terms of such a clause where it exists) under the terms of the arrangement, as accurately delineated, is arm's length.

9.81. The accurate delineation of the transaction will identify whether an indemnification clause or arrangement is in place upon termination, non-renewal or re-negotiation of the arrangements. In order to do so, the starting point should be a review of whether an indemnification clause or similar provision for termination, non-renewal or renegotiation is provided for, and of whether the conditions for termination, non-renewal or renegotiation of the contract were respected (e.g. with regard to any required notice period). However, the examination of the terms of the contract between the associated enterprises may not suffice from a transfer pricing perspective as the mere fact that a given terminated, non renewed or renegotiated contract did not provide an indemnification or similar provision does not necessarily mean that this is arm's length, as discussed below.

9.82. As noted in paragraph 1.46, in transactions between independent enterprises, the divergence of interests between the parties ensures that: (i) contractual terms are concluded that reflect the interest of both parties, (ii) the parties will ordinarily seek to hold each other to the terms of the contract, and (iii) that contractual terms will be ignored or modified after the fact generally only if it is in the interests of both parties. However, this same divergence of interest may not exist in the case of associated enterprises or any such divergences may be managed in ways facilitated by the relationship between the associated enterprises and not solely or mainly through contractual agreements. For this reason, when the facts of the case differ from the written terms of the agreement between the parties or when no written terms exist, the absence or existence (and its terms) of an indemnification clause should be deduced from the conduct of the parties. For instance, it may be that, on the basis of the facts of the case and of the actual conduct of the associated enterprises, it is determined that the term of the contract is longer than established in the written contract, which would entitle the terminated party to some indemnification in case of early termination.

9.83. Once the existence or absence of an indemnification clause in favour of the restructured entity upon termination, non-renewal or substantial renegotiation of the agreements has been determined, the analysis should then focus on assessing whether such indemnification clause and its terms (or absence thereof) are arm's length. Where comparables data evidence a similar indemnification clause (or absence thereof) in comparable circumstances, the indemnification clause (or absence thereof) in a controlled transaction will be regarded as arm's length.

9.84. However, in those cases where such comparables data are not found, the determination of whether the indemnification clause (or absence thereof) is arm's length should take into account the rights and other assets of the parties at the time of entering into the arrangement and of its termination or renegotiation. This analysis might also be assisted by an examination of the options realistically available to the parties, as in some situations, it may be the case that, in comparable circumstances, an independent party would not have had any option realistically available that would be clearly more attractive to it than to accept the conditions of the termination or substantial renegotiation of the contract. The guidance in Section D of Chapter I, as well as the Guidance in Section B of this Part, are applicable.

9.85. Another aspect that may be necessary to examine in assessing whether the conditions of an arrangement in relation to an indemnification clause are arm's length, is the remuneration of the transactions that are the object of the arrangement and the financial conditions of the termination thereof, as both can be inter-related. In effect, the terms of a termination clause (or the absence thereof) may be a significant element of the functional analysis of the transactions and specifically of the analysis of the risks of the parties, and may accordingly need to be taken into account in the determination of an arm's length remuneration for the transactions. Similarly, the remuneration of the transactions will affect the determination of whether the conditions of the termination of the arrangement are at arm's length.

9.86. Business restructurings may lead to the termination of the employment contracts of members of an assembled workforce. In this regard, in determining whether the restructuring is undertaken on arm's length terms, the analysis should consider the facts and circumstances before and after the restructuring related to the assembled workforce, including whether something of value has been transferred upon termination of the arrangements between associated enterprises and, for example, whether there are implicit or explicit restrictive covenants (e.g. non-compete clause) in the employment contracts of the workforce members, which should be reflected in the amount of any indemnification that should be paid to the party previously undertaking the activities through that workforce.

9.87. One circumstance that deserves particular attention, is the situation where the now-terminated contract required one party to make a significant investment for which an arm's length return might only be reasonably expected if the contract was maintained for an extended period of time. This created a financial risk for the party making the investment in case the contract was terminated before the end of such period of time. The degree of the risk would depend on whether the investment was highly specialised or could be used (possibly subject to some adaptations) for other clients. Where the risk was material, it would have been reasonable for independent parties in comparable circumstances to take it into account when negotiating the contract.

9.88. An example would be where a manufacturing contract between associated enterprises requires the manufacturer to invest in a new manufacturing unit. Assume an arm's length return on the investment can reasonably be anticipated by the manufacturer at the time the contract is concluded, subject to the manufacturing contract lasting for at least five years, for the manufacturing activity to produce at least × units per year, and for the remuneration of the manufacturing activity to be calculated on a basis (e.g. USD/unit) that is expected to generate an arm's length return on the total investment in the new manufacturing unit. Assume that after three years, the associated enterprise terminates the contract in accordance with its terms in the context of a group-wide restructuring of the manufacturing operations. Assume the manufacturing unit is highly specialised and the manufacturer further to the termination would have no other choice than to write off the assets.

9.89. At arm's length, the manufacturer may mitigate the risks inherent in the investment by:

- Including in the contract an appropriate indemnification clause or penalties in case of early termination, or an option for the party making the investment to transfer it at a given price to the other party in case the investment becomes useless to the former due to the early termination of the contract by the latter.
- Factoring the risk linked with the possible termination of the contract into the determination of the remuneration of the activities covered by the contract (e.g. by factoring the risk into the determination of

the remuneration of the manufacturing activities where third party comparables that bear comparable risks can be identified, perhaps by including front-end loaded fee structures). In such a case the party making the investment consciously accepts the risk and is rewarded for it; no separate indemnification for the termination of the contract seems necessary.

9.90. As a general matter, mitigation of risk inherent in the investment by a manufacturer is relevant to consider only if the manufacturer assumes the risk. In practice, the investment by an associated enterprise in a manufacturing plant where that enterprise is wholly dependent on another associated enterprise for the capability to generate returns is likely to require careful scrutiny in relation to the identification of risks and how those risks are controlled. As explained in Example 2 in paragraphs 1.84 and 1.102 where significant risks associated with generating a return from the manufacturing activities are controlled solely by another party (which also has the financial capacity to bear that risk), then that other party is allocated the upside and downside consequences of those risks, including under-utilisation, write-down, and closure costs. In that case, the manufacturer should not suffer the financial consequences of an early termination, as it did not control the economically significant risks that contributed to the closure, and in such a case the manufacturer would also not be expected to mitigate risks it did not in fact assume.

9.91. A similar issue may arise in the case where a party has undertaken development efforts resulting in losses or low returns in the early period and above-normal returns are expected in periods following the termination of the contract. In such a case, it will be necessary to analyse the actual arrangements very carefully to determine whether the party in substance takes a stake in the results of the development efforts or has merely accepted deferred payment terms. In performing the analysis the guidance relating to control over risk in Section D.1.2.1 of Chapter I will be relevant. If the party does control the risks, it might be expected that the party would seek to protect itself from the risk of non-recovery through penalty or indemnification terms. If the party did not control the risks of non-recovery, then the terms are unlikely to be arm's length.

9.92. In the case where the conditions made or imposed between associated enterprises with respect to the termination, non-renewal or substantial renegotiation of their existing arrangements differ from the conditions that would be made between independent enterprises, then any profits that would, but for those conditions, have accrued to one of the enterprises, but, by reason of those conditions, have not so accrued, may be included in the profits of that enterprise and taxed accordingly.

F.3. Which party should ultimately bear the costs related to the indemnification of the party that suffers from the termination or re-negotiation of the agreement

9.93. The transfer pricing analysis of the arm's length nature of the conditions of the termination or substantial renegotiation of an agreement should take account of both the perspectives of the transferor and of the transferee. Taking account of the transferee's perspective is important both to value the amount of an arm's length indemnification, if any, and to determine what party should bear it. It is not possible to derive a single answer for all cases and the response should be based on an examination of the facts and circumstances of the case, and in particular of the rights and other assets of the parties, of the risks assumed by the parties, of the economic rationale for the termination, of the determination of what party(ies) is (are) expected to benefit from it, and of the options realistically available to the parties. This can be illustrated as follows.

9.94. Assume a manufacturing contract between two associated enterprises, entity A and entity B, is terminated by A (B being the manufacturer). Assume A decides to use another associated manufacturer, entity C, to continue the manufacturing that was previously performed by B. As noted in paragraph 9.78, there should be no presumption that all contract terminations or substantial renegotiations should give a right to indemnification at arm's length. Assume that it is determined, based on the guidance in this section, that in the circumstances of the case at arm's length, B would be in a position to claim an indemnification for the detriment suffered from the termination. The question arises as to which party should ultimately bear the indemnification to be paid to B: A (i.e. the party terminating the contract), C (i.e. the party taking over the manufacturing activity previously performed by B), or another party in the MNE group benefitting from the restructuring. The analysis should start from the accurate delineation of the actual transactions comprising the business restructuring, and take into account economically related transactions with other enterprises in the MNE group that may help to delineate the controlled transaction (see paragraphs 1.36-1.38).

9.95. There can be situations where A would be willing to bear the indemnification costs at arm's length, for instance because it expects that the termination of its agreement with B will make it possible for it to derive costs savings through its new manufacturing agreement with C, and that the present value of these expected costs savings is greater than the amount of the indemnification.

9.96. There can be situations where C would be willing to pay an up-front fee to obtain the rights to the manufacturing contract from A, e.g. if the present value of the expected profits to be derived from its new manufacturing contract makes it worth the investment for C. In such situations, the payment by C might be organised in a variety of ways, for instance it might be that C would be paying A, or that C would be constructively paying A by meeting A's indemnification obligation to B. It is also possible that C would pay B, for example, in the circumstances where B had certain rights and C would pay B for the transfer of those rights.

9.97. There can be cases where at arm's length A and C would be willing to share the indemnification costs. In cases where the benefits arising from the restructuring accrue to another party in the MNE group, then that other party may bear the costs of indemnification, either directly or indirectly.

Part II: Remuneration of post-restructuring controlled transactions

A. Business restructurings versus "structuring"

A.1. General principle: no different application of the arm's length principle

9.98. The arm's length principle and these Guidelines do not and should not apply differently to post-restructuring transactions as opposed to transactions that were structured as such from the beginning. Doing otherwise would create a competitive distortion between existing players who restructure their activities and new entrants who implement the same business model without having to restructure their business.

9.99. Comparable situations must be treated in the same way, regardless of whether or not they came into existence as a result of a business restructuring of a previously existing structure. The selection and practical application of an appropriate transfer pricing method must be based on the economically relevant characteristics of the transaction leading to the accurate delineation of the actual transaction.

9.100. However, business restructuring situations involve change, and the arm's length principle must be applied not only to the post-restructuring transactions, but also to additional transactions that comprise the business restructuring. The application of the arm's length principle to those additional transactions is discussed in Part I of this chapter.

9.101. In addition, the comparability analysis of an arrangement that results from a business restructuring might reveal some factual differences compared to the one of an arrangement that was structured as such from the beginning, as discussed below. These factual differences do not affect the arm's length principle or the way the guidance in these Guidelines should be interpreted and applied, but they may affect the comparability analysis and therefore the outcome of this application. See Section D on comparing the pre- and post-restructuring situations.

A.2. Possible factual differences between situations that result from a restructuring and situations that were structured as such from the beginning

9.102. Where an arrangement between associated enterprises replaces an existing arrangement (restructuring), there may be factual differences in the starting position of the restructured entity compared to the position of a newly set up operation. Sometimes, the post-restructuring arrangement is negotiated between parties that have had prior contractual and commercial relationships. In such a situation, depending on the facts and circumstances of the case and in particular on the rights and obligations derived by the parties from these prior arrangements, this may affect the options realistically available to the parties in negotiating the terms of the new arrangement and therefore the conditions of the restructuring and of the post-restructuring arrangements (see paragraphs 9.27-9.31 for a discussion of options realistically available in the context of determining the arm's length compensation for the restructuring itself). For instance, assume a party has proved in the past to be able to perform well as a full-fledged distributor performing a whole range of marketing and selling functions, employing and developing valuable marketing intangible assets and assuming a range of risks associated with its activity such as inventory risks, bad debt risks and market risks. Assume that its distribution contract is re-negotiated and converted into a "limited risk distribution" contract whereby it will perform limited marketing activities under the supervision of a foreign associated enterprise, employ limited marketing intangibles and assume limited risks in its relationship with the foreign associated enterprise and customers. In such a situation, the restructured distributor would not be in the same position as a newly established distributor.

9.103. Where there is an ongoing business relationship between the parties before and after the restructuring, there may also be an inter-relationship between on the one hand the conditions of the pre-restructuring activities and/or of the restructuring itself, and on the other hand the conditions for the post-restructuring arrangements, as discussed in Section C below.

9.104. Some differences in the starting position of the restructured entity compared to the position of a newly set up operation can relate to the established presence of the operation. For instance, if one compares a situation where a long-established full-fledged distributor is converted into a limited risk distributor with a situation where a limited risk distributor is established in a market where the group did not have any previous commercial presence, market penetration efforts might be needed for the new entrant which are not needed for the converted entity. This may affect the comparability analysis and the determination of the arm's length remuneration in both situations.

9.105. When one compares a situation where a long-established full-fledged distributor is converted into a limited risk distributor with a situation where a limited risk distributor has been in existence in the market for the same duration, there might also be differences because the full-fledged distributor may have performed some functions, borne some expenses (e.g. marketing expenses), assumed some risks and contributed to the development of some intangibles before its conversion that the long-existing "limited risk distributor" may not have performed, borne, assumed or contributed to. The question arises whether at arm's length such additional functions, assets and risks should only affect the remuneration of the distributor before its being converted, whether they should be taken into account to determine a remuneration of the transfers that take place upon the conversion (and if so how), whether they should affect the remuneration of the restructured limited risk distributor (and if so how), or a combination of these three possibilities. For instance, if it is found that the pre-restructuring activities led the full-fledged distributor to own some intangibles while the long-established limited risk distributor does not, the arm's length principle may require these intangibles either to be remunerated upon the restructuring if they are transferred by the full-fledged distributor to a foreign associated enterprise, or to be taken into account in the determination of the arm's length remuneration of the post-restructuring activities if they are not transferred (see Section E.2 of Part I above and Chapter VI of these Guidelines).

9.106. Where a restructuring involves a transfer to a foreign associated enterprise of risks that were previously assumed by a taxpayer, it may be important to examine whether the transfer of risks only concerns the future risks that will arise from the post-restructuring activities or also the risks existing at the time of the restructuring as a result of pre-conversion activities, i.e. there is a cut-off issue. For instance, consider a situation in which a distributor was assuming bad debt risks which it will no longer assume after its being restructured as a "limited risk distributor", and that it is being compared with a long-established "limited risk distributor" that never assumed bad debt risk. It may be important when comparing both situations to examine, based on the guidance in Section D.1.2.1 of Chapter I, whether the "limited risk distributor" that results from a conversion still assumes the risks associated with bad debts that arose before the restructuring at the time it was full-fledged, or whether all the bad debt risks including those that existed at the time of the conversion were transferred.

9.107. The same remarks and questions apply for other types of restructurings, including other types of restructuring of sales activities as well as restructurings of manufacturing activities, research and development activities, or other services activities.

B. Application to business restructuring situations: selection and application of a transfer pricing method for the post-restructuring controlled transactions

9.108. The selection and application of a transfer pricing method to post-restructuring controlled transactions must derive from the analysis of the economically relevant characteristics of the controlled transaction as accurately delineated. It is essential to understand what the functions, assets and risks involved in the post-restructuring transactions are, and what party performs, uses or assumes them. This requires information to be available on the functions, assets and risks of both parties to a transaction, e.g. the restructured entity and the foreign associated enterprise with which it transacts. The analysis should go beyond the label assigned to the restructured entity, as an entity that is labelled as a "commissionnaire" or "limited risk distributor" can sometimes be found to own valuable local intangibles and to continue to assume significant market risks, and an entity that is labelled as a "contract manufacturer" can sometimes be found to pursue significant development activities or to own and use unique intangibles. In post-restructuring situations, particular attention should be paid to the identification of the valuable intangibles and the economically significant risks that effectively remain with the restructured entity (including, where applicable, local non-protected intangibles), and to whether such an allocation of intangibles and risks satisfies the arm's length principle. The form of remuneration cannot dictate inappropriate risk allocations. It is the determination of how the parties actually control risks, and whether they have the financial capacity to assume the risks, as set out in the process of analysing risk in Chapter I, which will determine the assumption of risks by the parties, and consequently dictate the selection of the most appropriate transfer pricing method. Issues regarding risks and intangibles are discussed in Part I of this chapter.

9.109. Post-restructuring arrangements may pose certain challenges with respect to the identification of potential comparables in cases where the restructuring implements a business model that is hardly found between independent enterprises. It should be noted that the mere fact that an arrangement is not seen between independent enterprises does not in itself mean that it is not arm's length nor commercially irrational. Furthermore, every effort should be made to determine the pricing for the restructuring transactions as accurately delineated under the arm's length principle.

9.110. There are cases where comparables (including internal comparables) are available, subject to possible comparability adjustments being performed. One example of a possible application of the CUP method would be the case where an enterprise that used to transact independently with the MNE group is acquired, and the acquisition is followed by a restructuring of the now controlled transactions. Subject to a review of the five economically relevant characteristics or comparability factors and of the possible effect of the controlled and uncontrolled transactions taking place at different times, it might be the case that the conditions of the pre-acquisition uncontrolled transactions provide a CUP for the post-acquisition controlled transactions. Even where the conditions of the transactions are restructured, it might still be possible, depending on the facts and circumstances of the case, to adjust for the transfer of functions, assets and/or risks that occurred upon the restructuring. For instance, a comparability adjustment might be performed to account for the fact that a different party assumes bad debt risk.

9.111. Another example of a possible application of the CUP method would be the case where independent parties provide manufacturing, selling or service activities comparable to the ones provided by the restructured affiliate. Given the recent development of outsourcing activities, it may be possible in some cases to find independent outsourcing transactions that provide a basis for using the CUP method in order to determine the arm's length remuneration of post-restructuring controlled transactions. This of course is subject to the condition that the outsourcing transactions qualify as uncontrolled transactions and that the review of the five economically relevant characteristics or comparability factors provides sufficient comfort that either no material difference exists between the conditions of the uncontrolled outsourcing transactions and the conditions of the post-restructuring controlled transactions, or that reliable enough adjustments can be made (and are effectively made) to eliminate such differences.

9.112. Whenever a comparable is proposed, it is important to ensure that a comparability analysis of the controlled and uncontrolled transactions is performed in order to identify material differences, if any, between them and, where necessary and possible, to adjust for such differences. In particular, the comparability analysis might reveal that the restructured entity continues to perform valuable and significant functions and/or the presence of local intangibles and/or of economically significant risks that remain in the "stripped" entity after the restructuring but are not found in the proposed comparables. See Section A on the possible differences between restructured activities and start-up situations.

9.113. The identification of potential comparables has to be made with the objective of finding the most reliable comparables data in the circumstances of the case, keeping in mind the limitations that may exist in availability of information and the compliance costs involved (see paragraphs 3.2 and 3.80). It is recognised that the data will not always be perfect. There are also cases where comparables data are not found, for instance where the restructuring has led to fragmentation of integrated functions across several group companies in a way that is not found between unrelated parties. This does not necessarily mean that the conditions of the controlled transaction as accurately delineated are not arm's length. Notwithstanding the difficulties that can arise in the process of searching comparables, it is necessary to find a reasonable solution to all transfer pricing cases. Following the guidance in paragraph 2.2, even in cases where comparables data are scarce and imperfect, the choice of the most appropriate transfer pricing method to the circumstances of the case should be consistent with the nature of the controlled transaction, determined in particular through a functional analysis.

C. Relationship between compensation for the restructuring and post-restructuring remuneration

9.114. There may in some circumstances be an important inter-relationship between the compensation for the restructuring and an arm's length reward for operating the business post-restructuring. This can be the case where a taxpayer disposes of business operations to an associated enterprise with which it must then transact business as part of those operations. One example of such a relationship is found in paragraph 9.74 regarding outsourcing.

9.115. Another example would be where a taxpayer that operates a manufacturing and distribution activity restructures by disposing of its distribution activity to a foreign associated enterprise to which the taxpayer will in the future sell the goods it manufactures. The foreign associated enterprise would expect to be able to earn an arm's length reward for its investment in acquiring and operating the business. In this situation, the taxpayer might agree with the foreign associated enterprise to forgo receipt of part or all of the up-front compensation for the business that may be payable at arm's length, and instead obtain comparable financial benefit over time through selling its goods to the foreign associated enterprise at prices that are higher than the latter would otherwise agree to if the up-front compensation had been paid. Alternatively, the parties might agree to set an up-front compensation payment for the restructuring that is partly offset through future lower transfer prices for the manufactured products than would have been set otherwise. See Part I of this chapter for a discussion of situations where compensation would be payable at arm's length for the restructuring itself.

9.116. In other words, in this situation where the taxpayer will have an ongoing business relationship as supplier to the foreign associated enterprise that carries on an activity previously carried on by the taxpayer, the taxpayer and the foreign associated enterprise have the opportunity to obtain economic and commercial benefits through that relationship (e.g. the sale price of goods) which may explain for instance why compensation through an up-front capital payment for transfer of the business was foregone, or why the future transfer price for the products might be different from the prices that would have been agreed absent a restructuring operation. In practice, however, it might be difficult to structure and monitor such an arrangement. While taxpayers are free to choose the form of compensation payments, whether up-front or over time, tax administrations when reviewing such arrangements would want to know how the compensation for the post-restructuring activity was possibly affected to take account of the foregone compensation, if any, for the restructuring itself. Specifically, in such a case, the tax administration would want to look at the entirety of the arrangements, while being provided with a separate evaluation of the arm's length compensation for the restructuring and for the post-restructuring transactions.

D. Comparing the pre- and post-restructuring situations

9.117. A relevant question is the role if any of comparisons that can be made of the profits actually earned by a party to a controlled transaction prior to and after the restructuring. In particular, it can be asked whether it would be appropriate to determine a restructured entity's post-restructuring profits by reference to its pre-restructuring profits, adjusted to reflect the transfer or relinquishment of particular functions, assets and risks.[5]

9.118. One important issue with such before-and-after comparisons is that a comparison of the profits from the post-restructuring controlled transactions with the profits made in controlled transactions prior to the restructuring would not suffice given Article 9 of the OECD Model Tax Convention provides for a comparison to be made with uncontrolled transactions. Comparisons of a taxpayer's controlled transactions with other controlled transactions are irrelevant to the application of the arm's length principle and therefore should not be used by a tax administration as the basis for a transfer pricing adjustment or by a taxpayer to support its transfer pricing policy.

9.119. Another issue with before-and-after comparisons is the likely difficulty of valuing the basket of functions, assets and risks that were lost by the restructured entity, keeping in mind that it is not always the case that these functions, assets and risks are transferred to another party.

9.120. That being said, in business restructurings, before-and-after comparisons could play a role in understanding the restructuring itself and could be part of a before-and-after comparability (including functional) analysis to understand the changes that accounted for the changes in the allocation of profit/loss amongst the parties. In effect, information on the arrangements that existed prior to the restructuring and on the conditions of the restructuring itself could be essential to understand the context in which the post-restructuring arrangements were put in place and to assess whether such arrangements are

5. This is a different question from the one of profit potential that is discussed in Part I of this chapter.

arm's length. It can also shed light on the options realistically available to the restructured entity.[6]

9.121. The analysis of the business before and after the restructuring may reveal that while some functions, assets and risks were transferred, other functions may still be carried out by the "stripped" entity. Typically, as part of the restructuring the entity may have been purportedly stripped of intangibles or risk, but after the restructuring it continues to carry out some or all of the functions it previously performed. Following the restructuring, however, the "stripped" entity performs those functions under contract to a foreign associated enterprise. The accurate delineation of the actual transaction between the foreign associated enterprise and the "stripped" entity will determine the actual commercial or financial relations between them, including whether the contractual terms are consistent with the conduct of the parties and other facts of the case. Arm's length compensation for each party should be consistent with its actual functions performed, assets used and risks assumed after the restructuring.

9.122. For example, an MNE manufactures and distributes products the value of which is not determined by the technical features of the products, but rather by consumer recognition of the brand.[7] The MNE wants to differentiate itself from its competitors through the development of brands with great value, by implementing a carefully developed and expensive marketing strategy. The trademarks, trade names and other intangibles represented by the brand are owned by Company A in Country A and Company A assumes the risks associated with the ownership, development and exploitation of those intangibles. The development, maintenance and execution of a worldwide marketing strategy are the main value drivers of the MNE, performed by 125 employees at Company A's head office. The value of the intangibles results in a high consumer price for the products. Company A's head office also provides central services for the group affiliates (e.g. human resource management, legal, tax). The products are manufactured by affiliates under contract manufacturing arrangements with Company A. They are distributed by affiliates who purchase them from Company A. The profits derived by Company A after having allocated an arm's length remuneration to the contract manufacturers and distributors are

6. See paragraphs 9.27-9.9.31 for a discussion of options realistically available; see also paragraphs 9.102-9.106 for a discussion of possible factual differences between situations that result from a restructuring and situations that were structured as such from the beginning and of how such differences may affect the options realistically available to the parties in negotiating the terms of the new arrangement and therefore the conditions of the restructuring and/or of the post-restructuring arrangements.

7. For an explanation of the term "brand", please see paragraph 6.23.

considered to be the remuneration for the intangibles, marketing activities and central services of Company A.

9.123. Then a restructuring takes place. Legal ownership of the trademarks, trade names and other intangibles represented by the brand is transferred by Company A to a newly set up affiliate, Company Z in Country Z in exchange for a lump sum payment. After the restructuring, Company A is remunerated on a cost plus basis for the services it performs for Company Z and the rest of the group. The remuneration of the affiliated contract manufacturers and distributors remains the same. The remaining profits after remuneration of the contract manufacturers, distributors, and Company A head office services are paid to Company Z. The accurate delineation of the transactions before and after the restructuring determines that:

- Company Z is managed by a local trust company. It does not have people (employees or directors) who have the capability to perform, and who in fact do not perform control functions in relation to the risks associated with the ownership or the strategic development of the trademarks, trade names or other intangibles represented by the brand. It also does not have the financial capacity to assume these risks.
- High ranking officials from Company A's head office fly to Country Z once a year to formally validate the strategic decisions necessary to operate the company. These decisions are prepared by Company A's head office in Country A before the meetings take place in Country Z. The MNE considers that these activities are service activities performed by Company A's head office for Z. These strategic decision-making activities are remunerated at cost plus in the same way as the central services are remunerated (e.g. human resource management, legal, tax).
- The development, maintenance and execution of the worldwide marketing strategy are still performed by the same employees of Company A's head office and remunerated on a cost plus basis.

9.124. Based on these findings, it can be concluded that Company A continues to perform the same functions and assume the same risks as before the restructuring took place. In particular, Company A continues to have the capability and actually performs control functions in relation to the risk of exploitation of the intangibles. It also carries on the functions related to the development, maintenance and execution of the worldwide marketing strategy. Company Z has no capability to perform control functions, and does not in fact perform the control functions needed to assume the intangible related risks. Accordingly, the accurate delineation of the transaction after the restructuring may lead to the conclusion that this is in substance a funding arrangement between Company A and Company Z, rather than a restructuring for the centralisation of intangible management. An assessment may be necessary of the commercial rationality of the transaction based on the guidance in Section D.2 of Chapter I taking into account the full facts and circumstances of the transaction[8].

9.125. There will also be cases where before-and-after comparisons can be made because the transactions prior to the restructuring were not controlled, for instance where the restructuring follows an acquisition, and where adjustments can reliably be made to account for the differences between the pre-restructuring uncontrolled transactions and the post-restructuring controlled transactions. See example in paragraph 9.110. Whether such uncontrolled transactions provide reliable comparables would have to be evaluated in light of the guidance in paragraph 3.2.

E. Location savings

9.126. Location savings can be derived by an MNE group that relocates some of its activities to a place where costs (such as labour costs, real estate costs, etc.) are lower than in the location where the activities were initially performed, account being taken of the possible costs involved in the relocation (such as termination costs for the existing operation, possibly higher infrastructure costs in the new location, possibly higher transportation costs if the new operation is more distant from the market, training costs of local employees, etc.). Where a business strategy aimed at deriving location savings is put forward as a business reason for restructuring, the discussion in Section D.1.5 of Chapter I is relevant.

9.127. Where significant location savings are derived further to a business restructuring, the question arises of whether and if so how the location savings should be shared among the parties. In addressing this matter, the guidance in Section D.6 of Chapter I is relevant.

9.128. Take the example of an enterprise that designs, manufactures and sells brand name clothes. Assume that the manufacturing process is basic and that the brand name is famous and represents a highly valuable intangible. Assume that the enterprise is established in Country A where the labour costs are high and that it decides to close down its manufacturing activities in Country A and to relocate them in an affiliate company in Country B where labour costs are significantly lower. The enterprise in Country A retains the rights on the brand name and continues designing the clothes. Further to this restructuring, the clothes will be manufactured by the affiliate in Country B under a contract manufacturing arrangement. The arrangement

8. This is notwithstanding any possible application of general anti-avoidance rules and notwithstanding the question about Company Z's place of effective management.

does not involve the use of any significant intangible owned by or licensed to the affiliate or the assumption of any significant risks by the affiliate in Country B. Once manufactured by the affiliate in Country B, the clothes will be sold to the enterprise in Country A which will on-sell them to third party customers. Assume that this restructuring makes it possible for the group formed by the enterprise in Country A and its affiliate in Country B to derive significant location savings. The question arises whether the location savings should be attributed to the enterprise in Country A, or its affiliate in Country B, or both (and if so in what proportions).

9.129. In such an example, given that the relocated activity is a highly competitive one, it is likely that the enterprise in Country A has the option realistically available to it to use either the affiliate in Country B or a third party manufacturer. As a consequence, it should be possible to find comparables data to determine the conditions in which a third party would be willing at arm's length to manufacture the clothes for the enterprise. In such a situation, a contract manufacturer at arm's length would generally be attributed very little, if any, part of the location savings. Doing otherwise would put the associated manufacturer in a situation different from the situation of an independent manufacturer, and would be contrary to the arm's length principle.

9.130. As another example, assume now that an enterprise in Country X provides highly specialised and quality engineering services to independent clients. It charges a fee to its independent clients based on a fixed hourly rate that compares with the hourly rate charged by competitors for similar services in the same market. Suppose that the wages for qualified engineers in Country X are high. The enterprise subsequently subcontracts a large part of its engineering work to a new subsidiary in Country Y. The subsidiary in Country Y hires equally qualified engineers to those in Country X for substantially lower wages, thus deriving significant location savings for the group formed by the enterprise and its subsidiary Clients continue to deal directly with the enterprise in Country X and are not necessarily aware of the sub-contracting arrangement. For some period of time, the well-known enterprise in Country X can continue to charge its services at the original hourly rate despite the significantly reduced engineer costs. After a certain period of time, however, it is forced due to competitive pressures to decrease its hourly rate (at an amount that would not allow the company in Country X to cover the wages for qualified engineers in Country X, but that would still yield a benefit if those services are provided by qualified engineers in Country Y). Part of the location savings are passed on to its clients. In this case also, the question arises of which party(ies) within the MNE group should, at arm's length, be attributed the part of the location savings not passed on to the clients: the subsidiary in Country Y, the enterprise in Country X, or both (and if so in what proportions).

9.131. In determining which party(ies) should be attributed the location savings at arm's length, it will be important to consider the functions, risks and assets of the parties, as well as the options realistically available to each of them. In this example, assume that there is a high demand for the type of engineering services that the company in Country X sells. Assume also that the subsidiary in Country Y is the only company operating in a lower-cost location that is able to provide such services with the required quality standard, and Company Y is able to withstand competitive pricing pressures because the technical know-how it has established acts as a barrier to competition. Furthermore, the company in Country X does not have the option of engaging qualified engineers in Country X to provide these services, as the cost of their wages would be too high compared to the hourly rate charged to clients. Considering this, the enterprise in Country X does not have many other options available to it than to use this service provider. The remuneration payable by Company X to Company Y should take into account the location savings created by Company Y, in addition to the value of its services including any intangibles used in providing those services. In some instances, the nature of the contributions made by the enterprise in Country X and its subsidiary in Country Y may meet the criteria for the use of a transactional profit split method.

Chapter X

Transfer pricing aspects of financial transactions

A. Introduction

10.1. The purpose of this chapter is to provide guidance for determining whether the conditions of certain financial transactions between associated enterprises are consistent with the arm's length principle.

10.2. Section B describes the application of the principles of Section D.1 of Chapter I to financial transactions. Section C provides guidance on determining the arm's length conditions for treasury activities including intra-group loans, cash pooling and hedging. Section D examines financial guarantees, and Section E outlines the analysis of captive insurance companies.

10.3. The conditions of financial transactions between independent enterprises will be the result of various commercial considerations. In contrast, an MNE group has the discretion to decide upon those conditions within the MNE group. Thus, in an intra-group situation, other considerations such as tax consequences may also be present.

B. Interaction with the guidance in Section D.1 of Chapter I

B.1. Determination of whether a purported loan should be regarded as a loan[1]

10.4. It may be the case that the balance of debt and equity funding of a borrowing entity that is part of an MNE group differs from that which would exist if it were an independent entity operating under the same or similar

1. The guidance contained in this subsection is consistent with the Commentary on Article 9 of the 2017 OECD Model Tax Convention and also with the Commentary as it would read with proposed changes that have been agreed by Working Party No. 1. The guidance might be revised in the event that those proposals are materially changed at any stage.

circumstances. This situation may affect the amount of interest payable by the borrowing entity and so may affect the profits accruing in a given jurisdiction.

10.5. Commentary to Article 9 of the OECD Model Tax Convention notes in paragraph 3(b) that Article 9 is relevant "not only in determining whether the rate of interest provided for in a loan contract is an arm's length rate, but also whether a prima facie loan can be regarded as a loan or should be regarded as some other kind of payment, in particular a contribution to equity capital."[2]

10.6. In the context of the preceding paragraphs, this subsection elaborates on how the concepts of Chapter I, in particular the accurate delineation of the actual transaction under Section D.1, may relate to the balance of debt and equity funding of an entity within an MNE group.

10.7. Where it is considered that the arrangements made in relation to the transaction, viewed in their totality, differ from those which would have been adopted by independent enterprises behaving in a commercially rational manner in comparable circumstances, the guidance in Section D.2 of Chapter I may also be relevant.

10.8. Although this guidance reflects an approach of accurate delineation of the actual transaction in accordance with Chapter I to determine the amount of debt to be priced, it is acknowledged that other approaches may be taken to address the issue of the balance of debt and equity funding of an entity under domestic legislation before pricing the interest on the debt so determined. These approaches may include a multi-factor analysis of the characteristics of the instrument and the issuer.

10.9. Accordingly, this guidance is not intended to prevent jurisdictions from implementing approaches to address the balance of debt and equity funding of an entity and interest deductibility under domestic legislation, nor does it seek to mandate accurate delineation under Chapter I as the only approach for determining whether purported debt should be respected as debt.

10.10. Although jurisdictions may have different views on the application of Article 9 to determine the balance of debt and equity funding of an entity within an MNE group, the purpose of this section is to provide guidance for jurisdictions that use the accurate delineation under Chapter I to determine whether a purported loan should be regarded as a loan for tax purposes (or should be regarded as some other kind of payment, in particular a contribution to equity capital).

2. As discussed in the Committee on Fiscal Affairs' Report on "Thin Capitalisation" adopted by the Council of the OECD on 26 November 1986 and reproduced in Volume II of the full version of the OECD MTC at page R (4)-1.

10.11. Particular labels or descriptions assigned to financial transactions do not constrain the transfer pricing analysis. Each situation must be examined on its own merits, and subject to the prefatory language in the previous paragraph, accurate delineation of the actual transaction under Chapter I will precede any pricing attempt.

10.12. In accurately delineating an advance of funds, the following economically relevant characteristics may be useful indicators, depending on the facts and circumstances: the presence or absence of a fixed repayment date; the obligation to pay interest; the right to enforce payment of principal and interest; the status of the funder in comparison to regular corporate creditors; the existence of financial covenants and security; the source of interest payments; the ability of the recipient of the funds to obtain loans from unrelated lending institutions; the extent to which the advance is used to acquire capital assets; and the failure of the purported debtor to repay on the due date or to seek a postponement.

10.13. For example, consider a situation in which Company B, a member of an MNE group, needs additional funding for its business activities. In this scenario, Company B receives an advance of funds from related Company C, which is denominated as a loan with a term of 10 years. Assume that, in light of all good-faith financial projections of Company B for the next 10 years, it is clear that Company B would be unable to service a loan of such an amount. Based on facts and circumstances, it can be concluded that an unrelated party would not be willing to provide such a loan to Company B due to its inability to repay the advance. Accordingly, the accurately delineated amount of Company C's loan to Company B for transfer pricing purposes would be a function of the maximum amount that an unrelated lender would have been willing to advance to Company B, and the maximum amount that an unrelated borrower in comparable circumstances would have been willing to borrow from Company C, including the possibilities of not lending or borrowing any amount (see comments upon "The lender's and borrower's perspectives" in Section C.1.1.1 of this chapter). Consequently, the remainder of Company C's advance to Company B would not be delineated as a loan for the purposes of determining the amount of interest which Company B would have paid at arm's length.

B.2. Identifying the commercial or financial relations

10.14. In determining the arm's length conditions of financial transactions, the same principles apply as described in Chapters I-III of these Guidelines for any other controlled transaction.

10.15. As with any controlled transaction, the accurate delineation of financial transactions requires an analysis of the factors affecting the performance of businesses in the industry sector in which the MNE group operates. Because differences exist among industry sectors, factors such as the particular point of an economic, business or product cycle, the effect of government regulations, or the availability of financial resources in a given industry are relevant features that have to be considered to accurately delineate the controlled transaction. This examination will take account of the fact that MNE groups operating in different sectors may require, for example, different amounts and types of financing due to different capital intensity levels between industries, or may require different levels of short-term cash balances due to different commercial needs between industries. Where the relevant MNEs are regulated, such as financial services entities subject to regulations consistent with recognised industry standards (e.g. Basel requirements), due regard should be had to the constraints those regulations impose upon them.[3]

10.16. As described in Chapter I, the process of accurate delineation of the actual transaction also requires an understanding of how the particular MNE group responds to those identified factors. In this regard, the MNE group's policies may inform the accurate delineation of the actual transaction through the consideration of, for instance, how the MNE group prioritises the funding needs among different projects; the strategic significance of a particular MNE within the MNE group; whether the MNE group is targeting a specific credit rating or debt-equity ratio; or whether the MNE group is adopting a different funding strategy than the one observed in its industry sector (see Section B.3.5).

10.17. In accordance with the guidance established in Chapter I, the accurate delineation of the actual transaction should begin with a thorough identification of the economically relevant characteristics of the transaction – consisting of the commercial or financial relations between the parties and the conditions and economically relevant circumstances attaching to those relations –, including: an examination of the contractual terms of the transaction, the functions performed, assets used, and risks assumed, the characteristics of the financial instruments, the economic circumstances of the parties and of the market, and the business strategies pursued by the parties.

10.18. In common with the analysis of any other transaction between associated enterprises, in applying the arm's length principle to a financial transaction it is necessary to consider the conditions that independent parties would have agreed to in comparable circumstances.

10.19. Independent enterprises, when considering whether to enter into a particular financial transaction, will consider all other options realistically available to them, and will only enter into the transaction if they see no

3. See footnote in Section D.1.2.1 of Chapter I of these Guidelines.

alternative that offers a clearly more attractive opportunity to meet their commercial objectives (see paragraph 1.38 of Chapter I). In considering the options realistically available, the perspective of each of the parties to the transaction must be considered. For instance, in the case of an entity that advances funds, other investment opportunities may be contemplated, taking account of the specific business objectives of the lender and the context in which the transaction takes place. From the borrower's perspective, the options realistically available will include broader considerations than the entity's ability to service its debt, for example, the funds it actually needs to meet its operational requirements. In some instances, although an entity may have the capacity to borrow and service an additional amount of debt, it may choose not to do so to avoid placing negative pressure on its credit rating and increasing its cost of capital, and jeopardising its access to capital markets and its market reputation (see comments upon "The lender's and borrower's perspectives" in Section C.1.1.1 of this chapter).

10.20. In an ideal scenario, a comparability analysis would enable the identification of financial transactions between independent parties which match the tested transaction in all respects. With the many variables involved, it is more likely that potential comparables will differ from the tested transaction. Where differences exist between the tested transaction and any proposed comparable, it will be necessary to consider whether such differences will have a material impact on the price. If so, it may be possible, where appropriate, to make comparability adjustments to improve the reliability of a comparable. This is more likely to be achievable where the adjustment is based on a quantitative factor and there is good quality data easily available (e.g. on currency differences) than, for instance, in trying to compare loans to borrowers with qualitative differences or where data is not so readily available (e.g. borrowers with different business strategies).

B.3. The economically relevant characteristics of actual financial transactions

10.21. To inform an analysis of the terms and conditions of a financial transaction as part of the accurate delineation of the actual transaction or seeking to price the accurately delineated actual transaction, the following economically relevant characteristics should be considered.

B.3.1. Contractual terms

10.22. The terms and conditions of a financial transaction between independent enterprises are usually explicitly stated in a written agreement. However, between associated enterprises the contractual arrangements may not always provide information in sufficient detail or may be inconsistent with the actual conduct of the parties or other facts and circumstances. It is therefore necessary to look to other documents, the actual conduct of the parties – notwithstanding that such consideration may ultimately result in the conclusion that the contractual form and actual conduct are in alignment – and the economic principles that generally govern relationships between independent enterprises in comparable circumstances in order to accurately delineate the actual transaction in accordance with Section D.1.1 of Chapter I.

B.3.2. Functional analysis

10.23. In accurately delineating the actual financial transaction, a functional analysis is necessary. This analysis seeks to identify the functions performed, the assets used and the risks assumed by the parties to that controlled transaction.

10.24. For instance, in the particular case of an intra-group loan, the key functions performed by a lender to decide whether and under which terms to advance funds would typically include an analysis and evaluation of the risks inherent in the loan, the capability to commit capital of the business to the investment, determining the terms of the loan and organising and documenting the loan. This may also include any ongoing monitoring and periodic review of the loan. Such a functional analysis is likely to include consideration of similar information to that which a commercial lender or ratings agency would consider in determining the creditworthiness of the borrower. An associated lender will not necessarily perform all of the same functions at the same intensity as an independent lender. However, in considering whether a loan has been advanced on conditions which would have been made between independent enterprises, the same commercial considerations and economic circumstances are relevant (see comments on "The lender's and borrower's perspectives" and "Use of credit ratings" in Sections C.1.1.1 and C.1.1.2 of this chapter).

10.25. When, under accurate delineation, the lender is not exercising control over the risks associated to an advance of funds, or does not have the financial capacity to assume the risks, such risks should be allocated to the enterprise exercising control and having the financial capacity to assume the risk (see paragraph 1.98 of Chapter I). For instance, consider a situation where Company A advances funds to Company B. Consider further that the accurate delineation of the actual transaction indicates that Company A does not exercise control functions related to the advance of funds but that Company P, the parent company of the MNE group, is exercising control over those risks, and has the financial capacity to assume such risks. Under Chapter I analysis, Company P will bear the consequences of the playing out of such risks and Company A will be entitled to no more than a risk-free return (see Section D.1.2.1 in Chapter I).

10.26. From the perspective of the borrower, the relevant functions would usually refer to ensuring the availability of funds to repay the principal and the interest on the loan in due time; providing collateral, if needed; and monitoring and fulfilling any other obligation derived from the loan contract (see comments upon “The lender’s and borrower’s perspectives” in Section C.1.1.1 of this chapter).

10.27. In some instances, the functions of the lender and the borrower may be undertaken by the same entity in different transactions. That could be the case, for example, of centralised treasury activities within an MNE group where the treasury entity raises and provides funds to other members of the MNE group. In those circumstances, the functional analysis should consider the applicability of the guidance in Section C of this chapter, and, in particular, paragraphs 10.44 and 10.45.

B.3.3. Characteristics of financial instruments

10.28. There is a wide variety of financial instruments in the open market that present very different features and attributes, which may affect the pricing of those products or services. Consequently, when pricing controlled transactions, it is important to document the transactions’ features and attributes.

10.29. For instance in the case of a loan, those characteristics may include but are not limited to: the amount of the loan; its maturity; the schedule of repayment; the nature or purpose of the loan (trade credit, merger/acquisition, mortgage, etc.); level of seniority and subordination, geographical location of the borrower; currency; collateral provided; presence and quality of any guarantee; and whether the interest rate is fixed or floating.

B.3.4. Economic circumstances

10.30. To achieve comparability requires that the markets in which the independent and associated enterprises operate do not have differences that have a material effect on price or that appropriate adjustments can be made.

10.31. The prices of financial instruments may vary substantially on the basis of underlying economic circumstances, for example, across different currencies, geographic locations, local regulations, the business sector of the borrower and the timing of the transaction.

10.32. Macroeconomic trends such as central bank lending rates or interbank reference rates, and financial market events like a credit crisis, can affect prices. In this regard, the precise timing of the issue of a financial instrument in the primary market or the selection of comparable data in the secondary market can therefore be very significant in terms of comparability. For instance, it is not likely that multiple year data on loan issuances will provide useful comparables. The opposite is more likely to be true, i.e. that the closer in timing a comparable loan issuance is to the issuance of the tested transaction, the less the likelihood of different economic factors prevailing, notwithstanding that particular events can cause rapid changes in lending markets.

10.33. Currency differences are another potentially important factor. Economic factors such as growth rate, inflation rate, and the volatility of exchange rates, mean that otherwise similar financial instruments issued in different currencies may have different prices. Moreover, prices for financial instruments in the same currency may vary across financial markets or jurisdictions due to regulations such as interest rate controls, exchange rate controls, foreign exchange restrictions and other legal and practical restrictions on financial market access.

B.3.5. Business strategies

10.34. Business strategies must also be examined in accurately delineating the actual financial transaction and in determining comparability for transfer pricing purposes since different business strategies can have a significant effect on the terms and conditions which would be agreed between independent enterprises.

10.35. For example, independent lenders may be prepared to lend on terms and conditions to an enterprise undertaking a merger or acquisition which might otherwise not be acceptable to the lender for the same business if it were in a steady state. In this kind of scenario, the lender may take a view over the term of the loan and consider the borrower's business plans and forecasts, effectively acknowledging that there will be temporary changes in the financial metrics of the business for a period as it undergoes changes. Section D.1.5 of Chapter I gives other examples of business strategies that must be examined in accurately delineating the actual transaction and determining comparability.

10.36. The analysis of the business strategies will also include consideration of the MNE group's global financing policy, and the identification of existing relationships between the associated enterprises such as pre-existing loans and shareholder interests (see Annex I to Chapter V of these Guidelines about the information to be included in the master file).

10.37. For example, consider that Company A, a member of AB Group, advances funds with a term of 10 years to an associated enterprise, Company B, which will use the funding for short-term working capital purposes. This advance is the only loan in Company B's balance sheet. AB Group's policy and practices demonstrate that the MNE group uses a one-year revolving loan to manage short-term working capital. In this scenario, under the prevailing facts and circumstances, the accurate delineation of the actual transaction may conclude that an unrelated borrower under the same conditions of Company B would not enter into a 10-year loan agreement to manage its short-term working capital needs and the transaction would be accurately delineated as a one-year revolving loan rather than a 10-year loan. The consequences of this delineation would be that assuming the working capital requirements continue to exist, the pricing approach would be to price a series of refreshed one-year revolver loans.

10.38. In any case, the reliability of results is generally improved to the extent comparable borrowers pursue similar business strategies to the tested borrower involved in an intra-group transaction.

C. Treasury function

10.39. For MNE groups, the management of group finances is an important and potentially complex activity where the approach adopted by individual businesses will depend on the structure of the business itself, its business strategy, place in the business cycle, industry sector, currencies of operation, etc.

10.40. The organisation of the treasury will depend on the structure of a given MNE group and the complexity of its operations. Different treasury structures involve different degrees of centralisation. In the most decentralised form, each MNE within the MNE group has full autonomy over its financial transactions. Decentralised treasury structures may be present, for instance, in MNE groups with multiple operating divisions that operate in discrete industries or with regional hub structures, or in MNE groups required to comply with specific local regulations. At the opposite end of the scale, a centralised treasury has full control over the financial transactions of the MNE group, with entities within the MNE group responsible for operational but not financial matters.

10.41. A key function of a corporate treasury may be, for example, to optimise liquidity across the MNE group to ensure that the business has sufficient cash available and that it is in the right place when it is needed and in the right currency. In general, efficient management of MNE group liquidity is driven by considerations above the level of individual entities, and acts to help mitigate risk across a number of entities.

10.42. Whilst the treasury's cash and liquidity management function is concerned with day-to-day operations, corporate financial management is concerned with development of strategies and planning for investment decisions in the longer term. Financial risk management requires identification and analysis of, and responses to, the financial risks to which the business is exposed. By identifying and taking action to address financial risk, treasury can help to optimise the cost of capital to the advantage of the users of the MNE group's treasury services.

10.43. Other examples of activities which the treasury may have responsibility for include raising debt (through bond issuances, bank loans or otherwise) and raising equity, and managing the relationship with the MNE group's external bankers and with independent credit rating agencies.

10.44. When evaluating the transfer pricing issues related to treasury activities, as with any case, it is important to accurately delineate the actual transactions and determine exactly what functions an entity is carrying on rather than to rely to any extent upon a general description such as "treasury activities".

10.45. Generally, the treasury function is part of the process of making the financing of the commercial business of the MNE group as efficient as possible. As such, the treasury function will usually be a support service to the main value-creating operation as in the case, for example, of the services provided by a cash pool leader (see Section C.2.3). Depending on the facts and circumstances of each case, such activities may be services in which case the pricing guidance on intra-group services at Chapter VII applies.

10.46. Similarly, the treasury may act as the contact point to centralise the external borrowing of the MNE group. External funds would then be made available within the MNE group through intra-group lending provided by the treasury. On prevailing facts and circumstances, guidance in paragraph 1.188 of Chapter I would apply to these situations and the treasury would be expected to receive an arm's length fee for its coordination activities.

10.47. In other situations, the treasury may be found to perform more complex functions and, therefore, it should be compensated accordingly.

10.48. Another key concern regarding treasury activities is the identification and allocation of the economically significant risks in accordance with Chapter I.

10.49. The activities of the treasury function take into account issues at a group level and follow the vision, strategy and policies set out by MNE group management. Accordingly, the approach of the treasury to risk will depend on the MNE group's policy where certain objectives may be specified, such as targeted levels of investment return (e.g. the yield must exceed the cost of capital), reduced cash flow volatility, or targeted balance sheet ratios (e.g. assets to liabilities). Therefore, it is important to note that usually the higher strategic decisions will generally be the result of policy set at group level rather than determined by the treasury itself.

10.50. The following sections outline the transfer pricing considerations which arise from some relevant treasury activities that are often performed within MNE groups, i.e. the provision of intra-group loans, cash pooling, and hedging activities.

Caveat

The following sections deal with specific issues related to determining whether the rate of interest provided for in a loan contract is an arm's length rate. The analysis included in these sections is based on the assumption that the transactions are respected as loans pursuant to an accurate delineation under Chapter I or domestic legislation, as the case may be.

C.1. Intra-group loans

C.1.1. General considerations

C.1.1.1. The lender's and borrower's perspectives

10.51. In considering the commercial and financial relations between the associated borrower and lender, and in an analysis of the economically relevant characteristics of the transaction, both the lender's and borrower's perspectives should be taken into account, acknowledging that these perspectives may not align in every case.

10.52. As in any other transfer pricing scenarios, the guidance in Section D.1 of Chapter I applies to determine whether the lender and the borrower assume risks related to intra-group loans. In particular, it is important to consider the risks that the funding arrangements carry for the party providing the funds, and the risks related to the acceptance and use of the funds from the perspective of the recipient. These risks will relate to repayment of the amount transferred, compensation expected for the use of that amount over time, and compensation for other associated risk factors.

10.53. The lender's perspective in the decision of whether to make a loan, how much to lend, and on what terms, will involve evaluation of various factors relating to the borrower, wider economic factors affecting both the borrower and the lender, and other options realistically available to the lender for the use of the funds.

10.54. An independent lender will carry out a thorough credit assessment of the potential borrower to enable the lender to identify and evaluate the risks involved and to consider methods of monitoring and managing these risks. That credit assessment will include understanding the business itself as well as the purpose of the loan, how it is to be structured and the source of its repayment which may include analysis of the borrower's cash flow forecasts and the strength of the borrower's balance sheet.

10.55. When an enterprise is making a loan to an associated enterprise, it will not necessarily follow all of the same processes as an independent lender. For example, it may not need to go through the same process of information gathering about the borrower's business, as the required information may already be readily available within the MNE group. However, in considering whether the loan has been made on conditions which would have been made between independent enterprises, the same commercial considerations such as creditworthiness, credit risk and economic circumstances are relevant.

10.56. In the case of a loan from the parent entity of an MNE group to a subsidiary, the parent already has control and ownership of the subsidiary, which would make the granting of security less relevant to its risk analysis as a lender. Therefore, in evaluating the pricing of a loan between associated enterprises it is important to consider that the absence of contractual rights over the assets of the borrowing entity does not necessarily reflect the economic reality of the risk inherent in the loan. If the assets of the business are not already pledged as security elsewhere, it will be appropriate to consider under Chapter I analysis whether those assets are available to act as collateral for the otherwise unsecured loan and the consequential impact upon the pricing of the loan.

10.57. Credit risk for the lender is the potential that the borrower will fail to meet its payment obligations in accordance with the terms of the loan. In deciding whether a prospective loan is a good commercial opportunity, a lender will also consider the potential impact of changes which could happen in economic conditions affecting the credit risk it bears, not only in relation to the conditions of the borrower but in relation to potential changes in economic conditions, such as a rise in interest rates, or the exposure of the borrower to movements in exchange rates.

10.58. Borrowers seek to optimise their weighted average cost of capital and to have the right funding available to meet both short-term needs and long-term objectives. When considering the options realistically available to it, an independent business seeking funding operating in its own commercial interests will seek the most cost effective solution, with regard to the business strategy it has adopted. For example in respect of collateral, in some circumstances, assuming that the business has suitable collateral to offer, this would usually be secured funding, ahead of unsecured funding, recognising that a business's collateral assets and its funding requirements may differ over time, e.g. because collateral is finite, the decision to pledge collateral on a particular borrowing precludes the borrower from pledging that same collateral on a subsequent borrowing. Therefore, an MNE pledging collateral would take into account its options realistically available regarding its overall financing (e.g. possible subsequent loan transactions).

10.59. Borrowers will also consider the potential impact of changes in economic conditions such as interest rates and exchange rates, as well as the risk of not being able to make timely payments of interest and principal on the loan if the borrower's business encounters unexpected difficulties, and the risk of not being able to raise more capital (either debt or equity) if necessary.

10.60. Macroeconomic circumstances may lead to changes in the financing costs in the market. In such a context, a transfer pricing analysis with regard to the possibilities of the borrower or the lender to renegotiate the terms of the loan to benefit from better conditions will be informed by the options realistically available to both the borrower and the lender.

10.61. The economic conditions of loans should also be viewed in the context of regulations that may affect the position of the parties. For example, insolvency law in the jurisdiction of the borrower may provide that liabilities towards associated enterprises are subordinated to liabilities towards unrelated parties.

C.1.1.2. Use of credit ratings

10.62. The creditworthiness of the borrower is one of the main factors that independent investors take into account in determining an interest rate to charge. Credit ratings can serve as a useful measure of creditworthiness and therefore help to identify potential comparables or to apply economic models in the context of related party transactions. Furthermore, in the case of intra-group loans and other financial instruments that are the subject of controlled transactions, the effect of group membership may be an economically relevant factor that affects the pricing of these instruments. Accordingly, this subsection elaborates on the use of credit ratings and the effect of group membership in the context of pricing intra-group loans. Where appropriate, reference to this subsection will be made in other parts of this guidance.

10.63. Credit ratings can be determined for the overall creditworthiness of an MNE or MNE group[4] or for a specific issuance of debt. As detailed in the following paragraphs, determining credit ratings requires consideration of quantitative – e.g. financial information – and qualitative factors – e.g. industry and jurisdiction in which the MNE or MNE group operates.

C.1.1.2.1. The credit rating of an MNE or MNE group

10.64. The credit rating of an MNE or MNE group (usually referred to as the "issuer credit rating") is an opinion about its general creditworthiness. Such an opinion is usually premised on the MNE or MNE group's capacity and willingness to meet its financial obligations in accordance with the terms of those obligations. The credit rating of an MNE or MNE group is effectively a form of relative ranking of the creditworthiness in comparison

4. For the purpose of this guidance, the credit rating of an MNE group is intended to refer to the credit rating of the ultimate parent entity of the MNE group calculated on consolidated financial statements.

to other borrowers. In general, a lower credit rating will indicate a greater risk of default and be expected to result in a higher rate of return for lenders.

10.65. Information is readily available in many lending markets on the different rates of interest charged for differently rated enterprises and such information may usefully contribute to performing comparability analyses. Financing transactions that the borrowing MNE or another MNE within the group has with external lenders may also be reliable comparables for interest rates charged by associated enterprises (see paragraphs 10.94 and 10.95). Financing transactions undertaken by the borrowing MNE or another entity in the MNE group, for example the MNE group parent, will be reliable comparables only where the differences between the controlled and uncontrolled transactions do not materially affect the interest rate or reasonably accurate adjustments can be made.

10.66. As a credit rating depends on a combination of quantitative and qualitative factors, there is still likely to be some variance in creditworthiness between borrowers with the same credit rating. In addition, when making comparisons between borrowers using the kind of financial metrics typically seen as important to lenders, such as debt-earnings or debt-equity ratios, it is important to note that the same financial metrics will not necessarily result in the same credit rating if there are other differences between the rated parties. For example, it may require stronger financial metrics to obtain a given rating in some industries than to obtain the same rating for a borrower in other industries. More intrinsically risky industries and those with less stable revenue streams tend to require better financial ratios in order to obtain the same rating.

10.67. There may be special circumstances, such as in the case of start-up entities, or those that have recently been part of a merger, that may have an impact on the credit rating of a group entity. These special situations should be taken into consideration.

10.68. It is important that the MNE group appropriately documents the reasons and selection of the credit rating used for a particular MNE when pricing intra-group loans and other controlled financial transactions.

C.1.1.2.2. The credit rating of a specific debt issuance

10.69. The credit rating of a particular debt issuance ("issue rating") is an opinion about the creditworthiness of the issuer with respect to a specific financial instrument. The issue rating considers specific features of the financial instrument, for instance, guarantees, securities and level of seniority.

10.70. The credit rating of an MNE or MNE group may differ from an issue rating due to the fact that the credit risk of a financial instrument is linked to its specific features and not only to the risk profile of the borrowing MNE.

On prevailing facts and circumstances, and provided there is comparability between the third party debt issuance and the controlled transaction, when both an issuer and issue ratings are available, the issue rating of the particular debt issuance would be more appropriate to use to price the controlled financial transaction.

C.1.1.2.3. Credit rating determinations

10.71. Particular considerations should be borne in mind when determining a credit rating for a specific MNE within an MNE group for the purpose of assessing controlled transactions. Where an MNE has a publicly available credit rating published by an independent credit rating agency, that rating may be informative for an arm's length analysis of the MNE's controlled financing transactions. However, in most cases, publicly available credit ratings are only available for the MNE group. An approach often used for a specific MNE is to apply quantitative and qualitative analyses of the individual characteristics of the MNE using publicly available financial tools or independent credit rating agencies' methodologies to seek to replicate the process used to determine the credit rating of the MNE group. This approach also involves taking into account improvements in creditworthiness that the specific MNE would be assumed to receive as a result of being part of the MNE group.

C.1.1.2.4. The use of publicly available financial tools or methodologies to approximate credit ratings

10.72. Publicly available financial tools are designed to calculate credit ratings. Broadly, these tools depend on approaches such as calculating the probability of default and of the likely loss should default occur to arrive at an implied rating for the borrowing. This can then be compared to a market database in a search for comparables to arrive at a price or price range for the borrowing. In considering whether the application of these tools results in a reliable assessment of the credit rating of controlled transactions, potential issues that need to be borne in mind include that the results are not based on a direct comparison with transactions between independent parties but are subject to the accuracy of the input parameters, a tendency to rely more on quantitative inputs at the expense of qualitative factors, and a lack of clarity in the processes (i.e. the workings of the underlying algorithms and processes may not be transparent).

10.73. The credit rating methodology used in publicly available financial tools may differ significantly in certain respects from the credit rating methodologies applied by independent credit rating agencies to determine official credit ratings and the impact of any such differences should be carefully considered. For instance, publicly available tools generally use only a limited sample of quantitative data to determine a credit rating. Official credit ratings published by independent credit rating agencies are derived as a result of far more rigorous analysis that includes quantitative analysis of historic and forecast entity performance as well as detailed qualitative analysis of, for instance, management's ability to manage the entity, industry specific features and the entity's market share in its industry.

10.74. For these reasons, the reliability of credit rating results derived from the use of publicly available financial tools may be improved to the extent the analysis can reproducibly demonstrate consistency of ratings using such tools with those provided by independent credit rating agencies.

10.75. In conducting a credit rating analysis, it is important to note that the financial metrics may be influenced by current and past controlled transactions (such as sales, or interest expenses). If it appears that such controlled transactions are not in accordance with the arm's length principle, the credit rating derived in light of such intra-group transactions may not be reliable. (See also guidance in Section B). These considerations apply both to controlled transactions that may affect the current earnings of the MNE and to previous funding and other intra-group transactions that may have had an impact on the measures of income and capital of the MNE that are the subject of quantitative analysis.

C.1.1.3. Effect of group membership

10.76. The effect of group membership is relevant for informing the conditions under which an MNE would have borrowed from an independent lender at arm's length in two ways in particular. Firstly, the external funding policies and practices of group management will assist in informing the form and terms and conditions of the debt the MNE would have entered into with an independent lender, including the pricing (i.e. interest rate paid), and all economically relevant characteristics such as the type of loan, its term, currency, security, covenants, business strategies, and so forth. Secondly, the MNE may receive support from the group to meet its financial obligations in the event of the borrower getting into financial difficulty. Paragraph 1.178 of Chapter I of these Guidelines is relevant to analyse the effect of group membership on the terms and conditions of a borrowing when the borrowing MNE obtains an incidental benefit arising solely by virtue of group affiliation, i.e. passive association.

10.77. In the context of intra-group loans, this incidental benefit that the MNE is assumed to receive solely by virtue of group affiliation, is referred to as implicit support. The effect of potential group support on the credit rating of an entity and any effect on that entity's ability to borrow or the interest rate paid on those borrowings would not require any payment or comparability adjustment. See Example 1 in paragraphs 1.184-1.186 of Chapter I and Section D.3.

10.78. Implicit support from the group may affect the credit rating of the borrower or the rating of any debt which it issues. The relative status of an entity within the group may help determine what impact that potential group support has on the credit rating of a debt issuer. Entities of an MNE group will be more or less likely to receive group support according to the relative importance of the entity to the MNE group as a whole and the linkages between the entity and the rest of the MNE group, either in its current form or in terms of future strategy. An MNE group member with stronger links, that is integral to the group's identity or important to its future strategy, typically operating in the group's core business, would ordinarily be more likely to be supported by other MNE group members and consequently have a credit rating more closely linked to that of the MNE group. Conversely, it may be reasonable to assume that an entity would be likely to receive support from the rest of the MNE group in more limited circumstances where it does not show those same indicators or the linkages are weaker. In the case of an entity where there is evidence that no support would be provided by the MNE group, it may be appropriate on the prevailing facts and circumstances to consider the entity on the basis of its own stand-alone credit rating only.

10.79. Another key consideration would be the likely consequences for other parts of the MNE group of supporting or not supporting the borrower. The criteria used to determine the status of an entity in this regard may include such considerations as legal obligations (e.g. regulatory requirements), strategic importance, operational integration and significance, shared name, potential reputational impacts, negative effects on the overall MNE group, general statement of policy or intent, and any history of support and common behaviour of the MNE group with respect to third parties. The relative relevance of those factors may vary from one industry to another.

10.80. The impact of an assessment of implicit support is a matter of judgement. The kind of information on which the MNE group would base a decision of whether or not to provide support to a borrower in particular circumstances may not be available to a tax administration, as is frequently the case in transfer pricing examinations, and the existence of information asymmetry may affect the ability of tax administrations to establish the likelihood of support (see Section B.2 in Chapter IV). Furthermore, changing facts and circumstances affecting the willingness or ability of the MNE group to provide support may mean that there is no decision by the MNE group itself until the eventuality for such support arises. This contrasts, for example, where the MNE receives a formal guarantee from another group member. The past behaviour of an MNE group as regards providing support may be a useful indicator of likely future behaviour but an appropriate analysis should be undertaken to identify whether different conditions apply.

C.1.1.4. Use of MNE group credit rating

10.81. It is also important to note that although there are established approaches to estimate a credit rating for a particular group member or debt issuance, the considerations detailed above mean that a pricing approach based on the separate entity credit ratings that are derived from publicly available financial tools (see paragraph 10.72), the implicit support analysis, the difficulties of accounting for controlled transactions reliably and the presence of information asymmetry may pose challenges that, if not resolved, may result in outcomes that are not reliable.

10.82. Where this is the case, the credit rating of the MNE group may also be used for the purpose of pricing the accurately delineated loan where the facts so indicate, particularly in situations such as where the MNE is important to the group as described in paragraphs 10.78 and 10.79 and where the MNE's indicators of creditworthiness do not differ significantly from those of the group. An MNE group credit rating is unaffected by controlled transactions and reflects the actual basis on which the group seeks external funding from independent lenders. In situations where an MNE group does not have an external credit rating, consideration may be given to conducting the credit rating analysis at the MNE group level for assessing the controlled transaction. In all cases, the MNE group credit rating, like any other credit rating, will be appropriate only if it is determined to be the most reliable indicator of the MNE credit rating in light of all the facts and circumstances.

C.1.1.5. Covenants

10.83. The purpose of covenants in a loan agreement is generally to provide a degree of protection to the lender and so limit its risk. That protection may be in the form of incurrence covenants or maintenance covenants.

10.84. Incurrence covenants require or prohibit certain actions by the borrower without the consent of the lender. Incurrence covenants may, for example, prohibit the borrower from taking on additional debt, creating any charge on the assets of the entity or disposing of particular assets of the entity, thus giving some degree of certainty over the balance sheet of the borrower.

10.85. Maintenance covenants refer typically to financial indicators which have to be met at regular, predetermined intervals during the life of a covenanted loan. Maintenance covenants can act as an early warning system so that in the event of financial underperformance by the borrower, the borrower and/or lender can move to take remedial action at an early stage. This can help to protect unrelated lenders against information asymmetry.

10.86. There may be less information asymmetry between entities (that is, better visibility) in the intra-group context than in situations involving unrelated parties. Intra-group lenders may choose not to have covenants on loans to associated enterprises, partly because they are less likely to suffer information asymmetry and because it is less likely that one part of an MNE group would seek to take the same kind of action as an independent lender in the event of a covenant breach, nor would it usually seek to impose the same kind of restrictions. Where there is an absence of covenants in any written agreement between the parties, it will be appropriate to consider under Chapter I guidance whether there is, in practice, the equivalent of a maintenance covenant between the parties and the consequential impact upon the pricing of the loan.

C.1.1.6. Guarantees

10.87. A guarantee from another party may be used to support the borrower's credit. A lender placing reliance on a guarantee or guarantees would need to evaluate the guarantor(s) in a similar way to that in which it evaluates the original borrower. For the lender to take a guarantee into account in setting or adjusting the terms and conditions of a loan, it would need to be reasonably satisfied that the guarantor(s) would be able to meet any shortfall resulting from the borrower being unable to meet its obligations in full in the event of a default. Guarantees are discussed in more detail in Section D.

C.1.2. Determining the arm's length interest rate of intra-group loans

10.88. The following paragraphs present different approaches to pricing intra-group loans. As in any other transfer pricing situation, the selection of the most appropriate method should be consistent with the actual transaction as accurately delineated, in particular, through a functional analysis (see Chapter II).

C.1.2.1. Comparable uncontrolled price method (CUP method)

10.89. Once the actual transaction has been accurately delineated, arm's length interest rates can be sought based on consideration of the credit rating of the borrower or the rating of the specific issuance taking into account all of the terms and conditions of the loan and comparability factors.

10.90. The widespread existence of markets for borrowing and lending money and the frequency of such transactions between independent borrowers and lenders, coupled with the widespread availability of information and analysis of loan markets may make it easier to apply the CUP method to financial transactions than may be the case for other types of transactions. Information available often includes details on the characteristics of the loan and the credit rating of the borrower or the rating of the specific issuance. Characteristics which will usually increase the risk for the lender, such as long maturity dates, absence of security, subordination, or application of the loan to a risky project, will tend to increase the interest rate. Characteristics which limit the lender's risk, such as strong collateral, a high quality guarantee, or restrictions on future behaviour of the borrower, will tend to result in a lower interest rate.

10.91. The arm's length interest rate for a tested loan can be benchmarked against publicly available data for other borrowers with the same credit rating for loans with sufficiently similar terms and conditions and other comparability factors. With the extent of competition often present within lending markets, it might be expected that, given the characteristics of the loan (amount, maturity, currency, etc.) and the credit rating of the borrower or the rating of the specific issuance (see Section C.1.1.2.), there would be a single rate at which the borrower could obtain funds and a single rate at which a lender could invest funds to obtain an appropriate reward. In practice, however, there is unlikely to be a single "market rate" but a range of rates although competition between lenders and the availability of pricing information will tend to narrow the range.

10.92. In the search for comparability data, a comparable is not necessarily restricted to a stand-alone entity. In examining commercial loans, where the potentially comparable borrower is a member of an MNE group and has borrowed from an independent lender, provided all other economically relevant conditions are sufficiently similar, a loan to a member of a different MNE group or between members of different MNE groups could be a valid comparable.

10.93. Arm's length interest rates can also be based on the return of realistic alternative transactions with comparable economic characteristics. Depending on the facts and circumstances, realistic alternatives to intra-group loans could be, for instance, bond issuances, loans which are uncontrolled transactions, deposits, convertible debentures, commercial papers, etc. In the evaluation of those alternatives as potential comparables it is important to bear in mind that, based on facts and circumstances, comparability adjustments may be required to eliminate the material effects of differences between the controlled intra-group loan and the selected alternative in terms of, for instance, liquidity, maturity, existence of collateral or currency.

10.94. When considering issues of comparability, the possibility of internal CUPs should not be overlooked.

10.95. Whereas it is unlikely that an MNE group's average interest rate paid on its external debt meets the comparability requirements to be considered as an internal CUP, it may be possible to identify potential comparable loans within the borrower's or its MNE group's financing with an independent lender as the counterparty. As with external CUPs, it may be necessary to make appropriate adjustments to improve comparability. See Example 1 at 1.164-1.166.

C.1.2.2. Loan fees and charges

10.96. In considering arm's length pricing of loans, the issue of fees and charges in relation to the loan may arise. Independent commercial lenders will sometimes charge fees as part of the terms and conditions of the loan, for example arrangement fees or commitment fees in relation to an undrawn facility. If such charges are seen in a loan between associated enterprises, they should be evaluated in the same way as any other intra-group transaction. In doing so, it must be borne in mind that independent lenders' charges will in part reflect costs incurred in the process of raising capital and in satisfying regulatory requirements, which associated enterprises might not incur.

C.1.2.3. Cost of funds

10.97. In the absence of comparable uncontrolled transactions, the cost of funds approach could be used as an alternative to price intra-group loans in some circumstances. The cost of funds will reflect the borrowing costs incurred by the lender in raising the funds to lend. To this would be added the expenses of arranging the loan and the relevant costs incurred in servicing the loan, a risk premium to reflect the various economic factors inherent in the proposed loan, plus a profit margin, which will generally include the lender's incremental cost of the equity required to support the loan.

10.98. One consideration to be kept in mind with the cost of funds approach is that it should be applied by considering the lender's cost of funds relative to other lenders operating in the market. The cost of funds can vary between different prospective lenders, so the lender cannot simply charge based on its cost of funds, particularly if there is a potential competitor who can obtain funds more cheaply. A lender in a competitive market may seek to price at the lowest possible rate in order to win business. In the commercial environment, this will mean that lenders drive operating costs as low as possible and seek to minimise the cost of obtaining funds to lend.

10.99. The application of the cost of funds approach requires consideration of the options realistically available to the borrower. On prevailing facts and circumstances, a borrowing MNE would not enter into a transaction priced under the cost of funds approach if it could obtain the funding under better conditions by entering into an alternative transaction.

10.100. In some intra-group transactions, the cost of funds approach may be used to price loans where capital is borrowed from an unrelated party which passes from the original borrower through one or more associated intermediary enterprises, as a series of loans, until it reaches the ultimate borrower. In such cases, where only agency or intermediary functions are being performed, as noted in paragraph 7.34, "it may not be appropriate to determine the arm's length pricing as a mark-up on the costs of the services but rather on the costs of the agency function itself."

C.1.2.4. Credit default swaps

10.101. Credit default swaps reflect the credit risk linked to an underlying financial asset. In the absence of information regarding the underlying asset that could be used as a comparable transaction, taxpayers and tax administrations may use the spreads of credit default swaps to calculate the risk premium associated to intra-group loans.

10.102. As financial instruments traded in the market, credit default swaps may be subject to a high degree of volatility. This volatility may affect the reliability of credit default swaps as proxies to measure the credit risk associated to a particular investment in isolation, since the credit default spreads may reflect not only the risk of default but also other non-related factors such as the liquidity of the credit default swaps contracts or the volume of contracts negotiated. Those circumstances could lead to situations where, for instance, the same instrument may have different credit default swaps spreads.

10.103. Accordingly, the use of credit default swaps to approximate the risk premium associated to intra-group loans will require careful consideration of the above-mentioned circumstances to arrive at an arm's length interest rate.

C.1.2.5. Economic modelling

10.104. Certain industries rely on economic models to price intra-group loans by constructing an interest rate as a proxy to an arm's length interest rate.

10.105. In their most common variation, economic models calculate an interest rate through a combination of a risk-free interest rate and a number of premiums associated with different aspects of the loan – e.g. default risk, liquidity risk, expected inflation or maturity. In some instances, economic models would also include elements to compensate the lender's operational expenses.

10.106. The reliability of economic models' outcomes depends upon the parameters factored into the specific model and the underlying assumptions adopted. In evaluating the reliability of economic models as an approach to pricing intra-group loans it is important to note that economic models' outcomes do not represent actual transactions between independent parties and that, therefore, comparability adjustments would be likely required. However, in situations where reliable comparable uncontrolled transactions cannot be identified, economic models may represent tools that can be usefully applied in identifying an arm's length price for intra-group loans, subject to the same constraints regarding market conditions discussed in paragraph 10.98.

C.1.2.6. Bank opinions

10.107. In some circumstances taxpayers may seek to evidence the arm's length rate of interest on an intra-group loan by producing written opinions from independent banks, sometimes referred to as a "bankability" opinion, stating what interest rate the bank would apply were it to make a comparable loan to that particular enterprise.

10.108. Such an approach would represent a departure from an arm's length approach based on comparability since it is not based on comparison of actual transactions. Furthermore, it is also important to bear in mind the fact that such letters do not constitute an actual offer to lend. Before proceeding to make a loan, a commercial lender will undertake the relevant due diligence and approval processes that would precede a formal loan offer. Such letters would not therefore generally be regarded as providing evidence of arm's length terms and conditions.

C.2. Cash pooling

C.2.1. Cash pooling structures

10.109. The use of a cash pool is popular among multinational enterprises as a way of achieving more efficient cash management by bringing together, either physically or notionally, the balances on a number of separate bank accounts. Depending on the particular arrangements in place, a cash pool can help to achieve more effective liquidity management, whereby reliance on external borrowing can be reduced or, where there is a cash surplus, an enhanced return may be earned on any aggregated cash balance. Financing costs may also be reduced by eliminating the bank spread embedded in the interest which would be payable or receivable on a number of separate debit or credit account balances and by reducing banking transaction costs.

10.110. In the context of this section, cash pooling is the pooling of cash balances as part of a short-term liquidity management arrangement. Cash pool arrangements are complex contracts which may involve controlled and uncontrolled transactions. For instance, one common structure is that the participating members of the MNE group conclude a contract with an unrelated bank that renders cash pooling services, and each participating member opens a bank account with that bank.

10.111. Although there are two basic types of cash pooling arrangements – physical and notional – other variations and combinations may be arranged to meet specific business needs. For example, a number of physical pools might be held, one for each currency in which the business operates, along with a notional pool which then combines those individual currency pools.

C.2.1.1. Physical pooling

10.112. In a typical physical pooling arrangement, the bank account balances of all the pool members are transferred daily to a single central bank account owned by the cash pool leader. Any account in deficit is brought to a target balance (usually zero) by a transfer from the master account to the relevant sub account. Depending on whether there is a surplus or a deficit after the members' accounts have been adjusted to the target balance, the cash pool leader may borrow from the bank to meet the net funding requirement of the pool or deposit any surplus as appropriate.

C.2.1.2. Notional pooling

10.113. In a notional cash pool, some of the benefits of combining credit and debit balances of several accounts are achieved without any physical transfer of balances between the participating members' accounts although the bank will usually require cross-guarantees from pool participants to enable the right to set off between accounts if necessary. The bank notionally aggregates the various balances of the individual accounts of participating members and pays or charges interest according to the net balance, either to a designated master account or to all participating accounts under a formula determined in the cash pooling agreement.

10.114. With no physical transfers of funds, the transactional costs of operating a notional pool are likely to be less than transactional costs of operating a physical pool. Functions carried out by the bank would be accounted for in the charges or interest rate of the bank. With minimal functions carried out by the pool leader (because functions are primarily performed by the bank), there will be little, if any, value added by the pool leader to be reflected in the intra-group pricing. An appropriate allocation of the benefit created as a result of the elimination of the bank spread and/or the optimisation of a single debit or credit position would need to consider the contribution or burden of each pool participant.

C.2.2. Accurate delineation of cash pooling transactions

10.115. The accurate delineation of the cash pooling transactions will depend on the particular facts and circumstances of each case. As cash pooling is not undertaken regularly, if at all, by independent enterprises, the application of transfer pricing principles requires careful consideration. As paragraph 1.11 notes "Where independent enterprises seldom undertake transactions of the type entered into by associated enterprises, the arm's length principle can be difficult to apply because there is little or no direct evidence of what conditions would have been established by independent enterprises."

10.116. The accurate delineation of cash pooling arrangements would need to take into account not only the facts and circumstances of the balances transferred but the wider context of the conditions of the pooling arrangement as a whole. For example, a cash pool is likely to differ from a straightforward overnight deposit with a bank or similar financial institution in that a cash pool member with a credit position is not depositing money as a transaction in isolation with a view to a simple depositor return.

10.117. The cash pool member is likely to be participating in providing liquidity as part of a broader group strategy, an arrangement in which the member can have a credit or debit position, which may include among its aims a range of benefits that can only be achieved as part of a collective strategy involving the pool members, done for the benefit of all of the pool participants, and the membership of which is limited to entities within the MNE group. Pool participants deposit cash to the pool (or withdraw cash from the pool), and not to (or from) a particular cash pool member.

10.118. No member of the pooling arrangement would expect to participate in the transaction if it made them any worse off than their next best option. The analysis of an MNE's decision to participate in a cash pool arrangement should be done with reference to its options realistically available, taking into account that an MNE can obtain benefits as a member of the cash pool other than an improved interest rate (see paragraph 10.146).

10.119. In delineating the cash pool transactions, it may be that the savings and efficiencies achieved are determined to arise as a result of group synergies created through deliberate concerted action (as discussed in Section D.8 of Chapter I).

10.120. As indicated in paragraph 1.179, the determination of the results that arise from deliberate concerted group actions must be established through a thorough functional analysis. Accordingly, in the context of cash pooling arrangements, it is necessary to determine (i) the nature of the advantage or disadvantage, (ii) the amount of the benefit or detriment provided, and (iii) how that benefit or detriment should be divided among members of the MNE group.

10.121. An advantage of a cash pooling arrangement may be the reduction of interest paid or the increase of interest received, which results from netting credit and debit balances. The amount of that group synergy benefit, calculated by reference to the results that the cash pool members would have obtained had they dealt solely with independent enterprises, would generally be shared by the cash pool members, provided that an appropriate reward is allocated to the cash pool leader for the functions it provides in accordance with Section C.2.3. of this chapter.

10.122. Another key consideration in analysing intra-group funding arrangements which might be described as cash pooling are situations where members of an MNE group maintain debit and credit positions which, rather than functioning as part of a short-term liquidity arrangement, become more long term. It would usually be appropriate to consider whether, on accurate delineation, it would be correct to treat them as something other than a short-term cash pool balance, such as a longer term deposit or a term loan.

10.123. One of the practical difficulties in such situations will be deciding how long a balance should be treated as part of the cash pool before it could potentially be treated as something else, for example a term loan. As cash pooling is intended to be a short-term, liquidity-driven arrangement, it may be appropriate to consider whether the same pattern is present year after year and to examine what policies the MNE group's financial management has in place, given that yield on cash balances is a key financial management issue.

10.124. A potential difficulty for tax administrations in analysing cash pooling arrangements is that the various entities in a cash pool may be resident across a number of jurisdictions, potentially making it difficult to access sufficient information to verify the position as set out by the taxpayer. It would be of assistance to tax authorities if MNE groups would provide information on the structuring of the pool and the returns to the cash pool leader and the members in the cash pool as part of their transfer pricing documentation. (See Annex I to Chapter V of these Guidelines about the information to be included in the master file).

10.125. Before any attempt is made to determine the remuneration of the cash pool leader and participants, it is central to the transfer pricing analysis to identify and examine under Chapter I guidance the economically significant risks associated to the cash pooling arrangement. These could include liquidity risk and credit risk. These risks should be analysed taking into account the short-term nature of the credit and debit positions within the cash pooling arrangement (see paragraph 10.123).

10.126. Liquidity risk in a cash pool arrangement arises from the mismatch between the maturity of the credit and debit balances of the cash pool members. Assuming the liquidity risk associated to a cash pool requires the exercise of control functions beyond the mere offsetting of the credit and debit positions of the cash pool members. Therefore, an analysis of the decision-making process related to the amounts of the debit and credit positions within the cash pool arrangement will be required to allocate the liquidity risk under Chapter I.

10.127. Credit risk refers to the risk of loss resulting from the inability of cash pool members with debit positions to repay their cash withdrawals. From the cash pool leader's perspective, there needs to be a probability for it to incur losses derived from the default of cash pool members with debit positions to bear the credit risk. Therefore, an examination under Chapter I guidance will be required to determine, under the specific facts and circumstances, which entity within the MNE group is exercising control functions and has the financial capacity to assume the credit risk associated with the cash pool arrangement.

C.2.3. Determining the arm's length price of cash pooling transactions

10.128. As with many types of financial transactions, different intent and understanding can be ascribed to the labels or descriptions attached to particular transactions. Each case must be considered on its own facts and circumstances and in each case accurate delineation of the actual transactions in accordance with the principles of Chapter I will be needed before any attempt to decide on an approach to pricing a transaction.

C.2.3.1. Rewarding the cash pool leader function

10.129. The appropriate reward of the cash pool leader will depend on the facts and circumstances, the functions performed, the assets used and the risks assumed in facilitating a cash pooling arrangement.

10.130. In general, a cash pool leader performs no more than a co-ordination or agency function with the master account being a centralised point for a series of book entries to meet the pre-determined target balances for the pool members. Given such a low level of functionality, the cash pool leader's remuneration as a service provider will generally be similarly limited.

10.131. Where accurate delineation of the actual transactions determines that a cash pool leader is carrying on activities other than co-ordination or agency functions, the pricing of such transactions would follow the approaches included in other parts of this guidance, as appropriate.

10.132. The following examples illustrate the principles described above.

Example 1

10.133. X is the parent entity of an MNE group which has subsidiaries H, J, K, and L which participate in a physical cash pooling arrangement with fellow subsidiary M acting as cash pool leader. All participants have the same functional currency and that is the only currency in the pool.

10.134. M sets up an intra-group cash pooling arrangement with an unrelated bank. Legal arrangements are put in place for all participants which allow transfers to or from M's cash concentration account to meet a specified target balance for each pool participant.

10.135. Under the cash management services agreement the bank makes any transfers necessary to meet the target balance for each pool participant with any net surplus deposited by M or any net overdrawn position being met by the bank lending to M. The facility that M may draw on is guaranteed by X. The third-party bank pays interest to, or receives interest from M based on the overall, pooled, position. In this instance, M receives surplus funds from MNE group members H and J and provides funds to MNE group members K and L which have a funding need. Interest on the balances of the pool participants is charged or paid in accordance with the pooling agreements.

10.136. As a result of the arrangements in place, M pays less interest to the bank or receives more interest than would have been the case absent the pooling arrangements.

10.137. A functional analysis shows that M is not subject to credit risk, which remains with the cash pool members, but merely performs a co-ordination function. Furthermore M is not performing the functions or assuming the risks that a bank would. Therefore M would not earn the kind of reward that a bank would earn such as retaining the interest spread between deposits and loans. Accordingly, M would earn a reward commensurate with the service functions it provides to the pool.

Example 2

10.138. Company T, a member of MNE Group Y, performs as the MNE group treasury entity and undertakes a range of different financial transactions both intra-group and externally. Company T's main purpose is to provide treasury services to the other entities within the MNE group including strategy and management of group liquidity. T is responsible for raising finance across the MNE group by issuing bonds or borrowing from third party banks and arranges intra-group loans to meet the funding needs of other group members as necessary.

10.139. As part of the group liquidity arrangements, T operates an MNE group cash pooling arrangement and is responsible for deciding how to invest surplus funds or fund any shortfall. T sets the intra-group interest rates and is at risk for any differences between the rates it sets with other group members and the rates at which it transacts with the independent lenders. T also bears credit risk, liquidity risk and currency risk for intra-group finance and decides on how or whether to hedge such risks.

10.140. The analysis under the guidance in Section D.1 of Chapter I indicates that the actual transactions should be accurately delineated as intra-group loans in the context of the treasury activities undertaken by Company T since Company T is performing functions and assuming risks that go beyond the co-ordination role of a cash pool leader. In particular, the functional analysis shows that Company T controls the financial risks contractually allocated to it and has the financial capacity to bear those risks.

10.141. Accordingly, T should be compensated for the functions it performs and the risks it assumes in accordance with the guidance in Section C.1. This may include earning part or all of the spread between the borrowing and lending positions which it adopts.

10.142. It should be borne in mind that the other group members which transact with T would still only do so if this left them no worse off than their next best option.

C.2.3.2. Rewarding the cash pool members

10.143. The remuneration of the cash pool members will be calculated through the determination of the arm's length interest rates applicable to the debit and credit positions within the pool. This determination will allocate the synergy benefits arising from the cash pool arrangement amongst the pool members and it will generally be done once the remuneration of the cash pool leader has been calculated.

10.144. Eventually, the remuneration of the cash pool members will depend upon the specific facts and circumstances and the functions, assets and risks of each of the pool members. Therefore, this guidance does not intend to provide a prescriptive approach for allocating the cash pooling benefits to the participating cash pool members in any given situation but rather lays down the principles that should guide that allocation.

10.145. Determining the arm's length interest rates for the cash pool intra-group transactions may be a difficult exercise due to the lack of comparable arrangements between unrelated parties. In this context, banking arrangements involving the cash pool leader, taking into account functional differences between the bank and the cash pool leader, and the options realistically available to the cash pool members may inform the identification of comparable interest rates in the transfer pricing analysis.

10.146. It is expected that all cash pool participants will be better off than in the absence of the cash pool arrangement. Under prevailing facts and circumstances that could imply, for instance, that all cash pool participants would benefit from enhanced interest rates applicable to debit and credit position within the cash pooling arrangement compared to the rates that they would expect to obtain from borrowing or depositing cash outside of the pool.

However, it is important to note that cash pool members might be willing to participate in cash pool arrangements to access benefits from the membership of the cash pool other than an enhanced interest rate like, for instance, access to a permanent source of financing; reduced exposure to external banks; or access to liquidity that may not be available otherwise.

C.2.3.3. Cash pooling guarantees

10.147. As part of the cash pooling arrangement, cross-guarantees and rights of set-off between participants in the cash pool may be required. This raises the question of whether guarantee fees should be payable. It will always be appropriate to consider the particular facts and circumstances in any situation but there are certain factors which are likely to be common to many cash pools: there will be numerous members of the pool, there may be both entities with debit positions and entities with credit positions in the pool, each pool member may have a different stand-alone credit rating, and the pooling agreement with the bank is likely to require full cross-guarantees and rights of set-off between all pool participants.

10.148. These cross-guarantees and set-off rights are a feature of an arrangement which would not occur between independent parties. Each guarantor is providing a guarantee for all members of the pool but will not have control over membership of the pool, has no control over the quantum of the debt which it is guaranteeing, and may not be able to access information on the parties for whom it is providing a guarantee. With other parties providing guarantees on the same loans, it may not be possible for the guarantor to evaluate its real risk in the event of a default. Thus, the practical result of the cross-guaranteeing arrangement is such that the formal guarantee may represent nothing more than an acknowledgement that it would be detrimental to the interests of the MNE group not to support the performance of the cash pool leader and so, by extension, the borrower. In such circumstances the guaranteed borrower may not be benefitting beyond the level of credit enhancement attributable to the implicit support of other group members. If the prevailing facts and circumstances support such a conclusion, no guarantee fee would be due, and any support, in case of a default from another group member, should be regarded as a capital contribution.

C.3. Hedging

10.149. Intra-group financial transactions may include instruments by which risk is transferred within the MNE group. For example, hedging arrangements are frequently used, in the ordinary course of business, as a means of mitigating exposure to risks such as foreign exchange or commodity price movements. An independent entity may decide to assume such risks or hedge against them according to its own policies. However, in an MNE group, such risks might be treated differently depending on the MNE group's approach to risk management and hedging.

10.150. Often an MNE group will centralise treasury functions and implement risk mitigation strategies relating to interest rate and currency risks in order to improve efficiency and effectiveness with the result that individual entities may not contractually enter into hedging arrangements although their risk is hedged from the perspective of the MNE as a whole.

10.151. Possible mechanisms by which an MNE group may centralise the hedging of risk include:

- delegation of responsibility for hedging to an MNE group treasury entity, with the hedging contracts arranged for and in the name of the relevant operating companies;
- delegation of responsibility for hedging to an MNE group treasury entity, with the hedging contracts made by and in the name of another MNE group entity;
- identification of the existence of natural hedges within the MNE group, in which case no formal hedging contracts are made.

10.152. Where the centralised treasury function arranges a hedging contract that the operating entity enters into, that centralised function can be seen as providing a service to the operating entity, for which it should receive compensation on arm's length terms.

10.153. More difficult transfer pricing issues may arise, however, if the contract instrument is entered into by the treasury entity or another MNE group entity, with the result that the positions are not matched within the same entity, although the MNE group position is protected. Where off-setting hedging contract instruments exist within the MNE group but not within the same entity, or where contract instruments do not exist within the MNE group but the MNE group position is protected (as may be the case with a natural hedge, for example), it would be inappropriate to match the hedges within the same entity or recognise hedging transactions where written contracts do not exist without a comprehensive analysis of the accurate delineation of the actual transactions under Section D.1 of Chapter I (for example, the existence of a deliberate concerted action to engage in a hedge of a specific risk) and the commercial rationality of the transactions under Section D.2 of Chapter I.

D. Financial guarantees

10.154. This section considers financial guarantees on certain intra-group transactions. To consider any transfer pricing consequences of a financial guarantee, it is first necessary to understand the nature and extent of the obligations guaranteed and the consequences for all parties, accurately delineating the actual transaction in accordance with Section D.1 of Chapter I.

10.155. In general, a financial guarantee provides for the guarantor to meet specified financial obligations in the event of a failure to do so by the guaranteed party. There are various terms in use for different types of credit support from one member of an MNE group to another. At one end of the spectrum is the formal written guarantee and at the other is the implied support attributable solely to membership in the MNE group. In the context of this section, a guarantee is a legally binding commitment on the part of the guarantor to assume a specified obligation of the guaranteed debtor if the debtor defaults on that obligation. The situation likely to be encountered most frequently in a transfer pricing context is that in which an associated enterprise (guarantor) provides a guarantee on a loan taken out by another associated enterprise from an unrelated lender.

D.1. Accurate delineation of financial guarantees

D.1.1. Economic benefit derived from a financial guarantee

10.156. The accurate delineation of financial guarantees requires initial consideration of the economic benefit arising to the borrower beyond the one that derives from passive association, as explained in the Section C.1.1.3.

10.157. From the borrower perspective, a financial guarantee may affect the terms of the borrowing – for instance, the existence of a guarantee may allow the guaranteed party to obtain a more favourable interest rate since the lender has access to a wider pool of assets –, or the amount of the borrowing – for instance, enabling the borrower to access a larger amount of funds.

D.1.1.1. Enhancement of the terms of the borrowing

10.158. From the perspective of a lender, the consequence of one or more explicit guarantees is that the guarantor(s) are legally committed; the lender's risk would be expected to be reduced by having access to the assets of the guarantor(s) in the event of the borrower's default. Effectively, this may mean that the guarantee allows the borrower to borrow on the terms that would be applicable if it had the credit rating of the guarantor rather than the terms it could obtain based on its own, non-guaranteed, rating. The principles and methodologies of pricing a guarantee in these circumstances are similar to those explained for loan pricing in Section C.1.2.

10.159. Where the effect of an intra-group guarantee as accurately delineated is to reduce the cost of debt-funding for the borrower, it might be prepared to pay for that guarantee, provided it was in no worse a position overall. In considering the borrower's overall financial position as a result of the guarantee, its cost of borrowing with the guarantee (including the cost of the guarantee and any associated costs of arranging the guarantee) would be measured against its non-guaranteed cost of borrowing, taking into account any implicit support. Borrowing with a guarantee might also affect terms and conditions of the loan other than price; each case will depend on its own facts and circumstances.

10.160. Alternatively, Chapter I analysis may indicate that the purported financial guarantee is not providing any benefit to the borrower but merely recognising the benefit that the guaranteed party would have obtained in any case by being part of the MNE group. In such situations, based on facts and circumstances, an unrelated enterprise in comparable circumstances would be unwilling to pay for the provision of a financial guarantee, and the guarantor would be found as providing no more than an administrative service to the borrower (see paragraph 10.164 and guidance in Chapter VII).

D.1.1.2. Access to a larger amount of borrowing

10.161. Where the effect of a guarantee is to permit a borrower to borrow a greater amount of debt than it could in the absence of the guarantee, the guarantee is not simply supporting the credit rating of the borrower but could be acting both to increase the borrowing capacity and to reduce the interest rate on any existing borrowing capacity of the borrower. In such a situation there may be two issues – whether a portion of the loan from the lender to the borrower is accurately delineated as a loan from the lender to the guarantor (followed by an equity contribution from the guarantor to the borrower), and whether the guarantee fee paid with respect to the portion of the loan that is respected as a loan from the lender to the borrower is arm's length. The conclusion of an analysis of such transactions may be, taking into account the full facts and circumstances, that the evaluation of the guarantee fee should be limited to a fee on the portion that has been accurately delineated as a loan, and the remainder of the loan granted should be regarded as effectively a loan to the guarantor followed by an equity contribution by the guarantor to the borrower.

D.1.2. Effect of group membership

10.162. This section elaborates on the effect of group membership on determining the arm's length price of financial guarantees, building upon the principles laid out in Section C.1.1.

10.163. By providing an explicit guarantee the guarantor is exposed to additional risk as it is legally committed to pay if the borrower defaults. Anything less than a legally binding commitment, such as a "letter of comfort" or other lesser form of credit support, involves no explicit assumption of risk. Each case will be dependent on its own facts and circumstances but generally, in the absence of an explicit guarantee, any expectation by any of the parties that other members of the MNE group will provide support to an associated enterprise in respect of its borrowings will be derived from the borrower's status as a member of the MNE group. For this purpose, whether a commitment from one MNE group member to another MNE group member to provide funding to meet its loan obligations, constitutes a letter of comfort or a guarantee depends on all the facts and circumstances, including whether the commitment provides the creditor relevant legal rights to enforce the commitment. The benefit of any such support attributable to the borrower's MNE group member status would arise from passive association and not from the provision of a service for which a fee would be payable. See paragraph 7.13 on passive association.

10.164. A borrower would not generally be prepared to pay for a guarantee if it did not expect to obtain an appropriate benefit in return. Even an explicit guarantee will not necessarily confer a benefit on the borrower; for example, banking covenants applicable to a parent or other MNE group member's debt facilities can include the default of another MNE group member as an event that may cause the termination of a facility or other adverse consequences. Other legal, financial or operational ties may mean that it would not be possible to abandon the borrower if it encounters financial difficulty without the MNE group suffering a credit rating downgrade. Any of these circumstances may produce the practical result that MNE group members are financially interdependent quite apart from any formal guarantee arrangement, so that the economic risk of the guarantor may not change materially on it giving an explicit guarantee. In other words, the formal guarantee may represent nothing more than an acknowledgement that it would be detrimental to the interests of the MNE group not to support the performance of the borrower. In such circumstances the guaranteed borrower is not benefitting beyond the level of credit enhancement attributable to the implicit support of other MNE group members and no guarantee fee would be due.

10.165. A similar issue arises in respect of cross-guarantees, where two or more entities in an MNE group guarantee each other's obligations. From the lender's perspective, it has access to the assets of every cross-guaranteeing entity in the event of a default by a guaranteed borrower. This potentially gives the lender greater comfort than a single guarantee as it can choose where within the cross-guaranteeing MNE group it seeks, if necessary, to make its recoveries. The effect of a cross-guarantee from a borrower's perspective is that it now has multiple guarantees on its borrowings and may stand as guarantor for multiple borrowings itself. This can give rise to questions on how to evaluate each guarantee. Not only is this complex from the perspective of potentially large numbers of guarantees to be evaluated but also because each party providing a guarantee may in turn be guaranteed by the party for whom it is now acting as guarantor. Evaluating the effect of a cross-guarantee arrangement is difficult and as the number of parties involved increases, may be practically impossible. It may not be possible to determine the effect of the guarantee between any two parties where the same risk is subject to multiple guarantees. An analysis of the facts may lead to the conclusion that such an arrangement does not enhance the credit standing of an MNE group member beyond the level of passive association, in which case any support in the event of default from another MNE group member should then be regarded as a capital contribution.

D.1.3. Financial capacity of the guarantor

10.166. The examination of financial guarantees under accurate delineation needs also to consider the financial capacity of the guarantor to fulfill its obligations in case of default of the borrower. This requires an evaluation of the credit rating of the guarantor and the borrower, and of the business correlations between them.

10.167. A lender would benefit from the stronger credit rating of the guarantor (compared to the borrower's credit rating) and/or the guarantor's asset pool (in addition to the borrower's asset pool), and the borrower accordingly may expect a benefit in the form of a lower interest rate. Thus, based on facts and circumstances, a guarantee may provide a benefit to the borrower that has the same or higher credit rating as the guarantor, if the guarantee effectively allows the lender to access wider recourse and, therefore, reduces the interest rate despite the guarantor not having a higher credit rating. In determining the credit rating of the guarantor and the borrower, the effect of implicit support must be considered as explained in Section C.1.1.

10.168. Likewise, the financial capacity of the guarantor to meet its obligations requires an analysis of the correlation between the guarantor's and borrower's businesses. In situations where the guarantor and the borrower operate under similar market conditions, an adverse market event that affects the performance of the borrower and increases its risk of default might also affect the guarantor and its capacity to fulfill its obligations.

D.2. Determining the arm's length price of guarantees

10.169. This section describes a number of pricing approaches for those circumstances where a guarantee is found to be appropriate. However, when the accurate delineation of the actual transaction indicates that the purported guarantee is not a guarantee, other pricing approaches should be considered, in particular the guidance in Chapter VII. As in any other transfer pricing situation, the selection of the most appropriate method should be consistent with the actual transaction as accurately delineated, in particular, through a functional analysis. (See Chapter II).

D.2.1. CUP method

10.170. The CUP method could be used where there are external or internal comparables; independent guarantors providing guarantees in respect of comparable loans to other borrowers or where the same borrower has other comparable loans which are independently guaranteed.

10.171. In considering whether controlled and uncontrolled transactions are comparable, regard should be had to all the factors which may affect the guarantee fee including: the risk profile of the borrower, terms and conditions of the guarantee, term and conditions of the underlying loan (amount, currency, maturity, seniority etc.), credit rating differential between guarantor and guaranteed party, market conditions, etc. When available, uncontrolled guarantees are the most reliable comparable to determine arm's length guarantee fees.

10.172. The difficulty with using the CUP method is that publicly available information about a sufficiently similar credit enhancing guarantee is unlikely to be found between unrelated parties given that unrelated party guarantees of bank loans are uncommon.

10.173. An independent entity providing a financial guarantee would expect to receive a fee to compensate it for the risk it is taking in accepting the contingent liability and to reflect any value it is providing to the borrower in respect of the guarantee. However, it must be borne in mind that an independent guarantor's charges will in part reflect costs incurred in the process of raising capital and in satisfying regulatory requirements. Those are costs which associated enterprises might not incur.

D.2.2. Yield approach

10.174. This approach quantifies the benefit that the guaranteed party receives from the guarantee in terms of lower interest rates. The method calculates the spread between the interest rate that would have been payable by the borrower without the guarantee and the interest rate payable with the guarantee. The first step is to determine the interest rate that would have been payable by the borrower on its own merits, taking into account the impact of implicit support as a result of its group membership. See Section C.1.2.

10.175. The next step would be to determine, by a similar process (unless directly observable in the case of a loan from a third party), the interest rate payable with the benefit of the explicit guarantee. The interest spread can be used in quantifying the benefit gained by the borrower as a result of the guarantee. In determining the extent of the benefit provided by the guarantee, it is important to distinguish the impact of an explicit guarantee from the effects of any implicit support as a result of group membership. See Example 2 in paragraph 1.187. The benefit to be priced is not the difference between the cost to the unguaranteed borrower on a stand-alone basis and the cost with the explicit guarantee but the difference between the cost to the borrower after taking into account the benefit of any implicit support and the cost with the benefit of the explicit guarantee.

10.176. The benefit of implicit support will be the difference between the borrowing terms attainable by the borrowing entity based on its credit rating as a member of the MNE group and those attainable on the basis of the stand-alone credit rating it would have had if it were an entirely unaffiliated enterprise. If the borrower has its own independent credit rating from an unrelated credit rating agency, this will usually reflect its membership of the MNE group and so ordinarily no adjustment would be needed to this credit rating to reflect implicit support.

10.177. The result of this analysis sets a maximum fee for the guarantee (the maximum amount that the recipient of the guarantee will be willing to pay), namely, the difference between the interest rate with the guarantee and the interest rate without the guarantee but with the benefit of implicit support (and taking into account any costs). The borrower would have no incentive to enter into the guarantee arrangement if, in total, it pays the same to the bank in interest and to the guarantor in fees as it would have paid to the bank in interest without the guarantee. Therefore this maximum fee does not of itself necessarily reflect the outcome of a bargain made at arm's length but represents the maximum that the borrower would be prepared to pay.

D.2.3. Cost approach

10.178. This method aims to quantify the additional risk borne by the guarantor by estimating the value of the expected loss that the guarantor incurs by providing the guarantee (loss given default). Alternatively the expected cost could be determined by reference to the capital required to support the risks assumed by the guarantor.

10.179. There are a number of possible models for estimating the expected loss and capital requirement. Popular pricing models for this approach work on the premise that financial guarantees are equivalent to another financial instrument and pricing the alternative, for example, treating the guarantee as a put option and using option pricing models, credit default swap pricing models, etc. For instance, publicly available data of credit default swaps spreads may be used to approximate the default risk associated to the borrowing and, therefore, the guarantee fee. When using this type of data, the identification of the default event (e.g. bankruptcy) is central to the comparability analysis between the controlled transaction and the potentially comparable credit default swap (See Section C.1.2, on the reliability of credit default swap data).

10.180. Pricing under each model will be sensitive to the assumptions made in the modelling process. Whatever valuation model is used, the evaluation of cost method sets a minimum fee for the guarantee (the minimum amount that the provider of the guarantee will be willing to accept) and does not of itself necessarily reflect the outcome of a bargain made at arm's length. The arm's length amount should be derived from a consideration of the perspectives (taking into account options realistically available) of the borrower and guarantor.

D.2.4. Valuation of expected loss approach

10.181. The valuation of expected loss method would estimate the value of a guarantee on the basis of calculating the probability of default and making adjustments to account for the expected recovery rate in the event of default. This would then be applied to the nominal amount guaranteed to arrive at a cost of providing the guarantee. The guarantee could then be priced based on an expected return on this amount of capital based on commercial pricing models such as the Capital Asset Pricing Model (CAPM).

D.2.5. Capital support method

10.182. The capital support method may be suitable where the difference between the guarantor's and borrower's risk profiles could be addressed by introducing more capital to the borrower's balance sheet. It would be first necessary to determine the credit rating for the borrower without the guarantee (but with implicit support) and then to identify the amount of additional notional capital required to bring the borrower up to the credit rating of the guarantor. The guarantee could then be priced based on an expected return on this amount of capital to the extent that the expected return so used appropriately reflects only the results or consequences of the provision of the guarantee rather than the overall activities of the guarantor-enterprise.

D.3. Examples

10.183. The following examples build on the principles discussed in Section D.8 of Chapter I, in particular in paragraph 1.187.

D.3.1. Example 1

10.184. Company M, the parent entity of an MNE group, maintains an AAA credit rating based on the strength of the MNE group's consolidated balance sheet. Company D, a member of the same MNE group, has a credit rating of only BBB on a stand-alone basis, and needs to borrow EUR 10 million from an independent lender.

10.185. Assume that the accurate delineation of the actual transaction shows that the effect of passive association raises Company D's credit standing from BBB to A, and that the provision of the explicit guarantee additionally enhances the credit standing of Company D to AAA. Assume further that independent lenders charge an interest rate of 8% to entities with a credit rating of A, and of 6% to entities with a credit rating of AAA. Assume further that Company M charges Company D a fee of 3% for the provision of the guarantee so the guarantee fee more than completely offsets the benefit of Company D's enhanced credit standing derived from the provision of such guarantee.

10.186. In that situation, the analysis under Chapter I may indicate that an independent enterprise borrowing under the same conditions as Company D would not be expected to pay a guarantee fee of 3% to Company M for the provision of the explicit guarantee since Company D is better off in the absence of the guarantee.

D.3.2. Example 2

10.187. Consider the same fact pattern as described in Example 1, but in this case assume that under the guidance in Section D.2, comparable uncontrolled transactions can be identified showing that the arm's length price of a comparable guarantee would be in the range of 1% to 1.5%.

10.188. The accurate delineation of the actual transaction indicates that the enhancement of Company D's credit standing from A to AAA is attributable to a deliberate concerted group action, i.e. the guarantee provided by Company M. Company D would be expected to be willing to pay an arm's length guarantee fee to Company M for the provision of the explicit guarantee since Company D is better off than in the absence of the guarantee.

E. Captive insurance

E.1. Definition and rationale for a captive insurance and reinsurance

10.189. There are many ways that MNE groups may manage risks within the group. For example, they may choose to set aside funds in reserves, pre-fund potential future losses, self-insure, acquire insurance from third parties or simply elect to retain the specific risk. In some other cases an MNE group may choose to consolidate certain risks through a so-called "captive" insurance.

10.190. In this guidance, the term captive insurance is intended to refer to an insurance undertaking or entity substantially all of whose insurance business is to provide insurance policies for risks of entities of the MNE group to which it belongs.

10.191. In contrast, in this guidance the term reinsurance refers to a reinsurance undertaking or entity the purpose of which is to provide reinsurance policies for risks of unrelated parties that are in the first instance insured by entities of the MNE group to which it belongs.[5] (The situation in which risks of entities within an MNE group are insured in the first instance by an unrelated party but then reinsured by an entity within the MNE group is discussed in Section E.2.4).

10.192. Captive insurances may be subject to regulation in the same way as other insurance and reinsurance companies.[6] The precise requirements of insurance regulation will vary from one jurisdiction to the next but typically include certain actuarial, accounting and capital requirements. While insurance regulation is intended to protect policyholders, local regulators may impose a lighter regulatory regime where the captive insurance provides insurance exclusively to members of the MNE group.

10.193. There are multiple reasons for an MNE group to use a captive insurance such as: to stabilise premiums paid by entities within the MNE group; to benefit from tax and regulatory arbitrage; gaining access to reinsurance markets; mitigating the volatility of market capacity; or because the MNE group considers that retaining the risk within the group is more cost effective.

10.194. Another possible reason for the use of a captive insurance by an MNE group in addition to those listed is the difficulty or impossibility of getting insurance coverage for certain risks. Where such risks are insured by a captive insurance this may raise questions as to whether an arm's length price can be determined and the commercial rationality of such an arrangement (see Section D.2 of Chapter I).

E.2. Accurate delineation of captive insurance and reinsurance

10.195. The principles of accurate delineation of the actual transactions and allocation of risk detailed in Chapter I of these Guidelines apply to captive insurance and reinsurance in the same manner that they apply to any other intra-group transactions. However, this section addresses mainly captive insurance (as well as captive reinsurance-fronting). In particular, it should be borne in mind that:

- the carrying on of risk mitigation functions falls within the wider concept of risk management but not within that of control of risk (see paragraphs 1.61 and 1.65);

5. For this section, insurance and reinsurance undertakings are defined by reference to insurance and reinsurance business as described in Part IV of the *Report on the Attribution of Profits to Permanent Establishments.* This description, which covers the general scheme of insurance, is not intended to exclude from this guidance risks which the insured has some ability to influence, such as product liability risk.
6. See paragraph 10.3.

- there is a difference between the specific risk being insured (the party taking the decision to insure – i.e. mitigate – or not, controls this risk; that party will usually be the insured but may be another entity within the MNE group) and the risk taken on by the insurer in providing insurance to the insured party.

10.196. Although the quantum of the risk reward for the insured party and the insurer might be dependent upon exactly the same events in both cases, that quantum could be significantly different (for example, if the insured risk materialises and a claim is made, the insured party could potentially receive significant upside relative to the premium paid whereas the insurer's income will be limited to the insurance premiums and investment income it has received regardless of the quantum of risk reward received by the insured party).

10.197. The insurer is carrying out a risk mitigation function in respect of the insured party's risk but not actually assuming that risk. It is assuming the risk of insuring (i.e. mitigating) the insured party's risk. That risk will be controlled by either the insurer or (more likely in a captive insurance scenario) another entity within the MNE group that makes the decision that the risk should be assumed by the insurer. (See paragraph 10.223). The insurer (or other entity) can make decisions as to how to respond to this risk – in accordance with paragraph 1.61 (ii) – by, for example, further diversifying its portfolio of insured risks or by reinsuring.

10.198. Captive insurances may be self-managed from within the MNE group, or managed by an unrelated service provider (often a division of a large insurance broker). Typically this management would include ensuring compliance with local law, issuing policy documents, collecting premiums, paying claims, preparing reports and providing local directors. If the captive insurance is managed from within the MNE group it is necessary to determine which entity manages it (if such management is not exercised by employees of the captive insurance) and to appropriately reward that management.

10.199. A frequent concern when considering the transfer pricing of captive insurance transactions is whether the transaction concerned is genuinely one of insurance, i.e. whether a risk exists and, if so, whether it is allocated to the captive insurance in light of the facts and circumstances. The following are indicators, all or substantially all of which would be found if the captive insurance was found to undertake a genuine insurance business:

- there is diversification and pooling of risk in the captive insurance;
- the economic capital position of the entities within the MNE group has improved as a result of diversification and there is therefore a real economic impact for the MNE group as a whole;

- both the captive insurance and any reinsurer are regulated entities with broadly similar regulatory regimes and regulators that require evidence of risk assumption and appropriate capital levels;
- the insured risk would otherwise be insurable outside the MNE group;
- the captive insurance has the requisite skills, including investment skills, and experience at its disposal (see paragraph 10.213);
- the captive insurance has a real possibility of suffering losses.

10.200. In order to consider the transfer pricing implications of a transaction with a captive insurance, it is first necessary to identify the commercial or financial relations between the associated enterprises and the conditions and economically relevant circumstances attaching to those relations in order that the actual transaction is accurately delineated. The initial question will therefore be whether the transaction under consideration is one of insurance, as defined above. This analysis requires consideration of whether the risk has been assumed by the insurer and whether risk diversification has been achieved.

E.2.1. Assumption of risk and risk diversification

10.201. Insurance requires the assumption of insurance risk by the insurer. In the event of a claim, the insured does not suffer the financial impact of a potential economic loss to the extent that insurance risk has been assumed by the insurer, because the loss is offset by the insurance payment.

10.202. From the captive insurance's perspective, the fact that the captive insurance is exposed to the downside outcome of the insured risk and to the possibility of significant loss could be an indicator that the insurance risk has been assumed by the captive insurance. In addition, the assumption of the insurance risk can only take place if the captive insurance has a realistic prospect of being able to satisfy claims in the event of the risk materialising, i.e. the captive insurance needs to have access to funding to bear the consequences of the playing out of the insured risk. Determining whether the captive insurance has the financial capacity to assume the risk requires consideration of the capital readily available to the captive and its options realistically available. In particular, when the captive insurance invests the premiums into the insured entities within the MNE group, the relation between the captive insurance's capacity to satisfy the claims and the financial positions of those other MNEs would be central to Chapter I analysis.

10.203. Insurance also requires risk diversification. Risk diversification is the pooling of a portfolio of risks by which the insurer achieves an efficient use of capital. Large commercial insurers rely on having sufficiently large numbers of policies with similar probabilities of loss to allow statistical laws of averages to apply and permit accuracy of modelling of the likelihood of claims. The insurer also maintains a portfolio of risks for which it has a capital reserve based on regulatory needs and rating agency requirements.

10.204. Risk diversification is at the core of insurance business. Combining non-correlated risk and varied geographical exposures lead to an efficient use of capital, allowing the insurer to have a lower level of capital than that the insured parties would have been required to maintain to face the consequences of risk materialisation.

10.205. A captive insurance may achieve risk diversification by insuring not only internal risks of its MNE group, but also including within its portfolio a significant proportion of external, non-group risks (while still staying within the definition of captive insurance in paragraph 10.190).

10.206. Alternatively, risk diversification may be achieved by covering internal risks when the breadth and depth of the MNE group allows the captive insurance to cover non-correlated or less than fully correlated risks and varied geographical exposures. Situations where a captive insurance only covers internal risks require a thorough analysis under Chapter I guidance to determine whether risk diversification actually occurred, i.e. whether a sufficient quantum and variety of risks are covered by the captive insurance. In this context, determining whether risk diversification occurred is a question of threshold and the conclusion of the analysis would be dependent upon the specific facts and circumstances.

10.207. Notably, internal risk diversification might generate lower capital efficiencies than those achieved through external risk diversification. Therefore, the remuneration of a captive insurance that exclusively covers internal risks might be lower than when risk diversification is achieved by insuring external, non-group risks, or by reinsuring a significant proportion of the MNE group's risks outside of the group. In addition, when the accurate delineation of the actual transaction indicates that the capital efficiencies achieved through the pooling of internal risks in the captive insurance arise from the result of group synergies created through deliberate concerted group actions, the benefits of such synergies should generally be shared by the MNEs that contributed to the creation of those synergies (see Section D.8 of Chapter I and paragraphs 10.222 and 10.223).

10.208. In situations where the captive insurance lacks the scale to achieve significant risk diversification or lacks sufficient reserves to meet additional risks represented by the relatively less diversified portfolio of the MNE group, the accurate delineation of the actual transaction may indicate that the captive insurance is operating a business other than an insurance one (see guidance in Chapter VII).

E.2.2. The assumption of the economically significant risks

10.209. In the process of accurately delineating the actual transaction involving a captive insurance, the economically relevant risks associated with issuing insurance policies, i.e. underwriting, must be identified with specificity. Part IV of the *Report on the Attribution of Profits to Permanent Establishments*[7] provides a description of those risks that include, inter alia, insurance risk, commercial risk or investment risk. These descriptions remain valid for the purpose of this guidance.

10.210. The accurate delineation of the actual transaction in scenarios involving captive insurance requires identifying whether the captive insurance is performing control functions regarding the economically significant risks associated to the underwriting function – in particular the insurance risk – to determine whether those risks should be allocated to the captive.

10.211. Part IV of the *Report on the Attribution of Profits to Permanent Establishments* describes the activities that form part of the underwriting function such as setting the underwriting policies, classifying and selecting the insured risk, setting the premiums (pricing), the analysis of risk retention and the acceptance of the insured risk. These activities would imply, inter alia, deciding to underwrite a risk or not and under what terms and conditions, or whether reinsurance protection should be purchased or not. On prevailing facts and circumstances, those activities may be considered as control functions as described in paragraph 1.65 of Chapter I and, if exercised by a captive insurance that possesses the financial capacity to assume the risk, would lead to the allocation of risk to the captive insurance under Chapter I analysis. Notably, the mere setting of parameters or the policy environment for the risk would not qualify as control functions for this purpose (see paragraph 1.66 of Chapter I, and paragraph 94 of Part IV of the *Report on the Attribution of Profits to Permanent Establishments*).

10.212. When the captive insurance does not have access to the appropriate skills, expertise and resources and, therefore, the captive insurance is not found to exercise control functions related to the risks associated to the underwriting, an analysis under Chapter I, based on facts and circumstances, may conclude that the risk has not been assumed by the captive insurance or that another MNE is exercising these control functions. In this latter case, the return derived from the investment of the premiums would be allocated to the member(s) of the MNE group that are assuming the risk associated with the underwriting in accordance with the guidance in Chapter I.

7. Report on the Attribution of Profits to Permanent Establishments, approved by the Committee on Fiscal Affairs on 22 June 2010 and by the Council for publication on 22 July 2010.

E.2.3. Outsourcing the underwriting function

10.213. In many cases, outsourcing certain aspects of the underwriting function would be inconsistent with the minimum regulatory standards required to operate an insurance business. However, in those situations where the captive insurance is permitted to outsource some of the activities that constitute the underwriting function (for instance, a captive insurance may be allowed to outsource the acceptance of insurance risk to an associated enterprise that acts as a broker and receives an arm's length remuneration), special consideration of the retention by the captive insurance of the control functions would be required in order to conclude whether the risk is allocated to the captive insurance. A captive insurance that outsources all aspects of the underwriting process without performing control functions would not assume the insurance risk under Chapter I analysis.

E.2.4. Reinsurance captives – Fronting

10.214. A reinsurance captive is a particular type of captive insurance which does not issue policies directly but operates as a reinsurance under an arrangement known as "fronting". Captive insurance may not be able to underwrite insurance policies in the same way as traditional insurance companies. For instance, certain insurance risks must be placed with regulated insurers as a legal requirement. This may lead to the use of a fronting arrangement in which the first contract of insurance is between the insured member of an MNE group and an unrelated insurer (the fronter); the fronter then reinsures with the captive insurance most or all of the risk of the first contract. The fronter may remain responsible for claims handling and other administrative functions or these functions may be handled by a member of the same MNE group as the captive. The fronter retains a commission to cover its costs and to compensate for any portion of the insured risk which it retains. The majority of the fronter's premium passes to the captive insurance as part of the reinsurance contract.

10.215. In accurately delineating fronting arrangements, the same principles stated for captive insurance apply. It is important to note, however, that fronting arrangements represent particularly complex controlled transactions to price as they involve the participation of a third party that is indifferent to the levels of the price of the insurance and reinsurance transactions. The key issues which are likely to arise in fronting cases are whether the transactions involved amount to genuine insurance or reinsurance and, if there is genuine insurance, whether the premiums payable (ultimately to the reinsurance captive) are on arm's length terms.

E.3. Determining the arm's length price of captive insurance and reinsurance

10.216. The following paragraphs outline different approaches to pricing intra-group transactions involving captive insurance and reinsurance. Each case must be considered on its own facts and circumstances and in each case accurate delineation of the actual transactions in accordance with the principles of Chapter I will be needed before any attempt to decide on an approach to pricing a transaction. As in any other transfer pricing situation, the most appropriate method should be selected under the guidance of Chapter II.

E.3.1. Pricing of premiums

10.217. Comparable uncontrolled prices may be available from comparable arrangements between unrelated parties. These may be internal comparables if the captive insurance has suitably similar business with unrelated customers, or there may be external comparables.

10.218. The application of the CUP method to a transaction involving a captive insurance may encounter practical difficulties to determine the need for and quantification of comparability adjustments. In particular, account should be taken of potential differences between the controlled and uncontrolled transactions that may affect the reliability of the comparables. Those differences may refer, for instance, to situations where the functional analysis indicates that a captive insurance performs less functions than a commercial insurer (e.g. a captive insurance that only insures internal risks within the MNE group may not need to perform distribution and sales functions). Similarly, differences between the captive insurance and the potential comparables in business volume or in the level of capital between the captive insurance and unrelated parties may require comparability adjustments (see paragraph 10.221).

10.219. Alternatively, actuarial analysis may be an appropriate method to independently determine the premium likely to be required at arm's length for insurance of a particular risk. In setting prices for an insurance premium, an insurer will seek to cover its expected losses on claims, its costs associated with writing and administering policies and dealing with claims, plus a profit to provide a return on capital, taking into account any investment income it expects to receive on the excess of premiums received less claims and expenses paid. The practical application of actuarial analysis may be a complex exercise. In evaluating the reliability of actuarial analysis to determine the arm's length price of premiums it is important to note that actuarial analyses do not represent actual transactions between independent parties and that, therefore, comparability adjustments would be likely required.

E.3.2. Combined ratio and return on capital

10.220. The remuneration of the captive insurance can be arrived at by considering the arm's length profitability of the captive insurance by reference to a two staged approach which takes into account both profitability of claims and return on capital. The first step would be to identify the captive insurance's combined ratio. This can be determined by expressing claims and expenses payable as a percentage of premiums receivable. The benchmarked combined ratio achieved by unrelated insurance companies indemnifying similar insurance risks can be identified. The benchmarked combined ratio can then be applied to the tested party's claims and expenses paid to arrive at an arm's length measure of annual premiums and thus underwriting profit (premiums receivable less claims and expenses). The second step is to assess the investment return achieved by the captive insurance against an arm's length return. This step requires two further considerations: (a) the amount of capital held by the captive insurance, and (b) to the extent to which the captive insurance invests in controlled investments (e.g. intra-group bonds, loans, etc.), the rate of investment return achieved by the captive insurance on those investments. The sum of underwriting profit from step one and investment income from step two gives total operating profit (see Section B.5 of Chapter III on multiple year data).

10.221. It is important to recognise that the capital adequacy requirements of a captive insurance are likely to be significantly lower than an insurer writing policies for unrelated parties. This factor should be considered and, if necessary, adjusted for in order to determine the appropriate level of capital to use when calculating the investment return. Differences in capital adequacy between captive insurance and arm's length insurers typically arise because of regulatory and commercial factors. Insurance regulators frequently set lower regulatory capital requirements for captive insurances. A primary commercial driver for arm's length insurers is capital efficiency. In order to attract investors and customers, arm's length insurers will target a strong credit rating by holding a level of operating capital which is in excess of the regulatory minimum. At the same time, arm's length insurers will attempt to maximise their return on capital results. They will try to hold the optimum amount of capital to meet these opposing drivers. Captive insurances have no commercial imperative to seek a credit rating nor to optimise their return on capital in order to attract investors. Reasonable adjustments may need to be made to ensure that the comparable investment return is restricted to the capital that the captive insurance needs under relevant regulatory requirements (plus a reasonable operating buffer to minimise the possibility of inadvertently breaching the regulatory requirement) to accept the insurance risk rather than the level of capital that might be needed by an independent insurer. Adjustments may be needed to account for differing capital adequacy requirements between different regulators and different categories of insurance business.

E.3.3. Group synergy

10.222. Where a captive insurance is used so that the MNE group can access the reinsurance market to divest itself of risk through insuring risk outside the MNE group, whilst making cost savings over using a third party intermediary, by pooling risks within the MNE group, the captive arrangement harnesses the benefits of collective negotiation on any reinsured risks and more efficient allocation of capital in respect of any risks retained. These benefits arise as a result of the concerted actions of the MNE policyholders and the captive insurance. The insured participants jointly contribute with the expectation that each of them will benefit through reduced premiums. This is similar to the type of group-wide arrangements that might exist for other group functions such as purchasing of goods or services. Where the captive insurance insures the risk and reinsures it in the open market, it should receive an appropriate reward for the basic services it provides. The remaining group synergy benefit should be allocated among the insured participants by means of discounted premiums.

10.223. For example, a manufacturing MNE group has 50 subsidiaries in different locations around the world, all in locations with substantial risk of earthquake, each insures against earthquake damage at its manufacturing plant, with each plant in a different location, assessed on its individual level of risk. The MNE group sets up a captive insurance which accepts the risk from all of the subsidiaries and reinsures it with independent reinsurers. By bringing together a portfolio of insurance risks across different geographical zones, the MNE group already represents a diversified risk to the market. The synergy benefit arises from the collective purchasing arrangement, not from value added by the captive insurance. It should be allocated amongst the insured according to the level of premium they contributed.

E.3.4. Agency sales

10.224. Where an insurance contract is not sold directly from insurer to insured, recompense will usually be due to the party who arranges the original sale. In certain circumstances a higher rate of profit might be earned on the third party sale than would otherwise be expected from comparison with similar transactions. Where the sales agent and insurer or reinsurer are associated, any comparability analysis as part of the process of determining the arm's length level of reward for the parties would need to consider the circumstances that give rise to the high level of profit. Competition would usually work to limit the amount of profit which can be earned on a transaction both on the part of the sales agent and on that of the insurer or reinsurer. The availability of alternative providers may also influence the ability of each party to negotiate a higher level of profit as part of the overall transaction.

10.225. For example Company A is a high street retailer of high value new technology consumer goods. At the point of sale, A offers insurance policies to third party customers which provide accidental damage and theft cover for a 3-year period. The policies are insured by Company B, an insurer which is part of the same MNE group as A. A receives a commission with substantially all of the profit on the insurance contract going to B. A full factual and functional analysis shows that the insurance contracts are very profitable and that there is an active market for insurance and reinsurance of the type of risks covered by the policies. Benchmarking studies show that the commission paid to A is in line with independent agents selling similar cover as a standalone product. The profit B earns is above the level of insurers providing similar cover.

10.226. In considering how the conditions of the transaction between A and B differ from those which would be made between independent enterprises, it is important to consider how the high level of profitability of the insurance policies is achieved and the contributions of each of the parties to that value creation. The product sold to the third party is an insurance policy substantially the same as that which any other insurer in the general market could provide. The sales agent has the advantage of offering the insurance policy to its customer alongside the sale of the goods to be insured. It is the advantage of intervening at the point of this sale which provides the opportunity to earn a high level of profit. A could sell policies underwritten by another insurer and retain most of the profit for itself. B could not find another agent that has the advantage of point of sale contact with the customer. The ability to achieve the very high level of profit on the sale of the insurance policies arises from the advantage of customer contact at the point of sale. The arm's length remuneration for B would be in line with the benchmarked return for insurers insuring similar risks and the balance of the profit should be allocated to A.

List of annexes

Annex to the OECD Transfer Pricing Guidelines

Guidelines for monitoring procedures on the OECD Transfer Pricing Guidelines and the involvement of the business community

A. Background

1. In July 1995, the OECD Council approved for publication the *Transfer Pricing Guidelines for Multinational Enterprises and Tax Administrations* ("the Guidelines"), submitted by the Committee on Fiscal Affairs ("the Committee"). At the same time, the OECD Council endorsed the Committee's recommendation that the Guidelines be reviewed and up-dated periodically as appropriate based upon the experience of member countries and the business community with the application of the principles and methods set forth in the Guidelines. For this purpose, and to facilitate on-going clarifications and improvements, the OECD Council instructed the Committee to undertake a period of monitoring international transfer pricing experience. The monitoring role is seen as an integrated part of the agreement reached in July 1995 and its successful implementation is a key feature to getting a consistent application of the Guidelines. The Council Recommendation "instructs the Committee on Fiscal Affairs to monitor the implementation of the 1995 Report in co-operation with the tax authorities of member countries and with the participation of the business community and to recommend to the Council to amend and update, if necessary, the 1995 Report in the light of this monitoring".

2. To summarise, the main purpose of the monitoring is to examine how far member countries' legislation, regulations and administrative practices are consistent with the Guidelines and to identify areas where the Guidelines may require amendments or additions. The monitoring should not only lead to identification of problematic issues, but also to the identification of practices followed by one or more member countries in applying the Guidelines which could be usefully extended to other countries. The monitoring is not intended to arbitrate on particular cases.

3. The monitoring is expected to be an on-going process and to cover all aspects of the Guidelines but with particular emphasis on the use of transactional profit methods. The purpose of this note is to set forth some procedures for carrying out the monitoring, thereby implementing the instruction of the OECD Council. These procedures will be implemented gradually. Further revisions may be necessary once the procedures have been put into practice.

4. In line with the Council's Recommendation, there will be a role for the business community in the monitoring and this role is set out in Section C.

B. Process

5. The monitoring process will be carried out through four related projects: 1. peer reviews of member country practices; 2. identification and analysis of difficult case paradigms; 3. review of changes in legislation, regulations, and administrative practices; and 4. development of examples. Each of these is discussed below.

B.1. Peer reviews

6. The Working Party No. 6 on Taxation of Multinational Enterprises ("the Working Party") has been undertaking peer reviews of the transfer pricing practices of member countries over the course of the last few years. The peer reviews aim to gain detailed information on legislation, practices and experiences of transfer pricing in member countries. The Delegates of the Working Party jointly decide which country should be reviewed and which countries would conduct the review. The reviews follow guidelines approved by the Committee.

7. The peer review guidelines call for a report to be submitted to the Working Party for each reviewed country. The report covers the legal basis for dealing with transfer pricing issues, any country guidelines to direct enforcement practices, approaches commonly used to address a complex transfer pricing problem, administrative arrangements for handling transfer pricing cases, case law principles, and experience with data gathering and taxpayer documentation. The report also is to describe experiences with administrative approaches to avoiding and resolving transfer pricing disputes (e.g. mutual agreement procedure, advance pricing arrangements and safe harbours).

8. Peer reviews will continue to be carried out but at three different levels:

1. The first level would be an "*issue review*", which would look at the approach taken by all member countries to a particular issue of widespread significance. Ideally, the review should link up with

other aspects of the monitoring process. For example, the best way to solve any problems emerging from such a review may be to analyse the issue in more detail by developing difficult case paradigms (see Section B.2 of this annex) or to develop practical examples for insertion in the Guidelines (see Section B.4 of this annex).

2. The second level would be a "*limited review*" in that it would only look at the approach of a particular country or countries in relation to a specific and relatively narrow issue. The review would be carried out by two reviewers for each country and the level of input necessary would depend on the nature of the issue

3. The third level would be a "*full review*" of a particular country which would be carried out according to the existing peer review guidelines referred to in paragraph 7 of this annex. A "full review" would therefore address directly the interpretation and application of the Guidelines in the particular member country.

Selection criteria

9. To improve the effectiveness of the peer review process it is essential that the reviews are undertaken selectively and concentrate on the areas of greatest difficulty in applying the Guidelines. The final decision to undertake any of the three types of review will be made by the full Working Party having regard both to the overall usefulness of any review to the work of the Working Party in monitoring the application of the Guidelines and to whether there are sufficient resources available to undertake the proposed review. It is important that any review, once undertaken, is completed to a high standard so that worthwhile conclusions can be drawn from it.

B.2. Identification and analysis of difficult case paradigms

10. A key aspect of monitoring will be to identify and then to analyse difficult fact patterns and problem areas which may be illustrated by practical examples and which present obstacles to an internationally consistent application of the transfer pricing methods set out in the Guidelines. Monitoring will also include areas where the Guidelines appear to offer no or inadequate guidance to tax authorities or taxpayers. All member countries will be actively involved in this process and recognise that resources will be required to ensure its success. The business community will also be involved in the monitoring (see Section C of this annex).

11. The first issue is the procedure to be used and the responsibility assigned for identifying the difficult case paradigms, focusing on issues and situations where the Guidelines may provide no or inadequate guidance or where member countries might be interpreting the Guidelines differently and

therefore presenting obstacles to an internationally consistent application of the Guidelines. Member countries can identify areas where, in their view, the Guidelines might not address or adequately address a particular issue.

12. In the context of the regular meetings of tax inspectors organised by the Committee on Fiscal Affairs, the Working Party will arrange biennial meetings of tax examiners to discuss difficult case paradigms and to provide an input to any appropriate updates to the Guidelines. OECD will consider the difficult case paradigms only from the perspective of monitoring the application of the Guidelines.

13. Individual countries would take responsibility at meetings of Working Party No. 6 for leading discussions of the difficult case paradigms and of problematic areas that can be illustrated with practical examples.

14. The outcomes envisaged by the Working Party from the identification and analysis of difficult case paradigms could include the development of examples illustrating the application of the Guidelines in cases (identified for discussion) where the principles already contained within the Guidelines can be applied. It could also include identification of areas where the Guidelines could be amended to provide clearer guidance or where new material could be inserted into the Guidelines.

B.3. Updates of legislation and practice

15. The Secretariat will solicit from member countries reports on developments in their domestic transfer pricing legislation, regulations, and administrative practices, consistent with the invitation of the Council.

B.4. Development of examples

16. The foregoing monitoring procedures will parallel the development of additional hypothetical examples to be added to the Guidelines. The examples are not intended to develop new principles or to cover new issues but rather to assist in interpreting principles and in addressing difficult issues already discussed in the Guidelines. To ensure that they are of practical value and avoid being overly prescriptive the examples will be short, based on stated facts and relatively straightforward so that their scope is not so confined that the guidance they provide is of narrow and limited application. The examples will fall into two broad categories. The first will consist of illustrations of the application of the methods and approaches described in the Guidelines. The second set of examples will be designed to aid in the selection of a suitable transfer pricing method or methods. Although hypothetical, the examples will draw on the practical experiences of tax administrations and taxpayers in applying the arm's length principle under the Guidelines, and will contribute to the establishing of good practices.

C. Involvement of the business community

17. It is not intended that the OECD should intervene in the resolution of transfer pricing disputes between a taxpayer and a tax administration. The monitoring process is not intended to be a form of arbitration and so taxpayers will not be able to present individual cases for resolution by the Working Party. Nevertheless, as foreseen in the Guidelines and the Council Recommendation, the business community will be encouraged to identify problematic issues (preferably illustrated with practical but hypothetical examples) which raise questions about the internationally consistent application of the Guidelines.

18. The Business Industry Advisory Committee ("BIAC") will be invited to present practical difficulties in monitoring the application of the Guidelines to the Working Party for its consideration of the adequacy of the guidance provided in the Guidelines in relation to such areas, respecting confidentiality of the information.

19. In contributing to the OECD role of monitoring the implementation of the Guidelines, the business community would be encouraged to take particular note of the guidance given in paragraph 17 of this annex. It should therefore focus on issues that give rise to either theoretical or practical difficulties and not on specific and unresolved transfer pricing cases. However, it may be useful to illustrate a particular issue by reference to a hypothetical example. In constructing such an example, which could draw upon features taken from a number of real cases, care should be taken to ensure it remains hypothetical and does not resemble a current case, and that the features described should be restricted to the problematic issues concerned in order to avoid an impression of setting any general precedent for the resolution of an individual case.

C.1. Peer reviews

20. It is felt that one of the strengths of the peer review process is that the review is conducted solely by peers i.e. in this case the other member countries. That way the process is conducted in a positive and constructive manner so that best practice can be passed on and worse practice improved. However, the general guidance to the business community encourages them to identify problematic issues which may be suitable for further analysis and the Working Party will be able to take account of this input when making its final selection of issues for the revised peer review.

21. It is also envisaged that once an issue or a country has been selected by the Working Party for further review, the BIAC will be notified of the decision so that they have the opportunity to comment. If the issue is one originally identified by the BIAC – particularly in the context of issue

reviews – they would be kept informed of the Working Party's discussion on these issues and asked, if necessary, to provide additional clarification. However, a further role for the BIAC in the peer review process beyond that already described is not contemplated at the moment.

C.2. Identification and analysis of difficult case paradigms and the development of examples

22. The difficult case paradigms are intended to illustrate issues and situations where the Guidelines provide no or inadequate guidance. Practical examples when complete will be inserted into the Guidelines to provide illustrations of particular principles. There is a clear role for the business community in assisting in the development of paradigms or examples by contributing the practical experience of their members. The Working Party will ask for comments on both the difficult case paradigms and the practical examples at regular stages in their development. BIAC may also initiate paradigms or examples, provided the caveats in paragraph 17 of this annex are followed so that there can be no question of the process being used to resolve a particular transfer pricing case.

C.3. Updates of legislation and practice

23. The aim of this element in the monitoring process is to keep the member countries informed about developments in each others' countries. There are usually well established ways at the national level by which the business community can make an input into any developments in the transfer pricing legislation, regulations and administrative practices of a member country. At the level of the OECD, the BIAC will have an opportunity to bring to the attention of the Working Party changes in legislation or practices in both member and non-member countries, which it considered were inconsistent with the Guidelines or which it felt could give rise to practical problems in terms of implementation without, of course, referring to individual cases.

24. The input from the BIAC will be discussed at the regular joint meetings between the BIAC and the Working Party.

Annex I to Chapter II

Sensitivity of gross and net profit indicators

See Chapter II, Part III, Section B of these Guidelines for general guidance on the application of the transactional net margin method.

The assumptions about arm's length arrangements in the following examples are intended for illustrative purposes only and should not be taken as prescribing adjustments and arm's length arrangements in actual cases of particular industries. While they seek to demonstrate the principles of the sections of the Guidelines to which they refer, those principles must be applied in each case according to the specific facts and circumstances of that case.

Furthermore, the comments below relate to the application of a transactional net margin method in the situations where, given the facts and circumstances of the case and in particular the comparability (including functional) analysis of the transaction and the review of the information available on uncontrolled comparables, such a method is found to be the most appropriate method to be used.

1. It is recognised that the transactional net margin method can be less sensitive to some differences in the characteristics of products than the comparable uncontrolled price or resale price methods. In practice when applying the transactional net margin method a greater emphasis is generally placed on functional comparability than on the characteristics of products. The transactional net margin method can however be less sensitive to some differences in functions which are reflected in variations in operating expenses as illustrated below.

Illustration 1: Effect of a difference in the extent and complexity of the marketing function performed by a distributor

The example below is for illustration only. It is not intended to provide any guidance on the selection of the transfer pricing method or of comparables, on the efficiency of distributors or on arm's length rates of return, but only to illustrate the effects of differences between the extent and complexity of the marketing function of a distributor and of comparables.

	Case 1 **The distributor performs a limited marketing function**	**Case 2** **The distributor performs a more significant marketing function**
Sales of product (For illustration purposes, assume both sell the same volume of the same product on the same market at the same price)	1 000	1 000
Purchase price from manufacturer taking account of the significance of the marketing function in accordance to the functional analysis	600	480 *
Gross margin	400 (40%)	520 (52%)
Marketing expenses	50	150
Other expenses (overheads)	300	300
Net profit margin	50 (5%)	70 (7%)

* Assume that in this case the difference of 120 in transaction price corresponds to the difference in the extent and complexity of the marketing function performed by the distributor (additional expense of 100 plus remuneration of the function of the distributor)

2. In Illustration 1, if a taxpayer is operating with an associated manufacturer as in case 2 while the third party "comparables" are operating as in case 1, and assuming that the difference in the extent and complexity of the marketing function is not identified because of for instance insufficiently detailed information on the third party "comparables", then the risk of error when applying a gross margin method could amount to 120 (12% × 1 000), while it would amount to 20 (2% × 1 000) if a net margin method was applied. This illustrates the fact that, depending on the circumstances of the case and in particular of the effect of the functional differences on the cost structure and on the revenue of the "comparables", net profit margins can be less sensitive than gross margins to differences in the extent and complexity of functions.

Illustration 2: Effect of a difference in the level of risk assumed by a distributor

The example below is for illustration only. It is not intended to provide any guidance on the selection of the transfer pricing method or of comparables, on the efficiency of distributors or on arm's length rates of return, but only to illustrate the effects of differences between the level of risk assumed by a distributor and by comparables.

	Case 1 **The distributor does not assume the risk of obsolescence of products because it benefits from a "buy-back" clause whereby all unsold inventory is purchased back by the manufacturer.**	**Case 2** **The distributor assumes the risk of obsolescence of products. It does not benefit from a "buy-back" clause in its contractual relationship with the manufacturer.**
Sales of product (For illustration purposes, assume both sell the same volume of the same product on the same market at the same price)	1 000	1 000
Purchase price from manufacturer taking account of the obsolescence risk in accordance with the functional analysis	700	640 *
Gross margin	300 (30%)	360 (36%)
Loss on obsolete inventory	0	50
Other expenses (overheads)	250	250
Net profit margin	50 (5%)	60 (6%)

* Assume that in this case the difference of 60 in transaction price corresponds to the difference in the allocation of the obsolescence risk between the manufacturer and the distributor (additional loss estimated 50 plus remuneration of the risk of the distributor), i.e. it is the price for the contractual "buy-back" clause.

3. In Illustration 2, if a controlled transaction is performed as in case 1 while the third party "comparables" are operating as in case 2, and assuming that the difference in the level of risks is not identified due to insufficiently detailed information on the third party "comparables", then the risk of error when applying a gross margin method could amount to 60 (6% × 1 000) instead of 10 (1% × 1 000) if a net margin method is applied. This illustrates the fact that, depending on the circumstances of the case and in particular of the effect of the differences in the level of risks on the cost structure and on the revenue of the "comparables", net profit margins can be less sensitive than gross margins to differences in the level of risks (assuming the contractual allocation of risks is arm's length).

4. Consequently, enterprises performing different functions may have a wide range of gross profit margins while still earning broadly similar levels of net profits. For instance, business commentators note that the transactional net margin method would be less sensitive to differences in volume, extent and complexity of functions and operating expenses. On the other hand, the transactional net margin method may be more sensitive than the cost plus or resale price methods to differences in capacity utilisation, because differences in the levels of absorption of indirect fixed costs (e.g. fixed manufacturing costs or fixed distribution costs) would affect the net profit but may not affect the gross margin or gross mark-up on costs if not reflected in price differences, as illustrated below.

Illustration 3: Effect of a difference in manufacturers' capacity utilisation

The example below is for illustration only and is not intended to provide any guidance on the selection of the transfer pricing method or of comparables, or on arm's length rates of return, but only to illustrate the effects of differences between the capacity utilisation of a manufacturer and of comparables.

In monetary units (m.u.)	Case 1 The manufacturer operates at full capacity: 1 000 units per year	Case 2 The manufacturer operates at excess capacity i.e. only manufactures 80% of what it could manufacture at full capacity: 800 units per year
Sales of manufactured products (For illustration purposes, assume both manufacturers have the same total capacity, and that they both manufacture and sell the same product on the same market which have the same price of 1 m.u. per manufactured product).*	1 000	800
Cost of goods sold: direct costs plus standard allocation of indirect manufacturing costs. (For illustration purposes, assume both manufacturers have the same variable cost of goods sold per manufactured unit, i.e. 0.75 m.u. per manufactured product, and fixed personnel costs of 50).	Variable: 750 Fixed: 50 Total: 800	Variable: 600 Fixed: 50 Total: 650
Gross mark-up on cost of goods sold	200 (25%)	150 (23%)
Indirect costs (For illustration purposes, assume both manufacturers have the same indirect costs)	150	150
Net profit margin	50 (5%)	Break-even

* This assumes that the arm's length price of the manufactured products is not affected by the manufacturer's capacity utilisation.

5. In Illustration 3, if a controlled transaction is performed as in case 1 while the third party "comparables" are operating as in case 2, and assuming that the difference in the capacity utilisation is not identified due to insufficiently detailed information on the third party "comparables", then the risk of error when applying a gross margin method could amount to 16 (2% × 800) instead of 50 (5% × 1 000) if a net margin method is applied. This illustrates the fact that net profit indicators can be more sensitive than gross mark-ups or gross margins to differences in the capacity utilisation, depending on the facts and circumstances of the case and in particular on the proportion of fixed and variable costs and on whether it is the taxpayer or the "comparable" which is in an over-capacity situation.

Annex II to Chapter II

Examples to illustrate the guidance on the transactional profit split method

See Chapter II, Part III, Section C of these Guidelines for general guidance on the application of the profit split method.

The adjustments and assumptions about arm's length arrangements in the examples that follow are intended for illustrative purposes only and should not be taken as prescribing adjustments and arm's length arrangements in actual cases or particular industries. They are necessarily presented with limited facts. The identification of the presence of one of the three factors (as identified in paragraphs 2.125 to 2.143) indicating that the transactional profit split method may be the most appropriate transfer pricing method, does not mean that one or both of the other factors may not also be present. For example, in a situation in which unique and valuable contributions are identified as being made by each party to the transaction, the business operations of the parties may also be highly integrated and the parties may also share the assumption of economically significant risks or separate assumption of closely related risks.

While the examples seek to demonstrate the principles of the sections of the Guidelines to which they refer, those principles must be applied in each case according to the specific facts and circumstances of that case. As such, the examples should not be used to interpret superficially similar cases.

Example 1

1. Company A is the parent company of an MNE group in the pharmaceutical sector. Company A owns a patent for a new pharmaceutical formulation. Company A designed the clinical trials and performed the research and development functions during the early stages of the development of the product, leading to the granting of the patent.

2. Company A enters into a contract with Company S, a subsidiary of Company A, according to which Company A licenses the patent rights

relating to the potential pharmaceutical product to Company S. In accordance with the contract, Company S conducts the subsequent development of the product and performs important enhancement functions. Company S obtains the authorisation from the relevant regulatory body. The development of the product is successful and it is sold in various markets around the world.

3. The accurate delineation of the transaction indicates that the contributions made by both Company A and Company S are unique and valuable to the development of the pharmaceutical product.

4. Under these circumstances, the transactional profit split method is likely to be the most appropriate method for determining the compensation for the patent rights licensed by Company A to Company S.

Example 2

5. A Co, a member of T Group, is a company incorporated in Country A whose principal activity is the growing and processing of tea. A Co identifies, acquires and cultivates land with extremely good soil for growing tea. A Co has developed extensive knowhow in respect of tea-growing, including maximising the desirable qualities of the tea it grows through its cultivation methods. The properties of the soil together with the cultivation methods give A Co's tea a highly sought after flavour.

6. A Co processes tea by undertaking the following activities: sorting leaf, grading, full or partial fermenting, and blending and packaging for export as per customer order specifications. Blending entails using extensive proprietary know-how to mix the various teas in order to get blends with the unique tastes appreciated by customers of T Group. Tea produced by A Co has won international acclaim for its unique taste and aroma.

7. A Co sells its tea to B Co, its parent company located in Country B. B Co then repackages and brands the teas for sale in the target markets.

8. B Co owns and has, by its own efforts, developed the tradename and trademark which are both unique and valuable. However, the branding features the origin of the tea and the unique blend developed by A Co. B Co has carried out extensive advertising campaigns through electronic media, internet, trade fairs and publications in industry magazines resulting in the product range becoming market leader in a number of geographic markets. Tea sold by T Group commands a premium price.

9. The accurate delineation of the transaction in this particular case determines that both A Co and B Co are making a unique and valuable contribution and the most appropriate transfer pricing method is likely to be the transactional profit split method.

Example 3

10. Company A and Company B are members of an MNE group that sells electronic appliances. For the launch of a new line of products, Company A will be responsible for its design, development and manufacturing whereas Company B will undertake the marketing functions and the global distribution of the goods.

11. In particular, Company A performs the research and development functions and decides on the lines of research and the timelines. For the manufacturing of the new line of products, Company A decides on the levels of production and performs the quality controls. In doing so, Company A uses its valuable know-how and expertise regarding the manufacturing of electronic appliances.

12. Once the products are manufactured, they are sold to Company B, which develops and executes cutting-edge global marketing activities relating to the new line of products. In particular, Company B is responsible for designing the marketing strategy, deciding on the level of marketing expenditure in each jurisdiction where the products will be released, and validating the impact of the marketing campaigns on a monthly basis. The marketing activities performed by Company B result in a valuable trademark and associated goodwill by which the new line of products is favourably differentiated from competitors' alternatives in the market.

13. Company B is also responsible for the global distribution of the products. The distribution activities performed by Company B are a key source of economic advantage over competitors. Company B has performed the R&D activities and assumed the risks associated with the development of a sophisticated proprietary algorithm to get feedback from customers on the performance of the products. This information is highly valuable in accurately forecasting demand and managing inventory and distribution logistics so that customers are assured of receiving their orders within 48 hours.

14. The accurate delineation of the transaction indicates that the contributions of Company A and Company B are unique and valuable to the potential success of the new line of products.

15. Under these circumstances, the transactional profit split method is likely to be the most appropriate method for determining the compensation for the products sold by Company A to Company B as both parties make unique and valuable contributions to the transaction.

Example 4

16. The facts in this example are the same as in Example 3, except that the marketing activities performed by Company B are more limited and do not significantly enhance the goodwill or reputation associated with the trademark. Company B has a mechanism whereby customer feedback on the products it sells is relayed to Company A, but this is a relatively simple process, and does not constitute a unique and valuable contribution. In sum, its distribution activities are not a particular source of competitive advantage in its industry. In particular, the potential success of the new line of products is largely dependent on its technical specifications, its design, and the price at which the products are sold to final customers.

17. The functional analysis concludes that Company A assumes the risks associated with the design, development and manufacturing of the product and Company B assumes the risks relating to marketing and distribution.

18. Marketing and distribution risks assumed by Company B may impact on the ultimate profitability of Company A. However, the functional analysis determines that the risks assumed by Company B are not economically significant for the business operations and that Company B does not make any unique and valuable contributions in relation to the controlled transaction.

19. Under these circumstances, the transactional profit split method may not be the most appropriate method as it is likely that the arm's length compensation for the contribution of Company B can be reliably benchmarked by reference to comparable uncontrolled transactions and the application of a one-sided transfer pricing method or methods.

Example 5

20. WebCo is a member of an MNE group that develops IT solutions for business customers. Recently, WebCo designed the architecture of a web crawler to collect pricing data from internet sites. WebCo has written the code of the programme so it is able to systematically scan web pages in a more efficient and faster way than any other similar search engines available in the market.

21. At this stage, WebCo licenses the programme to ScaleCo, a company in the same MNE group. ScaleCo is responsible for scaling-up the web crawler and for deciding the crawling strategy. ScaleCo is a specialist in designing add-ons for the web crawler and in customising the product to address gaps in the market. Without these contributions, the system would not be able to meet potential customers' needs.

22. Under the terms of the licence, WebCo will continue developing the underlying base technology and ScaleCo will use these developments to scale up the web crawler.

23. The functional analysis concludes that the economically significant risk in relation to the transaction is the development risk, i.e. the risk that the web crawler being developed is unsuccessful. In accordance with the risk analysis framework described in Section D.1.2.1 of Chapter I of these Guidelines, it is determined that WebCo and ScaleCo assume the development risk of the software.

24. The accurate delineation of the transaction indicates that WebCo's and ScaleCo's contributions are unique and valuable to the creation and potential success of the web crawler.

25. Under these circumstances, the transactional profit split method is likely to be the most appropriate method for determining the arm's length compensation for the licence between WebCo and ScaleCo.

Example 6

26. ASSET Co is the parent company of an MNE group that provides asset management services to unrelated parties. It has two subsidiaries, Company A in Country A and Company B, in Country B.

27. FUND Co is an independent asset management company that offers collective investment vehicles to retail investors in Country A and Country B. The investment vehicles commercialised by FUND Co are mirror funds that contain equity holdings from both Country A and Country B.

28. FUND Co hires ASSET Co to provide portfolio management services for the funds. FUND Co pays ASSET Co a fee based on the combined assets under management of the funds sold to retail investors in Country A and Country B.

29. ASSET Co enters into a contract with Company A and Company B such that both companies will provide the portfolio management services. Company A employs portfolio managers who specialise in Country A equity and Company B employs portfolio managers who specialise in Country B equity. ASSET Co acts as a nominee for Companies A and B. It does not perform any functions in relation to the FUND Co contract, nor has it contributed any assets or assumed any risks.

30. An investment management committee composed of equal numbers of portfolio managers from Company A and Company B decides on the funds' investment management. This committee meets regularly and determines the composition of the funds. The composition of the funds between equities of Countries A and B will vary according to the decisions of the committee.

31. The functional analysis concludes that the economically significant risk in relation to the transaction relates to retail investors withdrawing their deposits from the FUND Co mirror funds, in particular as a result of poor performance. In accordance with the risk analysis framework described in Section D.1.2.1 of Chapter I of these Guidelines, it is determined that Company A and Company B share the assumption of risks related to the performance of the funds and perform the portfolio management services in a highly integrated fashion.

32. While Company A and Company B provide valuable services, an active arm's length market for portfolio management services indicates that these services are not unique. Comparables for such portfolio management services (i.e. the services performed by Company A and B together) may be available, but would provide no information on how to split the arm's length fee between Company A and Company B.

33. Under these circumstances, the transactional profit split method is found to be the most appropriate method for determining the compensation for Company A and Company B as their operations are highly integrated and interdependent such that it is not possible to use a one-sided method to determine an arm's length outcome for either of their respective contributions. The arm's length fee received by ASSET Co from FUND Co will form the revenue portion of the relevant profits to be split between Company A and Company B. The arm's length compensation to ASSET Co will be zero.

Example 7

34. Company L, a resident of Country L, and Company M, a resident of Country M, are part of an MNE group, LM Corporation. Companies L and M offer international trade facilitation, freight forwarding and customs broking services to unrelated customers. Together, Companies L and M, provide customers with services including receipt of goods in the exporting country, customs clearance in the exporting country, containerisation, organising shipment of the container, delivery of containers to and from the ship, de-containerisation, customs clearance in the importing country, and delivering the goods to their destination. Customers may be importers or exporters and Companies L and M facilitate imports and exports from both countries. Customers typically pay for these services based on a combination of the volume and weight of the goods.

35. The accurate delineation of the transaction determines that Companies L and M perform the same trade facilitation, freight forwarding and customs broking services jointly in a highly integrated manner. Companies L and M are highly dependent on each other for the successful completion of each transaction with a customer. Companies L and M also

perform similar marketing and customer relationship functions, depending on the location of the customer. Companies L and M jointly use an integrated goods-tracking IT system. The system was initially purchased jointly by Companies L and M from an unrelated supplier. Companies L and M each make incremental improvements to the system where possible. LM Corporation's value proposition to its customers lies in its competitive pricing, which is made possible by its efficiency and economies of scale and scope, and its seamless integration across international boundaries.

36. Companies L and M jointly perform the same key value-adding functions and jointly use and contribute to the MNE group's most important assets. Although arm's length pricing for their joint activities is readily available, their operations are highly integrated and interdependent such that it is not possible to use a one-sided method to determine an arm's length outcome for either of their respective contributions. In this case, therefore, it is likely that a transactional profit split will be the most appropriate method of determining the arm's length compensation due to Companies L and M.

37. If Companies L and M also share the assumption of the economically significant risks associated with the transactions, a profit split of actual profits is likely to be appropriate.

Example 8

38. Company A is the parent company of M Group, an MNE group engaged in the manufacturing and distribution of electronic devices. Company A has the exclusive right to sell the devices in all territories.

39. Company A decides to subcontract the manufacturing of the electronic devices to Company B, another member of M Group. Under the terms of the contract, Company B will follow the directions of Company A to produce the devices. Company B will source and supply the materials necessary to produce the different parts of the final products. A key component in the manufacturing process is sourced from Company A. Company B sells the finished goods to Company A, which in turn will market and distribute the product to unrelated customers.

40. To perform the manufacturing activities, Company B has invested in machinery and tooling that is specifically adapted to the production of the electronic devices sold by M Group. Company B has no other customer than Company A so its entire output is acquired by Company A.

41. The accurately delineated transaction shows that Company B does not make any unique and valuable contributions in relation to the controlled transactions and the business of M Group. Furthermore, the risks assumed by Company B are not economically significant for the business operations

of the group. While the operations of Company B are integrated to some degree with those of Company A and are dependent upon Company A, arm's length compensation for the contributions of Company B can be reliably benchmarked by reference to comparable uncontrolled transactions and the application of a one-sided transfer pricing method or methods. Under these circumstances, the transactional profit split method is unlikely to be the most appropriate method.

Example 9

42. ACo, resident in Country A, and BCo, resident in Country B, are members of AB Inc, an MNE Group. ACo owns worldwide patents on Compound A and BCo owns worldwide patents on Enzyme B. Compound A and Enzyme B are both unique. ACo and BCo have each developed their respective compound or enzyme by their own efforts, for different purposes, but each found that they were not able to be used as they had originally intended. As a result, neither Compound A nor Enzyme B has significant value at this time.

43. However, engineers from ACo and BCo working together subsequently determine that the combination of Compound A and Enzyme B creates a unique and valuable drug which is very effective in treating a specific disease and is likely to be highly valuable.

44. ACo and BCo enter into a contract according to which ACo grants BCo the right to use Compound A. BCo will combine both components to develop the new drug and will market it.

45. Under these circumstances, the high level of integration and interdependency between the contributions of ACo and BCo affects the value of those contributions such that each contribution is unique and valuable when considered in combination with the other. As a result, the transactional profit split method is found to be the most appropriate method for determining the compensation at which the rights to use Compound A are transferred by ACo to BCo.

Example 10

46. Company A designs, develops and produces a line of high technology industrial products. A new generation of the product line incorporates a key component developed and created by Company B, an associated enterprise of Company A. This key component is highly innovative, incorporating unique and valuable intangibles. This innovation represents the key point of difference in the new generation of products. The success of the new generation of products is heavily dependent upon the performance of the key

component made by Company B. The key component is specifically tailored for the new generation of products and cannot be used in any other products.

47. The key component was developed entirely by Company B. The accurate delineation of the transaction determines that Company B performs all the control functions and assumed all the risks in relation to the development of the component, with no involvement by Company A.

48. The accurate delineation of the transaction also finds that Company A performs all the control functions and assumed all the risks in relation to the overall production and sale of the new generation of products. Company A cannot control (and thus does not assume) the risks relating to the performance of the key component.

49. In this example, it is determined that while Company A and Company B each assumes separate economically significant risks, those risks are highly inter-dependent. As a result, it is determined that the transactional profit split method is the most appropriate method.

50. If it is also found that the most appropriate way of applying the transactional profit split method in this case is by splitting revenues or gross profits from Company A's sales of the new generation product, each party would bear the consequences of the playing out of risks relating to their own operating costs.

Example 11

51. The success of an electronics product is linked to the innovative technological design both of its electronic processes and of its major component. That component is designed and manufactured by associated company A; is transferred to associated company B which designs and manufactures the rest of the product; and is distributed by associated company C. Information exists to verify by means of a resale price method that the distribution functions, assets and risks of Company C are being appropriately rewarded by the transfer price of the finished product sold from B to C.

52. The most appropriate method to price the component transferred from A to B may be a CUP, if a sufficiently similar comparable could be found. See paragraph 2.15 of the Guidelines. However, since the component transferred from A to B reflects the innovative technological advance enjoyed by company A in this market, which is found to be a unique and valuable contribution by company A, in this example it proves impossible (after the appropriate functional and comparability analyses have been carried out) to find a reliable CUP to estimate the correct price that A could command at arm's length for its product. Calculating a return on A's manufacturing costs could however provide an estimate of the profit element which would reward

A's manufacturing functions, ignoring the profit element attributable to the unique and valuable intangible used therein. A similar calculation could be performed on company B's manufacturing costs, to give an estimate of B's profit derived from its manufacturing functions, ignoring the profit element attributable to its unique and valuable intangible. Since B's selling price to C is known and is accepted as an arm's length price, the amount of the residual profit accrued by A and B together from the exploitation of their respective unique and valuable intangibles can be determined. At this stage the proportion of this residual profit properly attributable to each enterprise remains undetermined.

53. The residual profit may be split based on an analysis of the facts and circumstances that might indicate how the additional reward would have been allocated at arm's length. The R&D activity of each company is directed towards technological design relating to the same class of item, and it is established for the purposes of this example that the relative amounts of R&D expenditure reliably measure the relative value of the companies' contributions. See paragraph 2.145 of the Guidelines. This means that each company's unique and valuable contribution may reliably be measured by their relative expenditure on research and development, so that, if A's R&D expenditure is 15 and B's 10, giving a combined R&D expenditure of 25, the residual could be split 15/25 for A and 10/25 for B.

54. Some figures may assist in following the example:

a) Profit & loss of A and B

	A		B	
Sales		50		100
Less:				
Purchases		(10)		(50)
Manufacturing costs		(15)		(20)
Gross profits		25		30
Less:				
R&D	15		10	
Operating expenses	10	(25)	10	(20)
Net profit		0		10

b) Determine routine profit on manufacturing by A and B, and calculate total residual profit

55. It is established, for both jurisdictions, that third-party comparable manufacturers without unique and valuable intangibles earn a return on manufacturing costs (excluding purchases) of 10% (ratio of net profit to the direct and indirect costs of manufacturing).[1] A's manufacturing costs are 15, and so the return on costs would attribute to A a manufacturing profit of 1.5. B's equivalent costs are 20, and so the return on costs would attribute to B a manufacturing profit of 2.0. The residual profit is therefore 6.5, arrived at by deducting from the relevant net profit of 10 the combined manufacturing profit of 3.5.

c) Allocate residual profit

56. The initial allocation of profit (1.5 to A and 2.0 to B) rewards the manufacturing functions of A and B, but does not recognise the value of their respective unique and valuable contributions that have resulted in a technologically advanced product. Since in this case it is determined that the relative share of total R&D costs incurred by A and B in relation to the product is a reliable proxy for the value of their respective unique and valuable contributions, the residual can be split between A and B on that basis. The residual is 6.5 which may be allocated 15/25 to A and 10/25 to B, resulting in a share of 3.9 and 2.6 respectively, as below:

A's share $6.5 \times 15/25 = 3.9$

B's share $6.5 \times 10/25 = 2.6$

d) Recalculate profits

57. A's net profits would thus become $1.5 + 3.9 = 5.4$.

B's net profits would thus become $2.0 + 2.6 = 4.6$.

1. This 10% return does not technically correspond to a cost plus mark-up in its strictest sense because it yields net profit rather than gross profit. But neither does the 10% return correspond to a TNMM margin in its strictest sense, since the cost base does not include operating expenses. The net return on manufacturing costs is being used as a convenient and practical first stage of the profit split method, because it simplifies the determination of the amount of residual net profit attributable to the unique and valuable intangibles contributed by A and B.

The revised P & L for tax purposes would appear as:

		A		B
Sales		55.4		100
Less:				
Purchases		(10)		(55.4)
Manufacturing costs		(15)		(20)
Gross profit		30.4		24.6
Less:				
R& D	15		10	
Operating expenses	10	(25)	10	(20)
Net profit		5.4		4.6

Note: The example is intended to exemplify in a simple manner the mechanisms of a residual profit split and should not be interpreted as providing general guidance as to how the arm's length principle should apply in identifying arm's length comparables and determining an appropriate split. It is important that the principles that it seeks to illustrate are applied in each case taking into account the specific facts and circumstances of the case. In particular, it should be noted that the allocation of the residual profit may need considerable refinement in practice in order to identify and quantify the appropriate basis for the split. Where R&D expenditure is used, differences in the types of R&D conducted may need to be taken into account, e.g. because different types of R&D may have different levels of risk associated with them, which would lead to different levels of expected returns at arm's length. Relative levels of current R&D expenditure also may not adequately reflect the contribution to the earning of current profits that is attributable to intangible property developed or acquired in the past. See Section C.5.3.2 of Chapter II of these Guidelines.

Example 12

58. Company A, resident in Country A, Company B, resident in Country B, and Company C, resident in Country C, are members of an MNE group. Companies A and B undertake the design and manufacturing of products and their activities in this regard are highly integrated. Additionally, Company A and Company B are responsible for the marketing and distribution of the products to unrelated customers in Country A and in Country B, respectively. Company C is responsible for the benchmarkable marketing and distribution of products purchased from Company A and Company B to unrelated customers in Country C.

59. Company A and Company B enter into an agreement to buy and sell pieces, moulds and components to manufacture the different models of the products. These transactions may also relate to semi-finished products

to effectively meet customers' demands in a timely fashion. As a result of their broad experience in the sector, Company A and Company B have each developed unique and valuable know-how and other intangibles in their respective design and manufacturing processes. In contrast, the accurate delineation of the transaction shows that Company C does not make any unique and valuable contribution. Instead, Company C performs benchmarkable marketing and distribution functions.

60. Design and manufacturing are identified as the key value drivers for the MNE group and the functional analysis shows the economically significant risks are the strategic and operational risks relating to the design and manufacturing functions. Company A and Company B are engaged in a complex web of intragroup transactions where the performance of each company heavily depends on the capacity of the other to provide the different components and other inputs. The manufacturing and design activities of Company A and Company B are highly interdependent and the entities both perform relevant control functions in relation to the economically significant risks. In accordance with the risk analysis framework described in Section D.1.2.1 of Chapter I of these Guidelines, it is determined that Company A and Company B share the assumption of the risks relating to design and manufacturing. Both Companies A and B make unique and valuable contributions to the manufacturing and design processes.

61. Under these circumstances, the transactional profit split method is likely to be the most appropriate method for determining the compensation for Companies A and B in relation to their intra-group transactions. However, a one-sided transfer pricing method such as a resale price method or a TNMM is likely to be the most appropriate to determine an arm's length return for Company C.

62. In applying the transactional profit split method, the sales of products in Countries A, B and C should be taken into account in determining the relevant profits to be split. In the case of Country C, this will be calculated by reference to the sales revenue of Company C, less the arm's length return to Company C (as established above) for its contributions.

63. Under a residual approach to the transactional profit split method, the first step of the process would be to determine an arm's length return for the less complex, benchmarkable contributions of each of the parties (i.e. Companies A and B). These amounts are then deducted from the pool of relevant profits to identify the residual profits to be split. Under the second step of the residual analysis, the residual profits would then be split between Company A and Company B on the basis of their relative contributions to those residual profits.

Example 13

64. Company A, resident in Country A, is the parent company of Retail Group, an MNE group engaged in the retail fashion industry. Over the years, Company A has developed know-how and has enhanced the value of the trademark and associated goodwill of its business through intensive marketing activities. In this case, the intangibles developed and owned by Company A do not qualify as hard-to-value intangibles.

65. To expand the business into the Country B market, Company A enters into an agreement with Company B, a member of Retail Group resident in Country B. Under this agreement, Company A grants to Company B the rights to utilise the know-how and to use the trademarks for the purpose of fashion retailing in Country B. Company B has extensive experience in retail fashion distribution and has a strong track record in building brand recognition and loyalty in Country B through its in-house team which develops and implements innovative marketing strategies and activities.

66. The accurate delineation of the transaction indicates that the contributions of both companies are unique and valuable to the Retail Group's business in Country B.

67. In the scenarios presented below, the transactional profit split is found to be the most appropriate method for determining the compensation for the rights granted by Company A to Company B on the basis that both parties to the transaction are making unique and valuable contributions.

Scenario 1

68. The accurately delineated transaction shows that Company A does not share in the assumption of any of the economically significant risks associated with the marketing and exploitation activities of Company B related to the licensed intangibles.

69. Under these circumstances, the application of the transactional profit split should be based on the profits anticipated to be generated by Company B from commercialising the products over an appropriate period (e.g. using a discounted cash flow valuation technique as described in Chapter VI, Sections D.2.6.3 and D.2.6.4 of these Guidelines).

70. The relative value of the contributions made by Company A and Company B will be used to determine a split of the anticipated profits of Company B resulting from the combined contributions of the enterprises. The payment for the transaction may take a variety of forms, including a lump sum payment to Company A or a sales-based royalty.

Scenario 2

71. In this scenario the accurately delineated transaction shows that:

- Company A and Company B agree to a split of the actual profits from the sale of the products by Company B
- Company A and Company B will jointly perform the marketing and distribution activities related to the trademarked products, and
- Both Company A and Company B assume risks associated with the success or otherwise of the marketing and commercialisation of the products by Company B

72. Under these circumstances, the transactional profit split method applies to the actual profits achieved from the sales of the products and the relative value of the contributions made by Company A and Company B will be used to determine the split of those profits.

Example 14

73. Below are some illustrations of the effect of choosing a measure of profits to determine the relevant profits to be split when applying a transactional profit split method.

Scenario 1

74. Assume A and B are two associated enterprises situated in two different tax jurisdictions. Both manufacture the same widgets and incur expenditure that results in the creation of a unique and valuable intangible which they can mutually use. For the purpose of this example, it is assumed that the nature of this particular unique and valuable intangible is such that the value of A and B's respective unique and valuable contributions in the year in question is proportional to A and B's relative expenditure on the intangible in that year. (It should be noted that this assumption will not always be true in practice.) Assume A and B exclusively sell products to third parties. Assume that it is determined that the most appropriate method to be used is a residual profit split method; that the manufacturing activities of A and B are less complex, non-unique transactions that should be allocated an initial return of 10% of the Cost of Goods Sold; and that the residual profit should be split in proportion to A's and B's expenditure in relation to the unique and valuable intangible. The following figures are for illustration only.

	A	B	A + B combined
Sales	100	300	400
Cost of Goods Sold	60	170	230
Gross profit	40	130	170
Overhead expenses	3	6	9
Other operating expenses	2	4	6
Expenditure in relation to the unique and valuable intangible	30	40	70
Operating profit	5	80	85

Step one: determining the initial return for the non-unique manufacturing transactions (Cost of Goods Sold + 10% in this example)

A	60 + (60 × 10 %) = 66	→ Initial return for the manufacturing transactions of A =	6
B	170 + (170 × 10 %) = 187	→ Initial return for the manufacturing transactions of B =	17
		Total profit allocated through initial returns (6 + 17) =	23

Step two: determining the residual profit to be split

a) If it is determined as the operating profit:

Combined Operating Profit	85
Profit already allocated (initial returns for manufacturing transactions)	23
Residual profit to be split in proportion to A's and B's expenditure in relation to the unique and valuable intangible	62

Residual profit allocated to A:	62 × 30/70	26.57
Residual profit allocated to B:	62 × 40/70	35.43

Total profits allocated to A:	6 (initial return) + 26.57 (residual)	32.57
Total profits allocated to B:	17 (initial return) + 35.43 (residual)	52.43
Total		85

b) If it is determined as the operating profit before overhead expenses (assuming it is determined that the overhead expenses of A and B do not relate to the transaction examined and should be excluded from the determination of the relevant profits to be split):

	A	B	A + B combined
Sales	100	300	400
Cost Of Goods Sold	60	170	230
Gross profit	40	130	170
Other operating expenses	2	4	6
Expenditure in relation to the unique and valuable intangible	30	40	70
Operating profit before overhead expenses	8	86	94
Overhead expenses	3	6	9
Operating profit	5	80	85

Combined Operating Profit before overhead expenses	94
Profit already allocated (initial returns for manufacturing transactions)	23
Residual profit before overhead expenses to be split in proportion to A's and B's expenditure in relation to the unique and valuable intangible	71

Residual profit allocated to A:	71 × 30/70	30.43
Residual profit allocated to B:	71 × 40/70	40.57

Total profits allocated to A:	6 (initial return) + 30.43 (residual) – 3 (overhead expenses)	33.43
Total profits allocated to B:	17 (initial return) + 40.57 (residual) – 6 (overhead expenses)	51.57
Total		85

75. As shown in the above example, excluding some specific items from the determination of the relevant profits to be split implies that each party remains responsible for its own expenses in relation to it. As a consequence, the decision whether or not to exclude some specific items must be consistent with the accurate delineation of the transaction.

Scenario 2

76. As another example, in some cases it may be appropriate to back out a category of expenses to the extent that the profit splitting factor(s) used in the residual profit split analysis relies on those expenses. For example, in cases where relative expenditure contributing to the development of a unique and valuable intangible is determined to be the most appropriate profit splitting factor, residual profits can be based on operating profits before that expenditure. After determining the split of residual profits, each associated enterprise then subtracts its own expenditure. This can be illustrated as follows. Assume the facts are the same as in Scenario 1 to this example in paragraph 74 above and assume the overhead expenses are not excluded from the determination of the residual profit to be split.

Step one: determining the basic return for the manufacturing activities (Cost of Goods Sold + 10% in this example)

Same as in Scenario 1, Step 1 above.

Step two: determining the residual profit to be split

a) If it is determined as the operating profit after expenditure in relation to the unique and valuable intangible:

Same as in Scenario 1, Step 2, case a.

b) If it is determined as the operating profit before expenditure in relation to the unique and valuable intangible:

	A	B	A + B combined
Sales	100	300	400
Cost Of Goods Sold	60	170	230
Gross Profit	40	130	170
Overhead expenses	3	6	9
Other operating expenses	2	4	6
Operating profit before expenditure in relation to the unique and valuable intangible	35	120	155
Expenditure in relation to the unique and valuable intangible	30	40	70
Operating Profit	5	80	85

Relevant Operating Profit before Expenditure in relation to the unique and valuable intangible	155
Profit already allocated (initial returns for manufacturing transactions)	23
Residual profit before Expenditure in relation to the unique and valuable intangible to be split in proportion to A's and B's expenditure in relation to the unique and valuable intangible	132

Residual profit allocated to A:	132 × 30/70	56.57
Residual profit allocated to B:	132 × 40/70	75.43

Total profits allocated to A:	6 (initial return) + 56.57 (residual) – 30 (expenditure in relation to the unique and valuable intangible)	32.57
Total profits allocated to B:	17 (initial return) + 75.43 (residual) – 40 (expenditure in relation to the unique and valuable intangible)	52.43
Total		85

i.e. A and B are allocated the same profits as in the case where the relevant profit to be split is determined as the operating profit after expenditure in relation to the unique and valuable intangible, see case a) above.

77. This example illustrates the fact that, when the profit splitting factor used to split the residual profit relies on a category of expenses incurred during the period, it is irrelevant whether the residual profit to be split is determined before the expenses are deducted by each party, or whether the residual profit to be split is determined after the expenses are deducted. The outcome can however be different in the case where the splitting factor is based on the accumulated expenditure of the prior as well as current years.

Example 15

78. Company A, resident in Country A, and Company B, resident in Country B, are members of an MNE group. Both companies undertake the design and manufacturing of products and their activities in this regard are highly integrated. Additionally, Company A and Company B are responsible for the marketing and distribution of the products to unrelated customers in Country A and in Country B, respectively.

79. Company A and Company B enter into an agreement to buy and sell pieces, moulds and different components to manufacture various different models of products. These transactions may also relate to semi-finished products to effectively meet customers' demands in a timely fashion. As a

result of their broad experience in the sector, Company A and Company B have each developed unique and valuable know-how and other intangibles in their respective design and manufacturing processes.

80. The functional analysis shows the economically significant risks are the strategic and operational risks in relation to the design and manufacturing functions and that Company A and Company B are engaged in a complex web of intragroup transactions where the performance of each company heavily depends on the capacity of the other to provide the different components and other inputs. The manufacturing and design activities of Company A and Company B are highly interdependent and the entities both perform relevant control functions in relation to the economically significant risks. In accordance with the risk analysis framework described in Section D.1.2.1 of Chapter I of these Guidelines, it is determined that Company A and Company B share the assumption of the risks relating to design and manufacturing. Both Companies A and B make unique and valuable contributions to the design and manufacturing processes.

81. Under these circumstances, the transactional profit split method is likely to be the most appropriate method for determining the compensation for Companies A and B in relation to their intra-group transactions

82. In the absence of comparable uncontrolled transactions or direct evidence of how independent parties would have split the profits in comparable circumstances, the profit split can be applied based on the relative value of the contributions of Company A and Company B. In particular, an asset-based splitting factor may be appropriate, provided that the functional analysis concludes that there is a strong correlation between the assets of Company A and Company B and the creation of value in the context of their controlled transactions.

Example 16

83. Company A, Company B and Company C, members of the same MNE group, jointly agree to share the "greenfield" development of a new product. In this regard, none of the entities brings existing contributions of value such as pre-existing intangibles to the project. Each associated enterprise will be responsible for developing and manufacturing one of the three key components of the product.

84. In this case, assume that the transactional profit split is found to be the most appropriate method for determining the profits of the three companies from the sale of the new product. The functional analysis concludes that the relative contributions of the parties may be measured by reference to the relative expenses incurred by each company in the development of the

components as there is a direct correlation between these relative expenses and the relative value contributed by each company. Accordingly, the relevant profits (losses) in relation to the sales of the new product can be split based on the relative development costs incurred by each of the parties.

85. In this example, the splitting of profits based on relative development costs will yield results similar to those which would have resulted under an analogous cost contribution arrangement, since parties performing activities with similar economic characteristics should receive similar expected returns, irrespective of whether the contractual arrangement in a particular case is termed as a CCA or not (see paragraph 8.4).

Annex to Chapter III

Example of a working capital adjustment

See Chapter III, Section A.6 of these Guidelines for general guidance on comparability adjustments.

The assumptions about arm's length arrangements in the following examples are intended for illustrative purposes only and should not be taken as prescribing adjustments and arm's length arrangements in actual cases of particular industries. While they seek to demonstrate the principles of the sections of the Guidelines to which they refer, those principles must be applied in each case according to the specific facts and circumstances of that case.

This example is provided for illustration purposes as it represents one way, but not necessarily the only way, in which such an adjustment can be calculated.

Furthermore, the comments below relate to the application of a transactional net margin method in the situations where, given the facts and circumstances of the case and in particular the comparability (including functional) analysis of the transaction and the review of the information available on uncontrolled comparables, such a method is found to be the most appropriate method to be used.

Introduction

1. This simple example shows how to make an adjustment in recognition of differences in levels of working capital between a tested party (TestCo) and a comparable (CompCo). See paragraphs 3.47-3.54 of these Guidelines for general guidance on comparability adjustments. Working capital adjustments may be warranted when applying the transactional net margin method. In practice they are usually found when applying a transactional net margin method, although they might also be applicable in cost plus or resale price methods. Working capital adjustments should only be considered when the reliability of the comparables will be improved and reasonably accurate adjustments can be made. They should not be automatically made and would not be automatically accepted by tax administrations.

Why make a working capital adjustment?

2. In a competitive environment, money has a time value. If a company provided, say, 60 days trade terms for payment of accounts, the price of the goods should equate to the price for immediate payment plus 60 days of interest on the immediate payment price. By carrying high accounts receivable a company is allowing its customers a relatively long period to pay their accounts. It would need to borrow money to fund the credit terms and/or suffer a reduction in the amount of cash surplus which it would otherwise have available to invest. In a competitive environment, the price should therefore include an element to reflect these payment terms and compensate for the timing effect.

3. The opposite applies to higher levels of accounts payable. By carrying high accounts payable, a company is benefitting from a relatively long period to pay its suppliers. It would need to borrow less money to fund its purchases and/or benefit from an increase in the amount of cash surplus available to invest. In a competitive environment, the cost of goods sold should include an element to reflect these payment terms and compensate for the timing effect.

4. A company with high levels of inventory would similarly need to either borrow to fund the purchase or reduce the amount of cash surplus which the company is able to invest. Note that the interest rate might be affected by the funding structure (e.g. where the purchase of inventory is partly funded by equity) or by the risk associated with holding specific types of inventory.

5. Making a working capital adjustment is an attempt to adjust for the differences in time value of money between the tested party and potential comparables with an assumption that the difference should be reflected in profits. The underlying reasoning is that:

- A company will need funding to cover the time gap between the time it invests money (i.e. pays money to supplier) and the time it collects the investment (i.e. collects money from customers)
- This time gap is calculated as: the period needed to sell inventories to customers + (plus) the period needed to collect money from customers – (less) the period granted to pay debts to suppliers.

6. The process of calculating working capital adjustments:

   a) Identify differences in the levels of working capital. Generally trade receivables, inventory and trade payables are the three accounts considered. The transactional net margin method is applied relative to an appropriate base, for example costs, sales or assets (see paragraph 2.64 of the Guidelines). If the appropriate base is sales, for example, then any differences in working capital levels should be measured relative to sales.

   b) Calculate a value for differences in levels of working capital between the tested party and the comparable relative to the appropriate base and reflecting the time value of money by use of an appropriate interest rate.

c) Adjust the result to reflect differences in levels of working capital. The following example adjusts the comparable's result to reflect the tested party's levels of working capital. Alternative calculations are to adjust the tested party's results to reflect the comparables levels of working capital or to adjust both the tested party and the comparable's results to reflect "zero" working capital.

A practical example of calculating working capital adjustments:

7. The following calculation is hypothetical. It is only to demonstrate how a working capital adjustment can be calculated.

TestCo	Year 1	Year 2	Year 3	Year 4	Year 5
Sales	$179.5 mln	$182.5 mln	$187 mln	$195 mln	$198 mln
Earnings Before Interest & Tax (EBIT)	$1.5 mln	$1.83 mln	$2.43 mln	$2.54 mln	$1.78 mln
EBIT/Sales (%)	0.8%	1%	1.3%	1.3%	0.9%

Working Capital (at end of year)*					
Trade Receivables (R)	$30 mln	$32 mln	$33 mln	$35 mln	$37 mln
Inventories (I)	$36 mln	$36 mln	$38 mln	$40 mln	$45 mln
Trade Payables (P)	$20 mln	$21 mln	$26 mln	$23 mln	$24 mln
Receivables (R) + Inventory (I) – Payables (P)	$46 mln	$47 mln	$45 mln	$52 mln	$58 mln
(R + I – P) / Sales	25.6%	25.8%	24.1%	26.7%	29.3%

CompCo	Year 1	Year 2	Year 3	Year 4	Year 5
Sales	$120.4 mln	$121.2 mln	$121.8 mln	$126.3 mln	$130.2 mln
Earnings Before Interest & Tax (EBIT)	$1.59 mln	$3.59 mln	$3.15 mln	$4.18 mln	$6.44 mln
EBIT/Sales (%)	1.32%	2.96%	2.59%	3.31%	4.95%

Working Capital (at end of year)*					
Trade Receivables (R)	$17 mln	$18 mln	$20 mln	$22 mln	$23 mln
Inventory (I)	$18 mln	$20 mln	$26 mln	$24 mln	$25 mln
Trade Payables (P)	$11 mln	$13 mln	$11 mln	$15 mln	$16 mln
Receivables (R) + Inventory (I) – Payables (P)	$24 mln	$25 mln	$35 mln	$31 mln	$32 mln
(R + I – P) / Sales	19.9%	20.6%	28.7%	24.5%	24.6%

* See comment in paragraph 8.

Working Capital Adjustment	Year 1	Year 2	Year 3	Year 4	Year 5
Testco's (R + I – P) / Sales	25.6%	25.8%	24.1%	26.7%	29.3%
Compco's (R + I – P) / Sales	19.9%	20.6%	28.7%	24.5%	24.6%
Difference (D)	5.7%	5.1%	-4.7%	2.1%	4.7%
Interest Rate (I)	4.8%	5.4%	5.0%	5.5%	4.5%
Adjustment (D × I)	0.27%	0.28%	-0.23%	0.12%	0.21%
Compco's Ebit/Sales (%)	1.32%	2.96%	2.59%	3.31%	4.95%
Working Capital Adjusted Ebit / Sales For Compco	1.59%	3.24%	2.35%	3.43%	5.16%

8. Some observations:

- An issue in making working capital adjustments is what point in time are the Receivables, Inventory and Payables compared between the tested party and the comparables. The above example compares their levels on the last day of the financial year. This may not, however, be appropriate if this timing does not give a representative level of working capital over the year. In such cases, averages might be used if they better reflect the level of working capital over the year.
- A major issue in making working capital adjustments involves the selection of the appropriate interest rate (or rates) to use. The rate (or rates) should generally be determined by reference to the rate(s) of interest applicable to a commercial enterprise operating in the same market as the tested party. In most cases a commercial loan rate will be appropriate. In cases where the tested party's working capital balance is negative (that is Payables > Receivables + Inventory), a different rate may be appropriate. The rate used in the above example reflects the rate at which TestCo is able to borrow funds in its local market. This example also assumes that the same interest rate is appropriate for payables, receivables and inventory, but that may or may not be the case in practice. Where different rates of interest are found to be appropriately applicable to individual classes of assets or liabilities, the calculation may be considerably more complex than shown above.
- The purpose of working capital adjustments is to improve the reliability of the comparables. There is a question whether working capital adjustments should be made when the results of some comparables can be reliably adjusted while the results of some others cannot.

Annex I to Chapter IV

Sample Memoranda of Understanding for Competent Authorities to establish bilateral safe harbours

Introduction

This Annex contains sample Memoranda of Understanding (MOUs) for use by Competent Authorities in negotiating bilateral safe harbours for common categories of transfer pricing cases involving low risk distribution functions, low risk manufacturing functions, and low risk research and development functions. It is intended to provide jurisdictions with a tool to adapt and use in addressing, through bilateral safe harbours, important classes of transfer pricing cases that now take up a great deal of time and effort when processed on a case by case basis. Competent authorities are of course free to modify, add or delete any provision of the sample agreement when concluding their own bilateral agreements.

Reasons for concluding a bilateral safe harbour MOU

As described in Chapter IV, Section E.4 of these Guidelines, one of the potential problems arising from the use of unilateral transfer pricing safe harbours is that they may increase the risk of double taxation and double non-taxation. This can occur if the jurisdiction granting the unilateral safe harbour shades the safe harbour towards the high end of an acceptable arm's length profit range, while a treaty partner on the other end of the transaction disagrees with the assertion that the defined safe harbour profit level reflects arm's length dealing. Some critics contend that there is a tendency for safe harbour profit ranges to increase over time, exacerbating this potential problem. It is also sometimes suggested that unilateral safe harbours can tend to force taxpayers into reporting higher than arm's length levels of income, and to incur some resulting double taxation, as the price to be paid for administrative convenience and simplicity. Finally, unilateral safe harbours can, at times, provide a windfall to taxpayers whose specific facts might suggest that income above the safe harbour level would be more consistent with arm's length dealing.

These double tax and windfall issues would likely be quite pronounced in connection with safe harbours directed at some of the most common types of transfer pricing transactions. Transactions such as sales of goods to a local distribution affiliate for resale on a limited risk basis in the local market, contract manufacturing arrangements, and contract research arrangements could clearly raise these issues. It is perhaps for this reason that few jurisdictions, if any, have developed functioning safe harbours for dealing with these common types of transfer pricing issues.

Distribution margins and manufacturing mark-ups can sometimes be quite consistent across geographies and across many industries. Therefore guidance on normal settlement ranges for these types of cases could have the effect of reducing the number of transfer pricing audits and reducing competent authority dockets and other transfer pricing controversy by a substantial margin if reasonable ranges of results could be agreed bilaterally and published.

These types of cases could potentially be addressed through bilateral MOUs adopted and publicised by competent authorities. Some jurisdictions have adopted such arrangements on a bilateral basis. The general view of such jurisdictions is that treaty provisions based on Article 25(3) of the OECD Model Tax Convention provide sufficient authority to support a bilateral competent authority agreement on a safe harbour rule that would apply to numerous similarly situated taxpayers. Article 25(3) provides: "The competent authorities of the Contracting States shall endeavour to resolve by mutual agreement any difficulties or doubts arising as to the interpretation or application of the Convention. They may also consult together for the elimination of double taxation in cases not provided for in the Convention." A competent authority agreement on a bilateral transfer pricing safe harbour should properly be characterised as a "mutual agreement" that "resolves difficulties or doubts arising as to the interpretation or application" of Article 9 of the Treaty.

Although nothing would prevent the jurisdictions' competent authorities from adopting safe harbour provisions under Article 25(3) on a multilateral basis if the conditions and circumstances so allow, the particular types of transactions described above are such that jurisdictions will often adopt a bilateral approach.

If such MOUs existed, qualifying taxpayers would be able to manage their financial results to fall within the agreed safe harbour range, secure in the understanding that those results would be accepted in both jurisdictions agreeing to the MOU concerned. A commonly cited precedent for this type of approach is the agreement between the United States and Mexico regarding safe harbour profit ranges for maquiladora operations.

A bilateral approach to the development of safe harbours would have a number of advantages over unilateral transfer pricing safe harbours:

- A bilateral approach executed through competent authority MOUs could increase the likelihood that safe harbour provisions do not result in double taxation or double non-taxation.
- Bilateral safe harbours could be tailored to the economics of a particular market and circumstances, and thus be compatible with the arm's length principle.
- Bilateral safe harbours could be entered into on a selective basis with jurisdictions having similar tax rates, thus minimising the possibility that the safe harbour provision itself would create opportunities for transfer pricing manipulation and providing a means for limiting the application of the safe harbour to situations where transfer pricing risk is quite low.
- If the relevant jurisdictions desire, bilateral safe harbours could initially be limited to small taxpayers and/or small transactions in order to limit exposures to government tax revenue that might otherwise be created by the safe harbour.
- Safe harbours adopted by means of a competent authority MOU could be reviewed and modified from time to time by competent authority agreement, thus assuring that the provisions stay up to date and reflect developments in the broader economy.
- For developing countries with serious resource constraints, bilateral MOUs entered into with a number of treaty partners could provide a means of protecting the local tax base in common transfer pricing fact patterns without an inordinate enforcement effort.

The following elements may be of relevance in the negotiation and conclusion of an MOU.

1. Description of and criteria to be fulfilled by the qualifying enterprises. These could include:
   a) A description of the functions required to be performed (or to be disallowed) as a condition to application of the safe harbour;
   b) The risks to be assumed by the participating enterprises as a condition to application of the safe harbour;

c) The mix of assets permitted to be used by the participating enterprises as a condition of application of the safe harbour;

d) A description of classes of entities excluded from the safe harbour provision (by virtue of size, industry, etc.).

2. Description of the qualifying transactions covered by the MOU;
3. Determination of the arm's length range of tested party compensation;
4. The years to which the MOU applies;
5. Statement that the MOU is binding on both of the tax administrations involved;
6. Reporting and monitoring procedures for the MOU;
7. Documentation and information to be maintained by the participating enterprises:
8. A mechanism for resolving disputes.

Set forth below are sample MOUs for three types of transactions: (i) performance of low risk manufacturing services; (ii) performance of low risk distribution services; and (iii) performance of low risk contract research and development services.

Sample Memorandum of Understanding on Low Risk Manufacturing Services

Preamble

1. The Competent Authorities of [State A] and [State B] have reached an understanding relating to the arm's length remuneration applicable to low risk manufacturing services performed by a Qualifying Enterprise resident in [State A] on behalf of an associated enterprise resident in [State B], and by a Qualifying Enterprise resident in [State B] on behalf of an associated enterprise resident in [State A] in the circumstances described herein. The purpose of this memorandum of understanding is to provide legal certainty to Qualifying Enterprises by establishing specific procedures to comply with the transfer pricing rules in [State A] and [State B] and to eliminate double taxation.

2. This memorandum of understanding is entered into under authority of Article [25] of the [Tax Treaty] (the "Treaty") between [State A] and [State B]. It implements the principles of Article [9] of the Treaty in the circumstances described herein. It applies to taxable years of Qualifying Enterprises ending in calendar years [20__] through [20__]. This term will be extended for another five years unless either State notifies the other, in writing, of its intent to terminate this memorandum of understanding on or prior to December 31 [20__]. Expiration of this memorandum of understanding will have effect for taxable years of Qualifying Enterprises ending after the last day of the calendar year in which the application of this memorandum of understanding terminates.

3. For purposes of this memorandum of understanding, an "enterprise" means the enterprise defined in Article [3], paragraph [1] of the Treaty.

Qualifying Enterprise

4. For purposes of this memorandum of understanding, a Qualifying Enterprise must have each of the characteristics described in this paragraph.

a) The Qualifying Enterprise shall be a resident of a Contracting State for purposes of the Treaty and shall conduct business operations predominantly in such State.

b) The principal business activity of the Qualifying Enterprise shall be either the performance of manufacturing services in its State of residence on behalf of an associated enterprise (within the meaning of Article [9] of the Treaty) resident in the other Contracting State, or alternatively, the production of manufactured products for sale to such associated enterprise.

c) The Qualifying Enterprise shall have entered into a written agreement with the associated enterprise, prior to the commencement of the relevant taxable year of the Qualifying Enterprise, pursuant to which the associated enterprise assumes the principal business risks associated with the manufacturing activities of the Qualifying Enterprise and agrees to compensate the Qualifying Enterprise for its manufacturing activities at levels consistent with this memorandum of understanding.

d) Annual research, development, and product engineering expense of the Qualifying Enterprise shall, in the aggregate, be less than [__] percent of its net sales revenue.

e) The Qualifying Enterprise shall not engage in advertising, marketing and distribution functions, credit and collection functions, or warranty administration functions with regard to the products it manufactures.

f) The Qualifying Enterprise shall not retain title to finished products after they leave its factory, shall not bear any transportation or freight expense with respect to such finished products, and shall not bear any risk of loss with respect to damage or loss of finished products in transit.

g) The Qualifying Enterprise shall not engage in managerial, legal, accounting, or personnel management functions other than those directly related to the performance of its manufacturing activities.

h) At least [__] percent of the assets of the Qualifying Enterprise shall consist of manufacturing plant and equipment, raw material inventory, and work in process inventory, calculated on the basis of the average of assets held on the last day of each of the four quarterly periods during the relevant taxable year of the Qualifying Enterprise.

i) The finished product inventory of the Qualifying Enterprise shall not exceed [__] percent of the annual net sales of the Qualifying Enterprise, calculated on an average asset basis in the manner described in paragraph (h) above.

5. A Qualifying Enterprise may not:

a) Conduct its principal business activity in any of the following industries: [__].

b) Have annual net sales in excess of [__].

c) Have total assets in excess of [__].

d) Derive more than [__] percent of its net revenues from transactions other than Qualifying Transactions.

e) Have undergone a transfer pricing audit in either [State A] or [State B] within the past [__] years which resulted in adjustments in excess of [__].

Qualifying Transactions

6. For purposes of this memorandum of understanding, a Qualifying Transaction shall be (i) the rendering of manufacturing services by the Qualifying Enterprise on behalf of an associated enterprise resident in the other Contracting State and/or (ii) the sale of manufactured products produced by the Qualifying Enterprise to an associated enterprise resident in the other Contracting State, in each case without the interposition of other transactions or parties.

Determination of the Taxable Income of the Qualifying Enterprise

7. In the event a Qualifying Enterprise elects to apply the provisions of this memorandum of understanding:

a) In the event the Qualifying Enterprise holds title to raw materials and work in process inventory related to the Qualifying Transactions, the net income before tax of the Qualifying Enterprise with respect to its Qualifying Transactions for the taxable year shall be in the range of [equal to] [__ to __] percent of the total costs of the Qualifying Enterprise, excluding from the base for computing the profit percentage only net interest expense, currency gain or loss, and any non-recurring costs.

b) In the event the associated enterprise holds title to raw materials and work in process inventory related to the Qualifying Transactions, the net income before tax of the Qualifying Enterprise with respect to the Qualifying Transactions for the taxable year shall be in the range of [equal to] [__ to __] percent of the total costs of the Qualifying Enterprise, excluding from the base for computing the profit percentage only net interest expense, currency gain or loss, and any non-recurring costs.

c) Accounting terms utilised in this memorandum of understanding shall be defined in accordance with generally accepted financial accounting principles in the residence jurisdiction of the Qualifying Enterprise.

8. Each of [State A] and [State B] agree that compensation for Qualifying Transactions calculated in accordance with this memorandum of understanding shall be deemed to constitute an arm's length level of compensation for purposes of applying the transfer pricing rules of such State and the provisions of Article [9] of the Treaty.

Permanent Establishment

9. The Competent Authorities of [State A] and [State B] agree that the associated enterprise which is party to a Qualifying Transaction shall not be deemed to have a permanent establishment in the jurisdiction of residence of the Qualifying Enterprise by virtue of the performance of low risk manufacturing services on its behalf by the Qualifying Enterprise or by virtue of such associated enterprise taking title to products produced by the Qualifying Enterprise in the jurisdiction of residence of the Qualifying Enterprise.

Election and Reporting Requirements

10. A Qualifying Enterprise and the relevant associated enterprise may elect to apply the provisions of this memorandum of understanding consistently in [State A] and [State B] by filing a notice with [__] of [State A] and [__] of [State B] no later than [__] covering the Qualifying Transactions.

11. The required notice shall include:

- An affirmative statement that the taxpayers intend to apply and be bound by this memorandum of understanding [for the current year] [for a period of (__) years beginning with the current year];

- An affirmative statement that income and expense from Qualifying Transactions will be reported on a consistent basis in [State A] and [State B] in accordance with this agreement;
- A narrative description of the Qualifying Transactions;
- Identification of each of the associated enterprises that are parties to the Qualifying Transactions;
- Audited financial statements of the Qualifying Enterprise for the relevant year and sufficient additional financial and accounting information to demonstrate the status of the Qualifying Enterprise as a Qualifying Enterprise;
- A detailed calculation of the income of the Qualifying Enterprise from Qualifying Transactions applying the principles of this memorandum of understanding;
- A statement that the Qualifying Enterprise will respond within 60 days to any request of the tax authority of its jurisdiction of residence for information deemed necessary by such tax authority to verify qualification of the enterprise for treatment under this memorandum of understanding.

12. Satisfaction of the election and reporting requirements of this memorandum of understanding, and reporting income calculated in accordance with its terms in a timely filed tax return for the year, shall relieve the Qualifying Enterprise and its relevant associated enterprise from the obligation to comply with the otherwise applicable transfer pricing documentation requirements of [State A] and [State B] with respect to the Qualifying Transactions.

13. A Qualifying Enterprise and its relevant associated enterprise not electing treatment of their Qualifying Transactions under this memorandum of understanding shall be subject to the application of the transfer pricing and documentation rules of [State A] and [State B] as if this memorandum of understanding were not in force.

14. All disputes with regard to the application of this memorandum of understanding shall be referred to the competent authorities of [State A] and [State B] for resolution by mutual agreement.

15. The competent authorities of [State A] and [State B] may exchange information where necessary to carry out this agreement under the provisions of Article [26] of the Treaty.

Termination of the Agreement

16. Either [State A] or [State B] may terminate this memorandum of understanding at any time upon written notice to the competent authority of the other Contracting State and publication of such notice. Such termination will have effect for taxable years of Qualifying Enterprises beginning after the last day of the calendar year in which delivery and publication of such notice of termination occurs.

Sample Memorandum of Understanding on Low Risk Distribution Services

Preamble

17. The Competent Authorities of [State A] and [State B] have reached an understanding relating to the arm's length remuneration applicable to low risk distribution services performed by a Qualifying Enterprise resident in [State A] on behalf of an associated enterprise resident in [State B], and by a Qualifying Enterprise resident in [State B] on behalf of an associated enterprise resident in [State A] in the circumstances described herein. The purpose of this memorandum of understanding is to provide legal certainty to Qualifying Enterprises by establishing specific procedures to comply with the transfer pricing rules in [State A] and [State B] and to eliminate double taxation.

18. This memorandum of understanding is entered into under authority of Article [25] of the [Tax Treaty] (the "Treaty") between [State A] and [State B]. It implements the principles of Article [9] of the Treaty in the circumstances described herein. It applies to taxable years of Qualifying Enterprises ending in calendar years [20__] through [20__]. This term will be extended for another five years unless either State notifies the other, in writing, of its intent to terminate this memorandum of understanding on or prior to December 31 [20__]. Expiration of this memorandum of understanding will have effect for taxable years of Qualifying Enterprises ending after the last day of the calendar year in which the application of this memorandum of understanding terminates.

19. For purposes of this memorandum of understanding, an "enterprise" means the enterprise defined in Article [3], paragraph [1] of the Treaty.

Qualifying Enterprise

20. For purposes of this memorandum of understanding, a Qualifying Enterprise must have each of the characteristics described in this paragraph.

a) The Qualifying Enterprise shall be a resident of a Contracting State for purposes of the Treaty and shall conduct business operations predominantly in such State.

b) The principal business activity of the Qualifying Enterprise shall be either the performance of marketing and distribution services in its State of residence on behalf of an associated enterprise (within the meaning of Article [9] of the Treaty) resident in the other Contracting State, or alternatively, the purchase by the Qualifying Enterprise of products from an associated enterprise resident in the other Contracting State for resale to unrelated customers in its jurisdiction of residence.

c) The Qualifying Enterprise shall have entered into a written agreement with the associated enterprise, prior to the commencement of the relevant taxable year of the Qualifying Enterprise, pursuant to which the associated enterprise assumes the principal business risks associated with the marketing and distribution activities of the Qualifying Enterprise and agrees to assure that the Qualifying Enterprise is compensated for its marketing and distribution activities at levels consistent with this memorandum of understanding.

d) Annual research, development, and product engineering expense of the Qualifying Enterprise shall, in the aggregate, be less than [__] percent of its net sales revenue.

e) The Qualifying Enterprise shall not engage in manufacturing or assembly functions with regard to the products it markets and distributes.

f) The total marketing and advertising expense of the Qualifying Enterprise shall not exceed [__] percent of its net sales.

g) The Qualifying Enterprise shall not engage in managerial, legal, accounting, or personnel management functions other than those directly related to the performance of its marketing and distribution activities.

h) The finished product inventory of the Qualifying Enterprise shall not exceed [__] percent of the annual net sales of the Qualifying Enterprise, calculated on the basis of the average inventory held on the last day of each of the four quarterly periods during the relevant taxable year of the Qualifying Enterprise.

21. A Qualifying Enterprise may not:

a) Conduct its principal business activity in any of the following industries: [__].

b) Have annual net sales in excess of [__].

c) Have total assets in excess of [__].

d) Derive more than [__] percent of its net revenues from transactions other than Qualifying Transactions.

e) Have undergone a transfer pricing audit in either [State A] or [State B] within the past [__] years which resulted in adjustments in excess of [__].

Qualifying Transactions

22. For purposes of this memorandum of understanding, a Qualifying Transaction shall be (i) the rendering of marketing and distribution services by the Qualifying Enterprise on behalf of an associated enterprise resident in the other Contracting State and/or (ii) the sale of products to unrelated customers purchased by the Qualifying Enterprise from an associated enterprise resident in the other Contracting State, in each case without the interposition of other transactions or parties.

Determination of the Taxable Income of the Qualifying Enterprise

23. In the event a Qualifying Enterprise elects to apply the provisions of this memorandum of understanding:

a) The net income before tax of the Qualifying Enterprise with respect to its Qualifying Transactions for the taxable year shall be in the range of [equal to] [__ to __] percent of the total net sales of the Qualifying Enterprise.

b) Accounting terms utilised in this memorandum of understanding shall be defined in accordance with generally accepted financial accounting principles in the jurisdiction of residence of the Qualifying Enterprise.

24. Each of [State A] and [State B] agree that compensation for Qualifying Transactions calculated in accordance with this memorandum of understanding shall be deemed to constitute an arm's length level of compensation for purposes of applying the transfer pricing rules of such State and the provisions of Article [9] of the Treaty.

Permanent Establishment

25. The Competent Authorities of [State A] and [State B] agree that the associated enterprise that is party to a Qualifying Transaction shall not be deemed to have a permanent establishment in the jurisdiction of residence of the Qualifying Enterprise by virtue of the performance of low risk marketing and distribution services on its behalf by the Qualifying Enterprise or by virtue of the Qualifying Enterprise purchasing products from such associated enterprise in Qualifying Transactions for resale to unrelated customers.

Election and Reporting Requirements

26. A Qualifying Enterprise and the relevant associated enterprise may elect to apply the provisions of this memorandum of understanding consistently in [State A] and [State B] by filing a notice with [__] of [State A] and [__] of [State B] no later than [__] covering the Qualifying Transactions.

27. The required notice shall include:

- An affirmative statement that the taxpayers intend to apply and be bound by this memorandum of understanding [for the current year] [for a period of (__) years beginning with the current year];
- An affirmative statement that income and expense from Qualifying Transactions will be reported on a consistent basis in [State A] and [State B] in accordance with this agreement;
- A narrative description of the Qualifying Transactions;
- Identification of each of the associated enterprises that are parties to the Qualifying Transactions;
- Audited financial statements of the Qualifying Enterprise for the relevant year and sufficient additional financial and accounting information to demonstrate the status of the Qualifying Enterprise as a Qualifying Enterprise;
- A detailed calculation of the income of the Qualifying Enterprise from Qualifying Transactions applying the principles of this memorandum of understanding;
- A statement that the Qualifying Enterprise will respond within 60 days to any request of the tax authority of its jurisdiction of residence for information deemed necessary by such tax authority to verify qualification of the enterprise for treatment under this memorandum of understanding.

28. Satisfaction of the election and reporting requirements of this memorandum of understanding, and reporting income calculated in accordance with its terms in a timely filed tax return for the year, shall relieve the Qualifying Enterprise and its relevant associated enterprise from the obligation to comply with the otherwise applicable transfer pricing documentation requirements of [State A] and [State B] with respect to the Qualifying Transactions.

29. A Qualifying Enterprise and its relevant associated enterprise not electing treatment of their Qualifying Transactions under this memorandum of understanding shall be subject to the application of the transfer pricing and documentation rules of [State A] and [State B] as if this memorandum of understanding were not in force.

30. All disputes with regard to the application of this memorandum of understanding shall be referred to the competent authorities of [State A] and [State B] for resolution by mutual agreement.

31. The competent authorities of [State A] and [State B] may exchange information where necessary to carry out this agreement under the provisions of Article [26] of the Treaty.

Termination of the Agreement

32. Either [State A] or [State B] may terminate this memorandum of understanding at any time upon written notice to the competent authority of the other Contracting State and publication of such notice. Such termination will have effect for taxable years of Qualifying Enterprises beginning after the last day of the calendar year in which delivery and publication of such notice of termination occurs.

Sample Memorandum of Understanding on Low Risk Research and Development Services

Preamble

33. The Competent Authorities of [State A] and [State B] have reached an understanding relating to the arm's length remuneration applicable to low risk research and development services performed by a Qualifying Enterprise resident in [State A] on behalf of an associated enterprise resident in [State B], and by a Qualifying Enterprise resident in [State B] on behalf of an associated enterprise resident in [State A] in the circumstances described herein. The purpose of this memorandum of understanding is to provide legal certainty to Qualifying Enterprises by establishing specific procedures to comply with the transfer pricing rules in [State A] and [State B] and to eliminate double taxation.

34. This memorandum of understanding is entered into under authority of Article [25] of the [Tax Treaty] (the "Treaty") between [State A] and [State B]. It implements the principles of Article [9] of the Treaty in the circumstances described herein. It applies to taxable years of Qualifying Enterprises ending in calendar years [20__] through [20__]. This term will be extended for another five years unless either State notifies the other, in writing, of its intent to terminate this memorandum of understanding on or prior to December 31 [20__]. Expiration of this memorandum of understanding will have effect for taxable years of Qualifying Enterprises ending after the last day of the calendar year in which the application of this memorandum of understanding terminates.

35. For purposes of this memorandum of understanding, an "enterprise" means the enterprise defined in Article [3], paragraph [1] of the Treaty.

Qualifying Enterprise

36. For purposes of this memorandum of understanding, a Qualifying Enterprise must have each of the characteristics described in this paragraph.

c) The Qualifying Enterprise shall be a resident of a Contracting State for purposes of the Treaty and shall conduct business operations predominantly in such State.

d) The principal business activity of the Qualifying Enterprise shall be the performance of research and development services in its State of residence on behalf of an associated enterprise (within the meaning of Article [9] of the Treaty) resident in the other Contracting State.

e) The Qualifying Enterprise shall have entered into a written agreement with the associated enterprise, prior to the commencement of the relevant taxable year of the Qualifying Enterprise, pursuant to which: (i) the associated enterprise assumes the principal business risks associated with the research and development services of the Qualifying Enterprise, including the risk that the research and development will not be successful; (ii) the Qualifying Enterprise agrees that all interests in intangibles developed through its research and development services shall belong to the associated enterprise; and (iii) the associated enterprise agrees to compensate the Qualifying Enterprise for its research and development services at levels consistent with this memorandum of understanding.

f) The Qualifying Enterprise shall not engage in product manufacturing and assembly functions, advertising, marketing and distribution functions, credit and collection functions, or warranty administration functions.

g) The Qualifying Enterprise shall not utilise proprietary patents, know-how, trade secrets, or other intangibles in performing its research and development services other than those made available to it by the associated enterprise.

h) The Qualifying Enterprise shall not engage in managerial, legal, accounting, or personnel management functions other than those directly related to the performance of its research and development services.

i) The research and development programme carried out by the Qualified Enterprise shall be designed, directed and controlled by the associated enterprise.

37. A Qualifying Enterprise may not:

j) Conduct its principal business activity in any of the following industries: [__].

k) Have annual payroll and other operating expenses in excess of [__].

l) Have total assets in excess of [__].

m) Derive more than [__] percent of its net revenues from transactions other than Qualifying Transactions.

n) Have undergone a transfer pricing audit in either [State A] or [State B] within the past [__] years which resulted in adjustments in excess of [__].

Qualifying Transactions

38. For purposes of this memorandum of understanding, a Qualifying Transaction shall be the rendering of research and development services by the Qualifying Enterprise on behalf of an associated enterprise resident in the other Contracting State without the interposition of other transactions or parties.

Determination of the Taxable Income of the Qualifying Enterprise

39. In the event a Qualifying Enterprise elects to apply the provisions of this memorandum of understanding:

o) The net income before tax of the Qualifying Enterprise with respect to its Qualifying Transactions for the taxable year shall be in the range of [equal to] [__ to __] percent of the total costs of the Qualifying Enterprise incurred in performing research and development services, excluding from the base for computing the profit percentage only net interest expense, currency gain or loss, and any non-recurring costs.

p) Accounting terms utilised in this memorandum of understanding shall be defined in accordance with generally accepted financial accounting principles in the jurisdiction of residence of the Qualifying Enterprise.

40. Each of [State A] and [State B] agree that compensation for Qualifying Transactions calculated in accordance with this memorandum of understanding shall be deemed to constitute an arm's length level of compensation for purposes of applying the transfer pricing rules of such State and the provisions of Article [9] of the Treaty.

Permanent Establishment

41. The Competent Authorities of [State A] and [State B] agree that the associated enterprise that is party to a Qualifying Transaction shall not be deemed to have a permanent establishment in the jurisdiction of residence of the Qualifying Enterprise by virtue of the performance of low risk research and development services on its behalf by the Qualifying Enterprise.

Election and Reporting Requirements

42. A Qualifying Enterprise and the relevant associated enterprise may elect to apply the provisions of this memorandum of understanding consistently in [State A] and [State B] by filing a notice with [__] of [State A] and [__] of [State B] no later than [__] covering the Qualifying Transactions.

43. The required notice shall include:

- An affirmative statement that the taxpayers intend to apply and be bound by this memorandum of understanding [for the current year] [for a period of (__) years beginning with the current year];
- An affirmative statement that income and expense from Qualifying Transactions will be reported on a consistent basis in [State A] and [State B] in accordance with this agreement;
- A narrative description of the Qualifying Transactions;
- Identification of each of the associated enterprises that are parties to the Qualifying Transactions;
- Audited financial statements of the Qualifying Enterprise for the relevant year and sufficient additional financial and accounting information to demonstrate the status of the Qualifying Enterprise as a Qualifying Enterprise;
- A detailed calculation of the income of the Qualifying Enterprise from Qualifying Transactions applying the principles of this memorandum of understanding;
- A statement that the Qualifying Enterprise will respond within 60 days to any request of the tax authority of its jurisdiction of residence for information deemed necessary by such tax authority to verify qualification of the enterprise for treatment under this memorandum of understanding.

44. Satisfaction of the election and reporting requirements of this memorandum of understanding, and reporting income calculated in accordance with its terms in a timely filed tax return for the year, shall relieve the

Qualifying Enterprise and its relevant associated enterprise from the obligation to comply with the otherwise applicable transfer pricing documentation requirements of [State A] and [State B] with respect to the Qualifying Transactions.

45. A Qualifying Enterprise and its relevant associated enterprise not electing treatment of their Qualifying Transactions under this memorandum of understanding shall be subject to the application of the transfer pricing and documentation rules of [State A] and [State B] as if this memorandum of understanding were not in force.

46. All disputes with regard to the application of this memorandum of understanding shall be referred to the competent authorities of [State A] and [State B] for resolution by mutual agreement.

47. The competent authorities of [State A] and [State B] may exchange information where necessary to carry out this agreement under the provisions of Article [26] of the Treaty.

Termination of the Agreement

48. Either [State A] or [State B] may terminate this memorandum of understanding at any time upon written notice to the competent authority of the other Contracting State and publication of such notice. Such termination will have effect for taxable years of Qualifying Enterprises beginning after the last day of the calendar year in which delivery and publication of such notice of termination occurs.

Annex II to Chapter IV

Guidelines for conducting Advance Pricing Arrangements under the Mutual Agreement Procedure (MAP APAs)

A. Background

A.1. Introduction

1. Advance Pricing Arrangements ("APAs") are the subject of extensive discussion in the *Transfer Pricing Guidelines for Multinational Enterprises and Tax Administrations* at Chapter IV, Section F. The development of working arrangements between competent authorities is considered in paragraph 4.175:

> Between those jurisdictions that use APAs, greater uniformity in APA practices could be beneficial to both tax administrations and taxpayers. Accordingly, the tax administrations of such jurisdictions may wish to consider working agreements with the competent authorities for the undertaking of APAs. These agreements may set forth general guidelines and understandings for the reaching of mutual agreement in cases where a taxpayer has requested an APA involving transfer pricing issues.

It should be noted that the use of the term "agreement" in the above quotation is not intended to give any status to such procedural arrangements above that provided for by the Mutual Agreement Article of the OECD Model Tax Convention. Additionally, the Committee on Fiscal Affairs stated in paragraph 4.171 of the Guidelines that it intended "to monitor carefully any expanded use of APAs and to promote greater consistency in practice amongst those countries that choose to use them."

2. This annex follows up on the above recommendations. The objective is to improve the consistency of application of APAs by providing guidance to tax administrations on how to conduct mutual agreement procedures involving APAs. Although the focus of the annex is on the role of tax administrations, the opportunity is taken to discuss how best the taxpayer can

contribute to the process. This guidance is intended for use by those countries – both OECD members and non-members – that wish to use APAs.

A.2. Definition of an APA

3. Many jurisdictions have had, for some time, procedures (e.g. rulings) enabling the taxpayer to obtain some degree of certainty regarding how the law will be applied in a given set of circumstances. The legal consequences of the proposed action are determined in advance, based on assumptions about the factual basis. The validity of this determination is dependent upon the assumptions being supported by the facts when the actual transactions take place. The term APA refers to a procedural arrangement between a taxpayer or taxpayers and a tax administration intended to resolve potential transfer pricing disputes in advance. The APA differs from the classic ruling procedure, in that it requires the detailed review and to the extent appropriate, verification of the factual assumptions on which the determination of legal consequences is based, before any such determination can be made. Further, the APA provides for a continual monitoring of whether the factual assumptions remain valid throughout the course of the APA period.

4. An APA is defined in the first sentence of paragraph 4.134 of the Guidelines as "an arrangement that determines, in advance of controlled transactions, an appropriate set of criteria (e.g. method, comparables and appropriate adjustments thereto, critical assumptions as to future events) for the determination of the transfer pricing for those transactions over a fixed period of time." It is also stated in paragraph 4.142 that "The concept of APAs also may be useful in resolving issues raised under Article 7 of the OECD Model Tax Convention relating to allocation problems, permanent establishments, and branch operations."

5. In the Guidelines (see paragraph 4.140) the arrangements solely between a taxpayer or taxpayers and a tax administration are referred to as "unilateral APAs". The Guidelines encourage bilateral APAs and recommend in paragraph 4.173 that "Wherever possible, an APA should be concluded on a bilateral or multilateral basis between competent authorities through the mutual agreement procedure of the relevant treaty." A bilateral APA is based on a single mutual agreement between the competent authorities of two tax administrations under the relevant treaty. A multilateral APA is a term used to describe a situation where there is more than one bilateral mutual agreement.

6. Although, commonly an APA will cover cross-border transactions involving more than one taxpayer and legal enterprise, i.e. between members of a MNE group, it is also possible for an APA to apply to only one taxpayer and legal enterprise. For example, consider an enterprise in Country A that

trades through branches in Countries B, C and D. In order to have certainty that double taxation will not occur, Countries A, B, C and D will need to share a common understanding of the measure of profits to be attributed to each jurisdiction in respect of that trading activity under Article 7 of the OECD Model Tax Convention. This certainty could be achieved by the negotiation of a series of separate, but mutually consistent, bilateral mutual agreements, i.e. between A and B, A and C and A and D. The existence of multiple bilateral mutual agreements raises a number of special issues and these are discussed further in Section B, paragraphs 21-27 of this annex.

7. It is important to distinguish the different types of APAs and so the bilateral or multilateral APAs, which are the main subject of this annex, are hereafter referred to as "MAP APAs". The APAs that do not involve a mutual agreement negotiation are referred to as "unilateral APAs". The generic term "APA" is used where the feature to be discussed applies to both types of APA. It should be noted that, in the vast majority of cases a bilateral APA will be concluded under the mutual agreement procedure of a double tax convention. However, in some cases where a bilateral APA has been sought and the treaty is not appropriate, or where a treaty is not applicable, the competent authorities of some jurisdictions may nevertheless conclude an arrangement using the executive power conferred on the heads of tax authorities. The term MAP APA should be interpreted, with the necessary adaptations, as including such exceptional agreements.

8. The focus of this annex is on providing guidance to enable tax authorities to resolve disputes through the mutual agreement procedure, thereby helping to eliminate the risk of potential double taxation and providing the taxpayer with reasonable certainty of tax treatment. However, it should be noted that there are other mechanisms for achieving the same goals which are not discussed in this annex.

A.3. Objectives of the APA process

9. It has been the experience of a number of jurisdictions that the resolution of transfer pricing disputes by traditional audit or examination techniques has often proved very difficult and also costly for taxpayers and tax authorities both in terms of time and resources. Such techniques inevitably examine transfer prices (and the surrounding conditions) some time after they were set and there can be genuine difficulties in obtaining sufficient information to evaluate properly whether arm's length prices were used at the time they were set. These difficulties led in part to the development of the APA process as an alternative way of solving transfer pricing issues in some cases in order to avoid some of the problems described above. The objectives of an APA process are to facilitate principled, practical and co-operative negotiations, to resolve transfer pricing issues expeditiously and prospectively, to use the

resources of the taxpayer and the tax administration more efficiently, and to provide a measure of predictability for the taxpayer.

10. To be successful, the process should be administered in a non-adversarial, efficient and practical fashion and requires the co-operation of all the participating parties. It is intended to supplement, rather than replace, the traditional administrative, judicial, and treaty mechanisms for resolving transfer pricing issues. Consideration of an APA may be most appropriate when the methodology for applying the arm's length principle gives rise to significant questions of reliability and accuracy, or when the specific circumstances of the transfer pricing issues being considered are unusually complex.

11. One of the key objectives of the MAP APA process is the elimination of potential double taxation. Unilateral APAs give rise to considerable concerns in this area, which is why "most jurisdictions prefer bilateral or multilateral APAs" (paragraph 4.141 of the Guidelines). However, some kind of confirmation or agreement between the taxpayer and the tax administration is necessary in order to give effect to the MAP APA in each of the participating jurisdictions. The exact form of such confirmation or agreement depends on the domestic procedures in each jurisdiction (discussed in more detail in paragraphs 65-66 of this annex). Such a confirmation or agreement also provides a mechanism to ensure that the taxpayer complies with the terms and conditions of the MAP APA on which this confirmation or agreement is based.

12. Further, in order to meet the objectives described in this section, the MAP APA process needs to be conducted in a neutral manner. In particular, the process should be neutral as regards the residence of the taxpayer, the jurisdiction in which the request for the MAP APA was initiated, the audit or examination status of the taxpayer and the selection of taxpayers in general for audit or examination. The guidance in paragraph 4.167 of the Guidelines on possible misuse by tax administrations in their examination practices of information obtained in the APA process should also be borne in mind. The guidance given in this annex is intended to assist in attaining the objectives described in this section.

B. Eligibility for a MAP APA

B.1. Treaty issues

13. The first question that arises is whether it is possible for there to be an APA. The eligibility of a taxpayer to apply for a unilateral APA will be determined by the specific domestic requirements of the relevant tax administration. MAP APAs are governed by the mutual agreement procedure of the applicable double tax agreement, Article 25 of the OECD Model Tax Convention, and are administered at the discretion of the relevant tax

administrations. The work pursuant to Action 14 of the BEPS Action Plan to ensure the timely, effective and efficient resolution of treaty-related disputes recommended, as non-binding best practice 4, that jurisdictions should implement bilateral APA programmes as soon as they have the capacity to do so, recognising that APAs provide a greater level of certainty in both treaty partner jurisdictions, lessen the likelihood of double taxation and may proactively prevent transfer pricing disputes. In this regard, it should be noted that the country mutual agreement procedure profiles prepared pursuant to element 2.2 of the Action 14 minimum standard include information on the bilateral APA programmes.

14. In some cases the taxpayer will only request a unilateral APA. The reasons for the taxpayer not requesting a MAP APA should be explored. Following the guidance given by the Guidelines in paragraph 4.173 that "wherever possible, an APA should be concluded on a bilateral or multilateral basis", the tax authorities should encourage the taxpayer to request a MAP APA if the circumstances so warrant. Some jurisdictions if they determine that another tax administration should be involved may refuse to enter into unilateral negotiations with the taxpayer, even though the taxpayer still insists on a unilateral approach.

15. The negotiation of a MAP APA requires the consent of the relevant competent authorities. In some cases, the taxpayer will take the initiative by making simultaneous requests to the affected competent authorities. In other cases the taxpayer may file a request with one jurisdiction under the relevant domestic procedure and ask it to contact the other affected jurisdiction(s) to see if a MAP APA is possible. Consequently, as soon as is administratively practicable, the competent authority in that jurisdiction should notify the relevant tax treaty partner(s) to determine whether they want to participate. The other tax administration should respond to the invitation as quickly as practicable, bearing in mind the need to have sufficient time to evaluate whether their participation is possible or feasible.

16. However, Article 25 does not oblige the competent authorities to enter into MAP APAs at the request of the taxpayer. The willingness to enter into MAP APAs will depend on the particular policy of a jurisdiction and how it interprets the mutual agreement article of its bilateral treaties. Some competent authorities will only consider such an agreement for cases that require the resolution of "difficulties or doubts arising as to the interpretation or application of the Convention". The desire of the taxpayer for certainty of treatment is therefore not, in isolation, sufficient to pass the above threshold. Other competent authorities apply a less restrictive threshold for entering into MAP APAs, based on their view that the MAP APA process should be encouraged. Additionally, the taxpayer must qualify for the benefit of a particular treaty (e.g. by qualifying as a resident of one of the Contracting States) and must satisfy any other criteria contained in the mutual agreement article.

B.2. Other factors

17. The fact that a taxpayer may be under audit or examination should not prevent the taxpayer from requesting a MAP APA in respect of prospective transactions. The audit or examination and the mutual agreement procedure are separate processes and generally can be resolved separately. Audit or examination activities would not normally be suspended by a tax administration whilst the MAP APA is being considered, unless it is agreed by all parties that the audit or examination should be held in abeyance because the obtaining of the MAP APA would assist with the completion of the audit or examination. Nevertheless, the treatment of the transactions being audited or examined may be informed by the methodology agreed to be applied prospectively under the MAP APA, provided that the facts and circumstances surrounding the transaction under audit or examination are comparable with those relating to the prospective transactions. This issue is discussed further in paragraph 69 below.

18. The ability to conclude a MAP APA is predicated on full co-operation by the taxpayer. The taxpayer and any associated enterprises should: a) provide their full co-operation in assisting the tax administrations with the evaluation of their proposal; and b) provide, upon request, any additional information necessary for that evaluation, for example, details of their transfer pricing transactions, business arrangements, forecasts and business plans, and financial performance. It is desirable that this commitment from the taxpayer be sought before commencing the MAP APA process.

19. In some cases the freedom of one or both competent authorities to agree to a MAP APA may be limited, for example by a legally binding decision affecting issues subject to the APA proposals. In such circumstances, as the MAP APA process is by definition consensual, it is within the discretion of the affected competent authorities (subject to the domestic laws and policies of each jurisdiction) whether to engage in MAP APA discussions. For example, a competent authority may decline to enter into discussions if it determines that such a limitation on the position of the other competent authority unacceptably reduces the likelihood of mutual agreement. However, it is likely that in many cases MAP APA discussions would be viewed as desirable even though the flexibility of one or both competent authorities is restricted. This is a matter for the competent authorities to determine on a case by case basis.

20. When deciding whether a MAP APA is appropriate, a key consideration is the extent of the advantage to be gained by agreeing a method for avoiding the risk of double taxation in advance. This requires the exercise of judgement and the need to balance the efficient use of limited resources, both financial and human, with the desire to reduce the likelihood of double taxation. Tax administrations might consider the following items as relevant:

a) Does the methodology and the other terms and conditions of the proposal respect the guidance given by the Guidelines? If not, it will be desirable to get the taxpayer to revise the proposal accordingly, in order to increase the chances of reaching a mutual agreement. As paragraph 17 of the preface to the Guidelines states "these guidelines are also intended primarily to govern the resolution of transfer pricing cases in mutual agreement proceedings".

b) Are any "difficulties or doubts as to the interpretation or application of the Convention" likely to significantly increase the risk of double taxation and so justify the use of resources to settle any problems in advance of the proposed transactions?

c) Would the transactions covered by the proposal be ongoing in nature and is there a significant part of any limited life project left?

d) Are the transactions in question seriously contemplated and not of a purely hypothetical nature? The process should not be used to find out the likely views of the tax administration on a general point of principle – there are other established methods for doing this in many jurisdictions.

e) Is a transfer pricing audit already in progress in relation to past years where the fact pattern was substantially similar? If so, the outcome of the audit may be expedited by participating in a MAP APA, the terms of which could then be applied to inform or resolve the audit and any unresolved mutual agreement for earlier years.

B.3. Multilateral MAP APAs

21. The desire for certainty has resulted in an emerging trend for taxpayers to seek multilateral MAP APAs covering their global operations. The taxpayer approaches each of the affected jurisdictions with an overall proposal and suggests that it would be desirable if the negotiations be conducted on a multilateral basis involving all the affected jurisdictions, rather than by a series of separate negotiations with each tax authority. It should be noted that there is no multilateral method of implementing any agreement that may be reached, except by concluding a series of separate bilateral MAP APAs. The successful negotiation of a series of bilateral MAP APAs in this way would provide greater certainty and lower costs to the MNE group than if separate MAP APAs were undertaken bilaterally and in isolation of each other.

22. Although, as described above, there are potential benefits to having multilateral MAP APAs, a number of issues need to be considered. First,

it is unlikely to be appropriate for a single transfer pricing methodology to be applied to the wide variety of facts and circumstances, transactions and jurisdictions likely to be the subject of a multilateral MAP APA, unless the methodology can be appropriately adapted to reflect the particular facts and circumstances found in each jurisdiction. Therefore, care would need to be taken by all the participating jurisdictions to ensure that the methodology, even after such adaptation, represented a proper application of the arm's length principle in the conditions found in their jurisdiction.

23. Second, issues also arise because under a multilateral MAP APA several competent authorities are effectively involved in a process that was designed for a bilateral process. One issue is the extent to which it may be necessary to exchange information between all the affected jurisdictions. This could be problematic in cases where there are no transaction flows or common transactions between two or more of the affected treaty partners, so creating doubts as to whether the information is relevant to the particular bilateral MAP APA being discussed. However, in cases where similar transactions are conducted by different parts of the MNE or in which the area considered relates to trading on an integrated basis, there may be a need to have information about flows between other parties in order to be able to understand and evaluate the flows that are the subject of the particular bilateral MAP APA. Another problem is that it may be difficult to judge whether such information is indeed relevant prior to obtaining it.

24. Further, even if the information is relevant to the particular bilateral MAP APA, there may still be potential problems of confidentiality preventing the exchange of that information, either under the terms of the exchange of information article(s) of the relevant treaty or under the domestic law of one of the participating tax administrations. Given the wide range of possible circumstances likely to be found in multilateral MAP APAs, no general solution to these problems can be prescribed. Rather such issues need to be addressed specifically in each of the separate bilateral MAP APAs.

25. In cases where information about flows between other parties is found to be relevant, some exchange of information problems could possibly be overcome by not relying on treaty information exchange provisions, but instead asking the taxpayer to assume responsibility for providing information to all the affected tax administrations (though procedures would still be needed to verify that the same information is in fact provided to all tax administrations). Finally, in some cases the mutual agreement articles of the relevant treaties may not provide an adequate basis for such multilateral consideration and discussion, although the mutual agreement article of the OECD Model Tax Convention is designed to assist in the elimination of double taxation in a wide variety of circumstances, and therefore would, if applicable, appear to provide adequate authority in most situations.

26. In summary, as discussed in Section A, the desire by the taxpayer for certainty is not by itself sufficient to oblige a tax administration to enter into a MAP APA where this might be inappropriate. An invitation to participate in a multilateral MAP APA would therefore be evaluated in accordance with the usual criteria for determining whether a bilateral MAP APA could be pursued and each proposed bilateral APA would also be separately evaluated. A decision would then be taken whether the completion of the negotiations for the bilateral MAP APAs that the administration has decided to pursue, would best be served by its participation in multilateral negotiations. This evaluation will be made on a case-by-case basis.

27. The development of multilateral MAP APAs is at a relatively early stage, except perhaps in the global trading field. Indeed, where global trading is conducted on a fully integrated basis (i.e. the trading and risk management of a book of financial products takes place in a number of different locations, usually at least three), a multilateral, as opposed to a bilateral, APA has become the norm[1]. It is intended to monitor closely further developments in the area of multilateral MAP APAs.

C. Request for MAP APAs

C.1. Introduction

28. Although a MAP APA by its nature involves an agreement between tax administrations, the process needs considerable involvement by the taxpayer or taxpayers in order to be successful. This section looks at the first stages in this process, namely the request for the MAP APA which is normally initiated by the taxpayer(s). (N.B. Some tax administrations consider that they should take the initiative and actively encourage taxpayers to make requests in appropriate cases, for example following completion of an audit or risk assessment analysis.) Once it has been decided that a MAP APA is indeed appropriate, the primary responsibility for providing the participating tax administrations with sufficient information for them to be able to conduct mutual agreement negotiations will inevitably rest with the taxpayer(s). Consequently, the taxpayer should submit a detailed proposal for review by the relevant tax administration and be prepared to provide further information as requested by the tax administration.

1. For more details see OECD (1998), *The Taxation of Global Trading of Financial Instruments,* OECD, Paris.

C.2. Preliminary discussions

29. A feature of many domestic procedures for the obtaining of a unilateral APA is the ability to have a preliminary meeting (or meetings) before a formal request is made. Such a meeting (or meetings) provides a taxpayer with an opportunity to discuss with the tax administration the suitability of an APA, the type and extent of information which may be required and the scope of any analyses required for the completion of a successful APA. (For example, the extent of any functional analysis of affiliated enterprises; identification, selection and adjustment of comparables; and the need for, and the scope of, market, industry and geographic analyses.) The process also provides the taxpayer with an opportunity to discuss any concerns regarding disclosure and confidentiality of data, the term of the APA and the like. Experience has generally shown that the ability to have such preliminary discussions expedites the processing of any subsequent formal MAP APA proposal.

30. In the context of a MAP APA, the ability of the relevant competent authorities to have preliminary discussions with the taxpayer(s) may also be useful. In addition to the matters mentioned above, the discussions could usefully explore whether the circumstances were suitable for a MAP APA, for example whether there were sufficient "difficulties or doubts as to the interpretation or application of the Convention".

31. The preliminary meeting may also have a useful role in clarifying the expectations and objectives of the taxpayer(s) and the tax administration. It also provides an opportunity to explain the process, the policy of the tax administration on MAP APAs and to give details of any procedures for giving effect in domestic law to the agreement when completed. At the same time, the tax administration could provide guidance as to the content of the proposal, and the time frame for evaluating and concluding the mutual agreement. Tax administrations should publish general guidance on the MAP APA process in accordance with the recommendation for other types of mutual agreements in paragraphs 4.62-4.63 of the Guidelines.

32. The preliminary meeting process may be conducted on either an anonymous or a named basis, depending on domestic custom and practice. If on an anonymous basis, however, sufficient information about the operations will be required in order to make any discussion meaningful. The form of any meetings should be agreed between the parties and a preliminary meeting may range from an informal discussion to a formal presentation. Typically, it is in the taxpayer's interest to provide the tax administration with a memorandum outlining the topics for discussion. More than one preliminary meeting may be required in order to achieve the objective of having an informal discussion of the potential suitability of a MAP APA request, its

likely scope, the appropriateness of a methodology or the type and extent of information to be provided by the taxpayer.

33. As well as informal discussions with its taxpayer(s), it may be useful for the respective competent authorities to have an early exchange of views on whether a MAP APA would be appropriate. This could avoid unnecessary work if it is unlikely that one of the competent authorities will participate. These discussions may be of an informal nature and do not necessarily require a formal face to face meeting. Also there may be opportunities to have such exchanges during the course of regular competent authority meetings and negotiations.

C.3. MAP APA proposals

C.3.1. Introduction

34. If the taxpayer wishes to pursue a MAP APA request, it will need to make a detailed proposal to the relevant tax administration, pursuant to any domestic procedural requirements, e.g. a requirement to file the request with a designated part of the domestic tax administration. For a MAP APA, the purpose of the taxpayer's proposal is to give the relevant competent authorities all the information needed to evaluate the proposal and to undertake mutual agreement discussions. Jurisdictions have a number of ways of ensuring the competent authorities get the necessary information. One way is for the taxpayer to be able to make the proposal directly to the competent authority. Another way of achieving this goal is for the taxpayer to make available a copy of any domestic APA proposal to the other participating jurisdictions. Ideally, the exact form and content of the proposal will have been established at any preliminary meetings.

C.3.2. Activities usually covered in a MAP APA process

35. The scope of the MAP APA would depend on the wishes of the participating jurisdictions, as well as those of the taxpayer. It can apply to resolve issues covered by Articles 7 and 9 of the OECD Model Convention and would determine to what extents profits would arise in the tax jurisdictions involved.

36. The MAP APA may cover all of the transfer pricing issues of a taxpayer (or of the members of a MNE group) or may be more limited, for example to a particular transaction, sets of transactions, product lines or to only some members of a MNE group. Some jurisdictions, whilst recognising the need for flexibility in the process, have concerns over the appropriateness of specific issue APAs. It may be difficult to evaluate some issues in isolation, for example where the transactions covered by the proposal are

highly interrelated with transactions not covered by the proposal, or where there is a need to analyse transfer pricing issues in a wider context because intentional set offs are involved (see paragraphs 3.13-3.17 of the Guidelines).

37. A MAP APA may also cover issues other than the transfer pricing methodology, provided that these other issues are sufficiently clearly connected to the underlying transfer pricing issues so as to make it worthwhile attempting to resolve them in advance and provided that the other issues come within the terms of the mutual agreement article in the relevant treaty. That will be something to be decided between the affected parties for each individual case.

C.3.3. Content of a MAP APA proposal

38. The content of the proposal and the extent of the necessary supporting information and documentation will depend on the facts and circumstances of each case and the requirements of the individual participating tax administrations. It is therefore not considered practicable to list or define exactly what should be provided. The guiding principle, however, should be to provide the information and documentation necessary to explain the facts relevant to the proposed methodology and to demonstrate its application in accordance with the appropriate Article of the relevant treaty. The proposal should therefore be consistent with any general guidance given by the Commentary of the OECD Model Tax Convention on the corresponding Articles, together with the guidance on the application of the arm's length principle of Article 9 given by the Guidelines in cases involving transfer pricing between associated enterprises.

39. In terms of the supporting information and documentation to be included, the guidance in Chapter IV (paragraphs 4.165-4.168) and Chapter V of the Guidelines on documentation requirements should be borne in mind. However, because of the prospective nature of the agreement sought, different types of information may need to be supplied than in mutual agreement cases, which only relate to transactions already undertaken. As a guide, the following information may be of general relevance for MAP APAs, although it should be stressed that the list below is not intended to be exhaustive or prescriptive in nature:

a) The transactions, products, businesses or arrangements that will be covered by the proposal; (including, if applicable, a brief explanation of why not all of the transactions, products, businesses or arrangements of the taxpayer(s) involved in the request have been included);

b) The enterprises and permanent establishments involved in these transactions or arrangements;

c) The other jurisdiction or jurisdictions which have been requested to participate;

d) Information regarding the world-wide organisational structure, history, financial statement data, products, functions and assets (tangible and intangible) of any associated enterprises involved;

e) A description of the proposed transfer pricing methodology and details of information and analyses supporting that methodology, e.g. identification of comparable prices or margins and expected range of results etc.;

f) The assumptions underpinning the proposal and a discussion of the effect of changes in those assumptions or other events, such as unexpected results, which might affect the continuing validity of the proposal;

g) The accounting periods or tax years to be covered;

h) General description of market conditions (e.g. industry trends and the competitive environment);

i) A discussion of any pertinent ancillary tax issues raised by the proposed methodology;

j) A discussion of, and demonstration of compliance with, any pertinent domestic law, tax treaty provisions and OECD guidelines that relate to the proposal; and

k) Any other information which may have a bearing on the current or proposed transfer pricing methodology and the underlying data for any party to the request.

The rest of this section discusses some of the most important items from the above list in more detail.

C.3.4. Comparable pricing information

40. The taxpayer should include a discussion of the availability and use of comparable pricing information. This would include a description of how the search for comparables was carried out (including search criteria employed), what data relating to uncontrolled transactions was obtained and how such data was accepted or rejected as being comparable. The taxpayer should also include a presentation of comparable transactions along with adjustments to account for material differences, if any, between controlled and uncontrolled transactions. In cases where no comparables can be identified, the taxpayer should demonstrate, by reference to relevant market and financial data (including the internal data of the taxpayer), how the chosen methodology accurately reflects the arm's length principle.

C.3.5. Methodology

41. The MAP APA proposal should provide a full description of the chosen methodology. In cases involving associated enterprises, the chosen methodology should also respect the guidance found in the Guidelines on applying the arm's length principle of Article 9 of the OECD Model Tax Convention. It is stated in paragraph 2.11 of the Guidelines that "further, any method should be permitted where its application is agreeable to the members of the MNE group involved with the transaction or transactions to which the methodology applies and also to the tax administrations in the jurisdictions of all those members." That guidance on use of transfer pricing methods is particularly relevant in the context of a MAP APA, because of the opportunity to obtain advance agreement on the method to be used. The application of the methodology should be supported by data which can be obtained and updated over the period of the MAP APA without imposing too great a burden on the taxpayer, and which can be reviewed and verified effectively by the tax administrations.

42. The taxpayer should, to the extent possible, provide an analysis of the effect of applying the chosen methodology or methodologies during the proposed period of the agreement. Such an analysis necessarily will have to be based on projected results and so details of the assumptions on which those projections were made will be needed. It may also be helpful to illustrate the effect of applying the APA methodology or methodologies to the periods immediately before the APA period. The usefulness of this analysis, even as an illustration, will depend on the facts and circumstances surrounding the transactions in question being comparable to those applying to the prospective transactions contemplated under the proposal.

C.3.6. Critical assumptions

43. In entering into a MAP APA relating to the arm's length pricing of controlled transactions that have not yet occurred, it is necessary to make certain assumptions about the operational and economic conditions that will affect those transactions when they take place. The taxpayer should describe in the proposal the assumptions on which the ability of the methodology to accurately reflect the arm's length pricing of future transactions is based. Additionally, the taxpayer should explain how the chosen methodology will satisfactorily cope with any changes in those assumptions. The assumptions are defined as "critical" if the actual conditions existing at the time the transactions occur could diverge from those that were assumed to exist, to the extent that the ability of the methodology reliably to reflect arm's length pricing is undermined. One example might be a fundamental change to the market arising from new technology, government regulations, or widespread

loss of consumer acceptance. In such a case, the divergence may mean that the agreement would need to be revised or cancelled.

44. To increase the reliability of the MAP APA methodology, taxpayers and tax administrations should attempt to identify critical assumptions that are, where possible, based on observable, reliable and independent data. Such assumptions are not limited to items within the control of the taxpayer. Any set of critical assumptions needs to be tailored to the individual circumstances of the taxpayer, the particular commercial environment, the methodology, and the type of transactions covered. They should not be drawn so tightly that certainty provided by the agreement is jeopardised, but should encompass as wide a range of variation in the underlying facts as the parties to the agreement feel comfortable with. In general, however, and by way of example only, critical assumptions might include:

a) Assumptions about the relevant domestic tax law and treaty provisions.

b) Assumptions about tariffs, duties, import restrictions and government regulations.

c) Assumptions about economic conditions, market share, market conditions, end-selling price, and sales volume.

d) Assumptions about the nature of the functions and risks of the enterprises involved in the transactions.

e) Assumptions about exchange rates, interest rates, credit rating and capital structure.

f) Assumptions about management or financial accounting and classification of income and expenses; and

g) Assumptions about the enterprises that will operate in each jurisdiction and the form in which they will do so.

45. It may also be helpful to set parameters for an acceptable level of divergence for some assumptions in advance, in order to provide the necessary flexibility. These parameters would need to be set individually for each particular MAP APA and would form part of the negotiations between the competent authorities. Only if the divergence from the prediction exceeded the parameter would the assumption become "critical" and action considered. Any action to be taken might also depend on the nature of the assumption and the level of divergence.

46. If the reliability of the proposed transfer pricing methodology is known to be sensitive to exchange rate fluctuations, it would seem sensible to design a methodology that was capable of accommodating a certain degree of expected

fluctuation, perhaps by providing for prices to be adjusted to take into account exchange rate movements. Also it could be agreed in advance that movements in either direction of up to X% would require no action, that movements greater than X% but less than Y% would trigger a prospective review of the methodology to make sure it remained appropriate, whilst a movement of more than Y% would mean that a critical assumption had been breached and it would be necessary to prospectively re-negotiate the MAP APA. These parameters would need to be set individually for each particular MAP APA and would form part of the negotiation between the competent authorities.

C.3.7. Unexpected results

47. A problem may arise when the results of applying the transfer pricing methodology agreed in the MAP APA do not fulfil the expectations of one of the parties, as that party may question whether the critical assumptions, and the methodology which they support, are still valid. The resolution of such questions may take a considerable amount of time and effort, thereby negating one of the objectives of the whole process. One possible solution to this problem is to include enough flexibility in the proposal to cope with likely changes in the facts and circumstances so that unexpected results are less likely to occur so that there is less risk that the MAP APA agreement based upon the proposal will need to be renegotiated. The proposal must still, of course, conform to the arm's length principle.

48. One way of achieving the above objective is to design a methodology that appropriately takes into account likely changes in facts and circumstances; for example, some variation between projected and actual sales volume can be built in to the pricing methodology at the outset by including prospective price adjustment clauses or allowing pricing to vary with volume. The allowable level of deviation should be set by reference to what would have been accepted by independent parties.

49. Another possible way of achieving the objective of increasing certainty, is to agree an acceptable range of results from applying the method of the MAP APA. In order to conform with the arm's length principle, the range should be agreed by all affected parties in advance, thereby avoiding the use of hindsight, and based on what independent parties would have agreed to in comparable circumstances (see paragraphs 3.55-3.66 for discussion of the range concept). For example, the quantum of an item, such as a royalty, would be accepted so long as it remained within a certain range expressed as a proportion of the profits.

50. If the results fall outside the agreed range, the action to be taken would depend on what had been negotiated in the proposal in accordance with the wishes of the parties. Some parties may not wish to take the risk that the results will be significantly different from what they expected. Accordingly,

they would use the range concept simply as a means of determining whether a critical assumption had been breached as described in paragraph 46. Other parties may place more emphasis on certainty of treatment than on avoiding unexpected results and so may agree that the MAP APA should contain a mechanism for adjusting the results so that they fall within the range agreed in advance.

C.3.8. Duration of the MAP APA

51. By its nature, an APA applies to prospective transactions and so one issue to be decided is how long it will last. There are two sets of conflicting objectives that affect the negotiation of the appropriate term. On the one hand, it is desirable to have a sufficiently long period so as to grant a reasonable degree of certainty of treatment. Otherwise, it may not be worth making the initial effort of resolving potential transfer pricing problems in advance, as opposed to tackling problems only when they arise through the normal audit or tax return examination procedures. On the other hand, a long period makes the predictions as to future conditions on which the mutual agreement negotiations are based less accurate, thereby casting doubt on the reliability of the MAP APA proposals. The optimal trade-off between these two sets of objectives will depend on a number of factors, such as the industry, the transactions involved and the economic climate. The term should therefore be negotiated between the competent authorities on a case-by case basis. Experience to date has shown that a MAP APA might, on average, last for 3-5 years.

D. Finalisation of the MAP APA

D.1. Introduction

52. The success of the MAP APA process, as an alternative to relying solely on traditional audit or examination techniques, depends to a large extent on the commitment of all the participants. The ability of the relevant competent authorities to reach agreement in a prompt manner will be determined both by their actions and importantly by the willingness of the taxpayer(s) to provide all the necessary information as promptly as possible. The usefulness of the process, both for taxpayers and tax authorities, will be significantly diminished if the MAP APA is not agreed until the period proposed to be covered in the taxpayer's request has nearly expired. Such delay may also make it more difficult to avoid the use of hindsight when evaluating the proposal because the results of applying the methodology will be known for most of the period proposed by the MAP APA. Understandably, given the relatively early stage in the evolution of the MAP APA process, the goal of prompt prospective resolution has not always been met in the past. To

some extent, of course, some delay in the process is inevitable; MAP APAs tend to deal with large taxpayers, complex fact patterns, and difficult legal and economic issues, all of which require time and resources in order to understand and evaluate.

53. Tax authorities are encouraged, where possible, to devote sufficient resources and skilled personnel to the process to ensure that cases are settled promptly and efficiently. Some tax authorities may wish to improve the efficiency of their MAP APA programmes by setting informal goals for the length of time taken to complete the process and by publishing the average completion time. Particular treaty partners may also agree to set informal goals for completion of their bilateral negotiations. Given the often complex and difficult fact patterns, the possible need for translations and the relative novelty of such arrangements, it is not felt desirable to set more specific or binding targets for concluding MAP APAs at this stage. However, it will be appropriate to set more specific targets for completion time in the future, once more experience with the MAP APA process has been gained.

54. Once a taxpayer's proposal has been received by the tax administrations, they should mutually agree on the co-ordination of the review, evaluation and negotiation of the MAP APA. The MAP APA process can conveniently be broken up into two main stages; a) fact finding, review and evaluation and b) the competent authority discussions, each of which is discussed in greater detail below.

D.2. Fact finding, review and evaluation

D.2.1. General

55. In reviewing the MAP APA proposal, the tax administrations may undertake whatever steps they deem appropriate in the circumstances to conduct the mutual agreement procedure. These include, but are not limited to: requests for further information deemed relevant to review and evaluate the taxpayer's proposal, the carrying out of fieldwork (e.g. visits to taxpayer's premises, interviews with staff, review of financial or managerial operations, etc.) and the engaging of necessary experts. Tax administrations may also have recourse to information collected from other sources, including information and data on comparable taxpayers.

56. The aim of this stage of the MAP APA process is for the participating competent authorities to have all relevant information, data, and analyses they need for the negotiations. Where one tax administration obtains additional information from the taxpayer relevant to the subject of the MAP APA, for example at a meeting with the taxpayer's staff, both the taxpayer and the tax administration should ensure the information reaches the other participating tax

administration(s). The relevant competent authorities should arrange, amongst themselves and the taxpayers, for an appropriate mechanism to corroborate the completeness and details of documents and information supplied by the taxpayer(s). The requirements of the participating competent authorities should be respected. For example, many jurisdictions require that not only is the same factual information provided to all participating competent authorities but that it should, as far as is practicable, be made available at the same time.

57. The prospective nature of a MAP APA often involves the provision by the taxpayer of commercial information relating to forecasts which is likely to be even more sensitive to disclosure than information supplied after the event. Accordingly, in order to ensure that taxpayers have confidence in the MAP APA process, tax administrations should ensure that taxpayer information provided during the course of the MAP APA process is subject to the same secrecy, confidentiality and privacy safeguards of the relevant domestic law as any other taxpayer information. Further, where information is exchanged between competent authorities under the terms of the tax treaty, that information can be disclosed only in accordance with the specified terms of the treaty, and any exchange must comply with the exchange of information article(s) of the relevant treaty.

58. Generally, the competent authorities would conduct simultaneous, independent reviews and evaluations of the taxpayer's proposal, assisted in this task, where necessary, by transfer pricing, industry, or other specialists from elsewhere in their tax administration. However, it may be more efficient in appropriate cases to have some degree of joint fact finding. This could take a variety of forms ranging from an occasional joint fact finding meeting or site visit, to the preparation of a joint report by delegated caseworkers.

D.2.2. Role of taxpayer in the fact finding, review and evaluation process

59. In order to expedite the process, taxpayers should take responsibility for ensuring that the competent authorities, before they start to negotiate, are in possession of the same facts, have all the information they need and have a thorough understanding of the issues. This can be achieved by the taxpayer routinely making information requested by one tax administration available, at broadly the same time, to the other tax administration, preparing and transmitting notes of fact finding meetings by one tax administration to the other tax administration and where logistically and economically practical, facilitating joint fact finding meetings. The taxpayer should also arrange for any necessary translations to be made and ensure there is no undue delay in responding to requests for further relevant information. The taxpayer should also be entitled to confer with its tax administrations when mutually appropriate and convenient while the proposal is undergoing review and evaluation, and should be kept informed of progress.

D.3. Conduct of Competent Authority discussions

D.3.1. Co-ordination amongst the Competent Authorities

60. Many jurisdictions prefer to be fully involved in the process as soon as it commences and wish to work closely with the other competent authorities. Other countries prefer to confine their involvement to reviewing and commenting upon the MAP APA proposals as they near completion. However, the involvement of all participating tax administrations in the process at an early stage is recommended, subject to resource constraints, as this should maximise the efficiency of the process and help forestall unnecessary delays in concluding the mutual agreement.

61. The competent authorities should conduct the mutual agreement discussions in a timely manner. This requires the devotion of sufficient resources and appropriately skilled personnel to the process. It is desirable that the competent authorities discuss and co-ordinate an appropriate plan of action with regards to such matters as: designating authorised officers, exchanging of information, co-ordination of the review and evaluation of the proposal, tentative scheduling of dates for further consultations, negotiation and conclusion of a suitable agreement. The level of input and resources required should be tailored to the individual requirements of the case.

62. Experience has also shown that early and frequent discussion between the competent authorities as problems arise can be helpful and can avoid unpleasant surprises during the process. Given the nature of MAP APAs, there will often be significant issues which cannot be resolved simply by exchange of position papers and so more formal exchanges, such as face to face meetings between the competent authorities may be required. Use of conference calls or video conferencing may be helpful.

D.3.2. Role of the taxpayer in Competent Authority discussions

63. The role of the taxpayer in this process is necessarily more limited, than in the fact finding process, given that the finalisation of a MAP APA is a government to government process. The competent authorities may agree to have the taxpayer make a presentation of the factual and legal issues before the discussions themselves commence, when the taxpayer would leave. It also may be helpful to arrange to have the taxpayer available, on call, to answer any factual questions that may arise during the discussions. The taxpayer should avoid presenting new factual information or making supplementary representations at this meeting. The tax authorities will require time to review such matters and this will necessitate a postponement of a final decision on the proposed MAP APA. Such information should have been supplied prior to the commencement of the discussions.

D.3.3. Withdrawal from the APA process

64. The taxpayer or tax administration may withdraw from the MAP APA process at any time. However, withdrawal from the process, especially at a late stage and without good cause, should be discouraged because of the inevitable waste of resources caused by such action. When a MAP APA request is withdrawn neither the taxpayer nor the tax administrations should have any obligations to each other, and any previous undertakings and understandings between the parties would be of no further force and effect, unless otherwise required by domestic law (e.g. APA user fee may not be refundable). If a tax administration proposes to withdraw, the taxpayer should be advised of the reasons for such action and given an opportunity to make further representations.

D.3.4. Mutual agreement document

65. Participating competent authorities should prepare a draft mutual agreement when they have agreed on the methodology and other terms and conditions. It may be that, despite the best efforts of the competent authorities, the proposed mutual agreement does not completely eliminate double taxation. The taxpayer(s) should therefore be given an opportunity to say whether such a draft MAP APA is acceptable before it is finalised; there can be no question of imposing such an agreement in advance without the taxpayer's consent.

66. The MAP APA will be in the form of a written document and the content, layout etc. will be decided by the participating competent authorities. In order to achieve the objective of providing a clear record of the mutual agreement and for the agreement to be effectively implemented, the mutual agreement should contain the following minimum information or should refer to where this information is provided in the MAP APA proposal documentation:

a) The names and addresses of the enterprises that are covered by the arrangement;

b) The transactions, agreements or arrangements, tax years or accounting periods covered;

c) A description of the agreed methodology and other related matters such as agreed comparables or a range of expected results;

d) A definition of relevant terms which form the basis of applying and calculating the methodology (e.g. sales, cost of sales, gross profit, etc.);

e) Critical assumptions upon which the methodology is based, the breach of which would trigger renegotiation of the agreement;

f) Any agreed procedures to deal with changes in the factual circumstances which fall short of necessitating the renegotiation of the agreement;

g) If applicable, the agreed tax treatment of ancillary issues;

h) The terms and conditions that must be fulfilled by the taxpayer in order for the mutual agreement to remain valid together with procedures to ensure that the taxpayer is fulfilling those terms and conditions;

i) Details of the taxpayer's obligations to the tax administrations as a result of the domestic implementation of the MAP APA (e.g. annual reports, record keeping, notification of changes in critical assumptions etc.); and

j) Confirmation that, in order to secure the confidence of taxpayers and competent authorities in a MAP APA process in which information is exchanged freely, all information submitted by a taxpayer in a MAP APA case (including the identity of the taxpayer) will be protected from disclosure to the fullest extent possible under the domestic laws of the respective jurisdictions and all information exchanged between the competent authorities involved in such a case will be protected in accordance with the relevant bilateral tax treaty and applicable domestic laws.

D.4. Implementation of the MAP APA

D.4.1. Giving effect to the MAP APA and providing confirmation to the taxpayer

67. Once the MAP APA has been finally agreed, the participating tax authorities need to give effect to the agreement in their own jurisdiction. The tax administrations should enter into some kind of a confirmation or agreement with their respective taxpayers consistent with the mutual agreement entered into by the participating competent authorities. This confirmation or agreement would provide the taxpayer with the certainty that the transfer pricing transactions covered by the MAP APA would not be adjusted, so long as the taxpayer complies with the terms and conditions of the mutual agreement, as reflected in the domestic confirmation or agreement and has not made materially false or misleading statements during the process, including statements made in annual compliance reports. The terms and conditions would include certain assumptions which, if not met, might require an adjustment to be made or the agreement to be reconsidered.

68. The way this confirmation or agreement is given will vary from jurisdiction to jurisdiction and the exact form will depend on the particular domestic law and practice. In some jurisdictions the confirmation or agreement will take the form of an APA under the relevant domestic procedure. To implement the mutual agreement effectively, the domestic confirmation or agreement must be consistent with the MAP APA and give the taxpayer, as a minimum, the same benefits as negotiated in the mutual agreement. Additionally, where it was not possible to completely eliminate double taxation, it is open to one of the participating jurisdictions to give unilateral relief from the remaining double taxation in its domestic confirmation procedure. Also, that confirmation or agreement may cover additional matters to those contained in the MAP APA, for example the domestic tax treatment of other or ancillary issues, additional record keeping or documentation requirements and the filing of reports. Care should be taken to ensure that none of the additional terms of the domestic confirmation or agreement conflict with the terms of the MAP APA.

D.4.2. Possible retroactive application ("Roll back")

69. Neither the tax administrations nor the taxpayer are in any way obliged to apply the methodology agreed upon as part of the MAP APA to tax years ending prior to the first year of the MAP APA (often referred to as "rolling back"). Indeed, to do so might be impossible if a different fact pattern then prevailed. However, the methodology to be applied prospectively under the MAP APA may be instructive in determining the treatment of comparable transactions in earlier years. In some cases, the transfer prices may already be under enquiry by one tax administration in accounting periods prior to the MAP APA period and that tax administration and the taxpayer may wish to take the opportunity to use the agreed methodology to resolve the enquiry, or, pursuant to domestic law requirements, the tax administration may choose to make such an adjustment even without the taxpayer's request or agreement. Element 2.7 of the Action 14 minimum standard states that jurisdictions with bilateral APA programmes should provide for the roll-back of APAs (to previous filed tax years not included within the original scope of the APA) in appropriate cases, subject to the applicable time limits (such as domestic law statutes of limitation for assessments) where the relevant facts and circumstances in the earlier tax years are the same and subject to the verification of these facts and circumstances on audit.

E. MAP APA monitoring

70. It is essential that the tax administrations are able to establish that the taxpayer is abiding by the terms and conditions on which the mutual agreement is based, throughout its duration. As the mutual agreement is made between the tax administrations and the taxpayer is not a party to

such arrangements, the tax administrations have to rely on the domestic confirmation or agreement procedure described above in order to monitor the taxpayer's compliance. If the taxpayer fails to abide by the terms and conditions of the MAP APA, then it no longer need be applied. This section therefore focuses on the aspects of the domestic procedures necessary for the successful implementation of the MAP APA and on the necessary measures to ensure the taxpayer's compliance with all of its terms and conditions.

E.1. Record keeping

71. The taxpayer and the tax administrations should agree the types of documents and records (including any necessary translations) that the taxpayer must maintain and retain for the purposes of verifying the extent of the taxpayer's compliance with the MAP APA. The guidance in Chapters IV and V of the Guidelines should be followed in order to avoid the documentation requirements becoming overly burdensome. Provisions regarding the retention period and the response time for producing the documents and records may also be included.

E.2. Monitoring mechanisms

E.2.1. Annual reports

72. For each tax year, or accounting period, covered by the MAP APA, the taxpayer may be required to file, in addition to its tax return, an annual report describing the taxpayer's actual operations for the year and demonstrating compliance with the terms and conditions of the MAP APA, including the information necessary to decide if the critical assumptions, or other safeguards, have been met. This information should be made available by the taxpayer to the tax administration with which it has concluded the domestic confirmation or agreement, in the manner provided for under the relevant domestic law or procedure.

E.2.2. Audit

73. A MAP APA applies only to the parties specified in the agreement and in respect of the specified transactions. The existence of such an agreement would not prevent the participating tax administrations from undertaking audit activity in the future, although any audit of transactions that are covered by the MAP APA would be limited to determining the extent of the taxpayer's compliance with its terms and conditions and whether the circumstances and assumptions necessary for the reliable application of the chosen methodology continue to exist. The affected tax administrations may require the taxpayer to establish that:

a) The taxpayer has complied with the terms and conditions of the MAP APA;

b) The representations in the proposal, the annual reports and in any supporting documentation, remain valid and that any material changes in facts or circumstances have been included in the annual reports;

c) The methodology has been accurately and consistently applied in accordance with the terms and conditions of the MAP APA; and

d) The critical assumptions underlying the transfer pricing methodology remain valid.

E.3. Consequences of non-compliance or changes in circumstances

74. In general, the consequences of non-compliance with the terms and conditions of a MAP APA, or the failure to meet a critical assumption, will turn on a) the terms of the MAP APA, b) any further agreement between the competent authorities as to how to deal with such non-compliance or failure, and c) any applicable domestic law or procedural provisions. That is, the MAP APA itself may explicitly prescribe procedures to follow, or describe the consequences that will arise, in situations of non-compliance or failure. In such situations, the competent authorities may, at their discretion, enter into discussions of what action to take on a case by case basis. Finally, domestic law or procedural provisions may impose consequences or obligations on the taxpayer and affected tax administration. The following paragraphs provide suggested guidelines similar to procedures that have been adopted in some jurisdictions and which have, on the whole, proved workable. It should be emphasised, however, that some tax administrations may wish to adopt different procedures and approaches.

75. If the tax administrations determine that any requirement of the MAP APA has not been met, they may nevertheless agree, based on the terms and conditions of the MAP APA, to continue to apply it, for example where the effect of the failure to comply is not material. If they do not agree to continue to apply the MAP APA, there are three options that a tax administration could take. The nature of the action to be taken is likely to depend on the seriousness of the non compliance.

76. The most drastic action is revocation, which has the effect that the taxpayer is treated as if the MAP APA had never been entered into. Less serious is cancellation, which means the taxpayer is treated as if the MAP APA had been effective and in force but only up to the cancellation date and not for the whole of the proposed period. If the MAP APA is cancelled or revoked, then for those tax years or accounting periods for which the

cancellation or revocation is effective, the relevant tax administrations and taxpayers will retain all their rights under their domestic laws and treaty provisions, as though the MAP APA had not been undertaken. Finally, the MAP APA may be revised, which means that the taxpayer will still have the benefit of the MAP APA for the whole of the proposed period, albeit that different terms apply before and after the revision date. Further details are provided below.

E.3.1. Revoking a MAP APA

77. A tax administration may revoke a MAP APA (either unilaterally or by mutual agreement) if it is established that:

a) There was a misrepresentation, mistake or omission that was attributable to the neglect, carelessness, or wilful default of a taxpayer when filing the MAP APA request and submission, the annual reports, or other supporting documentation or in supplying any related information; or

b) The participating taxpayer(s) failed to materially comply with a fundamental term or condition of the MAP APA.

78. When a MAP APA is revoked, the revocation is retroactive to the first day of the first tax year or accounting period for which the MAP APA was effective and the MAP APA will no longer have any further force and effect on the affected taxpayer(s) and the other tax administration. Because of the serious effect of this action, the tax administration proposing to revoke a MAP APA should only do so after a careful and thorough evaluation of the relevant facts and should inform and consult with the affected taxpayer(s) and other tax administration(s) on a timely basis.

E.3.2. Cancelling a MAP APA

79. A tax administration may cancel a MAP APA (either unilaterally or by mutual agreement) if it is established that one of the following situations has arisen:

a) There was a misrepresentation, mistake or omission that was not attributable to the neglect, carelessness, or wilful default of a taxpayer when filing the MAP APA request and submission, the annual reports, or other supporting documentation or in supplying any related information; or

b) The participating taxpayer(s) failed to materially comply with any term or condition of the MAP APA; or

c) There was a material breach of one or more of the critical assumptions; or

d) There was a change in tax law, including a treaty provision materially relevant to the MAP APA; and it has not proved possible to revise the agreement (see paragraphs 80-82 below) to take account of the changed circumstances.

80. When a MAP APA is cancelled the date of cancellation will be determined by the nature of the event that led to the cancellation. This may be a specific date, for example if the event giving rise to the cancellation was a material change in tax law (although the MAP APA may still provide for there to be a period of transition between the date of change in the law and the cancellation date). In other cases, the cancellation will be effective for a particular tax year or accounting period, for example where there was a material change in one of the critical assumptions which could not be ascribed to a particular date in that tax year or accounting period. The MAP APA will no longer have any further force on the affected taxpayer(s) and the other tax administration from the date of cancellation.

81. The tax administration may waive cancellation if the taxpayer can show reasonable cause, to the satisfaction of the tax administration, and if the taxpayer agrees to make any adjustment proposed by the tax administration to correct the misrepresentation, mistake, omission or non-compliance, or take into account the changes in critical assumptions, tax law or treaty provision relevant to the APA. Such action may give rise to the revision of the MAP APA (see below).

82. The tax administration proposing the cancellation should inform and consult with the affected taxpayer(s) and the other tax administration(s) in a timely manner. This consultation should include an explanation of the reasons for proposing that the APA be cancelled. The taxpayer should be given an opportunity to respond before any final decision is taken.

E.3.3. Revising a MAP APA

83. The validity of the transfer pricing methodology is dependent on the critical assumptions continuing to apply for the duration of the MAP APA. The MAP APA and any domestic confirmation or agreement should therefore require the taxpayer to notify the affected tax administrations of any changes. If, after evaluation by the tax administrations, it is established that there has been a material change in conditions noted in a critical assumption, the MAP APA may be revised to reflect the change. As discussed above, the MAP APA may also contain assumptions, which although falling short of being critical to the validity of the MAP APA, nevertheless warrant a review by the affected parties. One result of such a review may again be a revision of the MAP APA. However,

in many cases the terms and conditions of the MAP APA may be sufficiently flexible to account for the effects of such changes without the need for revision.

84. The taxpayer's notification to the tax administrations that such a change has taken place should be filed as soon as practicable after the change occurs, or the taxpayer becomes aware of the change, and in any event no later than the date for filing, if required, the annual report for that year or accounting period. Early notification is encouraged in order to give the affected parties more time to try to reach agreement on revising the MAP APA, thereby reducing the likelihood of cancellation.

85. The revised MAP APA should state the date from which the revision is effective and also the date on which the original MAP APA is no longer effective. If the date of the change can be precisely identified, then normally the revision should take effect from that date but if a precise date cannot be identified, then normally the MAP APA would be revised with effect from the first day of the accounting period following the one in which the change took place. If the tax administrations and the taxpayer cannot agree on the need for a revised MAP APA or how to revise the MAP APA, the MAP APA will be cancelled and will no longer have any further force and effect on the participating taxpayers and tax administrations. The determination of the effective date of the cancellation of the MAP APA will normally follow the same principles as applied to determine the date of revision.

E.4. Renewing a MAP APA

86. A request to renew a MAP APA should be made at the time prescribed by the participating tax administrations, bearing in mind the need for sufficient lead time for the taxpayer(s) and tax administrations to review and evaluate the renewal request and to reach agreement. It may be helpful to commence the renewal process well before the existing MAP APA has expired.

87. The format, processing, and evaluation of the renewal application would usually be similar to those for an initial MAP APA application. However, the necessary level of detail may be reduced with the agreement of the participating tax administrations, particularly if there have not been material changes in the facts and circumstances of the case. Renewal of a MAP APA is not automatic and depends on the consent of all parties concerned and on the taxpayer demonstrating, among other things, compliance with the terms and conditions of the existing MAP APA. The methodology and terms and conditions of the renewed MAP APA may, of course, differ from those of the previous MAP APA.

Annex I to Chapter V

Transfer pricing documentation – Master file

The following information should be included in the master file:

Organisational structure

- Chart illustrating the MNE group's legal and ownership structure and geographical location of operating entities.

Description of MNE group's business(es)

- General written description of the MNE group's business including:
  - Important drivers of business profit;
  - A description of the supply chain for the group's five largest products and/or service offerings by turnover plus any other products and/or services amounting to more than 5% of group turnover. The required description could take the form of a chart or a diagram;
  - A list and brief description of important service arrangements between members of the MNE group, other than research and development (R&D) services, including a description of the capabilities of the principal locations providing important services and transfer pricing policies for allocating services costs and determining prices to be paid for intra-group services;
  - A description of the main geographic markets for the group's products and services that are referred to in the second bullet point above;
  - A brief written functional analysis describing the principal contributions to value creation by individual entities within the group, i.e. key functions performed, important risks assumed, and important assets used;

- A description of important business restructuring transactions, acquisitions and divestitures occurring during the fiscal year.

MNE group's intangibles (as defined in Chapter VI of these Guidelines)

- A general description of the MNE group's overall strategy for the development, ownership and exploitation of intangibles, including location of principal R&D facilities and location of R&D management.
- A list of intangibles or groups of intangibles of the MNE group that are important for transfer pricing purposes and which entities legally own them.
- A list of important agreements among identified associated enterprises related to intangibles, including cost contribution arrangements, principal research service agreements and licence agreements.
- A general description of the group's transfer pricing policies related to R&D and intangibles.
- A general description of any important transfers of interests in intangibles among associated enterprises during the fiscal year concerned, including the entities, jurisdictions, and compensation involved.

MNE group's intercompany financial activities

- A general description of how the MNE group is financed, including important financing arrangements with unrelated lenders.
- The identification of any members of the MNE group that provide a central financing function for the group, including the jurisdiction under whose laws the entity is organised and the place of effective management of such entities.
- A general description of the MNE group's general transfer pricing policies related to financing arrangements between associated enterprises.

MNE group's financial and tax positions

- The MNE group's annual consolidated financial statement for the fiscal year concerned if otherwise prepared for financial reporting, regulatory, internal management, tax or other purposes.
- A list and brief description of the MNE group's existing unilateral advance pricing agreements (APAs) and other tax rulings relating to the allocation of income among jurisdictions.

Annex II to Chapter V

Transfer pricing documentation – Local file

The following information should be included in the local file:

Local entity

- A description of the management structure of the local entity, a local organisation chart, and a description of the individuals to whom local management reports and the jurisdiction(s) in which such individuals maintain their principal offices.
- A detailed description of the business and business strategy pursued by the local entity including an indication whether the local entity has been involved in or affected by business restructurings or intangibles transfers in the present or immediately past year and an explanation of those aspects of such transactions affecting the local entity.
- Key competitors.

Controlled transactions

For each material category of controlled transactions in which the entity is involved, provide the following information:

- A description of the material controlled transactions (e.g. procurement of manufacturing services, purchase of goods, provision of services, loans, financial and performance guarantees, licences of intangibles, etc.) and the context in which such transactions take place.
- The amount of intra-group payments and receipts for each category of controlled transactions involving the local entity (i.e. payments and receipts for products, services, royalties, interest, etc.) broken down by tax jurisdiction of the foreign payor or recipient.

- An identification of associated enterprises involved in each category of controlled transactions, and the relationship amongst them.
- Copies of all material intercompany agreements concluded by the local entity.
- A detailed comparability and functional analysis of the taxpayer and relevant associated enterprises with respect to each documented category of controlled transactions, including any changes compared to prior years.[1]
- An indication of the most appropriate transfer pricing method with regard to the category of transaction and the reasons for selecting that method.
- An indication of which associated enterprise is selected as the tested party, if applicable, and an explanation of the reasons for this selection.
- A summary of the important assumptions made in applying the transfer pricing methodology.
- If relevant, an explanation of the reasons for performing a multi-year analysis.
- A list and description of selected comparable uncontrolled transactions (internal or external), if any, and information on relevant financial indicators for independent enterprises relied on in the transfer pricing analysis, including a description of the comparable search methodology and the source of such information.
- A description of any comparability adjustments performed, and an indication of whether adjustments have been made to the results of the tested party, the comparable uncontrolled transactions, or both.
- A description of the reasons for concluding that relevant transactions were priced on an arm's length basis based on the application of the selected transfer pricing method.
- A summary of financial information used in applying the transfer pricing methodology.
- A copy of existing unilateral and bilateral/multilateral APAs and other tax rulings to which the local tax jurisdiction is not a party and which are related to controlled transactions described above.

1. To the extent this functional analysis duplicates information in the master file, a cross-reference to the master file is sufficient.

Financial information

- Annual local entity financial accounts for the fiscal year concerned. If audited statements exist they should be supplied and if not, existing unaudited statements should be supplied.
- Information and allocation schedules showing how the financial data used in applying the transfer pricing method may be tied to the annual financial statements.
- Summary schedules of relevant financial data for comparables used in the analysis and the sources from which that data was obtained.

Annex III to Chapter V

Transfer pricing documentation – Country-by-Country Report

A. Model template for the Country-by-Country Report

Table 1. **Overview of allocation of income, taxes and business activities by tax jurisdiction**

Name of the MNE group: Fiscal year concerned: Currency used:											
Tax Jurisdiction	Revenues			Profit (Loss) before Income Tax	Income Tax Paid (on Cash Basis)	Income Tax Accrued – Current Year	Stated Capital	Accumulated Earnings	Number of Employees	Tangible Assets other than Cash and Cash Equivalents
	Unrelated Party	Related Party	Total							

Table 2. **List of all the Constituent Entities of the MNE group included in each aggregation per tax jurisdiction**

Name of the MNE group: Fiscal year concerned:															
			Main Business Activity(ies)												
Tax Jurisdiction	Constituent Entities Resident in the Tax Jurisdiction	Tax Jurisdiction of Organisation or Incorporation if Different from Tax Jurisdiction of Residence	Research and Development	Holding or Managing Intellectual Property	Purchasing or Procurement	Manufacturing or Production	Sales, Marketing or Distribution	Administrative, Management or Support Services	Provision of Services to Unrelated Parties	Internal Group Finance	Regulated Financial Services	Insurance	Holding Shares or Other Equity instruments	Dormant	Other[1]
	1.														
	2.														
	3.														
	1.														
	2.														
	3.														

1. Please specify the nature of the activity of the Constituent Entity in the "Additional Information" section.

Table 3. **Additional Information**

Name of the MNE group: Fiscal year concerned:
Please include any further brief information or explanation you consider necessary or that would facilitate the understanding of the compulsory information provided in the Country-by-Country Report.

B. Template for the Country-by-Country Report – General instructions

Purpose

This Annex III to Chapter V of these Guidelines contains a template for reporting a multinational enterprise's (MNE) group allocation of income, taxes and business activities on a tax jurisdiction-by-tax jurisdiction basis. These instructions form an integral part of the model template for the Country-by-Country Report.

Definitions

Reporting MNE

A Reporting MNE is the ultimate parent entity of an MNE group.

Constituent Entity

For purposes of completing Annex III, a Constituent Entity of the MNE group is (i) any separate business unit of an MNE group that is included in the Consolidated Financial Statements of the MNE group for financial reporting purposes, or would be so included if equity interests in such business unit of the MNE group were traded on a public securities exchange; (ii) any such business unit that is excluded from the MNE group's Consolidated Financial Statements solely on size or materiality grounds; and (iii) any permanent establishment of any separate business unit of the MNE group included in (i) or (ii) above provided the business unit prepares a separate financial statement for such permanent establishment for financial reporting, regulatory, tax reporting, or internal management control purposes.

Treatment of Branches and Permanent Establishments

The permanent establishment data should be reported by reference to the tax jurisdiction in which it is situated and not by reference to the tax jurisdiction of residence of the business unit of which the permanent establishment is a part. Residence tax jurisdiction reporting for the business unit of which the permanent establishment is a part should exclude financial data related to the permanent establishment.

Consolidated Financial Statements

The Consolidated Financial Statements are the financial statements of an MNE group in which the assets, liabilities, income, expenses and cash flows of the ultimate parent entity and the Constituent Entities are presented as those of a single economic entity.

Period covered by the annual template

The template should cover the fiscal year of the Reporting MNE. For Constituent Entities, at the discretion of the Reporting MNE, the template should reflect on a consistent basis either (i) information for the fiscal year of the relevant Constituent Entities ending on the same date as the fiscal year of the Reporting MNE, or ending within the 12 month period preceding such date, or (ii) information for all the relevant Constituent Entities reported for the fiscal year of the Reporting MNE.

Source of data

The Reporting MNE should consistently use the same sources of data from year to year in completing the template. The Reporting MNE may choose to use data from its consolidation reporting packages, from separate entity statutory financial statements, regulatory financial statements, or internal management accounts. It is not necessary to reconcile the revenue, profit and tax reporting in the template to the consolidated financial statements. If statutory financial statements are used as the basis for reporting, all amounts should be translated to the stated functional currency of the Reporting MNE at the average exchange rate for the year stated in the Additional Information section of the template. Adjustments need not be made, however, for differences in accounting principles applied from tax jurisdiction to tax jurisdiction.

The Reporting MNE should provide a brief description of the sources of data used in preparing the template in the Additional Information section of the template. If a change is made in the source of data used from year to year, the Reporting MNE should explain the reasons for the change and its consequences in the Additional Information section of the template.

C. Template for the Country-by-Country Report – Specific instructions

Overview of allocation of income, taxes and business activities by tax jurisdiction (Table 1)

Tax Jurisdiction

In the first column of the template, the Reporting MNE should list all of the tax jurisdictions in which Constituent Entities of the MNE group are resident for tax purposes. A tax jurisdiction is defined as a State as well as a non-State jurisdiction which has fiscal autonomy. A separate line should be included for all Constituent Entities in the MNE group deemed by the Reporting MNE not to be resident in any tax jurisdiction for tax purposes. Where a Constituent Entity is resident in more than one tax jurisdiction, the applicable tax treaty tie breaker should be applied to determine the tax jurisdiction of residence. Where no applicable tax treaty exists, the Constituent Entity should be reported in the tax jurisdiction of the Constituent Entity's place of effective management. The place of effective management is the place where key management and commercial decisions that are necessary for the conduct of the entity's business as a whole are in substance made. All relevant facts and circumstances must be examined to determine the place of effective management. An entity may have more than one place of management, but it can have only one place of effective management at any one time.

Revenues

In the three columns of the template under the heading Revenues, the Reporting MNE should report the following information: (i) the sum of revenues of all the Constituent Entities of the MNE group in the relevant tax jurisdiction generated from transactions with associated enterprises; (ii) the sum of revenues of all the Constituent Entities of the MNE group in the relevant tax jurisdiction generated from transactions with independent parties; and (iii) the total of (i) and (ii). Revenues should include revenues from sales of inventory and properties, services, royalties, interest, premiums and any other amounts. Revenues should exclude payments received from other Constituent Entities that are treated as dividends in the payor's tax jurisdiction.

Profit (Loss) before Income Tax

In the fifth column of the template, the Reporting MNE should report the sum of the profit (loss) before income tax for all the Constituent Entities resident for tax purposes in the relevant tax jurisdiction. The profit (loss) before income tax should include all extraordinary income and expense items.

Income Tax Paid (on Cash Basis)

In the sixth column of the template, the Reporting MNE should report the total amount of income tax actually paid during the relevant fiscal year by all the Constituent Entities resident for tax purposes in the relevant tax jurisdiction. Taxes paid should include cash taxes paid by the Constituent Entity to the residence tax jurisdiction and to all other tax jurisdictions. Taxes paid should include withholding taxes paid by other entities (associated enterprises and independent enterprises) with respect to payments to the Constituent Entity. Thus, if company A resident in tax jurisdiction A earns interest in tax jurisdiction B, the tax withheld in tax jurisdiction B should be reported by company A.

Income Tax Accrued (Current Year)

In the seventh column of the template, the Reporting MNE should report the sum of the accrued current tax expense recorded on taxable profits or losses of the year of reporting of all the Constituent Entities resident for tax purposes in the relevant tax jurisdiction. The current tax expense should reflect only operations in the current year and should not include deferred taxes or provisions for uncertain tax liabilities.

Stated Capital

In the eighth column of the template, the Reporting MNE should report the sum of the stated capital of all the Constituent Entities resident for tax purposes in the relevant tax jurisdiction. With regard to permanent establishments, the stated capital should be reported by the legal entity of which it is a permanent establishment unless there is a defined capital requirement in the permanent establishment tax jurisdiction for regulatory purposes.

Accumulated Earnings

In the ninth column of the template, the Reporting MNE should report the sum of the total accumulated earnings of all the Constituent Entities resident for tax purposes in the relevant tax jurisdiction as of the end of the year. With regard to permanent establishments, accumulated earnings should be reported by the legal entity of which it is a permanent establishment.

Number of Employees

In the tenth column of the template, the Reporting MNE should report the total number of employees on a full-time equivalent (FTE) basis of all the Constituent Entities resident for tax purposes in the relevant tax jurisdiction. The number of employees may be reported as of the year-end, on the basis of average employment levels for the year, or on any other basis consistently applied across tax jurisdictions and from year to year. For this purpose, independent contractors participating in the ordinary operating activities of the Constituent Entity may be reported as employees. Reasonable rounding or approximation of the number of employees is permissible, providing that such rounding or approximation does not materially distort the relative distribution of employees across the various tax jurisdictions. Consistent approaches should be applied from year to year and across entities.

Tangible Assets other than Cash and Cash Equivalents

In the eleventh column of the template, the Reporting MNE should report the sum of the net book values of tangible assets of all the Constituent Entities resident for tax purposes in the relevant tax jurisdiction. With regard to permanent establishments, assets should be reported by reference to the tax jurisdiction in which the permanent establishment is situated. Tangible assets for this purpose do not include cash or cash equivalents, intangibles, or financial assets.

List of all the Constituent Entities of the MNE group included in each aggregation per tax jurisdiction (Table 2)

Constituent Entities Resident in the Tax Jurisdiction

The Reporting MNE should list, on a tax jurisdiction-by-tax jurisdiction basis and by legal entity name, all the Constituent Entities of the MNE group which are resident for tax purposes in the relevant tax jurisdiction. As stated above with regard to permanent establishments, however, the permanent establishment should be listed by reference to the tax jurisdiction in which it is situated. The legal entity of which it is a permanent establishment should be noted (e.g. XYZ Corp – Tax Jurisdiction A permanent establishment).

Tax Jurisdiction of Organisation or Incorporation if Different from Tax Jurisdiction of Residence

The Reporting MNE should report the name of the tax jurisdiction under whose laws the Constituent Entity of the MNE is organised or incorporated if it is different from the tax jurisdiction of residence.

Main Business Activity(ies)

The Reporting MNE should determine the nature of the main business activity(ies) carried out by the Constituent Entity in the relevant tax jurisdiction, by ticking one or more of the appropriate boxes.

Business Activities
Research and Development
Holding or Managing Intellectual Property
Purchasing or Procurement
Manufacturing or Production
Sales, Marketing or Distribution
Administrative, Management or Support Services
Provision of Services to Unrelated Parties
Internal Group Finance
Regulated Financial Services
Insurance
Holding Shares or Other Equity Instruments
Dormant
Other[1]

1. Please specify the nature of the activity of the Constituent Entity in the "Additional Information" section.

Annex IV to Chapter V

Country-by-Country Reporting Implementation Package

Introduction

In order to facilitate a consistent and swift implementation of the Country-by-Country Reporting developed under Action 13 of the Base Erosion and Profit Shifting Action Plan (BEPS Action Plan, OECD, 2013), a Country-by-Country Reporting Implementation Package has been developed. This implementation package consists of (i) model legislation which could be used by jurisdictions to require the ultimate parent entity of an MNE group to file the Country-by-Country Report in its jurisdiction of residence including backup filing requirements and (ii) three model Competent Authority Agreements that are to be used to facilitate implementation of the exchange of Country-by-Country Reports, respectively based on the 1) Convention on Mutual Administrative Assistance in Tax Matters, 2) bilateral tax conventions and 3) Tax Information Exchange Agreements (TIEAs). It is recognised that developing countries may require support for the effective implementation of Country-by-Country Reporting.

Model legislation

The model legislation contained in the Country-by-Country Reporting Implementation Package takes into account neither the constitutional law and legal system, nor the structure and wording of the tax legislation of any particular jurisdiction. Jurisdictions will be able to adapt this model legislation to their own legal systems, where changes to current legislation are required.

Competent Authority Agreements

The *Convention on Mutual Administrative Assistance in Tax Matters* (the "Convention'), by virtue of its Article 6, requires the Competent Authorities of the Parties to the Convention to mutually agree on the scope of the automatic exchange of information and the procedure to be complied with. In the context of the Common Reporting Standard, this requirement has been translated into a Multilateral Competent Authority Agreement, which defines the scope, timing, procedures and safeguards according to which the automatic exchange should take place.

As the implementation of the automatic exchange of information by means of a Multilateral Competent Authority Agreement in the context of the Common Reporting Standard has proven both time- and resource-efficient, the same approach could be used for the purpose of putting the automatic exchange of information in relation to Country-by-Country Reports in place. Therefore, the Multilateral Competent Authority Agreement on the Exchange of Country-by-Country Reports (the "CbC MCAA") has been developed, based on the Convention and inspired by the Multilateral Competent Authority Agreement concluded in the context of the implementation of the Common Reporting Standard. In addition, two further model competent authority agreements have been developed for exchanges of Country-by-Country Reports, one for exchanges under Double Tax Conventions and one for exchanges under Tax Information Exchange Agreements.

In line with paragraph 5 of Chapter V of these Guidelines, one of the three objectives of transfer pricing documentation is to provide tax administrations with the information necessary to conduct an informed transfer pricing risk assessment, while paragraph 10 of Chapter V of these Guidelines states that effective risk identification and assessment constitute an essential early stage in the process of selecting appropriate cases for transfer pricing audit. The Country-by-Country Reports exchanged on the basis of the model competent authority agreements contained in the present Country-by-Country Reporting Implementation Package, represent one of the three tiers of the transfer pricing documentation and will, in accordance with paragraphs 16, 17 and 25 of Chapter V of these Guidelines, provide tax administrations with relevant and reliable information to perform an efficient and robust transfer pricing risk assessment analysis. Against that background, the model competent authority agreements aim to provide the framework to make the information contained in the Country-by-Country Report available to concerned tax authorities, such information being foreseeably relevant for the administration and enforcement of their tax laws through the automatic exchange of information.

The purpose of the CbC MCAA is to set forth rules and procedures as may be necessary for Competent Authorities of jurisdictions implementing BEPS Action 13 to automatically exchange Country-by-Country Reports prepared by the Reporting Entity of an MNE Group and filed on an annual basis with the tax authorities of the jurisdiction of tax residence of that entity with the tax authorities of all jurisdictions in which the MNE Group operates.

For most provisions, the wording is substantially the same as the text of the Multilateral Competent Authority Agreement for the purpose of exchanges under the Common Reporting Standard. Where appropriate, the wording has been complemented or amended to reflect the Guidance on Country-by-Country Reporting set out in Chapter V of these Guidelines.

An XML Schema and a related User Guide has also been developed to accommodate the electronic exchange of Country-by-Country Reports.

Model legislation related to Country-by-Country Reporting

Article 1
Definitions

For purposes of this [title of the law] the following terms have the following meanings:

1. The term "Group" means a collection of enterprises related through ownership or control such that it is either required to prepare Consolidated Financial Statements for financial reporting purposes under applicable accounting principles or would be so required if equity interests in any of the enterprises were traded on a public securities exchange.

2. The term "MNE Group" means any Group that (i) includes two or more enterprises the tax residence for which is in different jurisdictions, or includes an enterprise that is resident for tax purposes in one jurisdiction and is subject to tax with respect to the business carried out through a permanent establishment in another jurisdiction, and (ii) is not an Excluded MNE Group.

3. The term "Excluded MNE Group" means, with respect to any Fiscal Year of the Group, a Group having total consolidated group revenue of less than [750 million Euro]/[insert an amount in local currency approximately equivalent to 750 million Euro as of January 2015] during the Fiscal Year immediately preceding the Reporting Fiscal Year as reflected in its Consolidated Financial Statements for such preceding Fiscal Year.

4. The term "Constituent Entity" means (i) any separate business unit of an MNE Group that is included in the Consolidated Financial Statements of the MNE Group for financial reporting purposes, or would be so included if equity interests in such business unit of an MNE Group were traded on a public securities exchange; (ii) any such business unit that is excluded from the MNE Group's Consolidated Financial Statements solely on size or materiality grounds; and (iii) any permanent establishment of any separate business unit of the MNE Group included in (i) or (ii) above provided the business unit prepares a separate financial statement for such permanent establishment for financial reporting, regulatory, tax reporting, or internal management control purposes.

5. The term "Reporting Entity" means the Constituent Entity that is required to file a Country-by-Country Report conforming to the requirements in Article 4 in its jurisdiction of tax residence on behalf of the MNE Group. The Reporting Entity may be the Ultimate Parent Entity, the Surrogate Parent Entity, or any entity described in paragraph 2 of Article 2.

6. The term "Ultimate Parent Entity" means a Constituent Entity of an MNE Group that meets the following criteria:

i) it owns directly or indirectly a sufficient interest in one or more other Constituent Entities of such MNE Group such that it is required to prepare Consolidated Financial Statements under accounting principles generally applied in its jurisdiction of tax residence, or would be so required if its equity interests were traded on a public securities exchange in its jurisdiction of tax residence; and

ii) there is no other Constituent Entity of such MNE Group that owns directly or indirectly an interest described in subsection (i) above in the first mentioned Constituent Entity.

7. The term "Surrogate Parent Entity" means one Constituent Entity of the MNE Group that has been appointed by such MNE Group, as a sole substitute for the Ultimate Parent Entity, to file the Country-by-Country Report in that Constituent Entity's jurisdiction of tax residence, on behalf of such MNE Group, when one or more of the conditions set out in subsection (ii) of paragraph 2 of Article 2 applies.

8. The term "Fiscal Year" means an annual accounting period with respect to which the Ultimate Parent Entity of the MNE Group prepares its financial statements.

9. The term "Reporting Fiscal Year" means that Fiscal Year the financial and operational results of which are reflected in the Country-by-Country Report defined in Article 4.

10. The term "Qualifying Competent Authority Agreement" means an agreement (i) that is between authorised representatives of those jurisdictions that are parties to an International Agreement and (ii) that requires the automatic exchange of Country-by-Country Reports between the party jurisdictions.

11. The term "International Agreement" shall mean the Multilateral Convention for Mutual Administrative Assistance in Tax Matters, any bilateral or multilateral Tax Convention, or any Tax Information Exchange Agreement to which [Jurisdiction] is a party, and that by its terms provides legal authority for the exchange of tax information between jurisdictions, including automatic exchange of such information.

12. The term "Consolidated Financial Statements" means the financial statements of an MNE Group in which the assets, liabilities, income, expenses and cash flows of the Ultimate Parent Entity and the Constituent Entities are presented as those of a single economic entity.

13. The term "Systemic Failure" with respect to a jurisdiction means that a jurisdiction has a Qualifying Competent Authority Agreement in effect with [Jurisdiction], but has suspended automatic exchange (for reasons other than those that are in accordance with the terms of that Agreement) or otherwise persistently failed to automatically provide to [Jurisdiction] Country-by-Country Reports in its possession of MNE Groups that have Constituent Entities in [Jurisdiction].

Article 2
Filing Obligation

1. Each Ultimate Parent Entity of an MNE Group that is resident for tax purposes in [Jurisdiction] shall file a Country-by-Country Report conforming to the requirements of Article 4 with the [Jurisdiction Tax Administration] with respect to its Reporting Fiscal Year on or before the date specified in Article 5.

2. A Constituent Entity which is not the Ultimate Parent Entity of an MNE Group shall file a Country-by-Country Report conforming to the requirements of Article 4 with the [Jurisdiction Tax Administration] with respect to the Reporting Fiscal Year of an MNE Group of which it is a Constituent Entity, on or before the date specified in Article 5, if the following criteria are satisfied:

i) the entity is resident for tax purposes in [Jurisdiction]; and

ii) one of the following conditions applies:

a) the Ultimate Parent Entity of the MNE Group is not obligated to file a Country-by-Country Report in its jurisdiction of tax residence; or,

b) the jurisdiction in which the Ultimate Parent Entity is resident for tax purposes has a current International Agreement to which [Jurisdiction] is a party but does not have a Qualifying Competent Authority Agreement in effect to which [Jurisdiction] is a party by the time specified in Article 5 for filing the Country-by-Country Report for the Reporting Fiscal Year; or,

c) there has been a Systemic Failure of the jurisdiction of tax residence of the Ultimate Parent Entity that has been notified by the [Jurisdiction Tax Administration] to the Constituent Entity resident for tax purposes in [Jurisdiction].

Where there are more than one Constituent Entities of the same MNE Group that are resident for tax purposes in [Jurisdiction] and one or more of the conditions set out in subsection (ii) above apply, the MNE Group may designate one of such Constituent Entities to file the Country-by-Country Report conforming to the requirements of Article 4 with [Jurisdiction Tax Administration] with respect to any Reporting Fiscal Year on or before the date specified in Article 5 and to notify the [Jurisdiction Tax Administration] that the filing is intended to satisfy the filing requirement of all the Constituent Entities of such MNE Group that are resident for tax purposes in [Jurisdiction].

3. Notwithstanding the provisions of paragraph 2 of this Article 2, when one or more of the conditions set out in subsection (ii) of paragraph 2 of Article 2 apply, an entity described in paragraph 2 of this Article 2 shall not be required to file a Country-by-Country Report with [Jurisdiction Tax Administration] with respect to any Reporting Fiscal Year if the MNE Group of which it is a Constituent Entity has made available a Country-by-Country Report conforming to the requirements of Article 4 with respect to such Fiscal Year through a Surrogate Parent Entity that files that Country-by-Country Report with the tax authority of its jurisdiction of tax residence on or before the date specified in Article 5 and that satisfies the following conditions:

a) the jurisdiction of tax residence of the Surrogate Parent Entity requires filing of Country-by-Country Reports conforming to the requirements of Article 4;

b) the jurisdiction of tax residence of the Surrogate Parent Entity has a Qualifying Competent Authority Agreement in effect to which [Jurisdiction] is a party by the time specified in Article 5 for filing the Country-by-Country Report for the Reporting Fiscal Year;

c) the jurisdiction of tax residence of the Surrogate Parent Entity has not notified the [Jurisdiction Tax Administration] of a Systemic Failure;

d) the jurisdiction of tax residence of the Surrogate Parent Entity has been notified in accordance with paragraph 1 of Article 3 by the Constituent Entity resident for tax purposes in its jurisdiction that it is the Surrogate Parent Entity; and

e) a notification has been provided to [Jurisdiction Tax Administration] in accordance with paragraph 2 of Article 3.

Article 3
Notification

1. Any Constituent Entity of an MNE Group that is resident for tax purposes in [Jurisdiction] shall notify the [Jurisdiction Tax Administration] whether it is the Ultimate Parent Entity or the Surrogate Parent Entity, no later than [the last day of the Reporting Fiscal Year of such MNE Group].

2. Where a Constituent Entity of an MNE Group that is resident for tax purposes in [Jurisdiction] is not the Ultimate Parent Entity nor the Surrogate Parent Entity, it shall notify the [Jurisdiction Tax Administration] of the identity and tax residence of the Reporting Entity, no later than [the last day of the Reporting Fiscal Year of such MNE Group].

Article 4
Country-by-Country Report

1. For purposes of this [title of the law], a Country-by-Country Report with respect to an MNE Group is a report containing:

i) Aggregate information relating to the amount of revenue, profit (loss) before income tax, income tax paid, income tax accrued, stated capital, accumulated earnings, number of employees, and tangible assets other than cash or cash equivalents with regard to each jurisdiction in which the MNE Group operates;

ii) An identification of each Constituent Entity of the MNE Group setting out the jurisdiction of tax residence of such Constituent Entity, and where different from such jurisdiction of tax residence, the jurisdiction under the laws of which such Constituent Entity is organised, and the nature of the main business activity or activities of such Constituent Entity.

2. The Country-by-Country Report shall be filed in a form identical to and applying the definitions and instructions contained in the standard template set out at [Annex III of Chapter V of the OECD Transfer Pricing Guidelines as the same may be modified from time to time] / [Annex III of the Report *Transfer Pricing Documentation and Country-by-Country Reporting* on Action 13 of the OECD/G20 *Action Plan on Base Erosion and Profit Shifting*] / [the Appendix to this law].

Article 5
Time for filing

The Country-by-Country Report required by this [title of the law] shall be filed no later than 12 months after the last day of the Reporting Fiscal Year of the MNE Group.

Article 6
Use and Confidentiality of Country-by-Country Report Information

1. The [Jurisdiction Tax Administration] shall use the Country-by-Country Report for purposes of assessing high-level transfer pricing risks and other base erosion and profit shifting related risks in [Jurisdiction], including assessing the risk of non-compliance by members of the MNE Group with applicable transfer pricing rules, and where appropriate for economic and statistical analysis. Transfer pricing adjustments by the [Jurisdiction Tax Administration] will not be based on the CbC Report.

2. The [Jurisdiction Tax Administration] shall preserve the confidentiality of the information contained in the Country-by-Country Report at least to the same extent that would apply if such information were provided to it under the provisions of the Multilateral Convention on Mutual Administrative Assistance in Tax Matters.

Article 7
Penalties

This model legislation does not include provisions regarding penalties to be imposed in the event a Reporting Entity fails to comply with the reporting requirements for the Country-by-Country Report. It is assumed that jurisdictions would wish to extend their existing transfer pricing documentation penalty regime to the requirements to file the Country-by-Country Report.

Article 8
Effective Date

This [title of the law] is effective for Reporting Fiscal Years of MNE Groups beginning on or after [1 January 2016].

Multilateral Competent Authority Agreement on the Exchange of Country-by-Country Reports

Whereas, the jurisdictions of the signatories to the Multilateral Competent Authority Agreement on the Exchange of Country-by-Country Reports (the "Agreement") are Parties of, or territories covered by, the Convention on Mutual Administrative Assistance in Tax Matters or the Convention on Mutual Administrative Assistance in Tax Matters as amended by the Protocol (the "Convention") or have signed or expressed their intention to sign the Convention and acknowledge that the Convention must be in force and in effect in relation to them before the automatic exchange of country-by-country (CbC) reports takes place;

Whereas, a country that has signed or expressed its intention to sign the Convention will only become a Jurisdiction as defined in Section 1 of this Agreement once it has become a Party to the Convention;

Whereas, the jurisdictions desire to increase international tax transparency and improve access of their respective tax authorities to information regarding the global allocation of the income, the taxes paid, and certain indicators of the location of economic activity among tax jurisdictions in which Multinational Enterprise (MNE) Groups operate through the automatic exchange of annual CbC Reports, with a view to assessing high-level transfer pricing risks and other base erosion and profit shifting related risks, as well as for economic and statistical analysis, where appropriate;

Whereas, the laws of the respective Jurisdictions require or are expected to require the Reporting Entity of an MNE Group to annually file a CbC Report;

Whereas, the CbC Report is intended to be part of a three-tiered structure, along with a global master file and a local file, which together represent a standardised approach to transfer pricing documentation which will provide tax administrations with relevant and reliable information to perform an efficient and robust transfer pricing risk assessment analysis;

Whereas, Chapter III of the Convention authorises the exchange of information for tax purposes, including the exchange of information on an automatic basis, and allows the competent authorities of the Jurisdictions to agree on the scope and modalities of such automatic exchanges;

Whereas, Article 6 of the Convention provides that two or more Parties can mutually agree to exchange information automatically, albeit that the actual exchange of the information will take place on a bilateral basis between the Competent Authorities;

Whereas, the Jurisdictions will have, or are expected to have, in place by the time the first exchange of CbC Reports takes place, (i) appropriate safeguards to ensure that the information received pursuant to this Agreement remains confidential and is used for the purposes of assessing high-level transfer pricing risks and other base erosion and profit shifting related risks, as well as for economic and statistical analysis, where appropriate, in accordance with Section 5 of this Agreement, (ii) the infrastructure for an effective exchange relationship (including established processes for ensuring timely, accurate, and confidential information exchanges, effective and reliable communications, and capabilities to promptly resolve questions and concerns about exchanges or requests for exchanges and to administer the provisions of Section 4 of this Agreement) and (iii) the necessary legislation to require Reporting Entities to file the CbC Report;

Whereas, the Jurisdictions are committed to discuss with the aim of resolving cases of undesirable economic outcomes, including for individual businesses, in accordance with paragraph 2 of Article 24 of the Convention, as well as paragraph 1 of Section 6 of this Agreement;

Whereas, mutual agreement procedures, for instance on the basis of a double tax convention concluded between the jurisdictions of the Competent Authorities, remain applicable in cases where the CbC Report has been exchanged on the basis of this Agreement;

Whereas, the Competent Authorities of the jurisdictions intend to conclude this Agreement, without prejudice to national legislative procedures (if any), and subject to the confidentiality and other protections provided for in the Convention, including the provisions limiting the use of the information exchanged thereunder;

Now, therefore, the Competent Authorities have agreed as follows:

SECTION 1
Definitions

1. For the purposes of this Agreement, the following terms have the following meanings:

   a) the term **"Jurisdiction"** means a country or a territory in respect of which the Convention is in force and is in effect, either through ratification, acceptance or approval in accordance with Article 28, or through territorial extension in accordance with Article 29, and which is a signatory to this Agreement;

b) the term **"Competent Authority"** means, for each respective Jurisdiction, the persons and authorities listed in Annex B of the Convention;

c) The term **"Group"** means a collection of enterprises related through ownership or control such that it is either required to prepare consolidated financial statements for financial reporting purposes under applicable accounting principles or would be so required if equity interests in any of the enterprises were traded on a public securities exchange;

d) the term **"Multinational Enterprise (MNE) Group"** means any Group that (i) includes two or more enterprises the tax residence for which is in different jurisdictions, or includes an enterprise that is resident for tax purposes in one jurisdiction and is subject to tax with respect to the business carried out through a permanent establishment in another jurisdiction, and (ii) is not an Excluded MNE Group;

e) the term **"Excluded MNE Group"** means a Group that is not required to file a CbC Report on the basis that the annual consolidated group revenue of the Group during the fiscal year immediately preceding the reporting fiscal year, as reflected in its consolidated financial statements for such preceding fiscal year, is below the threshold defined in domestic law by the Jurisdiction and being consistent with the 2015 Report, as may be amended following the 2020 review contemplated therein;

f) the term **"Constituent Entity"** means (i) any separate business unit of an MNE Group that is included in the consolidated financial statements for financial reporting purposes, or would be so included if equity interests in such business unit of an MNE Group were traded on a public securities exchange, (ii) any separate business unit that is excluded from the MNE Group's consolidated financial statements solely on size or materiality grounds and (iii) any permanent establishment of any separate business unit of the MNE Group included in (i) or (ii) above provided the business unit prepares a separate financial statement for such permanent establishment for financial reporting, regulatory, tax reporting or internal management control purposes;

g) the term **"Reporting Entity"** means the Constituent Entity that, by virtue of domestic law in its jurisdiction of tax residence, files the CbC Report in its capacity to do so on behalf of the MNE Group;

h) the term **"CbC Report"** means the Country-by-Country Report to be filed annually by the Reporting Entity in accordance with the laws of its jurisdiction of tax residence and with the information required to be reported under such laws covering the items and reflecting the format set out in the 2015 Report, as may be amended following the 2020 review contemplated therein;

i) the term **"2015 Report"** means the consolidated report, entitled *Transfer Pricing Documentation and Country-by-Country Reporting*, on Action 13 of the OECD/G20 *Action Plan on Base Erosion and Profit Shifting*;

j) the term "**Co-ordinating Body**" means the co-ordinating body of the Convention that, pursuant to paragraph 3 of Article 24 of the Convention, is composed of representatives of the competent authorities of the Parties to the Convention;

k) the term **"Co-ordinating Body Secretariat"** means the OECD Secretariat that, pursuant to paragraph 3 of Article 24 of the Convention, provides support to the Co-ordinating Body;

l) the term **"Agreement in effect"** means, in respect of any two Competent Authorities, that both Competent Authorities have indicated their intention to automatically exchange information with each other and have satisfied the other conditions set out in paragraph 2 of Section 8. A list of Competent Authorities between which this Agreement is in effect is to be published on the OECD website.

2. As regards the application of this Agreement at any time by a Competent Authority of a Jurisdiction, any term not otherwise defined in this Agreement will, unless the context otherwise requires or the Competent Authorities agree to a common meaning (as permitted by domestic law), have the meaning that it has at that time under the law of the Jurisdiction applying this Agreement, any meaning under the applicable tax laws of that Jurisdiction prevailing over a meaning given to the term under other laws of that Jurisdiction.

SECTION 2
Exchange of Information with Respect to MNE Groups

1. Pursuant to the provisions of Articles 6, 21 and 22 of the Convention, each Competent Authority will annually exchange on an automatic basis the CbC Report received from each Reporting Entity that is resident for tax purposes in its jurisdiction with all such other Competent Authorities of Jurisdictions with respect to which it has this Agreement in effect, and

in which, on the basis of the information in the CbC Report, one or more Constituent Entities of the MNE Group of the Reporting Entity are either resident for tax purposes, or are subject to tax with respect to the business carried out through a permanent establishment.

2. Notwithstanding the previous paragraph, the Competent Authorities of the Jurisdictions that have indicated that they are to be listed as non-reciprocal jurisdictions on the basis of their notification pursuant to paragraph 1 b) of Section 8 will send CbC Reports pursuant to paragraph 1, but will not receive CbC Reports under this Agreement. Competent Authorities of Jurisdictions that are not listed as non-reciprocal Jurisdictions will both send and receive the information specified in paragraph 1. Competent Authorities will, however, not send such information to Competent Authorities of the Jurisdictions included in the aforementioned list of non-reciprocal Jurisdictions.

SECTION 3
Time and Manner of Exchange of Information

1. For the purposes of the exchange of information in Section 2, the currency of the amounts contained in the CbC Report will be specified.

2. With respect to paragraph 1 of Section 2, a CbC Report is first to be exchanged, with respect to the fiscal year of the MNE Group commencing on or after the date indicated by the Competent Authority in the notification pursuant to paragraph 1a) of Section 8, as soon as possible and no later than 18 months after the last day of that fiscal year. Notwithstanding the foregoing, a CbC Report is only required to be exchanged, if both Competent Authorities have this Agreement in effect and their respective Jurisdictions have in effect legislation that requires the filing of CbC Reports with respect to the fiscal year to which the CbC Report relates and that is consistent with the scope of exchange provided for in Section 2.

3. Subject to paragraph 2, the CbC Report is to be exchanged as soon as possible and no later than 15 months after the last day of the fiscal year of the MNE Group to which the CbC Report relates.

4. The Competent Authorities will automatically exchange the CbC Reports through a common schema in Extensible Markup Language.

5. The Competent Authorities will work towards and agree on one or more methods for electronic data transmission, including encryption standards, with a view to maximising standardisation and minimising complexities and costs and will notify the Co-ordinating Body Secretariat of such standardised transmission and encryption methods.

SECTION 4
Collaboration on Compliance and Enforcement

A Competent Authority will notify the other Competent Authority when the first-mentioned Competent Authority has reason to believe, with respect to a Reporting Entity that is resident for tax purposes in the jurisdiction of the other Competent Authority, that an error may have led to incorrect or incomplete information reporting or that there is non-compliance of a Reporting Entity with respect to its obligation to file a CbC Report. The notified Competent Authority will take appropriate measures available under its domestic law to address the errors or non-compliance described in the notice.

SECTION 5
Confidentiality, Data Safeguards and Appropriate Use

1. All information exchanged is subject to the confidentiality rules and other safeguards provided for in the Convention, including the provisions limiting the use of the information exchanged.

2. In addition to the restrictions in paragraph 1, the use of the information will be further limited to the permissible uses described in this paragraph. In particular, information received by means of the CbC Report will be used for assessing high-level transfer pricing, base erosion and profit shifting related risks, and, where appropriate, for economic and statistical analysis. The information will not be used as a substitute for a detailed transfer pricing analysis of individual transactions and prices based on a full functional analysis and a full comparability analysis. It is acknowledged that information in the CbC Report on its own does not constitute conclusive evidence that transfer prices are or are not appropriate and, consequently, transfer pricing adjustments will not be based on the CbC Report. Inappropriate adjustments in contravention of this paragraph made by local tax administrations will be conceded in any competent authority proceedings. Notwithstanding the above, there is no prohibition on using the CbC Report data as a basis for making further enquiries into the MNE Group's transfer pricing arrangements or into other tax matters in the course of a tax audit and, as a result, appropriate adjustments to the taxable income of a Constituent Entity may be made.

3. To the extent permitted under applicable law, a Competent Authority will notify the Co-ordinating Body Secretariat immediately of any cases of non-compliance with paragraphs 1 and 2 of this Section, including any remedial actions, as well as any measures taken in respect of non-compliance with the above-mentioned paragraphs. The Co-ordinating Body Secretariat will notify all Competent Authorities with respect to which this is an Agreement in effect with the first-mentioned Competent Authority.

SECTION 6
Consultations

1. In case an adjustment of the taxable income of a Constituent Entity, as a result of further enquiries based on the data in the CbC Report, leads to undesirable economic outcomes, including if such cases arise for a specific business, the Competent Authorities of the Jurisdictions in which the affected Constituent Entities are resident shall consult each other and discuss with the aim of resolving the case.

2. If any difficulties in the implementation or interpretation of this Agreement arise, a Competent Authority may request consultations with one or more of the Competent Authorities to develop appropriate measures to ensure that this Agreement is fulfilled. In particular, a Competent Authority shall consult with the other Competent Authority, before the first-mentioned Competent Authority determines that there is a systemic failure to exchange CbC Reports with the other Competent Authority. Where the first mentioned Competent Authority makes such a determination it shall notify the Co-ordinating Body Secretariat which, after having informed the other Competent Authority concerned, will notify all Competent Authorities. To the extent permitted by applicable law, either Competent Authority may, and if it so wishes through the Co-ordinating Body Secretariat, involve other Competent Authorities that have this Agreement in effect with a view to finding an acceptable resolution to the issue.

3. The Competent Authority that requested the consultations pursuant to paragraph 2 shall ensure, as appropriate, that the Co-ordinating Body Secretariat is notified of any conclusions that were reached and measures that were developed, including the absence of such conclusions or measures, and the Co-ordinating Body Secretariat will notify all Competent Authorities, even those that did not participate in the consultations, of any such conclusions or measures. Taxpayer-specific information, including information that would reveal the identity of the taxpayer involved, is not to be furnished.

SECTION 7
Amendments

This Agreement may be amended by consensus by written agreement of all of the Competent Authorities that have the Agreement in effect. Unless otherwise agreed upon, such an amendment is effective on the first day of the month following the expiration of a period of one month after the date of the last signature of such written agreement.

SECTION 8
Term of Agreement

1. A Competent Authority must provide, at the time of signature of this Agreement or as soon as possible thereafter, a notification to the Co-ordinating Body Secretariat:

a) that its Jurisdiction has the necessary laws in place to require Reporting Entities to file a CbC Report and that its Jurisdiction will require the filing of CbC Reports with respect to fiscal years of Reporting Entities commencing on or after the date set out in the notification;

b) specifying whether the Jurisdiction is to be included in the list of non-reciprocal Jurisdictions;

c) specifying one or more methods for electronic data transmission including encryption;

d) that it has in place the necessary legal framework and infrastructure to ensure the required confidentiality and data safeguards standards in accordance with Article 22 of the Convention and paragraph 1 and Section 5 of this Agreement, as well as the appropriate use of the information in the CbC Reports as described in paragraph 2 of Section 5 of this Agreement, and attaching the completed confidentiality and data safeguard questionnaire attached as Annex to this Agreement; and

e) that includes (i) a list of the Jurisdictions of the Competent Authorities with respect to which it intends to have this Agreement in effect, following national legislative procedures for entry into force (if any) or (ii) a declaration by the Competent Authority that it intends to have this Agreement in effect with all other Competent Authorities that provide a notification under paragraph 1e) of Section 8.

Competent Authorities must notify the Co-ordinating Body Secretariat, promptly, of any subsequent change to be made to any of the above-mentioned content of the notification.

2. This Agreement will come into effect between two Competent Authorities on the later of the following dates: (i) the date on which the second of the two Competent Authorities has provided notification to the Co-ordinating Body Secretariat under paragraph 1 that includes the other Competent Authority's Jurisdiction pursuant to subparagraph 1e) and (ii) the date on which the Convention has entered into force and is in effect for both Jurisdictions.

3. The Co-ordinating Body Secretariat will maintain a list that will be published on the OECD website of the Competent Authorities that have signed the Agreement and between which Competent Authorities this is an Agreement in effect. In addition, the Co-ordinating Body Secretariat will publish the information provided by Competent Authorities pursuant to subparagraphs 1a) and b) on the OECD website.

4. The information provided pursuant to subparagraphs 1c) through e) will be made available to other signatories upon request in writing to the Co-ordinating Body Secretariat.

5. A Competent Authority may temporarily suspend the exchange of information under this Agreement by giving notice in writing to another Competent Authority that it has determined that there is or has been significant non-compliance by the second-mentioned Competent Authority with this Agreement. Before making such a determination, the first-mentioned Competent Authority shall consult with the other Competent Authority. For the purposes of this paragraph, significant non-compliance means non-compliance with paragraphs 1 and 2 of Section 5 and paragraph 1 of Section 6 of this Agreement and/or the corresponding provisions of the Convention, as well as a failure by the Competent Authority to provide timely or adequate information as required under this Agreement. A suspension will have immediate effect and will last until the second-mentioned Competent Authority establishes in a manner acceptable to both Competent Authorities that there has been no significant non-compliance or that the second-mentioned Competent Authority has adopted relevant measures that address the significant non-compliance. To the extent permitted by applicable law, either Competent Authority may, and if it so wishes through the Co-ordinating Body Secretariat, involve other Competent Authorities that have this Agreement in effect with a view to finding an acceptable resolution to the issue.

6. A Competent Authority may terminate its participation in this Agreement, or with respect to a particular Competent Authority, by giving notice of termination in writing to the Co-ordinating Body Secretariat. Such termination will become effective on the first day of the month following the expiration of a period of 12 months after the date of the notice of termination. In the event of termination, all information previously received under this Agreement will remain confidential and subject to the terms of the Convention.

SECTION 9
Co-ordinating Body Secretariat

Unless otherwise provided for in the Agreement, the Co-ordinating Body Secretariat will notify all Competent Authorities of any notifications that it has received under this Agreement and will provide a notice to all signatories of the Agreement when a new Competent Authority signs the Agreement.

Done in English and French, both texts being equally authentic.

Annex to the Agreement – Confidentiality and Data Safeguards Questionnaire

1. Legal Framework

A legal framework must ensure the confidentiality of exchanged tax information and limit its use to appropriate purposes. The two basic components of such a framework are the terms of the applicable treaty, Tax Information Exchange Agreement (TIEA) or other bilateral agreement for the exchange of information, and a jurisdiction's domestic legislation.

1.1 Tax Conventions, TIEAs & Other Exchange Agreements	
Primary Check-list Areas	• Provisions in tax treaties, TIEAs and international agreements requiring confidentiality of exchanged information and restricting use to intended purposes
How do the exchange of information provisions in your Tax Conventions, TIEAs, or other exchange agreements ensure confidentiality and restrict the use of both outgoing information to other Contracting States and incoming information received in response to a request?	
1.2 Domestic Legislation	
Primary Check-list Areas	• Domestic law must apply safeguards to taxpayer information exchanged pursuant to a treaty, TIEA or other international agreement, and treat those information exchange agreements as binding, restrict data access and use and impose penalties for violations.
How do your domestic laws and regulations safeguard and restrict the use of information exchanged for tax purposes under Tax Conventions, TIEAs, or other exchange instruments? How does the tax administration prevent the misuse of confidential data and prohibit the transfer of tax information from the tax administrative body to non-tax government bodies?	

2. Information Security Management

The information security management systems used by each jurisdiction's tax administration must adhere to standards that ensure the protection of confidential taxpayer data. For example, there must be a screening process for employees handling the information, limits on who can access the information, and systems to detect and trace unauthorised disclosures. The internationally accepted standards for information security are known as the "ISO/IEC 27000-series". As described more fully below, a tax administration should be able to document that it is compliant with the ISO/IEC 27000-series standards or that it has an equivalent information security framework and that taxpayer information obtained under an exchange agreement is protected under that framework.

2.1.1 Background Checks and Contracts	
Primary Check-list Areas	• Screenings and background investigations for employees and contractors • Hiring process and contracts • Responsible Points of Contact
What procedures govern your tax administration's background investigations for employees and contractors who may have access to, use, or are responsible for protecting data received through exchange of information? Is this information publicly available? If so, please provide the reference. If not, please provide a summary of the procedures.	
2.1.2 Training and Awareness	
Primary Check-list Areas	• Initial training and periodic security awareness training based on roles, security risks, and applicable laws
What training does your tax administration provide to employees and contractors regarding confidential information including data received from partners through the Exchange of Information? Does your tax administration maintain a public version of the requirements? If so, please provide the reference. If not, please provide a summary of the requirement.	
2.1.3 Departure Policies	
Primary Check-list Areas	• Departure policies to terminate access to confidential information
What procedures does your tax administration maintain for terminating access to confidential information for departing employees and consultants? Are the procedures publicly available? If so, please provide the reference. If not, please provide a summary of the procedures.	
2.2.1 Physical Security: Access to Premises	
Primary Check-list Areas	• Security measures to restrict entry to premises: security guards, policies, entry access procedures
What procedures does your tax administration maintain to grant employees, consultants, and visitors access to premises where confidential information, paper or electronic, is stored? Are the procedures publicly available? If so, please provide the reference. If not, please provide a summary of the procedures.	

2.2.2 Physical Security: Physical Document Storage	
Primary Check-list Areas	• Secure physical storage for confidential documents: policies and procedures
What procedures does your tax administration maintain for receiving, processing, archiving, retrieving and disposing of hard copies of confidential data received from taxpayers or exchange of information partners? Does your tax administration maintain procedures employees must follow when leaving their workspace at the end of the day? Are these procedures publicly available? If yes, please provide the reference. If not, please provide a summary. Does your tax administration have a data classification policy? If so, please describe how your document storage procedures differ for data at all classification levels. Are these procedures publicly available? If yes, please provide the reference. If not, please provide a summary.	
2.3 Planning	
Primary Check-list Areas	• Planning documentation to develop, update, and implement security information systems
What procedures does your tax administration maintain to develop, document, update, and implement security for information systems used to receive, process, archive and retrieve confidential information? Are these procedures publicly available? If yes, please provide the reference. If not, please provide a summary. What procedures does your tax administration maintain regarding periodic Information Security Plan updates to address changes to the information systems environment, and how are problems and risks identified during the implementation of Information Security Plans resolved? Are these procedures publicly available? If yes, please provide the reference. If not, please provide a summary.	
2.4 Configuration Management	
Primary Check-list Areas	• Configuration management and security controls
What policies does your tax administration maintain to regulate system configuration and updates? Are the policies publicly available? If yes, please provide the reference. If not, please provide a summary.	
2.5 Access Control	
Primary Check-list Areas	• Access Control Policies and procedures: authorised personnel and international exchange of information
What policies does your tax administration maintain to limit system access to authorised users and safeguard data during transmission when received and stored? Please describe how your tax administration's access authorisation and data transmission policies extend to data received from an exchange of information partner under a treaty or TIEA or other exchange agreement. Are the policies publicly available? If yes, please provide the reference. If not, please provide a summary.	

2.6 Identification and Authentication	
Primary Check-list Areas	• Authenticating the identifying users and devices that require access to information systems
What policies and procedures does your tax administration maintain for each information system connected to confidential data? Are the policies and procedures publicly available? If so, please provide a reference. If not, please provide a summary. **What policies and procedures govern the authentication of authorised tax administration users by systems connected to confidential data? Are the policies and procedures publicly available? If so, please provide a reference. If not, please provide a summary.**	
2.7 Audit and Accountability	
Primary Check-list Areas	• Traceable electronic actions within systems • System audit procedures: monitoring, analysing, investigating, and reporting of unlawful/unauthorised use
What policies and procedures does your tax administration maintain to ensure system audits take place that will detect unauthorised access? Are the policies publicly available? If so, please provide a reference. If not, please provide a summary.	
2.8 Maintenance	
Primary Check-list Areas	• Periodic and timely maintenance of systems • Controls over: tools, procedures, and mechanisms for system maintenance and personnel use
What policies govern effective periodic system maintenance by your tax administration? Are these policies publicly available? If so, please provide a reference. If not, please provide a summary. **What procedures govern the resolution of system flaws identified by your tax administration? Are these procedures publicly available? If so, please provide a reference. If not, please provide a summary.**	
2.9 System and Communications Protection	
Primary Check-list Areas	• Procedures to monitor, control, and protect communications to and from information systems
What policies and procedures does your tax administration maintain for the electronic transmission and receipt of confidential data. Please describe the security and encryption requirements addressed in these policies. Are these policies publicly available? If so, please provide a reference. If not, please provide a summary.	

<table>
<tr><th colspan="2">2.10 System and Information Integrity</th></tr>
<tr><td>Primary Check-list Areas</td><td>• Procedures to identify, report, and correct information system flaws in a timely manner
• Protection against malicious code and monitoring system security alerts</td></tr>
<tr><td colspan="2">What procedures does your tax administration maintain to identify, report, and correct information system flaws in a timely manner? Please describe how these procedures provide for the protection of systems against malicious codes causing harm to data integrity. Are these procedures publicly available? If so, please provide a reference. If not, please provide a summary.</td></tr>
<tr><th colspan="2">2.11 Security Assessments</th></tr>
<tr><td>Primary Check-list Areas</td><td>• Processes used to test, validate, and authorise the security controls for protecting data, correcting deficiencies, and reducing vulnerabilities</td></tr>
<tr><td colspan="2">What policies does your tax administration maintain and regularly update for reviewing the processes used to test, validate, and authorise a security control plan? Is the policy publicly available? If so, please provide a reference. If not, please provide a summary.</td></tr>
<tr><th colspan="2">2.12 Contingency Planning</th></tr>
<tr><td>Primary Check-list Areas</td><td>• Plans for emergency response, backup operations, and post-disaster recovery of information systems</td></tr>
<tr><td colspan="2">What contingency plans and procedures does your tax administration maintain to reduce the impact of improper data disclosure or unrecoverable loss of data? Are the plans and procedures publicly available? If so, please provide a reference. If not, please provide a summary.</td></tr>
<tr><th colspan="2">2.13 Risk Assessment</th></tr>
<tr><td>Primary Check-list Areas</td><td>• Potential risk of unauthorised access to taxpayer information
• Risk and magnitude of harm from unauthorised use, disclosure, or disruption of the taxpayer information systems
• Procedures to update risk assessment methodologies</td></tr>
<tr><td colspan="2">Does your tax administration conduct risk assessments to identify risks and the potential impact of unauthorised access, use, and disclosure of information, or destruction of information systems? What procedures does your tax administration maintain to update risk assessment methodologies? Are these risk assessments and policies publicly available? If so, please provide a reference. If not, please provide a summary.</td></tr>
</table>

2.14 Systems and Services Acquisition	
Primary Check-list Areas	• Methods and processes to ensure third-party providers of information systems process, store and transmit confidential information in accordance with computer security requirements
What process does your tax administration maintain to ensure third-party providers are applying appropriate security controls that are consistent with computer security requirements for confidential information? Are the processes publicly available? If so, please provide a reference. If not, please provide a summary.	
2.15 Media Protection	
Primary Check-list Areas	• Processes to protect information in printed or digital form • Security measures used to limit media information access to authorised users only • Methods for sanitising or destroying digital media prior to disposal or reuse
What processes does your tax administration maintain to securely store and limit access to confidential information in printed or digital form upon receipt from any source? How does your tax administration securely destroy confidential media information prior to its disposal? Are the processes available publicly? If so, please provide a reference. If not, please provide a summary.	
2.16 Protection of Treaty-Exchanged data (formerly Prevention of Data Commingling)	
Primary Check-list Areas	• Procedures to ensure treaty-exchanged files are safeguarded and clearly labelled • Classification methods of treaty-exchanged files
What policies and processes does your tax administration maintain to store confidential information and clearly label it as treaty-exchanged after receipt from foreign Competent Authorities? Are these policies and processes publicly available? If so, please provide a reference. If not, please provide a summary.	
2.17 Information Disposal Policies	
Primary Check-list Areas	• Procedures for properly disposing paper and electronic files
What procedures does your tax administration maintain for the disposal of confidential information? Do these procedures extend to exchanged information from foreign Competent Authorities? Are the procedures publicly available? If so, please provide a reference. If not, please provide a summary.	

3. Monitoring and enforcement

In addition to keeping treaty-exchanged information confidential, tax administrations must be able to ensure that its use will be limited to the purposes defined by the applicable information exchange agreement. Thus, compliance with an acceptable information security framework alone is not sufficient to protect treaty-exchanged tax data. In addition, domestic law must impose penalties or sanctions for improper disclosure or use of taxpayer information. To ensure implementation, such laws must be reinforced by adequate administrative resources and procedures.

3.1 Penalties and Sanctions	
Primary Check-list Areas	• Penalties imposed for unauthorised disclosures • Risk mitigation practices
Does your tax administration have the ability to impose penalties for unauthorised disclosures of confidential information? Do the penalties extend to unauthorised disclosure of confidential information exchanged with a treaty or TIEA partner? Are the penalties publicly available? If so, please provide a reference. If not, please provide a summary.	
3.2.1 Policing Unauthorised Access and Disclosure	
Primary Check-list Areas	• Monitoring to detect breaches • Reporting of breaches
What procedures does your tax administration have to monitor confidentiality breaches? What policies and procedures does your tax administration have that require employees and contractors to report actual or potential breaches of confidentiality? What reports does your tax administration prepare when a breach of confidentiality occurs? Are these policies and procedures publicly available? If so, please provide a reference. If not, please provide a summary.	
3.2.2 Sanctions and Prior Experience	
Primary Check-list Areas	• Prior unauthorised disclosures • Policy/process modifications to prevent future breaches
Have there been any cases in your jurisdiction where confidential information has been improperly disclosed? Have there been any cases in your jurisdiction where confidential information received by the Competent Authority from an exchange of information partner has been disclosed other than in accordance with the terms of the instrument under which it was provided? Does your tax administration or Inspector General make available to the public descriptions of any breaches, any penalties/sanctions imposed, and changes put in place to mitigate risk and prevent future breaches? If so, please provide a reference. If not, please provide a summary.	

Competent Authority Agreement on the Exchange of Country-by-Country Reports on the basis of a Double Tax Convention ("DTC CAA")

Whereas, the Government of [Jurisdiction A] and the Government of [Jurisdiction B] desire to increase international tax transparency and improve access of their respective tax authorities to information regarding the global allocation of the income, the taxes paid, and certain indicators of the location of economic activity among tax jurisdictions in which Multinational Enterprise (MNE) Groups operate through the automatic exchange of annual CbC Reports, with a view to assessing high-level transfer pricing risks and other base erosion and profit shifting related risks, as well as for economic and statistical analysis, where appropriate;

Whereas, the laws of their respective Jurisdictions require or are expected to require the Reporting Entity of an MNE Group to annually file a CbC Report;

Whereas, the CbC Report is intended to be part of a three-tiered structure, along with a global master file and a local file, which together represent a standardised approach to transfer pricing documentation which will provide tax administrations with relevant and reliable information to perform an efficient and robust transfer pricing risk assessment analysis;

Whereas, Article [...] of the Income Tax Convention between [Jurisdiction A] and [Jurisdiction B] (the "Convention"), authorises the exchange of information for tax purposes, including the automatic exchange of information, and allows the competent authorities of [Jurisdiction A] and [Jurisdiction B] (the "Competent Authorities") to agree the scope and modalities of such automatic exchanges;

Whereas, [Jurisdiction A] and [Jurisdiction B] [have/are expected to have/have, or are expected to have,] in place by the time the first exchange of CbC Reports takes place (i) appropriate safeguards to ensure that the information received pursuant to this Agreement remains confidential and is used for the purposes of assessing high-level transfer pricing risks and other base erosion and profit shifting related risks, as well as for economic and statistical analysis, where appropriate, in accordance with Section 5 of this Agreement, (ii) the infrastructure for an effective exchange relationship (including established processes for ensuring timely, accurate, and confidential information exchanges, effective and reliable communications, and capabilities to promptly resolve questions and concerns about exchanges or requests for exchanges and to administer the provisions of Section 4 of this Agreement), and (iii) the necessary legislation to require Reporting Entities to file the CbC Report;

Whereas, [Jurisdiction A] and [Jurisdiction B] are committed to endeavour to mutually agree on resolving cases of double taxation in accordance with Article [25] of the Convention, as well as paragraph 1 of Section 6 of this Agreement;

Whereas, the Competent Authorities intend to conclude this Agreement on reciprocal automatic exchange pursuant to the Convention and subject to the confidentiality and other protections provided for in the Convention, including the provisions limiting the use of the information exchanged thereunder;

Now, therefore, the Competent Authorities have agreed as follows:

SECTION 1
Definitions

1. For the purposes of this Agreement, the following terms have the following meanings:

a) the term **"[Jurisdiction A]"** means [...];

b) the term **"[Jurisdiction B]"** means [...];

c) the term **"Competent Authority"** means in case of [Jurisdiction A], [...] and in case of [Jurisdiction B], [...];

d) The term "**Group**" means a collection of enterprises related through ownership or control such that it is either required to prepare consolidated financial statements for financial reporting purposes under applicable accounting principles or would be so required if equity interests in any of the enterprises were traded on a public securities exchange;

e) the term **"Multinational Enterprise (MNE) Group"** means any Group that (i) includes two or more enterprises the tax residence for which is in different jurisdictions, or includes an enterprise that is resident for tax purposes in one jurisdiction and is subject to tax with respect to the business carried out through a permanent establishment in another jurisdiction, and (ii) is not an Excluded MNE Group;

f) the term **"Excluded MNE Group"** means a Group that is not required to file a CbC Report on the basis that the consolidated group revenue of the Group during the fiscal year immediately preceding the reporting fiscal year, as reflected in its consolidated financial statements for such preceding fiscal year, is below the threshold defined in domestic law by the Jurisdiction and being consistent with the 2015 Report, as may be amended following the 2020 review contemplated therein;

g) the term **"Constituent Entity"** means (i) any separate business unit of an MNE Group that is included in the consolidated financial statements for financial reporting purposes, or would be so included if equity interests in such business unit of an MNE Group were traded on a public securities exchange (ii) any separate business unit that is excluded from the MNE Group's consolidated financial statements solely on size or materiality grounds and (iii) any permanent establishment of any separate business unit of the MNE Group included in (i) or (ii) above provided the business unit prepares a separate financial statement for such permanent establishment for financial reporting, regulatory, tax reporting or internal management control purposes;

h) the term **"Reporting Entity"** means the Constituent Entity that, by virtue of domestic law in its jurisdiction of tax residence, files the CbC Report in its capacity to do so on behalf of the MNE Group;

i) the term **"CbC Report"** means the Country-by-Country Report to be filed annually by the Reporting Entity in accordance with the laws of its jurisdiction of tax residence and with the information required to be reported under such laws covering the items and reflecting the format set out in the 2015 Report, as may be amended following the 2020 review contemplated therein; and

j) the term **"2015 Report"** means the consolidated report, entitled *Transfer Pricing Documentation and Country-by-Country Reporting*, on Action 13 of the OECD/G20 *Action Plan on Base Erosion and Profit Shifting*.

2. As regards to the application of this Agreement at any time by a Competent Authority of a Jurisdiction, any term not otherwise defined in this Agreement will, unless the context otherwise requires or the Competent Authorities agree to a common meaning (as permitted by domestic law), have the meaning that it has at that time under the law of the Jurisdiction applying this Agreement, any meaning under the applicable tax laws of that Jurisdiction prevailing over a meaning given to the term under other laws of that Jurisdiction.

SECTION 2
Exchange of Information with Respect to MNE Groups

Pursuant to the provisions of Article [...] of the Convention, each Competent Authority will annually exchange on an automatic basis the CbC Report received from each Reporting Entity that is resident for tax purposes in its Jurisdiction with the other Competent Authority, provided that, on the basis of the information provided in the CbC Report, one or more Constituent Entities of the MNE Group of the Reporting Entity are resident for tax purposes in the Jurisdiction of the other Competent Authority or, are subject to tax with respect to the business carried out through a permanent establishment situated in the Jurisdiction of the other Competent Authority.

SECTION 3
Time and Manner of Exchange of Information

1. For the purposes of the exchange of information in Section 2, the currency of the amounts contained in the CbC Report will be specified.

2. With respect to Section 2, a CbC Report is first to be exchanged with respect to fiscal years of MNE Groups commencing on or after [...]. Such CbC Report is to be exchanged as soon as possible and no later than 18 months after the last day of the fiscal year of the MNE Group to which the CbC Report relates. CbC Reports with respect to subsequent fiscal years are to be exchanged as soon as possible and no later than 15 months after the last day of the fiscal year of the MNE Group to which the CbC Report relates.

3. The Competent Authorities will automatically exchange the CbC Reports through a common schema in Extensible Markup Language.

4. The Competent Authorities will work towards and agree on one or more methods for electronic data transmission including encryption standards.

SECTION 4
Collaboration on Compliance and Enforcement

A Competent Authority will notify the other Competent Authority when the first-mentioned Competent Authority has reason to believe, with respect to a Reporting Entity that is resident for tax purposes in the Jurisdiction of the other Competent Authority, that an error may have led to incorrect or incomplete information reporting or that there is non-compliance of a Reporting Entity with the respect to its obligation to file a CbC Report. The notified Competent Authority will take all appropriate measures available under its domestic law to address the errors or non-compliance described in the notice.

SECTION 5
Confidentiality, Data Safeguards and Appropriate Use

1. All information exchanged is subject to the confidentiality rules and other safeguards provided for in the Convention, including the provisions limiting the use of the information exchanged.

2. In addition to the restrictions in paragraph 1, the use of the information will be further limited to the permissible uses described in this paragraph. In particular, information received by means of the CbC Report will be used for assessing high-level transfer pricing, base erosion and profit shifting related risks, and, where appropriate, for economic and statistical analysis. The information will not be used as a substitute for a detailed transfer pricing analysis of individual transactions and prices based on a full functional analysis and a full comparability analysis. It is acknowledged that information in the CbC Report on its own does not constitute conclusive evidence that transfer prices are or are not appropriate and, consequently, transfer pricing adjustments will not be based on the CbC Report. Inappropriate adjustments in contravention of this paragraph made by local tax administrations will be conceded in any competent authority proceedings. Notwithstanding the above, there is no prohibition on using the CbC Report data as a basis for making further enquiries into the MNE Group's transfer pricing arrangements or into other tax matters in the course of a tax audit and, as a result, appropriate adjustments to the taxable income of a Constituent Entity may be made.

3. To the extent permitted under applicable law, each Competent Authority will notify the other Competent Authority immediately regarding of any cases of non-compliance with the rules set out in paragraphs 1 and 2 of this Section, including any remedial actions, as well as any measures taken in respect of non-compliance with the above-mentioned paragraphs.

SECTION 6
Consultations

1. In cases foreseen by Article [25] of the Convention, the Competent Authorities of both Jurisdictions shall consult each other and endeavour to resolve the situation by mutual agreement.

2. If any difficulties in the implementation or interpretation of this Agreement arise, either Competent Authority may request consultations with the other Competent Authority to develop appropriate measures to ensure that this Agreement is fulfilled. In particular, a Competent Authority shall consult with the other Competent Authority before the first-mentioned Competent Authority determines that there is a systemic failure to exchange CbC Reports with the other Competent Authority.

SECTION 7
Amendments

This Agreement may be amended by consensus by written agreement of the Competent Authorities. Unless otherwise agreed upon, such an amendment is effective on the first day of the month following the expiration of a period of one month after the date of the last signature of such written agreement.

SECTION 8
Term of Agreement

1. This Agreement will come into effect on [.../the date of the later of the notifications provided by each Competent Authority that its Jurisdiction either has the necessary laws in place to require Reporting Entities to file a CbC Report].

2. A Competent Authority may temporarily suspend the exchange of information under this Agreement by giving notice in writing to the other Competent Authority that it has determined that there is or has been significant non-compliance by the other Competent Authority with this Agreement. Before making such a determination, the first-mentioned Competent Authority shall consult with the other Competent Authority. For the purposes of this paragraph, significant non-compliance means non-compliance with paragraphs 1 and 2 of Section 5 and paragraph 1 of Section 6 of this Agreement, including the provisions of the Convention referred to therein, as well as a failure by the Competent Authority to provide timely or adequate information as required under this Agreement. A suspension will have immediate effect and will last until the second-mentioned Competent Authority establishes in a manner acceptable to both Competent Authorities that there has been no significant non-compliance or that the second-mentioned Competent Authority has adopted relevant measures that address the significant non-compliance.

3. Either Competent Authority may terminate this Agreement by giving notice of termination in writing to the other Competent Authority. Such termination will become effective on the first day of the month following the expiration of a period of 12 months after the date of the notice of termination. In the event of termination, all information previously received under this Agreement will remain confidential and subject to the terms of the Convention.

Signed in duplicate in [...] on [...].

Competent Authority for [Jurisdiction A]	Competent Authority for [Jurisdiction B]

Competent Authority Agreement on the Exchange of Country-by-Country Reports on the basis of a Tax Information Exchange Agreement ("TIEA CAA")

Whereas, the Government of [Jurisdiction A] and the Government of [Jurisdiction B] intend to increase international tax transparency and improve access of their respective tax authorities to information regarding the global allocation of the income, the taxes paid, and certain indicators of the location of economic activity among tax jurisdictions in which Multinational Enterprise (MNE) Groups operate through the automatic exchange of annual CbC Reports, with a view to assessing high-level transfer pricing risks and other base erosion and profit shifting related risks, as well as for economic and statistical analysis, where appropriate;

Whereas, the laws of their respective Jurisdictions require or are expected to require the Reporting Entity of an MNE Group to annually file a CbC Report;

Whereas, the CbC Report is intended to be part of a three-tiered structure, along with a global master file and a local file, which together represent a standardised approach to transfer pricing documentation which will provide tax administrations with relevant and reliable information to perform an efficient and robust transfer pricing risk assessment analysis;

Whereas, Article [5A] of the Tax Information Exchange Agreement between [Jurisdiction A] and [Jurisdiction B] (the "TIEA"), authorises the exchange of information for tax purposes, including the automatic exchange of information, and allows the competent authorities of [Jurisdiction A] and [Jurisdiction B] (the "Competent Authorities") to agree the scope and modalities of such automatic exchanges;

Whereas, [Jurisdiction A] and [Jurisdiction B] [have/are expected to have/have, or are expected to have,] in place by the time the first exchange of CbC Reports takes place (i) appropriate safeguards to ensure that the information received pursuant to this Agreement remains confidential and is used for the purposes of assessing high-level transfer pricing risks and other base erosion and profit shifting related risks, as well as for economic and statistical analysis, where appropriate, in accordance with Section 5 of this Agreement, (ii) the infrastructure for an effective exchange relationship (including established processes for ensuring timely, accurate and confidential information exchanges, effective and reliable communications, and capabilities to promptly resolve questions and concerns about exchanges or requests for exchanges and to administer the provisions of Section 4 of this Agreement) and (iii) the necessary legislation to require Reporting MNEs to file the CbC Report;

Whereas, the Competent Authorities intend to conclude this Agreement on reciprocal automatic exchange pursuant to the TIEA and subject to the confidentiality and other protections provided for in the TIEA, including the provisions limiting the use of the information exchanged thereunder;

Now, therefore, the Competent Authorities have agreed as follows:

SECTION 1
Definitions

1. For the purposes of this Agreement, the following terms have the following meanings:

a) the term **"[Jurisdiction A]"** means [...];

b) the term **"[Jurisdiction B]"** means [...];

c) the term **"Competent Authority"** means in case of [Jurisdiction A], [...] and in case of [Jurisdiction B], [...];

d) The term **"Group"** means a collection of enterprises related through ownership or control such that it is either required to prepare consolidated financial statements for financial reporting purposes under applicable accounting principles or would be so required if equity interests in any of the enterprises were traded on a public securities exchange;

e) the term **"Multinational Enterprise (MNE) Group"** means any Group that (i) includes two or more enterprises the tax residence for which is in different jurisdictions, or includes an enterprise that is resident for tax purposes in one jurisdiction and is subject to tax with respect to the business carried out through a permanent establishment in another jurisdiction, and (ii) is not an Excluded MNE Group;

f) the term **"Excluded MNE Group"** means a Group that is not required to file a CbC Report on the basis that the consolidated group revenue of the Group during the fiscal year immediately preceding the reporting fiscal year, as reflected in its consolidated financial statements for such preceding fiscal year, is below the threshold defined in domestic law by the Jurisdiction and being consistent with the 2015 Report, as may be amended following the 2020 review contemplated therein;

g) the term **"Constituent Entity"** means (i) any separate business unit of an MNE Group that is included in the consolidated financial statements for financial reporting purposes, or would be so included if equity interests in such business unit of an MNE Group were traded on a public securities exchange (ii) any separate business unit that is excluded from the MNE Group's consolidated financial statements solely on size or materiality grounds and (iii) any permanent establishments of any separate business unit of the MNE Group included in (i) or (ii) above provided such business unit prepares a separate financial statement for such permanent establishment for financial reporting, regulatory, tax reporting or internal management control purposes;

h) the term **"Reporting Entity"** means the Constituent Entity that, by virtue of domestic law in its jurisdiction of tax residence, files the CbC Report in its capacity to do so on behalf of the MNE Group;

i) the term **"CbC Report"** means the Country-by-Country Report to be filed annually by the Reporting Entity in accordance with the laws of its jurisdiction of tax residence and with the information required to be reported under such laws covering the items and reflecting the format set out in the 2015 Report, as may be amended following the 2020 review contemplated therein; and

j) the term **"2015 Report"** means the consolidated report, entitled *Transfer Pricing Documentation and Country-by-Country Reporting*, on Action 13 of the OECD/G20 Action Plan on Base Erosion and Profit Shifting.

2. As regards to the application of this Agreement at any time by a Competent Authority of a Jurisdiction, any term not otherwise defined in this Agreement will, unless the context otherwise requires or the Competent Authorities agree to a common meaning (as permitted by domestic law), have the meaning that it has at that time under the law of the Jurisdiction applying this Agreement, any meaning under the applicable tax laws of that Jurisdiction prevailing over a meaning given to the term under other laws of that Jurisdiction.

SECTION 2
Exchange of Information with Respect to MNE Groups

Pursuant to the provisions of Article [5A] of the TIEA, each Competent Authority will annually exchange on an automatic basis the CbC Report received from each Reporting Entity that is resident for tax purposes in its Jurisdiction with the other Competent Authority, provided that, on the basis of the information provided in the CbC Report, one or more Constituent Entities of the MNE Group of the Reporting Entity are resident for tax purposes in the Jurisdiction of the other Competent Authority or, are subject to tax with respect to the business carried out through a permanent establishment situated in the Jurisdiction of the other Competent Authority.

SECTION 3
Time and Manner of Exchange of Information

1. For the purposes of the exchange of information in Section 2, the currency of the amounts contained in the CbC Report will be specified.

2. With respect to Section 2, a CbC Report is first to be exchanged with respect to fiscal years of MNE Groups commencing on or after […]. Such CbC Report is to be exchanged as soon as possible and no later than 18 months after the last day of the fiscal year of the Reporting Entity of the MNE Group to which the CbC Report relates. CbC Reports with respect to subsequent fiscal years are to be exchanged as soon as possible and no later than 15 months after the last day of the fiscal year of the MNE Group to which the CbC Report relates.

3. The Competent Authorities will automatically exchange the CbC Reports through a common schema in Extensible Markup Language.

4. The Competent Authorities will work towards and agree on one or more methods for electronic data transmission including encryption standards.

SECTION 4
Collaboration on Compliance and Enforcement

A Competent Authority will notify the other Competent Authority when the first-mentioned Competent Authority has reason to believe, with respect to a Reporting Entity that is resident for tax purposes in the Jurisdiction of the other Competent Authority, that an error may have led to incorrect or incomplete information reporting or that there is non-compliance of a Reporting Entity with the respect to its obligation to file a CbC Report. The notified Competent Authority will take all appropriate measures available under its domestic law to address the errors or non-compliance described in the notice.

SECTION 5
Confidentiality, Data Safeguards and Appropriate Use

1. All information exchanged is subject to the confidentiality rules and other safeguards provided for in the TIEA, including the provisions limiting the use of the information exchanged.

2. In addition to the restrictions in paragraph 1, the use of the information will be further limited to the permissible uses described in this paragraph. In particular, information received by means of the CbC Report will be used for assessing high-level transfer pricing, base erosion and profit shifting related risks, and, where appropriate, for economic and statistical analysis. The information will not be used as a substitute for a detailed transfer pricing analysis of individual transactions and prices based on a full functional analysis and a full comparability analysis. It is acknowledged that information in the CbC Report on its own does not constitute conclusive evidence that transfer prices are or are not appropriate and, consequently, transfer pricing adjustments will not be based on the CbC Report. Inappropriate adjustments in contravention of this paragraph made by local tax administrations will be conceded in any competent authority proceedings. Notwithstanding the above, there is no prohibition on using the CbC Report data as a basis for making further enquiries into the MNE's transfer pricing arrangements or into other tax matters in the course of a tax audit and, as a result, appropriate adjustments to the taxable income of a Constituent Entity may be made.

3. To the extent permitted under applicable law, each Competent Authority will notify the other Competent Authority immediately regarding of any cases of non-compliance with the paragraphs 1 and 2 of this Section, including any remedial actions, as well as any measures taken in respect of non-compliance with the above-mentioned paragraphs.

SECTION 6
Consultations

1. In case an adjustment of the taxable income of a Constituent Entity, as a result of further enquiries based on the data in the CbC Report, leads to undesirable economic outcomes, including if such cases arise for a specific business, both Competent Authorities shall consult each other and discuss with the aim of resolving the case.

2. If any difficulties in the implementation or interpretation of this Agreement arise, either Competent Authority may request consultations with of the other Competent Authority to develop appropriate measures to ensure that this Agreement is fulfilled. In particular, a Competent Authority shall consult with the other Competent Authority before the first-mentioned Competent Authority determines that there is a systemic failure to exchange CbC Reports with the other Competent Authority.

SECTION 7
Amendments

This Agreement may be amended by consensus by written agreement of the Competent Authorities. Unless otherwise agreed upon, such an amendment is effective on the first day of the month following the expiration of a period of one month after the date of the last signature of such written agreement.

SECTION 8
Term of Agreement

1. This Agreement will come into effect on [.../the date of the later of the notifications provided by each Competent Authority that its Jurisdiction either has the necessary laws in place to require Reporting Entities to file a CbC Report].

2. A Competent Authority may temporarily suspend the exchange of information under this Agreement by giving notice in writing to the other Competent Authority that it has determined that there is or has been significant non-compliance by the other Competent Authority with this Agreement. Before making such a determination, the first-mentioned Competent Authority shall consult with the other Competent Authority. For the purposes of this paragraph, significant non-compliance means non-compliance with paragraphs 1 and 2 of Section 5 and paragraph 1 of Section 6 of this Agreement and the provisions of the TIEA referred to therein, as well as a failure by the Competent Authority to provide timely or adequate information as required under this Agreement. A suspension will have immediate effect and will last until the second-mentioned Competent Authority establishes in a manner acceptable to both Competent Authorities that there has been no significant non-compliance or that the second-mentioned Competent Authority has adopted relevant measures that address the significant non-compliance.

3. Either Competent Authority may terminate this Agreement by giving notice of termination in writing to the other Competent Authority. Such termination will become effective on the first day of the month following the

expiration of a period of 12 months after the date of the notice of termination. In the event of termination, all information previously received under this Agreement will remain confidential and subject to the terms of the TIEA.

Signed in duplicate in […] on […].

Competent Authority for [Jurisdiction A]	Competent Authority for [Jurisdiction B]

Annex I to Chapter VI

Examples to illustrate the guidance on intangibles

Example 1

1. Premiere is the parent company of an MNE group. Company S is a wholly owned subsidiary of Premiere and a member of the Premiere group. Premiere funds R&D and performs ongoing R&D functions in support of its business operations. When its R&D functions result in patentable inventions, it is the practice of the Premiere group that all rights in such inventions be assigned to Company S in order to centralise and simplify global patent administration. All patent registrations are held and maintained in the name of Company S.

2. Company S employs three lawyers to perform its patent administration work and has no other employees. Company S does not conduct or control any of the R&D activities of the Premiere group. Company S has no technical R&D personnel, nor does it incur any of the Premiere group's R&D expense. Key decisions related to defending the patents are made by Premiere management, after taking advice from employees of Company S. Premiere's management, and not the employees of Company S, controls all decisions regarding licensing of the group's patents to both independent and associated enterprises.

3. At the time of each assignment of rights from Premiere to Company S, Company S makes a nominal EUR 100 payment to Premiere in consideration of the assignment of rights to a patentable invention and, as a specific condition of the assignment, simultaneously grants to Premiere an exclusive, royalty free, patent licence, with full rights to sub-licence, for the full life of the patent to be registered. The nominal payments of Company S to Premiere are made purely to satisfy technical contract law requirements related to the assignments and, for purposes of this example, it is assumed that they do not reflect arm's length compensation for the assigned rights to patentable inventions. Premiere uses the patented inventions in manufacturing and selling its products throughout the world and from time to time sublicenses patent

rights to others. Company S makes no commercial use of the patents nor is it entitled to do so under the terms of the licence agreement with Premiere.

4. Under the agreement, Premiere performs all functions related to the development, enhancement, maintenance, protection and exploitation of the intangibles except for patent administration services. Premiere contributes and uses all assets associated with the development and exploitation of the intangible, and assumes all or substantially all of the risks associated with the intangibles. Premiere should be entitled to the bulk of the returns derived from exploitation of the intangibles. Tax administrations could arrive at an appropriate transfer pricing solution by delineating the actual transaction undertaken between Premiere and Company S. Depending on the facts, it might be determined that taken together the nominal assignment of rights to Company S and the simultaneous grant of full exploitation rights back to Premiere reflect in substance a patent administration service arrangement between Premiere and Company S. An arm's length price would be determined for the patent administration services and Premiere would retain or be allocated the balance of the returns derived by the MNE group from the exploitation of the patents.

Example 2

5. The facts related to the development and control of patentable inventions are the same as in Example 1. However, instead of granting a perpetual and exclusive licence of its patents back to Premiere, Company S, acting under the direction and control of Premiere, grants licences of its patents to associated and independent enterprises throughout the world in exchange for periodic royalties. For purposes of this example, it is assumed that the royalties paid to Company S by associated enterprises are all arm's length.

6. Company S is the legal owner of the patents. However, its contributions to the development, enhancement, maintenance, protection, and exploitation of the patents are limited to the activities of its three employees in registering the patents and maintaining the patent registrations. The Company S employees do not control or participate in the licensing transactions involving the patents. Under these circumstances, Company S is only entitled to compensation for the functions it performs. Based on an analysis of the respective functions performed, assets used, and risks assumed by Premiere and Company S in developing, enhancing, maintaining, protecting, and exploiting the intangibles, Company S should not be entitled ultimately to retain or be attributed income from its licensing arrangements over and above the arm's length compensation for its patent registration functions.

7. As in Example 1 the true nature of the arrangement is a patent administration service contract. The appropriate transfer pricing outcome

can be achieved by ensuring that the amount paid by Company S in exchange for the assignments of patent rights appropriately reflects the respective functions performed, assets used, and risks assumed by Premiere and by Company S. Under such an approach, the compensation due to Premiere for the patentable inventions is equal to the licensing revenue of Company S less an appropriate return to the functions Company S performs.

Example 3

8. The facts are the same as in Example 2. However, after licensing the patents to associated and independent enterprises for a few years, Company S, again acting under the direction and control of Premiere, sells the patents to an independent enterprise at a price reflecting appreciation in the value of the patents during the period that Company S was the legal owner. The functions of Company S throughout the period it was the legal owner of the patents were limited to performing the patent registration functions described in Examples 1 and 2.

9. Under these circumstances, the income of Company S should be the same as in Example 2. It should be compensated for the registration functions it performs, but should not otherwise share in the returns derived from the exploitation of the intangibles, including the returns generated from the disposition of the intangibles.

Example 4

10. The facts related to the development of the patents are the same as described in Example 3. In contrast to Example 1, Company S in this example has employees capable of making, and who actually make, the decision to take on the patent portfolio. All decisions relating to the licensing programme were taken by Company S employees, all negotiations with licensees were undertaken by Company S employees, and Company S employees monitored compliance of independent licensees with the terms of the licenses. It should be assumed for purposes of this example that the price paid by Company S in exchange for the patents was an arm's length price that reflected the parties' respective assessments of the future licensing programme and the anticipated returns to be derived from exploitation of the patents as of the time of their assignment to Company S. For the purposes of this example, it is assumed that the approach for hard-to-value intangibles in Section D.4 does not apply.

11. Following the assignments, Company S licensed the patents to independent enterprises for a few years. Thereafter the value of the patents increases significantly because of external circumstances unforeseen at the time the patents were assigned to Company S. Company S then sells the

patents to an unrelated purchaser at a price exceeding the price initially paid by Company S to Premiere for the patents. Company S employees make all decisions regarding the sale of the patents, negotiate the terms of the sale, and in all respects manage and control the disposition of the patents.

12. Under these circumstances, Company S is entitled to retain the proceeds of the sale, including amounts attributable to the appreciation in the value of the patents resulting from the unanticipated external circumstances.

Example 5

13. The facts are the same as in Example 4 except that instead of appreciating, the value of the patents decreases during the time they are owned by Company S as a result of unanticipated external circumstances. Under these circumstances, Company S is entitled to retain the proceeds of the sale, meaning that it will suffer the loss.

Example 6

14. In Year 1, a multinational group comprised of Company A (a Country A corporation) and Company B (a Country B corporation) decides to develop an intangible, which is anticipated to be highly profitable based on Company B's existing intangibles, its track record and its experienced research and development staff. The intangible is expected to take five years to develop before possible commercial exploitation. If successfully developed, the intangible is anticipated to have value for ten years after initial exploitation. Under the development agreement between Company A and Company B, Company B will perform and control all activities related to the development, enhancement, maintenance, protection and exploitation of the intangible. Company A will provide all funding associated with the development of the intangible (the development costs are anticipated to be USD 100 million per year for five years), and will become the legal owner of the intangible. Once developed, the intangible is anticipated to result in profits of USD 550 million per year (years 6 to 15). Company B will license the intangible from Company A and make contingent payments to Company A for the right to use the intangible, based on returns of purportedly comparable licensees. After the projected contingent payments, Company B will be left with an anticipated return of USD 200 million per year from selling products based on the intangible.

15. A functional analysis by the Country B tax administration of the arrangement assesses the functions performed, assets used and contributed, and risks assumed by Company A and by Company B. The analysis through which the actual transaction is delineated concludes that although Company A

is the legal owner of the intangibles, its contribution to the arrangement is solely the provision of funding for the development of an intangible. This analysis shows that Company A contractually assumes the financial risk, has the financial capacity to assume that risk, and exercises control over that risk in accordance with the principles outlined in paragraphs 6.63 and 6.64. Taking into account Company A's contributions, as well as the realistic alternatives of Company A and Company B, it is determined that Company A's anticipated remuneration should be a risk-adjusted return on its funding commitment. Assume that this is determined to be USD 110 million per year (for Years 6 to 15), which equates to an 11% risk-adjusted anticipated financial return.[1] Company B, accordingly, would be entitled to all remaining anticipated income after accounting for Company A's anticipated return, or USD 440 million per year (USD 550 million minus USD 110 million), rather than USD 200 million per year as claimed by the taxpayer. (Based on the detailed functional analysis and application of the most appropriate method, the taxpayer incorrectly chose Company B as the tested party rather than Company A).

Example 7

16. Primero is the parent company of an MNE group engaged in the pharmaceutical business and does business in Country M. Primero develops patents and other intangibles relating to Product X and registers those patents in countries around the world.

17. Primero retains its wholly owned Country N subsidiary, Company S, to distribute Product X throughout Europe and the Middle East on a limited risk basis. The distribution agreement provides that Primero, and not Company S, is to bear product recall and product liability risk, and provides further that Primero will be entitled to all profit or loss from selling Product X in the territory after providing Company S with the agreed level of compensation for its distribution functions. Operating under the contract, Company S purchases Product X from Primero and resells Product X to independent customers in countries throughout its geographical area of operation. In performing its distribution functions, Company S follows all applicable regulatory requirements.

18. In the first three years of operations, Company S earns returns from its distribution functions that are consistent with its limited risk

1. For purposes of this example, it is not necessary to derive these results. The example assumes that making a funding "investment" of USD 100 million per year for five years in a project with this level of risk should earn at arm's length anticipated profits of USD 110 million per year for the following ten years. This corresponds to an 11% return on funding.

characterisation and the terms of the distribution contract. Its returns reflect the fact that Primero, and not Company S, is entitled to retain income derived from exploitation of the intangibles with respect to Product X. After three years of operation, it becomes apparent that Product X causes serious side effects in a significant percentage of those patients that use the product and it becomes necessary to recall the product and remove it from the market. Company S incurs substantial costs in connection with the recall. Primero does not reimburse Company S for these recall related costs or for the resulting product liability claims.

19. Under these circumstances, there is an inconsistency between Primero's asserted entitlement to returns derived from exploiting the Product X intangibles and its failure to bear the costs associated with the risks supporting that assertion. A transfer pricing adjustment would be appropriate to remedy the inconsistency. In determining the appropriate adjustment, it would be necessary to determine the true transaction between the parties by applying the provisions of Section D.1 of Chapter I. In doing so, it would be appropriate to consider the risks assumed by each of the parties on the basis of the course of conduct followed by the parties over the term of the agreement, the control over risk exercised by Primero and Company S, and other relevant facts. If it is determined that the true nature of the relationship between the parties is that of a limited risk distribution arrangement, then the most appropriate adjustment would likely take the form of an allocation of the recall and product liability related costs from Company S to Primero. Alternatively, although unlikely, if it is determined on the basis of all the relevant facts that the true nature of the relationship between the parties includes the exercising control over product liability and recall risk by Company S, and if an arm's length price can be identified on the basis of the comparability analysis, an increase in the distribution margins of Company S for all years might be made to reflect the true risk allocation between the parties.

Example 8

20. Primair, a resident of Country X, manufactures watches which are marketed in many countries around the world under the R trademark and trade name. Primair is the registered owner of the R trademark and trade name. The R name is widely known in countries where the watches are sold and has obtained considerable economic value in those markets through the efforts of Primair. R watches have never been marketed in Country Y, however, and the R name is not known in the Country Y market.

21. In Year 1, Primair decides to enter the Country Y market and incorporates a wholly owned subsidiary in Country Y, Company S, to act

as its distributor in Country Y. At the same time, Primair enters into a long-term royalty-free marketing and distribution agreement with Company S. Under the agreement, Company S is granted the exclusive right to market and distribute watches bearing the R trademark and using the R trade name in Country Y for a period of five years, with an option for a further five years. Company S obtains no other rights relating to the R trademark and trade name from Primair, and in particular is prohibited from re-exporting watches bearing the R trademark and trade name. The sole activity of Company S is marketing and distributing watches bearing the R trademark and trade name. It is assumed that the R watches are not part of a portfolio of products distributed by Company S in Country Y. Company S undertakes no secondary processing, as it imports packaged watches into Country Y ready for sale to the final customer.

22. Under the contract between Primair and Company S, Company S purchases the watches from Primair in Country Y currency, takes title to the branded watches and performs the distribution function in Country Y, incurs the associated carrying costs (e.g. inventory and receivables financing), and assumes the corresponding risks (e.g. inventory, credit and financing risks). Under the contract between Primair and Company S, Company S is required to act as a marketing agent to assist in developing the market for R watches in Country Y. Company S consults with Primair in developing the Country Y marketing strategy for R watches. Primair develops the overall marketing plan based largely on its experience in other countries, it develops and approves the marketing budgets, and it makes final decisions regarding advertising designs, product positioning and core advertising messages. Company S consults on local market issues related to advertising, assists in executing the marketing strategy under Primair's direction, and provides evaluations of the effectiveness of various elements of the marketing strategy. As compensation for providing these marketing support activities, Company S receives from Primair a service fee based on the level of marketing expenditure it incurs and including an appropriate profit element.

23. Assume for the purpose of this example that, based upon a thorough comparability analysis, including a detailed functional analysis, it is possible to conclude that the price Company S pays Primair for the R watches should be analysed separately from the compensation Company S receives for the marketing it undertakes on behalf of Primair. Assume further that based upon identified comparable transactions, the price paid for the watches is arm's length and that this price enables Company S to earn an arm's length level of compensation from selling the watches for the distribution function it performs, the assets it uses and the risks it assumes.

24. In Years 1 to 3, Company S embarks on a strategy that is consistent with its agreement with Primair to develop the Country Y market for

R watches. In the process, Company S incurs marketing expenses. Consistent with the contract, Company S is reimbursed by Primair for the marketing expenses it incurs, and is paid a mark-up on those expenses. By the end of Year 2, the R trademark and trade name have become well established in Country Y. The compensation derived by Company S for the marketing activities it performed on behalf of Primair is determined to be arm's length, based upon comparison to that paid to independent advertising and marketing agents identified and determined to be comparable as part of the comparability analysis.

25. Under these circumstances, Primair is entitled to retain any income derived from exploiting the R trademark and trade name in the Country Y market that exceeds the arm's length compensation to Company S for its functions and no transfer pricing adjustment is warranted under the circumstances.

Example 9

26. The facts in this example are the same as in Example 8, except as follows:

- Under the contract between Primair and Company S, Company S is now obligated to develop and execute the marketing plan for Country Y without detailed control of specific elements of the plan by Primair. Company S bears the costs and assumes certain of the risks associated with the marketing activities. The agreement between Primair and Company S does not specify the amount of marketing expenditure Company S is expected to incur, only that Company S is required to use its best efforts to market the watches. Company S receives no direct reimbursement from Primair in respect of any expenditure it incurs, nor does it receive any other indirect or implied compensation from Primair, and Company S expects to earn its reward solely from its profit from the sale of R brand watches to third party customers in the Country Y market. A thorough functional analysis reveals that Primair exercises a lower level of control over the marketing activities of Company S than in Example 8 in that it does not review and approve the marketing budget or design details of the marketing plan. Company S bears different risks and is compensated differently than was the case in Example 8. The contractual arrangements between Primair and Company S are different and the risks assumed by Company S are greater in Example 9 than in Example 8. Company S does not receive direct cost reimbursements or a separate fee for marketing activities. The only controlled transaction between Primair and Company S in Example 9 is the transfer of the branded watches. As a result,

Company S can obtain its reward for its marketing activities only through selling R brand watches to third party customers.

- As a result of these differences, Primair and Company S adopt a lower price for watches in Example 9 than the price for watches determined for purposes of Example 8. As a result of the differences identified in the functional analysis, different criteria are used for identifying comparables and for making comparability adjustments than was the case in Example 8. This results in Company S having a greater anticipated total profit in Example 9 than in Example 8 because of its higher level of risk and its more extensive functions.

27. Assume that in Years 1 through 3, Company S embarks on a strategy that is consistent with its agreement with Primair and, in the process, performs marketing functions and incurs marketing expenses. As a result, Company S has high operating expenditures and slim margins in Years 1 through 3. By the end of Year 2, the R trademark and trade name have become established in Country Y because of Company S's efforts. Where the marketer/distributor actually bears the costs and associated risks of its marketing activities, the issue is the extent to which the marketer/distributor can share in the potential benefits from those activities. Assume that the enquiries of the Country Y tax administrations conclude, based on a review of comparable distributors, that Company S would have been expected to have performed the functions it performed and incurred its actual level of marketing expense if it were independent from Primair.

28. Given that Company S performs the functions and bears the costs and associated risks of its marketing activities under a long-term contract of exclusive distribution rights for the R watches, there is an opportunity for Company S to benefit (or suffer a loss) from the marketing and distribution activities it undertakes. Based on an analysis of reasonably reliable comparable data, it is concluded that, for purposes of this example, the benefits obtained by Company S result in profits similar to those made by independent marketers and distributors bearing the same types of risks and costs as Company S in the first few years of comparable long-term marketing and distribution agreements for similarly unknown products.

29. Based on the foregoing assumptions, Company S's return is arm's length and its marketing activities, including its marketing expenses, are not significantly different than those performed by independent marketers and distributors in comparable uncontrolled transactions. The information on comparable uncontrolled arrangements provides the best measure of the arm's length return earned by Company S for the contribution to intangible value provided by its functions, risks, and costs. That return therefore reflects arm's length compensation for Company S's contributions and accurately measures its share of the income derived from exploitation of the trademark

and trade name in Country Y. No separate or additional compensation is required to be provided to Company S.

Example 10

30. The facts in this example are the same as in Example 9, except that the market development functions undertaken by Company S in this Example 10 are far more extensive than those undertaken by Company S in Example 9.

31. Where the marketer/distributor actually bears the costs and assumes the risks of its marketing activities, the issue is the extent to which the marketer/distributor can share in the potential benefits from those activities. A thorough comparability analysis identifies several uncontrolled companies engaged in marketing and distribution functions under similar long-term marketing and distribution arrangements. Assume, however, that the level of marketing expense Company S incurred in Years 1 through 5 far exceeds that incurred by the identified comparable independent marketers and distributors. Assume further that the high level of expense incurred by Company S reflects its performance of additional or more intensive functions than those performed by the potential comparables and that Primair and Company S expect those additional functions to generate higher margins or increased sales volume for the products. Given the extent of the market development activities undertaken by Company S, it is evident that Company S has made a larger functional contribution to development of the market and the marketing intangibles and has assumed significantly greater costs and assumed greater risks than the identified potentially comparable independent enterprises (and substantially higher costs and risks than in Example 9). There is also evidence to support the conclusion that the profits realised by Company S are significantly lower than the profit margins of the identified potentially comparable independent marketers and distributors during the corresponding years of similar long-term marketing and distribution agreements.

32. As in Example 9, Company S bears the costs and associated risks of its marketing activities under a long-term contract of exclusive marketing and distribution rights for the R watches, and therefore expects to have an opportunity to benefit (or suffer a loss) from the marketing and distribution activities it undertakes. However, in this case Company S has performed functions and borne marketing expenditures beyond what independent enterprises in potentially comparable transactions with similar rights incur for their own benefit, resulting in significantly lower profit margins for Company S than are made by such enterprises.

33. Based on these facts, it is evident that by performing functions and incurring marketing expenditure substantially in excess of the levels of

function and expenditure of independent marketer/distributors in comparable transactions, Company S has not been adequately compensated by the margins it earns on the resale of R watches. Under such circumstances it would be appropriate for the Country Y tax administration to propose a transfer pricing adjustment based on compensating Company S for the marketing activities performed (taking account of the risks assumed and the expenditure incurred) on a basis that is consistent with what independent enterprises would have earned in comparable transactions. Depending on the facts and circumstances reflected in a detailed comparability analysis, such an adjustment could be based on:

- Reducing the price paid by Company S for the R brand watches purchased from Primair. Such an adjustment could be based on applying a resale price method or transactional net margin method using available data about profits made by comparable marketers and distributors with a comparable level of marketing and distribution expenditure if such comparables can be identified.
- An alternative approach might apply a residual profit split method that would split the relevant profits from sales of R branded watches in Country Y by first giving Company S and Primair a basic return for the functions they perform and then splitting the residual profit on a basis that takes into account the relative contributions of both Company S and Primair to the generation of income and the value of the R trademark and trade name.
- Directly compensating Company S for the excess marketing expenditure it has incurred over and above that incurred by comparable independent enterprises including an appropriate profit element for the functions and risks reflected by those expenditures.

34. In this example, the proposed adjustment is based on Company S's having performed functions, assumed risks, and incurred costs that contributed to the development of the marketing intangibles for which it was not adequately compensated under its arrangement with Primair. If the arrangements between Company S and Primair were such that Company S could expect to obtain an arm's length return on its additional investment during the remaining term of the distribution agreement, a different outcome could be appropriate.

Example 11

35. The facts in this example are the same as in Example 9, except that Company S now enters into a three-year royalty-free agreement to market and distribute the watches in the Country Y market, with no option to renew.

At the end of the three-year period, Company S does not enter into a new contract with Primair.

36. Assume that it is demonstrated that independent enterprises do enter into short-term distribution agreements where they incur marketing and distribution expenses, but only where they stand to earn a reward commensurate with the functions performed, the assets used, and the risks assumed within the time period of the contract. Evidence derived from comparable independent enterprises shows that they do not invest large sums of money in developing marketing and distribution infrastructure where they obtain only a short-term marketing and distribution agreement, with the attendant risk of non-renewal without compensation. The potential short-term nature of the marketing and distribution agreement is such that Company S could not, or may not be able to, benefit from the marketing and distribution expenditure it incurs at its own risk. The same factors mean that Company S's efforts may well benefit Primair in the future.

37. The risks assumed by Company S are substantially higher than in Example 9 and Company S has not been compensated on an arm's length basis for bearing these additional risks. In this case, Company S has undertaken market development activities and borne marketing expenditures beyond what comparable independent enterprises with similar rights incur for their own benefit, resulting in significantly lower profit margins for Company S than are made by comparable enterprises. The short term nature of the contract makes it unreasonable to expect that Company S has the opportunity of obtaining appropriate benefits under the contract within the limited term of the agreement with Primair. Under these circumstances, Company S is entitled to compensation for its at risk contribution to the value of the R trademark and trade name during the term of its arrangement with Primair.

38. Such compensation could take the form of direct compensation from Primair to Company S for the anticipated value created through the marketing expenditures and market development functions it has undertaken. Alternatively, such an adjustment could take the form of a reduction in the price paid by Company S to Primair for R watches during Years 1 through 3.

Example 12

39. The facts in this example are the same as in Example 9 with the following additions:

- By the end of Year 3, the R brand is successfully established in the Country Y market and Primair and Company S renegotiate their earlier agreement and enter into a new long-term licensing agreement. The new agreement, which is to commence at the beginning of Year 4, is for five years with Company S having an option for a further five years. Under this agreement, Company S agrees to pay a royalty to Primair based on the gross sales of all watches bearing the R trademark. In all other respects, the new agreement has the same terms and conditions as in the previous arrangement between the parties. There is no adjustment made to the price payable by Company S for the branded watches as a result of the introduction of the royalty.

- Company S's sales of R brand watches in Years 4 and 5 are consistent with earlier budget forecasts. However, the introduction of the royalty from the beginning of year 4 results in Company S's profit margins declining substantially.

40. Assume that there is no evidence that independent marketers/distributors of similar branded products have agreed to pay royalties under similar arrangements. Company S's level of marketing expenditure and activity, from Year 4 on, is consistent with that of independent enterprises.

41. For transfer pricing purposes, it would not generally be expected that a royalty would be paid in arm's length transactions where a marketing and distribution entity obtains no rights for transfer pricing purposes in trademarks and similar intangibles other than the right to use such intangibles in distributing a branded product supplied by the entity entitled to the income derived from exploiting such intangibles. Furthermore, the royalty causes Company S's profit margins to be consistently lower than those of independent enterprises with comparable functions performed, assets used and risks assumed during the corresponding years of similar long-term marketing and distribution arrangements. Accordingly, a transfer pricing adjustment disallowing the royalties paid would be appropriate based on the facts of this example.

Example 13

42. The facts in this example are the same as those set out in Example 10 with the following additions:

- At the end of Year 3, Primair stops manufacturing watches and contracts with a third party to manufacture them on its behalf. As a result, Company S will import unbranded watches directly from the manufacturer and undertake secondary processing to apply the R name and logo and package the watches before sale to the final customer. It will then sell and distribute the watches in the manner described in Example 10.

- As a consequence, at the beginning of Year 4, Primair and Company S renegotiate their earlier agreement and enter into a new long term licensing agreement. The new agreement, to start at the beginning of Year 4, is for five years, with Company S having an option for a further five years.
- Under the new agreement, Company S is granted the exclusive right within Country Y to process, market and distribute watches bearing the R trademark in consideration for its agreement to pay a royalty to Primair based on the gross sales of all such watches. Company S receives no compensation from Primair in respect of the renegotiation of the original marketing and distribution agreement. It is assumed for purposes of this example that the purchase price Company S pays for the watches from the beginning of Year 4 is arm's length and that no consideration with respect to the R name is embedded in that price.

43. In connection with a tax audit conducted by Country Y tax administrations in Year 6, it is determined, based on a proper functional analysis, that the level of marketing expenses Company S incurred during Years 1 through 3 far exceeded those incurred by independent marketers and distributors with similar long term marketing and distribution agreements. It is also determined that the level and intensity of marketing activity undertaken by Company S exceeded that of independent marketers and distributors, and that the relatively greater activity has been successful in expanding volumes and/or increasing the Primair group's overall margins from sales in Country Y. Given the extent of the market development activities undertaken by Company S, including its strategic control over such activities, it is evident from the comparability and functional analysis that Company S has assumed significantly greater costs and assumed greater risks than comparable independent enterprises. There is also evidence that the individual entity profit margins realised by Company S are significantly lower than the profit margins of comparable independent marketers and distributors during the corresponding years of similar long-term marketing and distribution arrangements.

44. The Country Y audit also identifies that in Years 4 and 5, Company S bears the costs and associated risks of its marketing activities under the new long-term licensing arrangement with Primair, and because of the long-term nature of the agreement, Company S may have an opportunity to benefit (or suffer a loss) from its activities. However, Company S has undertaken market development activities and incurred marketing expenditure far beyond what comparable independent licensees with similar long-term licensing agreements undertake and incur for their own benefit, resulting in significantly lower anticipated profit margins for Company S than those of comparable enterprises.

45. Based on these facts, Company S should be compensated with an additional return for the market development functions it performs, the assets it uses and the risks it assumes. For Years 1 through 3, the possible bases for such an adjustment would be as described in Example 10. For Years 4 and 5 the bases for an adjustment would be similar, except that the adjustment could reduce the royalty payments from Company S to Primair, rather than the purchase price of the watches. Depending on the facts and circumstances, consideration could also be given to whether Company S should have received compensation in connection with the renegotiation of the arrangement at the end of Year 3 in accordance with the guidance in Part II of Chapter IX.

Example 14

46. Shuyona is the parent company of an MNE group. Shuyona is organised in and operates in Country X. The Shuyona group is involved in the production and sale of consumer goods. In order to maintain and, if possible, improve its market position, ongoing research is carried out by the Shuyona group to improve existing products and develop new products. The Shuyona group maintains two R&D centres, one operated by Shuyona in Country X and the other operated by Company S, a subsidiary of Shuyona operating in Country Y. The Shuyona R&D centre is responsible for the overall research programme of Shuyona group. The Shuyona R&D centre designs research programmes, develops and controls budgets, makes decisions as to where R&D activities will be conducted, monitors the progress on all R&D projects and, in general, controls the R&D function for the MNE group, operating under strategic direction of Shuyona group senior management.

47. The Company S R&D centre operates on a separate project by project basis to carry out specific projects assigned by the Shuyona R&D centre. Suggestions of Company S R&D personnel for modifications to the research programme are required to be formally approved by the Shuyona R&D centre. The Company S R&D centre reports on its progress on at least a monthly basis to supervisory personnel at the Shuyona R&D centre. If Company S exceeds budgets established by Shuyona for its work, approval of Shuyona R&D management must be sought for further expenditures. Contracts between the Shuyona R&D centre and the Company S R&D centre specify that Shuyona will bear all risks and costs related to R&D undertaken by Company S. All patents, designs and other intangibles developed by Company S research personnel are registered by Shuyona, pursuant to contracts between the two companies. Shuyona pays Company S a service fee for its research and development activities.

48. The transfer pricing analysis of these facts would begin by recognising that Shuyona is the legal owner of the intangibles. Shuyona

controls and manages both its own R&D work and that of Company S. It performs the important functions related to that work such as budgeting, establishing research programmes, designing projects and funding and controlling expenditures. Under these circumstances, Shuyona is entitled to returns derived from the exploitation of the intangibles developed through the R&D efforts of Company S. Company S is entitled to compensation for its functions performed, assets used, and risks assumed. In determining the amount of compensation due Company S, the relative skill and efficiency of the Company S R&D personnel, the nature of the research being undertaken, and other factors contributing to value should be considered as comparability factors. To the extent transfer pricing adjustments are required to reflect the amount a comparable R&D service provider would be paid for its services, such adjustments would generally relate to the year the service is provided and would not affect the entitlement of Shuyona to future returns derived from exploiting intangibles derived from the Company S R&D activities.

Example 15

49. Shuyona is the parent company of an MNE group. Shuyona is organised in and operates exclusively in Country X. The Shuyona group is involved in the production and sale of consumer goods. In order to maintain and, if possible, improve its market position, ongoing research is carried out by the Shuyona group to improve existing products and develop new products. The Shuyona group maintains two R&D centres, one operated by Shuyona in Country X, and the other operated by Company S, a subsidiary of Shuyona, operating in Country Y.

50. The Shuyona group sells two lines of products. All R&D with respect to product line A is conducted by Shuyona. All R&D with respect to product line B is conducted by the R&D centre operated by Company S. Company S also functions as the regional headquarters of the Shuyona group in North America and has global responsibility for the operation of the business relating to product line B. However, all patents developed through Company S research efforts are registered by Shuyona. Shuyona makes no or only a nominal payment to Company S in relation to the patentable inventions developed by the Company S R&D centre.

51. The Shuyona and Company S R&D centres operate autonomously. Each bears its own operating costs. Under the general policy direction of Shuyona senior management, the Company S R&D centre develops its own research programmes, establishes its own budgets, makes determinations as to when R&D projects should be terminated or modified, and hires its own R&D staff. The Company S R&D centre reports to the product line B management team in Company S, and does not report to the Shuyona R&D

centre. Joint meetings between the Shuyona and Company S R&D teams are sometimes held to discuss research methods and common issues.

52. The transfer pricing analysis of this fact pattern would begin by recognising that Shuyona is the legal owner/registrant of intangibles developed by Company S. Unlike the situation in Example 14, however, Shuyona neither performs nor exercises control over the research functions carried out by Company S, including the important functions related to management, design, budgeting and funding that research. Accordingly, Shuyona's legal ownership of the intangibles does not entitle it to retain or be attributed any income related to the product line B intangibles. Tax administrations could arrive at an appropriate transfer pricing outcome by recognising Shuyona's legal ownership of the intangibles but by noting that, because of the contributions of Company S in the form of functions, assets, and risks, appropriate compensation to Company S for its contributions could be ensured by confirming that Company S should make no royalty or other payment to Shuyona for the right to use any successfully developed Company S intangibles, so that the future income derived from the exploitation of those intangibles by Company S would be allocated to Company S and not to Shuyona.

53. If Shuyona exploits the product line B intangibles by itself, Shuyona should provide appropriate compensation to Company S for its functions performed, assets used and risks assumed related to intangible development. In determining the appropriate level of compensation for Company S, the fact that Company S performs all of the important functions related to intangible development would likely make it inappropriate to treat Company S as the tested party in an R&D service arrangement.

Example 16

54. Shuyona is the parent company of an MNE group. Shuyona is organised in and operates exclusively in Country X. The Shuyona group is involved in the production and sale of consumer goods. In order to maintain and, if possible, improve its market position, ongoing research is carried out by the Shuyona group to improve existing products and develop new products. The Shuyona group maintains two R&D centres, one operated by Shuyona in Country X, and the other operated by Company S, a subsidiary of Shuyona, operating in Country Y. The relationships between the Shuyona R&D centre and the Company S R&D centre are as described in Example 14.

55. In Year 1, Shuyona sells all rights to patents and other technology related intangibles, including rights to use those intangibles in ongoing research, to a new subsidiary, Company T, organised in Country Z. Company T establishes a manufacturing facility in Country Z and begins to supply products to members of the Shuyona group around the world. For purposes of this

example, it is assumed that the compensation paid by Company T in exchange for the transferred patents and related intangibles is based on a valuation of anticipated future cash flows generated by the transferred intangibles at the time of the transfer.

56. At the same time as the transfer of patents and other technology related intangibles, Company T enters into a contract research agreement with Shuyona and a separate contract research agreement with Company S. Pursuant to these agreements, Company T contractually agrees to bear the financial risk associated with possible failure of future R&D projects, agrees to assume the cost of all future R&D activity, and agrees to pay Shuyona and Company S a service fee based on the cost of the R&D activities undertaken plus a mark-up equivalent to the profit mark-up over cost earned by certain identified independent companies engaged in providing research services.

57. Company T has no technical personnel capable of conducting or supervising the research activities. Shuyona continues to develop and design the R&D programme related to further development of the transferred intangibles, to establish its own R&D budgets, to determine its own levels of R&D staffing, and to make decisions regarding whether to pursue or terminate particular R&D projects. Moreover, Shuyona continues to supervise and control the R&D activities in Company S in the manner described in Example 14.

58. The transfer pricing analysis begins by identifying the commercial or financial relations between the parties and the conditions and economically relevant circumstances attaching to those relations in order that the controlled transaction is accurately delineated under the principles of Chapter I, Section D.1. Key assumptions in this example are that Company T functions as a manufacturer and performs no activities in relation to the acquisition, development or exploitation of the intangibles and does not control risks in relation to the acquisition of the intangibles or to their further development. Instead, all development activities and risk management functions relating to the intangibles are performed by Shuyona and Company S, with Shuyona controlling the risk. A thorough examination of the transaction indicates that it should accurately be delineated as the provision of financing by Company T equating to the costs of the acquired intangibles and the ongoing development. A key assumption in this example is that, although Company T contractually assumes the financial risk and has the financial capacity to assume that risk, it does not exercise control over that risk in accordance with the principles outlined in paragraphs 6.63 and 6.64. As a result, in addition to its manufacturing reward, Company T is entitled to no more than a risk-free return for its funding activities. (For further guidance see Section D.1 of Chapter I, and in particular paragraph 1.103.)

Example 17

59. Company A is a fully integrated pharmaceutical company engaged in the discovery, development, production and sale of pharmaceutical preparations. Company A conducts its operations in Country X. In conducting its research activities, Company A regularly retains independent Contract Research Organisations (CROs) to perform various R&D activities, including designing and conducting clinical trials with regard to products under development by Company A. However, such CROs do not engage in the blue sky research required to identify new pharmaceutical compounds. Where Company A does retain a CRO to engage in clinical research activities, research personnel at Company A actively participate in designing the CRO's research studies, provide to the CRO results and information derived from earlier research, establish budgets and timelines for CRO projects, and conduct ongoing quality control with respect to the CRO's activities. In such arrangements, CROs are paid a negotiated fee for services and do not have an ongoing interest in the profits derived from sales of products developed through their research.

60. Company A transfers patents and related intangibles related to Product M, an early stage pharmaceutical preparation believed to have potential as a treatment for Alzheimer's disease to Company S, a subsidiary of Company A operating in Country Y (the transaction relates strictly to the existing intangibles and does not include compensation for future R&D services of Company A). It is assumed for purposes of this example that the payment of Company S for the transfer of intangibles related to Product M is based on a valuation of anticipated future cash flows. Company S has no technical personnel capable of designing, conducting or supervising required ongoing research activities related to Product M. Company S therefore contracts with Company A to carry on the research programme related to Product M in the same manner as before the transfer of intangibles to Company S. Company S agrees to fund all of the ongoing Product M research, assume the financial risk of potential failure of such research, and to pay for Company A's services based on the cost plus margins earned by CROs like those with which Company A regularly transacts.

61. The transfer pricing analysis of these facts begins by recognising that, following the transfer, Company S is the legal owner of the Product M intangibles under relevant contracts and registrations. However, Company A continues to perform and control functions and to manage risks related to the intangibles owned by Company S, including the important functions described in paragraph 6.56, and is entitled to compensation for those contributions. Under these circumstances, Company A's transactions with CRO's are not comparable to the arrangements between Company S and Company A related to Product M and may not be used as a benchmark for the arm's length compensation required to be provided to Company A for its

ongoing R&D activity with respect to the Product M intangibles. Company S does not perform or control the same functions or control the same risks in its transactions with Company A, as does Company A in its transactions with the CROs.

62. While Company S is the legal owner of the intangibles, it should not be entitled to all of the returns derived from the exploitation of the intangibles. Because Company S lacks the capability to control research related risks, Company A should be treated as bearing a substantial portion of the relevant risk and Company A should also be compensated for its functions, including the important functions described in paragraph 6.56. Company A should be entitled to larger returns than the CROs under these circumstances.

63. A thorough examination of the transaction in this example may show that it should accurately be delineated as the provision of financing by Company S equating to the costs of the acquired intangibles and the ongoing development. As a result, Company S is entitled to only a financing return. The level of the financing return depends on the exercising of control over the financing risk in accordance with the guidance in Section D.1 of Chapter I and the principles outlined in paragraphs 6.63 and 6.64. Company A would be entitled to retain the remaining income or losses.

Example 18

64. Primarni is organised in and conducts business in Country A. Company S is an associated enterprise of Primarni. Company S is organised in and does business in Country B. Primarni develops a patented invention and manufacturing know-how related to Product X. It obtains valid patents in all countries relevant to this example. Primarni and Company S enter into a written licence agreement pursuant to which Primarni grants Company S the right to use the Product X patents and know-how to manufacture and sell Product X in Country B, while Primarni retains the patent and know-how rights to Product X throughout Asia, Africa, and in Country A.

65. Assume Company S uses the patents and know-how to manufacture Product X in Country B. It sells Product X to both independent and associated customers in Country B. Additionally, it sells Product X to associated distribution entities based throughout Asia and Africa. The distribution entities resell the units of Product X to customers throughout Asia and Africa. Primarni does not exercise its retained patent rights for Asia and Africa to prevent the sale of Product X by Company S to the distribution entities operating in Asia and Africa.

66. Under these circumstances, the conduct of the parties suggests that the transaction between Primarni and Company S is actually a licence of

the Product X patents and know-how for Country B, plus Asia and Africa. In a transfer pricing analysis of the transactions between Company S and Primarni, Company S's licence should be treated as extending to Asia and Africa, and should not be limited to Country B, based on the conduct of the parties. The royalty rate should be recalculated to take into account the total projected sales by Company S in all territories including those to the Asian and African entities.

Example 19

67. Company P, a resident of Country A conducts a retailing business, operating several department stores in Country A. Over the years, Company P has developed special know-how and a unique marketing concept for the operation of its department stores. It is assumed that the know-how and unique marketing concept constitute intangibles within the meaning of Section A of Chapter VI. After years of successfully conducting business in Country A, Company P establishes a new subsidiary, Company S, in Country B. Company S opens and operates new department stores in Country B, obtaining profit margins substantially higher than those of otherwise comparable retailers in Country B.

68. A detailed functional analysis reveals that Company S uses in its operations in Country B, the same know-how and unique marketing concept as the ones used by Company P in its operations in Country A. Under these circumstances, the conduct of the parties reveals that a transaction has taken place consisting in the transfer from Company P to Company S of the right to use the know-how and unique marketing concept. Under comparable circumstances, independent parties would have concluded a license agreement granting Company S the right to use in Country B, the know-how and unique marketing concept developed by Company P. Accordingly, one possible remedy available to the tax administration is a transfer pricing adjustment imputing a royalty payment from Company S to Company P for the use of these intangibles.

Example 20

69. Ilcha is organised in Country A. The Ilcha group of companies has for many years manufactured and sold Product Q in countries B and C through a wholly owned subsidiary, Company S1, which is organised in Country B. Ilcha owns patents related to the design of Product Q and has developed a unique trademark and other marketing intangibles. The patents and trademarks are registered by Ilcha in Countries B and C.

70. For sound business reasons, Ilcha determines that the group's business in Countries B and C would be enhanced if those businesses were operated through separate subsidiaries in each country. Ilcha therefore organises in Country C a wholly owned subsidiary, Company S2. With regard to the business in Country C:

- Company S1 transfers to Company S2 the tangible manufacturing and marketing assets previously used by Company S1 in Country C.
- Ilcha and Company S1 agree to terminate the agreement granting Company S1 the following rights with relation to Product Q: the right to manufacture and distribute Product Q in Country C; the right to use the patents and trademark in carrying out its manufacturing and distribution activities in Country C; and, the right to use customer relationships, customer lists, goodwill and other items in Country C (hereinafter, "the Rights").
- Ilcha enters into new, long-term licence agreements with Company S2 granting it the Rights in Country C.

The newly formed subsidiary thereafter conducts the Product Q business in Country C, while Company S1 continues to conduct the Product Q business in Country B.

71. Assume that over the years of its operation, Company S1 developed substantial business value in Country C and an independent enterprise would be willing to pay for that business value in an acquisition. Further assume that, for accounting and business valuation purposes, a portion of such business value would be treated as goodwill in a purchase price allocation conducted with regard to a sale of Company S1's Country C business to an independent party.

72. Under the facts and circumstances of the case, there is value being transferred to Company S2 through the combination of (i) the transfer of part of Company S1's tangible business assets to Company S2 in Country C, and (ii) the surrendering by Company S1 of the Rights and the subsequent granting of the Rights by Ilcha to Company S2. There are three separate transactions:

- the transfer of part of Company S1's tangible business assets to Company S2 in Country C;
- the surrendering by Company S1 of its rights under the licence back to Ilcha; and
- the subsequent granting of a licence by Ilcha to Company S2.

For transfer pricing purposes, the prices paid by Ilcha and by Company S2 in connection with these transactions should reflect the value of the business which would include amounts that may be treated as the value of goodwill for accounting purposes.

Example 21

73. Första is a consumer goods company organised and operating in Country A. Prior to Year 1, Första produces Product Y in Country A and sells it through affiliated distribution companies in many countries around the world. Product Y is well recognised and attracts a premium compared to its competitors, to which Första is entitled as the legal owner and developer of the trademark and related goodwill giving rise to that premium.

74. In Year 2, Första organises Company S, a wholly owned subsidiary, in Country B. Company S acts as a super distributor and invoicing centre. Första continues to ship Product Y directly to its distribution affiliates, but title to the products passes to Company S, which reinvoices the distribution affiliates for the products.

75. Beginning in Year 2, Company S undertakes to reimburse the distribution affiliates for a portion of their advertising costs. Prices for Product Y from Company S to the distribution affiliates are adjusted upward so that the distribution affiliate operating profit margins remain constant notwithstanding the shift of advertising cost to Company S. Assume that the operating profit margins earned by the distribution affiliates are arm's length both before and after Year 2 given the concurrent changes in product pricing and the reimbursement of advertising costs. Company S performs no functions with regard to advertising nor does it control any risk related to marketing the products.

76. In Year 3, the prices charged by Första to Company S are reduced. Första and Company S claim such a reduction in price is justified because Company S is now entitled to income related to intangibles. It asserts that such income is attributable to intangibles in respect of Product Y created through the advertising costs it has borne.

77. In substance, Company S has no claim to income derived from the exploitation of intangibles with respect to Product Y. It performs no functions, assumes no risk, and in substance bears no costs related to the development, enhancement, maintenance or protection of intangibles. Transfer pricing adjustments to increase the income of Första in Year 3 and thereafter would be appropriate.

Example 22

78. Company A owns a government licence for a mining activity and a government licence for the exploitation of a railway. The mining licence has a standalone market value of 20. The railway licence has a standalone market value of 10. Company A has no other net assets.

79. Birincil, an entity which is independent of Company A, acquires 100% of the equity interests in Company A for 100. Birincil's purchase price allocation performed for accounting purposes with respect to the acquisition attributes 20 of the purchase price to the mining licence; 10 to the railway licence; and 70 to goodwill based on the synergies created between the mining and railway licences.

80. Immediately following the acquisition, Birincil causes Company A to transfer its mining and railway licences to Company S, a subsidiary of Birincil.

81. In conducting a transfer pricing analysis of the arm's length price to be paid by Company S for the transaction with Company A, it is important to identify with specificity the intangibles transferred. As was the case with Birincil's arm's length acquisition of Company A, the goodwill associated with the licences transferred to Company S would need to be considered, as it should generally be assumed that value does not disappear, nor is it destroyed as part of an internal business restructuring.

82. As such, the arm's length price for the transaction between Companies A and S should take account of the mining licence, the railway licence, and the value ascribed to goodwill for accounting purposes. The 100 paid by Birincil for the shares of Company A represents an arm's length price for those shares and provides useful information regarding the combined value of the intangibles.

Example 23

83. Birincil acquires 100% of the equity interests in an independent enterprise, Company T for 100. Company T is a company that engages in research and development and has partially developed several promising technologies but has only minimal sales. The purchase price is justified primarily by the value of the promising, but only partly developed, technologies and by the potential of Company T personnel to develop further new technologies in the future. Birincil's purchase price allocation performed for accounting purposes with respect to the acquisition attributes 20 of the purchase price to tangible property and identified intangibles, including patents, and 80 to goodwill.

84. Immediately following the acquisition, Birincil causes Company T to transfer all of its rights in developed and partially developed technologies, including patents, trade secrets and technical know-how to Company S, a subsidiary of Birincil. Company S simultaneously enters into a contract research agreement with Company T, pursuant to which the Company T workforce will continue to work exclusively on the development of the transferred technologies and on the development of new technologies on behalf of Company S. The agreement provides that Company T will be compensated for its research services by payments equal to its cost plus a mark-up, and that all rights to intangibles developed or enhanced under the research agreement will belong to Company S. As a result, Company S will fund all future research and will assume the financial risk that some or all of the future research will not lead to the development of commercially viable products. Company S has a large research staff, including management personnel responsible for technologies of the type acquired from Company T. Following the transactions in question, the Company S research and management personnel assume full management responsibility for the direction and control of the work of the Company T research staff. Company S approves new projects, develops and plans budgets and in other respects controls the ongoing research work carried on at Company T. All company T research personnel will continue to be employees of Company T and will be devoted exclusively to providing services under the research agreement with Company S.

85. In conducting a transfer pricing analysis of the arm's length price to be paid by Company S for intangibles transferred by Company T, and of the price to be paid for ongoing R&D services to be provided by Company T, it is important to identify the specific intangibles transferred to Company S and those retained by Company T. The definitions and valuations of intangibles contained in the purchase price allocation are not determinative for transfer pricing purposes. The 100 paid by Birincil for the shares of Company T represents an arm's length price for shares of the company and provides useful information regarding the value of the business of Company T. The full value of that business should be reflected either in the value of the tangible and intangible assets transferred to Company S or in the value of the tangible and intangible assets and workforce retained by Company T. Depending on the facts, a substantial portion of the value described in the purchase price allocation as goodwill of Company T may have been transferred to Company S together with the other Company T intangibles. Depending on the facts, some portion of the value described in the purchase price allocation as goodwill may also have been retained by Company T. Under arm's length transfer pricing principles, Company T should be entitled to compensation for such value, either as part of the price paid by Company S for the transferred rights to technology intangibles, or through the compensation Company T is paid in years following the transaction for the R&D services of its

workforce. It should generally be assumed that value does not disappear, nor is it destroyed, as part of an internal business restructuring. If the transfer of intangibles to Company S had been separated in time from the acquisition, a separate inquiry would be required regarding any intervening appreciation or depreciation in the value of the transferred intangibles.

Example 24

86. Zhu is a company engaged in software development consulting. In the past Zhu has developed software supporting ATM transactions for client Bank A. In the process of doing so, Zhu created and retained an interest in proprietary copyrighted software code that is potentially suitable for use by other similarly situated banking clients, albeit with some revision and customisation.

87. Assume that Company S, an associated enterprise of Zhu, enters into a separate agreement to develop software supporting ATM operations for another bank, Bank B. Zhu agrees to support its associated enterprise by providing employees who worked on the Bank A engagement to work on Company S's Bank B engagement. Those employees have access to software designs and know-how developed in the Bank A engagement, including proprietary software code. That code and the services of the Zhu employees are utilised by Company S in executing its Bank B engagement. Ultimately, Bank B is provided by Company S with a software system for managing its ATM network, including the necessary licence to utilise the software developed in the project. Portions of the proprietary code developed by Zhu in its Bank A engagement are embedded in the software provided by Company S to Bank B. The code developed in the Bank A engagement and embedded in the Bank B software would be sufficiently extensive to justify a claim of copyright infringement if copied on an unauthorised basis by a third party.

88. A transfer pricing analysis of these transactions should recognise that Company S received two benefits from Zhu which require compensation. First, it received services from the Zhu employees that were made available to work on the Bank B engagement. Second, it received rights in Zhu's proprietary software which was utilised as the foundation for the software system delivered to Bank B. The compensation to be paid by Company S to Zhu should include compensation for both the services and the rights in the software.

Example 25

89. Prathamika is the parent company of an MNE group. Prathamika has been engaged in several large litigation matters and its internal legal department has become adept at managing large scale litigation on behalf of Prathamika. In the course of working on such litigation, Prathamika has developed proprietary document management software tools unique to its industry.

90. Company S is an associated enterprise of Prathamika. Company S becomes involved in a complex litigation similar to those with which the legal department of Prathamika has experience. Prathamika agrees to make two individuals from its legal team available to Company S to work on the Company S litigation. The individuals from Prathamika assume responsibility for managing documents related to the litigation. In undertaking this responsibility they make use of the document management software of Prathamika. They do not, however, provide Company S the right to use the document management software in other litigation matters or to make it available to Company S customers.

91. Under these circumstances, it would not be appropriate to treat Prathamika as having transferred rights in intangibles to Company S as part of the service arrangement. However, the fact that the Prathamika employees had experience and available software tools that allowed them to more effectively and efficiently perform their services should be considered in a comparability analysis related to the amount of any service fee to be charged for the services of the Prathamika employees.

Example 26

92. Osnovni is the parent company of an MNE Group engaged in the development and sale of software products. Osnovni acquires 100% of the equity interests in Company S, a publicly traded company organised in the same country as Osnovni, for a price equal to 160. At the time of the acquisition, Company S shares had an aggregate trading value of 100. Competitive bidders for the Company S business offered amounts ranging from 120 to 130 for Company S.

93. Company S had only a nominal amount of fixed assets at the time of the acquisition. Its value consisted primarily of rights in developed and partially developed intangibles related to software products and its skilled workforce. The purchase price allocation performed for accounting purposes by Osnovni allocated 10 to tangible assets, 60 to intangibles, and 90 to goodwill. Osnovni justified the 160 purchase price in presentations to its Board of Directors by reference to the complementary nature of the existing products of the Osnovni group and the products and potential products of Company S.

94. Company T is a wholly owned subsidiary of Osnovni. Osnovni has traditionally licensed exclusive rights in all of its intangibles related to the European and Asian markets to Company T. For purposes of this example it is assumed that all arrangements related to the historic licences of European and Asian rights to Company T prior to the acquisition of Company S are arm's length.

95. Immediately following the acquisition of Company S, Osnovni liquidates Company S, and thereafter grants an exclusive and perpetual licence to Company T for intangible rights related to the Company S products in European and Asian markets.

96. In determining an arm's length price for the Company S intangibles licensed to Company T under the foregoing arrangements, the premium over the original trading value of the Company S shares included in the acquisition price should be considered. To the extent that premium reflects the complementary nature of Osnovni group products with the acquired products in the European and Asian markets licensed to Company T, Company T should pay an amount for the transferred Company S intangibles and rights in intangibles that reflects an appropriate share of the purchase price premium. To the extent the purchase price premium is attributable exclusively to product complementarities outside of Company T's markets, the purchase price premium should not be taken into account in determining the arm's length price paid by Company T for Company S intangibles related to Company T's geographic market. The value attributed to intangibles in the purchase price allocation performed for accounting purposes is not determinative for transfer pricing purposes.

Example 27

97. Company A is the Parent of an MNE group with operations in Country X. Company A owns patents, trademarks and know-how with regard to several products produced and sold by the MNE group. Company B is a wholly owned subsidiary of Company A. All of Company B's operations are conducted in Country Y. Company B also owns patents, trademarks and know-how related to Product M.

98. For sound business reasons related to the co-ordination of the group's patent protection and anti-counterfeiting activities, the MNE group decides to centralise ownership of its patents in Company A. Accordingly, Company B sells the Product M patents to Company A for a lump-sum price. Company A assumes responsibility to perform all ongoing functions and it assumes all risks related to the Product M patents following the sale. Based on a detailed comparability and functional analysis, the MNE group concludes that it is not able to identify any comparable uncontrolled transactions that can be used to

determine the arm's length price. Company A and Company B reasonably conclude that the application of valuation techniques represents the most appropriate transfer pricing method to use in determining whether the agreed price is consistent with arm's length dealings.

99. Valuation personnel apply a valuation method that directly values property and patents to arrive at an after-tax net present value for the Product M patent of 80. The analysis is based on royalty rates, discount rates and useful lives typical in the industry in which Product M competes. However, there are material differences between Product M and the relevant patent rights related to Product M, and those typical in the industry. The royalty arrangements used in the analysis would therefore not satisfy the comparability standards required for a CUP method analysis. The valuation seeks to make adjustments for these differences.

100. In conducting its analysis, Company A also conducts a discounted cash flow based analysis of the Product M business in its entirety. That analysis, based on valuation parameters typically used by Company A in evaluating potential acquisitions, suggests that the entire Product M business has a net present value of 100. The 20 difference between the 100 valuation of the entire Product M business and the 80 valuation of the patent on its own appears to be inadequate to reflect the net present value of routine functional returns for functions performed by Company B and to recognise any value for the trademarks and know-how retained by Company B. Under these circumstances further review of the reliability of the 80 value ascribed to the patent would be called for.

Example 28

101. Company A is the Parent company of an MNE group with operations in Country S. Company B is a member of the MNE group with operations in Country T, and Company C is also a member of the MNE group with operations in Country U. For valid business reasons the MNE group decides to centralise all of its intangibles related to business conducted outside of Country S in a single location. Accordingly, intangibles owned by Company B are sold to Company C for a lump sum, including patents, trademarks, know-how, and customer relationships. At the same time, Company C retains Company B to act as a contract manufacturer of products previously produced and sold by Company B on a full-risk basis. Company C has the personnel and resources required to manage the acquired lines of business, including the further development of intangibles necessary to the Company B business.

102. The MNE group is unable to identify comparable uncontrolled transactions that can be used in a transfer pricing analysis of the arm's

length price to be paid by Company C to Company B. Based on a detailed comparability and functional analysis, the MNE group concludes that the most appropriate transfer pricing method involves the application of valuation techniques to determine the value of the transferred intangibles. In conducting its valuation, the MNE group is unable to reliably segregate particular cash flows associated with all of the specific intangibles.

103. Under these circumstances, in determining the arm's length compensation to be paid by Company C for the intangibles sold by Company B, it may be appropriate to value the transferred intangibles in the aggregate rather than to attempt a valuation on an asset by asset basis. This would particularly be the case if there is a significant difference between the sum of the best available estimates of the value of individually identified intangibles and other assets when valued separately and the value of the business as a whole.

Example 29

104. Pervichnyi is the parent of an MNE group organised and doing business in Country X. Prior to Year 1, Pervichnyi developed patents and trademarks related to Product F. It manufactured Product F in Country X and supplied the product to distribution affiliates throughout the world. For purposes of this example assume the prices charged to distribution affiliates were consistently arm's length.

105. At the beginning of Year 1, Pervichnyi organises a wholly owned subsidiary, Company S, in Country Y. In order to save costs, Pervichnyi transfers all of its production of Product F to Company S. At the time of the organisation of Company S, Pervichnyi sells the patents and trademarks related to Product F to Company S for a lump sum. Under these circumstances, Pervichnyi and Company S seek to identify an arm's length price for the transferred intangibles by utilising a discounted cash flow valuation technique.

106. According to this valuation analysis, Pervichnyi could have generated after tax residual cash flows (after rewarding all functional activities of other members of the MNE group on an arm's length basis) having a present value of 600 by continuing to manufacture Product F in Country X. The valuation from the buyer's perspective shows that Company S could generate after tax residual cash flows having a present value of 1 100 if it owned the intangibles and manufactured the product in Country Y. The difference in the present value of Pervichnyi's after tax residual cash flow and the present value of Company S's after tax residual cash flow is attributable to several factors.

107. Another option open to Pervichnyi would be for Pervichnyi to retain ownership of the intangible, and to retain Company S or an alternative supplier to manufacture products on its behalf in Country Y. In this scenario,

Pervichnyi calculates it would be able to generate after tax cash flow with a present value of 875.

108. In defining arm's length compensation for the intangibles transferred by Pervichnyi to Company S, it is important to take into account the perspectives of both parties, the options realistically available to each of them, and the particular facts and circumstances of the case. Pervichnyi would certainly not sell the intangibles at a price that would yield an after tax residual cash flow with a present value lower than 600, the residual cash flow it could generate by retaining the intangible and continuing to operate in the manner it had done historically. Moreover there is no reason to believe Pervichnyi would sell the intangible for a price that would yield an after tax residual cash flow with a present value lower than 875. If Pervichnyi could capture the production cost savings by retaining another entity to manufacture on its behalf in a low cost environment, one realistically available option open to it would be to establish such a contract manufacturing operation. That realistically available option should be taken into account in determining the selling price of the intangible.

109. Company S would not be expected to pay a price that would, after taking into account all relevant facts and circumstances, leave it with an after tax return lower than it could achieve by not engaging in the transaction. According to the discounted cash flow valuation, the net present value of the after tax residual cash flow it could generate using the intangible in its business would be 1 100. A price might be negotiated that would give Pervichnyi a return equal to or greater than its other available options, and give Company S a positive return on its investment considering all of the relevant facts, including the manner in which the transaction itself would be taxed.

110. A transfer pricing analysis utilising a discounted cash flow approach would have to consider how independent enterprises dealing at arm's length would take into account the cost savings and projected tax effects in setting a price for the intangibles. That price should, however, fall in the range between a price that would yield Pervichnyi after tax residual cash flow equivalent to that of its other options realistically available, and a price that would yield Company S a positive return to its investments and risks, considering the manner in which the transaction itself would be taxed.

111. The facts of this example and the foregoing analysis are obviously greatly oversimplified by comparison to the analysis that would be required in an actual transaction. The analysis nevertheless reflects the importance of considering all of the relevant facts and circumstances in performing a discounted cash flow analysis, evaluating the perspectives of each of the parties in such an analysis, and taking into consideration the options realistically available to each of the parties in performing the transfer pricing analysis.

Annex II to Chapter VI

Guidance for tax administrations on the application of the approach to hard-to-value intangibles

1. Introduction

1. Action 8 of the BEPS Action Plan mandated the development of transfer pricing rules or special measures for transfers of hard-to-value intangibles aimed at preventing base erosion and profit shifting by moving intangibles among group members.

2. The outcome of this work is found in Section D.4 of the Revised Chapter VI of the Transfer Pricing Guidelines, contained in the 2015 Final Report for Actions 8-10, "Aligning Transfer Pricing Outcomes with Value Creation" (BEPS TP Report) and now formally adopted as part of the Guidelines. Section D.4 addresses the treatment of hard-to-value intangibles (HTVI) for transfer pricing purposes. That Section contains an "approach consistent with the arm's length principle that tax administrations can adopt to ensure that tax administrations can determine in which situations the pricing arrangements as set by the taxpayers are at arm's length and are based on an appropriate weighting of the foreseeable developments or events that are relevant for the valuation of certain hard-to-value intangibles, and in which situations this is not the case" (paragraph 6.188). The HTVI approach protects tax administrations from the negative effects of information asymmetry by ensuring that tax administrations can consider *ex post* outcomes as presumptive evidence about the appropriateness of the *ex-ante* pricing arrangements. Under the approach, the taxpayer has the possibility to rebut such presumptive evidence by demonstrating the reliability of the information supporting the pricing methodology adopted at the time the controlled transaction took place. There are a number of additional exemptions that, where the conditions governing those exemptions are met, render the approach inapplicable. Importantly, where the approach applies, a tax administration is entitled to use, in evaluating the *ex ante* pricing arrangements, the *ex post*

evidence about financial outcomes to inform the determination of the arm's length pricing arrangements that would have been made between independent enterprises at the time of the transaction (see paragraph 6.192). However, the *ex post* evidence should not be used without considering whether the information on which the *ex post* results are based could or should reasonably have been considered by the associated enterprises at the time the transaction was entered into (see paragraph 6.188).

3. The BEPS TP Report mandates the development of guidance for tax administrations on the implementation of the approach to HTVI. This guidance is aimed at reaching a common understanding and practice among tax administrations on how to apply adjustments resulting from the application of the approach to HTVI. This guidance should improve consistency and reduce the risk of economic double taxation.

4. The BEPS TP Report also states that the practical application of the exemptions listed in paragraph 6.193 of the BEPS TP Report, including the measurement of materiality and time periods contained in the current exemptions, will be reviewed by 2020 in the light of further experience.

5. Tackling information asymmetry between the extensive information available to the taxpayer and the absence of information available to the tax administration, other than what the taxpayer may present, is at the heart of the reason for HTVI guidance in Section D.4 of Chapter VI of the Guidelines. When a HTVI is transferred, each of the parties involved in the transaction are likely to prepare a valuation at the time of the transaction using assumptions based on its specialised knowledge, expertise and insight into the business environment in which the intangible is developed or exploited. The problem for the tax administration is that the valuation is extremely difficult to objectively evaluate since such evaluation may be wholly based on the information provided by the taxpayer. Such information asymmetry restricts the ability of tax administrations to establish or verify, at an early stage, the developments or events that might be considered relevant for the pricing of a transaction involving the transfer of intangibles or rights in intangibles, as well as the extent to which the occurrence of such developments or events, or the direction they take, might have been foreseen or reasonably foreseeable at the time the transaction was entered into.

6. The HTVI guidance aims at providing a tool for tax administrations to address this problem. In the case of intangibles which fall within the definition of HTVI found in paragraph 6.189, and under certain conditions, tax administrations are entitled to consider *ex post* outcomes as presumptive evidence about the appropriateness of the *ex ante* pricing arrangements. Where, the actual income or cash flows are significantly higher or lower than the anticipated income or cash flows on which the pricing was based, then there is presumptive evidence (from the perspective of the tax administration)

that the projected income or cash flows used in the original valuation should have been higher or lower, and that the probability-weighting of such an outcome requires scrutiny, taking into account what was known and could have been anticipated at the time of entering into the transaction involving the HTVI. However, it would be incorrect to base the revised valuation on the actual income or cash flows without also taking into account the probability, at the time of the transaction, of the income or cash flows being achieved.

7. This evaluation of the *ex ante* pricing arrangements based on the *ex post* outcomes will necessarily consider the guidance contained in Chapters I-III and, in particular, the guidance in Chapters VI and VIII of these Guidelines.

8. In performing such evaluation, tax administrations may consider not only the ex post outcomes taken as presumptive evidence (within the limits of Section D.4 of Chapter VI of these Guidelines) about the appropriateness of the ex ante pricing arrangement, but also any other relevant information related to the HTVI transaction that becomes available to the tax administrations and that could or should reasonably have been known and considered by the associated enterprises at the time the transaction was entered into (see Section B.5 of Chapter III).

9. Importantly even if the HTVI approach is not applicable to a particular transaction, an adjustment may still be appropriate under other parts of these Guidelines, including other sections of Chapter VI.

10. Any application of the HTVI approach should be done in a manner that promotes tax certainty for taxpayers, and reduces the risk of double taxation resulting from a primary adjustment, considering the jurisdiction's domestic law (for example, the applicable statute of limitations) and treaty framework. Tax administrations should identify and act upon HTVI transactions as early as possible.

11. The nature of the approach to HTVI inevitably requires some consideration of timing issues. In some cases, the elapsed time between the transfer of the HTVI and the emergence of ex post outcomes may not correspond with audit cycles or with administrative and statutory time periods. This problem may be more acute where an adjustment is appropriate under the HTVI approach in transactions involving intangibles qualifying as HTVI under paragraph 6.189 that have a long incubation period – that is, the period after the transfer and before the intangible can be exploited commercially and income can be derived (see paragraph 6.190).

12. The impact of timing issues should not be overstated since there is already a time lag in typical audit cycles. For example, assume an audit of Years 1-3 is carried out in Year 5; during the course of the audit, the tax administration may identify not only a transfer of a hard-to-value intangible in

Year 1 but also ex post outcomes of that transfer that may be evaluated during the audit process. Tax administrations are encouraged to identify transfers of potential HTVI, to evaluate the assumptions made by the taxpayer in valuing the intangible, and to seek information about developments that lead to ex post outcomes which may call into question those assumptions, even when those outcomes arise in years subsequent to those under audit, in order to be in a position to consider the appropriateness of the ex ante pricing.

13. Tax administrations should apply audit practices to ensure that HTVI transactions are identified and acted upon as early as possible. However, it should be kept in mind that in some cases it may be difficult for tax administrations to perform a risk assessment at the time of the transaction, or even shortly thereafter, to evaluate the reliability of the information on which pricing has been based, or to consider whether the transfer is priced at arm's length. Such analysis may only be possible some years after the transaction. Under the HTVI approach, the tax administration may, in particular circumstances, use ex post outcomes to consider the reasonableness of the projections and probability weightings taken into account in the valuation at the time of the transaction.

14. This guidance for tax administrations on the application of the HTVI approach should not be used to delay or bypass normal audit procedures. In fact, it remains important to identify transfers of HTVI as early as possible and to act on presumptive evidence promptly as a matter of good administrative practice, and in order to avoid running into difficulties with administrative or statutory time limits for audits and reassessment. Nothing in this guidance changes those time limits, which are a matter of sovereignty of jurisdictions.

15. To enhance tax certainty for taxpayers and reduce the risk of double taxation, it is desirable that the HTVI approach be applied consistently. However, some jurisdictions may encounter difficulties in applying the HTVI approach due, for example, to short audit cycles or a short statute of limitations. This guidance does not require jurisdictions to adopt legislation aimed at overcoming such difficulties, but it does not prevent jurisdictions from considering targeted changes to procedures or legislation (such as the introduction of a requirement to notify promptly the transfer or licence of an intangible falling within the HTVI definition, or amendment of the normal statute of limitations).

16. In applying the HTVI approach contained in Section D.4 of Chapter VI, tax administrations may make appropriate adjustments, including adjustments that reflect an alternative pricing structure that differs from that adopted by the taxpayer but reflects one which would have been made by independent enterprises in comparable circumstances to take account of the valuation uncertainty in the pricing of the transaction (for example, milestone payments, running royalties with or without adjustable elements, price adjustment clauses, or a combination of these characteristics). See

paragraph 6.185 and 6.192. Since hard to value intangibles are intangibles for which no reliable comparables exist, tax administrations cannot be expected to substantiate adjustments to the pricing structure by referring to uncontrolled transactions involving comparable intangibles.

17. Some of the practical ways in which the approach to HTVI can be applied are illustrated in the examples in the following section. The application of the approach to HTVI should be underpinned by the following principles:

- Where the HTVI approach applies, tax administrations can consider *ex post* outcomes as presumptive evidence about the reasonableness of the assumptions of the ex *ante* pricing arrangements.
- The *ex post* outcomes inform the determination of the valuation that would have been made at the time of the transaction; however, it would be incorrect to base the valuation on the actual income or cash flows without taking into account whether the associated enterprises could or should reasonably have known and considered, at the time of the transfer of the HTVI, the information related to the probability of achieving such income or cash flows.
- Where a revised valuation shows that the intangible was transferred at an undervalue or overvalue compared to the arm's length price, the revised price of the transferred intangible may be assessed to tax taking into account price adjustment clauses and/or contingent payments, irrespective of the payment profiles asserted by the taxpayer, consistently with paragraph 16.
- Tax administrations should apply audit practices to ensure that presumptive evidence based on *ex post* outcomes is identified and acted upon as early as possible.

2. Examples[1]

18. The following examples are aimed at illustrating the practical application of a transfer pricing adjustment arising from the application of the HTVI guidance. The assumptions made about arm's length arrangements

1. Please note that the fact that these examples are focused on the pharmaceutical sector should not be interpreted as limiting the application of the HTVI approach set out in Section D.4 of Chapter VI of the Guidelines or this guidance to this particular industry. The HTVI approach contained in Section D.4 of the Guidelines and this guidance are applicable to transactions involving intangibles qualifying as HTVI under paragraph 6.189, irrespective of the industry or sector in which they take place.

and transfer pricing adjustments determined in the examples are intended for illustrative purposes only and should not be taken as prescribing adjustments and arm's length arrangements in actual cases or particular industries. The HTVI guidance must be applied in each case according to the specific facts and circumstances of the case.

19. These examples make the following assumptions:

- The transaction involves the transfer of an intangible (or rights therein) meeting the criteria for HTVI in paragraph 6.189, that is (i) no reliable comparables exist; and (ii) at the time the transaction was entered into, the projections of future cash flows or income expected to be derived from the transferred intangible, or the assumptions used in valuing the intangible, are highly uncertain, making it difficult to predict the level of ultimate success of the intangible at the time of the transfer.
- The exemptions to the application of the HTVI approach contained in paragraph 6.193 are not applicable unless specifically discussed.
- As a result, the HTVI guidance is applicable and the tax administration may consider *ex post* outcomes as presumptive evidence about the appropriateness of the *ex ante* pricing arrangements.
- A transfer pricing adjustment is warranted for the transaction.

20. In addition, the examples make reference to valuation techniques using the discounted value of projected income or cash flows derived from the exploitation of the transferred intangible. Neither this application guidance nor the examples below are intended to mandate the use of valuation techniques using the discounted value of projected income or cash flows for determining the arm's length price of transactions involving HTVI. Therefore, references to such a valuation technique should not be interpreted as implying conclusions about the appropriateness of the technique in a particular case. The guidance on applying methods based on the discounted value of projected cash flows is contained in Chapter VI paragraphs 6.153-6.178, and this application guidance should be applied in a manner that is consistent with other relevant guidance contained in the Transfer Pricing Guidelines.

Example 1

21. Company A, a resident of Country A, has patented a pharmaceutical compound. Company A has concluded pre-clinical tests for the compound and has successfully taken the compound through Phases I and II of the clinical trials. Company A transfers in Year 0 the patent rights to an affiliate, Company S, a resident of Country S. Company S will be responsible for the

Phase III trials following the transfer. In order to determine the price for the patent on the partially developed drug, the parties made an estimation of expected income or cash flows that will be obtained upon exploitation of the drug once finalised over the remaining life of the patent. Assume the price so derived at the time of the transfer was 700 and that this was paid as a lump sum in Year 0.

22. In particular, the taxpayer assumed sales would not exceed 1 000 a year and that commercialisation would not commence until Year 6. The discount rate was determined by referring to external data analysing the risk of failure for drugs in a similar therapeutic category at the same stage of development. Even if the tax administration of Country A had been aware of these facts relating to the transfer of the patent rights in Year 0, it would have had little means of verifying the reasonableness of the taxpayer's assumptions relating to sales.

Scenario A

23. In Year 4, the tax administration of Country A audits Company A for Years 0-2 and obtains information that commercialisation in fact started during Year 3 since the Phase III trials were completed earlier than projected. Sales in Years 3 and 4 correspond to sales that were projected, at the time of the transfer, to be achieved in Years 6 and 7. The taxpayer cannot demonstrate that its original valuation took into account the possibility that sales would arise in earlier periods, and cannot demonstrate that such a development was unforeseeable.

24. The tax administration uses the presumptive evidence provided by the *ex post* outcome to determine that the valuation made at the time the transaction took place did not consider the possibility of sales occurring in earlier years. The taxpayer's original valuation is revised to include the appropriately risk-adjusted possibility of earlier sales resulting in a revised net present value of the drug in Year 0 of 1 000 instead of 700. The revised net present value also takes into account the functions performed, assets used and risks assumed in relation to the HTVI by each of the parties before the transaction and reasonably anticipated, at the time of the transaction, to be performed, used or assumed by each of the parties after the transaction. Therefore, assume for the purposes of the example that the arm's length price anticipated in Year 0 should have been 1 000. Note that the value of 1 000 is not necessarily the net present value of the transferred rights based solely on the actual outcome (see paragraph 6 of this guidance).

25. In accordance with the approach to HTVI, the tax administration is entitled to make an adjustment to assess the additional profits of 300 in Year 0.

Scenario B

26. The tax administration uses the presumptive evidence provided by the *ex post* outcomes to determine that the valuation made at the time the transaction took place, did not consider the possibility of sales occurring in earlier years. The taxpayer's original valuation is revised to include the appropriately risk-adjusted possibility of sales occurring in earlier years resulting in a revised net present value of the drug in Year 0 of 800 instead of 700. Therefore, assume for the purposes of the example that the arm's length price anticipated in Year 0 should have been 800. Note that the value of 800 is not necessarily the net present value of the transferred rights based solely on the actual outcome (see paragraph 6 of this guidance).

27. In accordance with the approach to HTVI, the tax administration is entitled to make an adjustment to assess the additional profits of 100 in Year 0. However, in this example, the exemption provided by item (iii) in paragraph 6.193 applies since the adjustment to the compensation for the transfer is within 20% of the compensation determined at the time of the transaction.

Example 2

28. The facts are the same as in paragraphs 21-22. Based on those facts, assume that in Year 7, the tax administration of Country A audits Company A for Years 3-5 and obtains information that sales in Years 5 and 6 of the product to which the patent relates were significantly higher than those projected. In the original valuation, the taxpayer had not projected sales any higher than 1 000 in any year, but outcomes in each of Years 5 and 6 show sales of 1 500. The taxpayer cannot demonstrate that its original valuation took into account the possibility that sales would reach these levels, and cannot demonstrate that reaching that level of sales was due to an unforeseeable development.

29. The tax administration uses the presumptive evidence provided by the *ex post* outcomes to determine that the possibility of higher sales should have been taken into account in the valuation. The taxpayer's original valuation is revised to include the appropriately risk-adjusted possibility of sales occurring in earlier years, resulting in a revised net present value of the drug in Year 0 of 1 300 instead of 700. The revised net present value also takes into account the functions performed, assets used and risks assumed in relation to the HTVI by each of the parties before the transaction and reasonably anticipated, at the time of the transaction, to be performed, used or assumed by each of the parties after the transaction. Therefore, assume for the purposes of the example that the arm's length price anticipated in Year 0 should have been 1 300. Note that the value of 1 300 is not necessarily the net present value of the transferred rights based solely on the actual outcome (see paragraph 6 of this guidance).

30. In accordance with the approach to HTVI, the tax administration is entitled to make an adjustment to assess the additional profits of 600. Assume for the purposes of this example that none of the exemptions listed in paragraph 6.193 of Chapter VI of the Guidelines applies.

31. One way to implement the adjustment is to re-assess the price paid in Year 0. However, the significant revision of the lump-sum payment highlights the risks posed by the high uncertainty in valuing the intangible and gives rise to consideration, in light of this significant uncertainty, of whether adjustments consistent with an alternative payment structure might be more consistent with what unrelated parties would have done (see paragraph 16 of this guidance and paragraph 6.183 of Chapter VI of the Guidelines).

32. Evidence of pricing arrangements for the transfer of intangibles in comparable circumstances to address high valuation uncertainty may point to appropriate alternatives to making the adjustment in Year 0. For example, assume that in the pharmaceutical sector it is common to transfer patent rights to independent parties through a combination of an initial lump sum payment and additional contingent payment arrangements based on the successful completion of development phases or regulatory approvals in a particular market. In this case, assume that the first market approvals were obtained in Year 3. The tax administration may, therefore, determine that it is consistent with arm's length practices in comparable circumstances to recover the underpayment through a further payment in Year 3. Note that this paragraph is not intended to, and does not, imply that modification of the payment form can only occur when there is a common practice in the relevant business sector regarding the form of payment for the transfer of a particular type of intangible.

33. The principles illustrated by this example apply irrespective of whether the tax administration in fact carries out an audit for Years 0-2 and then a second audit for Years 3-5, or whether it audits only for Years 3-5. In both scenarios, a revision to the original valuation is justified based on *ex post* evidence emerging in Year 7, and, subject to any treaty or domestic law limitations, the undervaluation may be recovered based on the HTVI approach contained in Section D.4 of Chapter VI (see paragraph 6.192).

3. Dispute prevention and resolution in relation to the HTVI approach

34. The purpose of this guidance is to improve consistency in the application of the HTVI approach by jurisdictions, thus reducing the risk of economic double taxation. In addition to this guidance, there may be other tools at the disposal of taxpayers to avoid instances of double taxation and enhance tax certainty in HTVI transactions.

35. In particular, Chapter IV of these Guidelines discusses in detail advance pricing arrangements (APAs), which if concluded bilaterally or multilaterally between treaty partner competent authorities provide an increased level of certainty in the jurisdictions involved, lessen the likelihood of double taxation, and may proactively prevent transfer pricing disputes. Recognising the role of APAs in preventing double taxation and providing certainty to taxpayers, paragraph 6.193 of these Guidelines prevents the application of the HTVI approach when the transfer of the HTVI is covered by a bilateral or multilateral APA in effect for the period in questions between the jurisdictions of the transferee and the transferor.

36. In this regard, the Final BEPS Report for Action 14 "Making Dispute Resolution Mechanisms More Effective" (BEPS Report on Action 14) recommends as a best practice the implementation of bilateral APAs, as soon as a jurisdiction has the capacity to do so (Best Practice no. 4). Furthermore, one of the elements of the BEPS Report on Action 14 is that jurisdictions with bilateral APA programmes provide for the rollback of APAs in appropriate cases, subject to the applicable time limits where the relevant facts and circumstances in the earlier tax years are the same and subject to the verification of these facts and circumstances on audit.

37. In the event that the application of the approach to HTVI leads to double taxation, the guidance in paragraph 6.195 states that it would be important to permit resolution of such cases through access to the mutual agreement procedure under the applicable treaty. Accordingly, this guidance should be read in conjunction with Article 25 and its Commentary and the commitment made in the Final BEPS Report on Action 14. That Report describes the minimum standard on dispute resolution to which the members of the Inclusive Framework on BEPS have committed, which consists of specific measures to remove obstacles to an effective and efficient mutual agreement procedure.

38. In the context of the HTVI approach it is especially relevant that under Article 25 the mutual agreement procedure "can be set in motion by the taxpayer without waiting until the taxation considered by him to be not in accordance with the Convention has been charged against or notified to him. To be able to set the procedure in motion, he must, and it is sufficient if he does, establish that the actions of one or both of the Contracting States will result in such taxation, and that this taxation appears as a risk which is not merely possible but probable" (see paragraph 14 of the Commentary to Article 25 of the Model Tax Convention). This possibility under the applicable tax treaty may alleviate some of the concerns arising in relation to timing issues and reduce the instances of unresolved double taxation.

39. Finally, one of the best practices recommended in the BEPS Report on Action 14 and that is relevant for HTVI transactions is that, subject to the

requirements of paragraph 1 of Article 25, jurisdictions implement appropriate procedures to permit, in certain cases and after an initial tax assessment, taxpayer requests for the multiyear resolution through the MAP of recurring issues with respect to filed tax years, where the relevant facts and circumstances are the same and subject to the verification of such facts and circumstances on audit.

Annex to Chapter VIII

Examples to illustrate the guidance on cost contribution arrangements

Example 1

1. Example 1 illustrates the general principle that contributions should be assessed at value (i.e. based on arm's length prices) in order to produce results that are consistent with the arm's length principle.

2. Company A and Company B are members of an MNE group and decide to enter into a CCA. Company A performs Service 1 and Company B performs Service 2. Company A and Company B each "consume" both services (that is, Company A receives a benefit from Service 2 performed by Company B, and Company B receives a benefit from Service 1 performed by Company A).

3. Assume that the costs and value of the services are as follows:

Costs of providing Service 1 (cost incurred by Company A)	100 per unit
Value of Service 1 (i.e. the arm's length price that Company A would charge Company B for the provision of Service 1)	120 per unit
Costs of providing Service 2 (cost incurred by Company B)	100 per unit
Value of Service 2 (i.e. the arm's length price that Company B would charge Company A for the provision of Service 2)	105 per unit

4. In Year 1 and in subsequent years, Company A provides 30 units of Service 1 to the group and Company B provides 20 units of Service 2 to the group. Under the CCA, the calculation of costs and benefits are as follows:

Cost to Company A of providing services (30 units × 100 per unit)	3 000	(60% of total costs)
Cost to Company B of providing services (20 units × 100 per unit)	2 000	(40% of total costs)
Total cost to group	5 000	

Value of contribution made by Company A (30 units × 120 per unit)	3 600	(63% of total contributions)
Value of contribution made by Company B (20 units × 105 per unit)	2 100	(37% of total contributions)
Total value of contributions made under the CCA	5 700	

Company A and Company B each consume 15 units of Service 1 and 10 units of Service 2:		
Benefit to Company A:		
Service 1: 15 units × 120 per unit	1 800	
Service 2: 10 units × 105 per unit	1 050	
Total	2 850	(50% of total value of 5 700)
Benefit to Company B		
Service 1: 15 units × 120 per unit	1 800	
Service 2: 10 units × 105 per unit	1 050	
Total	2 850	(50% of total value of 5 700)

5. Under the CCA, the value of Company A and Company B's contributions should each correspond to their respective proportionate shares of expected benefits, i.e. 50%. Since the total value of contributions under the CCA is 5 700, this means each party must contribute 2 850. The value of Company A's in-kind contribution is 3 600 and the value of Company B's in-kind contribution is 2 100. Accordingly, Company B should make a balancing payment to Company A of 750. This has the effect of "topping up" Company B's contribution to 2 850; and offsets Company A's contribution to the same amount.

6. If contributions were measured at cost instead of at value, since Companies A and B each receive 50% of the total benefits, they would have been required contribute 50% of the total costs, or 2 500 each, i.e. Company B would have been required to make a 500 (instead of 750) balancing payment to A.

7. In the absence of the CCA, Company A would purchase 10 units of Service 2 for the arm's length price of 1 050 and Company B would purchase 15 units of Service 1 for the arm's length price of 1 800. The net result would be a payment of 750 from Company B to Company A. As can be shown from the above, this arm's length result is only achieved in respect of the CCA when contributions are measured at value.

Example 1A

8. The facts are the same as Example 1. In accordance with the guidance in paragraph 8.27, an alternative way to achieve the identical result under Example 1 is through the use of a two-step process as set out below.

9. Step 1 (contributions measured at cost): Company A should bear 50% of the total cost of 5 000, or 2 500. The cost of Company A's in-kind contribution is 3 000. Company B should bear 50% of the total cost, or 2 500. The cost of Company B's in-kind contribution is 2 000. Company B should thus make an additional payment to Company A of 500. This reflects a balancing payment associated with current contributions.

10. Step 2 (accounting for additional contributions of value to the CCA): Company A produces 20 of value above costs per unit. Company B produces 5 of value above costs per unit. Company A consumes 10 units of Service 2 (50 of value over cost), and Company B consumes 15 units of Service 1 (300 of value over cost). Accordingly, Company A should be compensated 250 for the additional 250 of value that it contributes to the CCA. This reflects a balancing payment associated with pre-existing contributions.

11. The two-step method provides for a sharing of costs plus a separate and additional payment to the participant that makes an additional contribution of value to the arrangement. In general, the additional contribution of value might reflect pre-existing contributions, such as intangibles owned by one of the participants, that are relevant to the purpose of the CCA. Thus, the two-step method might be most usefully applied to development CCAs.

Example 2

12. The facts are the same as Example 1, except that the per-unit value of Service 1 is 103 (that is, both Service 1 and Service 2 are low-value services). Assume, therefore, that the calculation of the costs and value of the services is as follows:

Cost to Company A of providing services (30 units × 100 per unit)	3 000	(60% of total costs)
Cost to Company B of providing services (20 units × 100 per unit)	2 000	(40% of total costs
Total cost to group	5 000	

Value of contribution made by Company A (30 units × 103 per unit)	3 090	(59.5% of total contributions)
Value of contribution made by Company B (20 units × 105 per unit)	2 100	(40.5% of total contributions)
Total value of contributions made under the CCA	5 190	

Company A and Company B each consume 15 units of Service 1 and 10 units of Service 2:		
Benefit to Company A:		
Service 1: 15 units × 103 per unit	1 545	
Service 2: 10 units × 105 per unit	1 050	
Total	2 595	(50% of total value of 5 190)

Benefit to Company B		
Service 1: 15 units × 103 per unit	1 545	
Service 2: 10 units × 105 per unit	1 050	
Total	2 595	(50% of total value of 5 190)

13. Under the CCA, the value of Company A and Company B's contributions should each correspond to their respective proportionate shares of expected benefits, i.e. 50%. Since the total value of contributions under the CCA is 5 190, this means each party must contribute 2 595. The value of Company A's in-kind contribution is 3 090. The value of Company B's in-kind contribution is 2 100. Accordingly, Company B should make a balancing payment to Company A of 495. This has the effect of "topping up" Company B's contribution to 2 595; and offsets Company A's contribution to the same amount.

14. In this example, since all contributions to the CCA are low-value services, for practical reasons, contributions may be valued at cost since this will achieve results which are broadly consistent with the arm's length principle. Under this practical approach, the cost of Company A's in-kind contribution is 3 000; the cost of Company B's in-kind contribution is 2 000; and each participant should bear the costs associated with 50% of the total cost of contributions (2 500). Accordingly, Company B should make a balancing payment to Company A of 500.

Example 3

15. The facts are the same as Example 1, except that the per-unit value of Service 2 is 120 (that is, both Service 1 and Service 2 are equally valuable, and neither are low-value services).

Cost to Company A of providing services (30 units × 100 per unit)	3 000	(60% of total costs)
Cost to Company B of providing services (20 units × 100 per unit)	2 000	(40% of total costs)
Total cost to group	5 000	

Value of contribution made by Company A (30 units × 120 per unit)	3 600	(60% of total contributions)
Value of contribution made by Company B (20 units × 120 per unit)	2 400	(40% of total contributions)
Total value of contributions made under the CCA	6 000	

Company A and Company B each consume 15 units of Service 1 and 10 units of Service 2:		
Benefit to Company A:		
Service 1: 15 units × 120 per unit	1 800	
Service 2: 10 units × 120 per unit	1 200	
Total	3 000	(50% of total value of 6000)

Benefit to Company B		
Service 1: 15 units × 120 per unit	1 800	
Service 2: 10 units × 120 per unit	1 200	
Total	3 000	(50% of total value of 6000)

16. Under the CCA, the value of Company A and Company B's contributions should each correspond to their respective proportionate shares of expected benefits i.e. 50%. Since the total value of contributions under the CCA is 6 000, this means each party must contribute 3 000. The value of Company A's in-kind contribution is 3 600. The value of Company B's in-kind contribution is 2 400. Accordingly, Company B should make a balancing payment to Company A of 600. This has the effect of "topping up" Company B's contribution to 3 000; and offsets Company A's contribution to the same amount. Example 3 illustrates that, in general, assessing contributions at cost will not result in an arm's length outcome even in those situations in which the arm's length mark-up on the cost of contributions is identical.

Example 4

17. Company A and Company B are members of an MNE group and decide to undertake the development of an intangible through a CCA. The intangible is anticipated to be highly profitable based on Company B's existing intangibles, its track record and its experienced research and development staff. Company A performs, through its own personnel, all the functions expected of a participant in a development CCA obtaining an independent right to exploit the resulting intangible, including functions required to exercise control over the risks it contractually assumes in accordance with the principles outlined in paragraphs 8.14 to 8.18. The particular intangible in this example is expected to take five years to develop before possible commercial exploitation and if successful, is anticipated to have value for ten years after initial exploitation.

18. Under the CCA, Company A will contribute to funding associated with the development of the intangible (its share of the development costs are anticipated to be USD 100 million per year for five years). Company B will contribute the development rights associated with its existing intangibles,

to which Company A is granted rights under the CCA irrespective of the outcome of the CCA's objectives, and will perform all activities related to the development, maintenance, and exploitation of the intangible. The value of Company B's contributions (encompassing the performance of activities as well as the use of the pre-existing intangibles) would need to be determined in accordance with the guidance in Chapter VI and would likely be based on the anticipated value of the intangible expected to be produced under the CCA, less the value of the funding contribution by Company A.

19. Once developed, the intangible is anticipated to result in global profits of USD 550 million per year (Years 6 to 15). The CCA provides that Company B will have exclusive rights to exploit the resulting intangible in Country B (anticipated to result in profits of USD 220 million per year in Years 6 to 15) and Company A will have exclusive rights to exploit the intangible in the rest of the world (anticipated to result in profits of USD 330 million per year).

20. Taking into account the realistic alternatives of Company A and Company B it is determined that the value of Company A's contribution is equivalent to a risk-adjusted return on its R&D funding commitment. Assume that this is determined to be USD 110 million per year (for Years 6 to 15).[1] However, under the CCA Company A is anticipated to reap benefits amounting to USD 330 million of profits per year in Years 6 to 15 (rather than USD 110 million). This additional anticipated value in the rights Company A obtains (that is, the anticipated value above and beyond the value of Company A's funding investment) reflects the contribution of Company B's pre-existing contributions of intangibles and R&D commitment to the CCA. Company A needs to pay for this additional value it receives. Accordingly, balancing payments from Company A to Company B to account for the difference are required. In effect, Company A would need to make a balancing payment associated with those contributions to Company B equal in present value, taking into account the risk associated with this future income, to USD 220 million per year anticipated in Years 6 to 15.

1. For purposes of this example, it is not necessary to derive these results. The example assumes that making a funding "investment" of USD 100 million per year for five years in a project with this level of risk should earn at arm's length anticipated profits of USD 110 million per year for the following ten years. The results used herein are included for the purposes of demonstrating the principles illustrated in this example only and no guidance as to the level of arm's length returns to participants in CCAs should be inferred.

Example 5

21. The facts are the same as in Example 4 except that the functional analysis indicates Company A has no capacity to make decisions to take on or decline the risk-bearing opportunity represented by its participation in the CCA, or to make decisions on whether and how to respond to the risks associated with the opportunity. It also has no capability to mitigate the risks or to assess and make decisions relating to the risk mitigation activities of another party conducted on its behalf.

22. In accurately delineating the transactions associated with the CCA, the functional analysis therefore indicates that Company A does not control its specific risks under the CCA in accordance with the guidance in paragraph 8.15 and consequently is not entitled to a share in the output that is the objective of the CCA.

Appendix

Recommendation of the Council on the Determination of Transfer Pricing between Associated Enterprises [C(95)126/Final, as amended]

THE COUNCIL,

HAVING REGARD to Article 5(b) of the Convention on the Organisation for Economic Co-operation and Development of 14th December, 1960;

HAVING REGARD to the Declaration on International Investment and Multinational Enterprises and the Guidelines annexed thereto [C(76)99(Final)];

HAVING REGARD to the Declaration on Base Erosion and Profit Shifting ("BEPS") [C/MIN(2013)22/FINAL] and to the BEPS Explanatory Statement and the measures set out in the BEPS Final Reports (the BEPS package), endorsed by the Council on 1 October 2015 [C(2015)125/REV1] and the G20 Leaders at the Antalya Summit on 15-16 November 2015;

HAVING REGARD to the Transfer Pricing Guidelines for Multinational Enterprises and Tax Administrations, hereafter referred to as "Guidelines" as they may be modified by the Committee on Fiscal Affairs;

HAVING REGARD to the Recommendation of the Council on Base Erosion and Profit Shifting Measures Related to Transfer Pricing [C(2016)79] which recommends that Members and non-Members having adhered to it follow the guidance set out in the 2015 BEPS Reports on Actions 8-10 "Aligning Transfer Pricing Outcomes With Value Creation" [C(2015)125/ADD8] and on Action 13 "Transfer Pricing Documentation and Country-by-Country Reporting" [C(2015)125/ADD11] as incorporated in the Guidelines;

HAVING REGARD to the establishment of the Inclusive Framework on Base Erosion and Profit Shifting as agreed by the Committee on Fiscal Affairs [CTPA/CFA/NOE2(2016)1/REV3], reported to the Council [C/M(2016)3], and endorsed by the G20 Finance Ministers at their

26-27 February 2016 meeting in Shanghai, China, under which over 100 countries and jurisdictions have been invited to participate as members [C(2016)78], i.e. on an equal footing with OECD Members on the basis of the same commitments as OECD Members and existing Associates with regard to the BEPS Project;

CONSIDERING the fundamental need for co-operation among tax administrations to remove the obstacles that international double taxation presents to the free movement of goods, services and capital between jurisdictions;

CONSIDERING the equally fundamental need to effectively prevent double non-taxation as well as no or low taxation resulting from the misapplication of the international standards for transfer pricing rules leading to outcomes in which the allocation of profits is not aligned with the economic activity that produced the profits;

CONSIDERING that transactions between associated enterprises may take place under conditions differing from those taking place between independent enterprises;

CONSIDERING that the prices of such transactions between associated enterprises (usually referred to as transfer pricing) should, nevertheless, for tax purposes be in conformity with those which would be charged between independent enterprises (usually referred to as arm's length pricing) consistent with Article 9 (paragraph 1) of the OECD Model Tax Convention on Income and on Capital;

CONSIDERING that problems with regard to transfer pricing in international transactions assume special importance in view of the substantial volume of such transactions;

CONSIDERING the need to achieve consistency in the approaches of tax administrations, on the one hand, and of associated enterprises, on the other hand, in the determination of the income and expenses of a company that is part of a Multinational Enterprise Group that should be taken into account within a jurisdiction.

On the proposal of the Committee on Fiscal Affairs:

I. **RECOMMENDS** that Members and non-Members adhering to this Recommendation (hereafter the "Adherents"):

   i) follow, when reviewing, and if necessary, adjusting transfer pricing between associated enterprises for the purposes of determining taxable income, the Guidelines – considering the whole of the Guidelines and the interaction of the different chapters – for arriving at arm's length pricing for transactions between associated enterprises;

ii) encourage taxpayers to follow the Guidelines; to that effect Adherents should give the Guidelines publicity and have them translated, where necessary, into their national language(s);

iii) develop further co-operation, on a bilateral or multilateral basis, in matters pertaining to transfer pricing.

II. **INVITES** Adherents to notify the Committee on Fiscal Affairs of any modifications to the text of any laws or regulations that are relevant to the determination of transfer pricing or of the introduction of new laws or regulations.

III. **INVITES** Adherents and the Secretary-General to disseminate this Recommendation and the Guidelines.

IV. **INVITES** non-Adherents to take due account of and adhere to this Recommendation.

V. **INSTRUCTS** the Committee on Fiscal Affairs to:

i) pursue its work on issues pertinent to transfer pricing and modify the Guidelines as necessary;

ii) monitor the implementation of this Recommendation, in co-operation with the tax authorities of Adherents and with the participation of the business community and other stakeholders and report to Council in light of this monitoring every five years;

iii) develop its dialogue with jurisdictions that have not adhered to this Recommendation with the aim of assisting them to become familiar with the Guidelines, and to adhere to the present Recommendation.

www.ingramcontent.com/pod-product-compliance
Lightning Source LLC
LaVergne TN
LVHW072011300926
849160LV00003B/12